The
COMPREHENSION,
DECISION MAKING &
INTERPERSONAL SKILLS

COMPENDIUM

for IAS Prelims General Studies Paper 2 & State PSC Exams

- **Corporate Office :** 45, 2nd Floor, Maharishi Dayanand Marg, Corner Market, Malviya Nagar, New Delhi-110017

  Tel. : 011- 49404757/ 49404758/ 49404768

Printed at Repro Knowledgecast Limited, Thane

Typeset by Disha DTP Team

For further information about the books from DISHA,

Log on to **www.dishapublication.com** or email to **info@dishapublication.com**

CONTENTS

INTERPERSONAL SKILLS INCLUDING COMMUNICATION SKILLS

Interpersonal skills or people's skills constitute the ability to interact and communicate effectively with another individual or others within a group. People with strong interpersonal skills are often more successful and happy in both their professional and personal lives. Interpersonal skills form the foundation of organizational functioning. The Administrative Services on account of their direct dealing with people require officers who have strong people's skills.

Basically centred on effective **verbal communication**, i.e., efficacious speaking, focussed listening, and genuine questioning, interpersonal skills include **non-verbal communication** which pertains to correct perception of body language, gestures, facial expressions, eye contact, and the tone and tenor of speech. Apart from this, they also involve emotional intelligence (ability to understand and manage own and others' emotions) and team work (ability to work genially with others in a formal or informal group).To result in an agreeable outcome, team work requires

1. negotiation, persuasion and influencing skills,
2. conflict resolution and mediation skills,
3. problem solving and decision making skills

IMPORTANCE OF INTERPERSONAL SKILLS FOR A CIVIL SERVANT

Interpersonal skills are important to solve real life problems. They show a way out in critical and deadlocked situations. Effective communication enables one to reach a target audience. Good communicators can persuade people to favour their decision, win people over to their side and can build consensus on issues. An ineffective communication, on the other hand, may deal a severe blow to one's efforts and ruin the chances of the desired outcome. Civil servants have to deal with people from different strata of the society for the administration of public services. So, they must be equipped with efficient interpersonal skills to get the expected results from all quarters and to ascertain effective dispensation of their services.

The purpose of including Interpersonal Skills in the paper is to test the candidate's attitudes, behavioral patterns and ability to interact with a wide range of disparate personality types. A civil servant, in the dispensation of his duties, is required to meet a diverse section of people who can be broadly classified into four types.

Bureaucrats: Officers of all the services need to interact with their contemporary, junior and senior bureaucrats. It is indispensable to interact genially with them, avoiding any conflict.

Corporates: Officers need to meet senior executives of the corporate sector who will themselves be sharp, ambitious, dynamic and charismatic; will sport a high acumen in their field; and will possess a flair for imposing their ideas and having the last word. It is important to establish a rapport with them and tactfully safeguard their interests.

Politicians: Civil servants work under ministers who are often difficult to deal with. Good interpersonal skills are imperative to maintain a cordial relation with these bosses.

Public: Given the numerous diversities prevalent in the country, civil servants may have to deal with an ignorant, unlettered old villager or a disgruntled aggressive NRI. They need to be extremely patient and tolerant with everyone.

Communication is the force by which an individual transmits stimuli to modify the behavior pattern of other individuals.

–Howland

'Communication' comes from Latin *communicare* which means 'to share'. Communication is a process by which information is exchanged between different entities or groups through a mutually-understood system of symbols, signs, and behaviour. The channel of communication can be visual (sight), auditory (hearing), olfactory (smell) or haptic (touch)/ tactile (like Braille).

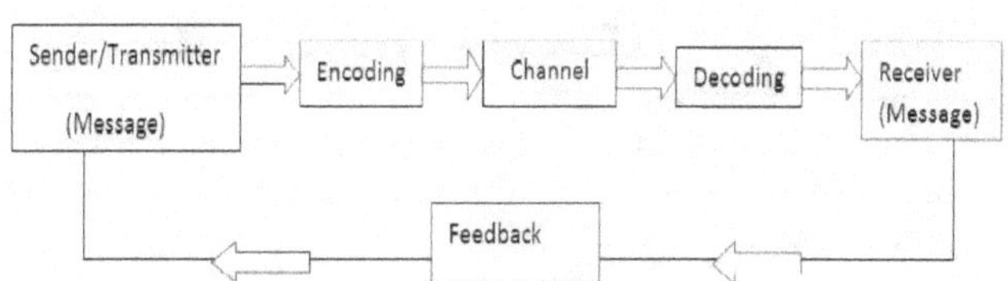

Communication works both ways—it involves putting across a point and receiving information and feedback. The receiving, however, is incomplete until the information has been accurately interpreted by the recipient.

COMMUNICATION

COMMUNICATION FLOWS AND NETWORKS

Communication flows in five directions.

1. Downward   2. Upward   3. Lateral
4. Diagonal   5. External

Communication channels accordingly form five kinds of networks. Create the figures below because they have been copied and therefore their labelling has to be changed. Text boxes will not change.

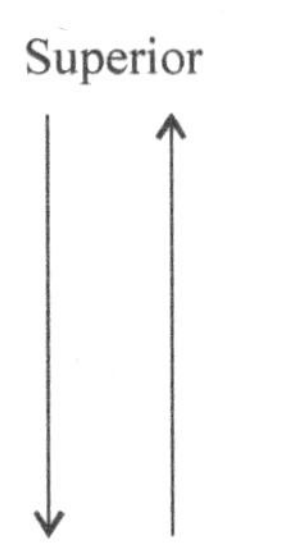

Vertical Network
Two-way, between the
superior and the subordinate

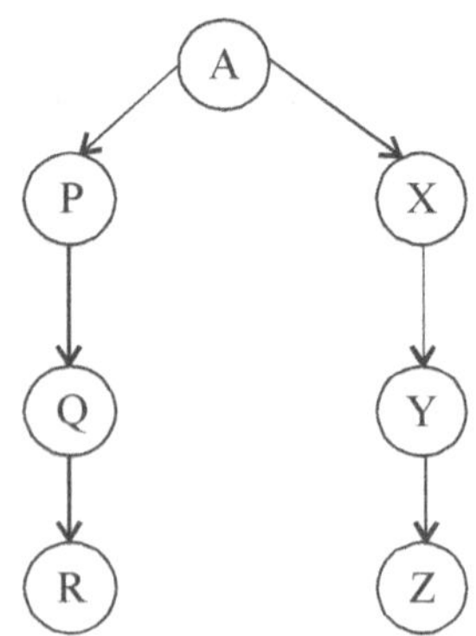

Chain of Command
From every superior to the
subordinate, in a hierarchy chain

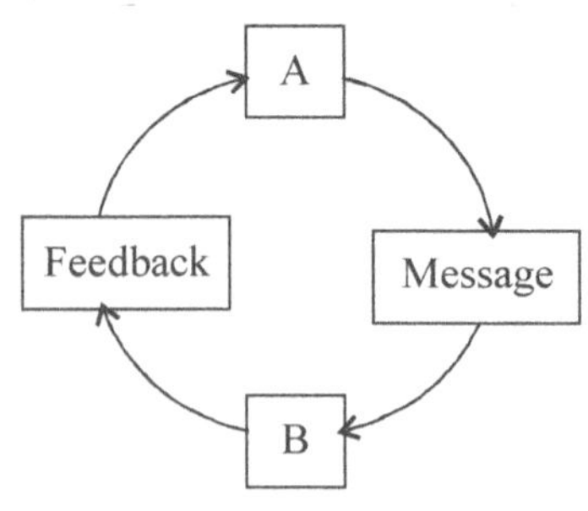

Circuit Network
Message from one to the
other and feedback to the
former, in a circuit

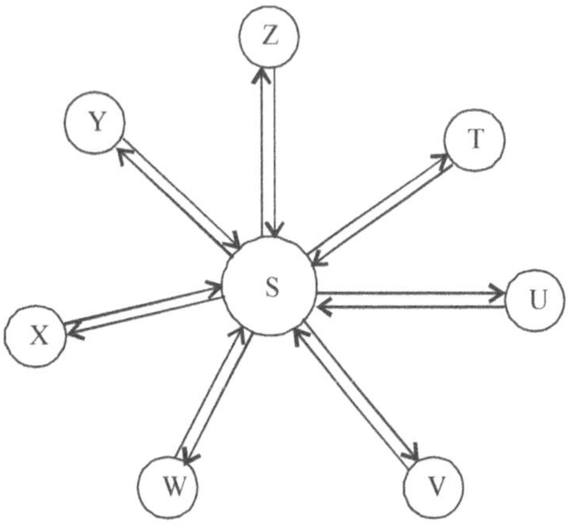

Wheel of Network
From one superior to
all subordinates

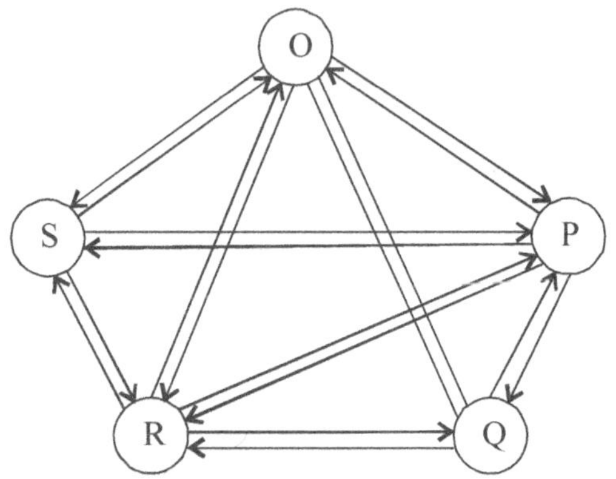

Star Channel
Each member of the group
communicates with another

TYPES OF INTERPERSONAL COMMUNICATION IN THE OFFICE

(a) **One Way Communication :** In one-way communication the manager or individual in charge of the workplace just gives a set of instructions to be followed by those who are working under him.

(b) **Two way Communication :** Two way communication is time consuming but it is more accurate and very rewarding in terms of higher productivity. In this case both the parties the worker and the person allotting work, spend time discussing the work procedures and work out a mutually acceptable method.

TYPES OF BUSINESS COMMUNICATION

There six different styles of communication used in business.

(A) Controlling Style

Managers use controlling style to impose discipline and get work done and to discourage employees from asking too many questions. This style is useful only during crises and that too if it is wielded by a respected and senior authority. Otherwise it only serves to alienate the workers.

(B) Structuring Style

Structuring style is used to impose schedules and discipline workers. Rules are cited with the objective of achieving goals. Here too alienation is created leading to resistance and low productivity.

(C) Egalitarian Style

Egalitarian style is a two way communication process where the other party is encouraged to come up with ideas and opinions. It is a very effective method of communication as it based on mutual understanding and respect.

(D) Withdrawing Style

Managers use the withdrawing style when they sit back and allow employees to do things their own ways. They exhibit a complete lack of interest and do not participate at all.

(E) Dynamic Style

In dynamic style the manager is a motivating factor trying to inspire his employees to deliver the desired results. This method is only effective if the employees are highly knowledgeable.

(F) Relinquishing Style

If employees are themselves knowledgeable, skillful and talented, relinquishing style is used. The manager is receptive to suggestions of his employees and adds his own ideas. The employees become team-mates of management.

BARRIERS/GAPS IN THE PROCESS OF BUSINESS COMMUNICATION

1. Complicated and obscure messages
2. Usage of jargon, slang, or unfamiliar terms
3. Misinterpretation of words, body language
4. Presumptions and prejudices
5. Personality conflicts
6. Emotional baggage
7. Generation gap
8. Mismatch of psychological, social or cultural contexts
9. Distractions like noise
10. Lack of follow up and feedback

Interaction between people does not happen in isolation; it is, indeed, a conglomeration of various contexts or environment, which are likely to give rise to conflict and stress in individuals and affect the group outcome.

1. **Psychical context:** the communicators' personality and background that governs individual thought and behaviour
2. **Relational context:** the relation between the communicators
3. **Cultural context:** the learned behaviours, norms and ethics that govern the interaction
4. **Social context:** the interrelation of social factors and site of the interaction
5. **Ethical contexts:** the set of ethics may differ for different parties

Management of conflict as well as stress is a prerequisite for effective team work.

CONFLICT MANAGEMENT

The different contexts, belief systems, values, needs, aspirations and ideas of individuals contribute to conflict which must be resolved for high productivity. So, conflict management skill is essential for high performance team work.

The following techniques help in conflict resolution:

1. Don't aim at winning or proving yourself right
2. Don't look to fix blame; find the root cause of problem
3. Acknowledge your emotions beforehand to identify the tangible cause of conflict
4. Collaborate with the other party on how to handle conflict
5. Keep your conversation goal-oriented
6. Recognise the other person's emotions and validate it aloud to assert that you're a good listener.
7. Admit if you go wrong or could have done better
8. Restrain yourself from directly accusing the other party for lapses; use terms like 'I guess', It appears', 'I believe', etc.
9. Focus on conduct rather than personality
10. Allow channels for open conversation to address conflict

STRESS MANAGEMENT

The disparity between the demands of the situation and the individual's capabilities for meeting those, leads to stress. Stress may be positive (*eustress*) when accompanied with high motivation and the sense of thrill in meeting challenges. Lack of drive and a feeling of utter hopelessness create negative stress (*distress*) and overstrain.

Research suggests the following strategies to manage negative stress:

1. Critically examine the problem from different angles to find a suitable way forward
2. Plan with prudence to minimize stressful situations
3. Regulate your breathing to relax your muscles and calm your mind
4. Fortify yourself by reflecting on your high values before facing a stressor
5. Employ your signature strength to find a novel way to counter the stressor
6. Maintain a balance of your top strengths; overuse as well as underuse of particular strengths leads to depression and stress
7. Forgive, let go and move on instead of lingering with the stressor
8. Take a pause and deliberate for a while on how best to tackle a stressor rather than reacting on a reflex

Honesty is important in interpersonal relations. If you say something and your body language conveys something else, you give out conflicting messages which erode trust. It is important to value others' time, space and comfort zone; wasting their valuable time through your ineffective communication or imposing yourself to the point of stifling them will only scuttle the chances of the desired outcome.

TIPS FOR EFFECTIVE VERBAL COMMUNICATION

1. Avoid wrong usage; choose your words carefully
2. Avoid ambiguity; be clear
3. Avoid cryptic or pompous words; use simple language for easy comprehension
4. Be coherent
5. Use courteous and respectful expressions
6. Use language that elicits a feedback
7. Allow others space and chance to voice their mind

TIPS FOR EFFECTIVE NON-VERBAL COMMUNICATION

1. Modulate your speech and wear a positive expression for **desired effect(paralanguage)**: The intonation, pitch and speed of speaking communicate your attitude and interest. Hesitation sounds like 'er..' mar the effect.
2. Regulate time of speaking and take desirable pauses (**chronemics**): Racing with your words will evoke negative emotions in the listener.
3. Be mindful of your posture, movements and gestures (**kinesics**): Leaning forward communicates receptiveness and interest. Slouching hints at disinterestedness. A nod or smile conveys encouragement. A frown, a straight look,

or rolling of your eyes communicates disapproval. Be sensitive to how the other person will interpret your motion. Inappropriate gestures send negative images.

4. Adopt friendly attitude: Friendly, flexible, respectful and open-minded attitude eases communication. Rigidity destroys headway.

5. Establish eye contact: It shows you're honest. Looking away hints at dishonesty in words.

6. Be focused: Avoid distractions. Lack of focus is noticeable and puts off the other person.

7. Touch the arm and shake hands (**haptics**): A firm handshake inspires trust; a two-handed shake expresses heartfelt emotions. A limp or clumsy handshake instills doubt. A high five establishes mutual approval. A touch on the arm or hand conveys empathy and assurance.

8. Allow comfortable space (**proxemics**): Be mindful of the other person's comfort zone. Moving too close may hint at a desire for intimacy. Being too far may suggest distancing and lack of feeling.

9. Adorn suitable attire and embellishments: The style and colour of your attire convey your outlook to life. The smell you wear conveys you attitude. Mild fragrance endears, strong can irritate and offend the other person. Make sensible choices to avoid conveying undesirable messages.

You may undertake periodic self-appraisal to assess and improve your interpersonal skills, including the art of communication. Record videos of your conversation with others and practice corrective steps to make your communication skills perfect.

TIPS TO BE A GOOD LISTENER

1. Avoid prejudice and presumption
2. Keep emotions in check, avoid over reaction
3. Wear a positive expression
4. Maintain good posture and lean forward
5. Be focussed
6. Establish eye contact
7. Nod in acknowledgement
8. Gently touch the other person's arm or squeeze, hand, to reassure that you understand and feel
9. Make good queries to demonstrate your involvement
10. Recapitulate the other person's words to assert that you are listening closely

PRINCIPLES OF EFFECTIVE INTERPERSONAL FOR CIVIL SERVANTS

Communication skills are a prerequisite for a civil servant given the high responsibility of public welfare that they shoulder and the challenges they face in dispensing their services to the complex social fabric of Indian diversities.

Certain principles can be laid out or effective Interpersonal Communication with all the four categories.

(A) As an officer and leader he should teach others to learn from their mistakes and not make an issue of it. The civil services environment demands that the officers should respect each others views on all topics.

(B) Instead of bickering or finding faults they should learn to put themselves in the other person's shoes and deal with them with affection and understanding. Such positive emotions will help not only others but also the officers themselves.

(C) While speaking to individuals it is not only important to express views clearly and succinctly but also to listen attentively to others. It would be better not to interrupt too frequently and wait till the opponent has had his say. To express ourselves clearly but briefly without going into a harangue should be our motto.

(D) If there are differences of opinion, it is important to ensure that there is no clash of egos. Just analyse the viewpoint only and not the person expressing it. Relationships are strengthened and bettered and not soured by such as approach.

(E) As a civil servant it would be expected that you would not divulge official secrets. This applies to interpersonal relationships also. Respect the confidentiality of not only your seniors but also your colleagues and your juniors. This will earn respect for you at your workplace.

Special rules for officers in the corporate environs: Officers who will hold high post in the corporate sector have to understand the different interpersonal communication styles employed in the business environment.

TIPS ON TACKLING QUESTIONS ON INTERPERSONAL SKILLS

You can score well provided you hone your own interpersonal communication skills. One of the most important aspects of building long, durable and stable relationships with people around you is development of the right attitude whether at work or play. We should be optimistic, be more empathetic than sympathetic in our dealings with others. A spiritual outlook towards life will help in developing these qualities. Just the understanding that life is ephemeral and that there is very limited time to do good in life, makes us more helpful and understanding. Another important thing to understand is that by helping others we only help ourselves. By making peace with all, we only increase the peace within. If we live life as if we were to die tomorrow, we will only be doing good to others and by default, to ourselves too. If you maintain such an atitude in life, you would likely not go wrong in the Inter Personal Communication questions.

TEST YOUR PERSONALITY

Answer the following questions by simply indicating your response (the number) from the suggestions given below:

Very frequently	Frequently	Often	Sometimes	Rarely	Never
1	2	3	4	5	6

Try to be as truthful as you can.
How often :

1. Are you sensitive to the moods of people you communicate with?

2. Do you lose your temper when people do not listen to you attentively?

3. Do you let your temper implode instead of exploding?

4. Do you ever sympathize or empathasize with the person who is telling you his problems ?

5. Can you express yourself clearly when you are facing an angry superior?

6. Do you observe the body language of the person you are speaking to?

7. How often do you interrupt a person who is speaking to you?

8. If a conversation does not interest you, do you get inattentive and irritable?

9. If someone gets dominating and bossy, do you start avoiding him ?

10. Are you an open book to all your acquaintances? Do you wear your heart on your sleeve?

11. If somebody hurts your feelings, are you strong enough to stand up for yourself?

12. Do you take criticism positively?

13. Do you try to overcome your faults by eliminating them ?

14. Do you enjoy a good equation with your boss at all the time?

15. Do you bring your workplace problems to your home?

16. When people working for you do not understand your point of your view, do you try to adjust yourself to their view point?

17. If a senior colleague has contradictory viewpoints do you deal with the situation diplomatically and tactfully ?

18. Are you flexible enough to control your moods based on the demands of the situation?

19. Do you have different ways of communicating with individuals coming from different backgrounds ?

20. Are you able to face pressures of meeting deadlines without tying your self up in knots?

21. Can you assess the mood of others by looking at them as you converse with them ?

22. Do you dominate conversations ?

23. Are you are able to resolve problems without showing emotions?

24. Do you find it easy to understand alternative point of views ?

25. While communicating with people, do you pay attention to their body language (ex. facial expression, hand movement, etc.) ?

26. Do you find yourself struggling to find the right words that expresses what you want to say ?

27. When you are angry, do you admit your anger ?

28. Can you sense when others are not able to understand what you are saying?

29. Are you completely at ease when a conversation shifts to topic of emotions?

30. Can you express your ideas clearly?

31. When you talk to others, do you put yourself in the other persons shoes?

32. Do you get caught up in what you have to say and become unaware of reactions of your listeners ?

33. When you know what the other person is going to say, do you complete the sentence for them?

34. Do you tend to misinterpret people's words?

35. Do you have difficulties in putting your thoughts into words?

36. Do emotionally charged situations make you uncomfortable?

37. People don't understand what you are conveying?

38. Do you fidget (e.g. play with hair, watch, pen) while listening to others?

39. You find it hard to express your feelings to others?

40. People tend to misinterpret what you say?

41. You postpone and avoid discussing touchy topics?

42. You have to repeat yourself often as people don't understand you the first time around?

43. If you don't understand someone's explanation the first time do you feel hesitant while asking for a clarification?

44. Are you able to confront someone who has hurt your feelings?

45. Do you flare up when dealing with someone you find intimidating?

46. You find it difficult to understand people who don't have the same point of view as you do?

47. You change the way you talk depending on who you are speaking to (e.g. speak slowly with someone whose first language isn't English; speak more professionally when in a meeting, etc.)?

48. You state your opinions, even if others disagree with you?

49. You believe that the best way to help others understand you is to be completely open about your feelings?

50. If you have something relevant to add, you'll interrupt and put forward your point of view.

51. When others become emotional, you are uncertain of your reaction?

52. People complain that you don't pay attention when they speak to you?

53. If you find a conversation boring, will you let your mind drift away ?

54. You are uncomfortable if you are not leading the conversation (e.g. choosing the topic, controlling the pace)?

55. You will stop a speaker mid-sentence if you disagree with a statement he has made ?

56. You try to divert or end conversations that don't interest you?

57. You are better off hiding your weaknesses so that no one will use the weakness against you?

58. You find it difficult to express your opinions when others don't share them?

ANALYSIS TABLE

100 - 200	→	Positive personality
between 200-250	→	Balanced personality
between 250 - 350	→	Negative personality

Exercise

Directions (Qs. 1-17) : *Fill in the blanks with the most appropriate answers :*

1. The ability to .... the feelings, emotions and problems conveyed by the opposite party is an important aspect of Interpersonal skills.
   (a) confront   (b) allay
   (c) understand   (d) remove

2. It is often surprising that the candidates who have academic excellence do not necessarily .... top positions in companies due to lack of interpersonal skills.
   (a) seek   (b) land
   (c) achieve   (d) upload

3. Technologically advanced methods of communication such as Email, audio and video conferencing require at least...................... interpersonal communication skills.
   (a) excellent   (b) improved
   (c) basic   (d) serious

4. All of us have our own needs to fulfil. The ability to .... the needs of others without completely sacrificing our own is an important aspect of interpersonal communication skills.
   (a) attenuate   (b) accommodate
   (c) focus on   (d) scrutinise

5. A successful leader has (i)...................... intercommunication skills; he is able to (ii)...................... his colleagues and juniors to his way of thinking without ruffling their feathers
   (a) (i) packed   (ii) argue
   (b) (i) colorful   (ii) conceptualize
   (c) (i) effective   (ii) persuade
   (d) (i) skeptical   (ii) rectify

6. In the metros especially in Delhi which is called a mini India people from diverse cultures and social backgrounds work together as a team adding their own (i)......................, insights, perspectives and skills to the (ii) .... whole.
   (a) (i) Knowledge (ii) coagulative
   (b) (i) Vocabulary (ii) collective
   (c) (i) Patience (ii) cognitive
   (d) (i) Ideology (ii) interactive

7. In the modern world of Information technology, where computers play a very important part, Interpersonal skills are useful not only in face to face communication but can also be put to good use in the .... world.
   (a) real   (b) scientific
   (c) virtual   (d) under

8. A leader has the ability to .... others through qualities such as a good personality, knowledge expertise, command of language, and the creation of mutual respect; all of which constitute interpersonal skills.
   (a) impact   (b) effect
   (c) control   (d) dominate

9. Interpersonal skills include the ability to .... the emotions, motivations, and behaviors of oneself and others during social interactions
   (a) influence   (b) affect
   (c) manage   (d) control

10. Those who have interpersonal skills are able to manage their behavior during social interactions and ....their goals to the goals of others while working as a team.
    (a) adjust   (b) align
    (c) put forth   (d) award

11. They are able to empathize and are ....to the needs of others and to the forces that mould the way that others feel and behave.
    (a) affected   (b) worried
    (c) sensitive   (d) bothered

12. They manage conflict effectively by devising win-win solutions, constructively influencing the behavior of others, and using effective communication ....
    (a) targets   (b) weapons
    (c) strategies   (d) goals

13. Many have wondered how it happens that persons with high IQs don't always get the top jobs: the answer often lies in ....skills.
    (a) intrapersonal   (b) interpersonal
    (c) orative   (d) writing

14. Modern teamwork often brings together individuals from diverse groups who may not share common norms, values, or salaries but who do offer .... expertise, insights, and perspectives.
    (a) strange   (b) unique
    (c) wonderful   (d) special

15. E-mail, voice mail, audio conferencing and videoconferencing, and the ....other technologies that enable individuals to communicate with each other not only increase the ways in which individuals can interact but also require a heightened sensitivity to the innuendos of interpersonal interactions.
    (a) myriad   (b) different
    (c) separate   (d) creative

16. This idea is particularly true in the worlds of virtual learning and virtual ...., where one cannot use hand gestures, facial expressions, or body language to fully express ideas.

(a) chatting   (b) teaching

(c) admissions   (d) communication

17. The challenge is to perfect interpersonal skills not only in .... interactions but in virtual interactions as well.

(a) real

(b) face-to-face

(c) social

(d) logical

II.   Directions (Qs. 18-65) : *The following questions are based on various situations that have been described in detail. Answers are to be given on the basis of these.*

SITUATION 1:

Wadekar was in charge of the Police station at Supriya Vihar. He was not only efficient and daring, but also tactful and diplomatic. So he was loved by one and all. He enjoyed an excellent equation with all those who worked at the police station. The public in Supriya Vihar also felt safe and secure due to his altruistic nature. One day, there was a burglary in the area. The whole area was searched but the culprits could not be found. Questions were raised on Wadekar's efficiency. Even his own colleagues did not spare him. Unable to bear the brunt of such criticism from the very people who he loved so much; Wadekar submitted his resignation.

18. Wadekar submitted his resignation because

(a) he was depressed.

(b) he felt insulted and let down.

(c) he was angry.

(d) he had no faith on anyone.

19. If you were Wadekar what would you have done?

(a) submitted your resignation

(b) fought with your detractors

(c) continued to work stoically

(d) complained to your superiors

20. According to you what was wrong with Wadekar's attitude?

(a) He was too sensitive.

(b) He was a loser.

(c) He was very egoistic.

(d) He lacked patience.

SITUATION 2:

Rakesh and Sameer were both health inspectors in charge of two adjacent constituencies in the Capital (New Delhi). They were not only colleagues from the same batch but also childhood friends. Both of them had to report to the commissioner who was equally happy with both. Dengue fever was spreading very rapidly in the capital. The government was beginning to get worried. The hospitals were overflowing. Even private hospitals reported lack of beds. Most patients were given prescriptions and asked to rest at home. Under such trying circumstances, people were attempting to gain admission into hospitals by hook or by crook. Health officials were inundated with requests. People would even stoop to offering bribes. Rakesh and Sameer being both honest and straightforward could not be easily lured by such tactics. Once it so happened that the son of the area MLA Mr. Rajesh Natarajan fell sick. He was diagnosed with dengue. The MLA who belonged to Rakesh's constituency sent an SOS expecting him to cooperate fully in such an enquiry. But Rakesh being Rakesh was not moved. The enraged MLA sought Sameer's help with promises of promotions in the future. Sameer could not withstand temptation; he gladly extended a helping hand. Rakesh reported the matter to the commissioner. Sameer was suspended for corrupt practices. The two friends became sworn enemies.

21. Why do you think Rakesh reported the matter to the commissioner?

(a) He did not like Sameer.

(b) He wanted to create an impression on the commissioner.

(c) He was so honest and principled that he could not tolerate Sameer's dishonesty.

(d) He hoped to get a promotion by exposing Sameer.

22. The two become sworn enemies when

(a) the MLA favored one over the other.

(b) they fought with each other.

(c) Sameer was suspended for corrupt practices.

(d) they developed different outlooks.

23. What would you have done had you been in Sameer's place?

(a) I would have requested the MLA to use his own resources.

(b) I would have sent him back to Rakesh.

(c) I would have expressed my inability to intervene in the given situation.

(d) both (a) and (c)

24. Do you think Rakesh did the right thing by complaining to the commissioner?

What would you have done ?

(a) No. I would have overloked the whole episode.

(b) Yes. I would want the guilty to be punished.

(c) No. I would have reasoned with Sameer.

(d) Yes. I would not want Sameer to get ahead of me.

SITUATION 3:

Aseema Ali was an LDC in the ministry of Defence. She had three children and her husband was an Inspector in the police. Her children were good at studies, well behaved and always smartly turned out. She was indeed a happy camper. Her lifestyle generated much envy among her neighbours and relatives. Under such circumstances it was surprising that her face always wore a frown. Something was obviously causing a nagging worry; Aseema was getting increasingly upset with the apathy of her section officer Mr. Hariharan. While some of her colleagues who were much junior to her were getting promoted as UDC's or even assistants, she had been working in the same post for the last twenty years. Her depression made her look for other avenues for peace. Her leaves were getting exhausted. She took many days off and started spending more and more time at home looking after her children, cooking for them. Cooking had been a childhood passion. She got selected in a cooking realty show on T.V. She took this opportunity to go on a long leave, away from her work.

25. Do you think she did the right thing by going on a long leave? Why?
    (a) No, she should have faced the problem.
    (b) Yes, it is better to avoid a confrontation.
    (c) No, she should have spoken to the media.
    (d) Yes, she needed a break.

26. What would you have done had you been in her place?
    (a) I would have gone in for voluntary retirement.
    (b) I would have reported the matter to my superiors.
    (c) I would have held a discussion with my section officer.
    (d) I would have applied for a transfer from the section.

SITUATION 4:

Kunjan was a hardworking and serious girl. She was an all-rounder who was equally good at academics and sports. So it was not surprising that she cleared the civil services exam with flying colours and opted for the Indian police service. Her firm and disciplinary attitude coupled with a high degree of physical fitness made her most suitable for the job. As the years passed by, her responsibilities went on increasing at the workplace. Her efficiency increased with each successive promotion. Her ideas, initiatives and their subsequent implementation earned her awards not only in India but also abroad. Her success caused envy among both male and female colleagues. She was soon competing for the post of police commissioner with two of her colleagues who were males. Almost every one was sure that she would be selected for the post. Unfortunately, one of her male colleagues was made the police commissioner. Kunjan resigned from the IPS in protest.

27. Kunjan resigned from the IPS in protest. Why?
    (a) She wanted to be the commissioner.
    (b) She was pressurised by her family.
    (c) Her superiors asked her to resign.
    (d) One of her male colleagues was made the commissioner.

28. Her chances of becoming the police commissioner was very bright because
    (a) she was ambitious.
    (b) she was loved by all.
    (c) her performance record was perfect.
    (d) she was competing with two male colleagues.

29. Do you think Kunjan reacted rightly? Why?
    (a) Yes, after all she had worked so hard for the country.
    (b) No, she should have been more patient. Talent never goes unrewarded.
    (c) Yes. There is something wrong with the system.
    (d) No. She should have protested in some other way.

SITUATION 5:

Rajat was absorbed as the finance officer in a bank. He belonged to a middle class family and was extremely happy to land such a lucrative job. As time passed he impressed all his superiors with his integrity and honesty. He was soon promoted to the post of manager. But there was a twist in this happy turn of events. He was transferred to a rural area. Rajat knew very well that if he refused the transfer, he would not get the promotion either. So he agreed to go leaving his old parents and an unmarried sister behind. Once Rajat took over the reigns of the village bank, he won the hearts of the villagers with his modest nature and compassionate heart. The farmers in the village were a worried lot. They were neck deep in debts and were being mercilessly exploited by the moneylenders. They approached Rajat seeking relief from such torture. Rajat promised to help them out. He sent an email to the head office explaining the predicament of the farmers and wanted loans sanctioned for at least some of them. His superiors were unmoved. There was no response; obviously they were more concerned about profits In the meantime five farmers attempted suicide. Two of them died while the other three were saved in the nick of time. A desperate Rajat decided to take matters into his own hands. Loans were quickly sanctioned to the surviving farmers. His seniors in the head office came to know of this. Rajat was suspended within a week's time.

30. Rajat's superiors were impressed with
    (a) his ability to work long hours.
    (b) the honesty and integrity in all his dealings.
    (c) his communication abilities.
    (d) his outstanding academic record.

31. His promotion as a manager was conditional because

(a) he could either accept or deny it.

(b) he would have to remain unmarried.

(c) he would now have to work in a far-flung village.

(d) he would have to leave family behind.

32. The villagers loved Rajat because

(a) he worked very hard.

(b) he was their guest.

(c) he held a powerful position.

(d) he was humble and sympathetic.

33. The farmers in the village were worried because

(a) the crops had failed that year.

(b) they were unable to pay their debts.

(c) they were being harassed by the money lenders.

(d) both (b) and (c).

34. Why do you think the farmer sought Rajat's help?

(a) He was the manager of the village bank.

(b) They knew he cared for them.

(c) He was kind and compassionate.

(d) both (a) and (c).

35. Rajat sought permission from the head office to

(a) get loans sanctioned to at least some of the farmers.

(b) help the farmers grow more crops.

(c) issue a warning to the money lenders.

(d) go on a long leave.

36. Rajat decided to take matters into his own hands because

(a) there was no response from the head office.

(b) one or two farmers had committed suicide.

(c) he was desperate.

(d) all of the above.

37. His seniors at the bank were so angry that they

(a) called him back.

(b) fired him.

(c) suspended him.

(d) filed an FIR against him.

38. Had you been in Rajat's shoes what would you have done?

(a) I would have made repeated appeals to the Head office.

(b) I would have gone down to the head office and spoken directly to the manager along with the evidence.

(c) I would have arranged for funds from elsewhere.

(d) I would have taken the money lenders to task.

SITUATION 6:

She seemed to turn out error-free work at an amazing pace. Her attention to detail was admired by all who used her services. She seldom committed even a minor typing error. Last month, Saritha was appointed as the officer in charge at the administrative department. It was her first management experience. But, very soon problems surfaced. Leela, a typist with four years of experience went to Sankar, the manager to complain about the 'unbelievable nit-picking'.

'I can't seem to do anything right, according to Saritha,' complained Leela. 'She checks everything I type. She is driving me nuts, not to mention the fact that my output has slowed down dramatically. Just yesterday, Mr. Desai, that new Vice President - Marketing made a wise crack about cobwebs growing on his report before he could get it out of typing.'

When Sankar asked about Leela's concern, Saritha flew off the hands. 'We are supposed to be the best typing pool in the company. After all, we type for the top people. The work has to be perfect.' She was almost screaming. Then she slumped in a chair in Sankar's office.

'Sankar, I am going nuts up there. None of my people seem to care about the quality of the work, the way I do. I have been working till nine or ten every night checking work and just trying to keep up. I am just about convinced that being a supervisor is just not worth it.'

39. According to you, why did Leela, complain about Saritha?

(a) She was acting bossy.

(b) Leela is jealous of Saritha.

(c) Saritha is making her work very hard.

(d) Professional differences.

40. Leela's concern about Saritha is because

(a) she is afraid of Saritha's growing authority.

(b) Saritha is a very tough boss.

(c) she perceives a threat to her job.

(d) she perceives a threat to her performance and career.

41. Saritha's reaction to Sankar's enquiry shows

(a) her devotion for the company.

(b) her concern for quality work.

(c) she is a perfectionist by nature.

(d) her frustration about the subordinates.

42. According to you, the problem with Saritha is that

(a) she has no management experience.

(b) she lacks leadership.

(c) she is too concerned about quality.

(d) she is obsessed with perfection.

43. If you were Sankar, what would you have done?

(a) Promoted Leela

(b) Demoted Leela

(c) Ignored the issue

(d) Introduced conflict-resolving interventions

SITUATION 7:

Vijesh, an Accountant of SP College was promoted as a Treasurer and Chief Accountant in charge of Finance. He was delegated with sufficient powers both regarding inflow and outflow of cash. He was accountable (for whatever he did) to the Director, Riteshan under whose direct control he functioned. Normally, no questions were asked by the Director on any expenditure incurred by Vijesh. However, there had been occasions when the Director had frowned upon some of the actions of Vijesh. Vijesh, therefore, had to take abundant caution at times, with regard to cash inflow and outflow.

Anshul was a colleague of Vijesh and he was incharge of the academic side of the college. Anshul and Vijesh were friends and were having excellent coordination and inter-personal relations. Anshul was also reporting to Riteshan, the Director. There were no problems between any of them since they were adopting a 'give and take' policy and usually discussed any problem and were coming to a mutually agreed solution.

Jivesh, is a great friend of Anshul. Jivesh had a college going son who was not brilliant but just above average. Jivesh's son was studying in a different college. Jivesh wanted to ensure a good career for his son. Because of campus interviews and selections in SP College, a good start was always available to its students that had earned a big name. Jivesh brought his son to Anshul for advice. Anshul, without a word, admitted the boy in SP College. Anshul also waived the tuition and other fees due to the college. He also promised Jivesh of further help regarding books, etc. When the report regarding this went to Vijesh, he was unhappy that at a time when there was a financial crunch Anshul sought to favour his friend so much. However, he did not express anything, controlled the feelings within himself and behaved as if nothing had happened.

After about two months, Anshul felt that his room needed a renovation and therefore, submitted to Vijesh, the Chief Accountant;a proposal with estimates, etc., to incur some expenditure in renovation. Vijesh felt that at that juncture the renovation expenditure was unnecessary and hence, did not accept the proposal and returned it back stating that this was an unnecessary expenditure. Anshul was very unhappy over this. He wanted somehow to get what he wanted. He therefore, approached the Director, Riteshan with his demand. Though Riteshan felt that the expenditure was not wholly justified, he passed orders allowing part renovation. Vijesh on seeing this, felt let down. He sent in his resignation.

Riteshan was puzzled on seeing the resignation letter and sent for Vijesh to discuss about it.

44. Vijesh turned down Anshul proposal for renovation because
    (a) renovation expenditure was unnecessary.
    (b) he wanted to show his displeasure.
    (c) Anshul was again trying to take unnecessary advantage/favour.
    (d) Vijesh wanted cut down cost for the college.

45. Director Riteshan partially approved Anshul's proposal because
    (a) he didn't want to disappoint Anshul.
    (b) Anshul's proposal was genuine.
    (c) partial renovation was required.
    (d) both (c) and (a)

46. According to you, this kind of confrontation can be best described as :
    (a) Inter-Individual
    (b) Intra-Individual
    (c) Inter-Personal
    (d) Organisational

SITUATION 8:

Ritesh has been a clerk in a business firm for over a decade. He feels that he has been doing his work efficiently. However, the promotion to a supervisory position, which he has been expecting, has never materialised. He feels sad about it, and a little angry with his manager, Krishnan, who is responsible for promotions.

Ritesh feels that a deserving promotion has been denied to him and he attributes it to the fact that Krishnan belongs to a community different from his. This feeling has gone to such an extent that Ritesh has become somewhat negligent in his work. He keeps a book of poems which he quietly reads in the office in moments of dullness. He has even begun to write poems - a practice of his college days - and now he does so even in his office occasionally and delights in it. He even thinks of giving up his clerical job and imagines himself sitting on the chair of the sub-editor of a magazine which has published two of his poems under a pseudonym (false name).

47. Ritesh's negligent behaviour is due to
    (a) Ritesh's not being promoted.
    (b) Ritesh's attitude toward Krishnan.
    (c) Krishnan's attitude toward Ritesh.
    (d) Ritesh's perception of injustice.

48. Ritesh's writing poetry in office is
    (a) his pastime.
    (b) his way to give vent to his feelings.
    (c) his serious decision to switch careers.
    (d) his reply to Krishnan's biased behaviour.

49. Ritesh's behaviour of neglecting work and writing poems is :

(a) Angry behaviour

(b) Frustrated behaviour

(c) Normal behaviour

(d) Constructive behaviour

50. Whose responsibility is it to break this deadlock between Ritesh and Krishnan?

(a) Only Krishnan's

(b) Only Ritesh's

(c) Both Ritesh's & Krishnan's

(d) There is no need

SITUATION 9:

'Sriram Industries' is a mechanical engineering establishment situated in Bombay. It has 15,000 workmen employed in first shift between 8-16 hours. This is a major shift and is known as the general shift. The workmen of Sriram Industries report for work from distant places such as Pune, Virar and also Karjat which are miles away from the place of work. The workers travel by Central Railway, Western Railway (suburban services) and by BEST buses (BEST is the local municipal bus transport organisation). Some also travel by petrol driven vehicles, or their own bicycles. A small number staying in surrounding areas of the factory, report for duty on foot.

On 27 June, 1990, there was a very heavy downpour which is not uncommon in Bombay. Vast areas were submerged under water. Central and Western suburban railway services, therefore, were completely disrupted. As a result of the heavy rains, train services were suspended between 7 and 8 a.m. Frequency of BEST buses dropped and in some areas there was no bus service at all. A few time keepers who somehow managed to reach the factory took the attendance. It was found that out of the total contingent, 4000 were in time, 2600 reached two hours late, 4800 were four hours late and the remaining 3600 did not attend.

As was obvious, neither the management nor the workmen were responsible for the aforesaid happening and the trade union, operating in the establishment requested the management to deal sympathetically with the employees. They requested that since it was beyond the control of workmen, even those who could not attend should not be marked 'absent'.

The union leader had produced a certificate from Railway authorities and also BEST authorities about complete dislocation between 7 and 8.30 a.m. and a partial dislocation till 2.30 p.m. As will be seen from the case, 4000 employees worked for the whole day, 2600 worked for six hours, 4800 worked for four hours only and 3600 did not report for duty at all. The issue was how to adjust the wages for the day. The General Manager called a meeting of the officers to discuss the issue. It was found that a good number of officers who stayed in long distance suburbs or were staying in remote areas could also not attend to work. Some of the officers who participated in the meeting, opined that 'no-work-no-pay' should be the only principle and at best, the only relief the management should give is not to take any disciplinary action, as such. Others expressed different views and there was no near-consensus even in the meeting. The General Manager adjourned the meeting without coming to any decision. Relations between the management and the three unions operating in the Company were generally satisfactory.

Only one of the three unions which had mainly white collared staff as members had a legalistic approach in all matters and was not easily satisfied.

51. The case deals with
(a) rain problems in Mumbai .
(b) distances causing difficulties to workers .
(c) absenteeism.
(d) worker-Management relations in solving issues .

52. 'A large number of workers reported late due to heavy downpour and disruption of transport services'. This shows

(a) the workers' commitment to work.

(b) their casual attitude toward work.

(c) their indiscipline and misbehaviour.

(d) their being opportunistic.

53. 'Some of the officers also didn't come to work due to rain.' This shows that

(a) the situation was really difficult.

(b) they were having a good time.

(c) they are not scared of management.

(d) rules for them are different.

54. Officers present that day pressed for 'No-Work-No-Pay' because

(a) they really felt that way

(b) they wanted to support the management

(c) they wanted to teach absenting workers a lesson

(d) they wanted to somehow harm the position of absenting officers

55. The General Manager seems to be
(a) a very professional man.
(b) a welfare loving man.
(c) a confused person.
(d) an able Manager faced with conflicting alternatives.

56. Legalist approach of one of the unions is reflective of
(a) their love of law & order.
(b) their perceived superiority over the other two unions because of their white collar membership.
(c) their being hand-in-glove with the management.
(d) their constant endeavour to show the other two unions down.

III   Direction (Qs. 57-150) : *Choose the correct response for each of these situations.*

57. On a particularly difficult day, you are the only officer available to deal with the public; you would
(a) ask for additional staff.
(b) take a leave.
(c) just do your portion of the work.
(d) do your level best to solve the problems of the people.

58. If you get angry due to unforeseen circumstances at the workplace, you would
(a) get violent.
(b) maintain a stony silence.
(c) try to occupy your mind with something else.
(d) walk away in a huff.

59. If you are an officer in the civil services and find that one of your juniors is not working properly you would
(a) suspend him.
(b) warn him.
(c) talk to your superiors about him.
(d) talk to him and try to find out his problem.

60. If someone from the underworld turns up with a request for revealing government secrets in exchange for an undisclosed very lucrative reward, you would
(a) postpone the matter.
(b) report the matter to your superiors.
(c) say yes without hesitation.
(d) say no without any hesitation.

61. Two of your closest colleagues are having strained relations. How will you handle the situation?
(a) you will speak to each of them separately.
(b) discuss the problem with them.
(c) ask them to avoid each other.
(d) pretend that you know nothing about it.

62. There was much ruckus created before the hosting of the Commonwealth Games about the poor conditions in the games village. The Chief Minister Sheila Dikshit was the main target of criticism. Had you been in her place, how you have reacted to the whole situation?
(a) I would have pulled up the media for unnecessary defamation of the country.
(b) I would have inspected the site and then supervised the renovation of the whole place.
(c) I would have held a meeting of heads all departments and requested them to rectify their mistakes.
(d) I would have threatened to stop payments to all people concerned unless the whole situation was rectified.

63. The government has banned the use of polythene bags but these bags are still being used rampantly. As an animal rights activist you are getting increasingly concerned with the death of cows due to consumption of plastic bags. How will you get people to follow the law?
(a) Bring up the matter in the media
(b) File a petition in the court
(c) Hold a public meeting on the issue
(d) both (a) and (b)

64. The CBSE grading system is not going down very well with parents, teachers and even a section of the students. This is brought to the notice of the CBSE chairman during a conference of the chairpersons from different states. He is quite disturbed and decides to do something about it. What do you think would be the best course of action?
(a) He should wait for a few more sessions and see how the system can be changed.
(b) He should call for a meeting and build a general consensus on the issue.
(c) He should make some modifications to the system.
(d) He should ignore the messages as nothing but rumours.

65. Recently there was a shocking incident about a sessions judge demanding dowry in his own marriage. The dowry system should be completely eradicated. It is quite clear that only making laws will not do. If you were in the judge's shoes how would you help to get rid of this evil system?
(a) I would ask my father in law to present a pen as dowry for my marriage.
(b) I would not take a single paisa but make sure that the marriage got wide media coverage.
(c) I would go in for a registered marriage.
(d) both (a) and (c)

66. Stories of adulterated foodstuff are, unfortunately, many. Perhaps this is one of the main reasons why the number of people falling sick is increasing day by day. As Food Inspector of your area what major steps would you take to bring this problem under control?
(a) The punishment to people caught in the act will be to cancel their licences and prevent them from supplying food in the future.
(b) Conduct regular raids on food factories.
(c) Take suspicious characters to the police station for questioning.
(d) both (a) and (b)

67. If your best friend and batchmate wants to borrow a certain sum of money from you, say, ₹50,000, you would
(a) refuse.
(b) try to postpone the matter.
(c) ask him/ her for what purpose the money is needed and then decide accordingly.
(d) give the money immediately; after all he is your best friend.

68. The Jessica Lall murder case once again caught the attention of the public when a film was made on the same. Had you been a member of the victim's family, would you have allowed such a film to be made? Why or why not?

(a) I would not allow such a film to be made as it would open up old wounds.

(b) I would allow the film to be made provided the scenes were depicted factually.

(c) I would allow it as it would serve as a lesson to the general public.

(d) both (b) and (c)

69. You had gone to visit Amritsar and happened to attend the function at the much talked about Wagah border. Due to strict security regulation you got separated from your spouse. How would you handle such a situation?

(a) I would wait for my spouse at the place where we deposited our belongings.

(b) I would wait at the entrance so that my spouse would join me soon.

(c) I would ask the security personnel to help me out.

(d) I would hold up a placecard to help my spouse locate me.

70. The day before the interview for the civil services is to take place, a neighbour who is an IAS officer tells you that it is extremely difficult to get through. You

(a) stop preparing and start calling up your coaching centre.

(b) console yourself saying that there are always other options available.

(c) go and visit all the nearby temples promising to offer God a gold coin if you get through.

(d) don't bother much as you are fully confident that you have prepared well.

71. What are your work habits like? You

(a) prefer to work during the day only

(b) you are a nightbird

(c) can work extra hours if required

(d) require an afternoon gap

72. You are holding a high position in the state government. A junior officer has the temerity to point out a few silly mistakes made by you while implementing a particular project.

(a) You get very angry and issue a suspension letter

(b) You just ignore him and ask him to mind his own business

(c) You feel very upset and miserable but deal with it tactfully

(d) You are thankful that you are getting a chance to rectify your errors.

73. Your arch-rival during your college days has met with an accident. You come to know of this from a common friend. Your immediate reaction is

(a) one of absolute indifference.

(b) you feel sorry for him but feel that life has to go on.

(c) you feel that he has only paid for his mistakes.

(d) you decide to go and meet him in the hospital.

74. Your immediate boss takes all the credit for an important project on which you had spent sleepless nights. You decide to

(a) take a transfer.

(b) continue working hard stoically.

(c) learn from your mistakes.

(d) tell all that it is you who did all the work.

75. Which would be the most important factor which will help you to decide whether to take up a job for which you have been selected?

(a) the salary

(b) chances for promotion and growth

(c) the freedom to implement some of your own ideas at the work place

(d) all the above

76. Ragging has been banned in colleges; still, one comes across instances of ragging especially in Engineering colleges. As Education Minister, what steps would you take to put a complete end to this practice?

(a) take more stringent legal action against the wrong doers

(b) debar them from pursuing further studies in India

(c) appoint special Inspectors in school to keep a check on ragging

(d) all of the above

77. The newly constructed Metro Railway services are beginning to report technical snags almost everyday. If you were in charge of the Metro Railway Corporation, what steps would you take to put a stop to these persistent problems?

(a) pull the metro staff up for inefficiency

(b) suspend the services for a few months

(c) educate the commuters about how to deal with such situations.

(d) employ highly skilled engineers for trouble shooting.

78. The U.S. President Obama visited India in 2010. One of his main purposes was to create more jobs for his countrymen. The Indian Prime Minister Dr. Manmohan Singh clearly stated that Indians were not trying to steal U.S. jobs. If you were the US President, what steps would you take to root out the problem of rising unemployment in your country?

(a) make strict laws to stop outsourcing

(b) tell Americans to stop all dealings with India.

(c) tell Americans to build their skills to bring them on par with other nations and to take more qualifications

(d) start sending Americans abroad to work.

79. One constantly hears of passwords being hacked on the internet. Suppose that you are the manager of a famous bank; and your site has been hacked. What immediate steps would you take?

(a) Close the site down for a few days

(b) change the passwords

(c) Install more efficient security software

(d) all of the above

80. Do you think that one should change one's job often and face new situation?
   (a) No, unless compelled one should not leave his old job.
   (b) Yes, every new job is challenging and one should accept the challenge
   (c) No, as it takes time to get adjusted
   (d) No, as the new situation may not suit you

81. What will you do if you find an aged person who has lost his road orientation?
   (a) avoid the matter totally
   (b) help him with some money
   (c) collect the necessary information related to his destination and guide him accurately
   (d) just show sympathy and give suggestion to contact the nearest police station.

82. You are suffering from diabetes. When you see a whole lot of chocolates, you are tempted to eat them. But you also realise that they are not good for you in the long run. What do you do?
   (a) You would not eat them because you know the harmful effects.
   (b) You decide not to eat them but keep thinking about them.
   (c) You would eat them but feel guilty about what you have done.
   (d) You would give in to the temptation and eat the chocolates without being bothered about the consequences.

83. You have worked hard on an idea which you believe would be a breakthrough. But the presentation does not go as you had hoped it would. You
   (a) ignore all the suggestions and believe that you were correct.
   (b) break down and get all emotional.
   (c) take this as a learning experience and convince yourself that you would do better next time.
   (d) feel like a loser.

84. Your colleague is not performing his duties up to the mark. You will
   (a) just do your part of the duties and enjoy your work.
   (b) take advantage of it to promote yourself.
   (c) report the matter to the seniors.
   (d) try and handle his customers to maintain the company's status

85. The Lajpat Nagar and Sarojini Nagar bomb blasts in the capital are hard to forget. Had you been among the survivors in such a bomb blast, what would have been your first instinct under such trying conditions?
   (a) I would have immediately started looking for my near and dear ones.
   (b) I would have been too shocked to react.
   (c) I would have tried to help save as many people as I could.
   (d) both (a) and (c).

86. Your boss has given you some urgent assignment at the last minute. What would you do?
   (a) Try to finish the job as per its requirement
   (b) Tell him that you would do it next day.
   (c) Request one of your colleagues to help you
   (d) None of these.

87. Your bathroom tap is leaking and is very noisy. You would
   (a) sleep with pillows upon your ears.
   (b) put a bucket underneath.
   (c) try to put up a cork upon the mouth of the tap.
   (d) call a plumber to repair the tap.

88. You are a social worker. On visiting an orphanage, you see a child who is not ready to let you go away.
   (a) You ignore the child because you have other kids to attend to.
   (b) You leave with no concern.
   (c) You decide to visit him every Sunday.
   (d) You talk to the authorities and arrange for parents who can adopt him.

89. You are a team leader and you are supposed to hold a convention on HR issues. But your team members are unable to get adequate sponsorship.
   (a) You put in your money and hold the event as scheduled.
   (b) You try and motivate them that they can do it.
   (c) You postpone the event and give them some more time.
   (d) You tell them things can not work out like this and cancel the event.

90. After your graduation, you are offered a well-paid government job. However, your friend says that you have to bribe to get the appointment order. You
   (a) go to some influential politician who can help.
   (b) accept the job by paying the bribe, consoling yourself that this is the present social setup.
   (c) accept the job by paying the bribe, but firmly resolve that this is the last time you will pay bribe.
   (d) flatly refuse the offer.

91. The Chief Minister of a state had a shoe hurled at him for the second time in four months. Many of our leaders have had to pass through this better experience of having shoes hurled at them. Had you been in their place, how would you have reacted to such harassment?
   (a) pulled up the security personnel for a lapse of duty on their part
   (b) would have put the culprits in prison
   (c) remained unfazed
   (d) used it as a weapon to gain publicity

92. When it was predicted that the world would be destroyed in 2012, experts came up with some scientific evidence to boot. The luminosity of the Northern Lights would increase and mobile phones, national grids and global positioning systems would trip. As Chairman of the ISRO, you would have been highly disturbed and would have resolved to
   (a) put corrective systems in place as fast as possible to prevent such an occurrence.
   (b) carry out a detailed research about the validity of such an argument
   (c) assess the extent of damage that may take place.
   (d) all of the above.

93. Human brain stem cells can be grown in rats; so there is hope for patients of epilepsy and Parkinson's disease. On hearing this news, as head of the neuroscience department of AIIMS, you resolve to
   (a) start research on this immediately.
   (b) approach the state government for funds for this research.
   (c) convey the good news to your patients
   (d) (a) and (b) only.

94. When you pass by a dead body, you
   (a) feel like crying and keep thinking about it for the rest of the day.
   (b) join hands in prayer.
   (c) don't fear death, so remain unperturbed.
   (d) get captured by the memory of a recent death in your family.

95. When communicating information on an important company policy change, what sort of medium would you choose?
   (a) Written communication alone
   (b) Oral communication alone
   (c) Written communication followed by oral communication
   (d) Oral communication followed by written communication

96. An angry customer wants to meet the senior manager for grievance reporting. What will you do as the manager?
   (a) Talk to him yourself and try to cool him down.
   (b) argue with him
   (c) try to remove his inconvenience by consulting seniors
   (d) tell him it is not easy to meet the senior manager.

97. You can manage your emotions well. You
   (a) get upset when others do not behave properly.
   (b) are least interested about what others are thinking about you.
   (c) can keep your face smiling even when you are terribly disgusted.
   (d) feel that you should not conceal your attitude from others.

98. Friendship to you is
   (a) a conditional relationship.
   (b) an emotional language.
   (c) a burden.
   (d) an understanding between two or more people.

99. Oprah Winfrey has been adjudged as the most charitable celebrity. If you were in Oprah's place, what precautions would you take to ensure that all the money was spent for the targeted causes?
   (a) ask my staff to do a complete research before the money is handed over
   (b) employ staff to keep a track of the money after it changes hands
   (c) give money only to highly reputed organisations
   (d) be happy to have been of use to someone and think no more about it.

100. Bill Gates is known the world over for having changed people's lives with technology. Almost everyone knows that Gates was a class IX drop out. Had you been in Gates place at that particular point of time, how would you have reacted?
   (a) I would have felt very demoralised and disheartened.
   (b) I would have resolved to continue my education.
   (c) I would have resolved to look for a job.
   (d) I would have been too absorbed in my computer to bother much about it.

101. The CFC'S in cans of perfume, hair spray, deodorants, etc., can damage the ozone layer. Under such conditions what would you do?
   (a) stop using cosmetics altogether
   (b) use them but not frequently
   (c) not be bothered at all
   (d) stop using such cosmetics and tell others to stop using them, too

102. The headlines say Sun Pharma eyes $ 300 million acquisition in U.S. Suppose you are the head of Sun Pharma. You would
   (a) throw a celebration party.
   (b) follow a wait and watch policy.
   (c) move out of India.
   (d) start making further plans.

103. The Logistic, Industry is having excellent growth prospect. So, from Reliance to Cafe Coffee Day, India is queuing up for a share of the logistics pie. If you were the Managing Director of Reliance, how would you react to this news?
   (a) start looking for quick acquisition
   (b) carry out a detailed study
   (c) be indifferent.
   (d) see what others do.

104. Saina Nehwal became world no. 1 in badminton rankings after beating the reigning champion from China. If you were Saina,
   (a) you would be deliriously happy.
   (b) you would resolve to work even harder.
   (c) you would accept that the No. 1 spot is tough to retain
   (d) all of the above

105. Your college has organised a blood donation camp. You
   (a) persuade your friends to donate.
   (b) donate your blood at the camp.
   (c) do not believe in donating blood and decide not to attend.
   (d) yourself donate blood and ask others to do so too.

106. You are in a new place and you want to go shopping. What is the most likely thing that you would do?
   (a) totally drop the idea of shopping
   (b) find out the place on your own
   (c) ask someone who knows the place, to come with you
   (d) ask someone else to do the shopping for you

107. You own a pharmaceutical company. You have received information that someone who is not an employee has tampered with certain types of tablets in a specific area, which has caused some deaths in that area. In such a crisis, what will you do?
   (a) not launch a campaign to alert the people, as this incident can have a negative effect on your company's reputation and earnings and can lead to losses.
   (b) launch a campaign to alert the public and recall tablets from the specific area
   (c) recall tablets from only the specific area and not the whole country
   (d) recall those tablets from the entire country despite the fact that the tampering of tablets occurred in a certain area

108. After having committed to your family that you would be taking them out on a vacation, you suddenly find yourself wanted in a board meeting which unfortunately clashes with the vacation. What would you do?

 (a) assuming it to be urgent, start making necessary arrangement to ensure that the objective of the meeting is fulfilled, thus cancelling the vacation

 (b) find out what the urgent meeting is all about and make necessary arrangements and postpone your vacation

 (c) proceed with your vacation plans without making any arrangement

 (d) try and get out of that situation by asking your colleague to cover up for you.

109. You are getting late for your college and no bus is available. In such a situation

 (a) you start walking

 (b) you drop the idea of going to college that day and return home

 (c) you think about other possible conveyance

 (d) you wait patiently for the bus though you are late for the class

110. Grandparents are getting young at heart, too. More and more grandparents are moving out of their children's homes and spending a happy post-retirement life. If you are such a grandparent yourself; what will be your take on the subject?

 (a) I would like to book a retirement home in Goa.

 (b) I would prefer to stay back with my children if they are fine with it.

 (c) I would first discuss this with my friends.

 (d) I believe that sacrifices are rewarded in heaven if not on earth.

111. R.K. Srivastava, secretary in charge of SC/ST/OBC and minority welfare was arrested to ensure his presence at a hearing. As R.K. Srivastava, what is your opinion on the matter?

 (a) I was not feeling well enough to attend the hearing.

 (b) This is not the way to treat a civil servant.

 (c) I will have to discuss the matter with my seniors

 (d) Even I have to follow rules, it was a lapse on my part.

112. According to the Centre for Science and Environmental studies the mix of ozone, Carbonmonoxide and Nitrogen Oxides in the atmosphere is pushing up pollution levels in the capital. As minister for environment, what steps are you going to take to control this?

 (a) Make it mandatory for all vehicles to use CNG only

 (b) Reduce the number of vehicles

 (c) Move factories outside NCT

 (d) (a) and (c) only

113. There are lots of stray dogs in the capital. The monkey menace too is assuming huge proportions. As chairman of the MCD, how will you help the people?

 (a) Employ staff to capture them and set them up in cages

 (b) Appeal to NGO's to step in and help solve the problem

 (c) Set up more hospitals for rabies

 (d) (a) and (b) only

114. The global crude oil prices have once again sent prices spiralling. What suggestions do you have to give to the homemaker who is fed up with rising inflation?

 (a) Maintain a tight budget

 (b) Economise your spends

 (c) Discipline the children regarding this

 (d) (b) and (c) only

115. You go for a date with your friend and he/she comments on your not looking good. You

 (a) get back at him/her telling him/her how bad he/she is looking .

 (b) make up some reason as to what went wrong.

 (c) take offence to it and estrange your relationship.

 (d) start crying.

116. The front office in the organisation you work for has a very uncomfortable physical set-up to work in. You will.

 (a) launch a campaign to set things right.

 (b) complain to seniors about it.

 (c) ignore everything and concentrate on your job.

 (d) manage somehow with reluctance.

117. There has been a recent death in your family, and you are still grieving. However, your quarterly appraisal is round the corner, and for this you have to catch up with a lot of work. What would you do?

 (a) Take the help of your organisation counsellor to overcome your emotions.

 (b) Ignore the appraisal and continue working since the appraisal happens every three months, you feel you can make up the next time.

 (c) Just try your best to wriggle out of the situation by asking your superior to postpone the appraisal for you this time.

 (d) Get back to work immediately.

118. You are a sincere and dedicated manager in a reputed five-star hotel. You have been appointed as the Chief Manager of the Guwahati branch which needs to be developed. Your salary has been hiked.

 (a) You give it a shot for two months and see how it goes.

 (b) You accept the challenge and go ahead with the project.

 (c) You accept another offer and leave the job.

 (d) You crib for limited resources and try to convince your superior to send somebody else instead of you.

119. Your new boss's wife/ husband offers you a cigarette knowing fully well that you are trying to quit smoking. What do you do?

 (a) You cannot resist it but think twice before taking it.

 (b) You accept and readily light it.

 (c) You accept but do not light the cigarette.

 (d) You politely decline her/ his offer.

120. You are in the middle of an important dinner party when the waiter spills steaming hot soup over the boss' lap. How would you react?

    (a) You panic and start shouting at the waiter

    (b) You arrange for the first-aid and make arrangements to rush him or her off to the hospital

    (c) You dab frantically at the ruined outfit with a napkin while screaming at the waiter

    (d) You pour the entire contents of a jug of water over his lap, explaining that your prompt action will prevent burns, and then lay out a change of clothes in the guest bedroom and return to the party while the boss changes

121. You have a new boss. You will

    (a) be indifferent to him.

    (b) welcome him warmly.

    (c) go and flatter him as he will help out in future.

    (d) have problems adjusting as you are still loyal to your old boss.

122. Suppose your friend visits your home on his way to office. You will

    (a) not offer anything as he is getting late.

    (b) compel him to listen to your personal problems.

    (c) request him to have some refreshment.

    (d) ask him to spend at least 15 minutes with you.

123. You are a guest at a dinner. The host asks you to take one more chapati after your stomach is full. You would

    (a) make a blunt refusal.

    (b) take the chapati.

    (c) politely say that the food was too good and you have already eaten much.

    (d) make a bad face at him.

124. You are in the parking area of a shopping complex. Suddenly, the electricity fails and there is total darkness. You will

    (a) try and take help from someone around.

    (b) grope your way towards your vehicle.

    (c) shout for help.

    (d) wait till the lights come.

125. You have received a gift early, which your aunt wants you to open on our birthday, which is two weeks away. You

    (a) really want to open it and keep thinking about it, but do not open it.

    (b) leave it for a while but eventually open it because you could not wait.

    (c) quickly open it because she would not come to know.

    (d) honour her wish because you know that the gift would not run way.

126. You are a manager of a company and an employee does not turn up for work because his son was ill. You will

    (a) tell him to come on time in future no matter what .

    (b) ask him how his son is and give him a day off.

    (c) give him a strict warning.

    (d) ask how his son is and tell him to call the office if ever in future he decides not to come.

127. You are a member of the sports team of your college. One day due to some misunderstanding, other members stop talking to you. You

    (a) ask someone to mediate.

    (b) go forward and start talking.

    (c) wait till they come and start talking again.

    (d) keep to yourself and let things take their time for improving.

128. You are desperately waiting for someone at home. You

    (a) don't give it a thought.

    (b) keep yourself busy at your work.

    (c) run out the minute you hear a car stop.

    (d) call up many times to find out why he/ she is taking so long.

129. If wrongly accused of something, you would

    (a) try to convince others, without harbouring any hope of it happening.

    (b) try your best to convince others and sincerely hope that you succeed.

    (c) not even try, as it would be of no use.

    (d) be able to convince others of your innocence easily.

130. A product launched by the company is having initial hiccups and complaints. You will

    (a) tell your boss this product should be withdrawn to save the company's reputation.

    (b) convince the customers about the working and positive aspects of the product.

    (c) warn the customers for initial hiccups.

    (d) try and convince the customers it is temporary.

131. The Chinese PM is going to visit India. Indo-Chinese ties are fragile. If you are the Indian PM, what will you do to improve the ties?

    (a) make sure that he is given a warm welcome

    (b) make it clear that India needs China's support

    (c) concentrate on long-term bilateral plans & reforms

    (d) (a) and (c) only

132. Crimes against women are increasing in the capital. Women here feel very unsafe. As Commissioner of police, what steps will you take to control this menace?

    (a) capture the culprits and punish them severely

    (b) put up Police vans at all vantage points

    (c) make sure that there are constables keeping a vigil throughout the night.

    (d) all of the above

133. Intel, the computer global giant wants to provide affordable PC's to the masses. After the disaster of the affordable car Nano, it comes as a great surprise. What steps will you take as a CEO of Intel to make sure that it succeeds?

    (a) Make the PC's available at competitive rates

    (b) Give the option of replacing them if they do not meet customer satisfaction

    (c) Use expensive components

    (d) (a) and (b) only

134. Any impasse in the Lok Sabha continues for a prolonged period. As the Speaker, how will you resolve this dilemma?
  (a) order the errant members out of the assembly
  (b) ask the President to pass an ordinance to end the 'logjam'
  (c) use your powers as the speaker to solve the problem
  (d) carry out a detailed study to ensure that you are taking the right decision

135. You start to work on a project
  (a) with a great deal of enthusiasm.
  (b) thinking you would rather plan an activity than take part in it.
  (c) taking lead in organizing the project.
  (d) by hiring a group of some kind.

136. When you eat a meal with others, you
  (a) entertain others.
  (b) are usually one of the last to finish.
  (c) just eat, drink and be merry.
  (d) eat quietly.

137. When you find that something you have bought is defective, you
  (a) demand an exchange.
  (b) hesitate to demand an exchange.
  (c) demand a refund.
  (d) keep quiet.

138. Thrown by chance with a stranger, you would
  (a) wait for the person to introduce himself.
  (b) find it difficult to chat about things in general.
  (c) introduce yourself first.
  (d) keep quiet throughout.

139. If someone asks you to take part in many social activities. You would
  (a) ask him to get lost.
  (b) pay him some money and excuse yourself.
  (c) participate with full enthusiasm.
  (d) can't say

140. If you hold an opinion that is radically different from that expressed by a lecturer, you would
  (a) argue right on the spot.
  (b) tell the person about it during the lecture.
  (c) tell the person about it after the lecture.
  (d) forget about it.

141. If you find the price at any retail shop is too much, yet you want to buy that product, you would
  (a) argue over the price with a clerk or sales person
  (b) ask for discounts.
  (c) as usual avoid arguing over the price with a clerk or sales person.
  (d) use your credit card and buy it.

142. If you have a deadline to submit an assignment in the morning, you
  (a) often find it difficult to go to sleep at night because you keep thinking of what will happen the next day.
  (b) just have a sound sleep without being worried about the work.
  (c) ask any colleague to do the job for you.
  (d) ask for more time.

143. If some of your friends are around and see what you are reading, you would
  (a) as usual, be bothered by people watching you.
  (b) ask them to leave you alone.
  (c) stop reading and start talking to them.
  (d) go to some other place and continue reading.

144. At the scene of an accident, you
  (a) take an active part in helping out.
  (b) wait and watch.
  (c) ask others for help.
  (d) just leave the place as soon as possible.

145. On any hectic day,
  (a) your mood often changes.
  (b) you shout at everyone without knowing why.
  (c) you ask others not to disturb.
  (d) you concentrate on your work and try to be patient.

146. When you are served stale or inferior food in a restaurant, you
  (a) complain to the manager.
  (b) don't pay the bill and leave.
  (c) ask to be served fresh food.
  (d) can't say

147. You usually keep cheerful even in the face of a trouble, because
  (a) being worried wouldn't help.
  (b) you don't like being worried.
  (c) you are confident enough to face any kind of situation.
  (d) don't know.

148. How should an immediate boss behave with his subordinates?
  (a) Permit subordinates to express their disagreement and resolve differences.
  (b) Be angry with a few and affectionate to others.
  (c) Maintain a distance from subordinates.
  (d) Make subordinates feel both scared and affectionate

149. What is appropriate behaviour of a Controlling Officer towards a new employee?
  (a) Not create close relationship immediately.
  (b) Meet him with an expression of unwillingness.
  (c) Advise him to work responsibly.
  (d) I introduce the new employee to all and request for cooperation.

150. What should be merits of the Head of a Department. He should have
  (a) knowledge of work.
  (b) an attitude of a leader.
  (c) honesty and expertise.
  (d) All of the above.

IV. Direction (Qs 151 - 185) : *Read the situation and choose the best course of action from the options provided.*

151. Your superior has asked you to give a presentation on a topic within two days. You burn the midnight oil and manage to finish it. However, during actual presentation, your superior is disappointed and rebukes you for the work done. What will be your reaction?

(a) Leave the place immediately.

(b) Resign from the job.

(c) React and shout at the superior.

(d) Ask for feedback and assure that you will rectify the errors.

152. You are working on a project report that needs to be completed and submitted the same day. Suddenly, there is disturbance in the office and everybody starts running out. What will you do?

(a) Try to find out the reason, and then sit calmly to continue your work.

(b) Become a part of the confusion.

(c) Sort out the outburst and then resume your work.

(d) Ignore the problem.

153. You and Gopal have been friends since childhood. You both share events in your lives with each other. However you have observed that Gopal has started avoiding you and does not answer your mobile calls. He is not even telling you his problem . What will you do?

(a) Try to find the reason and resolve the issues.

(b) Leave the situation as it is.

(c) Aggravate the situation by showing emotions.

(d) Let other friends solve the situation.

154. You own a factory. One day, there is noise in the factory and you are told that an iron rod has fallen on two workers. They are badly injured and are bleeding. Everybody is in panic. What should you do?

(a) Call the union leader and discuss the matter with him.

(b) Tell the labourers to mind their own business.

(c) Get immediate medical attention to the injured.

(d) Call the police to control the situation.

155. On your birthday, your friends have asked you to treat them. You take them to a restaurant. Once the bill arrives, you realise that you have left behind your wallet. What will you do?

(a) You will excuse yourself and disappear without telling anyone.

(b) Ask one of your friends to pay and pay him back when you reach home.

(c) You will convince the manager so that you can pay the bill later.

(d) Cry in front of your friends.

156. You are working on a project with a deadline. You have delegated specific work to every team members. You are informed about the sudden demise of the father of a team member. You have been entrusted with the responsibility of breaking the news to him. What will you do?

(a) Inform him at once and permit him to leave the important project.

(b) Inform him immediately but take his inputs about his work, and assure him that you will manage and take care of the rest. Then, you relieve him.

(c) Decide not to tell him as he will leave on receiving this news which would be detrimental to your project.

(d) Call off the project.

157. You are working in a company where you observe that the employees are working below their potential. They waste time and are bored with their monotonous jobs. You have an idea to improve productivity of the employees but your superiors have a low opinion of you. They are most likely to reject your idea. What will you do?

(a) Convey the idea to your superiors.

(b) Present data to strengthen your point and then share the idea.

(c) Ignore the superiors.

(d) Pass on the idea indirectly through your subordinates.

158. Your are in an organisation where you are required to communicate and interact daily with your subordinates and your peers; and, you report weekly to the management. Therefore, communication becomes an essential part of your work. How, should you communicate at the workplace?

(a) Should communicate minimally.

(b) Listen with one ear and speak distractedly with your subordinates as they do not require attention.

(c) Should be focused on personal work.

(d) Should always be attentive and clear in speech.

159. You have been shifted to a department as an officer with 50 employees. You observe that most employees come late to work. How would you communicate the need to come on time?

(a) Call for the attendance register and start crossing those coming late and send the message to everyone to come on time.

(b) Hold a staff meeting and tell them to be punctual and also convey to them that in the future action would be taken against them if they are late.

(c) Write a letter to all employees about coming on time.

(d) Prefer to observe and ask the establishment in-charge to speak to those coming late to be on time.

160. You have been employed in the service sector for the last two years. You have been reassigned the responsibility to look into marketing. After analysis, you find that the quality of customer service is low. How would you convey to your employees the need for improvement?

(a) Make a presentation to all employees about the declining levels of customer service and ask them to improve.

(b) Call for a meeting of key officials responsible for customer services and then issue a common letter to each employee expressing concerns of this declining trend and need for correction.

(c) Talk to all employees by rotation specifying the declining trend of customer service which becomes a critical concern for the organisation.

(d) Provide training to the employees to improve customer service.

161. You and your colleagues have gone for an investigation. While leaving the scene, you notice that one of the staff has picked up an article from the house and kept it into his pocket. You

(a) report the matter to your senior officer.

(b) warn your colleague to keep the article back or you will report the matter .

(c) ignore the act as it would spoil the image of your colleague.

(d) Shout at him reminding him of his duty.

162. You have to go for some important work but you find that your colleague has taken your official vehicle away. You

(a) call him and criticise him for his act.

(b) wait for him to return.

(c) arrange some alternative vehicle and talk to your colleague later.

(d) inform your superior.

163. A senior citizen has been making rounds of your office for getting his pension documents cleared. You have noticed him for over a week but the staff is not clearing his file as certain documents are missing. The elderly man gets angry after making so many rounds and shouts. You

(a) call the dealing clerk and ask him to deal with his file.

(b) call him to your office and try to pacify him explaining the necessity of documents.

(c) ask the concerned department/ to look for alternative solutions so that you can clear his file.

(d) wait for the matter to come upto you.

164. You are the head of your department. Your role is supervisory, and you are willing to work efficiently. You have always been anxious about your effective supervision abilities. Which of the following do you think is needed for effective supervision?

(a) Concern for employees, trust and warmth.

(b) Needs of supervisor and subordinates to be kept in mind.

(c) Personality of both the supervisor and subordinates to be considered.

(d) All of the above.

165. You are a Director and are addressing the department under your control on communication skills. You think that this is the mantra for efficient working and productive performance. Therefore, you issue guidelines to the staff. Which of the following is not a correct guideline?

(a) Be an active listener.

(b) Do not criticise.

(c) Create standards for improvements.

(d) Make your subordinates defensive.

166. You are the department head and want to streamline communication in your department. You have various options that are essential in creating effective communication. Which of the following will ensure effective formal communication?

(a) Rules, policies, procedures

(b) Computerised systems

(c) Manual systems

(d) Organisation structure

167. You are the IT expert in a consultancy but the work assigned to you pertains to Human Resources, an area in which you have limited knowledge. What do you do?

(a) At the time of assignment, you should inform the boss about not having relevant experience.

(b) Inform the senior in writing that this work is not of any concern to you.

(c) Do a limited job and send it to the boss.

(d) Take help from co-workers and after learning the ropes dispose the work and inform the senior that you have taken the help of a fellow worker to finish the job.

168. You are extremely punctual and always reach office on time. However, one day your vehicle breaks down, you get late and get caught with the late comers. You will

(a) inform the Boss about the reason in detail, both verbally and in writing.

(b) return home and submit a leave application.

(c) complain to fellow worker against the Boss that you come every day on time; so, if you are late for one day, it does not really matter.

(d) start working silently without undertaking any other action.

169. You are part of a delegation of CEOs from India. The leader of the delegation directs you to lead the group in a meeting in which your seniors will also be present.

(a) There will be initial hesitation while speaking before senior officials.

(b) You will be unhappy thinking why the boss assigned you the job when he knew about your limitations.

   (c) Without hesitating, though seniors are present, you will obey the orders of the boss and show your capability in the duty assigned.

   (d) You will request the boss himself to lead during the meeting.

170. Your senior is on leave due to his daughter's wedding and you have been assigned the work of overseeing the routine process in your branch by the zonal manager.

   (a) You will dispose of the work avoiding any change in the organisation.

   (b) You will create a favourable environment and permit the staff to work with initiative.

   (c) You will terrorise the staff and boss around showing your power.

   (d) You will introduce your new idea and method of work and show the good results when the boss returns.

171. After a long and successful period in your branch, your boss has been promoted and transferred to the head office. A new boss takes charge of your branch.

   (a) You will narrate a false sentimental story to seek his leniency.

   (b) You will speak against your colleagues to earn his favour.

   (c) You will work overtime to win his trust.

   (d) You will work honestly and efficiently no matter who your superior is.

172. Apart from being a works supervisor, you have the additional task of being a channel between the boss and employees to improve coordination. What would your strategy be?

   (a) Employees will submit their problems to you in writing.

   (b) Boss should meet everybody once a month in which he should listen to the problems and sort them out.

   (c) All demands should be raised before you through an employees' association and in case they are not met, they may demonstrate before the boss.

   (d) Don't tell the boss about employees' issues till you resolve them.

173. You are an investment banker in an organization that follows strict gender policy and has an equal number of male-female employees. What will be your attitude towards female coworkers?

   (a) You will maintain a distance from them.

   (b) You will treat them like any other employee.

   (c) You will assist them in their work.

   (d) You will show kindness to them as they are female.

174. In a factory, a machine has to be repaired for increasing output. Foreign engineers are hired for the task but, they are not able to complete the project. A skilled labourer gives a suggestion for enhancing the machine's performance. The company engineer agrees and raises the performance of the machine.

   (a) Credit should go to the local skilled labourer.

   (b) Credit should go to the Indian engineer.

   (c) Credit should go to both the skilled labourer and the Indian engineer.

   (d) Credit should go to all the three-skilled labour, Indian engineer and foreign engineer.

175. During peak time, excessive work load is created in your organisation. How will you deal with excessive work load?

   (a) You will ask your subordinates to work and give them overtime.

   (b) Allow them to leave office at closing time.

   (c) Request additional staff.

   (d) You will keep quiet.

176. You have been given a tight deadline within which you have to finish the work assigned to you. You will

   (a) achieve it without planning.

   (b) achieve it by planning.

   (c) refuse work assuming that it cannot be completed.

   (d) assure the senior official regarding completion of work on time and explain the delay later.

177. You have been assigned a target but you have not been given appropriate resources. There is lack of finances, manpower and government cooperation. What do you do in such a situation?

   (a) You will still try to achieve the target.

   (b) You will use the limited resources in an efficient manner.

   (c) You will request for more resources to achieve the target.

   (d) Use the limited resources and then demand resource at a later stage.

178. In a government job elated to financial matters, you will be

   (a) dependent on the Cashier.

   (b) direct the Cashier after acquiring full financial knowledge.

   (c) be aware about the work and follow all the financial rules.

   (d) not be obliged to follow the financial rules.

179. Which of the following describes a good employee most appropriately?

   (a) Comes to the office and does not work but chats.

   (b) Comes to the office daily, works according to rules and is obedient.

   (c) Comes to the office daily and forces the boss to do all the work according to the rules.

   (d) Comes to the office late and leaves early, but finishes all the work .

180. You are the Senior Production Manager of a Steel firm and have won the bid to supply steel for railway bridges across the river Ganga. You have been asked to ensure maximum production in the next eight months. You would

   (a) plan out a production strategy with your team and monitor production schedule at regular intervals.

    (b) pressurise the production team to meet the target anyhow.

    (c) relax, thinking that the work will be done anyway.

    (d) pass on the responsibility to higher management.

181. You are a senior advisor to a real estate company. You have to give your opinion on shortlisting an organisation to collaborate with your company for developing the athletes' village for the National Games. Which of the following will you shortlist?

    (a) Organization A, which has adequate resources for the project.

    (b) Organization B, which has goodwill but no past experience of such a project.

    (c) Organization C, which has enough experience and resources.

    (d) Organization D, which does not have experience or resources but has been recommended by your senior.

182. On Saturday, you are at home as you have taken leave to finish personal commitments and want to complete them so that you can go back to your official duties. An acquaintance, visits you and he is in a relaxed and gossiping mood. How would you react?

    (a) You will passively listen to his chitchat and ignore the conversation to discourage his gossip.

    (b) You enjoy his company and spend time with your friend relaxing then resume work.

    (c) You give him due respect but tell him that you are in a hurry and cannot spend time with him.

    (d) You sit and wait for his departure.

183. You are the head of your office. There are certain houses reserved for allotment to the office staff and you have been given the discretion to do so. A set of rules for the allotment of the houses has been laid down by you and has been made public. Your personal secretary, who is very close to you, comes to you and pleads that as his father is seriously ill, he should be given priority in allotment of a house. The office secretariat that examined the request as per the rules turns down the request and recommends the procedure to be followed according to the rules. You do not want to annoy your personal secretary. In such circumstances, what would you do?

    (a) Call him over to your room and personally explain why the allotment cannot be done.

    (b) Allot the house to him to win his loyalty.

    (c) Agree with the office note to show that you are not biased and that you do not indulge in favouritism.

    (d) Keep the file with you and not pass any orders.

184. While travelling in a Delhi-registered commercial taxi from Delhi to an adjacent city (another State), your taxi driver informs you that as he has no permit for running the taxi in that city, he will stop at its Transport Office and pay the prescribed fee of ₹ forty for a day. While he is paying the fee at the counter you find that the transport clerk is taking an extra fifty rupees for which no receipt is being given. You are in a hurry for your meeting. In such circumstances, what would you do?

    (a) Go up to the counter and ask the clerk to give back the money which he has illegally taken.

    (b) Do not interfere at all as this is a matter between the taxi driver and the tax authorities.

    (c) Take note of the incident and subsequently report the matter to the concerned authorities.

    (d) Treat it as a normal affair and simply forget about it.

185. A person lives in a far off village which is almost two hours by bus from your office. The villager's neighbour is a very powerful landlord who is trying to occupy the poor villager's land by force. You are the District Magistrate and are busy in a meeting called by a local Minister. The villager has come all the way, by bus and on foot, to see you and give an application seeking protection from the powerful landlord. The villager keeps on waiting outside the meeting hall for an hour. You come out of the meeting and are rushing to another meeting. The villager follows you to submit his application. What would you do?

    (a) Tell him to wait for another two hours till you come back from your next meeting.

    (b) Tell him that the matter is actually to be dealt by a junior officer and that he should give the application to him.

    (c) Call one of your senior subordinate officers and ask him to solve the villager's problem.

    (d) Quickly take the application from him, ask him a few relevant questions regarding his problem and then proceed to the meeting.

186. There is a shortage of sugar in your district of which you are the District Magistrate. The Government has ordered that only a maximum amount of 30 kg sugar is to be released for wedding celebrations. Your friend requests you to release at least 50 kg sugar for his son's wedding. He expresses annoyance when you tell him about the Government's restrictions on this matter. He feels that since you are the District Magistrate you can release any amount. You do not want to spoil your friendship with him. In such circumstances, how would you deal with the situation?

    (a) Release the extra amount of sugar which your friend has requested for.

    (b) Refuse your friend the extra amount and strictly follow the rules.

    (c) Show your friend the copy of the Government instructions and then persuade him to accept the lower amount as prescribed in the rules.

    (d) Advise him to directly apply to the allotting authority and inform him that you do not interfere in this matter.

187. You are in charge of implementing the Family Planning programme in an area where there is a strong opposition to this policy. You want to convince the residents of the need for having a small family. What would be the best way of communicating this message?

- (a) Logically explaining to the residents the need for family planning to improve the health and living standards.
- (b) Encouraging late marriages and proper spacing of children.
- (c) Offering incentives for adopting family planning devices.
- (d) Asking people who have been sterilized or are using contraceptives to directly talk to the residents.

188. You are a teacher in a University and are setting a question paper on a particular subject. One of your colleagues, whose son is preparing for the examination on that subject, comes to you and informs you that it is his son's last chance to pass that examination and asks whether you could help him by indicating what questions are going to figure in the examination paper. In the past, your colleague had helped you in another matter. He informs you that his son will suffer from depression if he fails in this examination. In such circumstances, what would you do?

- (a) Extend your help to him in view of the help he had given you.
- (b) Express regret that you cannot be of any help to him.
- (c) Explain that this would be violating the trust of the University authorities and you are not in a position to help him.
- (d) Report the conduct of your colleague to the higher authorities.

Solutions

ANSWER KEY

1	(c)	18	(b)	35	(a)	52	(a)	69	(a)	86	(a)	103	(b)	120	(d)	137	(a)	154	(c)	171	(d)
2	(b)	19	(c)	36	(d)	53	(a)	70	(d)	87	(d)	104	(d)	121	(b)	138	(c)	155	(b)	172	(d)
3	(c)	20	(a)	37	(c)	54	(a)	71	(c)	88	(d)	105	(a)	122	(c)	139	(c)	156	(b)	173	(b)
4	(b)	21	(c)	38	(b)	55	(d)	72	(d)	89	(b)	106	(c)	123	(c)	140	(c)	157	(b)	174	(c)
5	(c,d)	22	(d)	39	(a)	56	(b)	73	(d)	90	(d)	107	(b)	124	(d)	141	(c)	158	(d)	175	(a)
6	(a,b)	23	(c)	40	(d)	57	(d)	74	(b)	91	(c)	108	(b)	125	(d)	142	(d)	159	(b)	176	(b)
7	(c)	24	(b)	41	(d)	58	(c)	75	(d)	92	(d)	109	(c)	126	(d)	143	(d)	160	(b)	177	(b)
8	(c)	25	(a)	42	(d)	59	(d)	76	(d)	93	(d)	110	(b)	127	(d)	144	(a)	161	(b)	178	(c)
9	(c)	26	(c)	43	(d)	60	(d)	77	(d)	94	(b)	111	(d)	128	(b)	145	(a)	162	(c)	179	(b)
10	(b)	27	(d)	44	(d)	61	(a)	78	(c)	95	(d)	112	(d)	129	(b)	146	(c)	163	(c)	180	(a)
11	(c)	28	(c)	45	(d)	62	(b)	79	(d)	96	(c)	113	(d)	130	(d)	147	(c)	164	(d)	181	(c)
12	(c)	29	(b)	46	(c)	63	(d)	80	(d)	97	(c)	114	(d)	131	(d)	148	(d)	165	(d)	182	(c)
13	(b)	30	(b)	47	(a)	64	(b)	81	(c)	98	(d)	115	(b)	132	(d)	149	(c)	166	(d)	183	(a)
14	(b)	31	(c)	48	(b)	65	(d)	82	(a)	99	(a)	116	(a)	133	(d)	150	(a)	167	(d)	184	(c)
15	(a)	32	(d)	49	(b)	66	(d)	83	(c)	100	(d)	117	(a)	134	(d)	151	(d)	168	(a)	185	(d)
16	(d)	33	(d)	50	(c)	67	(c)	84	(d)	101	(d)	118	(b)	135	(a)	152	(c)	169	(c)	186	(d)
17	(b)	34	(d)	51	(d)	68	(d)	85	(d)	102	(d)	119	(c)	136	(d)	153	(a)	170	(d)	187	(a)
																				188	(c)

DETAILED EXPLANATIONS

151. (d) Gracefully accepting the feedback and rectifying one's own lapse is the best course of action.

152. (c) First, the cause of the commotion needs to be found and problem, resolved; then only the environment will be conducive for speedy completion of your work.

153. (a) Friendship is valuable and should not be allowed to die over misunderstandings or contentious issues. Going the extra mile to resolve issues and to maintain friendship is the best course of action.

154. (c) Saving life, and administering medical aid is the first course of action in case of any mishap.

155. (b) Paying the bill then and there is imperative; so, this is the best course of action. Options (a) and (c) are negative actions.

156. (b) Relieving the particular team member is necessary given his tragic situation. The best course of action, therefore, is to take report and inputs of his work and manage with the rest of the available resources.

157. (b) You have the best knowledge of the ground situation. So, subtantiating your claim with data and getting the idea approved to improve the situation is desirable action.

158. (d) Effective listening as well as speaking is essential for good communication.

159. (b) Personal communication has greater impact.

160. (b) It is the lower level officials who are crucial for improving quality.

161. (b) You have prevented a wrong act and helped a brother officer.

162. (c) The work assigned to you must be performed.

163. (c) Such help will enable the sufferer to get his pension without violating any rules.

164. (d) All the above points are essential for effective supervision.

165. (d) If the staff is always on the defensive, efficiency will be low.

166. (d) If the structure is well thought out then communication will flow easily.

167. (d) The boss is trusting you with this work. You must honour his trust.

168. (a) Your superior must be informed. He will understand based on your past record.

169. (c) Unless you rise above your limitations, you will never rise in life.

170. (d) Limited experimentation is never hurtful.

171. (d) Honest and efficient work is the only right means to be appreciated and to maintain good interpersonal relations with colleagues. No special effort with vested interest is desirable.

172. **(d)** When you have been designated as the channel between the boss and the employees, you will do all it takes to resolve issues; and then will inform the boss.

173. **(b)** Gender policy constitutes gender equality in all ways, i.e., no discrimination of any kind whatsoever.

174. **(c)** Credit is due to the skilled labourer for his suggestion and the Indian engineer for successfully implementing it.

175. **(a)** This is the best short term solution.

176. **(b)** Planning enables you to achieve most of the targets.

177. **(b)** This is the best approach as resources may not be given when they are demanded.

178. **(c)** In finance, all the laid down financial rules should be followed and no one should be blindly relied on.

179. **(b)** Punctuality and working honestly within rules is the mark of a good employee.

180. **(a)** Planning will take care of many problems in future.

181. **(c)** Experience in the concerned area and availability of resources are equally important for any real estate project.

182. **(c)** You are short of time, so, you will tell your friend about the situation.

183. **(a)** When it comes to declining a request, it is better done in private with proper explanation for not being able to do a favour so that it does not make the other person feel bad, especially when the person is very close to you.

184. **(c)** One should not ignore wrong doing or the wrong doer because that will set a wrong precedent. So, if on-the-spot action is not feasible, one must exercise restraint and make a mental note instead. Complaint can be lodged later but an urgent meeting need not be ignored or spoilt for any avoidable reason. Such unscrupulous people. can be taken to task later.

185. **(d)** The next meeting can be put on hold for a few minutes, but the person who has already made a lot of effort to reach the district magistrate's office in anticipation of help, must be heard first. This humane attitude towards common people and their problems will enhance the respect of the chair, the person and the district administration.

186. **(d)** This will make it very clear to him that doing favours is not part of your job. You hold a responsible position. The advise will show that you care for him and a direct approach to the allotting authority might work for him. This gives a lasting impression that you follow the rules.

187. **(a)** At a place where there is a strong opposition to family planning, it is not easy to implement any programme quickly or hastily. But persuasion and explanation can surely make a difference. So, by logically explaining the pros and cons of the progamme, people can be persuaded better though it may take longer.

188. **(c)** Extending a helping hand to someone for personal reasons while sitting in a responsible position is unethical and does not do justice to the trust and responsibility of the authority invested in you.

SECTION 1 : ADMINISTRATIVE COURSES OF ACTION

In this type of questions, a statement is given, followed by two or more decisions in the form of course of action. Candidates have to analyse the statement and then decide which of the courses of action logically follows.

What is a 'course of action'?

A 'course of action' is a step or administrative decision taken for improvement or follow-up or further action in regard to the problem, policy etc, on the basis of the information given in the statement. Courses of action should be feasible and should relate with the practical aspect of life.

Mostly, the given statement mentions a problem and the suggested course of action offers a solution. Thus, it is a 'problem-solving situation'. Sometimes, the statement merely gives a fact and the suggested course of action offers a way to improve the situation. Thus, it is a 'fact-follow-up action' situation.

TECHNIQUE FOR SOLVING

Always assume everything given in the statement to be true and only then choose the correct option among the given ones. Read the statement and the options very carefully. In such questions, generally, 2 types of options are given :

	Type A	Type B
(a)	if only I follows;	if only I follows
(b)	if only II follows;	if only II follows
(c)	if either I or II follows;	if either I or II follows
(d)	if both I and II follow.	if neither I nor II follows

Directions (Qs. 1-4) : *In each of the following questions, a statement is given followed by two courses of action numbered I and II. Decide which of the courses of action logically follows and give answer as :*

(a) if only I follows;
(b) if only II follows;
(c) if either I or II follows;
(d) if both I and II follow.

Illustration – 1

Statement : Most of the children in India are not able to get education because they get employed to earn livelihood in their childhood.

Courses of action : I. Education should be made compulsory for all children up to the age of 14.

II. Employment of children below the age of 14 years should be banned.

Solution :

(d) To educate all children, enforcement of education is necessary. Also, the reason is that they are employed. So, ban on such employment is also needed. Thus, both the courses follow.

Illustration – 2

Statement : India has been continuously experiencing military threats from its neighbouring countries.

Courses of action : I. India should engage in an all-out war to stop the nagging threats.

II. India should get the neighbours into a serious dialogue to reduce the tension at its borders.

Solution :

(b) War cannot be an answer to such problems, but dialogue can definitely lessen the problem. Engaging in war might bring in new problems and it might not be able to solve the problem at all.

Illustration – 3

Statement : At least 15 people were killed and many others injured when a bus fell into the river from the bridge.

Courses of action : I. The protection walls of the bridge should be made strong enough to avoid such accidents.

II. The bus driver should be arrested immediately to make necessary inquiry.

Solution :

(d) I is advisable because it will restrict cases of such accident further. II is advisable because that would help know the cause of the accident.

Directions: *In the following question, a statement is followed by three courses of action numbered I, II and III. Decide which of the three given courses of action logically follows and then give the answer.*

(a) Only either I or II
(b) Only II and III
(c) Only I
(d) None of these
(e) All the three

Illustration – 4

Statement : The Management of School 'M' has decided to give free breakfast from next academic year to all the students in its primary section through its canteen even though they will not get any government grant.

Courses of action : I. The school will have to admit many poor students who will seek admission for the next academic year.

II. The canteen facilities and utensils will have to be checked and new purchases to be made to equip it properly.

III. Funds will have to be raised to support the scheme for years to come.

Solution :

(b) I is redundant in the context of the statement. II and III clearly follow from the statement.

Exercise

Directions (Qs. 1-9) : *In each of the following questions, a statement is given followed by two courses of action numbered I and II. Decide which of the courses of action logically follows and give answer as :*

(a) if only I follows

(b) if only II follows

(c) if either I or II follows

(d) if neither I nor II follows

1. **Statement :**

The company 'X' has decided to give 10% increase in salary to its employees from next month.

Courses of action :

I. The accounts department will have to prepare new salary statement for all employees before due date.

II. Employees' association should ask for more rise in the salary considering the market condition.

2. **Statement :**

The meteorological department has predicted good monsoon this year for the tenth consecutive year and this will result in a good crop yield.

Courses of action :

I. The Government should off-load the stores before harvesting.

II. The Government should provide chemical fertilisers to farmers immediately.

3. **Statement :**

Most of the development plans develop in papers only.

Courses of action :

I. The officers-in-charge should be instructed to supervise the field work regularly.

II. The supply of paper to such departments should be cut short.

4. **Statement :**

The cinema halls are incurring heavy losses these days as people prefer to watch movies their homes on TV than to visit cinema halls.

Courses of action :

I. The cinema halls should be demolished and residential multistorey buildings should be constructed there.

II. The cinema halls should be converted into shopping malls.

5. **Statement :**

The alert villagers collectively caught a group of dreaded dacoits armed with murderous weapons.

Courses of action :

I. The villagers should be provided sophisticated weapons.

II. The villagers should be rewarded for their courage and unity.

6. **Statement :**

There was waterlogging in the major part of the city due to heavy rain during past few days and the people residing in those areas were forced to shift to other areas.

Courses of action :

I. The Government should arrange food and shelter for the displaced people.

II. The fire brigade should be put on high alert to cope with the situation.

7. **Statement :**

The 'M' State Government has decided henceforth to award the road construction contracts through open tenders only.

Courses of action :

I. The 'M' state will not be able to get the work done swiftly as it will have to go through tender and other procedures.

II. Henceforth, the quality of roads constructed may be far better.

8. **Statement :**

Many private sector banks have reduced interest rate on housing loans in comparison to public sector banks.

Courses of action :

I. The case should be raised before the regulatory authority for investigation by the public sector banks as they cannot follow such reduction.

II. Public sector banks must adopt such policy to remain in competition.

9. Statement :

The proposed strike by the transporters would paralyse day-to-day life of the people.

Courses of action :

I. City administrators should engage the transporters successfully in negotiations on their demands in order to pre-empt their strike.

II. City administrators should arrange for alternative public transportation system during the strike.

Directions (Qs. 10-17) : *In each of the following questions, a statement is given followed by two courses of action numbered I and II. Decide which of the courses of action logically follows and give your answer as :*

(a) if only I follows
(b) if only II follows
(c) if either I or II follows
(d) if both I and II follow

10. Statement :

ABC Ltd. company has decided to launch free education up to class X for the children of its employees from June 2000.

Courses of action :

I. The company should reduce its other expenditures to save money for the plan.

II. The company will have to prepare details for the execution of the plan.

11. Statement :

The meteorological department has issued a notification forecasting less rainfall during next year's monsoon.

Courses of action :

I. The farmers should be advised to be ready for the eventuality.

II. The Government should make arrangements to provide water to the affected areas.

12. Statement :

The Asian Development Bank has approved a $ 285 million loan to finance a project to construct coal ports by Paradip and Madras Port Trusts.

Courses of action :

I. India should use financial assistance from other international financial organisations to develop such ports in other places.

II. India should not seek such financial assistance from the international financial agencies.

13. Statement :

There are more than 200 villages in the hill area of Uttar Pradesh which are severely damaged due to cyclone and it causes an extra burden of Rs 200 crore on State Government for relief and rehabilitation work.

Courses of action :

I. People of hill area should be shifted to other safer places.

II. State Government should ask for more financial support from Central Government.

14. Statement :

Orissa and Andhra Pradesh have agreed in principle to set up a joint control board for better control, management and productivity of several inter-state multipurpose projects.

Courses of action :

I. Other neighbouring states should set up such control boards.

II. The proposed control board should not be allowed to function as such joint boards are always ineffective.

15. Statement :

Footpaths of a busy road are crowded with vendors selling cheap items.

Courses of action :

I. The help of police should be sought to drive them away.

II. Some space should be provided to them where they can earn their bread without blocking footpaths.

16. Statement :

A recent study shows that children below five years die in the cities of the developing countries mainly from diarrhoea and parasitic intestinal worms.

Courses of action :

I. Governments of the developing countries should take adequate measures to improve the hygienic conditions in the cities.

II. Children below five years in the cities of the developing countries need to be kept under constant medication.

17. Statement :

There has been a significant drop in the water level of all the lakes supplying water to the city.

Courses of action :

I. The water supply authority should impose a partial cut in supply to tackle the situation.

II. The Government should appeal to all the residents through mass media for minimum use of water.

Directions (Qs. 18-21) : *In each of the following questions, a statement is followed by three courses of action numbered I, II and III. Decide which of the three given courses of action logically follows and then give the answer.*

18. Statement :

Suicides are on the rise among the youth, particularly due to unemployment.

Courses of action :

I. A committee should be made to find out the main cause of the rise in cases of suicide.

II. People should be discouraged from indulging in love affairs and encouraged to get self-employed.

III. Parents should be instructed to nurse their wards if they observe them facing critical circumstances.

(a) All I, II and III   **(b)** Only I and II
(c) Only I and III   **(d)** None of these

19. Statement :

Indian Railways are absolutely dependent on government subsidies and lack concentration on transportation activities.

Courses of action :

I. A committee should be constituted to look into the matter.

II. Railways should explore new areas to generate more revenue.

III. Railways should concentrate on hiving off non-core activities such as design and manufacture of rolling stock, construction, housing etc., to private sectors.

(a) Only I   (b) Only I and II

(c) Only II and III   (d) All follow

20. Statement :

The chairman of the car company announced in the meeting that all trials of its first product – the new car model 'M' – are over and the company plans to launch the car in the market after six months.

Courses of action :

I. The network of dealers is to be finalised and all legal, financial and other matters in this connection will have to be finalised shortly.

II. The company will have to make plans for products other than a car.

III. Material, managerial and other resources will have to be in fine tune to maintain production schedule.

(a) Only I and II   (b) Only I

(c) All the three   (d) Only II

21. Statement :

The Deputy Mayor of city 'Z' has proposed to install a plant of mineral water and to supply citizens mineral water bottles at Rs 6 per litre as against Rs 10 per litre being sold by local private companies.

Courses of action :

I. The local private companies of city 'Z' will have to close their operation.

II. The Corporation of city Z will have to provide for losses in this project in its budget.

III. The tap water scheme of city Z will have to be stopped.

(a) Only I and III   (b) Only I and II

(c) Only II and III   (d) None of these

Directions (Qs. 22-28) : *In each of these questions, there is given a statement followed by two courses of action, numbered I and II. You have to assume everything in the statement to be true to decide which of the two suggested courses of action logically follows. Mark your answer as:*

(a) if only I follows,

(b) if only II follows,

(c) if either I or II follows,

(d) if neither I nor II follows.

22. Statement :

The Minister said that the teachers are still not familiarised with the need, importance and meaning of population education in the higher education system.

They are not even clearly aware about their role and responsibilities in the population education programme.

Courses of action:

I. Population education programme should be included in the college curriculum.

II. Orientation programme should be conducted for teachers of population education.

23. Statement :

Financial stringency prevented the state government from paying salaries to its employees since April this year.

Course of action:

I. The state government should immediately curtail the staff strength by at least 30%.

II. The state government should reduce wasteful expenditure and arrange to pay the salaries of its employees.

24. Statement :

One of the problems facing the food processing industry is the irregular supply of raw material. The producers of raw material are not getting a reasonable price.

Courses of action:

I. The government should regulate the supply of raw material to other industries also.

II. The government should announce an attractive package to ensure regular supply of raw material for food processing industry.

25. Statement :

The officer in charge of a Company had a hunch that some money was missing from the safe.

Courses of action:

I. He should get it recounted with the help of the staff and check it with the balance sheet.

II. He should inform the police.

26. Statement :

The government has decided not to provide financial support to voluntary organisations from the next Five-Year Plan and has communicated that all such organisations should raise funds to meet their financial needs.

Courses of action:

I. Voluntary organisations should collaborate with foreign agencies.

II. They should explore other sources of financial support.

27. Statement :

If the retired professors of an Institute are also invited to deliberate on restructuring of the organisation, then their contribution may be beneficial to the institute.

Courses of action:

I. Management may seek opinion of the employees before calling retired professors.

II. Management should involve experienced people for the systematic restructuring of the organisation.

28. **Statement:**

Youngsters are often found staring at obscene posters.

Courses of action:

I. Children should be punished and penalised if they are found doing so.

II. Any display of such material should be banned.

Directions (Qs. 29-33): *A statement is followed by three courses of action numbered I, II and III, You have to assume everything in the statement to be true. Decide which course(s) of action logically follow(s) from the given options marked (a), (b), (c), and (d):*

29. **Statement:**

In one of the worst accidents on railway level crossing, fifty people died when a bus carrying them collided with a running train.

Courses of action:

I. The train driver should immediately be suspended.

II. The driver of the bus should be tried in court for negligence on his part.

III. The railway authority should be asked to get all its level crossings manned.

(a) None follows   (b) Only I and II follow

(c) Only III follows   (d) Only II and III follow

30. **Statement:**

There was a spurt in criminal activities in the city during the recent festival season.

Courses of action:

I. The police should immediately investigate into the causes of this increase.

II. In future, the police should take adequate precaution to avoid recurrence of such situation during the festival season.

III. The known criminals should be arrested before any festive season.

(a) None follows

(b) Only I and II follow

(c) Only II and III follow

(d) All follow

31. **Statement:**

A mass mortality of shrimps in ponds on the entire Andhra coast has recently been reported due to the presence of a virus.

Courses of action:

I. The water of the ponds affected should immediately be treated for identifying the nature of the virus.

II. The catching of shrimps from the ponds should temporarily be stopped.

III. The fishermen should be asked to watch for the onset of such phenomenon in nature.

(a) Only I follows

(b) Only I and II follow

(c) All follow

(d) Only II and III follow

32. **Statement:**

The world will have to feed more than 10 billion people in the next century of whom half will be in Asia and will eat rice as their staple.

Courses of action:

I. More funds should immediately be allocated for rice research to help ensure adequate supplies.

II. The people in Asia should be encouraged to change their food habit.

III. The rice should be grown in countries outside Asia to meet the demand.

(a) Only I and II follow

(b) Only II and III follow

(c) All follow

(d) None follows

33. **Statement:**

If the faculty members also join the strike, then there is going to be a serious problem.

Courses of action:

I. The faculty members should be persuaded not to go on strike.

II. Those faculty members who join the strike should be suspended.

III. The management should not worry about such small things.

(a) None follows

(b) Only I follows

(c) Only I and II follow

(d) Only II and III follow

Directions (Qs. 34-40): *Each of these questions has a situation followed by three suggested courses of action numbered I, II and III. Assume everything in the statement to be true, and decide which of the given courses of action logically follows:*

34. **Statement:**

Drinking water supply to New Bombay has been suspended till further orders from Maharashtra Pollution Control Board following pollution of Patalganga river, caused by discharge of effluents from some chemical industries.

Courses of action:

I. The industries responsible for discharging effluents into the river should be asked to close down immediately.

II. The river water should immediately be treated chemically before resuming supply.

III. The Pollution Control Board should check the nature of effluents being discharged into the river by industries at regular intervals.

(a) All follow

(b) Only II and III follow

(c) Only I follows

(d) Only III follows

35. Statement :

The Department of Education has recommended that the primary level admission to Government and Government-aided schools should be done purely by random selection and not by admission tests. This is necessitated as the number of admission seekers are much more than the available seats.

Courses of action:

I. The Government should instruct the private schools also to follow the same practice.

II. The Government should set up an independent body to regulate the primary level admissions.

III. The schools should be asked to select students only from those who stay in the neighbouring areas of the school.

(a) None follows   (b) Only II and III follow

(c) Only I follows   (d) Only II follows

36. Statement :

The vehicular traffic has increased so much in the recent past that it takes at least two hours to travel between the city and the airport during peak hours.

Courses of action:

I. Non-airport bound vehicles should not be allowed to ply on the road connecting the city and the airport.

II. The load of vehicular traffic should be diverted through various link roads during peak hours.

III. The departure and arrival of flights should be regulated so as to avoid congestion during peak hours.

(a) Only I follows   (b) Only I and II follow

(c) Only II follows   (d) All follow

37. Statement :

Due to cancellation of a huge export order for not adhering to the time frame, the company is likely to get into incurring losses in the current financial year.

Courses of action:

I. The officer-in-charge of the production should be immediately suspended.

II. The goods manufactured for the export order should be sold to an other party.

III. The company should change its machinery to maintain the time frame.

(a) None follows   (b) Only I and II follow

(c) Only II follows   (d) All follow

38. Statement :

A devastating earthquake has ravaged the city killing hundreds of people and rendering many more homeless.

Courses of action:

I. The entry of outsiders into the city should be stopped.

II. The civic administration should immediately make alternate temporary housing arrangement for the victims.

III. The affected people should immediately be shifted to a safer place.

(a) Only I follows

(b) Only III follows

(c) Only II and III follow

(d) Either II or III follows

39. Statement :

The army has been alerted in the district following floods triggered by incessant rains.

Courses of action :

I. Relief to flood-affected people should be arranged.

II. Supply of food articles should be arranged.

III. Adequate medical facilities should be arranged.

(a) None follows   (b) Only I follows

(c) Only II follows   (d) All follow

40. Statement :

Higher disposal costs encourage those who produce waste to look for cheaper ways to get rid of it.

Courses of action :

I. The disposal costs should be made higher.

II. The disposal costs should be brought down.

III. A committee should be set up to study the details in this respect.

(a) All follow   (b) Only I follows

(c) Only II follows   (d) Only II and III 'follow

Directions (Qs. 41-46) : *In each question below is given a statement followed by two courses of action numbered I and II. You have to assume everything in the statement to be true, then decide which of the two given suggested courses of action logically follows. Mark answer as :*

(a) If only II follows

(b) If only I follows

(c) If neither I nor II follows

(d) If both I and II follow

41. Statement :

A large section of the population in the city is caught in the malaria epidemic.

Courses of action :

I. The municipal officials should be instructed to supervise extensive fumigation in the city.

II. Advisories to prevent mosquito bites should be issued.

42. Statement :

A large number of engineering graduates in the country are not in a position to have gainful employment at present and the number of such engineers is likely to grow in the future.

Courses of action :

I. The government should launch attractive employment generation schemes and encourage these graduates to opt for such schemes to use their expertise and knowledge effectively.

II. This happened due to proliferation of engineering colleges in the country and thereby lowered the quality of the engineering graduates. Those colleges which are not equipped to impart quality education should be closed down.

43. Statement:

The police department has come under a cloud with recent revelations that at least two senior police officials are suspected to have been involved in the illegal sale of a large quantity of weapons from the state police armoury.

Courses of action:

I. A thorough investigation should be ordered by the State Government to bring out all those who are involved in the illegal sale of arms.

II. State police armoury should be kept under Central Government's controls.

44. Statement:

The Committee has criticized the Institute for its failure to implement a dozen regular programmes despite an increase in the staff strength and for not drawing up a firm action plan for studies and research.

Courses of action:

I. The broad objectives of the Institute should be redefined to implement a practical action plan.

II. The Institute should give a report on reasons for not having implemented the planned programmes.

45. Statement:

The availability of imported fruits has increased in the indigenous market and so the demand for indigenous fruits has decreased.

Courses of action:

I. To help the indigenous producers of fruits, the government should impose high import duty on these fruits, even if these are not of good quality.

II. The fruit vendors should stop selling imported fruits so that the demand for indigenous fruits would be increased.

46. Statement:

Some serious blunders were detected in the accounts section of a factory.

Courses of action:

I. An efficient team of auditors should be appointed to check the Accounts.

II. A show cause notice should be issued to all the employees involved in the irregularity.

47. Statement:

In the last two weeks, stray dogs have attacked five people including a child of 6 years, in the colony. The people are scared of coming out of their homes.

Courses of action:

I. An FIR should be lodged by the Residents' Welfare Association of the colony so that police may take immediate action in this regard.

II. MCD should be informed immediately about the attacks by the stray dogs.

48. Statement:

There is a place of worship erected by local people in the outskirts of the city and the land on which it is built has been allotted to a company to open its manufacturing unit. Now, the company wants the structure to be removed from the land which has evoked public outrage.

Courses of action:

I. The company should offer to erect a similar structure on a nearby site, thereby, requesting permission to demolish the structure built on its land.

II. The company should start its working without removing the structure as demolishing it may become chaotic and will result in heavy public outcry by hurting their religious sentiments.

49. Statement:

Due to the heavy demand of milk during Diwali, there is a rumour that sweets hop owners are using adulterated milk or synthetic milk to make sweets.

Courses of action:

I. The district administration should direct the police to raid all the sweet shops and check the purity of the milk used to make sweets.

II. The district administration should issue a notice in the newspaper starting that if any adulteration is found in any product made by the shops, the shops will be heavily penalised along with cancellation of their licences.

50. Statement:

There has been a shortage of water in the state for the last four days as the neighbouring state has stopped the supply of water due to some inter-state problems.

Courses of action:

I. The Central Government should immediately intervene to discuss the matter with these two states and find the solution.

II. The CMs of both the states should take this matter seriously and discuss the matter in order to find a resolution to the issue of water crisis; and try to maintain a good relation with each other.

Solutions

ANSWER KEY

1	(a)	6	(a)	11	(d)	16	(d)	21	(d)	26	(b)	31	(b)	36	(c)	41	(d)	46	(d)
2	(a)	7	(d)	12	(a)	17	(d)	22	(b)	27	(b)	32	(d)	37	(b)	42	(d)	47	(a)
3	(a)	8	(b)	13	(d)	18	(d)	23	(b)	28	(b)	33	(c)	38	(d)	43	(b)	48	(b)
4	(d)	9	(a)	14	(a)	19	(d)	24	(b)	29	(c)	34	(a)	39	(d)	44	(a)	49	(a)
5	(b)	10	(d)	15	(c)	20	(b)	25	(a)	30	(d)	35	(d)	40	(d)	45	(c)	50	(a)

DETAILED EXPLANATIONS

1. **(a)** I is a reasonable course of action. Hence, it follows. Nothing about the market condition is known from the statement. Hence, II does not follow.

2. **(a)** I is advisable to be prepared for the storage of the new crop. II is not relevant as the statement says that there will be good crop and does not show any requirement of fertilisers.

3. **(a)** Clearly, proper supervision alone can see the development in practice. So, only course I follows. II will only aggravate the problem.

4. **(d)** I is not a proper way to tackle the problem. Because this action will not help reduce the problem. Hence, I is not advisable. On a similar basis, II is also not advisable. None of the two are able to solve the problem.

5. **(b)** I is not advisable because sophisticated weapons must not be provided in lay hands. Further, this can lead to villagers turning into dacoits or robbers. II is advisable because this will encourage the villagers.

6. **(a)** I follows because it will lessen the miseries of affected people. II does not follow. Fire brigade can't play any role in a problem caused by heavy rain.

7. **(d)** Neither of the courses of action talks about what should be done. Both only suggest the probable consequences.

8. **(b)** Only II follows as I does't provide solution to the problem. Rather, it talks about the contrary and will aggravate the problem further.

9. **(a)** The first course should be to try their best that transporters don't go on strike. Hence, I follows. II talks about alternative public transport which is out of context. The statement talks about transport (goods carriers) & not public transport (Bus, auto, ricksha etc.)

10. **(d)** Money is very important for the execution of any plan. Reduction in other expenditures will definitely help to raise money. Hence, I follows. Any programme can not succeed without a good planning. Hence, II follows.

11. **(d)** I is advisable because it will prepare the farmers to face the situation (in a better way) well in advance. II is also advisable because it will be helpful to cope with the problem related to water.

12. **(a)** Clearly, such projects shall be an asset and a source of income to the country later on. So, course I shall follow.

13. **(d)** Since severe damage has been caused by cyclone, people in affected villages ought to be shifted to safer places. Also, since relief work entails huge amounts, financial help from Central Government is a must. So, both the courses follow.

14. **(a)** The effectiveness of such Control Boards is established by the fact that Orissa and A.P. have agreed to it for better control of its multipurpose projects. So, only course I follows.

15. **(c)** The problem pointed out in the statement is the over crowdeness of the footpaths, which are meant for the pedestrians. So, the problem must be either lessened or completely solved for any of the courses to follow. I follows as this will completely solve the problem. II can also solve the problem as the pedestrians can move easily. Hence, either I or II follows.

16. **(d)** Clearly, the two diseases mentioned are caused by unhygienic conditions. So, improving the hygienic conditions is a step towards their eradication. Also, constant medication will help timely detection of the disease and hence, a proper treatment. So, both I and II follow.

17. **(d)** I is advisable because partial cut in supply will be useful when water crisis occurs. II is also advisable because minimal use of water by people will help conserve water and ensure smooth supply in future. Both the courses will lead to increase in the water level.

18. **(d)** I is not advisable because it is explicitly mentioned in the statement that unemployment is the main cause of raise in suicide cases. Love affair lead to suicidal death is out of context. Hence, II is not advisable. III is advisable because it will help minimise the problem. As none of the options shows only III so (d) is correct.

19. **(d)** The problem is that the railways are dependent on government subsidies as they lack funds/revenues due to lack of concentration on transportation activities. I follows as the committee would be the first step in lessening this problem.

II follows as this can help the railways in generating more revenues.

III follows as by living of non-core activities will help the railways in focussing an transportation activities.

20. (b) As mentioned in the statement, 'model M is its first product', so, it is necessary to finalise the network of dealers and all matters regarding the sale of the product. Hence, I follows. II has no connection with the statement. The statement talks about the launch of the car and not about the maintainence of production schedule. Hence, III does not follow.

21. (d) I is a final out come and not a course of action. II and III are redundant and out of context

22. (b) According to the statement, the teachers are not familiarised with the need, importance and meaning of population education. Hence, II is appropriate.

23. (b) The state government should pay salaries to the employees Hence, II is logical.

24. (b) The government should ensure regular supply of raw material for food processing industry. Hence, II is logical course of action.

25. (a) Since the offer has a hunch, therefore, it is logical that he verifies the balance sheet and cash balance. Hence I is appropriate.

26. (b) Logically the voluntary organizations should explore other sources of financial support.

27. (b) Management should involve experienced people for restructuring because their involvement would be beneficial.

28. (b) Display of obscene material should be banned.

29. (c) Train drivers are not supposed to, nor able to stop trains in such situations, hence I is ruled out. Due to collision with running train, chances of bus driver's survival is negligible, hence II is ruled out. III gives a preventive measure for such mishaps.

30. (d) All statements suggest a precautionary measure for future.

31. (b) Statement III puts all responsibility on fishermen alone. Watching a mishap is no cure for the mishap. Statement I is corrective measure and II is precautionary measure.

32. (d) Eating habit of a society develops through centuries and is impossible to change, hence, II can't be implemented. I and III will help address the growth in demand.

33. (c) Faculty members should be persuaded not to go on strike and an action against the members who join the strike should be taken.

34. (a) All the three courses of actions follow in this case. The chemical industries are discharging effluents into the river which may be hazardous hence, the chemical factories should be closed down. Now, that the water is polluted, it has to be treated chemically before resuming supply, otherwise it may affect those using it. This also gives an example to Pollution Control Board to keep a check to prevent any mishappening at regular intervals.

35. (d) To avoid testing at the primary level admissions, the government should take the course of action II .

36. (c) The best option in this case is to divert the load of vehicular traffic through various link roads during peak hours.

37. (b) The officer-in-charge of production should be suspended so as to ensure that this kind of a problem does not happen in future. Also the export order should be sold to the other party.

38. (d) If the entry of outsiders were stopped, how would the victims get the help. Hence, surely course of action (I) does not follow. Now, if the civic administration is making alternate housing arrangements for the victim there is no requirement to shift them and vice-versa. Hence II or III follow.

39. (d) After incessant rains, there will be many problems regarding shelter, food, and medical facilities of flood effected people.

40. (d) Both II & III follow.

41. (d) Fumigation by municipal body and prevention of mosquito bites undertaken by people, both are required to fight the epidemic.

42. (d) I is advisable because government employment generation scheme will encourage the talented student to opt for engineering stream. II is also advisable because without quality education, proliferation of sub-standard engineering colleges will generate unskilled engineers.

43. (b) I is advisable because thorough investigation would be helpful to bring out all those who are involved in the illegal sale of arms. II has no connection with the statement.

44. (a) II is advisable.

45. (c) I is not fully correlated with the statement, so, it is not advisable. II is not a practical course of action.

46. (d) I is advisable because it will be helpful to correct the blunders. II is also advisable because it will encourage employees to stop the irregularity.

47. (a) II follows because MCD is the concerned authority to take action in this type of cases, not the police.

48. (b) I follows because offering to build a similar structure on a nearby site appears to be a good initiative by the company, respecting the sentiments of the people. II is not a solution of the problem.

49. (a) II follows as issuing a warning letter will definitely help in stopping the use of synthetic on adulterated milk (if any). I doesn't follow as it is not feasible for the police to raid each and every shop and check the purity of the milk used to make sweets. This step is taken later, only on reports of violators despite the warning.

50. (a) II follows as the meeting between the heads of the concerned states will definitely help in working out a solution. I doesn't follow because the Centre never intervenes straightaway in case of inter-state disputes; it waits for the two states to resolve the issue on their own. The Centre intervenes only when the two states are not able to sort out the problems on their own.

SECTION 2: DECISION MAKING

DECISION MAKING—A MENTAL PROCESS

Decision Making is a mental process undertaken by an individual for selection of a course of action among many available options. Decision making will result in a final choice. Decisions are always taken in the context of a set of needs.

In this type of questions, a given situation is followed by four options of the decision to be made.

These questions are based on real-life situations that IAS officers encounter routinely. They gauge your ability to deal with similar situations and arrive at the best decisions. Thus, these questions are designed to judge your analytical skills and your ability to resolve a problem.

The questions may deal with different situations like land acquisition for a proposed economic zone; hurdles in setting up a power generation unit, etc. You have to decide on the best possible option in the given situation. There is no fixed rule for arriving at a decision. Your answer depends on your analytical ability and also on your interpersonal skills.

The idea underlying this test is to evaluate your ability to take decisions logically for exigencies, contingencies and emergencies with appropriate management of people. Therefore, real life situations have been framed as questions, to test your skills in dealing with the hypothetical crisis presented to you in the form to a query.

Take care while solving such questions. Never make assumptions of your own for the examiner wants you to solve the given problem within the ambit of its original premises.

Remember, analytical ability is the best tool to deal with such situations. You always use your personal abilities to analyse any crisis. The examiner wants to know your solution to the problems that as a civil servant you may have to deal with on a daily basis. Decision Making is difficult due to multiple alternatives available and, risky consequence involved in a particular decision. There is uncertainty, as well as complexity, and a need to evaluate issues involved in any decision. A major challenge during decision making is to settle interpersonal issues.

STEP TECHNIQUE FOR DECISION MAKING

1. Identification of objectives.
2. Classification of objectives.
3. Analysis of alternative actions.
4. Evaluation of alternatives.
5. Decision evaluated with respect to consequences.
6. Hindrances in implementing the decision.

EFFECTIVE LISTENING FOR DECISION MAKING

Listening helps you not only in problem solving, but also in image building in front of the interview board or the community. An attentive and smart listener listens to the question with utmost attention, answers it later on. This gives him/her enough time to recall the facts and figures to reply comprehensively. On the contrary, a poor listener never replies to a question properly. Thus, it is clear that listening is an ability that everyone must develop. Try the following steps to enhance your listening ability.

1. Pay attention to the speaker as long as he/she speaks. Make him/her feel that you are concentrating on him/her only and he/she is getting due attention. Try to show that you understand what he/she is trying to convey.

2. Try to make eye contact and observe the body language of the speaker. It will give you a chance to understand his/her posture as people often give out aggression or calmness through their body language.

3. Make the speaker feel that you are listening to him/ her. You can use your body language and small verbal communication such as 'yeah', or nod your head positively.

4. If you find anything difficult or miss any important point, ask the speaker to repeat that only after he/she completes his/her point.

5. Give feedback but only when a speaker—who may be a professor, a complainant, a student or anyone else—asks after he/she finishes his/her point. Every speaker solicits some feedback after he/she finishes his/her lecture.

6. Remember, your feedback should be balanced as it will define your image in the eyes of the speaker. Therefore, do not exaggerate, or understate your opinion. Try to summarize it precisely.

7. Try to guess where the discourse is leading.

If you are attentive, well focused, and you pay attention to minute details, you will gradually develop the ability of a good listener. It will help you in making decisions in your career, in your office and in your daily life.

There are three aspects of listening.

1. Receiving information
2. Solving problem
3. Sharing with others

When you receive information, you must pay utmost attention so that you collect right information. Civil servants often have to deal with tricky situations while probing an important case. Suppose that you are an IPS officer and receive the information that a station house officer has indulged in corruption. As a district police chief, it is your responsibility to ensure action against the officer to solve the problem. But before taking any decision, you would like to investigate the truth behind the complaint. You will share it with some of your juniors and people in the area where the SHO is posted. So, your listening ability will come to your great help in your decision making.

Exercise

Directions (Qs. 1–35): *Each item describes a situation and is followed by four possible responses. Indicate the response you find most appropriate. Choose only one response for each item. The responses will be evaluated based on the level of appropriateness for the given situation.*

Please attempt all the items. There is no penalty for wrong answers for these items.

1. The section officer had forgotten to inform you about a meeting you are required to attend. You were absent on that day and have been sent a notice by the deputy secretary. You are on very good terms with the section officer and do not want to expose him. You would
   (a) send a written reply offering some plausible excuse.
   (b) seek an appointment with the deputy secretary.
   (c) take the blame on yourself.
   (d) get philosophical about the whole thing.

2. You have a flat in south Delhi which has been rented out. As the tenant was your friend, you did not sign a lease agreement. Your father is soon retiring and you have to vacate government quarters within six months. Unfortunately, the tenant is refusing to move out. You would
   (a) report the matter to the police.
   (b) hire goons to get him thrown out.
   (c) file a case in the court.
   (d) buckle under pressure and sell the property.

3. An important document is missing from the office. The papers were handed over to an assistant in the department for safe-keeping. You would
   (a) suspend the assistant.
   (b) give him a week's time to locate the document.
   (c) Inform the headquarters
   (d) get him removed from service

4. You are in-charge of handing out compensation to the victims of the High Court bomb blast in September, 2011. The families of the victims are not happy with the way in which compensation cases are being handled. They accuse you of malpractices. You would
   (a) ask for an enquiry.
   (b) ignore the allegations.
   (c) refuse to work until matters are sorted out.
   (d) ask your seniors to hand over the responsibility to some body else.

5. You have been asked to establish asbestos shelters for the poor. You have invited bids from contractors. Unfortunately the bids are above the approved rates. You would
   (a) accept the lowest bid.
   (b) call for new bids.
   (c) refer the matter to your seniors.
   (d) send new tenders with better specifications.

6. You are in charge of administering polio drops in your area. The work is almost done. Just as you take a breather you are informed that a certain house in your locality has still not received the drops. You are in a dillema as stocks have been exhausted. You would
   (a) arrange for the drops from another area.
   (b) request the residents of that house to procure the drops privately.
   (c) procure a fresh stock of vaccines.
   (d) buy the vaccines from a doctor and send it to the house.

7. You have undertaken a project to create low cost homes for the poor. The project has taken off well. Some individuals have even moved in. They complain that the homes are not habitable due to presence of snakes. You would
   (a) continue with the project ignoring their complaints.
   (b) assure the residents of an enquiry.
   (c) ask them to lodge a written complaint.
   (d) ask them to re-consider their decision.

8. You have been approached by the parents of a girl who is being troubled by goons on her way to the college. As you are the M.L.A of the constituency, it is your duty to ensure the welfare of residents. You would
   (a) tell them to file an FIR.
   (b) take your own measures to catch the goons.
   (c) counsel the girl and her parents.
   (d) take the help of the Residents Welfare Association.

9. You are in charge of the police station. You are a very efficient officer. The resident feel safe and secure due to the efficient working of the police force. However, a dacoity taken place in your area. An old couple are attacked. People start criticizing you. You would
   (a) complain to your superiors.
   (b) submit your resignation.
   (c) continue to work.
   (d) work with your detractors.

10. You are an officer in the revenue department. One day as you are handling the cash, you realize that some money is missing from the safe. You would
    (a) get it recounted by the cashier and tally it with balance sheet.
    (b) appoint a private detective agency to look into the matter.
    (c) inform the police about the missing money.
    (d) inform your superiors and plead innocence.

11. You are the block development officer. The district has many matchbox factories. There is a report that the drinking water in a village is contaminated with arsenic making it unfit for human consumption. You would
    (a) get the residents shifted to another area.
    (b) make arrangements for the supply of safe drinking water.
    (c) get water from a nearby village.
    (d) ask for extra funds to tide over the crisis.

12. As an official in the ministry of Foreign Affairs you come to know that the U.S is not likely to grant India's request for a $ 500 million loan. A high level meeting has been called by the Ministry. What suggestions would you like to give ?

    (a) India should persuade U.S to grant the loan.
    (b) India should approach other countries for the loan.
    (c) India can approach the World Bank for redressal.
    (d) India should try to fall back upon its own resources in such a case.

13. The rainy season had not been good in Delhi last year. There was a major drop in the water table. The summers are going to be more difficult. As the mayor of the city, you are worried. You would
    (a) seek help from neighbouring states to get additional water supply.
    (b) take steps to control the situation by opting for rainwater harvesting.
    (c) instruct the water supply department to impose a partial cut in supply to conserve water.
    (d) use the media to appeal to all the residents to reduce water consumption.

14. You are in charge of a steel factory where a large stock of live ammunition has been found as scrap. You would
    (a) inform the police.
    (b) call the bomb squad.
    (c) close down the unit.
    (d) enquire into the matter and take corrective measures.

15. A woman stops you on your patrol and gives a wallet to you that contains ₹400 which she found on a cosmetic counter in a nearby store. There is nothing in the wallet which will help in its identification. What should you do ?
    (a) Ask her to keep the wallet.
    (b) Ask her to give the wallet back at the store's Lost and Found office.
    (c) Take the wallet, get her name, and give it to the police department's Lost and Found division.
    (d) None of the above.

16. You are the Chief Minister of U.P. Acquisition of land in Greater Noida has led to violence and death of many farmers. You are worried. You would
    (a) institute an enquiry to prevent further incidents.
    (b) pull up the administrative staff for negligence.
    (c) speak to the people involved in purchase of land.
    (d) take measures to ensure that farmers are paid reasonable dues.

17. You are an officer in Central Bureau of Investigation. You receive a complaint about a junior from a civilian. He is asking for a bribe. You are undecided. You would
    (a) suspend the assistant immediately.
    (b) institute an enquiry to find the truth of the matter.
    (c) give the assistant a warning.
    (d) inform the superiors giving them all the details.

18. You are the Municipal Commissioner of Delhi. It has been decided by the government to withdraw the mid-day meal scheme from primary schools. As a result, the number of dropouts has increased. To rectify the problem, you would
    (a) ask the government to reconsider its decision.
    (b) consider closing down some schools.
    (c) inquire into the reason for high rate of dropouts.
    (d) ignore the problem.

19. You are a health official of your locality. Dengue is spreading very rapidly. Private hospitals are reporting a shortage of beds. One of your relatives suffering from dengue requests you to get him a bed in any hospital. You would
    (a) help him out by talking to a friend in a nearby state.
    (b) request him to make his own arrangements as you are helpless in the matter.
    (c) use your influence to get him admitted to a private hospital.
    (d) take the help of a superior to get him admitted to a government hospital.

20. You have been working as a section officer in the Ministry for the past ten years. You deserve a promotion as a deputy secretary. You find that your juniors are being given preference over you. You would
    (a) go in for voluntary retirement.
    (b) discuss the issue with your immediate boss.
    (c) report the matter to superiors.
    (d) apply for a transfer.

21. You are a woman IPS officer selected for promotion as a commissioner along with two other males. If one of your male colleagues is made the commissioner and you are not promoted, you would
    (a) go in for voluntary retirement.
    (b) you would wait patiently as you have the ability.
    (c) you would protest formally.
    (d) you would take the help of media.

22. You are the manager of a village bank. The farmers are neck deep in debts. They are being exploited by the money lenders. An e-mail has been dispatched to the head office asking for permission to grant loans to such individuals but there has been no response. Two farmers have attempted suicide and the media is getting critical. You would
    (a) take the money lenders to task.
    (b) sanction loans at your own risk.
    (c) send another request to the headquarters.
    (d) arrange for funds from any other source.

23. Workers have gone on strike to protest against the company's unfair treatment of workers. As a CEO, how would you deal with such a situation? You would
    (a) fire the employees who are on strike.
    (b) negotiate a deal.
    (c) declare a lock-out till the situation becomes normal.
    (d) try to reason with workers.

24. You are the D.M. of the Southern Railways. There is a major accident near Chennai. 10 people get killed. You would
    (a) send men and equipment to begin rescue operations.
    (b) divert trains on the route.
    (c) send an SOS to enlist help from all sources.
    (b) expect that the local villagers would give relief.

25. The old style single screen cinema halls are incurring heavy losses as people prefer to watch movies at home or on computers. As the owner of one such hall, you are worried. You would
    (a) close down the hall.
    (b) set up a multiplex to attract more visitors.

   (c)   consider setting up a residential complex.

   (d)   advertise about the richness of cinematic experience.

26. As the Education Minister, you are worried as engineering graduates are not getting employment. Number of unemployed engineers is likely to grow in future. To stop this trend, you would

   (a)   close down the colleges which are not equipped properly.

   (b)   launch employment schemes specifically for such graduates.

   (c)   inform the public as to which colleges are good.

   (d)   request colleges to upgrade their facilities.

27. You have been asked to give an explanation for not attending an important official meeting. Your immediate boss who has not informed you about the meeting is now putting pressure on you not to place an allegation against him/her. You would

   (a)   send a written reply explaining the fact.

   (b)   seek an appointment with the top boss to explain the situation.

   (c)   admit your fault to save the situation.

   (d)   put the responsibility on the coordinator of the meeting for not informing.

28. You are an officer in the department of Disaster Management. An earthquake in Sikkim has destroyed four villages. It has come to light that this was mainly due to poor level of development and inadequate infrastructure. To prevent such large scale destruction in the future, you would

   (a)   replace all cemented buildings with wooden structures.

   (b)   educate the residents about disaster management during an earthquake

   (c)   call in the experts to improve existing infrastructure.

   (d)   ask for extra funds to face future calamities.

29. You are an administrative officer at MCD. The footpaths in your area are occupied by vendors. This is dangerous for pedestrians. Traffic jams are caused as vendors and shoppers spill over on the streets. To solve this problem you would

   (a)   round up the vendors and clear footpaths.

   (b)   impose licence fees so a lesser number of vendors will appear.

   (c)   get all the vendors shifted to an appropriate place.

   (d)   provide vendors with alternative work.

30. You are a secretary in the Ministry of Foreign affairs. You are concerned about military threats India is facing from its neighbours. In your opinion, India should

   (a)   go to war with her errant neighbours.

   (d)   call for a dialogue on border issues.

   (c)   get the support of the international community to counter such threats.

   (d)   should spend more on Defence to safeguard itself.

31. You are the manager of a bank. You notice that customers are not repaying loans on time. It is difficult to locate the defaulters. To protect the bank from such fraudulent transactions, you would

   (a)   appoint investigating officers to identify such transactions.

   (b)   appoint muscle men to recover loans.

   (c)   verify the customers before granting loans.

   (d)   stop advancing loans for the time being.

32. You are the CEO of a company where sale of a product has gone down. You want to reverse the trend. The first thing you would do is to

   (a)   ask you staff to examine rival products.

   (b)   reduce the price of the product and improve its quality.

   (c)   stop manufacturing the product.

   (d)   introduce a discount scheme to finish the existing stocks.

33. You are the police commissioner of your state. The department has come under a cloud as a senior police official has been involved in a criminal act. You would:

   (a)   initiate investigation to find the truth.

   (b)   suspend the official.

   (c)   issue a warming to staff about strict action.

   (d)   request the media not to give too much publicity to it.

34. You are the Chief Election Commissioner. There was very low voter turnout in Andhra Pradesh in the assembly elections. As Chief Election Commissioner you would

   (a)   cancel the election as this is not a good representation of votes.

   (b)   punish those who did not caste their votes.

   (c)   advertise the election details more effectively.

   (d)   hold fresh elections to ensure better voter turn out.

35. You are a D.M. in the Indian Railways. The AC class in trains are going half empty. This is caused by low fares offered by airlines. Passengers prefer to travel by air. To increase the rate of occupancy, you would

   (a)   reduce the fare to get back passengers.

   (b)   reduce the capacity of upper classes to match lower demand.

   (c)   ignore the problem thinking that it will solve itself.

   (d)   eliminate the upper class facility.

36. You have to accomplish a very important task for your Headquarters within the next two days. Suddenly, you meet with an accident. Your office insists that you complete the task. You would

   (a)   ask for an extension of deadline.

   (b)   inform Headquarters of your inability to finish on time.

   (c)   suggest alternate person to Headquarters who may do the needful.

   (d)   stay away till you recover.

37. You are an officer in Delhi Development Authority. You are concerned with the large number of legal cases pending in the courts. The courts are not able to decide important disputes. You feel that

   (a)   courts should be requested to speed up cases.

   (b)   special powers should be granted to speed up investigations.

   (c)   accept the situation as it is.

   (d)   request the courts not to accept any petitions till pending cases are disposed of .

38. You are an officer dealing with internet matters. There have been many cases of internet hacking among users. Internet users are getting wary of sharing personal details in cyber space, you would

(a)   trace the culprits and have them arrested.
(b)   advise internet users to be cautious till safety measures are undertaken.
(c)   develop more powerful software to deal with hackers.
(d)   seek additional staff to deal with the issue.

39. You are travelling in a bus and you see a lady standing, and some young boys sitting on seats reserved for ladies. You would

(a)   ask them to vacate the seat for the lady.
(b)   request them to leave the seat.
(c)   tell them that it is a reserved seat so they should get up.
(d)   ask someone else to vacate the seat for the lady.

40. You are a senior officer in the IAS. High prices of vegetables is of concern to the common man as well as the ruling party. What measures would you suggest to control vegetable prices?

(a)   Government should control prices of diesel.
(b)   Hoarding by traders should be prohibited.
(c)   Vegetables should be sold at government outlets.
(d)   Follow a wait and watch policy.

41. You are a senior official in the Ministry of Home Affairs. Fairs and festivals invariably have stampede resulting in deaths. What should be the steps taken by the government to prevent stampede?

(a)   Arrange for crowd control at all sensitive spots.
(b)   Give prompt compensation to the victims.
(c)   Ban all fairs and festivals.
(d)   Restrict the number of people coming to such events.

42. You are a secretary in the Ministry of Finance. Cases of corruption are being reported against microfinance companies. You would commend

(a)   banning all micro finance enterprises.
(b)   enacting a law to regulate and nationalise such companies.
(c)   appointing a committee to probe the issue.
(d)   imposing heavy penalty on directors of the company.

43. Cases of road accidents are increasing in urban areas. If you are the transport authority, what you would decide?

(a)   Impose tough norms for maintenance of vehicles.
(b)   Order the traffic police to punish those who are violating traffic rules.
(c)   convince people through seminars and meetings and make them more sensitive.
(d)   All of the above.

44. You are a secretary in the Ministry of Information and Broadcasting. You find that the lady employees are almost always late for work. What will you do in such a situation?

(a)   You will suspend the late comers.
(b)   Give late comers a warning.
(c)   Forgive them as they are females.
(d)   Analyse the problem to find out the real cause and then decide on further action.

45. You are a senior government officer. While traveling in your official car, your driver is involved in an accident. An individual is badly injured. You would

(a)   ask the driver to run away.
(b)   take the injured to the hospital.
(c)   ask the driver to surrender to the police
(d)   Put the blame for the accident on the driver

46. You are the chairman of a private bank which is going to be taken over. Your staff oppose this as they are sure that they will lose their jobs. You would

(a)   try to explain the situation from your point of view.
(b)   convince them that they will be safe.
(c)   try to prevent the takeover.
(d)   tell the staff to take voluntary retirement.

47. You are the project Manager for Project Tiger. The project has to be revamped and then relaunched. In spite of proper delegation and coordination, your subordinates are not able to meet the deadline, you would

(a)   suspend all subordinates.
(b)   resign from the post.
(c)   ask seniors to advance the deadline.
(d)   call for a meeting to isolate the problem and continue work.

48. You are a social activist. Corruption costs the economy around 3% of GDP every year. This equals the amount spent on education. What steps should the government take to control corruption?

(a)   Make strict laws to punish the culprits.
(b)   Amend existing laws to make them more effective.
(c)   Take action against guilty.
(d)   Try to improve the values in the administrative system.

49. You are head of transport authority in an urban area. Cases of road accidents are increasing in your area. You would

(a)   impose strict rules for maintenance of vehicles.
(b)   order the traffic police to punish violations.
(c)   spread the message of safe travel by using mass media.
(d)   deploy traffic policemen at accident prone spots.

50. You are the chairman of a committee looking into health status of poor children. You find that there are a large number of undernourished children. The first step that you would take to reverse the trend would be to

(a)   increase the rate of tax on the rich.
(b)   arrange for employment of parents of children.
(c)   introduce free meals at schools and give subsides in ration shops.
(d)   educate parents about good nutrition for children.

51. You are a senior official in the passport department. One of your friends has lost his passport and he has to reach the U.S in a week's time. You would

(a)   get things done as per rules and regulations.
(b)   take the initiative to help your friend at the earliest.
(c)   help him to procure documents without compromising on procedures.
(d)   shorten some of the procedures knowing he is your friend.

52. You are a senior police officer. There is a phone call to inform you that a bomb blast has taken place in the Lajpat Nagar market. You would
    (a) rush to the spot with a force.
    (b) call up the fire Department and the bomb disposal squad and then proceed to the market.
    (c) inform your superiors about the blast.
    (d) instruct the media not to spread rumours.

53. You are the principal of a public school. Accident of a private van transporting children from your school has angered both parents and teachers. The first step that you would take would be to
    (a) recruit new drivers for the school buses.
    (b) do away with private contracts.
    (c) go for government vehicles.
    (d) look into the problem area wise.

54. You are the chairman of Indian Airlines. Due to heavy fogs in winter, most flights from Delhi are delayed causing passengers a great deal of inconvenience. You would request the government to
    (a) construct a new runway which is fog free.
    (b) improve training of the pilots.
    (c) study the problem and take corrective measures.
    (d) fly new planes which can land in fog.

55. You are the CEO of a reputed organization. In the past few years, the job market has improved for both skilled and semi-skilled personnel. You are worried about cases where workers tend to move between jobs without prior notice thus, causing losses to the company. You would
    (a) ask the HR department to draw up a list of irresponsible employees so that strict action can be taken against them.
    (b) make strict rules for the staff for leave taking.
    (c) ask the staff to sign contracts before joining.
    (d) ignore the problem as a flash in the pan.

56. You are a senior official in the Ministry of Road Transport and Highways. Traffic jams during peak hours is a matter of concern. What measures do you think can be taken to reduce jams?
    (a) Improve public transport so that there are fewer private vehicles on roads.
    (b) Improve Metro services.
    (c) Ban private vehicles during peak hours.
    (d) Ask people to share vehicles to limit private vehicles on road.

57. Petroleum prices have increased twice during past one month. The middle class is reeling under the pressure of inflation. What measures do you suggest? They should
    (a) sell their cars.
    (b) write to editors.
    (c) cut down on usage of vehicles.
    (d) protest strongly by going on mass hunger strikes.

58. You are in charge of a police station in Delhi. You receive a radio message asking you to rush to an area where gang of goons are teasing girls. You rush to the spot and
    (a) arrest the goons.
    (b) let them off with a warning.
    (c) get the names and addresses of the eve teasers.
    (d) beat the eve teasers severely.

59. You are an officer in the Defence Ministry. You have to write down a confidential message given by your colleagues but other staff are within ear shot. To verify the message you have noted, you would
    (a) read the message back.
    (b) ask the colleague to call back later.
    (c) tell him that you will revert back.
    (d) ask him to repeat the message.

60. Many people die in stampede during fairs and festivals. What steps should be taken by the government?
    (a) Make arrangements to control crowds.
    (b) Give compensation to the injured and dead.
    (c) Ban celebration of such fairs and festivals.
    (d) Limit number of people who take part in these programmes.

61. You are driving your car. Suddenly, a child runs from the wrong side and is injured by your car. You know that it was not your fault. The parents of child and others appear on the spot.
    (a) You start shouting at them for their carelessness.
    (b) Start telling them that it was the fault of the child.
    (c) Run away from the accident.
    (d) Ask people to help you take the child to the hospital.

62. One morning when you are taking your morning walk, you see that an aircraft has crashed and fallen on the outskirts of the village. What would be your response?
    (a) Start shouting.
    (b) Go there and rescue those who are injured.
    (c) Go to police to inform them about the accident.
    (d) Go back to village to call people for help.

63. You and your friend are working in the office. Suddenly you hear the sound of firing. It was the sound of a bullet fired by your friend at your CEO. What is your reaction? You would
    (a) try to escape.
    (b) start shouting and create panic.
    (c) analyse and try to understand the act of your friend.
    (d) call the police and ask your friend to surrender.

64. You are the CEO of a real estate company. You are working on a project which will expand public facilities. But residents claim that your company has taken over their land without enough compensation. They are protesting against this. You would
    (a) call the police and get the protestors removed.
    (b) give them compensation based on their demand.
    (c) try to convince the protestors against extra compensation.
    (d) promise to consider their case again.

65. Government has raised the retirement age of the public sector workers. The young educated people protest as the government's plan to raise the retirement age will reduce the job opportunities open to them. The situation is out of control. In your opinion, government should

(a) convince the young people that this policy will not reduce opportunities available to them.

(b) take strong action against the protestors.

(c) reverse the decision.

(d) create other opportunities for the young.

66. Threat to air safety is high due to poor maintenance. In the current global airline passenger boom, competition is intense which compels airline to minimise cost and maximise revenue. What you will do to reduce the threat of under maintenance?

(a) Increase funds for maintenance.

(b) Reduce fares.

(c) Isolate the main factors causing problems and take best possible measures to improve air safety.

(d) maintain air safety even at higher cost.

67. You along with your mother are shopping in Sarojini Nagar Market for a wedding. Suddenly, you hear an explosion close by. You would

(a) run towards your mother and hold her tight.

(b) move away from the blast and start praying.

(c) locate the source of noise.

(d) start shouting for assistance.

68. The city has experienced lowest temperature in the last decade accompanied by heavy fog. Most flights from the airport have been delayed causing inconvenience to passengers. As the authority, you would

(a) plan for a new airport.

(b) improve training of pilots.

(c) judge the reasons for delay, prioritizes some areas and plan accordingly.

(d) upgrade the planes.

69. Recently, the job market has improved for professionally qualified youth. Yet, you have come across cases where many youngsters are still not able to get jobs. You would:

(a) raise the job availability.

(b) assist the youth with some money of your own but would not compromise on procedures.

(c) ignore some procedural steps to cater to the employment needs of the youth.

(d) go by rules and regulations to take steps like vocational training to create self-employment opportunities for unemployed youth

70. Supply of illegal, adulterated and local alcohol is a matter of concern for the citizens and administration. A meeting was called by local people and you also attended to discuss the situation. People claim that the administration is not doing enough to deal with the situation. You are representing the administration. What should be your reaction to such claims?

(a) Tell them that the real problem is with people as they buy illegal and adulterated alcohol, and not with the administration.

(b) Tell that citizens should refrain from buying local liquor.

(c) Tell that this problem occurs very frequently and it is the individuals in the city only who run these business and it is for them to stop such activity. It is not the duty of district administration to handle such situations.

(d) Begin by stating that district administration needs the cooperation of citizens to find a solution.

71. You are a police officer on patrol duty. You receive a call from another officer working in another area where a dacoity has occurred. He is calling the headquarters but cannot connect. He requires immediate assistance. You are on duty in the nearby area which is 10 km from where the dacoity has occured. The police wireless does not appear to be receiving his call for help. Which of the following should you do?

(a) Contact the police headquarters.

(b) Go to police headquarters and inform about the situation.

(c) Ignore the call.

(d) Go to the concerned officer to assist him in tackling the situation.

72. You get a complaint against a hospital which undertakes abortion illegally. The complainant wants to remain anonymous. She tells you the name of the hospital and its location. What should be your first step?

(a) Tell the complainant that you will handle the situation.

(b) Tell the complainant she should cooperate with you and give a formal complaint.

(c) Record all the details that she provides and assure her that you will pursue the case.

(d) Ignore the complaint.

73. Officer Vinod is taking free meals from a local restaurant owner in exchange for providing parking space in front of his business. He is permitting the parking of cars in the area marked by administration as non-parking area. A customer has complained to you about conduct of Vinod. Which of the following should you initially do?

(a) Go to your senior officer and complain to him about Vinod.

(b) Speak with the complainant and get the details about his alleged conduct.

(c) Go to Vinod and tell him about the complaint that has been received and the corrupt image he has.

(d) Not do anything immediately but observe officer Vinod to determine if there is any truth in the complaint.

74. A businessman contacts you and asks you to come to his shop as he has a confidential matter to discuss. When you reach the shop, he shows you that he has counterfeit notes. He tells you that he was deceived by one of the customers who cheated him. However, he does not want to report the matter as police will seize the counterfeit currency as evidence and he will end up losing all the money. He wants you to investigate the case but he does not want to surrender the counter-feit currency and says that he will pass them off. What should you tell the shopkeeper?

(a) That you will accept his request.

(b) That you cannot help him until and unless he registers the complaint formally.

(c) That he needs to surrender the entire amount of counterfeit notes so that he can investigate.

(d) That you're calling your supervisor and asking for assistance.

75. While on patrol duty, you came across people who were stalking and eve teasing a girl. They ran away when they noticed you. However, one of them did not see you coming and stayed back. When he saw the others gone, he yelled out for them to stop. By this time, you reach him. Which of the following actions should you do next?
   (a) Chase after the running persons.
   (b) Ask the girl if she is OK.
   (c) Arrest the guy who did not run.
   (d) Inform the nearest police station.

76. You are on patrol and you see a big crowd from a distance. When you reach the spot, you are told that fighting has taken place and a person has been injured. You see that a man is lying on the ground. When you approach him, he states that he was trying to break up a fight when someone hit him with a stick on the back. However, he is not in a condition to speak anything else. Suddenly, some people come forward and tell you that it is Vinod and Promod who are still in the crowd who have hit the man. What should your next action be under these circumstances?
   (a) Call for backup.
   (b) Shout out the names of Vinod and Promod telling them to come out of the crowd.
   (c) Move towards Vinod and Promod so that you can ask them about the incident.
   (d) Ask the people who are near them to hold them.

77. You are on duty and receive information that a bank dacoity is in progress. You rush to the station and take out your jeep to go to the site of crime. However, you realise that the road is blocked. What action should you first take?
   (a) Walk and reach the spot.
   (b) Call the superior and inform him of your circumstances.
   (c) Return to the police station.
   (d) Call your superior for assistance.

78. You are patrolling, and come across two boys fighting. You go towards them but when you reach there, they are laughing and patting each other. It appears that they were just joking. What should you do?
   (a) Arrest both of them.
   (b) Ask them why are they are causing a nuisance.
   (c) Approach them and ask them to explain what was happening.
   (d) Ignore the situation.

79. You have a case based on a complaint received from a shop keeper. You speak to that shop owner to whom a lady sells goods at wholesale rates. The shopkeeper tells you that the young woman in her 20s has been selling goods which could be stolen. She tells you that the woman is now in the store and has just handed over some goods. You look for the woman but she has fled the building. What action should you take?
   (a) Get a good description of the woman and go in pursuit.
   (b) Interview other salespersons to determine if they can identify her.
   (c) Ask the shopkeeper to collect more information as it could lead to the identity of the woman.

   (d) Ask the shopkeeper to give some material evidence that can be used to convict the woman.

80. You receive a complaint that a person has been accused of dacoity. You approach the house of that person and knock at the door. There is no response. Much later, a woman opens the door. Under these circumstances, what should you initially tell her?
   (a) Tell her to call the accused of the dacoity.
   (b) That you have come to arrest the person.
   (c) That you want to know who she is and what she is doing there.
   (d) That the police have a complaint that the individuals who has allegedly committed the recent dacoity is hiding inside.

81. While on duty, a dangerous situation comes to your notice that electrical wires have broken away from poles and are lying "live". You reach the spot but are alone and find that a car with two occupants is caught between the live wires. They do not know what to do and are frightened. What action should you take?
   (a) Block off the road for other vehicles and contact the electricity department.
   (b) Try to help those two occupants to get out.
   (c) Ask the occupants of the car to try and get out from there.
   (d) Use your mobile to call the electricity department and ask for help.

82. Your senior police officer is unhappy with your performance. He does not like the way you deal with cases. How should you react?
   (a) Complain to your colleagues and turn people against him
   (b) Meet the senior officer and discuss your problem
   (c) Meet the boss of your senior and register a formal complaint.
   (d) Meet everyone who is against him and complain against him

83. You have just been informed by your friend that he can manage the tickets for a cricket match that is being held the next day. It is an India-Pakistan match which is rare in your city and you are really keen to watch it. However, your boss does not ever grant leave on one-day notice. What should you do?
   (a) Inform your boss that you cannot attend office due to ill health.
   (b) Notify the supervisor that an emergency has occurred and you want avail of leave.
   (c) Ask your senior officer if he can suggest a way for you to be excused so you can attend the match.
   (d) Cook up a story and ask your senior officer for leave.

84. A citizen who lives in a rural area complains to you that she has seen two people with a rifle and their activities are suspicious. She does not like the fact that they have weapons and are in the area. Of the following, the action that you should first take is to tell her that
   (a) it is none of her business.

(b) you will investigate and that if they are carrying illegal weapons, or if they are trying to do something illegal, they will be arrested.

(c) unless those boys trespass on her property, they are not violating any law.

(d) None of the above.

85. You are on duty in a park. You find that several teenagers are creating a nuisance and raising a ruckus. All of them seem to be college students. What should be your initial course of action under such a situation?

(a) Ignore the situation.

(b) Ignore the incident as they are not bothering anyone.

(c) Arrest them and take them to the police station.

(d) Enquire about what is going on; ask them to stop creating nuisance and issue a warning.

86. You are posted as District Magistrate. The trustees of a Hanuman temple bring to your notice that on every Tuesday between 9-10 am a group numbering 20 to 25 gathers in front of the temple to protest against RSS-VHP and their aversion to occasions like Valentine's Day and Christmas. The trustees inform you that on one occasion, a devotee was insulted and assaulted. You know that a gathering of more than five persons can be regarded as unlawful assembly. What would be the most appropriate action for you to take under these circumstances?

(a) Tell the trustees that the group has a constitutional right to assemble but that they are violating the right of others and as soon as you identify the leader you will arrest the entire group.

(b) Tell the Trustees that you have to check with your superiors. The assembly is apparently an unlawful assembly and you need to investigate further.

(c) Tell the trustees that you will have a talk with the group when they assemble and ask them to disperse and tell them not to undertake such an activity in future as it disturbs others.

(d) Tell the trustees that it is a "controversial issue" and the police cannot get involved in it.

87. You are a police officer and you receive a complaint from a lady that the new occupant of the flat adjacent to hers appears very suspicious. He behaves strangely, goes out during night and returns at odd hours. The people who come to his house to meet him also appear to be of the same type. She is apprehensive that he might be engaged in some terrorist activity. What should you do?

(a) Tell her to keep calm and stop being apprehensive.

(b) Ask her for more details and act accordingly.

(c) Go to that house of the strange person and ask him to furnish his personal details.

(d) Do nothing as you have no evidence that the man is involved in unlawful activities.

88. A local thug (bad element) has started illegal construction on your vacant plot. He has refused your request to vacate and threatened you of dire consequences in case you do not sell the property at a cheap price to him. You would

(a) sell the property at a cheap price to him.

(b) go to the police to file a complaint and request for necessary action.

(c) ask your neighbours for help.

(d) negotiate with the goon to get a higher price.

89. You are an officer in charge of providing basic medical facilities to the survivors of an earthquake affected area. Despite your best possible efforts, people have made allegations against you for making money out of the funds given for relief. You would

(a) let an enquiry be set up to look into the matter.

(b) ask your senior to appoint some other person in your place.

(c) not pay attention to allegations.

(d) stop undertaking any initiative till the matter is resolved.

90. You have been made responsible to hire boats at a short notice to be used for an area under flood. On seeing the price mentioned by the boat owners, you found that the lowest price was approximately three times more than the approved rate of the Government. You would

(a) reject the proposal and call for a fresh price.

(b) accept the lowest price.

(c) refer the matter to the Government and wait.

(d) threaten the boat owners about a possible cancellation of the licence.

91. You are the officer in charge of administering distribution of vaccine in an isolated epidemic-hit village, and you are left with only one vital of vaccine. There is a requirement of that vaccine for the Gram Pradhan as well as a poor villager. You are being pressurised by the Gram Pradhan to issue the vaccine to him. You would

(a) initiate the procedure to expedite the next supply without issuing the vaccine to either.

(b) arrange vaccine for the poor villager from the distributor of another area.

(c) ask both to approach a doctor and get an input about the urgency of their respective cases.

(d) arrange vaccine for the Gram Pradhan from the distributor of another area.

92. You are competing with your batchmate for a prestigious award to be decided on the basis of an oral presentation. Ten minutes are allowed for each presentation. You have been asked by the committee to finish on time. Your friend, however, is allowed more than the stipulated time period. You would

(a) lodge a complaint to the chairperson against the discrimination.

(b) not listen to any justification from the committee.

(c) ask for withdrawal of your name.

(d) protest and leave the place.

93. You are the chairperson of a state sports committee. You have received a complaint and after a probe have found that an athlete in the junior age category who has won a medal has crossed the age criteria by 5 days. You would

(a) ask the screening committee for a clarification.

(b) ask the athlete to return the medal.

(c) ask the athlete to get an affidavit from the court declaring his/her age.

(d) ask the members of the sports committee for their views.

94. You are involved in setting up a water supply project in a remote area. Full recovery of cost is impossible in any case. The income levels in the area are low and 25% of the population is below poverty line (BPL). When a decision has to be taken on pricing, you would
    (a) recommend that the supply of water be free of charge in all respects.
    (b) recommend that the users pay a one time fixed sum for the installation of taps and the usage of water be free.
    (c) recommend that a fixed monthly charge be levied only on the non-BPL families and for BPL families, water be free.
    (d) recommend that the users pay a charge based on the consumption of water with differentiated charges for non-BPL and BPL families.

95. You have taken up a project to create night-shelters for homeless people during the winter season. Within a week of establishing the shelters, you have received complaints from the residents of the area about the increase in theft cases with a demand to remove the shelters. You would
    (a) ask them to lodge a written complaint in the police station.
    (b) assure residents of an enquiry into the matter.
    (c) ask residents to consider the humanitarian effort made.
    (d) continue with the project and ignore their complaint.

96. You, as an administrative authority, have been approached, by the daughter-in-law of an influential person regarding harassment by her in-laws on account of insufficient dowry. Her parents are not able to approach you because of social pressures. You would
    (a) call the in-laws for an explanation.
    (b) counsel the lady to adjust, given such a circumstance.
    (c) take action after her parents who approach you.
    (d) ask her to lodge a complaint with the police.

97. You have differences of opinion regarding the final report prepared by your subordinate that is to be submitted, urgently. The subordinate is justifying the information given in the report. You would
    (a) convince the subordinate that he is wrong.
    (b) tell him to reconsider the results.
    (c) revise the report on your own.
    (d) tell him not to justify the mistake.

98. You are handling a time-bound project. During the project review meeting, you find that the project is likely to get delayed due to lack of cooperation of the team members. You would
    (a) warn the team members for their non-cooperation.
    (b) look into reasons for non-cooperation.
    (c) ask for the replacement of team members.
    (d) ask for extension of time citing reasons.

99. You are handling a priority project for which have been meeting all the deadlines and are therefore planning your leave during the project. Your immediate boss does not grant your leave citing the urgency of the project. You would
    (a) proceed on leave without waiting for the sanction.
    (b) pretend to be sick and take leave.
    (c) approach higher authority to reconsider the leave application.
    (d) tell the boss that it is not justified and talk the matter out.

100. As a citizen, you have some work with a government department. The official calls you again and again, and without directly asking you, sends out feelers for a bribe. You want to get your work done. You would
    (a) give a bribe.
    (b) behave as if you have not understood the feelers and persist with your application.
    (c) go to the higher officer for help verbally complaining about feelers.
    (d) send in a formal complaint.

Solutions

ANSWER KEY																			
1	(b)	11	(b)	21	(b)	31	(a)	41	(a)	51	(c)	61	(d)	71	(a)	81	(a)	91	(c)
2	(c)	12	(a)	22	(c)	32	(d)	42	(c)	52	(b)	62	(d)	72	(c)	82	(b)	92	(a)
3	(b)	13	(c)	23	(b)	33	(a)	43	(d)	53	(c)	63	(d)	73	(b)	83	(c)	93	(b)
4	(a)	14	(a)	24	(a)	34	(c)	44	(d)	54	(c)	64	(d)	74	(c)	84	(b)	94	(d)
5	(c)	15	(b)	25	(b)	35	(b)	45	(b)	55	(c)	65	(a)	75	(b)	85	(d)	95	(a)
6	(a)	16	(d)	26	(b)	36	(b)	46	(b)	56	(a)	66	(c)	76	(a)	86	(c)	96	(d)
7	(b)	17	(c)	27	(b)	37	(b)	47	(d)	57	(c)	67	(c)	77	(b)	87	(b)	97	(c)
8	(a)	18	(a)	28	(c)	38	(b)	48	(a)	58	(a)	68	(c)	78	(c)	88	(b)	98	(b)
9	(c)	19	(d)	29	(c)	39	(c)	49	(c)	59	(d)	69	(d)	79	(c)	89	(a)	99	(d)
10	(a)	20	(b)	30	(d)	40	(b)	50	(c)	60	(a)	70	(d)	80	(d)	90	(b)	100	(d)

DETAILED EXPLANATIONS

1. **(b)** Meeting the deputy secretary and acknowledging him about the situation will be the best course of action.

2. **(c)** Filing a case in this matter will be the best course of action. Reporting the matter to the police won't help as they too will advise to file a case in the court.

3. **(b)** It would be humane on your part to at least give him time to locate the document.

4. **(a)** This will prove your honesty and your willingness to bring transparency in the system.

5. **(c)** This would be the best option. This would satisfy both the parties.

6. **(a)** This the best option because the process has to be completed.

7. **(b)** Thus means that you are ready to look into the matter and take proactive measures.

8. **(a)** Filing an FIR is the right course of action in such cases. They approached you because they were looking for some other forceful action from you but you need to counsel them about the right procedure.

9. **(c)** Work must continue. You should also solve the problem.

10. **(a)** There is a possibility of counting mistake so, getting the money recounted by the cashier and tallying it with the Balance sheet will be best course of action.

11. **(b)** You have to take quick action as it is a question of drinking water which is a basic necessity.

12. **(a)** Diplomatic exercise should be undertaken to persuade the U.S. for granting the loan. Option (b) and (c) are steps that can be taken only after the failure of persuasion.

13. **(c)** This is very first step to be taken. Self help is the best help.

14. **(a)** The police is to be informed immediately. They will further send the bomb squad.

15. **(b)** This will enable the person who has lost the wallet to get in back.

16. **(d)** It is the best way to calm down tempers and ensure no such incident occurs in future.

17. **(c)** It would be correct to give the junior a chance.

18. **(a)** Since the reason for the dropents is given so, no further enquiry is needed. You should ask the government to reconsider its decision.

19. **(d)** After all, he is your relative and it is your duty to help him. Charity begins at home.

20. **(b)** If you are on good terms with your boss then you can seek his advise in this matter.

21. **(b)** If you are truly deserving then there will be some other door which will open for you. In questions of this type, you have to apply a practical, rational and logical approach.

22. **(c)** Requesting the headquarters again seeking urgent response would be the best course of action.

23. **(b)** This the most positive and peaceful option satisfying every body. Production should not get disrupted.

24. **(a)** In this way, you will be taking responsibility into your own hands and not depend on others.

25. **(b)** This is the current trend. Cinema owners are converting

their halls into multiplexes.

26. (b) The problem is of unemployment so option (b) is the best course of action.

27. (b) (a) A little less positive. A written explanation is too formal and technical. It will not touch the heart. It may raise doubts about the veracity of your statement.

(b) It is only ethical to keep your boss informed of any kind of development in the office.

(c) It does not make sense to cower under pressure. One should be able to stand up for oneself.

(d) It is negative. Making someone else the scape goat means asking for trouble. It will ultimately expose you as a liar who cannot be trusted.

28. (c) This would be the most practical and cost-effective response.

29. (c) To ensure the safety of pedestrians and smooth movement of traffic, all the vendors should be shifted to an appropriate place.

30. (d) Indians are peaceful people. We would like to adopt a peaceful process towards any problem.

31. (a) This seems to be a long term solution to the problem.

32. (d) This would improve the cash flow. Other aspects should also be studied.

33. (a) Initiating an investigation to find the truth would be the best course of action.

34. (c) None of the other is described are legal. Hence, the commissioner can only give better publicity to subsequent elections.

35. (b) Air travel saves times. Hence, lower fares will not solve the problem. Reducing capacity is the best option.

36. (b) (a) A little negative. If the work is very urgent, the company may not be able to comply with your request. So, you must be prepared for both a yes or a no. Not a very happy state of affairs for either of you.

(b) It is better to leave the decision to the headquarters as to how the job should be done.

(c) The headquarters would like to take care of this themselves.

(d) This is a completely negative approach. You may even lose your job this way. Or even if you retain it you will lose the trust and faith that has been imposed upon you.

37. (b) This the most practical and legally correct response.

38. (b) Hackers are difficult to catch. Hence, the internet users have to be cautious.

39. (c) Educating the young boys thereby, providing a seat for the lady would be the best course of action.

40. (b) The smooth supply of vegetables should be ensured by preventing hoarding.

41. (a) This would be very helpful in controlling stampede.

42. (c) No action can be taken until guilt is proven in a probe.

43. (d) All the given options would be helpful in controlling road accidents.

44. (d) All the rules should be followed as you are a government officer.

45. (b) The basic approach should be to save the life of the victim.

46. (b) As the seniormost person, you should explain the right situation subordinates and assure them.

47. (d) Getting to the root cause is always essential.

48. (a) Strict laws may solve the problem.

49. (c) Making people aware of the safety measures to be followed while driving would be a good initiative to decrease the cases of road accidents.

50. (c) Availability of free midday meals increases attendance and improves health.

51. (c) Rules should be followed but delays can be reduced.

52. (b) Even a hoax call has to be taken seriously. Hence, your immediate reaction should be to reach the market.

53. (c) Govt-vehicles are safe and obey traffic rules.

54. (c) Fog is a natural phenomenon and cannot be solved by humans.

55. (c) Legally binding contracts will deter most workers from moving away.

56. (a) Good public transport will reduce congestion.

57. (c) reducing consumption is the best way to reduce the impact of high prices of any commodity.

58. (a) As eve teasing is a crime, arresting them is the best option.

59. (d) If the caller repeats the message the level of secrecy would remain high and the message would be verified.

60. (a) The government should make proper arrangements in order to control crowds during fairs and festivals.

61. (d) Saving the life of the child should be the first step so, option (d) is the best course of action.

62. (d) Saving the life of the people on the crashed aircraft should be the priority therefore, raising an alarm and calling the villagers for help should be the best course of action as they would be the first to help the victims. Police can be informed later on; waiting for police to control the situation may worsen the situation.

63. (d) Informing the police in such cases should be the first step one should take.

64. (d) People should be convinced that you will look into the matter and do the needful. In this way, you will win their faith as well as stop their protest. An investigation should be done to find the truth.

65. (a) convincing the youth will be the best course of action to control the situation.

66. (c) Taking best possible measures to improve air safety should be the priority.

67. (c) Locating the source of noise will help you find the place where the explosion has occurred. After locating the place, you may call the police and inform them about the blast; you can also stop other people from

   (b)   you will investigate and that if they are carrying illegal weapons, or if they are trying to do something illegal, they will be arrested.

   (c)   unless those boys trespass on her property, they are not violating any law.

   (d)   None of the above.

85. You are on duty in a park. You find that several teenagers are creating a nuisance and raising a ruckus. All of them seem to be college students. What should be your initial course of action under such a situation?

   (a)   Ignore the situation.

   (b)   Ignore the incident as they are not bothering anyone.

   (c)   Arrest them and take them to the police station.

   (d)   Enquire about what is going on; ask them to stop creating nuisance and issue a warning.

86. You are posted as District Magistrate. The trustees of a Hanuman temple bring to your notice that on every Tuesday between 9-10 am a group numbering 20 to 25 gathers in front of the temple to protest against RSS-VHP and their aversion to occasions like Valentine's Day and Christmas. The trustees inform you that on one occasion, a devotee was insulted and assaulted. You know that a gathering of more than five persons can be regarded as unlawful assembly. What would be the most appropriate action for you to take under these circumstances?

   (a)   Tell the trustees that the group has a constitutional right to assemble but that they are violating the right of others and as soon as you identify the leader you will arrest the entire group.

   (b)   Tell the Trustees that you have to check with your superiors. The assembly is apparently an unlawful assembly and you need to investigate further.

   (c)   Tell the trustees that you will have a talk with the group when they assemble and ask them to disperse and tell them not to undertake such an activity in future as it disturbs others.

   (d)   Tell the trustees that it is a "controversial issue" and the police cannot get involved in it.

87. You are a police officer and you receive a complaint from a lady that the new occupant of the flat adjacent to hers appears very suspicious. He behaves strangely, goes out during night and returns at odd hours. The people who come to his house to meet him also appear to be of the same type. She is apprehensive that he might be engaged in some terrorist activity. What should you do?

   (a)   Tell her to keep calm and stop being apprehensive.

   (b)   Ask her for more details and act accordingly.

   (c)   Go to that house of the strange person and ask him to furnish his personal details.

   (d)   Do nothing as you have no evidence that the man is involved in unlawful activities.

88. A local thug (bad element) has started illegal construction on your vacant plot. He has refused your request to vacate and threatened you of dire consequences in case you do not sell the property at a cheap price to him. You would

   (a)   sell the property at a cheap price to him.

   (b)   go to the police to file a complaint and request for necessary action.

   (c)   ask your neighbours for help.

   (d)   negotiate with the goon to get a higher price.

89. You are an officer in charge of providing basic medical facilities to the survivors of an earthquake affected area. Despite your best possible efforts, people have made allegations against you for making money out of the funds given for relief. You would

   (a)   let an enquiry be set up to look into the matter.

   (b)   ask your senior to appoint some other person in your place.

   (c)   not pay attention to allegations.

   (d)   stop undertaking any initiative till the matter is resolved.

90. You have been made responsible to hire boats at a short notice to be used for an area under flood. On seeing the price mentioned by the boat owners, you found that the lowest price was approximately three times more than the approved rate of the Government. You would

   (a)   reject the proposal and call for a fresh price.

   (b)   accept the lowest price.

   (c)   refer the matter to the Government and wait.

   (d)   threaten the boat owners about a possible cancellation of the licence.

91. You are the officer in charge of administering distribution of vaccine in an isolated epidemic-hit village, and you are left with only one vital of vaccine. There is a requirement of that vaccine for the Gram Pradhan as well as a poor villager. You are being pressurised by the Gram Pradhan to issue the vaccine to him. You would

   (a)   initiate the procedure to expedite the next supply without issuing the vaccine to either.

   (b)   arrange vaccine for the poor villager from the distributor of another area.

   (c)   ask both to approach a doctor and get an input about the urgency of their respective cases.

   (d)   arrange vaccine for the Gram Pradhan from the distributor of another area.

92. You are competing with your batchmate for a prestigious award to be decided on the basis of an oral presentation. Ten minutes are allowed for each presentation. You have been asked by the committee to finish on time. Your friend, however, is allowed more than the stipulated time period. You would

   (a)   lodge a complaint to the chairperson against the discrimination.

   (b)   not listen to any justification from the committee.

   (c)   ask for withdrawal of your name.

   (d)   protest and leave the place.

93. You are the chairperson of a state sports committee. You have received a complaint and after a probe have found that an athlete in the junior age category who has won a medal has crossed the age criteria by 5 days. You would

   (a)   ask the screening committee for a clarification.

   (b)   ask the athlete to return the medal.

   (c)   ask the athlete to get an affidavit from the court declaring his/her age.

   (d)   ask the members of the sports committee for their views.

94. You are involved in setting up a water supply project in a remote area. Full recovery of cost is impossible in any case. The income levels in the area are low and 25% of the population is below poverty line (BPL). When a decision has to be taken on pricing, you would

(a) recommend that the supply of water be free of charge in all respects.

(b) recommend that the users pay a one time fixed sum for the installation of taps and the usage of water be free.

(c) recommend that a fixed monthly charge be levied only on the non-BPL families and for BPL families, water be free.

(d) recommend that the users pay a charge based on the consumption of water with differentiated charges for non-BPL and BPL families.

95. You have taken up a project to create night-shelters for homeless people during the winter season. Within a week of establishing the shelters, you have received complaints from the residents of the area about the increase in theft cases with a demand to remove the shelters. You would

(a) ask them to lodge a written complaint in the police station.

(b) assure residents of an enquiry into the matter.

(c) ask residents to consider the humanitarian effort made.

(d) continue with the project and ignore their complaint.

96. You, as an administrative authority, have been approached, by the daughter-in-law of an influential person regarding harassment by her in-laws on account of insufficient dowry. Her parents are not able to approach you because of social pressures. You would

(a) call the in-laws for an explanation.

(b) counsel the lady to adjust, given such a circumstance.

(c) take action after her parents who approach you.

(d) ask her to lodge a complaint with the police.

97. You have differences of opinion regarding the final report prepared by your subordinate that is to be submitted, urgently. The subordinate is justifying the information given in the report. You would

(a) convince the subordinate that he is wrong.

(b) tell him to reconsider the results.

(c) revise the report on your own.

(d) tell him not to justify the mistake.

98. You are handling a time-bound project. During the project review meeting, you find that the project is likely to get delayed due to lack of cooperation of the team members. You would

(a) warn the team members for their non-cooperation.

(b) look into reasons for non-cooperation.

(c) ask for the replacement of team members.

(d) ask for extension of time citing reasons.

99. You are handling a priority project for which have been meeting all the deadlines and are therefore planning your leave during the project. Your immediate boss does not grant your leave citing the urgency of the project. You would

(a) proceed on leave without waiting for the sanction.

(b) pretend to be sick and take leave.

(c) approach higher authority to reconsider the leave application.

(d) tell the boss that it is not justified and talk the matter out.

100. As a citizen, you have some work with a government department. The official calls you again and again, and without directly asking you, sends out feelers for a bribe. You want to get your work done. You would

(a) give a bribe.

(b) behave as if you have not understood the feelers and persist with your application.

(c) go to the higher officer for help verbally complaining about feelers.

(d) send in a formal complaint.

going in that direction. So, option (c) will be the best course of action.

68. (c) Analysing the situation before taking any decision should be the best course of action. All other option are irrelevant in the context of the given situation.

69. (d) Vocational training helps in generating employment, especially among the youth. So, this would be the best course of action.

70. (d) Problem solving is a collective effort.

71. (a) The information should reach the correct authority.

72. (c) Getting the details is crucial.

73. (b) The initial details are always crucial.

74. (c) Asking the person to surrender the counterfeit notes would be the best course of action/suggestion (as per the law) then only, you can investigate the matter further.

75. (b) To know the condition of the victim, is very important.

76. (a) You are outnumbered and need help.

77. (b) You should always involve the superior in decision making.

78. (c) You should be aware of the total situation.

79. (c) Getting more information about the suspicious lady will help in tracking her and catching her red handed if she is engaged in any illegal or unlawful activity.

80. (d) This would be the truthful explanation of the purpose of your visit.

81. (a) In such situations, your first duty should be to help the victims and second, to raise an alarm so that others do not get in contact with the live-wire. After this, you should immediately contact the electricity department to stop the electricity supply to the affected area.

82. (b) Discussion is normally enough to solve most of the problems.

83. (c) Seniors have greater experience in solving such problems. This way, you take your senior into confidence and avail yourself of leave too.

84. (b) Only illegal activities can be looked into.

85. (d) Such actions on part of the youngsters can escalate anytime.

86. (c) The rights of every citizen have to be respected.

87. (b) Getting more information in such cases is essential and helps a lot; so, this would be the best course of action.

88. (b) There is no need to buckle under pressure, one can always approach the law enforcing agencies for justice.

89. (a) This is the most positive approach to the situation. The very fact that you are open to an enquiry being conducted on the matter proves that your are honest. It reveals your willingness to cooperate with the authorities. Only a courageous person will be willing to undergo such a painful process.

90. (b) [**TIP:** This type of question calls for social awareness and humanitarian concerns; and also, an understanding of the victims, situation and a practical approach]

    (a) If you reject the proposal and call for a fresh price, you will be taking matters into your own hands. This is not advisable when there are so many people senior to you. You will also be antagonising the boat-owners to some extent.

    (b) Since it is an emergency, it would be better to expedite the process.

    (c) There is not so much time left as to refer the matter to the government and then wait for a reply.

    (d) Threatening the boat owners means creating big trouble for you and your employers.

91. (c) This would ensure that you are not partial to either of them.

92. (a) This would be the most positive approach to the whole situation. Moreover, one has to follow the protocol. So, just lodge a complaint since the results are yet awaited.

93. (b) This is the best decision required.

    (a) Asking the screening committee for a clarification will make it a long drawn process. You have the authority to take action when the probe has revealed the truth.

    (b) Strict action has to be taken so that such incidents do not take place in the future.

    (c) This decision is based on the assumption that the athlete is telling the truth. It is not fair to all.

    (d) Unless quick action is taken, your authority as the chairman of the sports committee can also be questioned.

94. (d)

    (a) It would be practically feasable to make the supply of water free of cost.

    (b) A one time fee for taps can be easily afforded by the non – BPL families but not by the BPL families.

    (c) This is again not a very feasable solution for it may lead to a lopsided usage of water.

    (d) An extremely feasable option. This will at least ensure that the consumption of water is well regulated and the non – BPL families will not feel exploited.

95. (a) Written complaint to the police in the matter will lead to an inquiry.

96. (d) Anti-dowry laws have been designed to protect and safeguard the interest of women harassed for dowry. Social pressures exacerbate the pitiable situation of daughters-in-law harassed for dowry. Legal course of action is the only way for redressal of such complaints/issues.

97. (c) It would be most advisable to revise the report on your own. It would involve effort but it would be the most peaceful and positive means.

98. (b) (a) Warning the team-members for their non-cooperation would not yield much results. It is not so easy to change others.

    (b) If one can look into reasons for their non-cooperation; one has a chance to rectify the situation.

(c) A negative approach. There is no guarantee that the next set of team members will be cooperative.

(d) This is slightly negative. Extending the time will not change the attitude of the team members.

99. (d) This would be the best option. By discussing your problem directly with your boss, you both will be able to resolve the issue and reach a compromise. This will ensure a better working relationship.

100. (d) (a) By giving a bribe, you are accepting the situation for what it is. You are also inviting similar trouble in the future.

(b) If you behave as if you are ignorant of the feelers, they will not stop. On the contrary, the work will get postponed indefinitely.

(c) Going to the higher officer will not ensure that the matter will be looked into. The higher officer may himself be corrupt and may also be involved in the matter.

(d) By sending in a formal complaint, you can ensure that you will be given a hearing. The letter will reach the concerned authorities and can even be sent to the press.

○ ○ ○

GENERAL COMPREHENSION

HOW TO ATTEMPT READING COMPREHENSION?

Reading comprehension exercise judges your ability to understand the passage; to analyse the problem in a proper perspective; as well as, to answer quickly, correctly and systematically. Comprehension exercise measures your ability to read and understand the written passage.

The entire process of Reading Comprehension can be divided into 7 simple steps that are shown in the flow chart below:

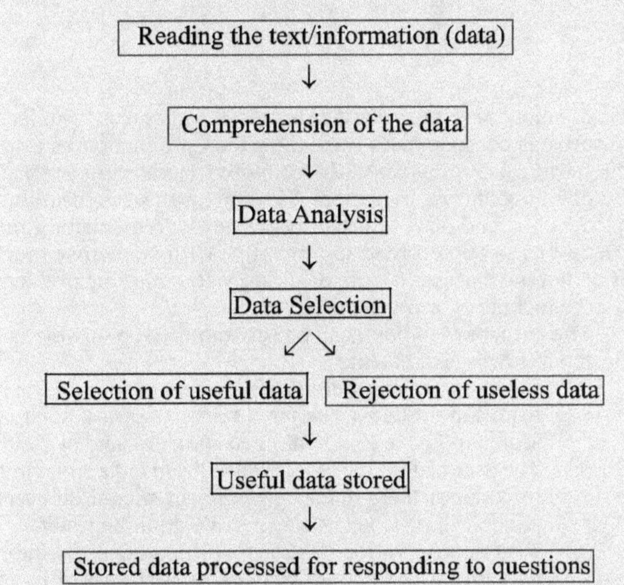

Though reading comprehension is what our brain practises all the time, we do not always perform very well when attempting a reading comprehension question; why ?

Because what the brain does is at an ordinary simplistic level and we are unaware of even that. But what is required of an aspiring students is a conscious, skilful, determined effort to master the art of reading comprehension.

To answer the questions based on reading the passage, it is important that they should be drawn from the information given in the passage. Your common sense, knowledge and presumption should not be taken into account while answering the questions. If you have some related information from your own experience and knowledge, you should not use it to answer the question. Even if you think that there is some mistake, you must still answer the question on the basis of the information given in the passage.

The following techniques a will help you in answering the questions based on the given passages.

IMPORTANT TECHNIQUES

(A) USE YOUR PENCIL AS A POINTER:

To begin with, use your pencil as a pointer. Using the pencil to guide your eyes along a line of text helps you to focus on the details given in the passage it holds your attention to the precise words in the passage. In a long test, attention may weaken. Fatigue may blunt your attention to details. But using your pencil as a pointer will help you preserve your attention to details.

(B) READ FASTER ALONG YOUR PENCIL:

Another benefit of using the pencil as a pointer is that it will probably speed up your reading. The steady flow of the pencil across the page with each line of text draws the eyes along at a steady pace. Do not go faster than you can grasp the text, but do try to keep your reading going at a steady pace set by the pencil.

(C) CIRCLE KEY WORDS AND PHRASES:

Remember, you are not reading just for a vague general understanding of the passage. You have to read for detailed understanding. Circle key words or phrases which will enable you to zero in on precise points needed to answer a question.

(D) KEEP FORGING AHEAD:

Do not get bogged down if there is a word or sentence you do not understand. You may get the main idea without knowing the individual word or sentence. Sometimes, you can sense the meaning of the word from the context. Sometimes, the word or sentence may not be the basis of any question. If there is some idea you need to answer a question but do not understand, read it one more time. If you still do not understand it, move on. You can come back to this question later if you have time left at the end of the test.

(E) FORMATION OF AN IDEA FROM THE QUESTIONS:

Another good reading comprehension strategy is to read the questions before starting the passage. This does not mean to read the answer choices as well. By reading the questions, you will have an idea of what information you will need after reading the passage. This may alert you to certain details, ideas and specific areas in the paragraph where the questions are drawn from.

RIGHT APPROACH

1. Questions are to be answered on the basis of the information provided in the passage and you are not expected to rely on outside knowledge of a particular topic. Your own views or opinions may sometimes conflict with the views expressed or the information provided in the passage. Be sure that you work within the context of the passage. You should not expect to agree with everything you encounter in reading passages.

2. You should analyse each passage carefully before answering the accompanying questions. As with any kind of close and thoughtful reading, look for clues that will help you understand less explicit aspects of the passage. Try to separate main ideas from supporting ideas or evidences.

3. Note transitions from one idea to the next, and examine the relationships among the different ideas or parts of the passage.

For example, are they contrasting? Are they complementary? Consider the points made by the author he conclusions drawn, and how and why those points are made or conclusions drawn.

4. Read each question carefully and be certain that you answer exactly what is being asked.

5. Always read all the answer choices before selecting the best answer.

6. The best answer is the one that most accurately and most completely answers the questions in accordance with the passage. Be careful not to pick an answer choice simply because it is a true statement. Be careful not to get misled by answer choices that are only partially true or only partially satisfy the problem posed in the question.

7. The methodology of eliminating wrong answers also works here. It simply means that if you are unable to judge the right choice or right answer, cross out the answers that are incorrect, so that the remaining one is the right choice.

Exercise

PASSAGE-1

India's National Biodiversity Action Plan (NBAP) recognises the importance of biodiversity for inclusive development. The Green Agriculture project implemented by the Indian government and the Food and Agricultural Organisation (FAO) takes a novel approach to support the NBAP and synergise biodiversity conservation, agriculture production and development. It is being implemented in five landscapes adjoining Protected Areas/ Biosphere Reserves. It envisages a transformation in Indian agriculture for global environmental benefits by addressing land degradation, climate change mitigation, sustainable forest management, and biodiversity conservation.

1. What is the most rational message that is implied from the above passage?
   (a) India is facing stiff competition in biodiversity conservation at the global level so, it has taken an initiative with various organisations to stay ahead.
   (b) Forecasting a transformation in its agricultural sector for global environmental benefits, India has started addressing various issues related to it.
   (c) For the betterment of India's agricultural products, India needs to have an action plan that checks the flaws in its agricultural development and biodiversity conservation initiatives.
   (d) Considering the significance of biodiversity in inclusive growth, government of India in collaboration with FAO is determined to make its biodiversity plan a success.

PASSAGE-2

Water conservation cannot brook delay any longer in India. According to a forecast by the Asian Development Bank, India will have a water deficit of 50% by 2030. India's water needs are basically met by rivers and groundwater. Water scarcity can lead to disastrous consequences impacting food production as most of the farming is rain-fed. With ground water catering to about 60% of the country's irrigation, 85% of rural water drinking requirements, and 50% of urban water needs, replenishing the aquifers has to be accorded top priority. Millions across India still do not have access to safe drinking water and this problem has to be tackled on a war footing.

2. The author's viewpoint can be best summed up in which of the following statements?
   (a) India's increasing scarcity of water has put an onus on it to take the issue seriously and start conserving water as soon as possible else, it may become a dry land by 2030.
   (b) The issue of drinking water availability in India is of prime importance thus, Indian government should do every possible thing to get its citizens safe drinking water.
   (c) Water conservation has been a difficult task for India which now can't be overlooked as the future of India in terms of drinking water availability seems pitiful.
   (d) In times to come, India will suffer with huge scarcity of drinking water therefore, it should start working on this immediately so that the people do not face problem in the future.

PASSAGE-3

Judiciary has become the centre of controversy, in the recent past, on account of the sudden 'Me' in the level of judicial intervention. The area of judicial intervention has been steadily expanding through the device of public interest litigation. The judiciary has shed its pro-status-quo approach and taken upon itself the duty to enforce the basic rights of the poor and vulnerable sections of society, by progressive interpretation and positive action. The Supreme Court has developed new methods of dispensing justice to the masses through the public interest litigation.

3. Which of the following can be inferred from the above passage?
   (a) The judiciary has become very conscious about enforcing the basic rights of the marginalized section of the society in the purview of which the apex court has come up with methods of providing justice through PIL.
   (b) Certain personal issues and agendas in recent past in the level of judicial intervention have put a question mark on the credibility of the apex court.
   (c) Public Interest Litigation is a boon for the poor and vulnerable sections of the society as far as the enforcement of their basic rights is concerned.
   (d) The Supreme Court is very concerned about the under-privileged sections of the society and thus, has come up with an innovative idea to dispensing justice.

PASSAGE-4

Judicial activism has arisen mainly due to the failure of the executive and legislatures to act. Sec-ondly, it has arisen also due to the fact that there is a doubt that the legislature and executive have failed to deliver the goods. Thirdly, it occurs because the entire system has been plagued by ineffectiveness and inactiveness. The violation of basic human rights has also led to judicial activism. Finally, due to the misuse and abuse of some of the provisions of the Constitution, judicial activism has gained significance.

4. Which of the following statements does not relate to the above passage?
   (a) Judicial activism has carried forward participative justice thereby justifying that the entire system has been plagued by ineffectiveness and inactiveness.
   (b) There is a suspicion on the executive and the legislative organ of the government as far as their working is concerned.
   (c) The failure of the other organs of the government has led to the emergence of judicial activism.
   (d) Violation of basic human rights has led to judicial activism.

PASSAGE-5

We should know what is right and wrong for us. Western culture is not altogether bad, although it has made our life faster but enhanced technology has also made our life easier and comfortable. We need to give importance to our Indian culture which taught us to live in peace and harmony with other by way of increasing our tolerance and patience. Many people of other countries are realizing the importance of Indian heritage and are adapting the goodness of Indian culture such as practice of Yoga and meditation, wisdom and teachings passed by the ancient saints. The knowledge of Indian wisdom helps human being of any race to enrich their life.

5. What is/are the most logical message(s) that is implied from the above passage?
   (I) The author is sceptical about Western culture.
   (II) Although Western culture has affected our lifestyle positively, Indian culture and its influence is no less than it.
   (III) India culture has an edge over Western culture in many ways therefore, it must be given more importance.
   (a) Only (I)   (b) Only (II)
   (c) Only (III)   (d) Both (II) and (III)

PASSAGE-6

Democracy functions only when all the stakeholders are heard and their views taken on board during decision-making. It thrives in an environment in which transparency and accountability are the norm. Our republic is threatened when freedom of speech is muzzled, when independent voices are subjected to suppression and non-believers coerced into silence. A state in which traditional professions become hazardous enterprises, where worldviews are attacked by obscurantist and fringe elements and where heartrending tales of violation of women and young girls abound, may have a functional electoral system but the other basic characteristics of democracy are missing. It makes us wonder about the quality of our journey as a republic.

6. The author's viewpoint can be best summed up in which of the following statements?
   (I) All the elements of democracy have equal say in decision making, the curtailment of which may weaken the functioning of the democracy in respect to transparency and accountability.
   (II) Despite India having a functional electoral system, its present shoddy condition exhibits that it still lacks in the basic characteristics of democracy thereby, putting a question mark on us as a republic.
   (III) Stakeholders of democracy being the key elements in decision making must be heard in order to maintain an environment full of accountability and transparency.
   (a) Both (I) and (III)   (b) Both (I) and (II)
   (c) Both (II) and (III)   (d) All (I), (II) and (III)

PASSAGE-7

The e-commerce industry been directly impacting the micro, small & medium enterprises (MSME) in India by providing means of financing, technology and training and has a favourable cascading effect on other industries as well. The Indian e-commerce industry has been on an upward growth trajectory and is expected to surpass the US to become the second largest e-commerce market in the world by 2034. Technology enabled innovations like digital payments, hyper-local logistics, analytics driven customer engagement and digital advertisements will likely support the growth in the sector. The growth in e-commerce sector will also boost employment, increase revenues from export, increase tax collection by ex-chequers, and provide better products and services to customers in the long-term.

7. What are the most crucial messages implied from the above passage?
   (I) E-commerce industry in India has jolted the MSME thus, its repercussions can't be neglected.
   (II) Indian e-commerce industry is highly supported by technological advancements and innovations that have led to its growth in recent times.
   (III) The growth in the e-commerce industry looks forward to inducing more jobs, increasing revenue and becoming customer supportive in long run.
   (a) Both (I) and (III)   (b) Both (I) and (II)
   (c) Both (II) and (III)   (d) All (I), (II) and (III)

PASSAGE-8

Today, space is not about weather prediction, DTH services, tele-education and tele-medicine alone, but also about the growing number of uses in the national security sector. Ignoring the growing requirements in the security domain can be detrimental to India's strategic interests. India's overarching space policy should also be the by-product of a larger national security strategy approach that would outline what kind of future warfare India expects to fight and the kind of space capabilities that may be required for such wars. Such an exercise is best undertaken by the political leadership than a sector-specific department. A policy developed in the absence of such a strategic interface could be seriously problematic.

8.   What is the most rational message that is implied from the above passage?
   (I)   India can tremendously use its space policies in wars against its enemies.
   (II)   In the contemporary time, the importance of space technology can't be overlooked as it is of prime importance in establishing a good international relations.
   (III) Apart from providing weather information, DTS services, tele-education etc., space technology is also contributing enormously in national security thus, its significance shouldn't be ignored while making India's space policy.
   (a) Only (I)   (b) Only (III)
   (c) Both (I) and (III) (d) All (I), (II) and (III)

PASSAGE-9

The Paris Agreement aims to keep global temperature rise in this century well below 2°C compared to pre-industrial levels and pursue efforts to limit the increase even further, to 1.5°C. The Intergovernmental Panel on Climate Change (IPCC) makes it clear that the human and economic costs of a 2°C rise are far greater than for 1.5°C, and the need for action is urgent. Human activity has warmed the world by 1°C over the pre-industrial level and with another half-degree rise, many regions will have warmer extreme temperatures, raising the frequency, intensity and amount of rain or severity of drought. Risks to food security and water, heat exposure, drought and coastal submergence all increase significantly even for a 1.5°C rise.

9.   What is the most rational message that is implied from the above passage?
   (a) It is the duty of each and every one of us to make sure that the global temperature does not cross 1.5°C.
   (b) The issue of rise in global temperature must be adhered seriously else, it will have an adverse effect on environment and mankind.
   (c) Human activities have been the main reason for the global rise in temperature by 2°C in last decade.
   (d) The Paris agreement solely aims to curb all human activities that result to the rise in global temperature.

PASSAGE-10

The Road Accidents in India report of the Ministry of Road Transport and Highways for 2017 comes as a disappointment. By reiterating poorly performing policies and programmes, it has failed to signal the quantum shift necessary to reduce death and disability on the roads. It expresses concern at the large number of people who die every year and the thousands who are crippled in accidents, but the remedies it highlights are weak, incremental and unlikely to bring about a transformation. The lack of progress in reducing traffic injuries is glaring, given that the Supreme Court is seized of the issue and has been issuing periodic directions in a public interest constituted by the Centre.

10. What is the most rational message that is implied from the above passage?
   (a) A large number of people die in road accidents in India therefore, the centre needs to take necessary steps to reduce these numbers.
   (b) The report on road accidents is worth praising as it expresses a deep concern at the large number of people who die every year and the thousands who are crippled in accidents.
   (c) The Supreme Court has taken the issue of road accidents seriously considering the large number of deaths occurring due it and has given strict directions to the centre to overcome these numbers.
   (d) The report on road accidents has not met expectations as on one hand, it expresses a concern over the number of deaths and injuries occurring in road accidents and on the other hand, its suggested solutions are useless.

PASSAGE-11

The Supreme Court has named a four-member Committee of Administrators to run the affairs of the Board of Control for Cricket in India as part of a continuing judicial exercise to reform the way the body is administering the game. While few will sympathise with the BCCI office-bearers who were removed for defying the court's well-intended reforms, there is no escaping the feeling that it should have found a way of reforming the body without appointing its own administrators. Only one of the four appointees has played representative cricket, and it is arguable whether a public auditor, a cricket chronicler or a financial sector executive are the most suitable candidates to administer a body that oversees a competitive sport.

11. What is the most rational message that is implied from the above passage?
   (a) Supreme Court's decision to appoint a member dominated by non-cricketers to administer BCCI is under scanner.
   (b) It's a good decision by the apex court of India to name a four-member Committee of Administrators to run the affairs of the Board of Control for Cricket in India.
   (c) While selecting an administrative committee to run the affairs of BCCI, the Supreme Court should have considered certain points.
   (d) BCCI's way of administering the game in India was suspicious hence, the Supreme Court stepped into it and has started an exercise to reform the way the body is administering the game.

PASSAGE-12

The Constitution protects religious freedom in two ways. It protects an individual's right to profess, practise and propagate a religion, and it also assures similar protection to every religious denomination to manage its own affairs. The legal challenge to the exclusion of women in the 10-50 age group from the Sabarimala temple in Kerala represented a conflict between the group rights of the temple authorities in enforcing the presiding deity's strict celibate status and the individual rights of women to offer worship there. The Supreme Court's ruling, by a 4:1 majority, that the exclusionary practice violates the rights of women devotees establishes the legal principle that individual freedom prevails over purported group rights, even in matters of religion.

12. What is the most rational message that is implied from the above passage?
  (a) Though the constitution gives religious freedom to all the citiizens of India, there are certain exceptions to it in the likes of the non-entry of women in 10-50 age group in the Sabrimala temple.
  (b) Since the constitution gives equal rights to every citizen therefore, exclusion of women in the 10-50 age group from the Sabarimala temple is unconstitutional.
  (c) According to the verdict of Supreme Court, now, women of all age group can enter into the Sabarimala temple and enjoy their religious freedom.
  (d) The Supreme Court's decison in connection to the women who were deprived of entering into Sabrimala temple is sceptical.

PASSAGE-13

The Centre's decision to increase customs duty on imports of 19 "non-essential" items amounts to tinkering at the margins to address a structural macro-economic issue. Using tariffs to curb imports of these items will not have a significant impact on narrowing the current account deficit (CAD), which is the Centre's stated objective. By its own admission, the aggregate value of these imported items in the last fiscal year was just Rs. 86,000 crore. At that level, these imports constituted a little less than 3% of the country's merchandise import bill in 2017-18. With the first six months of the current fiscal having elapsed, the impact of this tariff increase in paring the import bill and thus containing the CAD is at best going to be short-term and marginal. On the other hand, the decision to double import duties on a clutch of consumer durables to 20% could dampen consumption of these products, especially at a time when the rupee's slide against the dollar is already likely to have made these goods costlier.

13. What is the most rational message that is implied from the above passage?
  (a) The centre is trying every possible thing to narrow the CAD and increasing customs duty is one of them.
  (b) Considering last year's imports tariff which was Rs. 86,000 crore, the center has once again imposed high custom duty in order to gain more.
  (c) Center's decision to increase custom duty to narrow the CAD doesn't seem effective in the long run.
  (d) Increasing custom duty is an obligation upon the government to manage the Current Account Deficit.

PASSAGE-14

The Aadhaar project has survived a fierce legal challenge. Ever since a nine-judge Bench ruled unanimously last year that privacy is a fundamental right, opinion began to gain ground that the unique identification programme was vulnerable in the face of judicial scrutiny. It was projected by sceptics, detractors and activists as an intrusion on citizens' privacy, a byword for a purported surveillance system, a grand project to harvest personal data for commercial exploitation by private parties and profiling by the state. But the government has staved off the challenge by successfully arguing that it is essentially a transformative scheme primarily aimed at reaching benefits and subsidies to the poor and the marginalised.

14. What is the most rational message that is implied from the above passage?
  (a) Despite large hue and cry over Aadhaar project, the government has successfully justified its transformative scheme.
  (b) Despite Supreme Court's unanimous verdict about the vulnerability of Aadhaar project, the government has been successful in continuing the project by giving valid reasons.
  (c) Privacy is a fundamental right and Aadhaar project is totally in contrast to it so, it must be curbed.
  (d) Aadhaar details was used by private parties however, the government has taken care of it.

PASSAGE-15

Prime Minister's announcement that Ayushman Bharat sends out the signal that the government is finally recognising the linkages between health care and economic development. Political parties have not yet made the right to health a campaign issue, and the National Health Policy does not recommend such a right since it cannot be fulfilled. But there is increasing awareness that it is unsustainable for a country of 1.3 billion people to rely on household savings to pay for health care. The NHPM is an ambitious initiative, providing a coverage of Rs. 5 lakh per family a year to 10 crore families chosen through the Socio-Economic Caste Census, mainly rural poor and identified urban workers. State governments, which will administer it through their own agency, will have to purchase care from a variety of players, including in the private sector, at pre-determined rates.

15. What is the most rational message that is implied from the above passage?
  (a) National Health Policy can be seen as a good initiative by the central government to provide health care facilities to the people of India at an affordable price.
  (b) Ayushman Bharat is primarily aimed to help the rural poor and identified urban workers.
  (c) The center as well as the state government will be providing adequate health care facilities to the people under the Ayushman Bharat scheme.
  (d) Ayushman Bharat is an ambitious project aimed to empower the rural poor and identified urban workers.

PASSAGE-16

In a vital decision that will help secure the rights of Internet users in the country, the Telecom Commission has approved the recommendations of the Telecom Regulatory Authority of India (TRAI) on net neutrality. By endorsing steps that call for amendments to access services licences for Internet Service Providers (ISPs) and Telecom Operators, the Commission has made it clear that any violation of net neutrality will be treated as a violation of the licence conditions. It has said that some specialised and emerging services such as Voice over Internet Protocol (VoIP) may be exempt from the non-discriminatory principles, but these cannot be at the cost of the overall quality of Internet access. Combining this approval with the fact that TRAI had barred telecom service providers from charging differential rates for data services (zero rating, for example), India will now have among the strongest net neutrality regulations.

16. What is the most rational message that is implied from the above passage?
    (I) The approval of Telecom Commission on the recommendations TRAI on net neutrality makes sure that India will have a strongest net neutrality regulations.
    (II) TRAI's recommendations on neutrality safeguards the rights of Internet users in the country.
    (III) TRAI's recommendations on net neutrality ensures that any violation of the licence conditions by ISPs and Telecom Operators will be severe.
    (a) Only (I)   (b) Only (II)
    (c) Both (I) and (II)   (d) Both (I) and (III)

PASSAGE-17

In its report on higher education for the Twelfth Plan, the working group of the erstwhile Planning Commission identified expansion, inclusion and excellence as the three pillars for growth. The NDA government had the theme of excellence in its 2016 annual budget, with a proposal to make 10 institutions each in the public and private sectors globally competitive. The challenge of excellence is to develop liberal institutions founded on academic rigour, high scholarship and equitable access for all classes of students. Quite ambitiously, the HRD Ministry has taken the decision to give Institution of Eminence (IoE) status to six institutes, three each from the public and private sectors. Potentially, this will help the select few rise above the many State, Central and private universities, national-level institutes of technology, science, management and humanities, and attract talent.

17. What is the most crucial message that is implied from the above passage?
    (a) HRD ministry is looking forward to enhance the studies and nurture the students to get good marks in state, central and private universities.
    (b) The government seems very serious regarding education as it is giving its effort to enhance educational institutions and attract talented students.
    (c) The present government is copying what the NDA government did in its regime as far as education s concerned.
    (d) IoE status to six institutes by the government will encourage other private and government universities to increase their excellence level in order to get the IoE status.

PASSAGE-18

The decision of the Punjab Cabinet to recommend the death penalty to drug-peddlers is an example of insubstantial measure towards curbing the pervasive drug menace. Capital punishment is abhorrent. Given that there is evidence that suggests it is also no guarantee of deterring crime, this is more of an empty signal. What is required is a comprehensive war on drugs fought on several fronts, including interventions in the community to spread awareness and foster a culture against the use of drugs. The challenges faced by the State are huge. Estimates vary but by some accounts as many as two-thirds of all households in Punjab have a drug addict in their midst. Punjab's prisons are overcrowded with drug-users and peddlers, and its streets and farms witness the easy availability of narcotics and opiates.

18. What is the most rational message that is implied from the above passage?
    (a) Giving capital punishment for drug peddling may invite criticism to Punjab government because the challenges faced by the state are huge.
    (b) Capital punishment can't be a solution to check drug-peddling and stop people from drug abuse.
    (c) Punjab Cabinet's decision to give capital punishment to drug-peddlers is justified as the state is over crowded with drug addicts and narcotics and opiates are easily available anywhere in the state.
    (d) In order to stop drug abuse in the state, Punjab cabinet's decision to give death penalty to drug-peddlers is worth praising as this will definitely help curb the drug menace in the state.

PASSAGE-19

The trade wars have finally begun. After exchanging several threats over the last few months, both the United States and China implemented a tariff of 25% on imports worth $34 billion. This marks the official beginning of what China dubs as "the biggest trade war in economic history". While this trade war is far from the biggest the world has seen, it has the potential to cause some significant damage to the world economy. U.S. President Donald Trump, who began the year by imposing tariffs on imported solar panels and washing machines, has vowed to possibly tax all Chinese imports into the U.S., which last year added up to a little over $500 billion. Mr. Trump's tariffs against China will likely resonate with voters who believe in his "America First" campaign and perceive the trade deficit with China as a loss to the U.S. economy. China, not surprisingly, has responded by targeting American exports like soybean and automobiles, a move that could cause job losses in American states that accommodate Mr. Trump's voter base.

19. What is the most crucial message that is implied from the above passage?
    (a) Putting import tariff on Chinese products will help Trump get the support of his voters.
    (b) Putting import tariff by both USA and China will adversely affect their economies and people.
    (c) Trump's decision to put import tariff on Chinese products is an initiative to start 'America First' campaign in the USA.

(d) China and the USA, both are significant for the world economy hence, they must take economic decisions considering the whole world without being biased for themselves.

PASSAGE-20

In a judgment that essentially reaffirms the constitutional position, the Supreme Court has ruled that the Lt. Governor has to ordinarily act on the aid and advice of the Council of Ministers. At the same time, it has retained the Lt. Governor's powers to refer matters to the President for a decision. However - and this is the nub of the judgment - it has significantly circumscribed this power. The power to refer "any matter" to the President no longer means "every matter". Further, there is no requirement of the Lt. Governor's concurrence for any proposal. The 'reference' clause may give rise to conflict even now. However, the court has significantly limited its potential for mischief. It has not given an exhaustive list of matters that can be referred, but it has been indicated that it could "encompass substantial issues of finance and policy which impact upon the status of the national capital or implicate vital interests of the Union." Every trivial difference of opinion will not fall under the proviso. Overall, the verdict is an appeal to a sense of constitutional morality and constitutional trust among high functionaries.

20. What is the most rational message that is implied from the above passage?
   (a) As per the latest verdicts of Supreme Court, Lt. Governor will now be accountable to the Council of Ministers.
   (b) After the decision of Supreme Court, Lt. Governor can't take any decision without the consent of the Council of Ministers.
   (c) The Lt. Governor being a constitutional position can't come entirely under the purview of Council of Ministers.
   (d) Lt. Governor will have to ordinarily act on the aid and advice of the council of minister however, he is not answerable to the Council of Ministers for each and every decision he takes.

PASSAGE-21

Even as antibiotics lose their efficacy against deadly infectious diseases worldwide, it seems to be business as usual for governments, private corporations and individuals who have the power to stall a post-antibiotic apocalypse. In a recent investigation, it was found that the world's largest veterinary drug-maker, Zoetis, was selling antibiotics as growth promoters to poultry farmers in India, even though it had stopped the practice in the U.S. India is yet to regulate antibiotic-use in poultry, while the U.S. banned the use of antibiotics as growth-promoters in early 2017. So, technically, the drug-maker was doing nothing illegal and complying with local regulations in both countries.

21. What is the most logical message that is implied from the above passage?
   (a) India unlike the USA has allowed the use of antibiotics as growth promoters in poultry farming thus, Zoetis is doing nothing wrong in selling antibiotics to India.
   (b) Antibiotics are very useful in enhancing the growth of poultry animals.
   (c) USA is very concerned about the negative repercussions of the use of antibiotics in poultry farming therefore, it has banned its use in the country.
   (d) Antibiotics produced by Zoetis is no more useful in curing deadly infectious diseases worldwide therefore, they are used as growth promoters in poultry farming.

PASSAGE-22

India took extraordinary care to stay on Myanmar's right side by resisting any show of sympathy to the Rohingya people. On his first bilateral visit to the country, Indian Prime Minister said he shared the Myanmar government's concerns about "extremist violence" in Rakhine state, which has seen unprecedented violence over the past fortnight. Meanwhile, at the World Parliamentary Forum on Sustainable Development, Lok Sabha Speaker Sumitra Mahajan abstained from the Bali Declaration because of a reference to "violence in Rakhine state". New Delhi has traditionally been wary of internationalising the internal affairs of its neighbours; on Myanmar, it has concerns about keeping the country from spinning back into the Chinese orbit.

22. What is the most logical message that is implied from the above passage?
   (a) India's maintaining an amiable relation with Myanmar is its strategy so that, Myanmar doesn't spin back to China.
   (b) Though India had sympathy for the Rohingya people but, it resisted to show any in order not to break its healthy relations with Myanmar.
   (c) India never interferes in the internal affairs of its neighbouring countries.
   (d) India doesn't want Myanmar to have a friendly relation with China therefore, it supported Myanmar's say over Rohingya people.

PASSAGE-23

With the Rajya Sabha Chairman rejecting the notice given by 64 Opposition members for the impeachment of the Chief Justice of India, the focus has shifted to the presiding officer's power to admit or reject a motion. The Congress, spearheading the move, is planning to approach the Supreme Court. Section 3 of the Judges (Inquiry) Act, 1968, says the presiding officer may admit or refuse to admit the motion after holding consultations with such persons as he thinks fit, and considering the material before him. The law is open to interpretation on whether he can reject the motion on merits without sending the charges to a committee for investigation. A common sense view suggests the Chairman has to apply his mind to the nature of the charge. To argue that he should merely satisfy himself on the number of signatures appended to the motion and straightaway constitute a probe committee is unlikely to find judicial favour. However, it needs a court to delineate the contours of such an interpretation.

23. What is the most logical message that is implied from the above passage?
   (a) The Rajya Sabha Chairman can accept or reject a motions as per his will.
   (b) Rajya Sabha Chairman's power to accept or reject a motion requires more clarity.
   (c) It is mandatory for the Rajya Sabha Chairman to consult with such persons as he thinks fit before he rejects or accepts any motion.

(d) The chairman of Rajya Sabha has no authority to accept any motion that includes the impeachment of the Chief Justice of India.

PASSAGE-24

The Bombay High Court quashed an order by the Maharashtra Forest Department to shoot a tigress in the Bramhapuri region after she killed two persons. The death warrant was overturned as a result of a PIL petition by an animal rights activist, which argued that the tigress's behaviour had been forged by illegal human intrusion into her territory. Forest officials were then forced to capture the problem animal and re-release her in the Bor forest reserve, less than 200 km away, putting another set of villagers in harm's way. This is the latest in a series of instances where forest departments have gone against the advice of conservation researchers; the fact that they were arm-twisted into doing so by animal-lovers makes it even more worrisome. The released tigress went on to kill two others in Bor, and the authorities scrambled to capture her again. Such actions go against conservation science. Translocating a large carnivore as a response to conflict does not work. Large predators need a certain prey density and are territorial, and they would tend to find their way back, even over hundreds of kilometres, to their original habitat.

24. What is the most logical message that is implied from the above passage?
   (a) Humans should not trespass in the territory of carnivorous animals else, they might be killed as in the case of Bramhapuri region.
   (b) Sometimes, over enthusiasm from animal lovers results to the death of common people by dangerous animals.
   (c) Large carnivores should be translocated according to conservation science otherwise, the result may be fatal and severe.
   (d) Tigers are dangerous animals therefore, they shouldn't be allowed to roam free.

PASSAGE-25

The acquittal of five suspects in the Mecca Masjid bomb blast case is likely to reinforce public cynicism in the country about the state of the criminal justice system. Regardless of whether the acquittal was owing to the innocence of Swami Aseemanand and four others belonging to a Hindu right-wing group, or because the prosecuting agency lacked the resolve and freedom to obtain their conviction, the outcome is undoubtedly a substantial denial of justice for a crime that killed nine people and injured many others. It also shattered the lives of dozens of Muslims who were taken into custody by the Hyderabad police in the immediate aftermath of the blast in May 2007; their arbitrary incarceration, alleged custodial torture and the protracted court hearings amounted to grave miscarriage of justice.

25. What is the most logical message that is implied from the above passage?
   (a) The acquittal of five suspects in the Mecca Masjid blast case may result to huge public outrage in Hyderabad.
   (b) After the acquittal of the suspects of Mecca Masjid blast, people have started losing faith in the state's justice system.
   (c) The five suspects of the suspects of Mecca Masjid blast were acquitted due to the lack of evidence against them.

(d) The justice system should take robust approach while dealing with serious issues like Mecca Masjid bomb blast because any wrong decison may shatter the faith of common people in judiciary.

PASSAGE-26

In recent months, Madhya Pradesh, Rajasthan, Haryana and Arunachal Pradesh have sought to amend the law to prescribe the death penalty for the rape of a minor below the age of 12. There is a clear dichotomy of views on the desirability of prescribing a death penalty. Enlightened public opinion would not approve of a vengeful state response to individual brutality, even if outraged public opinion clamoured for it. Moreover, it should not be forgotten that the death penalty has never been a deterrent against any sort of crime. There is little empirical evidence to show that those about to commit a capital offence would stop themselves merely out of the fear of being hanged. Further, there is a legitimate concern that the country's judicial system has not been consistent in awarding the death penalty.

26. What is the most logical message that is implied from the above passage?
   (a) Awarding death penalty to the culprits is not a solution to stop crimes.
   (b) Rapists of minor below 12 years of age must be awarded death penalty as it will be an appropriate punisment for such brutality.
   (c) Capital punishment can't prove to be deterrent against any sort of crime.
   (d) Indian judiciary rarely awards death penalty.

PASSAGE-27

It is unfortunate that the Cauvery dispute is once again before the Supreme Court, barely weeks after the final verdict. The Centre is to blame for the dispute going into another round of litigation. While Tamil Nadu has moved the court to initiate contempt proceedings against the Centre for not complying with the direction to frame a scheme to implement the water-sharing arrangement set out in the previous judgment, the Centre has sought three more months and some clarifications in the court order. It is difficult to believe the issue at hand is so perplexing that the Centre had no option but to come back to the court. Political and electoral considerations appear to have dictated the Centre's action.

27. What is is the most logical message that is implied from the above passage?
   (a) The centre is responsible for another round of litigation.
   (b) Supreme Court wasn't able to dispense justice in the Cauvery dispute in its previous verdicts.
   (c) Certain political and electoral considerations have led Tamil Nadu to go against the centre in the court of law.
   (d) Centre's action in connection to Cauvery water dispute appears to be motivated by political and electoral considerations.

PASSAGE-28

Nine months after the Union Cabinet's in-principle nod for offloading the government's stake in Air India, the ball has finally been set rolling to privatise the bleeding airline. A preliminary information memorandum was unveiled last week by the Civil Aviation Ministry for prospective bidders. According to this, the Centre will divest 76% of its stake in AI. A 100% stake is being offered in its subsidiary Air India Express, and a 50% stake is on offer in its ground handling operations arm. Other subsidiaries, such as Alliance Air, Hotel Corporation of India, which owns the Centaur properties in New Delhi and Srinagar, Air India Air Transport Services and Air India Engineering Services, are not being sold - they will be transferred to a special purpose entity along with roughly a third of AI's Rs. 48,781 crore outstanding debt.

28. What is the most logical message that is implied from the above passage?
   (a) The Centre is looking forward to privatise Air India owing to its large outstanding debts.
   (b) Air India is on the verge of becoming bankrupt thus, it would be a good decision to privatise it.
   (c) Air India is in critical condition due to heavy outstanding debts.
   (d) The Civil Aviation Ministry is equally supporting the centre in its decision of divestment in Air India.

PASSAGE-29

More people are losing their love for Indian bonds. Foreign investors have been net sellers of over $1 billion in Indian debt this month, almost cancelling out inflows since the beginning of the year. Domestic investors were already spooked by a widening fiscal deficit, so foreign selling now has managed to add pressure on the market. The deserting of the Indian market by foreign investors comes at a time when the Centre is looking at tapping the bond market aggressively to finance its election-year spending. The yield on the benchmark 10-year bond has risen by almost 100 basis points since late-July amid lacklustre investor demand. The rise in yields is due to a variety of reasons that have pushed both foreign and domestic investors to re-price Indian sovereign bonds.

29. What is the most logical message that is implied from the above passage?
   (a) Foreign investors have overpowered Indian Money Market.
   (b) Due to the increasing fiscal deficit, people have started losing their interest in Indian bonds.
   (c) The value of Indian bonds is decresing day by day which is worrisome for the government.
   (d) Indian money market is being overburdened by foreign investors thereby feeling pressure.

PASSAGE-30

Many crimes committed in the name of defending the honour of a caste, clan or family may have their origin in India's abominable caste system, but there are other contributing factors as well. Entrenched social prejudices, feudal structures and patriarchal attitudes are behind what are referred to as 'honour killings'. While these cannot be eradicated overnight through law or judicial diktat, it is inevitable that a stern law and order approach is adopted as the first step towards curbing groups that seek to enforce such medieval notions of 'honour' through murder or the threat of murder, or ostracisation. It is in this context that the Supreme Court's strident observations against khap panchayats and guidelines to deal with them acquire significance. It is not the first time that the apex court has voiced its strong disapproval of khaps, or village assemblies that assume the authority to discipline what they deem behaviour that offends their notions of honour. Previous judgments have made it clear that the life choices of individual adults, especially with regard to love and marriage, do

not brook any sort of interference from any quarter.

30. What is the most logical message that is implied from the above passage?
   (a) Every adult in India has freedom to choose his/her partner for marriage therefore, killing them in the name of 'honour' is absurd hence, it should be condemned.
   (b) India needs to move away from its obnoxious caste system for the betterment of its youth as young people should not be killed in the name of 'Honour'.
   (c) 'Honour killing' which is an evil in Indian society can't be stopped all of a sudden, however, a stern law and order approach which are initiatives to stop it may prove to be helpful.
   (d) The Supreme Court has over the years been very critial to 'Honour killings' and has given adequate guidelines to Khaps and village assemblies to stop such incidents.

PASSAGE-31

For the second time, the Supreme Court has temporarily banned the sale of firecrackers in the National Capital Region. The idea is to test whether it cuts the deadly pollution levels seen in Delhi during and after Deepavali. In other words, to see whether they can be collapsed from the astronomical 1,000-plus micrograms per cubic metre of fine particulate matter seen in 2016 to merely life-threatening levels of a few hundred micrograms/cu.m that Delhi usually sees in winter. But that is a big if. Given that it came just about 10 days before the festival, it will be tough to impose the ban on an industry that has already produced stocks to order. Nor will it be easy to rein in revellers unconvinced by the court order.

31. What is the most logical message that is implied from the above passage?
   (a) Burning of firecrackers during Deepavali increases deadly pollution level which is life-threatening.
   (b) Rather than depending on the governemnt, it is our duty as well to stop burning firecrackers in order to save ourselves from the deadly smoke.
   (c) Putting a ban on the sale of firecrackers about 10 days before the festival will affect the firecracker industry adversely.
   (d) In order to decrease the level of pollution during Deepavali, the Supreme Court has taken a strict measure by putting a ban on the sale of firecrackers in the National Capital Region.

PASSAGE-32

The debate on allowing euthanasia as a means to protect the dignity of patients in a vegetative state has crystallised into a key question before a Constitution Bench of the Supreme Court. Should the law allow 'living wills'? These are advance directives that people can lay down while being sound of mind, on whether they should continue to get life-sustaining treatment after they reach a stage of total incapacitation, that is, a vegetative state. The question is fraught with legal, moral and philosophical implications. The court will have to resolve the question whether the right to life under Article 21 of the Constitution, which according to an earlier verdict does not include the right to die, is being voluntarily waived by a person giving such an advance directive. A living will, at the same time, may relieve the close family members and caregivers of a terminally ill patient of the moral burden of making a life-ending decision.

32. What is the most logical message that is implied from the above passage?
   (a) Laws regarding Euthanasia needs more clarity from the Supreme Court.
   (b) Euthanasia is still a confusing topic in India.
   (c) People should not be given permission to end their life as our constitution doesn't allow it.
   (d) A person should have the right either to live or to end his life according to his will.

PASSAGE-33

Plastics are now widely present in the environment, as visible waste along coastlines, in lakes and rivers, and even in the soil. The recent finding that microplastic particles are found even in 'safe' bottled water indicates the magnitude of the crisis. There is little doubt that the global production of plastics, at over 300 million tonnes a year according to the UN Environment Programme, has overwhelmed the capacity of governments to handle what is thrown away as waste. Microplastics are particles of less than 5 mm that enter the environment either as primary industrial products, such as those used in scrubbers and cosmetics, or via urban waste water and broken-down elements of articles discarded by consumers. Washing of clothes releases synthetic microfibres into water bodies and the sea. The health impact of the presence of polypropylene, polyethylene terephthalate and other chemicals in drinking water, food and even inhaled air may not yet be clear, but indisputably these are contaminants.

33. What is the most logical message that is implied from the above passage?
   (a) Plasics are health hazardous.
   (b) UN Environment Programme advocates to reduce the production of plastics for the betterment of human health.
   (c) Plastic contaminants are present everywhere right from food to drinking water.
   (d) We should be careful while eating and drinking as they may contain plastic contaminants.

PASSAGE-34

A survey helps determine usable rooftops, separating them from green spaces, and analyses the quality of the solar resource. With steady urbanisation, solar maps of this kind will help electricity utilities come up with good business cases and investment vehicles and give residents an opportunity to become partners in the effort. An initiative to rapidly scale up rooftop solar installations is needed if the target of creating 40 GW of capacity connected to the grid by 2022 is to be realised. Rooftop solar power growth has demonstrated an overall positive trend when tenders for 220 MW represented a doubling of the achievement in the previous quarter. But this will need to be scaled up massively to achieve the national target. Going forward, domestic policy has to evaluate the impact of factors such as imposition of safeguard duty and anti-dumping duty on imports, and levy of the goods and services tax on photovoltaic modules.

34. The author's viewpoint can be best summed up in which of the following statements?
   (a) All of us must contribute by taking an inititiave to install solar panels.
   (b) Rooftop solar power seems to have good future ahead if worked upon effectively.
   (c) Rooftop solar panels have capability to replace all other sources of power in India.
   (d) India's domestic policy should be changed if we want have an effective and economical power supply.

PASSAGE-35

Regardless of the provocation or the sequence of events, there is an urgent need for India and Pakistan to address allegations of harassment of each other's diplomats and interference in High Commission work. While surveillance of diplomats by intelligence agencies in New Delhi and Islamabad is not new, matters have escalated in the past month, and the treatment of diplomatic officials by both sides has dropped to new lows. The spark for this round of 'tit-for-tat' actions appears to be an incident when alleged ISI agents roughed up Pakistani construction workers headed for the Indian mission's new building site in Islamabad. While Pakistan's foreign office claimed they did not have security clearance to enter the diplomatic zone, India saw it as an attempt to stop the work, adding that power and water connections were tampered with. Then, the Pakistan High Commission in Delhi claimed that Indian security personnel warned repairmen and electricians against entering its premises. Both missions said personnel were being targeted on the road, with cars stopped and drivers intimidated.

35. The author's viewpoint can be best summed up in which of the following statements?
   (a) India and Pakistan are moving towards a war situation.
   (b) The diplomatic ties between India and Pakistan needs revival.
   (c) In order to maintain a good international relation, India and Pakistan should urgently work upon addressing the allegations they have made on each other.
   (d) The government of both India and Pakistan should go to the UNO to get the issue of allegations over each other resolved.

PASSAGE-36

Given the apparent ease with which economic offenders flee India and cock a snook at the banking and judicial systems, the proposed Fugitive Economic Offenders Bill to seize their wealth is undoubtedly a welcome measure. In fact, given the public disquiet over the apparent impunity enjoyed by billionaire fraudsters living in the safety of foreign climes, any new law is likely to be viewed in a positive light. However, its success rides on the slim hope that the threat of confiscation of property will act as a serious deterrent to those seeking to flee or as a big incentive for fugitives to return. Legal provisions to confiscate the assets of offenders already exist, but these are regarded as somewhat inadequate.

36. The author's viewpoint can be best summed up in which of the following statements?
   (a) The Fugitive Economic Offenders Bill seems to be a ray of hope in recovering the looted money by the economic offenders.
   (b) Confiscating the property of economic offenders is not a solution to punish them and recover the money.
   (c) The Fugitive Economic Offenders Bill aims to make up for the shortcomings and provide a legal framework

that would enable the confiscation of the property of those evading prosecution by fleeing the country or remaining abroad.

(d) The government should bring rules like the The Fugitive Economic Offenders Bill in order to check and control money thefts by economic fraudsters.

PASSAGE-37

The latest economic data from the Central Statistics Office reveal that India's GDP expanded at a brisk 7.2% pace in the three months ended December, an acceleration from the 6.5% posted in the second quarter. On the face of it, the numbers are cause for cheer and optimism, with gross fixed capital formation, a key measure of investment demand, showing a healthy improvement. Sectoral gross value added (GVA) figures also reflect a broad-based pickup in activity from the preceding quarter. The only three laggards last quarter were mining; utility services (including electricity, gas, and water supply); and trade, hotels, transport and communication services. The contraction in mining is of particular concern. The October-December quarter in 2016 was, however, the period when the Centre implemented the widely disruptive demonetisation of high-value currency notes, and so one has to bear in mind the base effect on the latest third-quarter data.

37. The author's viewpoint can be best summed up in which of the following statements?
    (a) Mining didn't contribute much in increasing India's GDP.
    (b) Despite some lagging sectors, India managed to increase its GDP with a rapid pace.
    (c) Demonetisation, somehow, was responsible for the slow and steady increase in India's GDP in 2017 compared to 2016
    (d) Sectors like mining. utility services, trade, hotels etc. need to contribute in India's GDP like other sectors so that India may generate more revenue.

PASSAGE-38

In what has been called India's MeToo moment, the social media is thick with women coming forth with stories of sexual harassment. In the quick aftermath of actor Tanushree Dutta's allegations of harassment on a film set a decade ago, women have been speaking of their experiences and the trauma, mostly on Twitter and Facebook. The testimonies so far have mostly concerned the film world and the mainstream media, and cover both the workplace and private spaces. They range from stories of assault to propositioning, suggestiveness to stalking. In the vast majority of cases, the naming is a result of the failure to receive a just response from the system, a signal that it is no longer possible for such behaviour to be breezily dismissed or excused because boys, after all, will be boys.

38. The author's viewpoint can be best summed up in which of the following statements?
    (a) Social media platforms have become a preferred medium for women, especially from films and mainstream media to share their experiences of sexual harassment both at their workplace and private spaces.
    (b) Majorly, people related to films and mainstream media are indulged in sexual harassment.

(c) Over the years, judiciary has not been able to dispense justice to women in cases of sexual harassment therefore, women have now chosen social media platforms to share their stories openly.
(d) Women should not hide their stories of sexual harassment rather, they should come up with them to get justice.

PASSAGE-39

Forty-five years after India nationalised its coal-mining industry, the Central government has allowed the re-entry of commercial mining firms into the sector, turning the clock back. India's coal industry was predominantly driven by the private sector after Independence until the Indira Gandhi government decided to transfer all coal holdings to Coal India through the Coal Mines (Nationalisation) Act, 1973. The key reason cited for taking coal out of the private sector's hands was that it was essential to meet power needs. Now, India's coal market is a virtual monopoly for the public sector behemoth. Coal India accounts for over 80% of the country's coal supply.

39. The author's viewpoint can be best summed up in which of the following statements?
    (a) Government's decision to allow the entry of private sector in coal-mining industry may affect the power generation capacity of the country.
    (b) Indira Gandhi government did a good job by nationalising India's coal-mining industry.
    (c) Allowing private players in coal-mining may not be a good decision by the government.
    (d) Coal India has monopoly over coal-mining in India.

PASSAGE-40

In purely bilateral terms, Iranian President's visit to India was pitch perfect in content and optics. After his meeting with India's Prime Minister, India and Iran signed agreements and memorandums of understanding on a wide variety of issues. Among the announcements was the decision to award India the contract to operate the Chabahar Shahid Beheshti port terminal after the project is completed. While no announcement was made on the Farzad-B gas field that India has expressed an interest in, the joint statement indicates that positive deliberations may follow. There were discussions on enhancing trade and investment and ease of doing business between India and Iran, including a double taxation avoidance agreement and an expert group to recommend "trade remedy measures".

40. The author's viewpoint can be best summed up in which of the following statements?
    (a) The meeting between two high dignitaries of Iran and India has proved to be fruitful for both the nations.
    (b) India will be benefitted more from the MoU that it signed with Iran.
    (c) Iran has been a good friend of India for the past many years.
    (d) Iranian President and Indian Prime Minister met each other to enhance business ties and trade agreements.

PASSAGE-41

The present government lost precious time in its first three years in initiating a health scheme that serves the twin purposes of achieving universal coverage and saving people from high health care costs. It announced two years ago in the Budget a health protection scheme offering a cover of Rs.1 lakh per family, but ultimately that did not extend beyond Rs. 30,000. Fresh hopes have been raised with the announcement of Ayushman Bharat in Budget 2018. The plan has the components of opening health centres for diagnostics, care and distribution of essential drugs as envisaged in the National Health Policy, and a National Health Protection Scheme (NHPS) to provide a cover of up to Rs. 5 lakh each for 10 crore poor and vulnerable families for hospitalisation.

41. The author's viewpoint can be best summed up in which of the following statements?
  (a)   Ayushman Bharat scheme aims to offer a cover of Rs. 1 lakh per family of the country.
  (b)   Health care should be the main focus of government in order to win public faith.
  (c)   The present government is very conscious about heath care services in India and has been taking regular initiatives to enhance them.
  (d)   Over the last three years, the government has failed to fulfill the aspirations of people, especially in the health care sector.

PASSAGE-42

As international oil prices head higher, India will have to brace itself for the economic risks of expensive energy. Brent crude oil futures were trading at about $70 a barrel, marking a four-year high and a price increase of close to 6% since the start of the year. The rise in international prices has been particularly sharp. This is a rally of about 55%. Oil price dynamics have often been explained by changes in the supply outlook influenced by the decisions of major oil producers. Oil trading at $70 should offer some respite to traditional oil producers like the OPEC members, which have suffered the onslaught of U.S. shale producers. The recent spurt in oil prices, however, seems to be more the result of a weakening of the U.S dollar than anything else.

42. The author's viewpoint can be best summed up in which of the following statements?
  (a)   Rising oil prices lead to economic crisis in India.
  (b)   Decrease in the value of U.S dollar often leads to the increase in the value of oil prices.
  (c)   India should be ready to face the adverse economic situations arising out of increasing oil prices.
  (d)   Change in demand of oil results to increase in its prices.

PASSAGE-43

In what may be the Centre's first strike in response to the rural distress read into the Gujarat Assembly poll outcomes, a 30% customs duty has been slapped on the import of chana dal and masoor dal. The official reasoning is clear. Cheap imports could hit farm incomes especially at a time when domestic production of pulses is at a record high and a bumper rabi crop is expected. With an adequate domestic stockpile of pulses and with international prices remaining low for a prolonged period, the Centre fears that traders may still prefer to import some pulses rather than buy the fresh crop from local farmers at higher prices.

43. The author's viewpoint can be best summed up in which of the following statements?
  (a)   Gujarat governemnt is taking care of the farmers so that it does not lose its voters.
  (b)   Though the government is trying to help the farmers by imposing a high cutome duty on the import of chana and masoor dal, it still fears that its this decision may not be fully successful.
  (c)   India is a rich producer of pulses and rabi crop however, sometimes farmers face problems in selling their productions due to the import of crops from outside.
  (d)   Indian traders should acknowledge the abundance of pulses in India and therefore, they should not import pulses from outside.

PASSAGE-44

Iraqi Prime Minister Haider al-Abadi declared victory over the Islamic State, signalling an end to more than three years of battle that saw Iraqi troops first fleeing without their weapons and then, with foreign assistance, regrouping to recover lost territory. At the peak of its influence, the IS controlled almost a third of Iraq, including Mosul, its second largest city. Mr. Abadi, who took over as Prime Minister in September 2014 when the country was in the middle of the civil war, adopted a cautious, gradualist approach with direct help from the United States and Iran to take on the IS. Iraqi troops first stopped the IS's southward expansion in the suburbs of Baghdad and then started offensive operations in the group's small pockets of influence.

44. The author's viewpoint can be best summed up in which of the following statements?
  (a)   The Islamic State after capturing Mosul moved towards Baghdad to expand its territory in Iraq.
  (b)   The US and Iran have directly helped Iraq whenever it was dealing with terrorism.
  (c)   In the initial years of battle, Iraqi troops were sacred of IS.
  (d)   Iraqi PM with the help of US and Iran was able to win over IS.

PASSAGE-45

The ghastly Dashara disaster at Amritsar that has left 59 people dead is a harsh reminder, if any were needed, that government departments have not yet taken official protocols for safety at mass gatherings seriously. In the aftermath of the entirely preventable carnage, in which spectators crowding a railway track to watch burning of effigies were mowed down by a train, there is a frantic effort to pin responsibility on agencies and individuals, and, deplorably, to exploit public anger for political ends. What happened in Amritsar points to the basic failure of the district administration and the police, which should have ensured law and order.

45. The author's viewpoint can be best summed up in which of the following statements?
  (a)   The state government can't be held responsible for the Dashara disaster as it was not aware of such mass gathering near the railway track.

   (c) Genetically modified crops produce more yield as compared to yield from the traditional methods.

   (d) Taking advantage of absence of regulatory standards, scientists have been dumping new products in the markets without appropriate approval.

69. Why according to the author, is genetic modification of crops not an answer to the problem of hunger in the world?

   1. People being highly doubtful of the long term effects of genetically modified crops, do not buy the products grown by such methods.

   2. The problem of hunger in the world is not due to inadequate production of food but due to unequal distribution of it.

   3. Many developing countries have banned genetically modified products as developed countries have been using these countries as dumping grounds for new genetically modified products.

   (a) 1 only   (b) 2 only

   (c) Both 2 and 3   (d) Both 1 and 3

70. The author of the given passage seems to be definitely

   (a) Suggesting the use of traditional methods of agriculture as against bio-technology by developing countries owing to their poor regulatory standards.

   (b) In favour of utilising bio-technology as a tool for alleviation of poverty from the world.

   (c) Urging the policy makers to improve infrastructural facilities so that farmers can maximise the benefits of genetically modified crops.

   (d) Unconvinced of the long term effects and rationale for immediate requirement of genetically modified products.

PASSAGE-56

A new analysis has determined that the threat of global warming can still be greatly diminished if nations cut emissions of heat-trapping green-house gases by 70% this century. The analysis was done by scientists at the National Centre for Atmospheric Research (NCAR). While global temperatures would rise, the most dangerous potential aspects of climate change, including massive losses of Arctic sea ice and permafrost and significant sea-level rise. could be partially avoided.

"This research indicates that we can no longer avoid significant warming during this century," said NCAR scientist Warren Washington, the study paper's lead author. "But, if the world were to implement this level of emission cuts, we could stabilise the threat of climate change", he added.

Average global temperatures have warmed by close to 1°C since the pre-industrial era. Much of the warming is due to human-produced emissions of greenhouse gases, predominantly carbon dioxide. This heat-trapping gas has increased from a pre-industrial level of about 284 parts per million (ppm) in the atmosphere to more than 380 ppm today. With research showing that additional warming of about 1°C may be the threshold for dangerous climate change, the European Union has called for dramatic cuts in emissions of carbon dioxide and other greenhouse gases.

To examine the impact of such cuts on the world's climate, Washington and his colleagues ran a series of global studies with the NCAR-based Community Climate System Model (CCSM). They assumed that carbon dioxide levels could be held to 450 ppm, at the end of this century. In contrast, emissions are now on track to reach about 750 ppm by 2100 if unchecked. The team's results showed that if carbon dioxide were held to 450 ppm. global temperatures would increase by 0.6°C above current readings by the end of the century. In contrast, the study showed that temperatures would rise by almost four times that amount, to 2.2°C above current readings, if emissions were allowed to continue on their present course. Holding carbon dioxide levels to 450 ppm would have other impacts, according to the climate modeling study.

Sea-level rise due to thermal expansion as water temperatures warmed would be 14 cm (about 5.5 inches) instead of 22 cm (8.7 inches). Also, Arctic ice in the summertime would shrink by about a quarter in volume and stabilise by 2100, as opposed to shrinking at least three-quarters and continuing to melt, and Arctic warming would be reduced by almost half.

71. What would be the impact of unchecked green-house gas and carbon dioxide emissions?

   (a) The temperature would rise from the current temperature by 2.2°C

   (b) The sea-level would rise by about 5.5 inches

   (c) The Arctic ice would stabilise by 2100

   (d) The Arctic ice would reduce by one-fourth

72. What can be the most appropriate title of the above passage?

   (a) A study of the rise in water level

   (b) A study of rise in temperatures

   (c) A study of the effects of green-house gas emissions

   (d) A study of the Arctic region

73. What does scientist Warren Washington mean when he says "we could stabilise the threat of climate change"?

   (a) Climate change can be stopped completely

   (b) Climate change can be regularised

   (c) Climate change and its effects can be studied extensively

   (d) The ill-effects of the change in climate can be minimised

74. Why did Washington and his colleagues conduct a series of studies?

   (a) Because they realised that the temperature increase was almost about 1°C

   (b) So that they could stabilise the climate change

   (c) So toot they could help the European Union in cutting the carbon dioxide emissions

   (d) None of the above

75. What would be the impact of holding the carbon dioxide level at 450 ppm at the end of this century?

   1. Global temperatures would increase by 0.6 degrees Celcius.

   2. Arctic warming would be reduced by half.

   3. Thermal expansion will stop completely.

   (a) 1 only   (b) 1 and 2

   (c) 2 and 3   (d) All 1, 2 and 3

PASSAGE-57

Financial markets in India have acquired greater depth and liquidity over the years. Steady reforms since 1991 have led to growing linkages and integration of the Indian economy and its financial system with the global economy. Weak global economic prospects and continuing uncertainties in the international financial markets therefore, have had their impact on the emerging market economies. Sovereign risk concerns, particularly in the Euro area, affected financial markets for the greater part of the year, with the contagion of Greece's soveregin debt problem spreading to India and other economies by way of higher-than-normal levels of volatility.

The funding constraints in international financial markets could impact both the availability and cost of foreign funding for banks and corporates. Since the Indian financial system is bank dominated, banks' ability to withstand stress is critical to overall financial stability. Indian banks, however, remain robust, notwithstanding a decline in capital to risk-weighted assets ratio and a rise in non-performing asset levels in the recent past. Capital adequacy levels remain above the regulatory requirements. The financial market infrastructure continues to function without any major disruption. With further globalization, consolidation, deregulation, and diversification of the financial system, the banking business may become more complex and riskier. Issue like risk and liquidity management and enhancing skill therefore assume greater significance.

76. According to the passage, the financial markets in the emerging market economies including India had the adverse impact in recent years due to
    1. weak global economic prospects.
    2. uncertainties in the international financial markets.
    3. sovereign risk concerns in the Euro area.
    4. bad monsoons and the resultant crop loss.
    Select the correct answer using the code given below:
    (a)　1 and 2 only　　　　(b)　1, 2 and 3
    (c)　2 and 3 only　　　　(d)　2, 3 and 4

77. The Indian financial markets are affected by global changes mainly due to the
    (a)　increased inflow of remittances from abroad
    (b)　enormous increases in the foreign exchange reserves.
    (c)　growing global linkages and integration of the Indian financial markets.
    (d)　contagion of Greece's sovereign debt problem.

78. According to the passage, in the Indian financial system, bank's ability to withstand stress is critical to ensure overall financial stability because Indian financial system is
    (a)　controlled by the Government of India
    (b)　less integrated with banks.
    (c)　controlled by the Reserve Bank of India.
    (d)　dominated by Banks.

79. Risk and liquidity management assume more importance in the Indian banking system in future due to
    1. further globalization.
    2. more consolidation and deregulation of financial system
    3. further diversification of the financial system.
    4. more financial inclusion in the economy.
    Select the correct answer using the code given below:
    (a)　1, 2 and 3　　　　(b)　2, 3 and 4
    (c)　1 and 2 only　　　(d)　3 and 4 only

PASSAGE-58

Net profits are only 2.2% of their total assets for central public sector undertakings, lower than for the private corporate sector. While the public sector or the State-led entrepreneurship played an important role in triggering India's industrialization, our evolving development needs, comparatively less-than-satisfactory performance of the public sector enterprises, the maturing of our

private sector, a much larger social base now available for expanding entrepreneurship and the growing institutional capabilities to enforce competition policies would suggest that the time has come to review the role of public sector.

What should the portfolio composition of the government be ? It should not remain static all times. The airline industry works well as a purely private affair. At the opposite end, rural roads, whose sparse traffic makes tolling unviable, have to be on the balance-sheet of the State. If the government did not own rural roads, they would not exist. Similarly, public health capital in our towns and cities will need to come from the public sector. Equally, preservation and improvement of forest cover will have to be a new priority for the public sector assets.

Take the example of steel. With near-zero tariffs, India is a globally competitive market for the metal. Indian firms export steel into the global market, which demonstrates there is no gap in technology. Indian companies are buying up global steel companies, which shows there is no gap in capital availability. Under these conditions, private ownership works best.

Private ownership is clearly desirable in regulated industries, ranging from finance to infrastructure, where a government agency performs the function of regulation and multiple competing firms are located in the private sector. Here, the simple and clean solution - government as the umpire and the private sector as the players is what works best. Inmany of these industries, we have a legacy of government ownership, where productivity tends to be lower, fear of bankruptcy is absent, and the risk of asking for money from the tax payer is ever present. There is also the conflict of interest between government as an owner and as the regulator. The formulation and implementation of competition policy will be more vigorous and fair if government companies are out of action.

80. According to the passage, what is/are the reason/reasons for saying that the time has come to review the role of public sector ?
    1. Now public sector has lost its relevance in the industrialization process.
    2. Public sector does not perform satisfactorily.
    3. Entrepreneurship in private sector is expanding.
    4. Effective competition policies are available now.
    Which of the statements given above is/are correct in the given context ?
    (a)　1and 3 only　　　　(b)　2 only
    (c)　2, 3 and 4 only　　(d)　1, 2, 3 and 4

81. According to the passage, rural roads should be in the domain of public sector only. Why ?
    (a)　Rural development work is the domain of government only.
    (b)　Private sector cannot have monetary gains in this.
    (c)　Government takes money from tax payers and hence it is the responsibility of government only.
    (d)　Private sector need not have any social responsibility.

82. The portfolio composition of the government refers to
    (a)　Public sector assets quality.
    (b)　Investment in liquid assets.
    (c)　Mix of government investment in different industrial sectors.
    (d)　Buying Return on Investment yielding capital assets.

83. The author prefers government as the umpire and private sector as players because
    (a)　Government prescribes norms for a fair play by the private sector.
    (b)　Government is the ultimate in policy formulation.
    (c)　Government has no control over private sector players.
    (d)　None of the above statements is correct in this context.

PASSAGE-59

In recent times, India has grown fast not only compared to its own past but also incomparison with other nations. But there cannot be any room for complacency because it is possible for the Indian economy to develop even faster and also to spread the benefits of this growth more widely than has been done thus far. Before going into details of the kinds of micro-structural changes that we need to conceptualize and then proceed to implement, it is worthwhile elaborating on the idea of inclusive growth that constitutes the defining concept behind this Government's various economic policies and decisions. A nation interested in inclusive growth views the same growth differently depending on whether the gains of the growth are heaped primarily on a small segment or shared widely by the population. The latter is cause for celebration but not the former. In other words, growth must not be treated as an end in itself but as an instrument for spreading prosperity to all. India's own past experience and the experience of other nations suggests that growth is necessary for eradicating poverty but it is not a sufficient condition. In other words, policies for promoting growth need to be complemented with policies to ensure that more and more people join in the growth process and, further, that there are mechanisms inplace to redistribute some of the gains to those who are unable to partake in the market process and, hence, get left behind.

A simple way of giving this idea of inclusive growth a sharper form is to measure a nation's progress in terms of the progress of its poorest segment, for instance the bottom 20 per cent of the population. One could measure the per capita income of the bottom quintile of the population and also calculate the growth rate of income; and evaluate our economic success in terms of these measures that pertain to the poorest segment. This approach is attractive because it does not ignore growth like some of the older heterodox criteria did. It simply looks at the growth of income of the poorest sections of the population. It also ensures that those who are outside of the bottom quintile do not get ignored. If that were done, then those people would in all likelihood drop down into the bottom quintile and so would automatically become a direct target of our policies. Hence the criterion being suggested here is a statistical summing up of the idea of inclusive growth, which, in turn, leads to two corollaries : to wish that India must strive to achieve high growth and that we must work to ensure that the weakest segments benefit from the growth.

84. The author's central focus is on.
- (a) applauding India's economic growth not only against its own past performance, but against other nations.
- (b) emphasizing the need for economic growth which is the sole determinant of a country's prosperity.
- (c) emphasizing inclusive growth where gains of growth are shared widely by the population.
- (d) emphasizing high growth.

85. The author supports policies which will help
- (a) develop economic growth.
- (b) better distribution of incomes irrespective of rate of growth.
- (c) develop economic growth and redistribute economic gains to those getting left behind.
- (d) put an emphasis on the development of the poorest segments of society.

86. Consider the following statements :
According to the author, India's economy has grown but there is no room for complacency as
1. growth eradicates poverty.
2. growth has resulted in prosperity for all.
Which of the statements given above is/are correct ?
- (a) 1 only
- (b) 2 only
- (c) Both 1 and 2
- (d) Neither 1 nor 2

PASSAGE-60

It is often forgotten that globalization is not only about policies on international economic relationships and transactions, but has ally to do with domestic policies of a nation. Policy changes necessitated by meeting the internationally set conditions (by WTO etc.) of free trade and investment flows obviously affect domestic producers and investors. But the basic philosophy underlying globalization emphasizes absolute freedom to markets to determine prices and production and distribution patterns, and view government interventions as processes that create distortions and bring in inefficiency. Thus, public enterprises have to be privatized through disinvestments and sales; sectors and activities hitherto reserved for the public sector have to be opened to the private sector. This logic extends to the social services like education and health. Any restrictions on the adjustments in workforce by way of retrenchment of workers should also be removed and exit should be made easier by removing any restrictions on closures. Employment and wages should be governed by free play of market forces, as any measure to regulate them can discourage investment and also create inefficiency in production. Above all, in line with the overall philosophy of reduction in the role of the State, fiscal reforms should be undertaken to have generally low levels of taxation and government expenditure should be kept to the minimum to abide by the principle of fiscal prudence. All these are policy actions on the domestic front and are not directly related to the core items of the globalization agenda, namely free international flow of goods and finance.

87. According to the passage, under the globalization, government interventions are viewed as processes leading to
- (a) distortions and inefficiency in the economy.
- (b) optimum use of resources.
- (c) more profitability to industries.
- (d) free play of market forces with regard to industries.

88. According to the passage, the basic philosophy of globalization is to
- (a) give absolute freedom to producers to determine prices and production.
- (b) give freedom to producers to evolve distribution patterns.
- (c) give absolute freedom to markets to determine prices, production and employment.
- (d) give freedom to producers to import and export.

89. According to the passage, which of the following is/are necessary for ensuring globalization ?
1. Privatization of public enterprises
2. Expansionary policy of public expenditure
3. Free play of market forces to determine wages and employment
4. Privatization of social services like education and health

Select the correct answer using the code given below :
(a)   1 only   (b)   2 and 3 only
(c)   1, 3 and 4   (d)   2, 3 and 4

90. According to the passage, in the process of globalization the State should have
(a)   expanding role.
(b)   reducing role.
(c)   statutory role.
(d)   None of the above roles.

PASSAGE-61

Today, India looks to be on course to join the league of developed nations. It is beginning to establish a reputation not just as the technology nerve-centre and back-office to the world, but also as its production centre. India's secularism and democracy serve as a role model to other developing countries. There is great pride in an India that easily integrates with a global economy, yet maintains a unique cultural identity.

But what is breathtaking is India's youth. For despite an ancient civilization that traces itself to the very dawn of human habitation, India is among the youngest countries in the world. More than half the country is under 25 years of age and more than a third is under 15 years of age.

Brought up in the shadow of the rise of India's service industry boom, this group feels it can be at least as good if not better than anyone else in the world. This confidence has them demonstrating a great propensity to consume, throwing away ageing ideas of asceticism and thrift. The economic activity created by this combination of a growing labour pool and rising consumption demand is enough to propel India to double-digit economic growth for decades. This opportunity also represents the greatest threat to India's future. If the youth of India are not properly educated and if there are not enough jobs created, India will have forever lost its opportunity.

India's Information Technology and Business Process Outsourcing industries are engines of job creation, but they still account for only 0.2 per cent of India's employment. The country has no choice but to dramatically industrialise and inflate its economy. According to a recent survey, more than half of India's unemployed within the next decade could be its educated youth.

91. Consider the following statements :
1.   India's rich cultural heritage prevents India from surging ahead to become an active partner in the global economy.
2.   By and large, India's youth still believe in a thrifty lifestyle.
Which of the statements given above is/are correct?
(a)   1 only   (b)   2 only
(c)   Both 1 and 2   (d)   Neither 1 nor 2

92. What is the approximate number of people in India who are in the age group 15-25 years?
(a)   500 million   (b)   350 million
(c)   210 million   (d)   180 million

93. In the recent past, which sector has witnessed a phenomenal growth?
(a)   Heavy industry   (b)   Service industry
(c)   Petrochemical industry (d)   Textile industry

94. Consider the following statements :
1.   Rising consumption demand will retard economic growth.
2.   India's youth are its greatest opportunity as well as threat.
Which of the statements given above is/are correct?
(a)   1 only   (b)   2 only
(c)   Both 1 and 2   (d)   Neither 1 nor 2

95. Consider the following statements :
1.   Information Technology sector provides a relatively large proportion of jobs in India.
2.   In the coming decade only uneducated youth will remain deprived of employment opportunity.
Which of the statements given above is/are correct?
(a)   1 only   (b)   2 only
(c)   Both 1 and 2   (d)   Neither 1 nor 2

PASSAGE-62

The US Senate's approval of an immigration Bill has been welcomed in India as well as in the IT industry in America because of the proposal of double H1-B visas for skilled foreign workers. However, the more important bit in the legislation, if approved by the House of Representatives, is the lifeline to millions of illegal immigrants in the US. Some of the key proposals in the Bill include allowing illegal immigrants, who have been in America for five years, to become legal residents by paying a certain amount in fines and back taxes. Those who have been in the country between two and five years can go to a point of entry at the US border and file an application. There is also a provision for creating a guest worker programme especially meant for farm workers. These are welcome moves to recognise the huge presence—according to some estimates 12 to 15 million —of illegal immigrants in the US and legitimising their existence. But it must be understood that the US is not considering this legislation out of a sense of altruism. The truth is that the bulk of immigrants are doing jobs that Americans simply don't want to do. They are employed in jobs that pay minimum wages and entail long working hours. But giving illegal immigrants the opportunity to become legal residents will at least ensure that they are not exploited by employers and that they are covered by social security benefits.

American legislators, however need to go beyond this. They must recognise that the US needs trained people in various fields, particularly in schools and hospitals. India with its vast population of educated youth is a natural source of such personnel. Instead of just targeting India for its best brains, The US should open up its labour market for more school teachers, nurses and technicians from India. Compared to Mexicans, the largest component of immigrants to the US, Indians have a natural advantage in that they know English. They would also be willing to work in America's inner cities and other supposedly 'hardship' stations. Along with nuclear deals and technology transfer, the two largest English-speaking democracies must realise that they could mutually benefit from bilateral employment agreements. India, with its one-billion plus and growing population, has the potential of supplying First World nations with declining birth rates much-needed labour.

Based on the passage given above, answer to the questions which follow:

96. Consider the following statements :
1. Besides for high technology areas, India can be an effective source of manpower in the health and education sectors of the United States of America.
2. Only those illegal immigrants can file an application for getting status of legal residents who have stayed in the US for over five years.

Which of the statement(s) given above is/are correct?
(a) Only 1   (b) Only 2
(c) Both 1 and 2   (d) Neither 1 nor 2

97. Consider the following statements :
1. The number of farm workers in the US is between 12 to 15 million.
2. The types of jobs which engage the immigrants are not sought after by the Americans.

Which of the statement(s) given above is/are correct?
(a) Only 1   (b) Only 2
(c) Both 1 and 2   (d) Neither 1 nor 2

98. Consider the following statements :
1. One of the shortcomings of the immigration Bill is that illegal immigrants will still be deprived of is that illegal immigrants will still be deprived of social security benefits.
2. India contributes the largest number of immigrants to the United States of America.

Which of the statement(s) given above is/are correct?
(a) Only 1   (b) Only 2
(c) Both 1 and 2   (d) Neither 1 nor 2

99. Consider the following statements :
1. The basic premise of the immigration Bill is a concern of the Federal Government of the United States of America for welfare of the mankind.
2. Both Mexican and Indian immigrants enjoy an advantage of good communication skills in English.

Which of the statement(s) given above is/are correct?
(a) Only 1   (b) Only 2
(c) Both 1 and 2   (d) Neither 1 nor 2

PASSAGE-63

The art of effective presentation is the fruit of persistent efforts and practice. Your personality is reflected in your presentation. Adequate planning and preparation are essential for a successful presentation. A thorough preparation is the best antidote for nervousness. If a person is not successful in presenting his views and ideas then it will become the greatest obstacle in his career and life. People form a perception about how competent you are by how you present yourself when you stand and speak.

A successful presentation can help a person in winning orders for the company he works for. Most people who work in organizations find that their effectiveness and success depend on their ability to organize their ideas and present them effectively. Delivering your message in person provides immediate feedback that helps you clarify points and answer questions.

Oral presentations are often more persuasive. As far as possible, one should never read a presentation or memorize it. Then the presentation will lose flexibility and communication will suffer. The spoken word wields great power. Face-to-face interaction demands thinking and speaking. Anecdotes, quotations and humorous touches often make a presentation interesting. One may consult his notes frequently when he is making his presentation. This may create a feeling among listeners that the speaker has taken pains to prepare for the occasion. A positive response will be generated and the speaker will be heard with respect. Speaker's enthusiasm and confidence can influence people to accept to reject an idea in a way that a written document cannot. A presentation should be persuasive and should change the audience's attitude. The topic of the presentation must be interesting to the audience. The topic should be of interest to the speaker also otherwise he will go through the motions of making a presentation. No perfunctory approach should ever be resorted to while making a presentation. It is very important that the speaker is perceived by the audience as credible and qualified to speak about the topic. Speaker must adapt to intellectual level of the audience.

100. Consider the following statements :
1. Persuasive skill-set is a prerequisite to an effective presentation.
2. At the end of a presentation, offering small gifts to the audience by the speaker is a good strategy.

Which of the statement(s) given above is/are correct?
(a) Only 1   (b) Only 2
(c) Both 1 and 2   (d) Neither 1 nor 2

101. Consider the following statements :
1. Innate stage fright of a speaker can be countered by meticulous preparation of his presentation.
2. Confidence of a speaker is generally taken by the audience as a sign of arrogance.

Which of the statement(s) given above is/are correct?
(a) Only 1   (b) Only 2
(c) Both 1 and 2   (d) Neither 1 nor 2

102. Consider the following statements :
1. Topic of the presentation must be of relevant interest to the audience to induce their responses.
2. Topic of the presentation may or may not be of intimate interest to the speaker.

Which of the statement(s) given above is/are correct?
(a) Only 1   (b) Only 2
(c) Both 1 and 2   (d) Neither 1 nor 2

103. Consider the following statements :
1. A speaker must memorize his talk so as to introduce more flexibility.
2. A written document is more efficacious than an oral presentation as it leaves a lasting impression on the reader.

Which of the statement(s) given above is/are correct?
(a) Only 1   (b) Only 2
(c) Both 1 and 2   (d) Neither 1 nor 2

104. Consider the following statements :
1. Presentations are not meant to change point of view of the audience about subject of the presentation.
2. Recounting of quotations in the presentation should be avoided as it makes the presentation appear superficial.
Which of the statement(s) given above is/are correct?
(a) Only 1   (b) Only 2
(c) Both 1 and 2   (d) Neither 1 nor 2

105. Consider the following statements :
1. One of the drawbacks of presentations is that they fails to provide a feedback from the audience.
2. While making a presentation one should, at times, refer to his written material.
Which of the statement(s) given above is/are correct?
(a) Only 1   (b) Only 2
(c) Both 1 and 2   (d) Neither 1 nor 2

106. Consider the following statements :
1. An effective presentation about the product of a company can help in increasing sales volumes.
2. Impromptu presentation can leave a more forceful impact on the audience.
Which of the statement(s) given above is/are correct?
(a) Only 1   (b) Only 2
(c) Both 1 and 2   (d) Neither 1 nor 2

PASSAGE-64

There are a great many people who have all the material conditions of happiness, i.e., health, sufficient income and clout, but who nevertheless, are profoundly unhappy. In such cases it would seem as if the fault must lie with a wrong theory as to how to live. We imagine ourselves more different from the animals than we are. Animals live on impulse and are happy as long as external conditions are favourable. Your needs are more complex than those of your pets but they still have their basis in instinct. In civilised societies, this is too apt to be forgotten. People propose to themselves some paramount objective and restrain all impulses that do not minister to it. A businessman may be so anxious to grow rich that to this end he sacrifices health and private affection. When at last he has become rich, no pleasure remains to him except harrying other people by exhortations to initiate his noble example.

107. Which one of the following is correct?
The "material conditions of happiness" do not include
(a) health   (b) money
(c) power   (d) hope

108. Which one of the following is correct? Modern man is very unhappy because he
(a) is always busy making money
(b) feels alienated from his fellow beings
(c) cannot communicate with animals
(d) suppresses his inner urges

109. Which one of the following is correct? The author is of the opinion that
(a) we are superior to animals
(b) animals are more impulsive than us
(c) we are really not very different from animals
(d) we have the unique ability to control our impulses

110. What does the phrase "do not minister to it" mean?
(a) Do not support it   (b) Do not oppose it
(c) Are ignorant about it   (d) Are careless about it

PASSAGE-65

The first of the political causes of war is war itself. Many wars have been fought, among other reasons, for the sake of seizing some strategically valuable piece of territory, or in order to secure a 'natural' frontier, that is to say, a frontier which is easy to defend and from which it is easy to launch attacks upon one's neighbours. Purely military advantages are almost as highly praised by the rulers of nations as economic advantages. The possession of an army, navy and air force is itself a reason for going to a war. "We must use our forces now', so runs the militarist's argument, 'in order that we may be in a position to use them to better effect next time.'

111. Why have wars been fought?
(a) To use weapons and make room for fresh purchase
(b) Because people want to show their neighbours that they are strong
(c) To capture some areas of another country which are of strategic importance
(d) To each neighbouring countries a good lesson

112. What does a 'natural' frontier mean?
(a) An area on the border from where you can keep watch on or attack your enemy
(b) Some place on the border of a country having beautiful natural scenery
(c) A borderline that has been naturally chosen by two neighbouring countries
(d) A sudden gift of land by nature because of sudden change in the course of a river

113. Which one of the following is correct? 'Military advantages' and 'economic advantages' :
(a) are the same for a country
(b) may or may not be the same but the rulers make them appear to be the same
(c) are completely different for a country
(d) go against each other

PASSAGE-66

Perhaps the best political epigram of recent years is the saying that this is the century of the common man. The coming of this century can be seen far back in the extension of the suffrage and later in the development of social legislation. For many years all men have been equal before the law, every adult man and woman has the vote. We are slowly creating economic democracy, that is, such a measure of economic freedom that poverty prevents no one from taking his part in public affairs or enjoying the facilities, educational and other which the state provides for all. It might seem that when this is achieved our work is done. In facts, it is only the beginning.

114. What does the term 'epigram' mean?
(a) A flattering remark
(b) An unsuitable remark
(c) A caustic remark
(d) A short and precise remark

115. Which one of the following is correct?
Extension of the suffrage indicates
(a) spread of suffering
(b) suffering of the common man
(c) right of vote for more and more people
(d) spread of crime in politics

116. What does 'economic democracy' stand for?
(a) Equal distribution of wealth
(b) Equal economic opportunity for all
(c) Application of democratic process in economic institutions
(d) Importance of money in political activities

PASSAGE-67

For more than 3 decades, I achieved great success as a lawyer, till a stroke left my right side totally paralysed. Despite the doctor's encouragement, I was consumed by rage and self-pity. I yearned to be active again. But what could a middle-aged cripple like me do? One day, glancing at some paintings I owned, I thought suddenly, " What about painting ? In fact, I had always wanted to paint, but had never had the time. Now, I had plenty of time. In the last 25 years, I have completed 300 paintings-one of them appeared on the cover of the Reader's Digest. The stroke, I realize, has helped me develop a latent talent and enjoy life.

117. Which one of the following is the correct statement ?
While in the hospital, the author was
(a) angry with himself for falling ill
(b) relieved at the successful treatment
(c) frustrated at his helpless situation
(d) resentful at being hospitalized

118. Why did the author consider himself a cripple?
(a) He could not go back to work
(b) He could not longer use his right hand
(c) He could not use his time properly
(d) He could not lead an active life

119. Which one of the following is the correct statement?
The paralytic stroke helped the author
(a) to face challenges in life successfully
(b) to realize his latent talent
(c) to learn a new hobby
(d) to earn more money

PASSAGE-68

We have built up an energy intensive society such that hundreds of daily acts are dependent on having energy at our ready command. Most of that energy comes from fossil fuels. Yet, within two centuries we will have used up nearly all of the fossil fuel that has been built up over millions of years of earth time. Furthermore, the extraction and consumption of fossil fuels is a major polluter of our environment. Our appetite for energy is seemingly insatiable. We are now searching for it in different places and using methods that inevitably upset and pollute the environment.

Since fossil energy will soon be gone we are searching for alternative sources.

120. Today we are dependent on energy for everything. What is the most likely factor that contributes to this situation?
(a) Sufficient quantity of energy is available at present
(b) We have developed a society which makes intensive use of energy
(c) Energy is most convenient and easy to use
(d) We have no alternatives

121. The author seems to disapprove further extraction and consumption of fossil fuels. Which of the following is the most likely reason for that?
(a) Further extraction of fossil fuel is a costly affair
(b) Further extraction and consumption of fossil fuel may lead to conflict between countries
(c) We do not have the technical know-how for further extraction of fossil fuels
(d) Further extraction and consumption of fossil fuels will lead to worldwide environmental pollution.

122. According to the author, we are searching for alternative sources of energy. What is the most likely reason for this?
(a) Alternative sources of energy are cheaper
(b) It is feared that fossil energy will soon be exhausted
(c) A number of alternative energy sources are easily available
(d) Alternative sources of energy will not cause any environmental problems

PASSAGE-69

A whole generation of Indians gave up everything and spent their lives in fighting in British in Gandhi's way without hurting, witho ut violence, without hatred. The hope that India would one day be free kept them going through very difficult times and gave them courage. When millions of people want the same thing very much, it is a great force which even the most powerful army cannot oppose.

123. The demand for freedom became a 'great force'. What is the most likely reason for it?
(a) Great leaders gave the call for freedom
(b) Millions of people wanted to get freedom
(c) The British rule did not permit any freedom
(d) Freedom is a noble ideal

124. Which is the 'most powerful army' referred to in the passage?
(a) The powerful army of the Government of India
(b) The powerful army of the British
(c) Any powerful army fighting against the wishes of millions of people
(d) The army formed by the freedom fighters

PASSAGE-70

There are eccentric people who enjoy saving money for no other reason than the pleasure of saving money. It is a passion like drinking, and a hobby like collecting of china. Does it usually begin with a money-box? Imagine a painter drawing the Miser's Progress in a number of scenes, with the first scene showing a benevolent grandfather holding out a harmless looking tin money-box to an infant scarcely able to walk. The gift should always be accompanied by a box of tools. As a young man the infant has grown into a miser. By the age of forty he has a substantial bank account. But he persuades himself that he is so poor that he never goes to the theatre, never invites a friend to dinner. But sixty he is a rich man and is convinced that he is all but a pauper.

125. Some people enjoy saving money because
  (a)   they are able to live a happy life
  (b)   saving is a passion with them
  (c)   they are able to enjoy the pleasures of life
  (d)   they can entertain others
126. If a money-box is given to a child, what should accompany it?
  (a)   Tips on the advantages of saving money
  (b)   Guidelines to preserve it
  (c)   Instructions on when and how to open it
  (d)   A box of tools to open it
127. A miserly man of forty does not go to the theatre because
  (a)   he has no liking for plays
  (b)   he does not want to waste his valuable time
  (c)   he persuades himself that he is very poor
  (d)   he is frightened by the darkness of the theatre hall

PASSAGE-71

No doubt, the 'green revolution' has led to self-sufficiency in food production but it has also brought with it the formidable problem of poisoning of food grains and other eatables. This is caused by excessive use of chemicals on crops and pesticide residues. It has also created havoc by exterminating the species of useful parasites and viruses which keep pests under control. Scientists are now worried about the resurgence of such formidable pests in menacing proportions which seem to undermine all that they have achieved in agricultural production.

128. From the reading of the passage, which one of these statements do you think is correct?
  (a)   The 'green revolution' has solved all problems in agriculture
  (b)   Application of chemical has resulted in everlasting preservation of grains
  (c)   The 'green revolution' is a mixed blessing
  (d)   Scientists are satisfied with achievements in agricultural production
129. The statement that "the green revolution has also created havoc by exterminating the species of useful parasites and viruses" means
  (a)   all parasites and viruses keep pests under control
  (b)   Pesticides and chemicals kill parasites and viruses, which control pests
  (c)   the pests are controlled by parasites
  (d)   application of chemicals to grains has created havoc
130. Which one of the following statements best reflects the underlying implication of the passage?
  (a)   Man's effort to control nature to his advantage has always created unseen dangers side by side
  (b)   Research in one area leads to a challenge for further research in the same field
  (c)   At present, research in preservation of agricultural production is at the cross-roads
  (d)   The excessive use of chemicals and pesticides is dangerous
131. Which one of these phrases best helps to bring out the precise meaning of 'menacing proportions?
  (a)   To and extent which becomes threatening
  (b)   Assuming dimension that cause concern
  (c)   Unimagined dangerous proportion
  (d)   Harmful size

PASSAGE-72

The importance of early detection of tuberculosis (TB), regular treatment and nutritious food are just not known widely enough. Often TB victims discontinue the treatment when the symptoms disappear, without waiting for a complete, cure; the next attack is more virulent from bacteria which have thus become drug-resistant. Anti- TB drugs are produced in India. The capability to meet the country's requirements of anti- TB drugs in full already exists. Yet millions of Indians suffer from TB and thousands of them die every year. Voluntary organizations and government agencies are doing commendable work. But we have so far tackled only the fringe of the problem. What is now needed is a nation-wide determination to fight TB. India eradicated smallpox with a national campaign. We can eradicate TB too.

132. Treatment is discontinued by TB victims, when
  (a)   they think that the disease is completely cured
  (b)   the apparent signs of TB are no longer visible to them
  (c)   they run out of resources like money or medicine
  (d)   they are attacked by drug-resistant bacteria
133. Millions of Indians suffer from TB, because
  (a)   people discontinue the treatment too soon or do not start the treatment early enough
  (b)   India does not produce anti-TB drugs of the required quality
  (c)   anti-TB drugs are not available at a reasonable price
  (d)   people do not have nutritious food
134. When the treatment of TB is discontinued too early
  (a)   the old symptoms reappear
  (b)   the patient gradually gets better, although slowly
  (c)   the disease appears in a new, more dangerous form
  (d)   the patient must get good, nutritious food
135. 'The fringe of the problem' means
  (a)   the basic cause of the problem
  (b)   the root of the problem
  (c)   the side effects of the drugs
  (d)   the edge of the problem, not the main point
136. Who or what become 'drug-resistant', according to the passage?
  (a)   TB patients who are treated for a long time
  (b)   People who do not want to take medicine for their illness
  (c)   TB bacteria that have not been fully eradicated
  (d)   Patients who have discontinued the treatment

PASSAGE-73

When we talk of education in our present age, we think largely in terms of schools and colleges. The man who is well-to-do spends money in sending his son to foreign lands, in the belief that some wonderful process will take place there transforming a dull fellow into a genius. Yet the products of expensive schools and universities often fail to make good. On the other hand, the poor man who has struggled against adversity often earns the highest honour. The fact is that the true background of early education is the home. The home, the influence of the mother, the inspiring examples that are held before the child at an age while he is impressionable, are the true groundwork of character.

137. According to the passage, who helps in our character-building?
  (a)   A foreign university
  (b)   A well-to-do man
  (c)   Examples that inspire
  (d)   A man who has earned honour
138. The proper background of early education is
  (a)   a school   (b) a college
  (c)   a religious institution   (d) the home

139. From the passage, we get an impression that the highest honour is earned by
  (a) a man who has received education in a foreign country
  (b) a man who has struggled against adversity
  (c) a man who has seen prosperity alone
  (d) the son of a prosperous man
140. A well-to-do man sends his son to foreign lands
  (a) because it is the fashion of the day
  (b) in the belief that his dull son will be transformed into a genius
  (c) so that the son may learn the customs of those countries
  (d) in order to make his son familiar with the persons and places of those countries
141. The expression "the products of expensive schools and universities often fail to make good" means
  (a) they fail to make a mark in life
  (b) they fail to become intelligent
  (c) they fail to earn proper living
  (d) they do not earn good reputation

PASSAGE-74

The functional declines of advancing age are depressing. The heart's ablity to pump blood drops about one per cent: blood flow to arms and legs decreases by thirty to forty per cent in old age. The amount of air a person can exhale after a deep breath lessens and the chest wall stiffens with age. However, recent studies have shown that most of these age-associated declines can be delayed by exercise. Exercise lowers the resting heart-rate and increases the amount of blood pumped with each beat in older people. When stress is placed on bones through exercise, calcium content rises, with the result that resistance to fracture is improved.

142. Old age is generally a depressing period because
  (a) old people worry more than others
  (b) old people tend to regret their past
  (c) various organs of the body function less efficiently
  (d) old people do very little work
143. The strength of bones can be increased by exercise, because it
  (a) increases the amount of blood pumped by the heart
  (b) increases calcium content in bones
  (c) increases the amount of air exhaled by a person
  (d) lessens the stiffness of the chest wall
144. The word 'exhale' means
  (a) breathe in   (b) breathe out
  (c) breathe slowly   (d) breathe fast
145. 'Which one of the following statements is correct?
  (a) Exercise delays natural decay of old age
  (b) Old age problems increase due to exercise
  (c) Exercise increases the heart-beat which is dangerous
  (d) Exercise creates stress which is harmful to bones
146. The chest wall becomes stiff in old age, because
  (a) the heart's ability to pump blood to it drops about one per cent
  (b) the blood flow to various organs decreases
  (c) the resting heart-rate becomes high
  (d) the person's ability to exhale sufficient air lessens

PASSAGE-75

When vegetation sprouts in the desert, it is a good sign but when the ice in the Arctic and Antarctic begins to turn green, there is something terribly wrong. Reports say that an iceberg, approximately the size of New York city, has broken off from the icy continent. An Argentine team discovered huge cracks in the polar ice caps. These developments can have serious implications. If polar ice fields melt, our coastal cities might be submerged, and sea levels across the world could rise between 3.65 and 6.09 metre in different parts of the earth. This is probably due to global warming.

147. What can be considered as a "good sign" in the desert?
  (a) When shrubs and trees grow there
  (b) When it snows in the desert·
  (c) When ice caps melt and there is water
  (d) When there is vegetation found in the desert
148. The melting of ice fields in the Arctic and Antarctic regions is dangerous because
  (a) the ice will turn green and poisonous
  (b) it will cause huge floods which will destroy coastal regions
  (c) it will create global warming and will badly affect our climate
  (d) huge cracks will develop all over the world
149. Polar ice caps develop huge cracks because
  (a) of the movement of the earth
  (b) of the breaking off of icebergs
  (c) of the crowding of cities like New York
  (d) of rising temperatures
150. What do you think the intention of the author is ?
  (a) To describe strange phenomena in nature
  (b) To report findings of research teams working in the polar regions
  (c) To make us aware of the dangers of global warming
  (d) To compare developments in deserts and Arctic regions caused by global warming

PASSAGE-76

Gandhi was not born great. He was a blundering boy, a mediocre student, a poor lawyer, 'an ordinary individual until he remade himself. He was a self-remade man. He had faith in himself, But above all, he had a deep, touching faith in the peasants, miners, labourers and young unformed men and women whom he drew into his work. He fed them all an elixir of growth which often transformed nameless, uneducated people into leonine heroes. The elixir was fearlessness.

151. Consider the following assumptions.
  1. Gandhi was a great man throughout his life.
  2. Men are not born great, but they are made great by self effort.
  3. Gandhi liked the ordinary people and neglected the rich?
  4. Gandhi transformed the ordinary masses into great heroes.
  Which of the above assumptions can be drawn from the above passage?
  (a) 2 and 4   (b) 1 and 2
  (c) 3 and 4   (d) None of these
152. Gandhi transformed the uneducated people by teaching them
  (a) work-mindedness   (b) self confidence
  (c) fearlessness   (d) heroism
153. Gandhi's attitude to the labour class was one of
  (a) generosity   (b) pity
  (c) compassion   (d) fearlessness

154. The word 'leonine' in the passage means
- (a) lean
- (b) courageous
- (c) timid
- (d) learning

PASSAGE-77

The dog fence in Australia has been erected to keep out hostile invaders, in this case hordes of yellow dogs called dingoes. The empire it preserves is that of wool growers. Yet the fence casts a much broader ecological shadow. For the early explorers, a kangaroo or a wallaby sighting marked a noteworthy event. Now try not to see one. Without a native predator there is no check on the marsupial population. The kangaroos are now cursed more than the dingoes. They have become rivals of sheep, competing for water and grass. The State Governments now cull more than three million kangaroos a year to keep Australia's natural symbol from over running the pastoral lands. *[2011-I]*

155. The 'fence' is meant to keep the
- (a) kangaroo in and the dingo out
- (b) kangaroo in and the sheep out
- (c) sheep in and the kangaroo out
- (d) sheep in and the dingo out

156. Australia's national symbol is
- (a) kangaroo
- (b) wallaby
- (c) sheep
- (d) dingo

157. What has led to the unchecked growth of the marsupial population ?
- (a) The building of fences
- (b) The absence of native predator
- (c) The culling of kangaroos
- (d) The availability of water and grass

158. The marsupial population is up in Australia because
- (a) both wallaby and kangaroo count as marsupials
- (b) the kangaroo consumes the water and grass of the sheep
- (c) the dingo cannot get at the kangaroo
- (d) the kangaroos are fenced out

PASSAGE-78

Not all nocturnal animals have good eyesight. Many of them concentrate on the other senses for finding their way about and for finding food. The sense of touch is very developed in many nocturnal animals, whether they have good eyes or not. The large hairs or whiskers on the faces of cats and mice are sense organs and the animals react rapidly if these whiskers are touched. The sense of smell is also very important for nocturnal animals such as hedgehogs and field mice. The moist night air holds scent much better than dry air does.

159. Which one of the following statements is correct ?
- (a) All nocturnal animals are blind
- (b) Many nocturnal animals do not have good eyesight
- (c) Most nocturnal animals can not see any thing in the dark
- (d) No nocturnal animals has good eyesight

160. The cat's whiskers are organs associated with the sense of
- (a) taste
- (b) touch
- (c) hearing
- (d) smell

PASSAGE-79

Elephants spray water over their ears to stay cool. The rhythm of an elephant's day is set largely by its watering routine. An adult needs about thirty gallons of water a day. When water is abundant there is no problem. But during droughts, elephants resort to an intriguing. technique: digging wells. In a dried- up river bed they scoop out holes with their forefeet until they reach water. After waiting patiently for the sand to settle, they drink in order of seniority, calves last.

161. According to the passage, water is
- (a) quite important for the elephant
- (b) vital for the elephant's survival
- (c) occasionally useful for the elephant
- (d) often a problem for the elephant

162. According to the passage, elephants spray water over themselves
- (a) to have fun
- (b) to ward off the heat
- (c) to cool their heels
- (d) to quench their thirst

163. During droughts, elephants
- (a) burrow in the sand to avoid heat
- (b) find water in rivers
- (c) dig holes in the river bed to reach the water
- (d) find new water holes

164. When the elephants find water
- (a) the baby elephants drink first
- (b) the oldest adult drinks first
- (c) the largest elephant drinks first
- (d) the youngest adult drinks first

PASSAGE-80

Even in the most primitive societies, the great majority of people satisfy a large part of their material needs by exchanging goods and services. Very few people indeed can make for themselves everything they need—all their food, their clothes, their housing, their tools. Ever since men started living in communities, they have been satisfying their needs by means of specialization and exchange; increasingly each individual has concentrated on what he can do best, and has produced more of the special goods or services in which he has concentrated, than he can consume himself. The surplus he has exchanged with other members of the community, acquiring, in exchange the things he needs that others have produced.

165. According to the passage, the great majority of people can satisfy their needs today by
- (a) providing things for themselves
- (b) exchanging goods and services
- (c) concentrating on what they can do best
- (d) individual specialization

166. Exchange of goods becomes possible only when
- (a) there is no specialization
- (b) goods are produced in surplus
- (c) primitive societies become modern
- (d) individuals make things for themselves

167. Specialization and exchange began when men started
- (a) big industries
- (b) concentrating on their work
- (c) producing things for individual use
- (d) living in communities

168. Exchange of goods and services becomes necessary because
(a) man is a social being
(b) reciprocity is the law of life
(c) trade and commerce are means of progress
(d) we cannot produce everything we need ourselves

PASSAGE-81

What interests many people is the possibility of finding an Earth-like planet, and many science fiction stories have been woven around the possibility of there existing a planet somewhere in the universe which is an exact replica of the Earth. There are too many variable quantities for this to be a possibility worth considering. What is possible, if planetary systems are common as they seem to be, is the existence of planets where the conditions are similar to conditions on the Earth and to which our form of life could rapidly adapt. If life had gained a foothold on such a planet, it is possible that life closely paralleling our own planet could have developed.

What sort of conditions is necessary for life as we know it to develop? First of all of course a suitable planetary body is essential. Given this, then two vital conditions must be satisfied. The temperature must be neither too hot nor too cold, since intense heat breaks down organic molecules and severe cold prevents activity from going on. Too much short-wave radiation also upsets living organisms. The other prerequisite is a suitable atmosphere sufficiently dense to give protection from radiation and meteorites and containing oxygen and water vapour in reasonable quantities.

169. This passage suggests that there
(a) cannot be another planet like the Earth
(b) are other planets like the Earth mentioned only in stories
(c) may be other planets like the Earth in this universe
(d) is a planet which is exactly like the Earth

170. The hypothesis about the possibility of planets parallel to the Earth gets its strength from the fact that
(a) the scientists have discovered them
(b) books have been written about them
(c) the planetary system exists
(d) many people have shown interest in it

171. The statement, "If life had gained a foothold on such a planet" means that
(a) if there is life on the planet, it would be like ours
(b) if we go there, we can develop it like this Earth
(c) even if we try, we cannot go and live there
(d) it is impossible for life to develop there

PASSAGE-82

It is no doubt true that we cannot go through life without sorrow. There can be no sunshine without shadow, we must not complain that roses have thorns but rather be grateful that thorns bear flowers. Our existence here is so complex that we must expect much sorrow and suffering. Yet it is certain that no man was ever discontented with the world who did his duty in it. The world is like a looking glass; if you smile, it smiles; if you frown, it frowns back. Always try, then, to look at the bright side of things. There are some persons whose very presence seems like a ray of sunshine and brightens the whole room. Life has been described as a comedy to those who think and a tragedy to those who feel.

172. The author says that we cannot go through life without sorrow because
(a) it is our fate
(b) we are always discontented
(c) life is a tragedy
(d) human life is very complex

173. According to the author no man can be discontented with the world if he
(a) is determined to be happy
(b) is sincere in discharging his duties
(c) has a healthy attitude to life
(d) likes sunshine

174. The expression "life is a tragedy to those who feel" means that it is a tragedy to those who
(a) think about the world
(b) believe in fate
(c) do not understand the world
(d) are sensitive and emotional

175. The author says, "There are some persons whose very presence seems like a ray of sunshine and brightens the whole room". The reason for this is that they
(a) have the capacity to love
(b) talk more of roses and less of thorns
(c) are happy and spread happiness
(d) look good and behave well

176. What is the author's message in this passage ?
(a) Look at the bright side of things
(b) Our existence is so complex
(c) The world is a looking glass
(d) Expect much sorrow and suffering

PASSAGE – 83

As civilization proceeds in the direction of technology, it passes the points of supplying all the basic essentials of life, food, shelter, cloth, and warmth.

Then we are faced with a choice between using technology to provide and fulfil needs which have hitherto been regarded as unnecessary or, on the other hand, using technology to reduce the number of hours of work which a man must do in order to earn a given standard of living. In other words, we either raise our standard of living above that necessary for comfort and happiness or we leave it at this level and work shorter hours.

I shall take it as axiomatic that mankind has, by that time, chosen the latter alternative. Men will be working shorter and shorter hours in their paid employment.

177. "Then we are faced with a choice ..." what does 'then' refer to?
(a) When automation takes over many aspects of human life
(b) The present state of civilization
(c) The past stage of civilization
(d) After having provided the basic essentials of life

178. What does the passage suggest about the use of technology?
(a) It creates new and essential needs for mankind
(b) It is opposed to the basic essentials of life
(c) It is complementary to a raised standard of living
(d) It is responsible for man's love of comfort and happiness

179. What does increased use of technology imply?
  (a) An advanced stage in human civilization
  (b) A backward step in human culture
  (c) Unnecessary comfort and happiness for mankind
  (d) Man's zest for more and more work
180. What does the author suggest ?
  (a) Man will gradually rise above his present stage in civilization
  (b) Man will gradually settle down to the same stage with fewer hours of work
  (c) Man will gradually raise his standard of living by working longer hours
  (d) Man will gradually earn a given standard of living with the help of technology

PASSAGE – 84

It is said that ideas are explosive and dangerous. To allow them unfettered freedom is, in fact, to invite disorder. But, to this position, there are at least two final answers. It is impossible to draw a line round dangerous ideas and any attempt at their definition involves monstrous folly. If views, moreover, which imply disorder are able to disturb the foundations of the state, there is something supremely wrong with the governance of the state. For disorder is not a habit of mankind. We cling so eagerly to our accustomed ways that, as even Burke insisted, popular violence is always the outcome of a deep popular sense of wrong.

181. What is the central point that the passage emphasizes ?
  (a) It is unnecessary to define dangerous ideas
  (b) Dangerous ideas are born out of the enjoyment of freedom
  (c) A well-governed state is unaffected by dangerous ideas
  (d) Dangerous ideas originate from man's preoccupation with politics
182. From a close study of the passage, which one of the following statements emerges most clearly ?
  (a) The author is against the exercise of political freedom
  (b) He is indifferent to dangerous and explosive ideas
  (c) He welcomes violence as a method to change governments
  (d) He warns that violence is the outcome of popular dissatisfaction with the government
183. The author says, "We cling so eagerly to our accustomed ways". Which one of the following statements may be considered as the assumption of the author ?
  (a) We are afraid of social changes
  (b) Mankind is averse to any disorder
  (c) We have developed inertia that makes us incapable of social action
  (d) There is an all round lack of initiative in the society
184. Which of the following statements may most correctly bring out the significance of the opinion of Burke quoted in the passage ?
  (a) Burke advocated violence against injustice
  (b) Burke's opinion coincides with the author's opinion on explosive and dangerous ideas
  (c) Burke hated any popular uprising
  (d) Burke had no belief in political liberty

PASSAGE – 85

What is to, be the limit of forgiveness? It would probably have been allowed by many of the ancients that an unforgiving temper was not to be commended.

They would have said, we are not to exact a penalty for every nice offence, we are to overlook some things, we are to be blind sometimes.
But they would have said at the same time, we must be careful to keep our self-respect, and to be on a level with the world. On the whole, they would have said, it is the part of a man fully to requite to his friends their benefits and to his enemies their injuries.

185. Which one of the following is the correct statement ? We must
  (a) be blind if we want to forgive others
  (b) be blind to the faults of our friends
  (c) be indifferent to what others do
  (d) overlook certain things
186. Which one of the following is the correct statement ? In ancient times people were
  (a) ordered to lose their tempers
  (b) permitted to lose their tempers and not forgive their enemies
  (c) told that it was not good to have an unforgiving temper
  (d) advised to forgive each and every offence committed by both friends and foes
187. What is the underlying tone of the passage?
  (a) We must be forgiving in general
  (b) We must forgive our friends
  (c) There is no limit whatsoever to our duty to forgive
  (d) We must always punish the wrong doer

PASSAGE – 86

The New Year is a time for resolutions. Mentally at least, most of us could compile formidable lists of do's and don'ts. The same old favourites recur year in and year out with monotonous regularity. Past experience has taught us that certain accomplishments are beyond attainment. If we remain inveterate smokers, it is only because we have so often experienced the frustration that results from failure. Most of us fail in our efforts at self improvement because our schemes are too ambitious and we never have time to carry them out. We also make the fundamental error of announcing our resolutions to everybody so that we look even more foolish when we slip back into our old bad ways.

188. The author seems to think that others
  (a) feel happy when we slip back to our old ways
  (b) do not really want us to improve ourselves
  (c) are ready to tease and laugh at our attempts if we fail
  (d) might embarrass us by praising our attempts
189. The author says that most of us fail in our attempts at self-improvement because
  (a) we set too high ambitions for ourselves
  (b) we do not have the persistence of mind
  (c) our nature is such that we cannot become perfect
  (d) certain imperfections have become a part and parcel of our lives
190. The author seems to imply that many are inveterate smokers because
  (a) they have not really tried to give up smoking
  (b) they know from past experience that they can never succeed in their attempt to give up
  (c) they want to forget the frustration of not smoking
  (d) they do not have the will power to stop smoking
191. The same old favourites recur ... with monotonous regularity' implies that
  (a) we want to be so perfect that we include some items regularly
  (b) we have been so regularly doing certain things that they have become monotonous

(c)   in spite of repeated failures, we still would like to try one more time

(d)   some favourite actions if repeated often could become monotonous

192. The phrase 'formidable lists of do's and don'ts' means that
    (a)   the bad points of our character are formidable
    (b)   the list is so long that it is frightening
    (c)   the things that need to be included is frightening
    (d)   the realisation that we are so imperfect is frightening

PASSAGE – 87

He dropped off to sleep. The cigarette slipped out of his mouth and burnt a great black hole in his only shirt. The smart of the burn awoke him, and he got up, cursing under his breath, and fumbled in the dark for a needle in order to sew up the hole. Otherwise his wife would see it in the morning and would hag away at him for a couple of hours. But he could not find a needle. He fell asleep again.

193. Which one of the following statements best sums up the man's reaction to his problem?
    (a)   The man is extremely upset to find the shirt burnt and frantically tries to repair the damage
    (b)   The hole in the shirt and the wife's anticipated nagging are minor problems, the greater one is that the man cannot find a needle
    (c)   Neither the shirt hole nor the nagging nor the lack of a needle is of great consequence
    (d)   The man is terrified of his wife and dreads her discovering the burnt shirt

194. The man wanted to sew the hole because
    (a)   he wanted to avoid being scolded by his wife
    (b)   he had nothing else to do
    (c)   he had no other shirt
    (d)   he wanted to sleep again

195. The man got up to search for a needle because
    (a)   his wife would be very upset
    (b)   the cigarette had damaged his only shirt
    (c)   he wanted to mend the shirt
    (d)   the burn-hole was huge and black

196. The man woke up in the dark because
    (a)   the cigarette had burnt his favourite shirt
    (b)   the cigarette had burnt his only shirt
    (c)   the cigarette had to be lit again
    (d)   the cigarette had burnt him

197. The cigarette fell out of the man's mouth because
    (a)   he fell off his stool
    (b)   he was surprised to see that it had made a hole in his shirt
    (c)   he fell asleep while smoking
    (d)   he fumbled in the dark for a needle

PASSAGE – 88

With the inevitable growth of specialization I see the universities facing two great dangers. First, it is very easy to get so involved in the technical details of education that the object of education is lost. And secondly, in an effort to condition a university to the needs of its students and to the needs of the state it may lose its power to make or mould those students into responsible men, capable of thinking for themselves and capable of expressing the results of their thoughts to others.

198. The author calls growth of specialisation 'inevitable'. Which one of the following statements is likely to be the most correct reason for this inevitability ?

    (a)   Universities give grants only to do specialised work in different disciplines
    (b)   The professors and researchers in universities are competent only for specialised work
    (c)   Specialization helps economic growth of the nation.
    (d)   In an age of science and technology specialization becomes necessary

199. Which one of the following statements most correctly suggests the central theme of the passage ?
    (a)   The aim of education is specialization
    (b)   The aim of education is to mould the youth to work for the state
    (c)   The aim of education is to make the youth capable of independent thought and expression
    (d)   The aim of education is to enable the youth to lead a comfortable living

200. Which one of the following statements most correctly suggests the warning implied in the passage ?
    (a)   University education should not be concerned with technical details.
    (b)   Universities should not subordinate themselves to the interests of the state.
    (c)   Universities should be concerned only with the needs of students.
    (d)   Universities should not go in for any specialization.

PASSAGE – 89

Popular illusion about birds extend further than the use of the word 'egg-shape' that would suggest that all eggs are alike. For instance, there is the popular idea that owls hoot. Actually, only very few owls hoot and these include the common brown or tawny wood owl. The white barn own screeches; the little own has a wailing cry; the long-earned owl barks; and the short-eared owl snorts! Another mistaken idea is that all ducks 'quack', because the common farmyard duck is a domesticated form of the common wild duck or mallard that quacks. Actually most wild ducks call with whistles.

201. The main purpose of this passage is
    (a)   to describe the life of popular birds.
    (b)   to show our incorrect ideas of bird life.
    (c)   to show our perfect knowledge about birds.
    (d)   to describe the calls of owls and ducks.

202. The impression created by repeating the terms, 'popular' and 'common' are
    (a)   human beings are closely attached to birds.
    (b)   our ideas about birds are derived from the most common types.
    (c)   owls and ducks are our favourite birds.
    (d)   domesticated birds are our source of information about the bird world.

203. The common duck is not a separate specie but a tamed version of wild variety because it
    (a)   whistles like most wild ducks.
    (b)   grunts like the tufted duck.
    (c)   has the same call as other ducks.
    (d)   quacks like the mallard.

PASSAGE – 90

"What is sixteen and three multiplied?" asked the teacher. The boy blinked. The teacher persisted, and the boy promptly answered: "twenty-four", with, as it seemed to the teacher, a wicked smile on his lips. The boy evidently was trying to fool him and was going contrary on purpose. He had corrected this error repeatedly, and now the boy persisted in saying "twenty-four". How could this fellow be made to obtain fifty in the classtest and go up by double-promotion to the first form, as his parents fondly hoped? At the mention of "twenty-four" the teacher felt all his blood rushing to his head. He controlled himself, and asked again: "How Much"? as a last chance. What the boy said the same thing obstinately, he felt as if his finger was releasing the trigger: he reached across the table, and delivered a wholesome slap on the youngster's cheek.

204. The boy answered the question
    (a) with fear and anxiety
    (b) with the intention to fail in the class test.
    (c) to make some fun in the class.
    (d) when the teacher persisted in asking.

205. The teacher felt blood rushing in his head because
    (a) there was no arrogant smile on the boy's lips.
    (b) he thought the boy was hopelessly dull.
    (c) he thought the boy made the mistake deliberately.
    (d) the boy gave a wrong answer to such as simple question.

206. The teacher controlled his anger because
    (a) he remembered the fond hopes of boys' parents.
    (b) he wanted to give another opportunity to the boy.
    (c) the boy was too young to pick up mathematics fast.
    (d) he believed that the boy must be taught the lesson again.

PASSAGE – 91

A village must have some trade; and this village has always been full of virility and power. Obscure and happy, its splendid energies had found employment in wrestling a livelihood out of the earth, whence had come a certain dignity, and kindliness, and love for other men. Civilization did not relax these energies, but it had diverted them; and all the special qualities, which might have helped to heal the world, had been destroyed. The family affection, the affection for the commune, the sane pastoral virtues – all had perished. No villain had done this thing: it was the work of ladies and gentlemen who were rich and often clever.

207. Village life is praised by the author because it
    (a) helps villagers to achieve material prosperity.
    (b) makes men complacent.
    (c) breeds humane virtues.
    (d) is free from the din and hurry of city life.

208. Civilization mainly destroys
    (a) the ability to create employment.
    (b) family affection and pastoral virtues.
    (c) medical facilities for the rural people.
    (d) agricultural trade.

PASSAGE – 92

It was Galileo and Newton – notwithstanding that Newton himself was a deeply religious man – who destroyed the old comfortable picture of a friendly universe governed by spiritual values. And this was effected, not by Newton's discovery of law of gravitation nor by any of Galileo's brilliant investigations, but by the general picture of the world which these men and others of their time made the basis of the science, not only of their own day, but of all succeeding generations down to the present. That is why the century immediately following Newton, the eighteenth century, was notoriously an age of religious skepticism. Skepticism did not have to wait for the discoveries of Darwin and the geologists in the nineteenth century. It flooded the world immediately after the age of the rise of science.

209. 'The old comfortable picture of a friendly universe' was:
    (a) a universe governed by religious beliefs
    (b) a universe with men like Newton who were deeply religious
    (c) a universe investigated by Galileo and Newton
    (d) the century immediately following Newton

210. Religious skepticism arose because:
    (a) Galileo and Newton were not religious, being scientists
    (b) Newton discovered the law of gravitation
    (c) of the discoveries of Darwin and the geologists of the nineteenth century
    (d) of the picture of the world that became the basis of science after the seventeenth century

PASSAGE – 93

Although Louis Braille died when he was only forty-three years old, he succeeded in devising a system of reading and writing for the blind which is now taught all over the world. Braille lost his sight accidentally as a child. Nevertheless, he was able to complete his education at a school for the blind in Paris and became a teacher. In his day, the few books that were available for blind people were printed in big, raised type; the letters used were those of the ordinary alphabet. The reading of such books required immense effort. Not only that, writing was almost impossible, for a blind person was still restricted to an alphabet which was extraordinarily difficult to reproduce on paper. Braille's idea was to use raised dots, instead of raised letters. He evolved a system, which made use of only six dots in all. By various combinations of these dots, it not only proved possible to represent each letter in the alphabet, but punctuation marks, numbers and musical notation as well. Reading and writing for the blind have thus become enormously simplified. The sensitive fingers of a blind person can travel rapidly over the dots; and there is a small machine, something like a typewriter, which enables the blind to write quickly and clearly.

211. Louis Braille:
    (a) was born blind
    (b) lost his sight when he was a child
    (c) lost his sight accidentally when he was forty-three years old
    (d) was not blind, but studies at a school for the blind

212. Before Braille's invention, the blind had difficulty in reading because:
    (a) there were only printed books
    (b) there were no schools for the blind
    (c) the few books available used the raised letters of the ordinary alphabet
    (d) the books meant for the blind were heavy

213. Braille's system uses:
    (a) only six dots
    (b) numbers and musical notation
    (c) ordinary alphabets in big raised type
    (d) a combination of alphabet and punctuation

214. Braille's system allows the blind
    (a) to write with ease
    (b) to read easily
    (c) to read as well as write with ease
    (d) to read easily but to write with great effort

PASSAGE – 94

The Indian culture of our times is in the making. Many of us are striving to produce a blend of all cultures that seem today to be in clash with one another. No culture can live, if it attempts to be exclusive. There is no such thing as pure Aryan culture in existence in India today. Whether the Aryans were indigenous to India or were unwelcome intruders, does not interest me much. What does interest me is the fact that my remote ancestors blended with one another with the utmost freedom and we of the present generation are a result of that blend.

I do not want my house to be walled in, on all sides and my windows to be stuffed. I want the cultures of all lands to be blown about my house as freely as possible. But I refuse to be blown off my feet by any. I would have any young men and women with literary tastes to learn as much of English and other world-languages as they like, and then expect them to give the benefits of their learning to India and the world alike like a Bose, a Ray or Tagore. But I would not have a single Indian forget, neglect or be ashamed of his mother tongue, or feel that he or she cannot think or express the best thoughts in his or her own vernacular. Mine is not a religion of the prison house.

215. The author views Indian Culture as:
   (a)   pure Aryan culture
   (b)   a clash of cultures
   (c)   a continual blend of cultures
   (d)   the culture of remote ancestors.

216. The author thinks that:
   (a)   The Aryans were indigenous to India.
   (b)   The Aryans were unwelcome intruders
   (c)   the question whether the Aryans were indigenous or not is not of interest
   (d)   the culture that we have inherited is the Aryan culture.

217. The author wants:
   (a)   the cultures of others to be kept out
   (b)   the cultures of others to replace our old culture
   (c)   the freedom to blend other cultures with our own
   (d)   the preservation of the culture of our ancestors.

218. The author wants Indians to:
   (a)   learn only English, as much as they like
   (b)   learn English and other world languages
   (c)   learn only the mother tongue or the vernacular
   (d)   learn English and other world languages in addition to the mother tongue.

PASSAGE – 95

The sky was already full of rusting wings. But when Jean stepped into the still lusterless water, he seemed to be swimming in an indeterminate darkness until he saw the streaks of red and gold over the horizon. Then he suddenly swam back to land and clambered up the winding path to his house. After a great deal of panting he reached a little gate, pushed it open and climbed a stairway. The house above the world had its huge bay-windows through which one could see the horizon from one edge to the other. Here, no one complained of exhaustion. Every one had his joy to conquer, every day.

219. Which of the following is/are indicated by the description in the passage ?
   1.   Time before sunrise   2.   Time after sunset
   3.   Clouds   4.   Birds
   Select the correct answer using the code given below :
   (a)   2 and 3 only   (b)   2 only
   (c)   2, 3 and 4 only   (d)   1 and 4 only

220. What do the words "great deal of panting" imply?
   1.   Jean was too weak to walk.
   2.   Jean's house was on a hill.

3.   Jean was too tired to walk after swimming.
4.   Jean's house was too far away from the shore.
Which of the statements given above is/are correct ?
(a)   1 and 2   (b)   2 only
(c)   2, 3 and 4   (d)   1 and 4

PASSAGE – 96

Fortunately it is as yet only through fantasy that we can see what the destruction of the scholarly and scientific disciplines would mean to mankind. From history we can learn what their existence has meant. The sheer power of disciplined thought is revealed in practically all the great intellectual and technological advances which the human race has made. The ability of the man of disciplined mind to direct this power effectively upon problems for which he has not specifically trained is proved by examples without number. The real evidence for the value of liberal education lies in history and in the biographies of men who have met the valid criteria of greatness. These support overwhelmingly the claim of liberal education that it can equip a man with fundamental powers of decision and action, applicable not only to boy-girl relationship, to tinkering hobbies, or to choosing the family dentist, but to all the great and varied concerns of human life ------------- not least, those that are unforeseen.

221. Liberal education enables a person to
   (a)   read with more discernment than others
   (b)   apply general principles to resolve issues
   (c)   gain prestige
   (d)   develop a clearer understanding of history than others

222. In this passage, the author stresses the importance of
   (a)   education for living
   (b)   technological advances
   (c)   increased interest in the study of history
   (d)   satisfying the desire for security

223. In this passage, the expression 'specifically trained' refers to
   (a)   characteristically trained (b)   particularly trained
   (c)   peculiarly trained   (d)   ostensibly trained

224. According to the author, 'the great and varied concerns of human life' are about
   (a)   fundamental rights
   (b)   challenges facing mankind
   (c)   tinkering hobbies
   (d)   liberal education

PASSAGE – 97

Young seekers after peace know that only trust shown to all the peoples of the earth and not just to a few of them, can lead to the healing of the wounds that tear them apart and so it is essential never to humiliate the members of a nation whose leaders have committed inhuman acts. Essential also is boundless concern for so many men and women who today, as exiles or immigrants, live on foreign soil. If every home was open to somebody of foreign origin, the racial problem would be partially solved.

225. For the reconciliation and unity it is essential.
   (a)   to have no discrimination in the trust shown to the peoples of the earth
   (b)   to have young seekers after peace
   (c)   to have confidence in at least a few of the peoples
   (d)   to punish the leaders who committed in human sins

226. To make the members of a nation responsible for the in human acts of their leaders is
   (a)   unimportant   (b)   understandable
   (c)   unjust   (d)   undesirable

227. Boundless concern should be shown to
  (a)   one's own country men alone
  (b)   the people belonging to our friendly nations only
  (c)   the foreigners who just visit our country
  (d)   all the exiles living away from their native lands

228. The theme of the passage is
  (a)   rigid nationalism alone can help peaceful co-existence
  (b)   trusting all the peoples of the earth may lead to serious problems
  (c)   being cautious of others is a must to live in peace
  (d)   concern for everyone irrespective of the race of country

PASSAGE – 98

One day we were becalmed among a group of small islands, most of which appeared to be uninhabited. As soon as we were in want of fresh water, the captain sent the boat ashore to bring off a cask or two. But we were mistaken in thinking there were no natives, for scarcely had we drawn near to the shore when a band of savages rushed out of the bush and assembled on the beach, brandishing their clubs and spears in a threatening manner.

229. The captain sent the boat to the shore to
  (a)   look for inhabitants
  (b)   find help
  (c)   find a place to settle there
  (d)   fetch some water

230. The savages brandished their spears in order to
  (a)   display their skill
  (b)   frighten the crew
  (c)   welcome the crew to the island
  (d)   tell the crew to leave

231. The inhabitants of the islands were
  (a)   man-eaters   (b)   pirates
  (c)   cruel people   (d)   primitive tribes

PASSAGE – 99

Nelson Mandela was appointed national volunteer-in-chief of the Defence Campaign; his deputy was Maulvi Cachalia, whose father had been one of the bravest resisters alongside Gandhi in 1907. Mandela toured the Cape, Natal and the Transvaal, visiting houses in the townships, explaining the plans, sometimes talking through the night. His task was to inspire people with confidence in their ability to overcome oppression through a direct non-violent challenge to the government. As always, there were the problems of being black in small towns, no hotels or taxis for Africans, nor were there telephone lines in township homes. This meant walking miles to the location and knocking on a likely looking door. Sometimes they were welcomed by an enthusiastic stranger, sometimes rebuffed by the cautious.

232. The purpose of Mandela's talks was to help people
  (a)   court arrests
  (b)   oppose oppression
  (c)   join him in his campaign tours
  (d)   get small town facilities

233. It is clear from the passage that the black Africans.
  (a)   enjoyed small town facilities .
  (b)   were helped by Gandhi in their freedom struggle.
  (c)   had an unfavourable government.
  (d)   liked visiting homes in townships

PASSAGE – 100

One day an army group won a land battle against the enemy. The commander feared that the enemy's powerful air force might bomb his camp that night in revenge. So he ordered all lights to be put out at 7.00 PM. At midnight the commander went round inspecting the camp. Seeing a light in a tent, he entered it. His son, an officer under him, was writing a letter. The son explained that he was writing to his mother about his brave deeds in battle. The commander told his son to add to his letter that by the time his mother received the letter he would have been shot dead for indiscipline.

234. The commander went round the camp at midnight because he
  (a)   was too tired from the day's battle to go to sleep
  (b)   wished to check if his soldiers had obeyed his order
  (c)   was too worried about the next day's battle
  (d)   wished to check if enemies hand entered his camp

235. The commander entered his son's tent because he
  (a)   wished to see and talk to his son
  (b)   suspected that enemies had entered his tent
  (c)   wished to send a message to his wife
  (d)   had to punish any soldier who disobeyed his order

236. The son was writing a letter because he
  (a)   wanted to write to his mother about his father's brave deeds in battle
  (b)   loved his mother so much that he had to write to her
  (c)   was eager to tell his mother about his own deeds
  (d)   did not care for orders since his father was the commander

PASSAGE – 101

The heat-wave deepened during the following few days while Jack and I lazed about in the house and yards, wearing ragged shirts and discarded garments, because the more presentable ones were being packed by Mother. She was obviously not strong enough to cycle down to Hemisphere, where Father and Jack had been one week-end, to see and rent a cottage in Ropley, near Alresford. From this prospective journey Jack had returned with half a dozen photographs taken with a plate-camera which he had made for himself, the aperture being a pinhole. This was only one of his many ingenious artefacts. I had studied the pictures, which included a church that leaned backwards, in the hope of finding the perpetually teasing certainty which we look for when about to take some adventurous step into the unknown. But Ropley remained unreal.

237. During the hot summer days the author and Jack
  (a)   were taking adventurous steps into the unknown
  (b)   went visiting several churches in Ropley
  (c)   were busy repairing a camera
  (d)   were passing their time in idleness

238. They were planning
  (a)   to move out Ropley
  (b)   a trekking expedition to Alresford
  (c)   to do some photography
  (d)   to make some artefacts

239. The author and Jack were wearing ragged shirts and discarded garments because
  (a)   they were very poor
  (b)   it was summer
  (c)   all their good clothes were already packed
  (d)   they were lazing about

240. The plate camera
   (a)   was the only artefact made by Father and Jack
   (b)   was the only artefact Jack had made for himself
   (c)   was only one of Jack's many such artefacts
   (d)   was borrowed by Jack from his friend for taking half a dozen photographs.

241. Father and Jack had been to Ropley one weekend
   (a)   to take photographs of the church that leaned backwards
   (b)   because Ropley was unreal
   (c)   to take some adventurous step into the unknown
   (d)   to see and rent a cottage there

PASSAGE – 102

Literature and history are twin sisters, inseparable. In the days of our own grandfathers, and for many generations before them, the basis of education was the Greek and Roman classics for the educated, and the Bible for all. In the classical authors and in the Bible, history and literature were closely intervolved, and it is that circumstance which made the old form of education so stimulating to the thought and imagination of our ancestors. To read the classical authors and to read the Bible was to read at once the history and the literature of the three greatest races of the ancient world. No doubt the classics and the Bible were read in a manner we now consider uncritical but they were read according to the best tenets of the time and formed a great humanistic education. Today the study both of the classics and of the Bible has dwindled to small proportions. What has taken their place? To some extent the vacuum has been filled by a more correct knowledge of history and a wider range of literature. But I fear that the greater part of it has been filled up with rubbish.

242. Which of the following statements best reflects the underlying tone of the passage ?
   (a)   Literature and history are mutually exclusive
   (b)   Literature and history are complementary to each other
   (c)   The study of literature is meaningless without any knowledge of history.
   (d)   Literature and history are inseparably linked together in the classics and the Bible

243. The author of the above passage says that in the past the basis of education for all people, irrespective of their intellectual calibre, was
   (a)   Greek and Roman classics
   (b)   The Bible
   (c)   A correct knowledge of history
   (d)   A wider range of literature

244. The author of the above passage says that the classics and the Bible were read by his ancestors
   (a)   methodically and with discretion.
   (b)   in a manner that broadened their view of life
   (c)   with great emphasis on their literary values
   (d)   without critical discrimination but in the light of their humanistic culture

245. According to the author of the above passage, the old form of education, based on the study of the classics and of the Bible, has
   (a)   succeeded in creating interest in history
   (b)   laid the basis of human civilization
   (c)   had a gradual decline in our time
   (d)   been rejuvenated in the context of modern education

246. The author of the above passage fears that the greater part of the vacuum created by lack of interest in the classics and the Bible had been filled up by

   (a)   a richer sense of history
   (b)   a wider range of literature
   (c)   worthless ideas
   (d)   a new philosophy of life

PASSAGE – 103

As the tortoise tucks its feet and head inside the shell and will not come out even though you may break the shell into pieces, even so the character of the man who has control over his motives and organs, is unchangeably establishment. He controls his own inner forces, and nothing can draw them out against his will. By this continuous reflex of good thoughts and good impressions moving over the surface of the mind, the tendency to do good becomes strong, and in consequence, we are able to control the Indriyas or sense organs.

247. The author uses the phrase 'inner forces' in this passage. Which of the following would be its most correct meaning in the context ?
   (a)   Emotional disturbances in man
   (b)   Strength of the internal organs
   (c)   Forces produced by sense organs
   (d)   Reflection of the intellect

248. Which of the following statements would illustrate the metaphor in the passage ?
   (a)   Man is slow-moving and slow-witted
   (b)   A man of character refuses to be influenced by outside compulsions against his will
   (c)   Man confines himself to a life of isolation
   (d)   Man cannot have a good character or strong will

249. Which of the following statements may be assumed to reflect the central theme of the passage ?
   (a)   Good thoughts lead to the control of the sense organs
   (b)   Control of the sense organs leads to good thoughts
   (c)   Character, though established, may be disturbed by outside forces
   (d)   No man can achieve success in destroying the inner forces

250. Which of the following statements would be most correct in explaining the metaphorical meaning of 'break the shell into pieces' ?
   (a)   Destruction of the human body
   (b)   Breaking of the physical environment of man
   (c)   Attempt to destroy the man's character
   (d)   Inflicting physical and mental agony on man

251. The passage consists of two long sentences and a short one. The purpose of this style could be to suggest that
   (a)   it is impossible for man to attain perfection of character
   (b)   the attainment of perfect character is the result of a long process of mental discipline
   (c)   the whole life process is clumsy
   (d)   there is a lot of confusion in our understanding of sense organs, character, etc.

PASSAGE – 104

One of the most serious problems confronting our country is that of a fast-growing population. In fact, it is at the root of many other problems. At the moment, thanks to planning, we are able to produce food and cloth sufficient for our people and even in some excess. But if the population continues to grow at this rate, it will not be long before the surplus turns into a bare minimum and even a deficit. The position in regard to accomodation is even now far from satisfactory in spite of our efforts.

252. "It is at the root of many other problems" means that
     (a)   it is found along with many other problems
     (b)   it is caused by many other problems
     (c)   it gives rise to many other problems
     (d)   it is buried under many other problems
253. The present satisfactory position in regard to food and cloth is due to
     (a)   the fact that the population has been controlled
     (b)   our good luck
     (c)   good rainfall
     (d)   our economic planning
254. If the population of India continues to increase at this rate, the situation in regard to food and cloth
     (a)   is likely to remain the same
     (b)   is likely to become less satisfactory
     (c)   is likely to improve
     (d)   is likely to vary up and down
255. The situation in respect of accommodation
     (a)   is less than satisfactory
     (b)   is quite satisfactory
     (c)   is improving rapidly
     (d)   is the result of total neglect
256. At present Indians have
     (a)   more provision for cloth than accommodation
     (b)   more provision for accommodation than cloth
     (c)   abundance of cloth and accommodation
     (d)   scarcity of cloth and accommodation

PASSAGE – 105

Even in the most primitive societies the great majority of people satisfy a large part of their material needs by exchanging goods and services. Very few people indeed can make for themselves everything they need–all their food, their clothes, their housing, their tools. Ever since men started living in communities, they have been satisfying their needs by means of specialization and exchange; increasingly each individual has concentrated on what he can do best, and has produced more of the special goods or services in which he has concentrated, than he can consume himself. The surplus he has exchanged with other members of the community, acquiring, in exchange the things he needs that others have produced.

257. Very few people can satisfy their needs today by
     (a)   providing things for themselves
     (b)   exchanging goods and services
     (c)   concentrating on what they can do best
     (d)   individual specialization
258. Exchange of goods becomes possible only when
     (a)   there is no specialization
     (b)   the goods are produced in surplus
     (c)   primitive societies become modern
     (d)   individuals make things for themselves
259. Specialization and exchange began when men started
     (a)   big industries
     (b)   concentrating on their work
     (c)   producing things for individual use
     (d)   living in communities
260. Exchange of goods and services becomes necessary because
     (a)   man is a social animal
     (b)   reciprocity is the law of life
     (c)   trade and commerce are means of progress
     (d)   we cannot produce everything we need ourselves

PASSAGE – 106

I came home from one vacation to find that my brother Ron had brought a dog while I was away. A big burly, choleric dog, he always acted as if he thought I wasn't one of the family. There was a slight advantage in being one of the family. For he didn't bite the family as often as he bit strangers. Mother used to send a box of candy every Christmas to the people he bit. The list finally contained forty or more names. Nobody could understand why we didn't get rid of the dog!

261. Which of the following descriptions fits the dog?
     (a)   The dog was tiny and delicate
     (b)   The dog was sturdy and short-tempered
     (c)   The dog was huge and cool
     (d)   The dog was small and sweet-tempered
262. The dog did not consider the writer as one of the family. What do you think was the consequence of this?
     (a)   The dog barked at him all the time
     (b)   The dog drove him out of his own house
     (c)   The dog behaved with him in an unfriendly way
     (d)   The dog bit him more than he bit others in the family
263. The Christmas list contained more than forty names. What does this suggest?
     (a)   The writer's mother had a lot of friends
     (b)   The writer's family celebrated Christmas well
     (c)   The writer's dog had bitten at least forty people
     (d)   The writer's mother sent them candy boxes

PASSAGE – 107

A little girl was learning a history lesson with her governess. All the morning she had been reading it over and hearing it explained by her governess, but no good came of either the reading or the teaching. The governess went over the lesson several times, explained the meaning, and for the last time, asked her pupil to read it over. After due time had been given, the girl was examined as to her knowledge of the lesson; but not a single answer could she give correctly. The governess lost patience with her, and threatened to punish her unless she could state where a certain treaty was signed.

264. According to the passage, the little girl read the lesson and heard it explained all the morning because
     (a)   the girl did not like her governess
     (b)   the governess could not explain it long enough
     (c)   the girl could not understand it
     (d)   the girl read the lesson only once
265. With reference to the passage, consider the following statements:
     1.   The governess taught the same lesson several times.
     2.   The governess wanted to complete her teaching work quickly.
     Which of the statements given above is/are correct?
     (a)   1 only   (b)   2 only
     (c)   Both 1 and 2   (d)   Neither 1 nor 2
266. After reading the whole passage, which of the following impressions do you think correct about the inability of the girl to answer questions correctly?
     (a)   The dullness of the girl
     (b)   The incompetence of the governess
     (c)   The difficulty of the language
     (d)   The lack of time
267. Which of the following correctly expresses the meaning of 'lost patience with her'?

(a) The inability of the governess to endure further the girl's failure to answer.
(b) The governess lost her enthusiasm to teach the girl
(c) The governess felt that the girl cannot be taught the lesson
(d) The governess felt that she was not good enough to teach the girl

PASSAGE – 108

Many doctors flatly refused to believe Jenner when he announced that he had found a preventive against smallpox. They declared vaccination to be a dangerous practice. But the dread of smallpox was in everybody's heart, and people flocked to Jenner to be vaccinated. The Latin word for cow is 'vacca'; it is the root from which the word vaccination was formed. Some of the 'vacca' used by Jenner were not pure and some harms were done; but when supplies of pure vaccine were available, the practice of vaccinating spread all over England and from England to other countries. We hardly hear of outbreaks of smallpox now.

268. The passage describes
(a) how smallpox may be treated
(b) how vaccines were manufactured in England
(c) the dangers of vaccination especially for children
(d) the gradual acceptance of vaccination as a preventive against smallpox

269. Vaccination sometimes proved harmful because
(a) vaccination was a dangerous practice
(b) some of the vaccines used were of a poor hygienic standard
(c) there are physiological difference between cows and human beings
(d) vaccination is given at a very early age

270. People hastened to get themselves vaccinoid because
(a) many doctors supported Jenner's claims
(b) fear of the terrible disease drove them to take the risk of vaccination
(c) supplies of pure vaccine had now become available
(d) the practice of vaccinating had spread all over the world

271. Vaccination was intended by Jenner to
(a) cure people suffering from smallpox
(b) delay the death of smallpox victims
(c) build up a defence against smallpox germs
(d) prevent cows from spreading the disease

272. With reference to the passage, consider the following statements:
1. Many doctors did not believe that Jenner was a doctor.
2. There are no outbreaks of smallpox nowadays.
Which of the statements given above is/are correct?
(a) 1 only   (b) 2 only
(c) Both 1 and 2   (d) Neither 1 nor 2

PASSAGE – 109

What were the early ideas of men about the sky and the earth? They naturally believed that the earth was motionless, and they also supposed that it was flat. These two ideas do not surprise us. Children now-a-days think the same until they are taught differently. How were men to know that the earth was a ball circling round the sun? They had no telescope for accurate observation. They had not travelled round the world. In fact, many parts of the world in those days were unexplored and unknown. They thought they lived on a kind of flat plate, and that the sky with the sun and the moon and the stars, was a kind of inverted bowl turning round above them. The sun, the moon and the stars were their lamps for day and night.

273. Unless children 'are taught differently they think that
(a) the earth is round and moving.
(b) the sun and the moon are motionless.
(c) the sun and the moon are moving.
(d) the sun and the moon are moving round the earth.

274. The early ideas of man were wrong because
(a) man did not use the telescope.
(b) man did not like to travel.
(c) man never had the scientific knowledge.
(d) man was foolish and lazy.

275. What was true for the early man ?
(a) The earth was round and moving.
(b) The telescope was accurate.
(c) Travelling and, exploring were the methods to gain knowledge.
(d) The sun was motionless.

276. What was the main cause of the early man's wrong ideas ?
(a) Lack of scientific knowledge
(b) Seeing and believing
(c) Lack of desire to know
(d) Lack of desire to observe and explore

PASSAGE – 110

George was a young man who had gone to the big city from a small rural community and, in a relatively short time, attained prominence in the business world. His sudden rise had gone into his head, however, and he became unbearably conceited.
Eventually, George returned home after a visit, halfway expecting everyone in town to be at the railway station to welcome him.
Much to his surprise, George saw that no one, not even his family, was around to meet him when he descended from the train. He looked very neat in a new suit and carried a bulky suitcase full of fashionable clothes.
After a little while, the station master came from his office and went over to the young fellow. "Well, hello there, George," he called out cheerily, "Are you going away "?

277. The station master's question implied that
(a) he offered help to George in climbing the train.
(b) he is known to George very intimately.
(c) he is making fun of George.
(d) George's absence from the town was not noticed by him.

278. George hoped for a big welcome because
(a) of his achievement and success.
(b) he is returning home after a very long time.
(c) people loved him.
(d) his community wanted dynamic leaders like him.

279. George's great expectations are an indication of his
(a) humility.   (b) optimism.
(c) pride.   (d) love of his community.

280. George's success was most clearly visible in
(a) the station master's words.
(b) his clothes.
(c) his being unbearably conceited.
(d) the manner in which he was received by the village.

PASSAGE – 111

The assault on the purity of the environment is the price that we pay for many of the benefits of modern technology. For the advantages of automotive transportation we pay a price in smog-induced diseases; for the powerful effects of new insecticides, we pay a price in dwindling wildlife and disturbances in the relation of living things and their surroundings; for nuclear power, we risk the biological hazards of radiation. By increasing agricultural production with fertilizers, we increase water pollution.

The highly developed nations of the world are not only the immediate beneficiaries of the good that technology can do, they are also the first victims of the environmental diseases that technology breeds. In the past, the environmental effects which accompanied technological progress were restricted to a small place and relatively a short time. The new hazards are neither local nor brief. Modern air pollution covers vast areas of continents. Radioactive fallout from nuclear explosions is worldwide. Radioactive pollutants now on the Earth's surface will be found there for generations, and in the case of Carbon-14, for thousands of years.

281. The passage emphasizes that modern technology
   (a) is totally avoidable.
   (b) has caused serious hazards to life.
   (c) has greater effect on developed countries.
   (d) is the source of the miseries of mankind.

282. The harmful effects of modern technology are
   (a) widespread but short lived.
   (b) widespread and long lasting.
   (c) local and long lasting.
   (d) severe but short lived.

283. With reference to the passage, the following assumptions have been made :
   1. The widespread use of insecticides has caused ecological imbalance.
   2. Conservation of natural flora and fauna is impossible in this age of modern technology.
   Which of the assumptions is/are valid ?
   (a) 1 only   (b) 2 only
   (c) Both 1 and 2   (d) Neither 1 nor 2

PASSAGE – 112

To what extent, though, are modern farming methods sustainable? There is abundant evidence that a high price has to be paid to sustain the high rates of food production achieved by farmed monocultures. For example, they offer ideal conditions for the epidemic spread of diseases such as mastitis, brucellosis and swine fever among livestock and coccidiosis among poultry. Farmed animals are normally kept at densities far higher than their-species would meet in nature with the result that disease transmission rates are magnified. In addition, high rates of transmission between herds occur as animals are sold from one farming enterprise to another; and it is easy for the farmers themselves, with mud on their-boots and their vehicles, to act as vectors of pests and disease.

284. With reference to the passage, consider the following statements :
   1. The modern practices of farming are undesirable for developing countries.
   2. Monoculture practices should be given up to eliminate disease transmission in animals.
   Which of the above statements is/are correct ?
   (a) 1 only   (b) 2 only
   (c) Both 1 and 2   (d) Neither 1 nor 2

285. What is the essence of this passage ?
   (a) Farming is a very costly affair.
   (b) Farmed animals are kept at higher densities in monocultures.
   (c) There is a widespread transmission of animal diseases now-a-days.
   (d) Human dependence of monoculture is fragile.

PASSAGE – 113

For days I trudged from one property-dealer to another, from one "to-let" notice to another, with the estimated advance money tucked safely in the inner lining of my handbag, but in vain. At one place they needed a couple, at another a young man, and at another they wished to know my employment status. And I realized that I was a freak called the single woman and the job status being nothing more than a freelance writer with hardly any assignments in hand, only dreams of making it some day. So the dream-house remained far away, gradually turning into a fantasy.

286. The author "trudged from one property dealer to another" means that the author
   (a) had to walk a lot of distance
   (b) had to do a brisk walk to save the time
   (c) visited several property-dealers without any success
   (d) acquired a good knowledge about the property-dealers of that area

287. According to the passage, the author was
   (a) a novelist
   (b) an independent writer
   (c) a publisher of journals
   (d) an unemployed person

288. Which of the following statements best reflects the underlying tone of the passage ?
   (a) People always let out their houses to well employed persons only
   (b) People always let out their houses only to couples
   (c) Single jobless women find it difficult to rent a house
   (d) Women always dream of a house

PASSAGE – 114

Many poor farmers had been compelled to take up indigo cultivation when the British settlers were given the right to purchase and cultivate land in India. Many whites, therefore, either acquired lanel or advanced loans to poor farmers and pressurised them to for sake the farming food grains and other cash crops for indigo cultivation. Indigo export to Europe was lucrative for the British settlers who held a monopoly of this business. Within a few years, most of the textile lands had undergone forcible indigo cultivation, resulting in a famine situation in Bengal. When the farmers declined to cultivate indigo, they were tortured, jailed and even killed.

289. The poor farmers in Bengal took up indigo cultivation because
   (a) the government encouraged them to do so
   (b) it was a money earning crop
   (c) they were forced to do so
   (d) this was the only crop that would grow in that region

290. British settlers bought land in Bengal in order to
   (a) introduce cultivation of cash crops in India
   (b) cultivatie indigo
   (c) settle down in India
   (d) promote export business in Bengal

291. Indigo export was profitable for the British settlers because
   (a) they had no competitors
   (b) the crop yield was good
   (c) they could oppress the farmers
   (d) the labour was cheap

PASSAGE – 115

Nationalism is only a curse when it becomes narrow and fanatical Like so many other things available to man, say, religion, it can easily lead men astray. Nationalism can lead people into thinking only of themselves, of their own struggles of their own misery. It can also cause a nation to become suspicious and fearful of its neighbours to look upon itself as superior, and to become aggressive and it is when nationalism impels a state to become expansionist and seek domination over others that it becomes a positive curse and harmful internationally.

292. From the passage, which of the following statements most correctly reflects the opinion of the author ?
(a) Nationalism makes people self centered and self-concelted
(b) It helps a nation to become superior to other nations
(c) It regulates international relationships
(d) It helps a nation to expand its territories and become powerful

293. Which of the following phrases most correctly suggests the central theme of the passage ?
(a) Nationalism and religion
(b) Nationalism as an inspiration for development
(c) Nationalism as a cause of war
(d) Evils of narrow and aggressive nationalism

294. From the passage which of the following statements can be assumed to be most likely to be true ?
(a) The author believes that nationalism is always a curse
(b) He believes that it is possible for men to misuse religion
(c) He thinks that religion always leads man astray
(d) He pleads for a mix-up of religion and nationalism

PASSAGE-116

Brown and his men, huddling round a fire, ate the last of the food that Kassim had brought them that day, Cornelius sat among them, half-asleep. Then one of the crew remembered that some tobacco had been left in the boat, and said he would go and fetch it. He didn't think there was any danger in going to the creek in the dark. He disappeared down the hillside, and a moment later he was heard climbing into the boat and then climbing out again.

295. Consider the following statements :
1. Brown and Cornelius sat round the fire.
2. Comelius lay half-asleep at a little distance from the fire.
3. All the people sat round the fire.
Which of the statements given above is/are correct ?
(a) 1 and 2   (b) 2 only
(c) 3 only   (d) 1 and 3

296. One of them disappeared down the hill implies that
(a) the slope of the hill was slippery
(b) he fell from the edge of the hill
(c) there was suddenly a sea beside the hill
(d) he walked down the hill

297. "He didn't think...in the dark". This sentence actually implies that he
(a) was bold and adventurous
(b) was addicted to smoking
(c) would face some trouble
(d) was the only person who knew where in the boat tobacco was

298. What does the word "huddling" imply ?
(a) Moving around   (b) Falling into a slumber
(c) Being close together   (d) Merrymaking

PASSAGE-117

As soon as I saw the elephant I knew with perfect certainty that I ought not to shoot him. It is a serious matter to shoot a working elephant – it is comparable to destroying a huge and costly piece of machinery – and obviously one ought not to do it if it can possibly be avoided. And at that distance, peacefully eating, the elephant looked no more dangerous than a cow.

299. The writer was against shooting the elephant because
(a) he suspected it to be a wild one and was afraid of it
(b) his heart was full of compassion for animals
(c) he was certain that the elephant was innocent
(d) it would amount to avoidable waste of useful property

300. The author compares the elephant to a costly machine because
(a) Ivory is very expensive
(b) it can do as much work as an expensive machine
(c) elephants look like big machines
(d) elephants and machines have similar prices

301. The elephant looked no more dangerous than a cow because
(a) it was quietly doing its work
(b) unlike lions, it is a vegetarian animal
(c) its tusks resemble the cow's horns
(d) cows can be very dangerous sometimes

PASSAGE-118

I was very fond of the old soldier in little town. He had only one leg, having lost the other somewhere in Assam in 1942. He used to tell me about his adventures. He told me that he had run away from home to join the army. He had experienced his first battle in the Libyan desert. Out of his dozens of war stories, the one I liked best was the one of his escape from a Japanese prison-of-war camp in Burma. He told me again and again how he walked two hundred miles in two weeks. On the way he was bitten on the toe by a poisonous snake and he had to cut off part of the toe in order to survive. But by the time he got to an Indian camp the wound had turned septic and the leg had to be amputated. He is, however, quite contented with his lot.

302. The author was very fond of the old soldier because
(a) He had lost one of his legs in war
(b) he used to tell the author about his adventures
(c) he was contented with his lot
(d) he had been to many countries

303. Why did the old soldier repeatedly tell that he walked two hundred miles ?
(a) He ran away from home to join the army
(b) He had to cross the Libyan desert
(c) He had to escape from a prison-of-war camp
(d) He was a strong soldier

304. The story of the old soldier that the author liked most was that about

(a)   his running away from home to join the army
(b)   his first battle in the Libyan desert
(c)   the loss of his leg in Assam
(d)   his escape from a Japanese prison-of-war camp

305. The old soldier, according to the author, was
(a)   unhappy about his life
(b)   satisfied with his lot
(c)   angry about his fate
(d)   disgusted with his misfortune

306. The soldier's leg had to be amputated because
(a)   he had walked two hundred miles in two weeks
(b)   he was wounded in war
(c)   the wounded toe turned septic
(d)   he was shot in the leg while escaping from the Japanese camp

PASSAGE – 119

On a surface which is free from obstacles, such as a clear road or a path, only two or three species of snakes can hope to catch up with a human being, even if they are foolish to try. A snake seems to move very fast but its movements are deceptive. Inspite of the swift, wave-like motions of its body, the snake crawls along the ground at no more than the speed of man's walk. It may, however, have an advantage inside a jungle, where the progress of a man is obstructed by thorny bushes. But in such places, the footsteps of a man are usually more than enough to warn snakes to keep away; Although they have no cars of the usual kind, they can feel slight vibrations of the ground through their bodies, and thus get an early warning of danger.

307. The snake has an advantage over men inside a jungle, because there:
(a)   it can crawl faster.
(b)   it gets advance warning.
(c)   man's movement is obstructed.
(d)   it is dark inside a jungle.

308. What helps the snakes to receive advance warning is their sensitivity to:
(a)   obstacles in the path.
(b)   smell of other beings.
(c)   sounds made by other beings.
(d)   movements of other beings.

PASSAGE-120

This rule of always trying to do things as well as one can do them has an important bearing upon the problem of ambition. No man or woman should be without ambition, which is the inspiration of activity. But if one allows ambition to drive one to attempt things which are beyond one's own personal capacity, then unhappiness will result. If one imagines that one can do everything better than other people, then envy and jealousy, those twin monsters, will come to sadden one's days. But if one concentrates one's attention upon developing one's own special capacities, the things one is best at, then one does not worry over much if other people are more successful.

309. Which one of the following alternatives brings out the meaning of 'to have a bearing upon' clearly?
(a)   to have an effect on
(b)   to carry the weight on oneself
(c)   to put up with
(d)   to decrease friction

310. Which one of 'the following statements is correct?
(a)   There is a close relationship between ambition and activity.
(b)   Ambition and activity belong to two different areas.
(c)   Ambition is useless.
(d)   Activity is responsible for ambition.

311. The statement 'if one allows ambition to drive one to attempt things which are beyond one's own personal capacity, then unhappiness will result, means that:
(a)   One must always try to do less than than one's capacity.
(b)   One must always try to do more than one's capacity.
(c)   Ambition must be consistent with one's capacity.
(d)   There should be no ambition at all.

312. Which one of the following statements best reflects the underlying tone of the passage ?
(a)   One must do everything as well as one can.
(b)   One must try to be better than others.
(c)   One must continuously worry about others.
(d)   One must try beyond one's capacity to get results.

313. Which one of the following statements can be assumed to be true ?
(a)   It is good to imagine oneself better than others.
(b)   One should not imagine oneself always to be better than others.
(c)   All persons have equal capacity.
(d)   One should have more ambition than others.

PASSAGE-121

An earthquake comes like a thief in the night, without warning. It was necessary, therefore, to invent instruments that neither slumbered nor slept. Some devices were quite simple. One, for instance, consisted of rods of various lengths and thicknesses which would stand up on end like ninepins. When a shock came it shook the rigid table upon which these stood. If it were gentle, only the more unstable rods fell. If it were severe, they all fell. Thus the rods by falling and by the direction in which they fell, recorded for the slumbering scientist, the strength of a shock that was too weak to waken him and the direction from which it came. But, instruments far more delicate than that were needed if any really serious advance was to be made. The ideal to be aimed at was to devise an instrument that could record with a pen on paper the movements, of the ground or of the table, as the quake passed by. While I write my pen moves but the paper keeps still. With practice, no doubt, I could, in time, learn to write by holding the pen still while the paper moved. That sounds a silly suggestion, but that was precisely the idea adopted in some of the early instruments (seismometers) for recording earthquake waves. But when table, penholder and paper are all moving how is it possible to write legibly? The key to a solution of that problem lay in an everyday observation. Why does a person standing in a bus or train tend to fall when a sudden start is made? It is because his feet move on, but his head stays still.

314. The passage says that early instruments for measuring earthquakes were:
(a)   faulty in design
(b)   expensive
(c)   not sturdy
(d)   not sensitive enough

315. Why was it necessary to invent instruments to observe an eqarthquake ?
(a)   Because an earthquake comes like a thief in the night.
(b)   To make people alert about earthquakes during their conscious as well as unconscious hours.

(c)   To prove that we are technically advanced.
(d)   To experiment with the control of man over nature.
316. A simple device which consisted of rods that stood up on end like ninepins was replaced by a more sophisticated one because it failed :
(a)   to measure a gentle earthquake.
(b)   to measure a severe earthquake.
(c)   to record the direction of the earthquake.
(d)   to record the facts with a pen on paper.
317. The everyday observation referred to in the passage relates to:
(a)   a moving bus or train.
(b)   the sudden start of a bus.
(c)   the tendency of a standing person to fall when a bus or train moves suddenly.
(d)   people standing in a bus or train.
318. The early seismometers adopted the idea that in order to record the earthquake, it is :
(a)   the pen that should move just as it moves when we write on paper.
(b)   the pen that should stay still and the paper should move.
(c)   both pen and paper that should move.
(d)   neither pen nor paper that should move.

PASSAGE-122

How can you improve your reading speed? By taking off the brakes. You wouldn't think of driving a car with the brake on. Yet as a reader you probably have several brakes slowing you down. One very common brake is regressing—looking back every now and then at something already read. It is like stepping backwards every few metres as you walk-hardly the way to move ahead quickly. Regression may arise from a lack of confidence, vocabulary deficiency, or actually missing a word or phrase. It makes a long sentence seem even more complex as the eyes frequently regress. Eye movement photographs of 12,000 readers in America showed that university students regress an average of 15 times in reading only 100 words. The average student of class four was found to look back 20 times. In short, regression consumes one-sixth of your precious reading time. Release this brake and enjoy a spurt in reading speed.
319. In the context of the passage, what does 'regression' mean ?
(a)   Lack of desire to improve the reading speed
(b)   Looking back at what is already read
(c)   Lack of proper understanding of what one reads
(d)   Comparing the reading speed of school and university students
320. In order to be a good reader you should
(a)   regress whenever necessary
(b)   be like a careful driver
(c)   not look back frequently while reading
(d)   test your vocabulary frequently
321. According to the author reading with regression is like
(a)   driving with poor quality brakes
(b)   stepping backwards while walking
(c)   using several brakes in order to slow down
(d)   making sudden spurts in reading speed

PASSAGE-123

Even in the most primitive societies the great majority of people satisfy a large part of their material needs by exchanging goods and services. Very few people indeed can make for themselves everything they need – all their food, their clothes, their housing,

their tools. Ever since men started living in communities,'they have been satisfying their needs by means of specialization and exchange; increasingly each individual has concentrated on what he can do best, and has produced more of the special goods or services in which he has concentrated, than he can consume himself. The surplus he has exchanged with other members of the community, acquiring, in exchange the things he needs that others have produced.
322. Very few people can satisfy their needs today by
(a)   providing things for themselves
(b)   exchanging goods and services
(c)   concentrating on what they can do best
(d)   individual specialization
323. Exchange of goods becomes possible only when
(a)   there is no specialization
(b)   goods are produced in surplus
(c)   primitive societies become modern
(d)   individuals make things for themselves
324. Specialization and exchange began when men started
(a)   big industries
(b)   concentrating on their work
(c)   producing things for individual use
(d)   living in communities
325. Exchange of goods and services becomes necessary because
(a)   man is a social being
(b)   reciprocity is the law of life
(c)   trade and commerce are means of progress
(d)   we cannot produce everything we need ourselves.

PASSAGE-124

Soil scientists have shown that the soil teems with millions of living things, many of them useful, others harmful. The living things which are useful include earthworms and various kinds of bacteria. Earthworms loosen the soil and so enable air and water to enter it. Bacteria, which are microscopic living things break down dead plants and animals and make humus, or take nitrogen from the air and change it into substances that plants use. The living things that do harm include other bacteria and fungi which cause diseases. Other harmful things are pests such as wire worms which feed on the roots of grass and other plants. While the farmer can usually keep weeds in check by careful cultivation, this alone may not protect his crops from insects, pests and diseases. Nowadays, however, he is much better able to control these enemies. He may plant specially resistant types of seeds or he may keep the pests and diseases-in check with chemicals. With better seeds farmers have been able to increase their crop yields. They can grow crops that ripen more quickly and have a stronger resistance to disease, frost or drought.
326. Scientists who study soil believe that
(a)   all insects and bacteria are harmful
(b)   only microscopic living things are useful
(c)   only earthworms are useful
(d)   not all worms and bacteria are harmful
327. The living things that do harm
(a)   break down plants and animals
(b)   use up the nitrogen from the air
(c)   cause disease in the plants
(d)   loosen up the soil from air and water
328. Farmers are always careful
(a)   to control insects and fungi that attack plants
(b)   to encourage pests in the soil

    (c)   to eliminate all bacteria from the soil
    (d)   to foster all kinds of worms in the earth

329. Nowadays it is possible to reduce the loss caused by pests and harmful bacteria
    (a)   with the use of chemical fertilisers
    (b)   throught the development of resistant seeds
    (c)   by using weeds as killers
    (d)   by controlling earthworms

330. The farmers today can also select seeds
    (a)   of slow ripening variety
    (b)   resistant to frost and drought
    (c)   for economy in costs
    (d)   of lower resistance to disease

PASSAGE - 125

The tigress was a mile away and the ground between her and us was densely wooded. scattered over with great rocks and cut up by a number of deep ravines, but she could cover the distance well within the half - hour — if she wanted to. The question I had to decide was, whether or not I should try to call her. If I called and she heard me, and came while it was still daylight and gave me a chance to shoot her, all would be well; on the other hand, if she came and did not give me a shot, some of us would not reach camp, for we had nearly two miles to go and the path the whole way ran through heavy jungle.

331. According to the author
    (a)   the tigress wanted to cover the distance within the half-hour
    (b)   the tigress did not wish to cover the distance within the-half-hour
    (c)   the tigress actually covered the distance within the half-hour
    (d)   there was a possibility of the tigress covering the distance within the half - hour

332. The author says, "Some of us would not reach camp" because
    (a)   it was two miles away
    (b)   the tigress would kill some of them
    (c)   the path is not suitable for walking
    (d)   the ground was scattered over with great rocks

333. The author found it difficult to decide the question because.
    (a)   he was afraid
    (b)   the tigress was only a mile away
    (c)   the ground between them was densely wooded
    (d)   there was uncertainty about the reaction of the tigress to his call

334. The time available to the author for shooting the tigress was
    (a)   the whole day
    (b)   one night
    (c)   a few hours
    (d)   thirty minutes

335. When the author says 'all would be well', he means
    (a)   that they would be able to hide themselves in the heavy jungle
    (b)   that the tigress would run away to the deep ravines
    (c)   that they would be able to shoot her down without difficulty
    (d)   that they would be able to return in daylight

PASSAGE - 126

After lunch, I felt at a loose end and roamed about the little flat. It suited us well enough when mother was with me, but now I was by myself it was too large and I'd moved the dining room table into my bedroom. That was now the only room I used ; it had all the furniture I needed; a brass bedstead, a dressing table, some cane chairs whose seats had more or less caved in, a wardrobe with a tarnished mirror. The rest of the flat was never used, so I didn't trouble to look after it.

336. The flat did not really suit him any more because
    (a)   the rooms were too small
    (b)   he was living on his own now
    (c)   his mother needed too much rooms
    (d)   the flat itself was too little

337. He did not look after the rest of the flat because
    (a)   he did not use it
    (b)   the bedroom was much too large
    (c)   he needed only the brass bedstead
    (d)   he had too much furniture

338. ".....now I was by myself it was too large".
The word *it* here refers to
    (a)   the dining room table
    (b)   the dining room
    (c)   the bedroom
    (d)   the flat

339. From the passage we learn that the writer was
    (a)   scared of living alone in the flat
    (b)   dissatisfied with the flat
    (c)   satisfied with the space in his bedroom
    (d)   an eccentric person

340. "After lunch I felt at a loose end" means
    (a)   he had nothing specific to do
    (b)   had a rope with a loose end
    (c)   had much work to do
    (d)   had a feeling of anxiety

PASSAGE- 127

The overwhelming vote given by the greater part of the public has so far been in favour of films which pass the time easily and satisfy that part of our imagination which depends on the more obvious kind of daydreams. We make up for what we secretly regard as our deficiencies by watching the stimulating adventures of the other people who are stronger, more effective, or more beautiful than we are. The conventional stars act out our daydreams for us in a constant succession of exciting situations set in the open spaces, in the jungles or in the underworld of great cities which abounds in crime and violence. We would not dare to be in such situations but the situations are very exciting to watch since our youth is being spent in day-to-day routine of school, office or home.

341. According to the passage, most of us prefer films which
    (a)   overwhelm our imagination
    (b)   depict our times
    (c)   fulfil our secret wishes
    (d)   appeal to our reason

342. By watching thrilling adventures in films we make up for
    (a)   the effectiveness of our desires
    (b)   the shortcomings in our life
    (c)   the stimulation of our everyday life
    (d)   the influence which we don't have

343. Film stars present situations
    (a)   which are familiar to us, the city dwellers
    (b)   which we have seen only in jungles
    (c)   which we meet everyday at work
    (d)   which excite us

344. Whether we admit it to ourselves or not, we are aware that
    (a)   we are weak and plain
    (b)   we are both powerful and handsome

    (c)   we are as strong as film heroes
    (d)   we are more beautiful than film stars

345. The daily life of students, office-goers and housewives is
    (a)   full of new adventures
    (b)   the same dull repetition
    (c)   stimulating to their imagination
    (d)   very exciting to them

PASSAGE- 128

It is possible to give wedding presents, birthday and Christmas presents, without any thought of affection at all, they can be ordered by postcard; but the unbirthday present demands the nicest care. It is therefore the best of all, and it is the only kind to which the golden rule of present-giving imperatively applies - the golden rule which insists that you must never give to another person anything that you would not rather keep: nothing that does not cost you a pang to part from. It would be better if this rule governed the choice also of those other three varieties of gifts, but they can be less exacting.

346. The author says that wedding, birthday and Christmas Presents
    (a)   are always indicators of the giver's affection.
    (b)   may not always be given with any thought of affection.
    (c)   are given only to flatter the recipient
    (d)   are given only to fulfil an obligation

347. 'They can be ordered by postcard' means that
    (a)   the present may only be a postcard
    (b)   the present would be an expensive one
    (c)   the choice does not involve much care
    (d)   the present would not be worth giving

348. The 'unbirthday' present is the best of all because
    (a)   it cannot be ordered by postcard
    (b)   it means giving expensive presents
    (c)   its choice needs the utmost care
    (d)   other occasions are better than birthdays for giving presents

349. A 'golden rule' is a rule which
    (a)   brings profit   (b)   is very important
    (c)   is very difficult   (d)   is very easy

350. The writer is of the view that one should give a present that
    (a)   one would like to possess oneself
    (b)   one would like to get rid of
    (c)   cannot be ordered by mail
    (d)   is highly expensive and attractive

PASSAGE-129

People project their mental processes into their handwriting. They subconsciously shape and organise their letters, words and lines in ways that directly reflect their personalities. This explains why no two handwritings are - or even can be - alike; the medium is just too personal. Everyday observation confirms the link between handwriting and personality, at least in an elementary way. Precise people construct their words with care, slowly and exactly; dynamic people dash them off. Flamboyant people boldly cover half a page with a few words and a signature, whose size fittingly reflects their expansive sense of self. Most of us have made such observations. But it takes a practiced eye to discern the scores of variations and interpret the subtle interplay of forces at work in any given handwriting. In fact in Europe, handwriting analysis known as graphology, now enjoys scientific acceptance and common use.

351. If you are a showy and colourful person, your-handwriting is likely to be
    (a)   neat and slow   (b)   dashing and careless
    (c)   bold and large   (d)   legible but small

352. Graphology is
    (a)   the study of graphs
    (b)   the analysis of handwriting
    (c)   a special branch of phonetics
    (d)   a graphical description of handwriting

353. Handwriting analysis is
    (a)   not useful to us
    (b)   an elementary study
    (c)   an imprecise science
    (d)   a means of studying personality

354. According to the author, people are:
    (a)   not conscious of what they write
    (b)   aggressive in the nature of their writing
    (c)   not conscious of the way they write
    (d)   not used to personal writing

355. The fact that handwriting is related to personality
    (a)   has been noticed by most people
    (b)   is appreciated by dynamic people
    (c)   is restricted to persons who write carefully
    (d)   is known only to graphologists

PASSAGE-130

The simplest method of welding two pieces of metal together is known as pressure welding. The ends of metal are heated to a white heat - for iron, the welding temperature should be about 1300°C - in a flame. At this temperature the metal becomes plastic. The ends are then pressed or hammered together, and the joint is smoothed off. Care must be taken to ensure that the surfaces are thoroughly clean first, for dirt will weaken the weld. Moreover, the heating of iron or steel to a high temperature cause oxidation, and a film of oxide is formed on the heated surfaces. For this reason, a flux is applied to the heated metal. At welding heat, the flux melts, and the oxide particles are dissolved in it together with any other impurities which may be present. The metal surfaces are pressed together, and the flux is squeezed out from the centre of the weld. A number of different types of weld may be used, but for fairly thick bars of metals, a vee-shaped weld should normally be employed. It is rather stronger than the ordinary butt weld.

356. The simplest way of welding two pieces of Metal together is
    (a)   heating the metal
    (b)   holding it in a flame
    (c)   coating the metal with plastic
    (d)   hammering heated pieces

357. Unless the surfaces are cleaned first
    (a)   the metal will not take white heat
    (b)   the resulting weld will be weak
    (c)   the joint will be rough
    (d)   the metal will be less plastic

358. When iron is heated to about 1300 degree centigrade
    (a)   flames turn from white to blue
    (b)   chemical reaction starts
    (c)   oxide film is found on its surfaces
    (d)   it turns into steel

359. The flux is used to
    (a)   make the metal plastic
    (b)   cool the heated metal

    (c)   cover up any dirt
    (d)   dissolve oxide and other impurities
360. For fairly thick bars of metals
    (a)   a vee shaped weld should be used
    (b)   ordinary butt weld should be used
    (c)   a number of different types of weld may be used
    (d)   a pressure weld may be used.

PASSAGE-131

To avoid the various foolish opinions to which mankind is prone, no superhuman brain is required. A few simple rules will keep you. not from all errors, but from silly errors.

If the matter is one that can be settled by observation, make the observation yourself. Aristotle could have avoided the mistake of thinking that women have fewer teeth than men. by the simple device of asking Mrs. Aristotle to keep her mouth open while he counted. Thinking that you know, when in fact you do not, is a bad mistake to which we are all prone. I believe myself that hedgehogs eat black beetles, because I have been told that they do, but if I were writing a book on the habits of hedgehogs, I should not commit myself until I had seen one enjoying this diet. Aristotle, however, was less cautious. Ancient and medieval writers knew all about unicorns and salamanders: not one of them thought it necessary to avoid dogmatic statements about them because he had never seen one of them .

361. The writer believes that
    (a)   most people could avoid making foolish mistakes if they were clever
    (b)   through observation we could avoid making many mistakes
    (c)   Aristotle made many mistakes because he was not observant
    (d)   All errors are caused by our own error in thinking
362. With reference to the passage, which one of the following is the correct statement ?
    (a)   Aristotle was able to avoid the mistake of thinking that women have fewer teeth than men
    (b)   Aristotle thought women have fewer teeth than men
    (c)   Aristotle proved that women have fewer teeth bv counting his wife's teeth
    (d)   Aristotle may have thought that women have fewer teeth because he never had a wife
363. The writer says that if he was writing a book on hedgehogs
    (a)   he would maintain that they eat black beetles because he had been told so
    (b)   he would first observe their eating habits
    (c)   he would think it unnecessary to verify that they are black beetles
    (d)   he would make the statement that they ate black beetles and later verify it
364. The writer is of the opinion that
    (a)   unicorns and salamanders were observed by ancient and medieval writers but were unknown to modern writers.
    (b)   ancient and medieval writers wrote authoritatively about unicorns and salamanders though they had never seen them
    (c)   unicorns and salamanders do not exist
    (d)   only those who had observed the habits of unicorns and salamanders wrote about them

365. A 'dogmatic statement' in the context means a statement which is
    (a)   convincing   (b)   proved
    (c)   unquestionable   (d)   doubtful

PASSAGE-132

Since I had nothing better to do. I decided to go to the market to buy a few handkerchiefs, the old ones had done vanishing trick. On the way I met an old friend of mine and I took him to a nearby restaurant for tea and snacks. Afterwards I went to the shop and selected a dozen handkerchiefs. I pulled out my purse to make the payment, and discovered that it was empty: I then realized that it was not my purse, it was a different purse altogether. How that happened is still a source of wonder to me and I refuse to believe that it was the work of my good old friend, for it was his purse that I held in my hand.

366. The man could not buy the handkerchiefs because
    (a)   he did not like the handkerchiefs
    (b)   his friend did not allow him to buy them
    (c)   the shop did not have any handkerchiefs
    (d)   he had no money in the purse
367. When he tried to take out the purse, he discovered that
    (a)   it was not there
    (b)   it was lost
    (c)   it was a new purse
    (d)   it was his friend's purse

PASSAGE-133

It is not luck but labour that makes men. Luck, says an American writer, is ever waiting for something to turn up; labour with keen eyes and strong will always turns up something, Luck lies in bed and wishes the postman would bring him news of a legacy: labour turns out at six and with busy pen and ringing hammer lays the foundation of competence. Luck whines, labour watches. Luck relies on chance; labour on character. Luck slips downwards to self-indulgence; labour strides upwards and aspires to independence. The conviction, therefore, is extending that diligence is the mother of good luck; in other words, that a man's success in life will be proportionate to his efforts, to his industry, to his attention to small things.

368. Which one of the following statements sums up the meaning of the passage ?
    (a)   Luck waits without exertion but labour exerts without waiting
    (b)   Luck waits and complains without working while labour achieves success although it complains
    (c)   Luck often ends in defeat but labour produces luck
    (d)   Luck is self-indulgent but labour is selfless
369. Which one of the following statements is true about the passage ?
    (a)   Luck is necessary for success
    (b)   Success depends on hard work and attention to details
    (c)   Expectation of good luck always meets with disappointment
    (d)   Success is exactly proportionate to hard work only
370. Labour turns out at six and with busy pen and ringing hammer lays the foundation fo competence. This statement means
    (a)   hard work of all kinds makes people efficient and skilled
    (b)   the labour lays the foundation of the building

    (c)   the writer and the labourer are the true eyes of the society

    (d)   there is no worker who works so hard as the labourer who begins his day at six in the morning

PASSAGE-134

The avowed purpose of the exact sciences is to establish complete intellectual control over experience in terms of precise rules which can be formally set out and empirically tested. Could that ideal be fully achieved, all truth and all error could henceforth be ascribed to an exact theory of the universe, while we who accept this theory would be relieved of any occasion for exercising our personal judgement. We should only have to follow the rules faithfully. Classical mechanics approaches this ideal so closely that it is often thought to have achieved it. But this leaves out of account the element of personal judgement involved in applying the formulae of mechanics to the facts of experience.

371. The purpose of the exact sciences is to
    (a)   form opinions about our experience
    (b)   formulate principles which will help us to exercise our personal judgement
    (c)   assert our intellectual superiority
    (d)   make formal and testable rules which can help verify experience

372. An exact theory of the universe is
    (a)   not desirable   (b)   improbable
    (c)   possible   (d)   yet to be made

373. In exact sciences
    (a)   personal judgements are set aside in favour of a mechanical theory
    (b)   one does not find answers to all questions and problems
    (c)   one reposes faith i n actual experience
    (d)   one interprets the universe according to one's wish

374. Classical mechanics
    (a)   has formulated precise rules based on experience
    (b)   has gained intellectual control over the world
    (c)   has formulated an exact theory of the universe
    (d)   just falls short of achieving intellectual control over experience

PASSAGE-135

One of the most important things to notice about the power of art is the way in which great works continue to exert their influence through the ages. Scientific discoveries which are of major importance at the time when they are made are superseded. Thus, Newton's theory of gravitation has been superseded by Einstein's theory of relativity. Hence the work of great scientists has value in stages on the way to a goal which supersedes them. Broadly speaking, the achievements of generals, politicians, and statesment have an importance only in their own time. Hence these people and their acts, great as they may have been are like milestones which mankind passes on its way to something else. But with works of art it is not so. The place which they occupy in the estimation of succeeding ages and the power which they exercise over men's spirits are as great as they were in the age which produced them; indeed, their power tends to increase with time, as they came to be better understood.

375. The power of art can be judged through
    (a)   its influence of a few individuals.
    (b)   its influence on the people over the years.

    (c)   the greatness of great artists.
    (d)   the opinions of great thinkers.

376. The statement 'Newton's theory of gravitation has been superseded by Einstein's theory of relativity" suggests that
    (a)   the theory of relativity has nothing to do with the theory of gravitation.
    (b)   the theory of relativity is new in comparison to the theory of gravitation.
    (c)   the theory of relativity is an improvement over the theory of gravitation.
    (d)   the theory of relativity has suppressed the theory of gravitation.

377. The achievements of generals, politicians and statement have been compared to milestones by the author because
    (a)   they are inscribed on the milestones.
    (b)   they have contemporary relevance.
    (c)   they have topical and historical interest.
    (d)   they are strong and lasting stones.

378. How is a work of art different from the work of a scientist?
    (a)   A work of art is as permanent as the work of a scientist.
    (b)   The influence of a work of art increases from age to age unlike the work of a scientist which diminishes in course of time.
    (c)   A work of art has no material value like the work of a scientist.
    (d)   A work of art is an expression of creative power while the work of a scientist is not.

PASSAGE - 136

Most disputes about whether or not men are stronger than women are meaningless because the word 'strong' may mean many things. Most men can surpass most women in lifting heavy weights, in striking an object, in running, jumping or doing heavy physical labour. But most women live longer than most men, they have a better chance of resisting disease, they can beat men at operations requiring finger dexterity and the ability to work accurately under monotonous conditions. So it would be legitimate to argue that women are stronger than men. The truth is that each gender can surpass the other in certain kinds of activities. To say that one is stronger than the other is to indulge in futile arguments.

379. Which one of the following statements best reflects the main contention of the author?
    (a)   In most cases men are stronger than women.
    (b)   Since women are healthier than men they are also stronger.
    (c)   In some activities men are stronger than women and in some others women are stronger than men.
    (d)   Men and women are equally strong.

380. The author says that any dispute about whether or not men are stronger than women is meaningless, because
    (a)   it is an already established fact that men are Stronger than women.
    (b)   the word 'stronger' can be interpreted in various ways.
    (c)   it is difficult to assess the comparative strength and women.
    (d)   it is a dispute that might harm the man-woman relationship in our society.

381. The author says it would be legitimate to argue that women are stronger than men, because
    (a)   the author believes in the superior strength of women.
    (b)   the author is not committed to any opinion.
    (c)   in some of the activities woman do give an impression that they are stronger than men.
    (d)   in fact women are inferior to men in every respect.

382. From the passage, which of the following statements is most likely to be correct?
- (a) Women live longer than men because they can resist diseases better than men.
- (b) Monotenous living conditions make women stronger than men.
- (c) All women are incapable of running, jumping and doing physical labour because they are not strong.
- (d) Statistically speaking, most women live longer than most men.

PASSAGE - 137

In national no less than in individual life there are no watertight compartments. No sharp lines can be drawn to mark off" the political from the moral, the social from the economic regions of life. Politicians often talk as though one has only to introduce certain political and economic changes for paradise to descend on earth, forgetful of the fact that the efficiency of an institution depends on the way it is worked, which itself is determined by the character and wisdom of the men who work it.

383. Which one of the following statements most clearly suggests the central theme of the passage?
- (a) Political and economic changes can solve all the problems facing the nation.
- (b) There is no difference between the political, moral, social and economic regions of life.
- (c) It is not the institutions that are important but the character and wisdom of the people who manage them.
- (d) National progress depends solely on the efficient running of our institutions.

384. Which one of the following phrases best helps to bring out the precise contextual meaning of 'watertight compartments"?
- (a) Activities of life unaffected by public opinion.
- (b) Spheres of life where no liberty of opinion is tolerated
- (c) Ways of life peculiar to each nation and each section of society.
- (d) Spheres of life which are independent and unconnected with one another.

385. Which one of the following statements most correctly reflects the attitude of the author towards politicians' opinions?
- (a) The author totally disbelieves what the politicians say.
- (b) The author believes what the politicians say.
- (c) The author is sceptical about the claims of the politicians.
- (d) The author thinks that the opinions of the politicians are contradictory.

386. Which one of the following statements most correctly indicates the implication of the phrase 'paradise to descend on earth'?
- (a) A world of perfect economic, political and social well-being.
- (b) A world ruled by religious persons.
- (c) A world of total liberty and equality.
- (d) A world in which nobody needs to labour.

PASSAGE - 138

Just as some men like to play football or cricket, so some men like to climb mountains. This is often very difficult to do, for mountains are not just big hills. Paths are usually very steep. Some mountainsides are straight up and down, so that it may take many hours to climb as little as one hundred feet. There is always the danger that you may fall off and be killed or injured. Men talk about conquering a mountain. It is a wonderful feeling to reach the top of a mountain after climbing for hours and may be even for days. You look down and see the whole country below you. You feel Godlike. Two Italian prisoners of war escaped from a prison camp in Kenya during the war. They did not try to get back to their own country, for they knew that was impossible. Instead they climbed to the top of Mount Kenya, and then they came down again and gave themselves up. They had wanted to get that feeling of freedom that one has, after climbing a difficult mountain.

387. Some men like to climb mountains because
- (a) they do not like to play football or cricket.
- (b) they know the trick of climbing.
- (c) they want to have a wonderful feeling.
- (d) they like to face danger.

388. To climb a mountain is often difficult because
- (a) mountains are big hills.
- (b) it consumes more time.
- (c) prisoners often escape from camps and settle there.
- (d) paths are steep and uneven.

389. It is a wonderful feeling .... 'It' refers to
- (a) the steep path
- (b) the prisoner
- (c) the mountain
- (d) mountaineering

390. Two Italian prisoners escaped the camp and climbed to the top of Mount Kenya to
- (a) escape to Italy.
- (b) come down and give up.
- (c) gain fame as mountaineers.
- (d) get the feeling of freedom.

PASSAGE - 139

Most of the people who appear most often and most gloriously in the history books are great conquerors and generals and soldiers, whereas the people who really helped civilization forward are often never mentioned at all we do not know who first set a broken leg, or launched a seaworthy boat, or calculated the length of the year, or manoeuvred a field; but we know all about the killers and destroyers People think a great deal of them, so much so that on all the highest pillars in the great cities of the world you will find the figure of a conqueror or a general or a soldier. And I think most people believed that the greatest countries are those that have beaten in battle the greatest number of other countries and ruled over them as conquerors.

391. People who are glorified often in history books are those
- (a) who contributed to the public health.
- (b) who contributed to the technical knowledge of man.
- (c) who made calendars.
- (d) who fought and won wars.

392. The words "the people who really helped civilization forward" suggest that conquerors, generals and soldiers
- (a) contributed a great deal to civilization.
- (b) contributed only towards civilization.
- (c) were least interested in the progress of civilization.
- (d) contributed little to civilization.

393. We will find the figure of a conqueror or a general or a soldier on all the highest pillars in great cities because

(a)   they sacrificed their lives for the benefit of humanity.

(b)   people have exaggerated notions about their achievements.

(c)   they had a deep concern for the welfare of humanity.

(d)   they built most cities.

394. The passage implies that the greatest countries are those that

(a)   have conquered many countries and ruled over them.

(b)   are very large in their size.

(c)   have the largest population.

(d)   are civilized

PASSAGE – 140

Urbanization and industrialization have often resulted in whole areas of forests being cleared to gain new land and to obtain timber for the various building projects. Large areas of fields and forests have disappeared to make way for concrete jungles many of which are fitted with huge plants and chimney stacks. Industrial growth has necessitated the increased demand for fuel oil to run the machines and in doing so produces industrial gases and fumes which belch through the chimney and pollute the atmosphere. The most evident elements in the contamination of the atmosphere are dust, sulphur dioxide, carbon monoxide and nitrous oxide.

395. The writer expresses the belief that

(a)   there is plenty of scope for further industrialization.

(b)   unplanned growth of industry has done more harm than good.

(c)   the change from rural to urban growth is a change for the better.

(d)   the timber obtained from the forests has been beneficially used.

396. The effect on forest areas produced by the activity described in the first sentence is called

(a)   devastation   (b)   deforestation

(c)   disfiguration   (d)   devaluation

397. The results of industrial development, according to the writer, are

(a)   urbanization.

(b)   no shortage of fuel oil.

(c)   greater availability of domestic gas.

(d)   greater fuel consumption and pollution.

398. The phrase 'concrete jungle' in the paragraph refers to the factories and houses built as a result of urbanization and industrialization. This phrase suggests that the author

(a)   regrets that fields and forests have been replaced by city buildings.

(b)   believes that too much cement has been used in building factories.

(c)   disapproves of modern industrial expansion.

(d)   would like to go back to life in the jungle.

PASSAGE – 141

I must say a word about the Eiffel Tower. I do not know what purpose it serves today. But I then heard it greatly disparaged as well as praised. I remember that Tolstoy was the chief among those who disparaged it. He said that the Eiffel Tower was a monument of man's folly, not of his wisdom. Tobacco, he argued, was the worst of all intoxicants, inasmuch as a man addicted to it was tempted to commit crimes which a drunkard never dared to do; liquor made a man mad, but tobacco clouded his intellect and

made him build castles in the air. The Eiffel Tower was one of the creations of a man under such influence. There is no art about the Eiffel Tower. In no way can it be said to have contributed to the real beauty of the Exhibition. Men flocked to see it and ascended it as it was a novelty and of unique dimensions. It was the toy of the Exhibition. So long as we are children we are attracted by toys, and the Tower was a good demonstration of the fact that we are children attracted by trinkets. That may be claimed to be the purpose served by the Eiffel Tower.

399. Why did Tolstoy disparage Eiffel Tower ?

   1.   Man was foolish to build it.

   2.   Huge man-made structures did not appeal to him.

   3.   Men flocked to see it.

Which of the statements given above is/are correct ?

(a)   1 only   (b)   1 and 2 only

(c)   1 and 3 only   (d)   2 and 3 only

400. Why did Tolstoy believe that tobacco was the Worst of all intoxicants ?

(a)   Man lost his intellectual abilities under the influence of tobacco.

(b)   Tobacco kept man in a state of inebriation.

(c)   People who commit crimes are invariably addicted to tobacco.

(d)   Statements (a) and (b) above are correct in this context.

401. Why did men flock to the Eiffel Tower ?

(a)   Men were attracted to the castles built in the air.

(b)   Men lost their wisdom under the influence of intoxicants.

(c)   Men were attracted to childish things.

(d)   Men were attracted to things of no value.

PASSAGE - 142

In its simple form, science has helped man to protect himself from Nature and to overcome natural obstacles to movement. But with the advance of science, a situation has arisen in which Nature need to be protected from man. He has used Nature's own gifts, not only of metal but even tha human brain, to attack Nature. Forests are being destroyed not only to satisfy need but to provide luxuries. The evil effects of deforestation are already making themselves clearly felt in climatic changes and soil erosion. Man has at last begun to learn that he has to protect if he wants Nature to protect him.

402. The use of science in its simple form has helped man to

(a)   do such things as building shelter and make carts, boats, etc.

(b)   make bombs and missiles

(c)   build factories using machinery

(d)   make planes

403. Nature now needs to be protected from man because

(a)   nature has become weak

(b)   man is rapidly destroying Nature

(c)   man is cruel to animals

(d)   man has become irrational

404. Forests are being destroyed in order to

(a)   provide land for agriculture

(b)   provide wood for fuel

(c)   kill dangerous animals

(d)   provide necessities as well as needless comforts and pleasures

405. The evil effect of destroying Nature instead of using it is seen in
    (a) the fall in production of our factories
    (b) the fall in our standard of living
    (c) the unfavourable changes in climate
    (d) frequent occurrence of epidemics

406. Climatic changes and soil erosion are results of
    (a) scientific developments   (b) nuclear explosion
    (c) natural calamity   (d) deforestation

PASSAGE - 143

According to the civil laws of most countries obedience is no longer the duty of a wife; every woman has the political right to vote; but these liberties remain theoretical as long as she does not have economic freedom. A woman supported by a man is not liberated from the male. It is through gainful employment that woman has travelled most of the distance that separated her from the male; and nothing else can guarantee her liberty in practice.

I once heard a maidservant declare, while cleaning the stone floor of a hotel lobby, "I never asked anybody for anything; I succeeded all by myself." She was as proud of her self-sufficiency as a Rockefeller, Ford or Birla.

However, the mere combination of the right to vote and a job does not mean complete liberation : working, today, is not a liberty. A recent study of women workers in a car factory shows that they would prefer to stay in the home rather than work in the factory. The majority of women do not escape from the traditional feminine world. Their jobs at the factory do not relieve them of housekeeping burdens; they get from neither society nor their husbands, the assistance they need to become in concrete fact the equals of men.

407. Which of the following helps women most to achieve equality with men?
    (a) The right to vote   (b) Civil liberties
    (c) A job   (d) Wealthy husbands

408. Why does the writer talk about the maidservant in the hotel lobby?
    (a) The servants of today will one day be freed from their rich masters
    (b) A servant can become as rich as Rockefeller or Birla
    (c) Even with a low paid job women can achieve equality
    (d) Economic independence is necessary for women's liberation

409. In which paragraph does the writer say that it is revealed that some women would not like to work in the factory?
    (a) In paragraph four   (b) In paragraph three
    (c) In paragraph two   (d) In paragraph one

410. "These liberties" in the first paragraph refer to
    (a) The right to vote, not to obey and right to a job
    (b) The right to vote and not to obey
    (c) The rights of servants to disobey their master and the right of the master to punish them
    (d) Women's right to vote and earn money

PASSAGE-144

During the past three generations the diseases affecting western societies have undergone dramatic changes. Polio, diphtheria, tuberculosis, commonly known as TB, are vanishing; one injection of an antibiotic often cures deadly diseases such as pneumonia or syphilis; and so many mass killes have come under control that two-thirds of all death are now associated with the diseases of old age. Those who die young are more often than not victims of accidents, violence or suicide.

These changes in health status are generally equated with the decrease in suffering and attributed to more or better medical care. Almost everyone believes that at least one of his friends would not be alive and well except for the skill of a doctor. But there is in fact no evidence of any direct relationship between this change in the pattern or nature of sicknesses on the one hand and the so-called progress of medicine on the other hand. These changes are the results of political technological changes. They are not related to the activities that require the preparation and status of doctors or the costly equipment in which doctors take pride. In addition, an increase in the number of new diseases in the last fifteen years are themselves the result for medical intervention. They are doctor-made or iatrogenic.

411. In the western societies, the occurrence of polio, diphtheria and tuberculosis has
    (a) increased   (b) completely stopped
    (c) decreased   (d) continued without changes

412. More death are now associated with old age than in the past because
    (a) iatrogenic diseases are spreading faster now
    (b) deadly diseases affecting the young have been well controlled
    (c) accidents, violence and suicide that killed many youths in the past are now under control
    (d) political and technological changes now take better care of the young than the old

413. The writer probably is arguing for
    (a) stopping the practice of western medicines completely
    (b) stopping the use of costly equipment and medicines
    (c) rethinking about the successes and failures of the western medicines
    (d) giving greater attention to new, iatrogenic diseases than to the old diseases such as polio, diphtheria and pneumonia

PASSAGE- 145

Poverty is a complex problem. It is far more than an economical condition. We measure it usually in terms of income but forget that poverty embraces a whole range of circumstances, including lack of access to information and to basic services like nutritional diet, health care and education. It results into a loss of cultural identity and destroys traditional knowledge. Poor people become marginalised and suffer from exploitation and loss of human dignity.

414. Which of the following sentences comes close to the meaning of the sentence, "Poverty embraces a whole range of circumstances."
    (a) There are lot of angles to poverty
    (b) They are several section in the society which are poor
    (c) There are several types of poverty
    (d) Poverty is solely an economic issue

415. What way do you think 'lack of access to information' affects poor people?
    (a) They don't get information about how to improve their conditions
    (b) They didn't get newspapers to read at all
    (c) They can't go to school and read books
    (d) They don't get information about schemes of getting rich

416. Why do you think 'cultural identify' is important?
- (a) A sense of cultural identify gives people self-respect and confidence
- (b) Cultural identify defines the character of poor people
- (c) It is important to have cultural identify to get jobs
- (d) It is useful to have cultural identity because it brings your success

417. Which of the following sentences comes closest to the sentence 'Poor people become marginalised'?
- (a) They are not given any benefit of any government schemes
- (b) They are ignored by the rich people
- (c) They are the most ignored elements of the society
- (d) They are the most disposed elements of the society

418. What do you think is the tone of the passage?
- (a) Objective but querulous
- (b) Descriptive and impassioned
- (c) Argumentative and critical
- (d) Objective and critical

PASSAGE - 146

Over-population is the most pressing of India's numerous and multi-faceted problems. In fact it has caused equally complex problems such as poverty, under-nourishment, unemployment and excessive fragmentation of land. Indisputably, this country has been facing a population explosion of crisis dimensions. It has largely diluted the fruits of the remarkable economic progress that the nation has made during the last four decades or so. The entire battle against poverty is thwarted by the rapid increase in the population. The tragedy is that while over-population accentuates poverty, the country's stark poverty itself is in many areas a major cause of over-population.

419. What is the irony behind the over-population of India?
- (a) Over-population gives birth to poverty, which (poverty) itself is the cause of over-population
- (b) Under nourishment and unemployment are outcomes of flawed economic progress
- (c) Fragmentation of land is leading to over-population
- (d) Fruits of the remarkable economic progress are trickling down to the poor

420. What is the general tone of the passage?
- (a) funny/humorous
- (b) sombre
- (c) didactic
- (d) tragic

421. What, in the author's view, severely affects the economic growth of our country?
- (a) poverty
- (b) illiteracy
- (c) over-population
- (d) None of the above

422. What, according to the author, is the biggest reason behind over-population?
- (a) under-nourishment
- (b) unemployment
- (c) excessive fragmentation of land
- (d) poverty

423. "It has largely <u>diluted</u> the fruits of the remarkable economic progress". Find antonym of the underlined word
- (a) coalesced
- (b) compounded
- (c) cheapened
- (d) consolidated

PASSAGE - 147

I have always opposed the idea of dividing the world into the Orient and the **Occident**. It is, however, the tremendous industrial growth that has made the West what it is. I think the difference, say, between India and Europe in the 12th or 13th century would not have been very great. Differences have been intensified by this process of industrialization which has promoted material well-being tremendously and which is destroying the life of the mind, which is in a process of deterioration, chiefly because the environment that has been created by it does not give time or opportunity to individuals to think. If the life of the mind is not encouraged, then inevitably civilization collapses.

424. The words "the Orient and the Occident" mean
- (a) the West and the East respectively
- (b) the East and the West respectively
- (c) the North and the South respectively
- (d) the South and the North respectively

425. The author believes that the difference between India and Europe in the 12th or 13th century was not very great because
- (a) Indians and Europeans mixed freely
- (b) Indians imitated the European way of living
- (c) Europeans imitated the Indian way of living
- (d) Industrialization had not yet taken place

426. In the opinion of the author, Industrialization is
- (a) an absolute blessing
- (b) an absolute curse
- (c) neither a blessing nor a curse
- (d) more of a curse than a blessing

427. The author says that the mental life of the world is in a process of deterioration because the modern generation is
- (a) endowed with low mental powers
- (b) too lazy to exert its mental powers
- (c) taught that physical activities are more important than mental
- (d) brought up in an environment unfavourable to the growth of the mental life

428. The title that best expresses the central idea of the passage is
- (a) difference between the Occident and the Orient
- (b) impact of Industrialization on our civilization
- (c) advantages of Industrialization
- (d) disadvantages of Industrialization

Directions *Read the following passages and answer the items that follow. Your answers to these items should be based on the passage only.*

PASSAGE - 148

Now India's children have a right-to receive at least eight years of education, the gnawing question is whether it will remain on paper or become a reality. One hardly needs a reminder that this right is different from the others enshrined in the Constitution, that the beneficiary – a six year old child cannot demand it, nor can she or he fight a legal battle when the right is denied or violated. In all cases, it is the adult society which must act on behalf of the child. In another peculiarity, where a child's right to education is denied, no compensation offered later can be adequate or relevant. This is so because childhood does not last. If a legal battle fought on behalf of a child is eventually won, it may be of little use to the boy or girl because the opportunity missed at school during childhood cannot serve the same purpose later in life. This may be painfully true for girls because our society permits them only a short childhood, if at all. The Right to Education (RTE) has become law at a point in India's history when the ghastly practice of female infanticide has resurfaced in the form of foeticide. This is "symptomatic of a deeper turmoil" in society which is compounding the traditional obstacles to the education of girls. Tenacious prejudice against the intellectual potential of girls runs across our cultural diversity and the system of education has not been able to address it.   *[2011 - II]*

429. With reference to the passage, consider the following statements :

1. When children are denied education, adult society does not act on behalf of them.
2. Right to Education as a law cannot be enforced in the country.

Which of the statements given above is/are correct?

(a) 1 only
(b) 2 only
(c) Both 1 and 2
(d) Neither 1 nor 2

430. According to the passage, what could be the traditional obstacles to the education of girls ?

1. Inability of parents to fight a legal battle when the Right to Education is denied to their children.
2. The traditional way of thinking about girls' role in society.
3. The prejudice against the intellectual potential of girls.
4. Improper system of education.

Select the correct answer from the codes given below :

(a) 1 and 2 only
(b) 2, 3 and 4 only
(c) 1, 3 and 4 only
(d) 1, 2, 3 and 4

431. On the basis of the passage, consider the following statements :

1. Right to Education is a legal right and not a fundamental right.
2. For realising the goal of universal education, the education system in the country must be made identical to that of developed countries.

Which of the statements given above is/are correct ?

(a) 1 only
(b) 2 only
(c) Both 1 and 2
(d) Neither 1 nor 2

432. Which one of the following statements conveys the key message of the passage ?

(a) India has declared that education is compulsory for its children.
(b) Adult society is not keen on implementing the Right to Education.
(c) The Right to Education, particularly of a girl child, needs to be safeguarded.
(d) The system of education should address the issue of Right to Education.

433. Which one of the following statements conveys the inference of the passage ?

(a) The society has a tenacious prejudice against the intellectual potential of girls.
(b) Adults cannot be relied upon to fight on behalf of children for their Right to Education.

(c) The legal fight to get education for children is often protracted and prohibitive.
(d) There is no sufficient substitute for education received in childhood.

PASSAGE - 149

For achieving inclusive growth there is a critical need to rethink the role of the State. The early debate among economists about the size of the Government can be misleading. The need of the hour is to have an enabling Government. India is too large and complex a nation for the State to be able to deliver all that is needed. Asking the Government to produce all the essential goods, create all the necessary jobs, and keep a curb on the prices of all goods is to lead to a large cumbersome bureaucracy and widespread corruption.

The aim must be to stay with the objective of inclusive growth that was laid down by the founding fathers of the nation and also to take a more modern view of what the State can realistically deliver.

This is what leads to the idea of an enabling State, that is, a Government that does not try to directly deliver to the citizens everything that they need. Instead, it (1) creates an enabling ethos for the market so that individual enterprise can flourish and citizens can, for the most part, provide for the needs of one another, and (2) steps in to help those who do not manage to do well for themselves, for there will always be individuals, no matter what the system, who need support and help. Hence we need a Government that, when it comes to the market, sets effective, incentive-compatible rules and remains on the sidelines with minimal interference, and at the same time, plays an important role in directly helping the poor by ensuring that they get basic education and health services and receive adequate nutrition and food.   *[2011 - II]*

434. According to the passage :

1. The objective of inclusive growth was laid down by the founding fathers of the nation.
2. Need of the hour is to have an enabling Government.
3. The Government should engage in maximum interference in market processes.
4. There is a need to change the size of the Government.

Which of the statements given above are correct ?

(a) 1 and 2 only
(b) 2 and 3 only
(c) 1 and 4 only
(d) 1, 2, 3 and 4

435. According to the passage, the strategy of inclusive growth can be effected by focusing on

(a) Meeting all the needs of every citizen in the country.
(b) Increasing the regulations over the manufacturing sector.
(c) Controlling the distribution of manufactured goods.
(d) Delivery of the basic services to the deprived sections of the society.

436. What constitutes an enabling Government?

1. A large bureaucracy.
2. Implementation of welfare programmes through representatives.
3. Creating an ethos that helps individual enterprise.

4. Providing resources to those who are underprivileged.
5. Offering direct help to the poor regarding basic services.

Select the correct answer from the codes given below :

(a) 1, 2 and 3 only   (b) 4 and 5 only
(c) 3, 4 and 5 only   (d) 1, 2, 3, 4 and 5

437. Why is the State unable to deliver "all that is needed"?
1. It does not have sufficient bureaucracy.
2. It does not promote inclusive growth.

Select the correct answer from the codes given below :

(a) 1 only   (b) 2 only
(c) Both 1 and 2   (d) Neither 1 nor 2

438. What is the essential message being conveyed by the author of the passage?
(a) The objectives of inclusive growth laid down by the founding fathers of the nation should be remembered.
(b) The Government needs to make available more schools and health services.
(c) The Government needs to establish markets and industries to meet the needs of the poor strata of the society.
(d) There is a need to rethink the role of the State in achieving inclusive growth.

PASSAGE - 150

The concept of 'creative society' refers to a phase of development of a society in which a large number of potential contradictions become articulate and active. This is most evident when oppressed social groups get politically mobilised and demand their rights. The upsurge of the peasants and tribals, the movements for regional autonomy and self-determination, the environmental movements, and the women's movements in the developing countries are signs of emergence of creative society in contemporary times. The forms of social movements and their intensity may vary from country to country and place to place within a country. But the very presence of movements for social transformation in various spheres of a society indicates the emergence of a creative society in a country. *[2011 - II]*

439. What does the author imply by "creative society" ?
1. A society where diverse art forms and literary writings seek incentive.
2. A society where social inequalities are accepted as the norm.
3. A society where a large number of contradictions are recognised.
4. A society where the exploited and the oppressed groups grow conscious of their human rights and upliftment.

Select the correct answer using the codes given below :

(a) 1, 2 and 3   (b) 4 only
(c) 3 and 4   (d) 2 and 4

440. What according to the passage are the manifestations of social movements ?
1. Aggressiveness and being incendiary.
2. Instigation by external forces.
3. Quest for social equality and individual freedom.

4. Urge for granting privileges and self-respect to disparaged sections of the society.

Select the correct answer using the codes given below :

(a) 1 and 3 only   (b) 2 and 4 only
(c) 3 and 4 only   (d) 1, 2, 3 and 4

441. With reference to the passage, consider the following statements :
1. To be a creative society, it is essential to have a variety of social movements.
2. To be a creative society, it is imperative to have potential contradictions and conflicts.

Which of the statements given above is/are correct ?

(a) 1 only   (b) 2 only
(c) Both 1 and 2   (d) Neither 1 nor 2

442. Consider the following three statements :
1. Only students can participate in the race.
2. Some participants in the race are girls.
3. All girl participants in the race are invited for coaching.

Which one of the following conclusions can be drawn from the above statements ?

(a) All participants in the race are invited for coaching.
(b) All students are invited for coaching.
(c) All participants in the race are students.
(d) None of the statements (a), (b) and (c) given above is correct.

PASSAGE - 151

A country under foreign domination seeks escape from the present in dreams of a vanished age, and finds consolation in visions of past greatness. That is a foolish and dangerous pastime in which many of us indulge. An equally questionable practice for us in India is to imagine that we are still spiritually great though we have come down in the world in other respects. Spiritual or any other greatness cannot be founded on lack of freedom and opportunity, or on starvation and misery. Many western writers have encouraged that notion that Indians are other-worldly. I suppose the poor and unfortunate in every country become to some extent other-worldly, unless they become revolutionaries, for this world is evidently not meant for them. So also subject peoples.

As a man grows to maturity he is not entirely engrossed in, or satisfied with, the external objective world. He seeks also some inner meaning, some psychological and physical satisfaction. So also with peoples and civilizations as they mature and grow adult. Every civilization and every people exhibit these parallel streams of an external life and an internal life. Where they meet or keep close to each other, there is an equilibrium and stability. When they diverge conflict arises and the crises that torture the mind and spirit. *[2011 - II]*

443. The passage mentions that "this world is evidently not meant for them". It refers to people who
1. seek freedom from foreign domination.
2. live in starvation and misery.
3. become revolutionaries.

Which of the statements given above is/are correct ?

(a) 1 and 2   (b) 2 only
(c) 2 and 3   (d) 3 only

444. Consider the following assumptions :
1. A country under foreign domination cannot indulge in spiritual pursuit.
2. Poverty is an impediment in the spiritual pursuit.
3. Subject peoples may become other-worldly.
   With reference to the passage, which of the above assumptions is/are valid ?
   (a) 1 and 2
   (b) 2 only
   (c) 2 and 3
   (d) 3 only

445. The passage thematically centres on
(a) the state of mind of oppressed people
(b) starvation and misery
(c) the growth of civilization
(d) body, mind and spirit of people in general

446. According to the passage, the torture of the mind and spirit is caused
(a) by the impact of foreign domination.
(b) by the desire to escape from foreign domination and find consolation in visions of past greatness.
(c) due to lack of equilibrium between an external life and an internal life.
(d) due to one's inability to be either revolutionary or other worldly.

PASSAGE - 152

A species that exerts an influence out of proportion to its abundance in an ecosystem is called a keystone species. The keystone species may influence both the species richness of communities and the flow of energy and materials through ecosystems. The sea star **Pisaster ochraceus**, which lives in rocky intertidal ecosystems on the Pacific coast of North America, is also an example of a keystone species. Its preferred prey is the mussel **Mytilus californianus**. In the absence of sea stars, these mussels crowd out other competitors in a broad belt of the intertidal zone. By consuming mussels, sea star creates bare spaces that are taken over by a variety of other species.

A study at the University of Washington demonstrated the influence of **Pisaster** on species richness by removing sea stars from selected parts of the intertidal zone repeatedly over a period of five years. Two major changes occurred in the areas from which sea stars were removed. First, the lower edge of the mussel bed extended farther down into the intertidal zone, showing that sea stars are able to eliminate mussels completely where they are covered with water most of the time. Second, and more dramatically, 28 species of animals and algae disappeared from the sea star removal zone. Eventually only **Mytilus,** the dominant competitor, occupied the entire substratum. Through its effect on competitive relationships, predation by **Pisaster** largely determines which species live in these rocky intertidal ecosystems.

[2011-II]

447. What is the crux of the passage ?
(a) Sea star has a preferred prey.
(b) A preferred prey determines the survival of a keystone species.
(c) Keystone species ensures species diversity.
(d) Sea star is the only keystone species on the Pacific coast of North America.

448. With reference to the passage, consider the following statements :
1. Mussels are generally the dominant species in intertidal ecosystems.
2. The survival of sea stars is generally determined by the abundance of mussels.
   Which of the statements given above is/are correct ?
   (a) 1 only
   (b) 2 only
   (c) Both 1 and 2
   (d) Neither 1 nor 2

449. Which of the following is/are implied by the passage?
1. Mussels are always hard competitors for sea stars.
2. Sea stars of the Pacific coast have reached the climax of their evolution.
3. Sea stars constitute an important component in the energy flow in intertidal ecosystem.
   Which of the statements given above is/are correct?
   (a) 1 and 2
   (b) 2 only
   (c) 1 and 3
   (d) 3 only

450. Consider the following assumptions:
1. The food chains/food web in an ecosystem are influenced by keystone species.
2. The presence of keystone species is a specific characteristic of aquatic ecosystems.
3. If the keystone species is completely removed from an ecosystem, it will lead to the collapse of the ecosystem. With reference to the passage, which of the above assumptions is/are valid ?
   (a) 1 only
   (b) 2 and 3 only
   (c) 1 and 3 only
   (d) 1, 2 and 3

PASSAGE - 153

Ecosystems provide people with a variety of goods and services; food, clean water, clean air, flood control, soil stabilization, pollination, climate regulation, spiritual fulfilment and aesthetic enjoyment, to name just a few. Most of these benefits either are irreplaceable or the technology necessary to replace them is prohibitively expensive. For example, potable fresh water can be provided by desalinating sea-water, but only at great cost.

The rapidly expanding human population has greatly modified the Earth's ecosystems to meet their increased requirements of some of the goods and services, particularly food, fresh water, timber, fibre and fuel. These modifications have contributed substantially to human well being and economic development. The benefits have not been equally distributed. Some people have actually been harmed by these changes. Moreover, short-term increases in some ecosystem goods and services have come at the cost of the long-term degradation of others. For example, efforts to increase the production of food and fibre have decreased the ability of some ecosystems to provide clean water, regulate flooding and support biodiversity.

[2011-II]

451. With reference to the passage, consider the following statements.
Expanding human population has an adverse effect on :
1. Spiritual fulfilment
2. Aesthetic enjoyment
3. Potable fresh water

4. Production of food and fibre
5. Biodiversity

Which of the statements given above are correct ?

(a) 1, 2 and 3 only   (b) 2, 4 and 5 only
(c) 3 and 5 only   (d) 1, 2, 3, 4 and 5

452. The passage mentions that "some people have actually been harmed by these changes". What does it imply ?

1. The rapid expansion of population has adversely affected some people:
2. Sufficient efforts have not been made to increase the production of food and fibre.
3. In the short term some people may be harmed, but in the long term everyone will benefit from modifications in the Earth's ecosystems.

Which of the statements given above is/are correct?

(a) 1 only   (b) 2 only
(c) 1 and 3   (d) None of the above

453. With reference to the passage, consider the following statements:

1. It is imperative to modify the Earth's ecosystems for the well being of mankind.
2. Technology can never replace all the goods and services provided by ecosystems.

Which of the statements given above is/are correct?

(a) 1 only   (b) 2 only
(c) Both 1 and 2   (d) Neither 1 nor 2

PASSAGE - 154

A moral act must be our own act; must spring from our own will. If we act mechanically, there is no moral content in our act. Such action would be moral, if we think it proper to act like a machine and do so. For, in doing so, we use our discrimination. We should bear in mind the distinction between acting mechanically and acting intentionally. It may be moral of a king to pardon a culprit. But the messenger carrying out the order of pardon plays only a mechanical part in the king's moral act. But if the messenger were to carry out the king's order considering it to be his duty, his action would be a moral one. How can a man understand morality who does not use his own intelligence and power of thought, but lets himself be swept along like a log of wood by a current ? Sometimes a man defies convention and acts on his own with a view to absolute good. *[2011 - II]*

454. Which of the following statements best describe/describes the thought of the writer ?

1. A moral act calls for using our discretion.
2. Man should react to a situation immediately
3. Man must do his duty.
4. Man should be able to defy convention in order to be moral.

Select the correct answer from the codes given below :

(a) 1 only   (b) 1 and 3
(c) 2 and 3   (d) 1 and 4

455. Which of the following statements is the nearest definition of moral action, according to the writer ?

(a) It is a mechanical action based on official orders from superiors.

(b) It is an action based on our sense of discretion.
(c) It is a clever action based on the clarity of purpose.
(d) It is a religious action based on understanding.

456. The passage contains a statement "lets himself be swept along like a log of wood by a current." Among the following statements, which is/are nearest in meaning to this ?

1. A person does not use his own reason.
2. He is susceptible to influence/pressure.
3. He cannot withstand difficulties/ challenges.
4. He is like a log of wood.

Select the correct answer using the codes given below :

(a) 1 only   (b) 1 and 2
(c) 2 and 3   (d) 1 and 4

PASSAGE - 155

Education, without a doubt, has an important functional, instrumental and utilitarian dimension. This is revealed when one asks questions such as 'what is the purpose of education?'. The answers, too often, are 'to acquire qualifications for employment/ upward mobility', 'wider/higher (in terms of income) opportunities', and 'to meet the needs for trained human power in diverse fields for national development'. But in its deepest sense education is not instrumentalist. That is to say, it is not to be justified outside of itself because it leads to the acquisition of formal skills or of certain desired psychological – social attributes. It must be respected in itself. Education is thus not a commodity to be acquired or possessed and then used, but a process of inestimable importance to individuals and society, although it can and does have enormous use value. Education then, is a process of expansion and conversion, not in the sense of converting or turning students into doctors or engineers, but the widening and turning out of the mind—the creation, sustenance and development of self-critical awareness and independence of thought. It is an inner process of moral-intellectual development.

[Prelims II- 2012]

457. What do you understand by the 'instrumentalist' view of education?

(a) Education is functional and utilitarian in its purposes.
(b) Education is meant to fulfil human needs.
(c) The purpose of education is to train the human intellect.
(d) Education is meant to achieve moral development.

458. According to the passage, education must be respected in itself because

(a) it helps to acquire qualifications for employment
(b) it helps in upward mobility and acquiring social status
(c) it is an inner process of moral and intellectual development
(d) All the (a), (b) and (c) given above are correct in this context.

459. Education is a process in which

(a) students are converted into trained professionals.
(b) opportunities for higher income are generated.
(c) individuals develop self-critical awareness and independence of thought.
(d) qualifications for upward mobility are acquired.

PASSAGE - 156

Chemical pesticides lose their role in sustainable agriculture if the pests evolve resistance. The evolution of pesticide resistance is simply natural selection in action. It is almost certain to occur when vast numbers of a genetically variable population are killed. One or a few individuals may be unusually resistant (perhaps because they possess an enzyme that can detoxify the pesticide). If the pesticide is applied repeatedly, each successive generation of the pest will contain a larger proportion of resistant individuals. Pests typically have a high intrinsic rate of reproduction, and so a few individuals in one generation may give rise to hundreds or thousands in the next, and resistance spreads very rapidly in a population.

This problem was often ignored in the past, even though the first case of DDT (dichlorodiphenyltrichloroethane) resistance was reported early as 1946. There is exponential increase in the numbers of invertebrates that have evolved resistance and in the number of pesticides against which resistance has evolved. Resistance has been recorded in every family of arthropod pests (including dipterans such as mosquitoes and house flies, as well as beetles, moths, wasps, fleas, lice and mites) as well as in weeds and plant pathogens. Take the Alabama leaf-worm, a moth pest of cotton, as an example. It has developed resistance in one or more regions of the world to aldrin, DDT, dieldrin, endrin, lindane and toxaphene.

If chemical pesticides brought nothing but, problems, — if their use was intrinsically and acutely unsustainable — then they would already have fallen out of widespread use. This has not happened. Instead, their rate of production has increased rapidly. The ratio of cost to benefit for the individual agricultural producer has remained in favour of pesticide use. In the USA, insecticides have been estimated to benefit the agricultural products to the tune of around $5 for every $1 spent.

Moreover, in many poorer countries, the prospect of imminent mass starvation, or of an epidemic disease, are so frightening that the social and health costs of using pesticides have to be ignored. In general the use of pesticides is justified by objective measures such as 'lives saved', 'economic efficiency of food production' and 'total food produced'. In these very fundamental senses, their use may be described as sustainable. In practice, sustainability depends on continually developing new pesticides that keep at least one step ahead of the pests – pesticides that are less persistent, biodegradable and more accurately targeted all the pests. *[Prelims II- 2012]*

460. "The evolution of pesticide resistance is natural selection in action." What does it actually imply?
   (a) It is very natural for many organisms to have pesticide resistance.
   (b) Pesticide resistance among organisms is a universal phenomenon.
   (c) Some individuals in any given population show resistance after the application of pesticides.
   (d) None of the statements (a), (b) and (c) given above is correct.

461. With reference to the passage, consider the following statements:
   1. Use of chemical pesticides has become imperative in all the poor countries of the world.
   2. Chemical pesticides should not have any role in sustainable agriculture.
   3. One pest can develop resistance to many pesticides.

Which of the statements given above is/are correct?
   (a) 1 and 2 only   (b) 3 only
   (c) 1 and 3 only   (d) 1, 2 and 3

462. Though the problems associated with the use of chemical pesticides is known for a long time, their widespread use has not waned. Why?
   (a) Alternatives to chemical pesticides do not exist at all.
   (b) New pesticides are not invented at all.
   (c) Pesticides are biodegradable.
   (d) None of the statements (a), (b) and (c) given above is correct.

463. How do pesticides act as agents for the selection of resistant individuals in any pest population?
   1. It is possible that in a pest population the individuals will behave differently due to their genetic makeup.
   2. Pests do possess the ability to detoxify the pesticides.
   3. Evolution of pesticide resistance is equally distributed in pest population.

Which of the statements given above is/are correct?
   (a) 1 only   (b) 1 and 2 only
   (c) 3 only   (d) 1, 2 and 3

464. Why is the use of chemical pesticides generally justified by giving the examples of poor and developing countries?
   1. Development countries can afford to do away with use of pesticides by adapting to organic farming, but it is imperative for poor and developing countries to use chemical pesticides.
   2. In poor and developing countries, the pesticide addresses the problem of epidemic diseases of crops and eases the food problem.
   3. The social and health costs of pesticide use are generally ignored in poor and developing countries.

Which of the statements given above is/are correct?
   (a) 1 only   (b) 1 and 2 only
   (c) 2 only   (d) 1, 2 and 3

465. What does the passage imply?
   (a) Alternative options to chemical pesticides should be promoted.
   (b) Too much use of chemicals is not good for the ecosystem.
   (c) There is no scope for the improvement of pesticides and making their use sustainable.
   (d) Both the statements (a) and (b) above are correct.

PASSAGE - 157

Today's developing economices use much less energy per capita than developed countries such as the United States did at similar incomes, showing the potential for lower-carbon growth. Adaptation and mitigation need to be integrated into a climate-smart development strategy that increases resilience, reduces the threat of further global warming, and improves development outcomes. Adaptation and mitigation measures can advance development, and prosperity can raise incomes and foster better institutions. A healthier population living in better-built houses and with access to bank loans and social security is better equipped to deal with a changing climate and its consequences. Advancing robust, resilient development policies that promote adaptation is needed today because changes in the climate, already begun, will increase even in the short term.

The spread of economic prosperity has always been interwined with adaptation to changing ecological conditions. But as growth has altered the environment and as environmental change has accelerated, sustaining growth and adaptability demands greater capacity to understand our environment, generate new adaptive technologies and practices, and diffuse them widely. As economic historians have explained, much of humankind's creative potential has been directed at adapting to the changing world. But adaptation cannot cope with all the impacts related to climate change, especially as larger changes unfold in the long term.

Countries cannot grow out of harm's way fast enough to match the changing climate. And some growth strategies, whether driven by the government or the market, can also add to vulnerability — particularly if they overexploit natural resources. Under the Soviet development plan, irrigated cotton cultivation expanded in water-stressed Central Asia and led to the near disappearance of the Aral Sea, threatening the livelihoods of fishermen, herders and farmers. And clearing mangroves — the natural coastal buffers against storm surges — to make way for intensive farming or housing development , increases the physical vulnerability of coastal settlements, whether in Guinea or in Louisiana.

[Prelims II-2012]

466. Which of the following conditions of growth can add to vulnerability?
1. When the growth occurs due to excessive exploitation of mineral resources and forests.
2. When the growth brings about a change in humankind's creative potential.
3. When the growth is envisaged only for providing houses and social security to the people.
4. When the growth occurs due to emphasis on farming only.

Select the correct answer using the codes given below:
(a) 1 only
(b) 2, 3 and 4 only
(c) 1 and 4 only
(d) 1, 2, 3 and 4

467. What does low-carbon growth imply in the present context?
1. More emphasis on the use of renewable sources of energy.
2. Less emphasis on manufacturing sector and more emphasis on agriculture sector.
3. Switching over from monoculture practices to mixed farming.
4. Less demand for goods and services.

Select the correct answer using the codes given below:
(a) 1 only
(b) 2, 3 and 4 only
(c) 1 and 4 only
(d) None of the above implies low-carbon growth

468. Which of the following conditions is/are necessary for sustainable economic growth?
1. Spreading of economic prosperity more.
2. Popularising/spreading of adaptive technologies widely.
3. Investing on research in adaptation and mitigation technologies.

Select the correct answer using the codes given below:
(a) 1 only
(b) 2 and 3 only
(c) 1 and 3 only
(d) 1, 2 and 3

469. Which of the following inferences can be made from the passage?
1. Rainfed crops should not be cultivated in irrigated areas.
2. Farming under water-deficient areas should not be a part of development strategy.

Select the correct answer using the codes given below:
(a) 1 only
(b) 2 only
(c) Both 1 and 2
(d) Neither 1 nor 2

470. Consider the following assumptions :
1. Sustainable economic growth demands the use of creative potential of man.
2. Intensive agriculture can lead to ecological backlash.
3. Spread of economic prosperity can adversely affect the ecology and environment.

With reference to the passage, which of the above assumptions is/are valid?
(a) 1 only
(b) 2 and 3 only
(c) 1 and 3 only
(d) 1, 2 and 3

471. Which one of the following statements constitutes the central theme of this passage?
(a) Countries with greater economic prosperity are better equipped to deal with the consequences of climate change.
(b) Adaptation and mitigation should be integrated with development strategies.
(c) Rapid economic growth should not be pursued by both developed and developing economies.
(d) Some countries resort to overexploitation of natural resources for the sake of rapid development.

PASSAGE - 158

Invasions of exotic species into new geographic areas sometimes occur naturally and without human agency. However, human actions have increased this trickle to a flood. Human-caused introductions may occur either accidentally as a consequence of human transport, or intentionally but illegally to serve some private purpose or legitimately to procure some hoped-for public benefit by bringing a pest under control, producing new agricultural products or providing novel recreational opportunities. Many introduced species are assimilated into communities without much obvious effect. However, some have been responsible for dramatic changes to native species and natural communities. For example, the accidental introduction of the brown tree snake *Boiga irregularis* into Guam, an island in the Pacific, has through nest predation reduced 10 endemic forest bird species to the point of extinction.

One of the major reasons for the world's great biodiversity is the occurrence of centers of endemism so that similar habitats in different parts of the world are occupied by different groups of species that happen to have evolved there. If every species naturally had access to everywhere on the globe, we might expect a relatively small number of successful species to become dominant in each biome. The extent to which this homogenization can happen naturally is restricted by the limited powers of dispersal of most species in the face of the physical barriers that exist to dispersal. By virtue of the transport opportunities offered by humans, these barriers have been breached by an ever-increasing number of exotic species. The effects of introductions have been to convert a hugely diverse range of local community compositions into something much more homogeneous.

It would be wrong, however, to conclude that introducing species to a region will inevitably cause a decline in species richness there. For example, there are numerous species of plants, invertebrates and vertebrates found in continental Europe but absent from the British Isles (many because they have so far failed to recolonize after the last glaciations). Their introduction would be likely to augment British biodiversity. The significant detrimental effect noted above arises where aggressive species provide a novel challenge to endemic biotas ill-equipped to deal with them. *[Prelims II- 2012]*

472. With reference to the passage, which of the following statements is correct?

(a) Introduction of exotic species into new geographical areas always leads to reduced biodiversity.

(b) Exotic species introduced by man into new areas have always greatly altered the native ecosystems.

(c) Man is the only reason to convert a hugely diverse range of local community compositions into more homogeneous ones.

(d) None of the statements (a), (b) and (c) is correct in this context.

473. Why does man introduce exotic species into new geographical areas?
1. To breed exotic species with local varieties.
2. To increase agricultural productivity.
3. For beautification and landscaping.
Which of the above statements is/are correct?
(a) 1 only   (b) 2 and 3 only
(c) 1 and 3 only   (d) 1, 2 and 3

474. How is homogenization prevented under natural conditions?
(a) Evolution of groups of species specific to local habitats.
(b) Presence of oceans and mountain ranges.
(c) Strong adaptation of groups of species to local physical and climatic conditions.
(d) All the statements (a), (b) and (c) given above are correct in this context.

475. How have the human beings influenced the biodiversity?
1. By smuggling live organisms.
2. By building highways.
3. By making ecosystems sensitive so that new species are not allowed.
4. By ensuring that new species do not have major impact on local species.
Which of the statements given above are correct?
(a) 1 and 2   (b) 2 and 3
(c) 1 and 3   (d) 2 and 4

476. What can be the impact of invasion of exotic species on an ecosystem?
1. Erosion of endemic species.
2. Change in the species composition of the community of the ecosystem.
Select the correct answer using the codes given below:
(a) 1 only   (b) 2 only
(c) Both 1 and 2   (d) Neither 1 nor 2

PASSAGE - 159

Most champions of democracy have been rather reticent in suggesting that democracy would itself promote development and enhancement of social welfare–they have tended to see them as good but distinctly separate and largely independent goals. The detractors of democracy, on the other hand, seemed to have been quite willing to express their diagnosis of what they see as serious tensions between democracy and development. The theorists of the practical split — "Make up your mind : do you want democracy, or instead, do you want development ?" — often came, at least to start with, from East Asian countries, and their voice grew in influence as several of these countries were immensely successful — through the 1970s and 1980s and even later — in promoting economic growth without pursuing democracy.

To deal with these issues we have to pay particular attention to both the content of what can be called development and to the interpretation of democracy (in particular to the respective roles of voting and of public reasoning). The assessment of development cannot be divorced from the lives that people can lead and the real freedom that they enjoy. Development can scarcely be seen merely in terms of enhancement of inanimate objects of convenience, such as a rise in the GNP (or in personal incomes), or industrialization – important as they may be as means to the real ends. Their value must depend on what they do to the lives and freedom of the people involved, which must be central to the idea of development.

If development is understood in a broader way, with a focus on human lives, then it becomes immediately clear that the relation between development and democracy has to be seen partly in terms of their constitutive connection, rather than only through their external links. Even though the question has often been asked whether political freedom is "conducive to development", we must not miss the crucial recognition that political liberties and democratic rights are among the "constituent components" of development. Their relevance for development does not have to be established indirectly through their contribution to be growth of GNP. *[Prelims II- 2012]*

477. According to the passage, why is a serious tension perceived between democracy and development by the detractors of democracy?
(a) Democracy and development are distinct and separate goals.
(b) Economic growth can be promoted successfully without pursuing a democratic system of governance.
(c) Non-democratic regimes deliver economic growth faster and far more successfully than democratic ones.
(d) All the statements (a), (b) and (c) given above are correct in this context.

478. According to the passage, what should be the ultimate assessment/aim/view of development?
(a) Rise in the per capita income and industrial growth rates.
(b) Improvement in the Human Development Index and GNP.
(c) Rise in the savings and consumption trends.
(d) Extent of real freedom that citizens enjoy.

479. What does a "constitutive" connection between democracy and development imply?
(a) The relation between them has to be seen through external links.
(b) Political and civil rights only can lead to economic development.
(c) Political liberties and democratic rights are essential elements of development.
(d) None of the statements (a), (b) and (c) given above is correct in this context.

PASSAGE - 160

The need for Competition Law becomes more evident when foreign direct investment (FDI) is liberalized. The impact of FDI is not always pro-competitive. Very often FDI takes the form of a foreign corporation acquiring a domestic enterprise or establishing a joint venture with one. By making such an acquisition the foreign investor may substantially lessen competition and gain a dominant position in the relevant market, thus charging higher prices. Another scenario is where the affiliates of two separate multinational companies (MNCs) have been established in competition with one another in a particular developing economy, following the liberalization of FDI. Subsequently, the parent companies overseas merge. With the affiliates no longer remaining independent, competition in the host country may be virtually eliminated and the prices of the products may be artificially inflated. Most of these adverse consequences of mergers and acquisitions by MNCs can be avoided if an effective competition law is in place. Also, an economy that has implemented an effective competition law is in a better position to attract FDI than one that has not. This is not just because most MNCs are expected to be accustomed to the operation of such a law in their home countries and know how to deal with such concerns but also that MNCs expect competition authorities to ensure a level playing field between domestic and foreign firms. *[Prelims II- 2012]*

480. With reference to the passage, consider the following statements:
1. It is desirable that the impact of Foreign Direct Investment should be pro-competitive.
2. The entry of foreign investors invariably leads to the inflated prices in domestic markets.

Which of the statements given above is/are correct?
(a) 1 only
(b) 2 only
(c) Both 1 and 2
(d) Neither 1 nor 2

481. According to the passage, how does a foreign investor dominate the relevant domestic market?
1. Multinational companies get accustomed to domestic laws.
2. Foreign companies establish joint ventures with domestic companies.
3. Affiliates in a particular market/sector lose their independence as their parent companies overseas merge.
4. Foreign companies lower the cost of their products as compared to that of products of domestic companies.

Which of the statements given above are correct?
(a) 1 and 2 only
(b) 2 and 3 only
(c) 1, 2 and 3 only
(d) 1, 2, 3 and 4

482. What is the inference from this passage?
(a) Foreign investors and multinational companies always dominate the domestic market.
(b) It is not in the best interests of the domestic economy to allow mergers of companies.
(c) With competition law, it is easy to ensure a level playing field between domestic and foreign firms.
(d) For countries with open economy, Foreign Direct Investment is essential for growth.

PASSAGE - 161

The poor especially in market economies, need the strength that collectivities offer for creating more economic, social and political space for themselves, for enhancing their socio-economic well-being and voice, and as a protection against free market individualism. It has been argued that a group approach to farming, especially in the form of bottom up agricultural production collectivities, offers substantial scope for poverty alleviation and empowering the poor as well as enhancing agricultural productivity. To realize this potential, however, the groups would need to be voluntary in nature, small in size, participative in decision making and equitable in work sharing and benefit distribution. There are many notable examples of such collectivities to be found in varied contexts, such as in the transition economies. All of them bear witness to the possibility of successful cooperation under given conditions. And although the gender impact of the family cooperatives in the transition economies are uncertain, the Indian examples of women-only groups farming offer considerable potential for benefiting women.
[Prelims II- 2012]

483. Agricultural collectivities such as group based farming can provide the rural poor
1. empowerment.
2. increased agricultural productivity.
3. safeguard against exploitative markets.
4. surplus production of agricultural commodities.
Select the correct answer using the codes given below:
(a) 1, 2, 3 and 4
(b) 1, 2 and 3 only
(c) 2 and 4 only
(d) 1, 3 and 4 only

484. What does the author imply by "gender impact"?
(a) Women are doubtful participants in cooperatives.
(b) Family cooperatives may not include women.
(c) Women benefiting from group farming.
(d) Women's role in transition economies is highly restrictive.

485. Consider the following assumptions:
1. It is imperative for transition economies to have agricultural collectivities.
2. Agricultural productivity can be increased by group approach to farming.
With reference to the above passage, which of these assumptions is/are valid?
(a) 1 only
(b) 2 only
(c) Both 1 and 2
(d) Neither 1 nor 2

PASSAGE - 162

In a typical Western liberal context, deepening of democracy invariably leads to consolidation of 'liberal values'. In the Indian context, democratization is translated into greater involvement of people not as 'individuals' which is a staple to liberal discourse, but as communities or groups. Individuals are getting involved in the public sphere not as 'atomized' individuals but as members of primordial communities drawn on religious or caste identity. Community-identity seems to be the governing force. It is not therefore surprising that the so-called peripheral groups continue to maintain their identities with reference to the social groups (caste, religion or sect) to which they belong while getting involved in the political processes despite the fact that their political goals remain more or less identical. By helping to articulate the political voice of the marginalized, democracy in India has led to 'a loosening of social strictures' and empowered the peripherals to be confident of their ability to improve the socio-economic conditions in which they are placed. This is a significant political process that had led to a silent revolution through a meaningful transfer of power from the upper caste elites to various subaltern groups within the democratic framework of public governance.

[Prelims II- 2012]

486. According to the passage, what does "deepening of democracy" mean in the Western context?
- (a) Consolidation of group and class identities.
- (b) Democratization translated as greater involvement of people.
- (c) Democratization as greater involvement of 'atomized' individuals in the public sphere.
- (d) None of the statements (a), (b) and (c) given above is correct in this context.

487. Greater democratization in India has not necessarily led to
- (a) the dilution of caste and communal identities in the public sphere.
- (b) irrelevance of community identity as a governing force in Indian politics.
- (c) marginalization of elite groups in society.
- (d) relative unimportance of hereditary identities over class identities.

488. What is the "silent revolution" that has occurred in the Indian democratic process?
- (a) Irrelevance of caste and class hierarchies in political processes.
- (b) Loosening of social strictures in voting behaviour and patterns.
- (c) Social change through transfer of power from upper caste elites to subaltern groups.
- (d) All the statements (a), (b) and (c) given above are correct in this context.

PASSAGE - 163

Ecological research over the last quarter of the century has established the deleterious effects of habitat fragmentation due to mining, highways and such other intrusions on forests. When a large block of forests gets fragmented into smaller bits, the edges of all these bits come into contact with human activities resulting in the degradation of the entire forests. Continuity of forested landscapes and corridors gets disrupted affecting several extinction-prone species of wildlife. Habitat fragmentation is therefore considered as the most serious threat to biodiversity conservation. Ad hoc grants of forest lands to mining companies coupled with rampant illegal mining is aggravating this threat.

[Prelims II- 2013]

489. What is the central focus of this passage ?
- (a) Illegal mining in forests
- (b) Extinction of wildlife
- (c) Conservation of nature
- (d) Disruption of habitat

490. What is the purpose of maintaining the continuity of forested landscapes and corridors?
1. Preservation of biodiversity.
2. Management of mineral resources.
3. Grant of forest lands for human activities.

Select the correct answer using the codes given below.
- (a) 1 only
- (b) 1 and 2
- (c) 2 and 3
- (d) 1, 2 and 3

PASSAGE - 164

The law in many parts of the world increasingly restricts the discharge of agricultural slurry into watercourses. The simplest and often the most economically sound practice returns the material to the land as semisolid manure or as sprayed slurry. This dilutes its concentration in the environment to what might have occurred in a more primitive and sustainable types of agriculture and converts pollutant into fertilizer. Soil microoganisms decompose the organic components of sewage and slurry and most of the mineral nutrients become available to be absorbed again by the vegetation.

The excess input of nutrients, both nitrogen and phosphorus – based, agricultural runoff (and human sewage) has caused many 'healthy' *oligotrophic* lakes (low nutrient concentrations, low plant productivity with abundant water weeds, and clear water) to change to *eutrophic* condition where high nutrient inputs lead to high phytoplankton productivity (sometimes dominated by bloom-forming toxic species). This makes the water turbid, eliminates large plants and, in the worst situations, leads to anoxia and fish kills; so called *cultural* eutrophication. Thus, important ecosystem services are lost, including the provisioning service of wild-caught fish and the cultural services associated with recreation.

The process of cultural eutrophication of lakes has been understood for some time. But only recently did scientists notice huge 'dead zones' in the oceans near river outlets., particularly those draining large catchment areas such as the Mississippi in North America and the Yangtze in China. The nutrient-enriched water flows through streams, rivers and lakes, and eventually to the estuary and ocean where the ecological impact may be huge, killing virtually all invertebrates and fish in areas up to $70,000 \text{ km}^2$ in extent. More than 150 sea areas worldwide are now regularly starved of oxygen as a result of decomposition of algal blooms, fuelled particularly by nitrogen from agricultural runoff of fertilizers and sewage from large cities. Oceanic dead zones are typically associated with industrialized nations and usually lie off countries that subsidize their agriculture, encouraging farmers to increases productivity and use more fertilizer.

[Prelims II- 2013]

491. According to the passage, why should the discharge of agricultural slurry into watercourses be restricted?
1. Losing nutrients in this way is not a good practice economically.
2. Watercourses do not contain the microorganisms that can decompose organic components of agricultural slurry.
3. The discharge may lead to the eutrophication of water bodies.

Select the correct answer using the codes given below:
- (a) 1 only
- (b) 2 and 3 only
- (c) 1 and 3 only
- (d) 1, 2 and 3

492. The passage refers to the conversion of "pollutant to fertilizer". What is pollutant and what is fertilizer in this context?
- (a) Decomposed organic component of slurry is pollutant and microorganisms in soil constitute fertilizer.
- (b) Discharged agricultural slurry is pollutant and decomposed slurry in soil is fertilizer.

   (c)   Sprayed slurry is pollutant and watercourses is fertilizer.

   (d)   None of the above expressions is correct in this context.

493. According to the passage, what are the effects of indiscriminate use of fertilizers?

   1.   Addition of pollutants to the soil and water.

   2.   Destruction of decomposer microorganism in soil.

   3.   Nutrient enrichment of water bodies.

   4.   Creation of algal blooms.

Select the correct answer from the codes given below:

   (a)   1, 2 and 3 only   (b)   1 , 3 and 4 only

   (c)   2 and 4 only   (d)   1, 2, 3 and 4

494. What is/are the characteristics of a water body with cultural eutrophication?

   1.   Loss of ecosystem services

   2.   Loss of flora and fauna

   3.   Loss of mineral nutrients

Select the correct answer using the code given below:

   (a)   1 only   (b)   1 and 2 only

   (c)   2 and 3 only   (d)   1, 2 and 3

495. What is the central theme of this passage?

   (a)   Appropriate legislation is essential to protect the environment.

   (b)   Modern agriculture is responsible for the destruction of environment.

   (c)   Improper waste disposal from agriculture can destroy the aquatic ecosystems.

   (d)   Use of chemical fertilizers is indesirable in agriculture.

PASSAGE - 165

The miseries of the world cannot be cured by physical help only. Until man's nature changes, his physical needs will always arise, and miseries will always be felt, and no amount of physical help will remove them completely. The only solution of the problem is to make mankind pure. Ignorance is the mother of evil and of all the misery we see. Let men have light, let them be pure and spiritually strong and educated; then alone will misery cease in the world. We may convert every house in the country into a charitable asylum, we may fill the land with hospitals, but human misery will continue until man's character changes.

[Prelims II- 2013]

496. According to the passage, which of the following statements is most likely to be true as the reason for man's miseries?

   (a)   The poor economic and social conditions prevailing in society.

   (b)   The refusal on the part of man to change his character.

   (c)   The absence of physical and material help from his society.

   (d)   Ever increasing physical needs due to changing social structure.

497. With reference to the passage, the following assumptions have been made"

   1.   The author gives primary importance to physical and material help in eradicating human misery.

   2.   Charitable homes, hospitals, etc. can remove human misery to a great extent.

Which of the assumption is/are valid?

   (a)   1 only   (b)   2 only

   (c)   Both 1 and 2   (d)   Neither 1 nor 2

PASSAGE - 166

The subject of democracy has become severely muddled because of the way the rhetoric surrounding it has been used in recent years. There is, increasingly, an oddly confused dichotomy between those who want to 'impose' democracy on countries in the non-Western world (in these countries' 'own interest', of course) and those who are opposed to such 'imposition' (because of the respect for the countries' 'own ways'). But the entire language of 'imposition', used by both sides, is extraordinarily inappropriate since it makes the implicit assumption that democracy belongs exclusively to the West, taking it to be a quintessentialy 'Wester' idea which has originated and flourished only in the West.

But the thesis and the pessimism it generates about the possibility of democratic practice in the world would be extremely hard to justify. There were several experiments in local democracy in ancient India. Indeed, in understanding the roots of democracy in the world, we have to take an interest in the history of people participation and public reasoning in different parts of the world. We have to look beyond thinking of democracy only in terms of European and American evolution. We would fail to understand the pervasive demands for participatory living, on which Aristotle spoke with far-reaching insight, if we take democracy to be a kind of a specialized cultural product of the West.

It cannot, of course, be doubted that the institutional structure of the contemporary practice of democracy is largely the product of European and American experience over the last few centuries. This is extremely important to recognize since these developments in institutional formats were immensely innovative and ultimately effective. There can be little doubt that there is a major 'Western' achievement here.   *[Prelims II- 2013]*

498. Which of the following is closest to the view of democracy as mentioned in the above passage?

   (a)   The subject of democracy is a muddle due to a desire to portray it as a Western concept, 'alien' to non-Western countries.

   (b)   The language of imposition of democracy is inappropriate. There is, however, a need to consider this concept in the backdrop of culture of 'own ways' of non-Western society.

   (c)   While democracy is not essentially a Western idea belonging exclusively to the West, the institutional structure of current democratic practices has been their contribution.

   (d)   None of the statements (a), (b) and (c) given above is correct.

499. With reference to the passage, the following assumption have been made:

   1.   Many of the non-Western countries are unable to have democracy because they take democracy to be a specialized cultural product of the West.

   2.   Western countries are always trying to impose democracy on non-Western countries.

Which of the above is/are valid assumption/assumptions?

   (a)   1 only   (b)   1 only

   (c)   Both 1 and 2   (d)   Neither 1 nor 2

PASSAGE - 167

Corporate governance is based on principles such as conducting the business with all integrity and fairness, being transparent with regard to all transactions, making all the necessary disclosures and decisions, complying with all the laws of the land, accountability and responsibility towards the stakeholders and commitment to conducting business in an ethical manner. Another point which is highlighted on corporate governance is the need for those in control to be able to distinguish between what are personal and corporate funds while managing a company.

Fundamentally, there is a level of confidence that is associated with a company that is known to have good corporate governance. The presence of an active group of independent directors on the board contributes a great deal towards ensuring confidence in the market. Corporate governance is known to be one of the criteria that foreign institutional investors are increasingly depending on when deciding on which companies to invest in. It is also known to have a positive influence on the share price of the company. Having a clean image on the corporate governance front could also make it easier for companies to source capital at more reasonable costs. Unfortunately, corporate governance often becomes the centre of discussion only after the exposure of a large scam.   *[Prelims II- 2013]*

500. According to the passage, which of the following should be the practice/practices in good corporate governance?
1. Companies should always comply with labour and tax laws of the land.
2. Every company in the country should have a government representative as one of the independent directors on the board to ensure transparency.
3. The manager of a company should never invest his personal funds in the company.

Select the correct answer using the codes given below:
(a) 1 only   (b) 2 and 3 only
(c) 1 and 3 only   (d) 1, 2 and 3

501. According to the passage, which of the following is/are the major benefit/benefits of good corporate governance?
1. Good corporate governance leads to increase in share price of the company.
2. A company with good corporate governance always increases its business turnover rapidly.
3. Good corporate governance is the main criterion for foreign institutional investors when they decide to buy a company.

Select the correct answer using the codes given below:
(a) 1 only   (b) 2 and 3 only
(c) 1 and 3 only   (d) 1, 2 and 3

PASSAGE - 168

Malnutrition most commonly occurs between the ages of six months and two years. This happens despite the child's food requirements being less than that of an older child. Malnutrition is often attributed to poverty, but it has been found that even in households where adults eat adequate quantities of food, more than 50 per cent of children-under-five do not consume enough food. The child's dependence on someone else to feed him/her is primarily responsible for the malnutrition. Very often the mother is working and the responsibility of feeding the young child is left to an older sibling. It is therefore crucial to increase awareness regarding the child's food needs and how to satisfy them.

[Prelims II- 2013]

502. According to the passage, malnutrition in children can be reduced.
(a) if the children have regular intake of food
(b) after they cross the age of five.
(c) if the food needs of younger children are known.
(d) if the responsibility of feeding younger children is given to adults.

503. According to the author, poverty is not the main cause of malnutrition, but the fact that
1. taking care of younger ones is not a priority for working mothers.
2. awareness of nutritional needs is not propagated by the Public Health authorities.

Select the correct answer using the codes given below:
(a) 1 only   (b) 2 only
(c) Both 1 and 2   (d) Neither 1 nor 2

PASSAGE - 169

A number of empirical studies find that farmers are risk-averse, though only moderately in many cases. There is also evidence to show that farmers' risk aversion results in cropping patterns and input use designed to reduce risk rather than to maximize income. Farmers adopt a number of strategies to manage and cope with agricultural risks. These include practices like crop and field diversification, non-farm 'employment storage of stocks and strategic migration of family members. There are also institutions ranging from share tenancy to kinship, extended family and informal credit agencies. One major obstacle to risk sharing by farmers is that the same type of risks can affect a large number of farmers in the region. Empirical studies show that the traditional methods are not adequate. Hence there is a need for policy interventions, especially measures that cut across geographical regions.

Polices may aim at tackling agricultural risks directly or indirectly. Examples of risk-specific policies are crop insurance, price stabilization and the development of varieties resistant to pests and diseases. Policies which affect risk indirectly are irrigation, subsidized credit and access to information. No single risk-specific policy is sufficient to reduce risk and is without side-effects, whereas policies not specific to risk influence the general situation and affect risks only indirectly. Crop insurance, as a policy measure to tackle agricultural risk directly, deserves careful consideration in the Indian context and in many other developing countries – because the majority of farmers depend on rain-fed agriculture and in many areas yield variability is the predominant cause of their income instability.   *[Prelims II- 2013]*

504. The need for policy intervention mitigate risks in agriculture is because
(a) farmers are extremely risk-averse.
(b) farmers do not know how to mitigate risks.
(c) the methods adopted by farmers and existing risk sharing institutions are not adequate.
(d) majority of farmers depend on rain-fed agriculture.

505. Which of the following observations emerges from the above passage?
- (a) One can identify a single policy that can reduce risk without any side-effect.
- (b) No single task-specific policy is sufficient to reduce agricultural risk.
- (c) Policies which affect risk indirectly can eliminate it.
- (d) Government's policy intervention can mitigate agricultural risk completely.

PASSAGE - 170

Financial markets in India have acquired greater depth and liquidity over the years. Steady reforms since 1991 have led to growing linkages and integration of the Indian economy and its financial system with the global economy. Weak global economic prospects and continuing uncertainties in the international financial markets therefore, have had their impact on the emerging market economies. Sovereign risk concerns, particularly in the Euro area, affected financial markets for the greater part of the year, with the contagion of Greece's soveregin debt problem spreading to India and other economies by way of higher-than-normal levels of volatility.

The funding constraints in international financial markets could impact both the availability and cost of foreign funding for banks and corporates. Since the Indian financial system is bank-dominated, banks' ability to withstand stress is critical to overall financial stability. Indian banks, however, remain robust, notwithstanding a decline in capital to risk-weighted assets ratio and a rise in non-performing asset levels in the recent past. Capital adequacy levels remain above the regulatory requirements. The financial market infrastructure continues to function without any major disruption. With further globalization, consolidation, deregulation, and diversification of the financial system, the banking business may become more complex and riskier. Issues like risk and liquidity management and enhancing skill therefore assume greater significance. *[Prelims II- 2013]*

506. According to the passage, the financial markets in the emerging market economies including India had the adverse impact in recent years due to
1. weak global economic prospects.
2. uncertainties in the international financial markets.
3. sovereign risk concerns in the Euro area.
4. bad monsoons and the resultant crop loss.
Select the correct answer using the code given below:
- (a) 1 and 2 only
- (b) 1, 2 and 3
- (c) 2 and 3 only
- (d) 2, 3 and 4

507. The Indian financial markets are affected by global changes mainly due to the
- (a) increased inflow of remittances from abroad
- (b) enormous increases in the foreign exchange reserves.
- (c) growing global linkages and integration of the Indian financial markets.

508. According to the passage, in the Indian financial system, bank's ability to withstand stress is critical to ensure overall financial stability because Indian financial system is
- (a) controlled by the Government of India
- (b) less integrated with banks.
- (c) controlled by the Reserve of Bank of India.
- (d) dominated by Banks.

509. Risk and liquidity management assumes more importance in the Indian banking system in future due to
1. further globalization.
2. more consolidation and deregulation of financial system
3. further diversification of the financial system.
4. more financial inclusion in the economy.
Select the correct answer using the code given below:
- (a) 1, 2 and 3
- (b) 2, 3 and 4
- (c) 1 and 2 only
- (d) 3 and 4 only

PASSAGE - 171

Crude mineral oil comes out of the earth as a thick brown or black liquid with a strong smell. It is a complex mixture of many different substances, each with its own individual qualities. Most of them are combinations of hydrogen and carbon in varying proportions. Such hydrocarbons are also found in other forms such as bitumen, asphalt and natural gas. Mineral oil originates from the carcasses of tiny animals and from plants that live in the sea. Over millions of years, these dead creatures form large deposits under the sea-bed; and ocean currents cover them with a blanket of sand and silt. As this mineral hardens, it becomes sedimentary rock and effectively shuts out the oxygen, so preventing the complete decomposition of the marine deposits underneath. The layers of sedimentary rock become thicker and heavier. Their pressure produces heat, which transforms the tiny carcasses into crude oil in a process that is still going on today. *[Prelims II- 2013]*

510. Mineral oil deposits under the sea do not get completely decomposed because they
- (a) are constantly washed by the ocean currents.
- (b) become rock and prevent oxygen from entering them.
- (c) contain a mixture of hydrogen and carbon.
- (d) are carcasses of organisms lying in saline conditions.

511. Sedimentary rock leads to the formation of oil deposits because
- (a) there are no saline conditions below it.
- (b) it allows some dissolved oxygen to enter the dead organic matter below it.
- (c) weight of overlying sediment layers causes the production of heat.
- (d) it contains the substances that catalyze the chemical reactions required to change dead organisms into oil.

PASSAGE - 172

Many nations now place their faith in capitalism and governments choose it as the strategy to create wealth for their people. The spectacular economic growth seen in Brazil, China and India after the liberalisation of their economies is proof of its enormous potential and success. However, the global banking crisis and the economic recession have left many bewildered. The debates tend to focus on free market operations and forces, their efficiency and their ability for self correction. Issues of justice, integrity and honesty are rarely elaborated to highlight the failure of the global banking system. The apologists of the system continue to justify the success of capitalism and argue that the recent crisis was a blip. Their arguments betray an ideological bias with the assumptions that an unregulated market is fair and competent, and that the exercise of private greed will be in the larger public interest.

Few recognize the bidirectional relationship between capitalism and greed; that each reinforces the other. Surely, a more honest conceptualisation of the conflicts of interest among the rich and powerful players who have benefited from the system, their biases and ideology is needed; the focus on the wealth creation should also highlight the resultant gross inequity.   *[Prelims II- 2013]*

512. The apologists of the "Free Market System", according to the passage, believe in

    (a)   market without control by government authorities.

    (b)   market without protection by the government.

    (c)   ability of market to self correct.

    (d)   market for free goods and services.

513. With reference to "ideological bias", the passage implies that

    (a)   free market is fair but not competent.

    (b)   free market is not fair but competent.

    (c)   free market is fair and competent.

    (d)   free market is neither fair nor biased.

514. The exercise of private greed will be in the larger public interest" from the passage

    1.   refers to the false ideology of capitalism.

    2.   underlies the righteous claims of the free market.

    3.   shows the benevolent face of capitalism.

    4.   ignores resultant gross inequity.

    Which of the statements given above is/are correct ?

    (a)   1 only   (b)   2 and 3

    (c)   1 and 4   (d)   4 only

PASSAGE - 173

Net profits are only 2.2% of their total assets for central public sector undertakings, lower than for the private corporate sector. While the public sector or the State-led entrepreneurship played an important role in triggering India's industrialization, our evolving development needs, comparatively less-than-satisfactory performance of the public sector enterprises, the maturing of our private sector, a much larger social base now available for expanding entrepreneurship and the growing institutional capabilities to enforce competition policies would suggest that the time has come to review the role of public sector.

What should the portfolio composition of the government be? It should not remain static all times. The airline industry works well as a purely private affair. At the opposite end, rural roads, whose sparse traffic makes tolling unviable, have to be on the balance-sheet of the State. If the government did not own rural roads, they would not exist. Similarly, public health capital in our towns and cities will need to come from the public sector. Equally, preservation and improvement of forest cover will have to be a new priority for the public sector assets.

Take the example of steel. With near-zero tariffs, India is a globally competitive market for the metal. Indian firms export steel into the global market, which demonstrates there is no gap in technology. Indian companies are buying up global steel companies, which shows there is no gap in capital availability. Under these conditions, private ownership works best.

Private ownership is clearly desirable in regulated industries, ranging from finance to infrastructure, where a government agency performs the function of regulation and multiple competing firms are located in the private sector. Here, the simple and clean solution

- government as the umpire and the private sector as the players is what works best. In many of these industries, we have a legacy of government ownership, where productivity tends to be lower, fear of bankruptcy is absent, and the risk of asking for money from the tax payer is ever present. There is also the conflict of interest between government as an owner and as the regulator. The formulation and implementation of competition policy will be more vigorous and fair if government companies are out of action.

[Prelims II- 2014]

515. According to the passage, what is/are the reason/reasons for saying that the time has come to review the role of public sector ?

    1.   Now public sector has lost its relevance in the industrialization process.

    2.   Public sector does not perform satisfactorily.

    3.   Entrepreneurship in private sector is expanding.

    4.   Effective competition policies are available now.

    Which of the statements given above is/are correct in the given context ?

    (a)   1 and 3 only   (b)   2 only

    (c)   2, 3 and 4 only   (d)   1, 2, 3 and 4

516. According to the passage, rural roads should be in the domain of public sector only. Why ?

    (a)   Rural development work is the domain of government only.

    (b)   Private sector cannot have monetary gains in this.

    (c)   Government takes money from tax payers and hence it is the responsibility of government only.

    (d)   Private sector need not have any social responsibility.

517. The portfolio composition of the government refers to

    (a)   Public sector assets quality.

    (b)   Investment in liquid assets.

    (c)   Mix of government investment in different industrial sectors.

    (d)   Buying Return on Investment yielding capital assets.

518. The author prefers government as the umpire and private sector as players because

    (a)   Government prescribes norms for a fair play by the private sector.

    (b)   Government is the ultimate in policy formulation.

    (c)   Government has no control over private sector players.

    (d)   None of the above statements is correct in this context.

PASSAGE - 174

Climate change poses potentially devastating effects on India's agriculture. While the overall parameters of climate change are increasingly accepted - a 1°C average temperature increase over the next 30 years, sea level rise of less than 10 cm in the same period, and regional monsoon variations and corresponding droughts - the impacts in India are likely to be quite site and crop specific. Some crops may respond favourably to the changing conditions, others may not. This emphasizes the need to promote agricultural research and create maximum flexibility in the system to permit adaptations.

The key ingredient for "drought proofing" is the managed recharge of aquifers. To ensure continued yields of important staple crops (e.g. wheat), it may also be necessary to shift the locations where these crops are grown, in response to temperature changes as well as to water availability. The latter will be a key factor in making long term investment decisions.

For example, water runoff from the Himalayas is predicted to increase over the next 30 years as glaciers melt, but then decline substantially thereafter. It will be critical to provide incentives to plan for these large-scale shifts in agro-ecological conditions. India needs to make long term investment in research and development in agriculture. India is likely to experience changed weather patterns in future. *[Prelims II- 2013]*

519. Consider the following statements :
Climate change may force the shifting of locations of the existing crops due to
1. melting of glaciers.
2. water availability and temperature suitability at other locations.
3. poor productivity of crops.
4. wider adaptability of crop plants.
Which of the statements given above are correct ?
(a) 1,2 and 3   (b) 2 and 3 only
(c) 1 and 4 only   (d) 1,2, 3 and 4

520. According to the passage, why is it important to promote agricultural research in India?
(a) To predict variations in monsoon patterns and to manage water resources
(b) To make long term investment decisions for economic growth
(c) To facilitate wider adaptability of crops
(d) To predict drought conditions and to recharge aquifers

PASSAGE - 175

It is essential that we mitigate the emissions of greenhouse gases and thus avoid some of the worst impacts of climate change that would take place in coming years and decades. Mitigation would require a major shift in the way we produce and consume energy. A shift away from overwhelming dependence on fossil fuels is now long overdue, but unfortunately, technological development has been slow and inadequate largely because government policies have not promoted investments in research and development, myopically as a result of relatively low prices of oil. It is now, therefore, imperative for a country like India treating the opportunity of harnessing renewable energy on a large scale as a national imperative. This country is extremely well endowed with solar, wind and biomass sources of energy. Where we have lagged, unfortunately, is in our ability to develop and to create technological solutions for harnessing these resources.

One particular trajectory for carryingout stringent mitigation of greenhouse gas emissions assessed by the Intergovernmental Panel on Climate Change (IPCC) clearly shows the need for ensuring that global emissions of greenhouse gases peak no later than 2015 and reduce rapidly thereafter. The cost associated with such a trajectory is truly modest and would amount, in the estimation of IPCC, to not more than 3 percent of the global GDP in 2030. In other words, the level of prosperity that the world would have reached without mitigation would at worst be postponed by a few months or a year at the most. This is clearly not a very high price to pay for protecting hundreds of millions of people from the worst risks associated with climate change. Any such effort, however, would require lifestyles to change appropriately also. Mitigation of greenhouse gas emissions is not a mere technological fix, and clearly requires changes in lifestyles and transformation of a country's economic structure,

whereby effective reduction in emissions is brought about, such as through the consumption of much lower quantities of animal protein. The Food and Agriculture Organization (FAO) has determined that the emissions from the livestock sector amount to 18 percent of the total. The reduction of emissions from this source is entirely in the hands of human beings, who have never questioned the impacts that their dietary habits of consuming more and more animal protein are bringing about. Mitigation overall has huge co-benefits, such as lower air pollution and health benefits, higher energy security and greater employment. *[Prelims II- 2014]*

521. According to the passage, which of the following would help in the mitigation of greenhouse gases ?
1. Reducing the consumption of meat
2. Rapid economic liberalization
3. Reducingthe consumerism
4. Modern management practices of livestock
Select the correct answer using the code given below :
(a) 1,2 and 3   (b) 2, 3 and 4
(c) 1 and 3 only   (d) 2 and 4 only

522. Why do we continue to depend on the fossil fuels heavily?
1. Inadequate technological development
2. Inadequate funds for research and development
3. Inadequate availability of alternative sources of energy
Select the correct answer using the code given below :
(a) 1 only   (b) 2 and 3 only
(c) 1 and 3 only   (d) 1,2 and 3

523. According to the passage, how does the mitigation of greenhouse gases help us ?
1. Reduces expenditure on public health
2. Reduces dependence on livestock
3. Reduces energy requirements
4. Reduces rate of global climate change
Select the correct answer using the code given below :
(a) 1,2 and 3   (b) 1, 3 and 4
(c) 2, 3 and 4   (d) 1 and 4 only

524. What is the **essential** message of the passage ?
(a) We continue to depend on fossil fuels heavily
(b) Mitigation of the greenhouse gases is imperative
(c) We must invest in research and development
(d) People must change their lifestyle

PASSAGE - 176

In recent times, India has grown fast not only compared to its own past but also incomparison with other nations. But there cannot be any room for complacency because it is possible for the Indian economy to develop even faster and also to spread the benefits of this growth more widely than has been done thus far. Before going into details of the kinds of micro-structural changes that we need to conceptualize and then proceed to implement, it is worthwhile elaborating on the idea of inclusive growth that constitutes the defining concept behind this Government's various economic policies and decisions. A nation interested in inclusive growth views the same growth differently depending on whether the gains of the growth are heaped primarily on a small segment or shared widely by the population. The latter is cause for celebration but not the former. In other words, growth must not be treated as an end in itself but as an instrument for spreading prosperity to all. India's own past experience and the experience of other nations suggests that growth is necessary for eradicating poverty but it is not a sufficient condition. In other words, policies for promoting growth need to be complemented with policies to ensure that more and more people join in the growth process and, further, that there are mechanisms in place to redistribute some of the gains to those who are unable to partake in the market process and, hence, get left behind.

A simple way of giving this idea of inclusive growth a sharper form is to measure a nation's progress in terms of the progress of its poorest segment, for instance the bottom 20 per cent of the population. One could measure the per capita income of the bottom quintile of the population and also calculate the growth rate of income; and evaluate our economic success in terms of these measures that pertain to the poorest segment. This approach is attractive because it does not ignore growth like some of the older heterodox criteria did. It simply looks at the growth of income of the poorest sections of the population. It also ensures that those who are outside of the bottom quintile do not get ignored. If that were done, then those people would in all likelihood drop down into the bottom quintile and so would automatically become a direct target of our policies. Hence the criterion being suggested here is a statistical summing up of the idea of inclusive growth, which, in turn, leads to two corollaries : to wish that India must strive to achieve high growth and that we must work to ensure that the weakest segments benefit from the growth.

[Prelims II- 2014]

525. The author's central focus is on.
- (a) applauding India's economic growth not only against its own past performance, but against other nations.
- (b) emphasizing the need for economic growth which is the sole determinant of a country's prosperity.
- (c) emphasizing inclusive growth where gains of growth are shared widely by the population.
- (d) emphasizing high growth.

526. The author supports policies which will help
- (a) develop economic growth.
- (b) better distribution of incomes irrespective of rate of growth.
- (c) develop economic growth and redistribute economic gains to those getting left behind.
- (d) put an emphasis on the development of the poorest segments of society.

527. Consider the following statements :
According to the author, India's economy has grown but there is no room for complacency as
1. growth eradicates poverty.
2. growth has resulted in prosperity for all.
Which of the statements given above is/are correct ?
- (a) 1 only
- (b) 2 only
- (c) Both 1 and 2
- (d) Neither 1 nor 2

PASSAGE - 177

It is easy for the government to control State-owned companies through nods and winks. So what really needs to be done as a first step is to put petrol pricing on a transparent formula - if the price of crude is x and the exchange rate y, then every month or fortnight, the government announces a maximum price of petrol, which anybody can work out from the x and the y. The rule has to be worked out to make sure that the oil-marketing companies can, in general, cover their costs. This will mean that if one company can innovate and cut costs, it will make greater profits. Hence,

firms will be more prone to innovate and be efficient under this system. Once the rule is announced, there should be no interference by the government. If this is done for a while, private companies will re-enter this market. And once a sufficient number of them are in the fray, we can remove the rule-based pricing and leave it truly to the market (subject to, of course, the usual regulations of anti-trust and other competition laws).

[Prelims II- 2014]

528. Consider the following statements :
According to the passage, an oil company can make greater profits, if a transparent formula for petrol pricing is announced every fortnight or month, by
1. promoting its sales.
2. undertaking innovation.
3. cutting costs.
4. selling its equity shares at higher prices.
Which of the statements given above is/are correct ?
- (a) 1 only
- (b) 2 and 3
- (c) 3 and 4
- (d) 1, 2 and 4

529. Consider the following statements :
According to the passage, private oil companies re-enter the oil producing market if
1. a transparent rule-based petrol pricing exists.
2. there is no government interference in the oil producing market.
3. subsidies are given by the government
4. regulations of anti-trust are removed.
Which of the statements given above are correct ?
- (a) 1 and 2
- (b) 2 and 3
- (c) 3 and 4
- (d) 2 and 4

PASSAGE - 178

The Himalayan ecosystem is highly vulnerable to damage, both due to geological reasons and on account of the stress caused by increased pressure of population, exploitation of natural resources and other related challenges. These aspects may be exacerbated due to the impact of climate change. It is possible that climate change may adversely impact the Himalayan ecosystem through increased temperature, altered precipitation patterns, episodes of drought and biotic influences. This would not only impact the very sustenance of the indigenous communities in uplands but also the life of downstream dwellers across the country and beyond. Therefore, there is an urgent need for giving special attention to sustain the Himalayan ecosystem. This would require conscious efforts for conserving all the representative systems. Further, it needs to be emphasized that the endemics with restricted distribution, and most often with specialized habitat requirements, are among the most vulnerable elements. In this respect the Himalayan biodiversity hotspot, with rich endemic diversity, is vulnerable to climate change. The threats include possible loss of genetic resources and species, habitats and concomitantly a decrease in ecosystem services. Therefore, conservation of endemic elements in representative ecosystems/ habitats assumes a great significance while drawing conservation plans for the region.

Towards achieving the above, we will have to shift toward contemporary conservation approaches, which include a paradigm of landscape level interconnectivity between protected area systems. The concept advocates a shift from the species-habitat focus to an inclusive focus on expanding the biogeographic range so that natural adjustments to climate change can proceed without being restrictive.   *[Prelims II- 2014]*

530. Consider the following statements :

According to the passage, the adverse impact of climate change on an ecosystem can be a

1. permanent disappearance of some of its flora and fauna.
2. permanent disappearance of ecosystem itself.

Which of the statements given above is/are correct ?

(a) 1 only   (b) 2 only
(c) Both 1 and 2   (d) Neither 1 nor 2

531. Which one of the following statements best implies the need to shift toward contemporary conservation approach?

(a) Exploitation of natural resources causes a stress on the Himalayan ecosystem.
(b) Climate change alters precipitation patterns, causes episodes of drought and biotic interference.
(c) The rich biodiversity, including endemic diversity, makes the Himalayan region a biodiversity hotspot.
(d) The Himalayan biogeographic region should be enabled to adapt to climate change smoothly.

532. What is the most important message conveyed by the passage ?

(a) Endemism is a characteristic feature of Himalayan region.
(b) Conservation efforts should emphasize on biogeographic ranges rather than on some species or habitats.
(c) Climate change has adverse impact on the Himalayan ecosystem.
(d) Without Himalayan ecosystem, the life of the communities of uplands and downstreams will have no sustenance.

533. With reference to the passage, the following assumptions have been made :

1. To maintain natural ecosystems, exploitation of natural resources should be completely avoided.
2. Not only anthropogenic but also natural reasons can adversely affect ecosystems.
3. Loss of endemic diversity leads to the extinction of ecosystems.

Which of the above assumptions is/are correct ?

(a) 1 and 2   (b) 2 only
(c) 2 and 3   (d) 3 only

PASSAGE - 179

It is often forgotten that globalization is not only about policies on international economic relationships and transactions, but has equally to do with domestic policies of a nation. Policy changes necessitated by meeting the internationally set conditions (by WTO etc.) of free trade and investment flows obviously affect domestic producers and investors. But the basic philosophy underlying globalization emphasizes absolute freedom to markets to determine prices and production and distribution patterns, and view government interventions as processes that create distortions and bring in inefficiency. Thus, public enterprises have to be privatized through disinvestments and sales; sectors and activities hitherto reserved for the public sector have to be opened to the private sector. This logic extends to the social services like education and health. Any restrictions on the adjustments in workforce by way of retrenchment of workers should also be removed and exit should be made easier by removing any restrictions on closures. Employment and wages should be governed by free play of market forces, as any measure to regulate them can discourage investment and also create inefficiency in production. Above all, in line with the overall philosophy of reduction in the role of the State, fiscal reforms should be undertaken to have generally low levels of taxation and government expenditure should be kept to the minimum to abide by the principle of fiscal prudence. All these are policy actions on the domestic front and are not directly related to the core items of the globalization agenda, namely free international flow of goods and finance.   *[Prelims II- 2014]*

534. According to the passage, under the globalization, government interventions are viewed as processes leading to

(a) distortions and inefficiency in the economy.
(b) optimum use of resources.
(c) more profitability to industries.
(d) free play of market forces with regard to industries.

535. According to the passage, the basic philosophy of globalization is to

(a) give absolute freedom to producers to determine prices and production.
(b) give freedom to producers to evolve distribution patterns.
(c) give absolute freedom to markets to determine prices, production and employment.
(d) give freedom to producers to import and export.

536. According to the passage, which of the following is/are necessary for ensuring globalization ?

1. Privatization of public enterprises
2. Expansionary policy of public expenditure
3. Free play of market forces to determine wages and employment
4. Privatization of social services like education and health

Select the correct answer using the code given below :

(a) 1 only   (b) 2 and 3 only
(c) 1, 3 and 4   (d) 2, 3 and 4

537. According to the passage, in the process of globalization the State should have

(a) expanding role.   (b) reducing role.
(c) statutory role.   (d) none of the above roles.

PASSAGE - 180

By 2050, the Earth's population will likely have swelled from seven to nine billion people. To fill all those stomachs - while accounting for shifting consumption patterns, climate change, and a finite amount of arable land and potable water – some experts say food production will have to double. How can we make the numbers add up? Experts say higher yielding crop varieties and more efficient farming methods will be crucial. So will waste reduction. Experts urge cities to reclaim nutrients and water from waste streams and preserve farmland. Poor countries, they say, can improve crop storage and packaging and rich nations could cut back on resource-intensive foods like meat.

538. Which one of the following statements best sums up the above passage? **[CSAT 2015]**
- (a) The population of the world is growing very fast.
- (b) Food security is a perennial problem only in developing countries.
- (c) The world does not have enough resources to meet the impending food scarcity.
- (d) Food security is increasingly a collective challenge.

PASSAGE - 181

The conflict between man and State is as old as State history. Although attempts have been made for centuries to bring about a proper adjustment between the competing claims of State and the individual, the solution seems to be' still far off. This is primarily because of the dynamic nature of human society where old values and ideas constantly yield place to new ones. It is obvious that if individuals are allowed to have absolute freedom of speech and action, the result would be chaos, ruin and anarchy.

539. The author's viewpoint can be best summed up in which of the following statements? **[CSAT 2015]**
- (a) The conflict between the claims of State and individual remains unresolved.
- (b) Anarchy and chaos are the obvious results of democratic traditions.
- (c) Old values, ideas and traditions persist despite the dynamic nature of human society.
- (d) Constitutional guarantee of freedom of speech is not in the interest of society.

PASSAGE - 182

We generally talk about democracy but when it comes to any particular thing, we prefer a belonging to our caste or community or religion. So long as we have this kind of temptation, our democracy will remain a phoney kind of democracy. We must be in a position to respect a man as a man and to extend opportunities for development to those who deserve them and not to those who happen to belong to our community or race. This fact of favouritism has been responsible for much discontent and ill-will in our country.

540. Which one of the following statements best sums up the above passage? **[CSAT 2015]**
- (a) Our country has a lot of diversity with its many castes, communities and religions.
- (b) True democracy could be established by providing equal opportunities to all.
- (c) So far none of us have actually understood the meaning of democracy.
- (d) It will never be possible for us to establish truly democratic governance in our country.

PASSAGE - 183

The existence/establishment of formal financial institutions that offer safe, reliable and alternative financial instruments is fundamental in mobilising savings. To save, individuals need access to safe and reliable financial institutions, such as banks, and to appropriate financial instruments and reasonable financial incentives. Such access is not always available to all people in developing countries like India and more so, in rural areas. Savings help poor households manage volatility in cash flow, smoothen consumption, and build working capital. Poor households without access to a formal savings mechanism encourage immediate spending temptations.

541. With reference to the above passage, consider the following statements:
1. Indian financial institutions do not offer any financial instruments to rural households to mobilise their savings.
2. Poor households tend to spend their earnings/savings due to lack of access to appropriate financial instruments.

Which of the statements given above is/are correct? **[CSAT 2015]**
- (a) 1 only
- (b) 2 only.
- (c) Both 1 and 2
- (d) Neither 1 nor 2

542. What is the crucial message conveyed in the passage?
- (a) Establish more banks. **[CSAT 2015]**
- (b) Increase the Gross Domestic Product (GDP) growth rate
- (c) Increase the interest rate of bank deposits
- (d) Promote financial inclusion

PASSAGE - 184

Historically, the biggest challenge to world agriculture has been to achieve a balance between demand for and supply of food. At the level of individual countries, the demand-supply balance can be a critical issue for a closed economy, especially if it is a populous economy and its domestic agriculture is not growing sufficiently enough to ensure food supplies, on an enduring basis; it is not so much and not always, of a constraint for an open, and growing economy, which has adequate exchange surpluses to buy food abroad. For the world as a whole, Spply-demand balance is always an inescapable prerequisite for warding off hunger and starvation. However, global availability of adequate supply does not necessarily mean that food would automatically move from countries of surplus to counteries of deficit if the latter lack in purchasing power. The uneven distribution of Hunger, starvation, under or malnourishment, etc., at the world-level, thus owes itself to the presence of empty-pock hungry mouths, overwhelmingly confined to the underdeveloped economies. Inasmuch as 'a two-square meal' is of elemental significance to basic human existence, the issue of worldwide supply` of food has been gaining significance, in recent times, both because the quantum and the composition of demand has been undergoing big changes, and because, in recent years, the capabilities individual countries to generate uninterrupted chain of food supplies have come under strain. Food production, marketing and prices, especially price-affordability by the poor in the developing world, have become global issues that need global thinking and global solutions.

543. According to the above passage, which of, the following are the fundamental solutions for the world food security problem?
1. Setting up more agro-based industries
2. Improving the price affordability by the poor
3. Regulating the conditions of marketing
4. Providing food subsidy to one and all

Select the correct answer using the code given below:
(a) 1 and 2
(b) 2 and 3 only
(c) 1, 3 an 4 only
(d) 1, 2, and 4

544. According to the above passage, the biggest challenge to world agriculture is:
(a) to find sufficient land for agriculture and to expand food processing industries
(b) to eradicate hunger in underdeveloped countries
(c) to achieve a balance between the production of food and non-food items
(d) to achieve a balance between demand for and supply of food

545. According to the above passage, which of the following helps/help in reducing hunger and starvation in the developing economies ?
1. Balancing demand and supply of food
2. Increasing imports of food
3. Increasing purchasing power of the poor
4. Changing the food consumption patterns and practices
Select the correct answer using the code given below:
(a) 1 only
(b) 2, 3 and 4 only
(c) 1 and 3 only
(d) 1, 2, 3 and 4

546. The issue of worldwide supply of food has gained importance mainly because of:
1. overgrowth of the population worldwide
2. sharp decline in the area of food production
3. limitation in the capabilities for sustained supply of food
Select the correct answer using the code given below:
(a) 1 and 2 only
(b) 3 only
(c) 2 and 3 only
(d) 1, 2 and 3

DIRECTIONS for the following 6 (six) items: *Read the following two passages and answer the items that follow each passage. Your answers to these items should be based on the passages only.*

PASSAGE - 185

Accountability, or the lack of it, in governance generally, and civil services, in particular, is a major factor underlying the deficiencies in governance and public administration. Designing an effective framework for accountability has been a key element of the reform agenda. A fundamental issue is whether civil services should be accountable to the political executive of the day or to society at large. In other words, how should internal and external accountability be reconciled? Internal accountability is sought to be achieved by internal performance monitoring, official supervision by bodies like the–Central–Vigilance Commission–and–Comptroller and Auditor– General, and judicial review of executive decisions. Articles 311 and 312 of the Indian Constitution provide job security and safeguards to the civil services, especially the All India Services. The framers of the Constitution had envisaged that provision of these safeguards would result in a civil service that is not totally subservient to the political executive but will have the strength to function in larger public interest. The need to balance internal and external accountability is thus built into the Constitution. The issue is where to draw the line. Over the years, the emphasis seems to have tilted in favour of greater internal accountability of the civil services to the political leaders of the day who in turn are expected to be externally accountable to the society at large through the election process. This system for seeking accountability to society has not worked out, and has led to several adverse consequences for governance.

Some special measures can be considered for improving accountability in civil services. Provisions of articles 311 and 312 should be reviewed and laws and regulations framed to ensure external accountability of civil services. The proposed Civil Services Bill seeks to address some of these requirements. The respective roles of professional civil services and the political executive should be defined so that professional managerial functions and management of civil services are depoliticized. For this purpose, effective statutory civil service boards should be created at the centre and in the states. Decentralization and devolution of authority to bring government and decision making closer to the people also helps to enhance accountability.

547. According to the passage, which of the following factor/ factors led to the adverse consequences for governance/ public administration?
1. Inability of civil services to strike a balance between internal and external accountabilities
2. Lack of sufficient professional training to the officers of All India Services
3. Lack of proper service benefits in civil services
4. Lack of Constitutional provisions to define the respective roles of professional civil services vis-a-vis political executive in this context
Select the correct answer using the code given below:
(a) 1 only
(b) 2 and 3 only
(c) 1 and 4 only
(d) 2, 3 and 4

548. With reference to the passage, the following assumptions have been made :
1. Political executive is an obstacle to the accountability of the civil services to the society
2. In the present framework of Indian polity, the political executive is no longer accountable to the society
Which of these assumptions is/are valid?
(a) 1 only
(b) 2 only
(c) Both 1 and 2
(d) Neither 1 nor 2

549. Which one of the following is the essential message implied by this passage?
(a) Civil services are not accountable to the society they are serving
(b) Educated and enlightened persons are not taking up political leadership
(c) The framers of the Constitution did not envisage the problems being encountered by the civil services
(d) There is a need and scope for reforms to improve the accountability of civil services

550. According to the passage, which one of the following is **not a** means of enhancing internal accountability of civil services?
- (a) Better job security and safeguards
- (b) Supervision by Central Vigilance Commission
- (c) Judicial review of executive decisions
- (d) Seeking accountability through enhanced participation by people in decision making process

PASSAGE - 186

In general, religious traditions stress our duty to god, or to some universal ethical principle. Our duties to one another derive from these. The religious concept of rights is primarily derived from our relationship to this divinity or principle and the implication it has on our other relationships. This correspondence between rights and duties is critical to any further understanding of justice. But, for justice to be practiced; viture, rights and duties cannot remain formal abstractions. They must be grounded in a community (common unity) bound together by a sense of common union (communion). Even as a personal virtue, this solidarity is essential to the practice and understanding of justice.

551. With reference to the passage, the following assumptions have been made :
1. Human relationships are derived from their religious traditions
2. Human beings can be duty bound only if they believe in god
3. Religious traditions are essential to practice and understand justice

Which of these assumption(s) is/are valid?
- (a) 1 only
- (b) 2 and 3 only
- (c) 1 and 3 only
- (d) 1, 2 and 3

552. Which one of the following is the crux of this passage?
- (a) Our duties to one another derive from our religious traditions
- (b) Having relationship to the divine principle is a great virtue
- (c) Balance between rights and duties is crucial to the delivery of justice in a society
- (d) Religious concept of rights is primarily derived from our relationship to god

---

DIRECTIONS for the following 5 (five) items : *Read the following two passages and answer the items that follow each passage. Your answers to these items should be based on the passages only.*

PASSAGE - 187

Biomass as fuel for power, heat, and transport has the highest mitigation potential of all renewable sources. It comes from agriculture and forest residues as well as from energy crops. The biggest challenge in using biomass residues is a long-term reliable supply delivered to the power plant at reasonable costs; the key problems are logistical constraints and the costs of fuel collection. Energy crops, if not managed properly, compete with food production and may have undesirable impacts on food prices. Biomass production is also sensitive to the physical impacts of a changing climate.

Projections of the future role of biomass are probably overestimated, given the limits to the sustainable biomass supply, unless breakthrough technologies substantially increase productivity. Climate -energy models project that biomass use could increase nearly four-fold to around 150 – 200 exajoules, almost a quarter of world primary energy in 2050. However the maximum sustainable technical potential of biomass resources (both residues and energy crops) without disruption of food and forest resources ranges from 80 – 170 exajoules a year by 2050, and only part of this is realistically and economically feasible. In addition, some climate models rely on biomass-based carbon capture and storage, an unproven technology, to achieve negative emissions and to buy some time during the first half of the century.

Some liquid biofuels such as corn-based ethanol, mainly for transport, may aggravate rather than ameliorate carbon emissions on a life-cycle basis. Second generation biofuels, based on ligno-cellulosic feedstocks – such as straw, bagasse, grass and wood – hold the promise of sustainable production that is high-yielding and emit low levels of greenhouse gases, but these are still in the R & D stage.

553. What is/are the present constraint/constraints in using biomass as fuel for power generation?
1. Lack of sustainable supply of biomass
2. Biomass production competes with food production
3. Bio-energy may not always be low carbon on a life-cycle basis

Select the correct answer using the code given below:
- (a) 1 and 2 only
- (b) 3 only
- (c) 2 and 3 only
- (d) 1, 2 and 3

554. Which of the following can lead to food security problem?
1. Using agricultural and forest residues as feedstock for power generation
2. Using biomass for carbon capture and storage
3. Promoting the cultivation of energy crops

Select the correct answer using the code given below:
- (a) 1 and 2 only
- (b) 3 only
- (c) 2 and 3 only
- (d) 1, 2 and 3

555. In the context of using biomass, which of the following is/are the characteristic/characteristics of the sustainable production of biofuel?
1. Biomass as a fuel for power generation could meet all the primary energy requirements of the world by 2050
2. Biomass as a fuel for power generation does not necessarily disrupt food and forest resources
3. Biomass as a fuel for power generation could help in achieving negative emissions, given certain nascent technologies

Select the correct answer using the code given below:
- (a) 1 and 2 only
- (b) 3 only
- (c) 2 and 3 only
- (d) 1, 2 and 3

556. With reference to the passage, following assumptions have been mad :
1. Some climate-energy models suggest that the use of biomass as a fuel for power generation helps in mitigating greenhouse gas emissions

2. It is not possible to use biomass as a fuel for power generation without disrupting food and forest resources

Which of these assumptions is/are valid?
(a) 1 only
(b) 2 only
(c) Both 1 and 2
(d) Neither 1 nor 2

PASSAGE - 188

A successful democracy depends upon widespread interest and participation in politics, in which voting is an essential part. To deliberately refrain from taking such an interest, and from voting, is a kind of implied anarchy; it is to refuse one's political responsibility while enjoying the benefits of a free political society.

557. This passage relates to   **[Prelim II-2017]**
(a) duty to vote
(b) right to vote
(c) freedom to vote
(d) right to participate in politics

PASSAGE - 189

In a free country, the man who reaches the position of leader is usually one of outstanding character and ability. Moreover, it is usually possible to foresee that he will reach such a position, since early in life one can see his qualities of character. But this is not always true in the case of a dictator, often he reaches his position of power through chance, very often through the unhappy state of his country.

558. The passage seems to suggest that   **[Prelim II-2017]**
(a) a leader foresees his future position
(b) a leader is chosen only by a free country
(c) a leader must see that his country is free from despair
(d) despair in a country sometimes leads to dictatorship

PASSAGE - 190

Many farmers use synthetic pesticides to kill infesting insects. The consumption of pesticides in some of the developed countries is touching 3000 grams/hectare. Unfortunately, there are reports that these compounds possess inherent toxicities that endanger the health of the farm operators, consumers and the environment. Synthetic pesticides are generally persistent in environment. Entering in food chain they destroy the microbial diversity and cause ecologcal imbalance. Their indiscriminate use has resulted in development of resistance among insects to insecticides, upsetting of balance in nature and resurgence of treated populations. Natural pest control using the botanical pesticides is safer to the user and the environment because they break down into harmless compounds within hours or days in the presence of sunlight Plants with pesticidal properties have been in nature for millions of years without any ill or adverse effects on the ecosystem. They are easily decomposed by many microbes common in most soils. They help in the maintenance of biological diversity of predators and the reduction of environmental contamination and human health hazards. Botanical pesticides formulated from plants are biodegradable and their use in crop protection is a practical sustainable alternative.

559. On the basis of the above passage, the following assumptions have been made :
1. Synthetic pesticides should never be used in modern agriculture.
2. One of the aims of sustainable agriculture is to ensure minimal ecological imbalance.
3. Botanical pesticides are more effective as compared to synthetic pesticides.

Which of the assumptions given above is/are correct?
(a) 1 and 2 only
(b) 2 only
(c) 1 and 3 only
(d) 1, 2 and3

560. Which of the following statements is/are correct regarding biopesticides?
1. They are not hazardous to human health.
2. They are persistent in environment.
3. They are essential to maintain the biodiversity of any ecosystem.

Select the correct answer using the code given below.
(a) 1 only
(b) 1 and 2 only
(c) 1 and 3 only
(d) 1, 2 and 3

PASSAGE - 191

It is no longer enough for us to talk about providing for universal access to education. Making available schooling facilities is an essential prerequisite, but is insufficient to ensure that all children attend school and participate in the learning process. The school may be there, but children may not attend or they may drop out after a few months. Through school and social mapping, we must address the entire gamut of social, economic, cultural and indeed linguistic and pedagogic issues, factors that prevent children from weaker sections and disadvantaged groups, as also girls, from regularly attending and complementing elementary education. The focus must be on the poorest and most vulnerable since these groups are the most disempowered and at a greatest risk of violation or denial of their right to education.

The right to education goes beyond free and compulsory education to include quality education for all. Quality is an integral part of the right to education. If the education process lacks quality, children are being denied their right. The Right of Children to Free and Compulsory Education Act lays down that the curriculum should provide for learning through activities, exploration and discovery. This places an obligation on us to change our perception of children as passive receivers of knowledge, and to move beyond the convention of using textbooks as the basis of examinations. The teaching-learning process must become stress-free; and a massive programme for curricular reform should be initiated to provide for a child-friendly learning system, that is more relevant and empowering. Teacher accountability systems and processes must ensure that children are learning, and that their right to learn in a child-friendly environment is not violated. Testing and assessment systems must be reexamined and redesigned to ensure that these do not force children to struggle between school and tuition centres, and bypass childhood.

561. According to the passage, which of the following is/are of paramount importance under the Right to education?
1. Sending of children to school by all parents
2. Provision of adequate physical infrastructure in schools
3. Curricular reforms for developing child-friendly learning system
Select the correct answer using the code given below.

[Prelim II-2018]
(a) 1 only
(b) 1 and 2 only
(c) 3 only
(d) None of the above

562. With reference to the above passage, the following assumptions have been made:
1. The Right to Education guarantees teachers' accountability for the learning process of children.
2. The Right to Education guarantees 100% enrolment of children in the schools.
3. The Right to Education intends to take full advantage of demographic dividend.
Which of the above assumptions is/are valid?

[Prelim II-2018]
(a) 1 only
(b) 2 and 3 only
(c) 3 only
(d) 1, 2 and 3

563. According to the passage, which one of the following is critical in bringing quality in education?

[Prelim II-2018]
(a) Ensuring regular attendance of children as well as teachers in school
(b) Giving pecuniary benefits to teachers to motivation them
(c) Understanding the socio-cultural background of children
(d) Inculcating learning through activities and discovery

564. What is the *essential message* in this passage?

[Prelim II-2018]
(a) The Right to Education now is a Fundamental Right.
(b) The Right to Education enables the children of poor and weaker sections of the society to attend schools.
(c) The Right to Free and Compulsory Education should include quality education for all.
(d) The Government as well a parents should ensure that all children attend schools.

PASSAGE - 192

Some people belive that leadership is a quality which you have at birth or not at all. This theory is false, for the art of leadership can be acquired and can indeed be taught. This discovery is made in time of war and the results achieved can surprise even the instructors. Faced with the alternatives of going left or right, every soldier soon grasps that a prompt decision either way is better than an endless discussion. A firm choice for direction has an even chance of being right while to do nothing will be almost certainly wrong.

565. The author of the passage holds the view that

[Prelim II-2018]
(a) leadership can be taught through war experience only
(b) leadership can be acquired as well as taught
(c) the results of training show that more people acquire leadership than are expected
(d) despite rigorous instruction few leaders are produced

ANSWER KEY

No.	Ans	No.	Ans	No.	Ans	No.	Ans	No.	Ans	No.	Ans	No.	Ans	No.	Ans	No.	Ans	No.	Ans	No.	Ans	No.	Ans
1	(d)	51	(b)	101	(a)	151	(a)	201	(b)	251	(b)	301	(a)	351	(c)	401	(c)	451	(c)	501	(a)	551	(a)
2	(d)	52	(d)	102	(a)	152	(c)	202	(b)	252	(c)	302	(b)	352	(b)	402	(a)	452	(a)	502	(c)	552	(c)
3	(a)	53	(c)	103	(d)	153	(c)	203	(d)	253	(d)	303	(d)	353.	(d)	403	(b)	453	(c)	503	(b)	553	(d)
4	(a)	54	(a)	104	(d)	154	(b)	204	(d)	254	(b)	304	(d)	354.	(c)	404	(d)	454	(d)	504	(c)	554	(b)
5	(b)	55	(c)	105	(b)	155	(d)	205	(c)	255	(a)	305	(b)	355	(d)	405	(c)	455	(b)	505	(b)	555	(b)
6	(d)	56	(c)	106	(a)	156	(a)	206	(a)	256	(a)	306	(c)	356	(d)	406	(d)	456	(b)	506	(b)	556	(a)
7	(c)	57	(d)	107	(d)	157	(b)	207	(c)	257	(a)	307	(c)	357	(b)	407	(b)	457	(a)	507	(c)	557	(a)
8	(a)	58	(d)	108	(d)	158	(a)	208	(b)	258	(b)	308	(d)	358	(c)	408	(d)	458	(c)	508	(d)	558	(d)
9	(b)	59	(d)	109	(c)	159	(b)	209	(a)	259	(d)	309	(a)	359	(d)	409	(a)	459	(c)	509	(a)	559	(b)
10	(d)	60	(c)	110	(a)	160	(b)	210	(d)	260	(d)	310	(a)	360	(a)	410	(b)	460	(c)	510	(b)	560	(c)
11	(c)	61	(b)	111	(c)	161	(a)	211	(b)	261	(b)	311	(c)	361	(b)	411	(c)	461	(b)	511	(c)	561	(c)
12	(c)	62	(d)	112	(a)	162	(b)	212	(c)	262	(d)	312	(a)	362	(b)	412	(b)	462	(d)	512	(c)	562	(d)
13	(c)	63	(b)	113	(b)	163	(c)	213	(a)	263	(c)	313	(b)	363	(b)	413	(c)	463	(b)	513	(c)	563	(d)
14	(a)	64	(a)	114	(d)	164	(b)	214	(c)	264	(c)	314	(d)	364	(d)	414	(a)	464	(c)	514	(c)	564	(c)
15	(b)	65	(d)	115	(c)	165	(b)	215	(c)	265	(a)	315	(b)	365	(c)	415	(a)	465	(d)	515	(c)	565	(b)
16	(c)	66	(a)	116	(b)	166	(b)	216	(c)	266	(a)	316	(d)	366	(d)	416	(a)	466	(a)	516	(b)		
17	(b)	67	(d)	117	(c)	167	(d)	217	(c)	267	(a)	317	(c)	367	(d)	417	(c)	467	(a)	517	(c)		
18	(b)	68	(c)	118	(d)	168	(d)	218	(d)	268	(d)	318	(b)	368	(a)	418	(d)	468	(b)	518	(a)		
19	(b)	69	(b)	119	(b)	169	(c)	219	(d)	269	(b)	319	(b)	369	(b)	419	(a)	469	(d)	519	(a)		
20	(d)	70	(d)	120	(b)	170	(c)	220	(c)	270	(b)	320	(c)	370	(b)	420	(b)	470	(d)	520	(c)		
21	(a)	71	(a)	121	(d)	171	(a)	221	(b)	271	(c)	321	(b)	371	(d)	421	(c)	471	(b)	521	(c)		
22	(a)	72	(c)	122	(b)	172	(d)	222	(a)	272	(b)	322	(c)	372	(d)	422	(d)	472	(d)	522	(a)		
23	(d)	73	(d)	123	(b)	173	(b)	223	(b)	273	(d)	323	(b)	373	(c)	423	(d)	473	(d)	523	(d)		
24	(c)	74	(d)	124	(b)	174	(d)	224	(b)	274	(c)	324	(d)	374	(c)	424	(b)	474	(b)	524	(b)		
25	(d)	75	(b)	125	(b)	175	(c)	225	(a)	275	(d)	325	(d)	375	(b)	425	(d)	475	(a)	525	(c)		
26	(c)	76	(b)	126	(d)	176	(a)	226	(d)	276	(a)	326	(d)	376	(d)	426	(b)	476	(c)	526	(c)		
27	(a)	77	(c)	127	(c)	177	(d)	227	(d)	277	(d)	327	(c)	377	(b)	427	(d)	477	(b)	527	(d)		
28	(a)	78	(d)	128	(c)	178	(c)	228	(d)	278	(a)	328	(a)	378	(b)	428	(b)	478	(d)	528	(b)		
29	(b)	79	(a)	129	(b)	179	(d)	229	(d)	279	(c)	329	(b)	379	(c)	429	(a)	479	(c)	529	(a)		
30	(c)	80	(c)	130	(d)	180	(b)	230	(b)	280	(c)	330	(b)	380	(b)	430	(b)	480	(a)	530	(d)		
31	(d)	81	(b)	131	(a)	181	(b)	231	(d)	281	(b)	331	(d)	381	(c)	431	(a)	481	(b)	531	(b)		
32	(a)	82	(c)	132	(b)	182	(d)	232	(b)	282	(b)	332	(b)	382	(d)	432	(c)	482	(c)	532	(b)		
33	(a)	83	(a)	133	(a)	183	(c)	233	(c)	283	(a)	333	(d)	383	(c)	433	(a)	483	(b)	533	(b)		
34	(b)	84	(c)	134	(c)	184	(a)	234	(b)	284	(d)	334	(a)	384	(a)	434	(a)	484	(c)	534	(a)		
35	(c)	85	(c)	135	(d)	185	(d)	235	(d)	285	(c)	335	(c)	385	(d)	435	(d)	485	(b)	535	(c)		
36	(c)	86	(d)	136	(c)	186	(c)	236	(c)	286	(c)	336	(b)	386	(a)	436	(b)	486	(c)	536	(c)		
37	(b)	87	(a)	137	(c)	187	(a)	237	(d)	287	(b)	337	(a)	387	(c)	437	(b)	487	(b)	537	(b)		
38	(a)	88	(c)	138	(d)	188	(c)	238	(b)	288	(c)	338	(d)	388	(d)	438	(d)	488	(c)	538	(d)		
39	(d)	89	(c)	139	(b)	189	(a)	239	(c)	289	(c)	339	(c)	389	(d)	439	(c)	489	(d)	539	(a)		
40	(a)	90	(b)	140	(b)	190	(b)	240	(c)	290	(b)	340	(a)	390	(d)	440	(b)	490	(a)	540	(b)		
41	(c)	91	(d)	141	(a)	191	(c)	241	(d)	291	(a)	341	(c)	391	(d)	441	(c)	491	(c)	541	(b)		
42	(c)	92	(d)	142	(c)	192	(b)	242	(d)	292	(a)	342	(b)	392	(d)	442	(c)	492	(b)	542	(d)		
43	(b)	93	(b)	143	(b)	193	(c)	243	(b)	293	(d)	343	(d)	393	(b)	443	(a)	493	(b)	543	(b)		
44	(d)	94	(b)	144	(b)	194	(a)	244	(d)	294	(b)	344	(a)	394	(a)	444	(c)	494	(b)	544	(d)		
45	(d)	95	(d)	145	(a)	195	(c)	245	(c)	295	(c)	345	(b)	395	(b)	445	(a)	495	(c)	545	(c)		
46	(c)	96	(d)	146	(d)	196	(b)	246	(c)	296	(d)	346	(b)	396	(b)	446	(c)	496	(b)	546	(b)		
47	(a)	97	(b)	147	(d)	197	(c)	247	(d)	297	(a)	347	(c)	397	(d)	447	(c)	497	(d)	547	(c)		
48	(a)	98	(a)	148	(b)	198	(d)	248	(b)	298	(c)	348	(c)	398	(a)	448	(d)	498	(c)	548	(d)		
49	(b)	99	(a)	149	(d)	199	(c)	249	(a)	299	(d)	349	(b)	399	(c)	449	(c)	499	(d)	549	(d)		
50	(b)	100	(a)	150	(c)	200	(a)	250	(c)	300	(b)	350	(a)	400	(a)	450	(c)	500	(a)	550	(d)		

Solutions

DETAILED EXPLANATIONS

1. (d) This can clearly be inferred from the first two lines of the passage.

2. (d) The fact that India will have a water deficit of 50% by 2030 and the last line clearly sums up the entire passage.

3. (a) It can clearly be inferred from the last two sentences of the paragraph.

4. (a) Apart from statement (a), every statement has been mentioned in the passage.

5. (b) In the passage, the author is of the view that Western culture has made our life faster, easier and comfortable so, it should not be criticized fully. However, Indian culture has impressed the people at global level and they are adapting its goodness, wisdom and teachings etc. thus, it must be given importance.

6. (d) All the statements can be inferred from the passage.

7. (c) These are clearly mentioned in the passage. The author is appraising the growth of e-commerce industry in India and expressing his positive insights about the effect of the growth in coming times.

8. (a) It can clearly be inferred from the third last line of the passage. Statement (I) is irrelevant in the context of the passage and statement (II) gives wrong information i.e. 'space' provides weather information, DTS services, tele-education etc. and not 'space technology'.

9. (b) This is the theme of the passage. Moreover, it can clearly be inferred from the last few sentences of the passage.

10. (d) It is inherent in the third sentence of the passage.

11. (c) The second half of the passage clearly states this fact.

12. (c) It can clearly be implied from the last sentence of the passage.

13. (c) It can be concluded from the last few sentences.

14. (a) It is inherent in the last line of the passage.

15. (b) This is the crux of the entire passage.

16. (c) It is implied from the first and last sentence of the passage.

17. (b) It is implied from the second half of the passage.

18. (b) It can easily be inferred from the passage.

19. (b) It is inherent in the passage that putting tariff on import by both the countries on each other's product will negatively affect both the countries and to some extent to the world thereby adversely affecting their economies.

20. (d) It is implied from the second half of the passage.

21. (a) This is theme of the passage and is clearly evident from it.

22. (a) It can clearly be summed up from the first and last sentences of the passage.

23. (d) It can be inferred from the last few sentences of the passage.

24. (c) It is implied from the last three sentences of the passage.

25. (d) The first and last sentence clearly exihibits this fact.

26. (c) It is evident from the second half of the passage.

27. (a) This is the theme of the passage. Option (d) appears to be correct as well, but in the option, 'Cauvery water dispute' is mentioned which is no where mentioned in the passage i.e. in the passage, only 'Cauvery' is mentioned. So, this option gets eliminated on the premsie that the answer should be picked on the basis of the passage and not on the basis of our general knowledge.

28. (a) This can be easily summed up from the passage.

29. (b) It is evident from the first few sentences of the passage.

30. (c) It can be summed up from third sentence onwards.

31. (d) It is evident from the second sentence of the passage.

32. (a) It is clearly evident from the first, second and fifth sentence.

33. (a) This is the ultimate theme of the passage.

34. (b) This is the crux of the whole passage. Rest options are irrelevant in the context of the passage.

35. (c) It is mentioned in the very first sentence of the passage.

36. (c) It can clearly be inferred from the first two sentences of the passage.

37. (b) It can be inferred from the first few sentences of the passage.

38. (a) It can be inferred from the first half of the passage.

39. (d) This is the gist of the passage.

40. (a) It is evident from the first and last sentence of the passage.

41. (c) It can easily be inferred from the passage that providing better health care services has been the aim of the present government especially, to the poor and vulnerable families.

42. (c) It is evident from the very first sentence of the passage. Moreover, India is the subject of the passage so, this can easily be summed up.

43. (b) It is evident from the entire passag.

44. (d) It can clearly be inferred from the last two sentences of the passage.

45. (d) It can clearly be inferred from the last sentence of the passage.

46. (c) It can easily be inferred from the second sentence onwards.

47. (a) This is the crux of the passage and it can clearly be

inferred from the last two sentences of the passage.

48. (a) This is clearly evident from the second, third and second last sentence of the passage.

49. (b) It is evident from the first and last sentence of the passage.

50. (b) This is the essence of the passage. Rest of the options are irrelevant in the context of the passage.

51. (b) The first paragraph in the passage conveys the message that the detractors of democracy are quite vocal about the fact that a number of non-democratic governments particularly in East Asia have successfully achieved economic development.

Options (a), (c) and (d) are automatically ruled out.

52. (d) The second and last paragraphs express the fact that freedom and liberty are essential components of development.

53. (c) The "constitutive" connection between democracy and development is political freedom and democratic rights.

54. (a) (A) follows because the passage talks of "water conflicts" between developing countries. However, we are told, such conflicts have not escalated into wars.

As for (C), the alteration has been done by water, not by water conflicts.

55. (c) Because they are logical developments.

56. (c) Highlight the seriousness of the threat posed by unresolved water conflicts.

57. (d) Note that the Prime Minister urges the state governments to show "an appreciation of the other's point of view".

58. (d) Water is a divisible resource.

59. (d) It is clearly given in the first line of the last paragraph.

60. (c) Statement 1 and 3 are true whereas statement 2 is false in the context of the passage.

61. (b) It is stated in the first paragraph.

62. (d) It is stated in the last paragraph.

63. (b) It is clearly mentioned in the third line of the passage.

64. (a) It can easily be inferred from the passage.

65. (d) This is not given in the passage so, it's untrue.

66. (a) It can be inferred from the starting lines of the second half of the passage.

67. (d) 68. (c) 69. (b) 70. (d)

71. (a) It is mentioned in the fourth paragraph.

72. (c) Since the entire passage is based on the effect of green house gas emissions thus, option (c) would be the appropriate title.

73. (d)

74. (d) None of these

75. (b) Statements 1 and 2 are clearly mentioned in the passage but not statement 3.

76. (b) According to the passage, weak global economic prospects and continuing uncertainties in the international markets as well as sovereign risk concerns, particular by in the Euro area have had their impact on the emerging market economies.

77. (c) The Indian financial markets are affected by global changes mainly due to the contagion of Greece's sovereign debt problem spreading to India.

78. (d) Since the Indian financial system is bank dominated banks ability to withstand stress is critical to overall financial stability.

79. (a) With further globalization, consolidation, deregulation and diversification, risk and liquidity management assumes more importance in the Indian banking system in future.

80. (c) According to the passage, net profits are only 2.2% as far as the central public sector undertakings are concerned. So, statement (2) is correct. The private sector has grown. There is a larger base with more educated and moneyed people around. Hence statement (3) is correct too from the paragraph point of view. The role of governmental institutions in encouraging competition among the private sector enterprises ensures the continuing growth of this sector.

81. (b) The rural roads should be in the domain of the public sector only because the sparse or the little traffic in these roads makes it impossible to make profits on the road tax or tolls as they are called.

82. (c) The government does invest in different industrial sectors. This is what the paragraph says. Indeed there is governmental investment in a variety of industries from airlines, roads, steel, and finance to industries where the private sector plays a prominent role. For in the latter it acts as the umpire or the regulating agency so as to create a competitive atmosphere for the growth of entrepreneurship.

83. (a) The government acts as a regulating agency by prescribing broad norms within which the private enterprises can conduct their business in an atmosphere of fair and fearless competition. That is why the government is made the umpire in a field of business players.

84. (c) In this passage, the author wants to convey that the best way to ensure the prosperity and further economic growth of the nation is by implementing inclusive growth where the benefits of growth are shared by the entire population and not by certain segments only.

85. (c) To make the process of inclusive growth more effective, the author suggests that we should not only concentrate on the poorer sections of society, but also ensure that the rich and middle class stand to gain certain points. In this way, it will be possible to

        redistribute the economic gains made by these sections of society to those getting left behind.

86. **(d)** According to the passage, eradication of poverty is not a sufficient condition for growth. So statement (1) is ruled out. Growth has to be treated as an instrument for ensuring prosperity for all. But this is yet to be attained. So, India has to strive on. So, statement (2) is also ruled out.

87. **(a)** According to the passage, government interference leads to distortions and inefficiency in the economy in the sense that there is room for corruption as well as a lack of interest in investment on the part of the entrepreneurs.

88. **(c)** The first paragraph states that the basic philosophy of globalization is to ensure absolute freedom for the markets, to set their prices, produce their goods, and distribute them as per their own criterion.

89. **(c)** The passage clearly states that in accordance with the conditions set by the WTO etc., for globalization, public sectors should be privatized. So statement (1) is correct. Employment and wages should be conditioned by the free play of the market forces involved, otherwise it might discourage investment as stated in statement (3). Even social services like heath and education should welcome private players as is correctly expressed in statement (4).

90. **(b)** The entire passage focuses on the fact that the state should play a reducing role in the process of globalization. This is elaborated in the last few lines of the passage with particular reference to India.

91. **(d)** Neither of the two statements are correct according to the passage, therefore, option (d) is the correct answer. The clue regarding this lies in the following lines of the passage – "There is a great pride in an Indian that easily integrates with a global economy, yet maintains a unique cultural identity". This line contradicts the idea mentioned in the first statements. The next clue is "this confidence has them demonstrating great propensity to consumer, throwing away ageing ideas of asceticism and thrift" This line contradicts the idea in the second statement.

92. **(d)** The approximate no : of people in India who are in the age group of 15 – 25 years is 180 million which is option (d), therefore, (d) is the correct answer. The clue regarding this lies in the following line of the passage – "more than half the country is under 25 years of age and more than a third under 5 years of age".

93. **(b)** In the recent past the service industry sector has witnessed a phenomenal growth which is option (b), therefore, (b) is the correct answers. The clue regarding this lies in the following line of the passage –'Brought up in the shadow of the rise of India's service industry boom this group … world."

94. **(b)** According to the given information in the passage , the information given in the first statement finds no mention in the passage. The second statements is correct which is option (b), therefore (b) is the correct answer. The clue regarding this lies in the following line of the passage 'India is among the youngest countries in the world. "If the youth of India are not properly educated and if there are not enough jobs created, India will have forever loss its opportunity.

95. **(d)** Neither (1) nor (2) statement is correct according to the passage, which is option (d), therefore, (d) is the correct answer.

96. **(d)** Neither 1st nor 2nd statement is correct which is marked option (d), therefore, (d) is the correct answer. The clue regarding this lies in the following lines of the passage "They must recognise that the US needs trained people in various fields "which implies that Indian can be a source of manpower, in any field be it high technology areas also. The second statement states that only those immigrants can file application who have stayed in the US for over five years. But the passage states" those who have been in the country between two and five years.

97. **(b)** Option (b) states that the types of jobs which engage the immigrants are not sougut after by the Americans. The clue regarding this lies in the following lines of the passage "the truth is that the bulk of immigrants are doing jobs that Americans simply don't want to do", therefore, (b) is the correct answer.

98. **(a)** Neither 1st nor 2nd statement is correct which is marked by option (d), therefore, (d) is the correct answer. The clue regarding this lies in the following lines of the passage – "But giving illegal immigrants gralts the opportunity to be come legal residents will at least ensure that they are not exploited by employers and that they are covered by social security benefits". The second statement states that India contributes the largest number of immigrants to the United States of America. But the passage says – "compared to Mexicans, the largest component of immigrants to the U.S, Indians have——".

99. **(a)** Neither 1st nor 2nd statement is correct which is marked by option (a), therefore, (a) is the correct answer. The clue regarding this lies in the following lines of the passage – "In US senate's approval of an immigration bill has been welcomed in the IT industry in America because of the proposal of double H1 – B visas for skilled foreign workers. Not for welfare of the mankind which is stated in the 1st statement. The second statement states that both Mexian and Indian immigrants enjoy good communication skills in English. But the passage states that – "that they know English" which means they have knowledge not good communication skills in English.

100. **(a)** Option (a) states that 'Persuasive skill - set is a prerequisite to an effective preseutation' The clue regarding this lies in the following lines of the passage "The art of effective presentation is the fruit of

persistent efforts and practice, therefore, (a) is the correct answer.

101. (a) Option (a) states that" innate stage fright of a speaker can be countered by meticulous preparation of his presentation. The clue regarding this lies in the following lines of the passage – "A thorough preparation is the best antidote for nervousness" therefore, (a) is the correct answer.

102. (a) Option (a) states "Topic of the presentation must be of relevant interest to the audience to induce there responses," The clue regarding this lies in the following lines of the passage – The topic of the presentation must be interesting to the audience " therefore, (a) is the correct answer.

103. (d) Neither (1) nor (2) statement is correct according to the information given in the passage, therefore, option (d) is the correct answer.

104. (d) Neither (1) nor (2) statement is correct according to the information given in the passage, therefore, option (d) is the correct answer.

105. (b) Option (b) states that "while making a presentation one should, at times, refer to his written material," The clue regarding this lies in the following lines of the passage "one may consult his notes frequently when he is making his presentation. Therefore, (b) is the correct answer.

106. (a) Option (a) states that "An effective presentation about the product of a company can help in increasing sales volumes" The clue regarding this lies in the following lines of the passage "A successful presentation can help a person in winning orders for the company he works for," therefore, option (a) is the correct answer.

107. (d) The "material conditions of happiness" does not include hope. This is mentioned in very first line of the passage. There are a great many people who have all the material conditions of happiness i.e. health, sufficient income and clout ...!. The word 'hope' is not mentioned.

108. (d) Modern man is very unhappy because he "suppresses his inner urges, which is option (d). The clue regarding this lies in the following lines of the passage. 'Your needs are more compare than those of your pets but they still have their basic in instict. 'In civilised societies, this is too apt to be forgotten.

109. (c) The author is of the opinion that 'we are really not very different from animals', which is option (c). The clue regarding this is in the following line of the passage - 'Animals live on impulse, your needs are more compare than those of your pets but still they have their basis in instinct'. The line shows that man is not very different form animals.

110. (a) The phrase "do not minister to it" means do not support it' which is option (a). The writer gives the clue regarding it when he says that 'people prose to themselves some paramount or important objective and restrain or stop all impulses that do not minister or support to it.'

111. (c) Wars have been fought 'to capture some areas of another country which are of strategic importance' which is option 'c', therefore, 'c' is the correct answer. The clue regarding this is given in the following line of the passage 'for the sake of seizing some strategically valuable piece of territory'.

112. (a) The 'natural' frontier means 'An area on the border from where you can keep watch on or attack your enemy which is option (a), so (a) is the correct answer. The writer has explained it in the following lines of the passage -
'natural frontier is frontier which is easy to defend and from which it is easy to launch attacks upon one's neighbours."

113. (b) Military advantages and economic advantages may or may not be the same but the rulers make them appear to be the same' which is option (b), so 'b' is the correct answer. The lines from the passage which give the clue regarding this are 'purely military advantages are almost as highly praised by the rulers of nations as economic advantages.'

114. (d) Epigram means a short, crisp and precise remark. Option 'd' has it all so that would be the correct answer.

115. (c) The dictionary meaning of suffrage is right to vote. So the extension of suffrage will certainly indicate the right to vote for more and more people. So option 'c' would be the correct answer.

116. (b) Democracy means, equal opportunity for everyone, so economic democracy would stand for equal economic opportunities for everyone. So option 'b' would be the correct answer.

117. (c) Author clearly says in 3rd line that when he was in the hospital, he was consumed by rage and self pity. So the correct statement would be like 'while in the hospital, the author was frustrated at his helpless situation.

118. (d) In advancing paragraph author expresses his wish that 'I yearned to be active again.' refer line 4 & 5. He is questioning himself that what could a middle-aged cripple like me do? So the answer would be 'he could not lead an active life'.

119. (b) In the concluding paragraph author says that the stoke (which paralysed him and got him hospitalised) made him realize, and helped him develop his latent talent (painting). So the correct statement would be, the paralytic stoke helped the author to realize his talent.

120. (b) Refer to the first line of the passage.

121. (d) Refer to the third line of the passage.

122. (b) Refer to the last line of the passage.

123. (b) Refer to the last line of the passage.

124. (b) Refer to the line that states 'it is a great .... oppose'.

125. (b) Refer to the second sentence 'It is a passion .... China'.

126. (d) Refer to the sentence 'The gift should always be accompanied by a box of tools'.

127. (c) Refer to the second last sentence 'But he persuades himself............. dinner.

128. (c) Refer to the first sentence that begins with 'No doubt ....food production'.

129. (b) Refer to the third sentence that 'It has created ....under control'.

130. (d) Refer to the fourth sentence that begins with 'scientists are now..........'.

131. (a) Refer to the last sentence of the passage.

132. (b) Refer to the second sentence of the passage that begins with 'often TB victims.............cure'.

133. (a) Refer to the second sentence of first para and third sentence of the second para of the passage.

134. (c) Refer to the last sentence of the first para of the passage.

135. (d) Refer to the fifth sentence of the second para of the passage.

136. (c) Refer to the third last sentence of the second para of the passage.

137. (c) Refer to the last sentence of the passage.

138. (d) Refer to the second last sentence of the passage.

139. (b) Refer to the middle part of the given passage.

140. (b) Refer to the second sentence of the passage.

141. (a) Refer to the third sentence of the passage.

142. (c) Refer to the first sentence of the passage.

143. (b) Refer to the last sentence of the passage.

144. (b) The word 'ex-'means out. Hence, exhale means to breathe out.

145. (a) Refer to the middle part of the passage.

146. (d) Refer to the second sentence of the passage.

147. (d) First sentence of passage in itself is satisfactory to answer the question.

148. (b) Option (a) is not mentioned in passage; option (b) can be inferred from the passage. Word - coastal regions to get submerged by melting ice is clearly written in passage. Global warming is the cause not the creation. Option (d) also is not the answer as cracks will develop before melting. Not after melting.

149. (d) Rising temperature although not written in the passage is the cause melting as ice melts only when the temperature rises.

150. (c) Author has, at last, described Global Warming as the cause of everything detailed in the passage so it can be his intention to warn against the dangers of global warming.

151. (a) Taking the example of Gandhi, it can be assumed that men are not born great but self effort can make them great. Second last sentence of the passage certifies what is given in (4). Assumption (1) is not true as per passage. And Assumption (3) is not even hinted in passage.

152. (c) Passage ends on this note. Fearlessness is described as the greatest virtue.

153. (c) This is best of the options. Although it is not clearly mentioned in the passage. Option (a) and (b) is out of context. Faith is direct word used. He taught them fearlessness not have a attitude of fearlessness for them.

154. (b) Leonine means like a lion. A lion is synonym to courage. See other words - vulpine (Like a wolf), Canine (like a dog), Asinine (Like an ass).

155. (d) First sentence of the passage clears that fence was meant to keep dingoes out. Second sentence clears that sheep (wool growers) are protected.

156. (a) Last sentence of the passage refers to the Kangaroos as the national symbol of Australia.

157. (b) It has been written in the passage clearly.

158. (a) Only this can be inferred from the passage other options are not true or irrelevant.

159. (b) Only option (b) is stated in the passage in the first sentence. This option is just presents the same thing in second way.

160. (b) Sense organs are which sense from the touch and obviously hairs or whiskers can not taste, hear or smell.

161. (a) 30 gallons/day is a large quantity; also it can be inferred that the lack of water creates problem. On this logical deduction, option (c) can be rejected. (d) is also not true. (b) is not clearly written, although might be true.

162. (b) First sentence of the passage gives the answer.

163. (c) What elephants do in the droughts - is explicitly given in the passage. Author calls it an intriguing technique - digging wells/holes.

164. (b) If they are drinking in order of seniority and seniority is counted according to age as per last two words of passage, definitely, oldest would drink first.

165. (b) exchanging goods and services

166. (b) goods are produced in surplus

167. (d) living in communities

168. (d) we cannot produce everything we need ourselves

169. (c) may be other planets like the Earth in the universe

170. (c) the planetary system exists

171. (a) if there is life on the planets, it would be like ours

172. (d) human life is very complex.

173. (b) is sincere in discharging his duties.

174. (d) are sensitive and emotional.

175. (c) are happy and spread happiness.

176. (a) Look at the bright side of things.

177. (d) The author is talking about the basic essentials of life, food, shelter, cloth, and warmth.

178. (c) The author is trying to suggest that increased use of technology implies unnecessary comfort and happiness for mankind and it is complementary to a raised standard of living.

179. (d) The increased use to technology suggests man's interest for more and more work.

180. (b) The author suggests that Man will be working shorter and shorter hours in his paid employment.

181. (b) The author talks of dangerous ideas which he says are born out of the enjoyment of freedom.

182. (d) The author warns that popular violence is always the outcome of a deep popular dissatisfaction with the government.

183. (c) The author is trying to highlight the developed laziness that makes us incapable of social action.

184. (a) Burke is highlighting the violence against injustice.

185. (d) The author says we need to overlook some certain things.

186. (c) The ancients said that an unforgiving temper was not to be commended.

187. (a) The author is highlighting the spirit of forgiveness.

188. (c) The author says that others are ready to tease and laugh at our attempts.

189. (a) The author says we fail in our attempts because we set high ambitations and never have time to carry them out.

190. (b) The word inveterate means having a particular habit that is long-established and unlikely to change.

191. (c) The author implies that despite our repeated failures we still try one more time.

192. (b) The word formidable means inspiring fear or respect and here the for middable list refers to the long list which was frigtening.

193. (c) The author's sentence "But he could not find a needle. He fell asleep again" describes the man's reaction to his problem.

194. (a) The man wanted to sew the hole because he didn't want to be scolded by his wife in the morning.

195. (c) The man was searching the needle to sew up the hole.

196. (b) The smell of burnt cigarette awoke the man and burnt his only shirt.

197. (c) As the man fell asleep, the cigarette fell from his mouth.

198. (d) In an age of science and technology, specialization becomes necessary.

199. (c) The central theme of the passage is that the aim of education is to make the youth capable of independent thought and expression.

200. (a) The major warning suggested in the passage is that University education should not be concerned with technical details rather it should embrace humanism.

201. (b) The author tries to highlight our misconception about common birds.

202. (b) Our ideas about birds are derived from the most common types.

203. (d) The common wild duck quacks like the mallard.

204. (d) The boy answered the question when the teacher asked the question again and again and persisted to answer.

205. (c) Since the boy was repeating the same mistake this made the teacher think that the boy was doing it intentionally.

206. (a) The teacher was trying to control his anger as the boy's parents had high hopes with the boy.

207. (c) The author praises village life as there is certain dignity, and kindliness, and love for other men.

208. (b) Civilization has mainly destroyed the family affection and pastoral virtues.

209. (a) The author mentions the old comfortable picture of a friendly universe governed by spiritual values.

210. (d) Religious skepticism rose immediately after the age of the rise of science.

211. (b) Braille lost his sight accidentally as a child.

212. (c) In those days, the few books that were available for blind people were printed in big, raised type; the letters used were those of the ordinary alphabet.

213. (a) Braille evolved a system, which made use of only six dots in all.

214. (c) Reading and writing for the blind have thus become enormously simplified by Braille's system.

215. (c) The author says that our ancestors blended with one another thus we are a result of a blended culture.

216. (c) The author is not interested whether the Aryans were indigenous to India or were unwelcome intruder.

217. (c) The author wishes to have the freedom to blend other cultures with our own.

218. (d) The author insists on learning English and other world languages in addition to the mother tongue.

219. (d) As the passage talks about sky being full with rusting wings and the streaks of red and golden in the sky, which implies times of sunrise and the sky being full with birds that is time before sunrise and birds. The answer should include both 1 and 4, thus the correct answer is (d).

220. (c) The word 'panting' means, 'not being able to breathe properly'; the passage talks about the struggle of Jean, who was really too tired with the swimming and climbing his way on the hill towards his home.

221. (b) The passage talks about the importance of liberal education and it's role in resolving fundamental issues.

222. (a) The author is highlighting the role of liberal education and its importance in present day.

223. (b) The synonym for word 'specifically' is 'particularly'.

224. (b) The author talks about the great and varied concerns of the humankind which are not daily concerns but a bigger picture which the mankind together is facing as a challenge.

225. (a) The author talks about the importance of equal trust shown to all people on earth for reconciliation.

226. (d) The author also tells not to humiliate the members of those nations whose leaders have committed inhuman crimes.

227. (d) The author is talking about the equality in treating people from different native lands.
228. (d) As the author is highlighting the importance of equal treatment for all people on earth, irrespective of their origin or races the answer is (d).
229. (d) As the Captain and his crew were lost on unknown islands; he sent his men in search of water.
230. (b) The savage brandished their spears to frighten the crew
231. (d) As the inhabitants of the islands had spears and clubs, this points that they were primitive tribes.
232. (b) The purpose of Mandela's talk was to help people oppose oppression.
233. (c) The passage clearly describes the struggle of black people with an unfavourable government.
234. (b) As the commander had ordered lights out by 7 p.m. he went to check whether his orders had been followed or not.
235. (d) The commander entered his son's tent because he wanted to punish any soldier who disobeyed his order.
236. (c) The son was eager to tell his mother about his own deeds and thus was writing a letter to her.
237. (d) During the hot summer days author and Jack were lazing around the house and yards.
238. (b) They were planning for some adventurous trip to an unknown place.
239. (c) Their mother had already packed all the good clothes for their upcoming trip.
240. (c) The plate camera was one of the ingenious artefacts made by Jack.
241. (d) The author mentions Father and Jack's trip to Ropley to see and rent a cottage there.
242. (d) Literature and history are inseparably linked together in the classics and the bible.
243. (b) The Bible
244. (d) Without critical discrimination but in the light of their humanistic culture.
245. (c) Had a gradual decline in our time
246. (c) Worthless ideas.
247. (d) Reflection of the intellect
248. (b) a man of character refuses to be influenced by outside compulsions against his will.
249. (a) Good thoughts lead to the control of the sense organs.
250. (c) attempt to destroy man's character
251. (b) the attainment of perfect character is the result of a long process of metal discipline.
252. (c) it gives rise to many other problems.
253. (d) our economic planning
254. (b) is likely to become less satisfactory.
255. (a) is less than satisfactory.
256. (a) more provision for cloth than accommodation.
257. (a) Providing things for themselves

258. (b) The goods are produced in surplus
259. (d) Living in communities
260. (d) We cannot produce everything we need ourselves.
261. (b) The dog was sturdy and short tempered.
262. (d) The dog bit him more than he bit other in the family.
263. (c) The writer's dog had bitten at least forty people.
264. (c) The girl could not understand it
265. (a) 1 only (the governess taught the same lesson several time)
266. (a) The dullness of the girl.
267. (a) The inability of the governess to endure further the girl's failure to answer.
268. (d) The gradual acceptance of vaccination as a preventive against small pox
269. (b) Some of the vaccines used were of a poor hygienic standard.
270. (b) Fear of the terrible disease drove them to take the risk of vaccination.
271. (c) Build up a defence against small pox germs.
272. (b) Only 2 (there is no outbreaks of smallpox nowadays).
273. (d) Unless the children are taught differently, they think that the sun and moon are moving round the earth.
274. (c) The early ideas of the man were wrong because they did not have any scientific knowledge as there were no telescopes or instruments to study the motion of earth and stars.
275. (d) Since the sun has been described as lamp in the passage, answer is (d).
276. (a) Lack of scientific knowledge was the main cause of wrong ideas.
277. (d) George's absence from the town was not noticed by the station master as he called out George asking if he was going away.
278. (a) George was expecting a big welcome because he thought that he had achieved a lot in a short span of time.
279. (c) George's expectations of people greeting him when he reaches his town shows his pride that he has achieved a lot in business.
280. (c) George's success was clearly visible in his being unbearably conceited and proud of himself.
281. (b) The passage highlights how with modern technology, serious life hazards are being accompanied.
282. (b) The harmful effects of modern technology are widespread and long lasting.
283. (a) Only first assumption is true. Second is in correct as conservation of flora and fauna can be done with efficient management.
284. (d) Both the statements are incorrect and incomplete.
285. (c) In order to achieve high food productions, monocultures and other modern farming methods are used. These is a widespread transmission of animal diseases now-a-days.

286. (c) The sentence means that the girl visited many property dealers over the last few days without any success.

287. (b) The girl was an independent freelance writer who is not particularly employed in any company.

288. (c) Single jobless women always face difficulty in renting an accommodation.

289. (c) It is hinted in the passage that farmers were pressurized to cultivate indigo and forsake cultivating other crops. Thus it means that they were forced to do it.

290. (b) In the passage the first sentence talks of Britishers' intention and their compelling farmers to take up indigo cultivation. This was their very intention to purchase land in Bengal.

291. (a) It is clearly evident from the passage as to why the indigo cultivation was profitable for Britishers. It was because they held monopoly over it. That means they had no competitors and only they could export it.

292. (a) Option (b), (c), and (d) are quite positive in idea whereas the author is talking about the negative perspective of extreme nationalism. How it becomes a curse for the nation when people think only about their own selves rather than others. Thus option (a) is the correct answer.

293. (d) In the first few sentences it has been suggested that nationalism becomes a curse for the nation when nationalism turns narrow and fanatical. Thus it is clear that option (d) the answer.

294. (b) In the second sentence, the author hints that in fanatical situation religion can lead men astray. This proves that religion sometimes can cause its misuse by some men. Thus option (b) is the answer.

295. (c) In the very first line it is clear that brown and his men sat around the fire. Thus option (c) is true.

296. (d) Option (a) is the correct answer as it is suggested in the last sentence that the man did not know about the danger and thus when he started walking down the hill, he vanished, means he slipped.

297. (a) The sentences 'He didn't think… in the dark' implies that he was bold and adventurous. Hence, option (a) is correct.

298. (c) The people were sitting beside the fire and eating hungrily. They were huddling round a fire means being close together. Thus option (c) is the answer.

299. (d) In the passage the author talks about not shooting the elephant because he feels it is a heavy and useful machinery. This phrase denotes that that the author considers it to be an important resource or property. Thus option (d) is the answer.

300. (b) The author denotes in the passage that killing a working elephant is like destroying a useful machine. Here the work done by elephant is compared to a heavy machinery. Thus option (b) is the correct answer.

301. (a) The author specifically compares the elephant to a cow here because although an elephant is wild animal, it was as quiet as a cow at that moment. Thus option (a) is the answer.

302. (b) In this item the author says in the second sentence that he was very fond of the old soldier and inspired by his adventurous stories. Thus option (b) is the answer.

303. (d) The author said that story of the soldier in which he walked 200 miles was his favourite because he had escaped from Japanese prison of war camp. He told it to the man many a times Thus, option (c) is the correct answer it shown he is a strong soldier.

304. (d) It has been mentioned by the author that he liked the story of Japanese prison of war the most. Thus option (d) is the answer.

305. (b) The passage discusses the author's life that though he had to face so many troubles, he was satisfied with his life. Thus option (b) is the answer.

306. (c) In the passage we notice that the soldier was bitten by a snake and he had cut his toe but the toe turned septic because of which he had to cut his leg. Thus option (c) is the correct answer.

307. (c) In the jungle, the snake has the added advantage over man. He is not obstructed by the thorns, trees and bushes as faced by the man.

308. (d) Movement of other beings causes small vibrations in the ground which the snake uses to decipher the danger

309. (a) Bearing upon means having an effect on.

310. (a) There is a close relationship between ambition and activity. Ambition is the inspiration for activity.

311. (c) Ambition must be consistent with one's capacities. If the capacities do not match with the ambition, then it results in failure.

312. (a) One must try to do their best in everything they do so as to achieve good results.

313. (b) One should not imagine oneself always to do be better than the others. Others should be treated as equal and one must concentrate on one's capacities instead of competing with others.

314. (d) The early instruments made were not delicate and were sensitive enough.

315. (b) Earthquake comes with a lot of destruction and takes a toll on infrastructure and people's lives. An instrument to observe an earthquake is the need of the hour so as to alert people about earthquakes beforehand during their conscious as well as unconcious hours.

316. (d) A device was needed that could record the parameters with a pen and paper.

317. (c) While travelling in a bus or train, a standing person has a tendency to fall when a bus or train moves suddenly.

318. (b) According to the early seismometers, the pen should stay still and the paper should move.

319. (b) According to the author, regressing back means looking back at the text that has already been read.

320. (c) In order to be a good reader, we must not look back frequently and instead grasp quickly what we are reading to avoid regression during the reading and enjoying a spurt in reading speed.

321. (b) The author describes regression as walking back a few meters while walking i.e looking back at the text already read again and again.

322. (c) In today's time, very few people can satisfy their needs all by themselves.

323. (b) Exchange of goods is possible when we produce a good in surplus such that apart from our personal use, we can share it.

324. (d) Specialisation and exchange began when men started living in communities.

325. (d) Exchange of goods and services is very important because we cannot produce and/or specialize in producing everything we need.

326. (d) Scientists who study soil believe that not all worms and bacteria are harmful. Some are useful as they helps in mixing up of nitrogen and air in the soil, while some help break down the decayed matter.

327. (c) The harmful pests and bacteria causes diseases in the plants.

328. (a) While farming, the farmers makes sure to avoid the weeds and pests that attack plants.

329. (b) With the advent in farming methods and technology, resistant seeds which fight weeds and pests are easily available that help farmers in controlling the loss caused by them.

330. (b) Nowadays, farmers can grow crops that ripen quickly and are resistant to frost, drought, disease.

331. (d) The tigress was miles away and according to how fast she runs, it is a possibility that she would cover the distance in half an hour.

332. (b) The author says that some of us won't reach the camp means that the tigress would kill few of them if she would hear them.

333. (d) The author found it difficult to decide the question because there was uncertainty whether or not she will hear them.

334. (a) The author had the time of whole day to kill the tigress but before the night they should be back to their camps.

335. (c) The author says that if the tigress comes in the daytime after hearing his voice, he would be able to shoot her down without any difficulty.

336. (b) The flat did not suit him much because unlike before, he was staying alone without his mother in the house.

337. (a) The author had put all the items and furniture of his utility into one room and never looked after the rest of the flat because he did not use it.

338. (d) The word 'it' refers to the flat.

339. (c) The author was satisfied with the space in his bedroom and made sure it had all the things of his utility.

340. (a) Be at a loose end means to have nothing to do.

341. (c) According to the passage, most of us prefer to watch films that satisfy and/or fulfil our secret wishes.

342. (b) By watching thrilling adventures, we make up for our shortcomings.

343. (d) Film stars present situations that are uncommon to our daily life and which excite us.

344. (a) We somehow admit to the fact that we are weak and plain and we try to find adventure by watching movie stars.

345. (b) The daily life of school, officegoers and home-makers make up for the same old repetition of routine.

346. (b) 347. (c) 348. (c)

349. (b) 350. (a) 351. (c)

352. (b) Graphology is the study of handwriting.

353. (d) 354. (c) 355. (d) 356. (d)

357. (b) 358. (c) 359. (d) 360. (a)

361. (b) 362. (b) 363. (b) 364. (d)

365. (c) dogmatic means inclined to lay down principles as undeniably true or unquestionable. Therefore in the given context dogmatic statement means a statement which is unquestionable.

366. (d) 367. (d) 368. (a)

369. (b) 370. (b) 371. (d) 372. (d) 373. (c)

374. (c)

375. (b) It is very clearly mentioned in the passage how power of out has exerted its influence through the ages. Hence, option (b) is the correct answer.

376. (d) The statement suggests that the theory of relativity has suppressed the theory of gravitation i.e. the theory of gravitation has been replaced by the theory of relativity. Hence option (d) is the correct answer.

377. (b) The passage clearly states that the achievements of these people had importance only in their own time. Hence option (b) is correct answer.

378. (b) The last few lines of the passage clearly suggest that the power of art increases with time and is better understood by people. Hence, option (b) is the correct choice.

379. (c) It is clearly mentioned in the passage how each gender can surpass the other in certain kinds of activities. Hence, option (c) is the correct answer.

380. (b) The very first line of the passage states that the word 'stronger' can be interpreted in many ways. Hence, option (b) is the correct answer.

381. (c) The author, in the passage, talks about how in certain activities, women are stronger than men. Most woman live longer than most men, they have better chance of resisting disease and work accurately under monotonous conditions etc. Hence, option (c) is the correct answer.

382. (d) Many instances are mentioned where women are stronger than men. The instances appears to be based on statistics. Hence, option (d) in the correct answer.

383. (c) It is clearly suggested in the passage that the efficiency of the institution depends on the way it is worked and the character and wisdom of the men who work it. Hence, option (c) is the correct answer.

384. (a) The contextual meaning of the phrase 'watertight compartments' is 'the activities of life unaffected by public opinion'.

385. (d) The author says that the politicians often talk about introducing certain political and economic changes. However, the author contradicts their view as the efficiency of an institution depends upon other factors as well. Hence, option (d) is the correct answer.

386. (a) In order to make earth a paradise to live in, everything from political, moral, social and economic well being should be perfectly synchronized with one another. Hence, option (a) is the correct answer.

387. (c) It is clearly mentioned in the passage that men talk about the wonderful feeling that they experience after reaching the top of mountain after climbing for hours and sometimes even days. Hence, the correct answer is option (c).

388. (d) The passage mentions that it is difficult to climb mountains as paths sides usually very steep. Moreover, some mountain sides are straight up and down. Hence, option (d) is the correct answer.

389. (d) In the sentence, ' It' refers to the act of climbing a mountain i.e. mountaineering. Hence, option (d) is the correct answer.

390. (d) The last few lines of the passage mentions that two Italian prisoners escaped the camp and climbed to the top of Mount Kenya to get the feeling of freedom. Hence, option (d) is the correct answer.

391. (d) It is clearly mentioned in the paragraph that great conquerors, generals and soldiers are glorified often in history books. Hence, option (d) is the correct answer.

392. (d) From the passage, it can be inferred that the war fighters i.e. the conquerors, generals and soldiers contributed more to the destruction and killing and less to civilization. Hence, option (d) is the best choice to pick.

393. (b) The author points out in the passage that people think a great deal of the conquerors, generals or soldiers, so much so that on all the hightest pillars in the great cities of the world, one will find the figure of one of these. Hence option (b) is the correct answer.

394. (a) In the passage, it is started that most people believe that the greatest countries are those, who have defeated other countries in battle and ruled over them. Hence, option (a) is the correct answer.

395. (b) After reading the passage, it is clear that the writer has expressed his viewpoint about how development has done more harm to environment than benefits to mankind.

396. (b) The action of clearing a wide area of trees is called 'deforestation' which is referred in the first sentence of the passage.

397. (d) Greater fuel consumption and pollution are some of the outcomes of industrial development according to the writer.

398. (a) The answer is given in first, second and third sentences of the passage.

399. (c) Only sentences 1 and 3 can be inferred after reading the passage. It is nowhere mentioned in the passage that huge man-made structure did not appeal Tolstoy.

400. (a) The answer is given in fifth sentence of the passage.

401. (c) The answer is given in last three sentences of the passage.

402. (a) The use of science has helped man in building shelter and making carts, boats, etc.

403. (b) Nature now needs to be protected because man is rapidly destroying nature.

404. (d) Forest are being destroyed in order to provide necessities as well as needless comforts and pleasures.

405. (c) The evil effect of destroying nature is seen in the unfavourable changes in climate.

406. (d) Climatic changes and soil erosion are results of deforestation.

407. (b) 'Civil liberties' helps women most achieve equality with men.

408. (d) The author talks about the maid servant in the hotel lobby to show that Economic independence is necessary for women's liberation.

409. (a) In paragraph four, the writer says that some women would not like to work in the factory.

410. (b) 'These liberties' in the first paragraph refers to the right of women to vote and not to obey.

411. (c) In the western societies, the occurrence of polio, diphtheria and tuberculosis has 'decreased'.

412. (b) More death are now associated with old age than in the past because deadly diseases affecting the young have been well controlled.

413. (c) The author probably is arguing for rethinking about the successes and failures of the western medicines.

414. (a) There are lots of angle 'to poverty' comes close to the meaning of the sentence 'poverty embraces a whole range of circumstance'.

415. (a) 'Lack of access to information' affects poor people a lot as it does not provide them the information about how to improve their condition.

416. (a) Cultural identiy is important because a sense of cultural identity gives people self-respect and confidence.

417. (c) 'Poor people become margenalised' can be explained in other words as 'they are the most ignored elements of the society'.

418. (d) The tone of the passage is objective and critical.

419. (a) It is clearly mentioned in the last line of the passage that over-population accentuates poverty, and the country's stark poverty itself is in many areas a major cause of over-population.

420. (b) The tone of the passage is sombre as the passage conveys a feeling of deep seriousness and sadness.

421. (c) It is clearly mentioned in the passage that over-population has largely diluted the fruits of the remarkable economic progress of the country.

422. (d) It is clearly stated in the last line of the passage.

423. (d) Dilute means to weaken or make thinner. Consolidated will be the correct antonym as it means to make stronger or more solid.

424. (b) 'Orient' means the countries of the East and 'Occident' means the countries of the West hence, option (b) is the correct answer.

425. (d) It is clearly mentioned in the passage that there was not much difference between Indian and Europe in the 12th and 13th century but, the differences got intensified by the process of Industrialisation.

426. (b) The second half of the passage clearly states that Industrialisation has proved to be a curse as "it is destroying the life of the mind, which is in process ....civilisation collapse".

427. (d) The last few lines of the passage clearly state this.

428. (b) The author, in the passage, has tried to explain the effect of Industrialisation on our civilization thus, option (b) i.e. impact of Industrialisation on our civilization is the central idea of the passage.

429. (a) Statement 1 is correct as passage clearly states "In all cases, it is the ... behalf of the child."

430. (b) Statement 1 is not correct as not stated by the passage. Statements 2 & 3 are correct as stated in passage "This is ... to the education of girls." Statement 4 is correct as the faulty education system.

431. (a) Statement 1 is correct as stated in the passage "one hardly needs .... denied or violated." Statement 2 is irrelevant as developed countries have not been mentioned in the passage.

432. (c) Statement (c) is correct as the passage clearly states that " This may be painfully ...if at all."

433. (a) Since girl's education is the key message, so, prejudice against the intellectual potential of girls.

434. (a) Statement 3 is eliminated as the government should sideline with minimal interference. Statement 4 is eliminated as change in size of government.

435. (d) Strategy of inclusive growth can be effected by focusing on delivery of the basic services to the deprived section of the society. It is clearly stated in the passage "The aim must be .... state can realistically deliver."

436. (b) According to given passage only 4 and 5 are that constitutes.

437. (b) State does not promote inclusive growth as stated in 2nd para " the aim ... realistically deliver."

438. (d) Options (a), (b) and (c) cannot be the message. The only sentence that talks of a message is option (d) which is the main idea of the passage.

439. (c) 1 is eliminated as " art form" is not mentioned in the passage. Social inequalities are not accepted. Only 3 and 4 are mentioned in the passage.

440. (b) According to passage Instigation by external forces (social group get politically ....) and "urge for granting privileges and self respect to disparaged section of the society" are manifestations of social movements.

441. (c) Statement 1 is correct as stated in the passage "The forms of .... in a country". Statement 2 is correct as "phase of development ..... active".

442. (c) Some participants in the race are girls (I - type)
All girl participants is the race are invited for coaching (A - type)
(I + A = I - type)
Thus, some participants in the race are invited for coaching
Hence, conclusions (a), (b) and (c) cannot be drawn from the above statements but conclusion (c) is the conversion of statement 1.
Hence, option (c) can be drawn.

443. (a) Only statements 1 and 2 are true as people who turn revolutionary are not 'other-wordly' unless world shows the contradiction.

444. (c) Only assumptions 2 and 3 are valid as for achieving anything great one has to be free of worries of basic needs and should be mentally as well as physically free.

445. (a) The passage thematically centres on the state of mind of oppressed people as they cannot dream of freedom or aspire for any kind of opportunity.

446. (c) Option (c) is the correct answer as stated in the passage " Every civilization.....life"

447. (c) Option (c) is correct answer as the author shows that not only mussels are affected but other 28 species also disappeared.

448. (d) Neither 1 nor 2 is correct as the dominant species is the keystone species and that is sea star. The sea stars do not live exclusively on mussels as their removal resulted in the disappearance of further 28 species.

449. (c) Only 1 and 3 are correct statements as the 'sea stars' are the keystone species which influences both richness of communities and flow of energy.

450. (c) Assumption 1 is correct as disappearance of 28 species along with mussels. Assumption 3 is also correct according to the passage.

451. (c) with reference to the passage, only 3 and 5 are adverse effect as potable fresh water and bio-diversity are drastically affected.

452. (a) Statement 2 is not correct as the efforts are being taken. 3 is also not correct as the short term gain have resulted into long term degradation of other.

453. (c) Both statements are correct as ecosystem provide people with variety of goods and benefits, they have to be modified considering the population expansion. Secondly technology will always remain expensive and nature is above man.

454. (d) Statement 1 is correct as the writer talks of 'moral act that should be done by our own will'. Statement 4 is also correct as the personal thinking and in order to be moral one can defy convention.

455. (b) According to the writer moral action is neither mechanical nor with clarity of purpose and religious action.

456. (b) Only statements 1 and 2 are correct as let himself be swept away means he does not hold his own ground.

457. (a) The passage clearly suggests that education is not instrumentalist in its deepest sense. But the opening sentence calls it to be functional, instrumental and utilitarian. Thus the instrumentalist view of education is the functional and utilitarian dimension in its purposes.

458. (c) The second part of the passage clearly states education is not a commodity but a process of expansion and conversion of the mind – the moral-intellectual development. Acquiring qualifications, upward mobility and social status are the basic utility values of education.

459. (c) Again the second part clearly states the answer. a, b & d are the utilitarian dimensions of education. But ultimately education leads to self-critical awareness and independence of thought.

460. (c) The sixth lines of the passage states, "one or few individuals may be usually resistant...". Hence, option (c) is correct.

461. (b) 1 is not correct because the passage does not talk about all the poor countries.

 2 is not correct because the passage talks about the role of pesticides in sustainable agriculture especially in poor countries.

 3 is correct as the 2nd para clearly illustrates Alabama leaf-worm developing resistance to aldrin, DDT, dieldrin, endrin, lindane and toxaphene.

462. (d) The widespread use of pesticides has not waned because the ratio of cost to benefit for the individual agricultural producer has remained in favour of pesticide use.

463. (b) Statement 1 finds in the paragraph 1. Statement 2 is mentioned in the paragraph which mentions pests may possess an enzyme that can detoxify the pesticide.

464. (c) 1 is not correct as organic farming is not mentioned in the passage. Further the passage justifies the cost benefit to developed countries like USA.

 2 is correct. Because of this problem it becomes imperative to use pesticides.

 3 is wrong as the social and health costs have to be ignored because of the frightening prospects of the epidemic diseases.

465. (d) The last paragraph states that sustainability depends on continually developing new pesticides. Option (b) states in last line of last paragraph that pesticides are more biodegrade.

 Therefore, option (a) and (b) both imply.

466. (a) Only 1 makes sense. According to the 3rd paragraph second line, 'And some growth .... natural resources.' 2, 3 & 4 are irrelevant statements.

467. (a) Low carbon implies renewable source of energy which are low on carbon and can be used and recycled. Whole passage emphasise on use of renewable sources of energy.

468. (b) 1 is not correct as economic prosperity can raise incomes and foster better institutions but it cannot foster sustainable economic growth. 2 is correct. Generating adaptive technologies can lead to a sustainable growth as discussed in para 2. 3 is correct. As investing on research in adaptation will help us in better handling of the changing climate.

469. (d) Neither statement 1 nor 2 can be inferred from the given passage.

470. (d) Statement 1 finds support in second paragraph: As economic/historians have explained, much of humankind's.....world.

 Statement 2 mentioned in last paragraph in the form of soviet development plan which led to ecological backlash.

 Statement 3 also mentioned in the last paragraph. Hence, (d) is correct choice.

471. (b) The central theme of the passage is clear that adaptation and mitigation should be integrated with development strategies. The author is not against development but a sustainable development what he is talking about.

472. (d) Option (a) is incorrect because the passage states that introduction of exotic species into geographical areas may increase biodiversity as well.

 Option (b) is incorrect because it cannot say that introduction of exotic species by man into new areas have always and greatly altered the ecosystems. Option (c) is incorrect because homogenization of local community population can also occur nationally.

473. (d) The first paragraph provides that human introduce exotic species to breed exotic species with local varieties (producing new agricultural products), to increase agricultural productivity (bringing pest under control) and for beautification and landscaping (recreational opportunities).

474. (b) The second paragraph provides that under natural conditions homogenization is prevented on account of natural barriers (ocean and mountain range).

475. (a) This obviously the correct answer, because it is the most practical one. It is humanly possible to smuggle live organisms and to build highways.

 (b) It is not easy nor practical to make ecosystems sensitive. So this option is ruled out.

 (c) This option is also ruled out for the above said reason.

 (d) It is very difficult and quite unnecessary to ensure new species do not have an impact on local species. So this option is also ruled out.

476. (c) Both the statements (1) and (2) are correct.

477. (b) The first paragraph in the passage conveys the message that the detractors of democracy are quite vocal about that fact that a number of non-democratic governments particularly in East Asia have successfully achieved economic development.

Options (a), (c) and (d) are automatically ruled out.

478. (d) The second and last paragraphs illustrate the fact that freedom and liberty are essential components of development.

479. (c) The "constitutive" connection between democracy and development is political freedom and democratic rights.

480. (a) The effect of FDI or Foreign Direct Investment should be to induce competition because this is ensured in most countries worldwide.

481. (b)
   (a) The first option of multinational companies getting accustomed to domestic laws is not mentioned at all. So, this is not the correct answer.
   (b) Foreign companies may establish joint ventures with domestic or companies may get stronger as the parent companies merge overseas. Both options are mentioned in the paragraph. So, this is the correct answer.
   (c) Since option (1) is included this is not the right answer.
   (d) Same as in (c). Moreover option (4) where foreign companies lower costs finds no mention in the paragraph.

482. (c) The message conveyed in the passage is that it is important to have a competition law in the country to ensure that both domestic and foreign firms have a level playing field.

483. (b) This is the first of the passage. Group farming helps remove poverty, increases agricultural productivity and secures the individual from exploitation.

There is no mention of surplus production. So the other options are ruled out.

484. (c) The last lines of passage mentioned that "the Indian examples of women only groups farming offer potential benefiting women". Hence, (c) is correct choice.

485. (b) (a) There is compulsion on the transition economies to go in for group farming. Therefore, this is not the correct answer.
   (b) The paragraph is all about the benefits of group approach to farming. This is the right answer.
   (c) Both options correct included.
   (d) Both cannot be negated.

486. (c) In the Western context "deepening of democracy" means the increased participation of the individuals in the democratic process.

So, the other options (a), (b) and (d) are automatically negated.

487. (b) Community-Identity seems to be the governing force mentioned in seventh line. Therefore option (b) is correct choice.

488. (c) The involvement of communities in the democratic process in India has led to a silent revolution. The upper castes held power in earlier days. This power is getting slowly, silently and surely transferred to the subaltern groups

In the context of this argument option (a), (b) and (d) are ruled out.

489. (d) The passage revolves around the problem of habitat fragmentation which poses a serious threat to biodiversity conservation.

490. (a) When forest lands get fragmented human activities start on the edges of these fragmented lands which results in degradation of entire forests. Therefore continuity of the forested landscapes and corridors should be maintained.

491. (c) The discharge of agricultural slurry into watercourses should be restricted because watercourses do not contain the microorganisms that can decompose organic components of agricultural slurry. Secondly, the discharge may lead to the eutrophication of water bodies.

492. (b) Discharged agricultural slurry has been referred to as pollutant and decomposed slurry in soil as fertilizer.

493. (b) The pollutants are added to both the soil and water. Soil doesn't get polluted as microorganisms convert pollutant into fertilizer. Water is enriched with the nutrient which flows through streams, rivers and lakes. These nutrients are responsible for eutrophication which results in decomposition of algal blooms.

494. (b) Cultural eutrophication will result in loss of flora and fauna as eutrophication of water bodies do not allow oxygen to pass through it.

495. (c) The theme of the passage is based on how the agricultural slurry when discharged in water causes cultural eutrophication resulting ecosystem service loss. The magnitude of the problem has been so much that the scientists have noticed huge 'dead zones' near big water bodies which means destruction of aquatic life.

496. (b) Man's physical need is never going to cease as long as man is craving for it. Desire brings along miseries. If man doesn't realize this and keeps on doing what he is doing then no physical help can reduce his miseries. It is man's nature which is responsible for all the miseries. The only solution to this is man's spiritual growth and bringing change in his character.

497. (d) The author gives primary importance to spiritual growth in man in eradicating human misery.

498. (c) The democracies in the west have evolved over a period of time because of people's participation in the democratic process. The western democracies have institutionalized the various instrument of governance. As a result their democracies are far more robust than the newly formed democracies.

499. (d) Statement 1 is incorrect.

Statement 2 is also incorrect because it can be inferred from the first paragraph that sometimes western nations are trying to impose democracy on non western nations but it cannot be inferred that western countries are always trying to impose democracy on non western.

500. (a) Statement 1 is correct as it can be inferred from the information given in the passage that companies shall comply with all the laws of land.

501. (a) Good corporate influence have positive influence on the share price of the company as mentioned in last few lines of paragraph. Corporate governance is one of criteria for the foreign institutional investors when they decide to buy a company.

502. (c) Malnutrition occurs due to not eating adequate quantity of food. The knowledge of the food needs of younger children can curb this problem.

503. (b) Taking care of a young child is often left to an older sibling by working mothers. Public health authorities do not find a mention in the passage hence (a) is correct.

504. (c) Policy intervention can save the farmers from agricultural risks. Because Indian farmers are risk averse. So they design inputs and cropping patterns to reduce risk not to maximize their profit.

505. (b) Agricultural risks can be tackled with many strategies like crop insurance, price stabilization, development of varieties resistant to pests and diseases. So no single risk specific policy is sufficient to reduce it.

506. (b) According to the passage, weak global economic prospects and continuing uncertainties in the international markets as well as sovereign risk concerns, particularly in the Euro area have had their impact on the emerging market economies.

507. (c) The Indian financial markets are affected by global changes mainly due to the contagion of Greece's sovereign debt problem spreading to India.

508. (d) Since the Indian financial system is bank dominated banks ability to withstand stress is critical to overall financial stability.

509. (a) With further globalization, consolidation, deregulation and diversification, risk and liquidity management assumes more importance in the Indian banking system in future.

510. (b) When Oxygen is shut from entering the decomposition doesn't take place completely. The Carcasses inside the sedimentary rocks get transformed into crude oil due to heat and pressure.

511. (c) The layers of Sedimentary rocks become thicker and heavier due to deposition and create pressure on the marine creatures under it, which in turn change the carcasses into crude oil.

512. (c) The apologists of the free market system believe in the ability of the market to self correct. Their discussions are generally about free market operations and forces, on the efficiency of such enterprises and their ability for self correction.

513. (c) Ideological bias means an opinion that is of a partial nature. Here the idea expressed in the passage is that an unregulated market is free and competent.

514. (c) It is clearly said that the arguments betray meaning give away a biased opinion. So statement (1) referring to the false ideology of capitalism is one of the options. It is also mentioned that a more honest analysis would reflect the resultant gross inequality. So statement (4) is also the correct option.

515. (c) According to the passage net profits are only 2.2% as far as the central public sector undertakings are concerned. So statement (2) is correct. The private sector has grown. There is a larger base with more educated and moneyed people around. Hence statement (3) is correct too from the point of view of the paragraph. The role of governmental institutions in encouraging competition among the private sector enterprises ensures the continuing growth of this sector. Hence, Statement (4) is also correct.

516. (b) The rural roads should be in the domain of the public sector only because the sparse or the little traffic in these roads makes it impossible to make profits on the road tax or tolls as they are called.

517. (c) The government does invest in different industrial sectors. This is what the paragraph says. Indeed there is governmental investment in a variety of industries from airlines, roads, steel, and finance to industries where the private sector plays a prominent role. For in the latter it acts as the umpire or the regulating agency so as to create a competitive atmosphere for the growth of entrepreneurship.

518. (a) The government acts as a regulating agency by prescribing broad norms within which the private enterprises can conduct their business in an atmosphere of fair and fearless competition. That is why the government is made the umpire in a field of business players.

519. (a) According to the passage the melting of glaciers from the Himalayas will lead to increased run-offs or flow of water in the next 30 years, after which it will decrease, so statement (1) is one of the factors which will force the shifting of location of existing crops due to climatic conditions. Temperatures will increase by 1 degree centigrade over the same period all over the world, and the sea level is expected to rise by 10 cm, so obviously very hot places cannot be suitable for certain crops. So statement (2) is also correct. Due to drought conditions and monsoon variations certain areas will give poor crop productivity. So crop production will have to be shifted to more suitable areas to adjust with ecological imbalances. Hence statement (3) has to be included in the answer too.

520. (c) As India is likely to experience changed weather patterns in the future it is important to invest in research and development in agriculture so that it is possible to locate and indentify the areas which will be most suitable for different crops.

521. (c) According to the passage there should be changes in lifestyle; especially the overuse of technology should be stopped at all costs as stated in statement (3). There should be less consumption of animal protein that is meat. The FAQ or the Food Administration Organization claims that nearly 18% of greenhouse gases are emitted from livestock. So statement (1) is also true.

522. (a) As Indians we continue to depend on fossil fuel heavily because of the lack of investment in research and development in other forms of energy which are so readily available. The lack of technological development prevents us from harnessing the resources of wind, solar and biomass energy, which are readily available.

523. (d) According to the passage the mitigation of greenhouse gases cause lower air pollution, this will lead to better health among the public, as a result there will be less expenditure on public health as stated in statement (1); scientists have already predicted that the emission of greenhouse gases will have disastrous impact on climate change in the next 30 years and worst still after that. So statement (4) is also correct.

524. (b) The essential message conveyed by the passage is that it is absolutely essential to reduce to a very great extent the emission of greenhouse gases into the atmosphere.

525. (c) In this passage the author wants to convey that the best way to ensure the prosperity and further economic growth of the nation is by implementing inclusive growth where the benefits of growth are shared by the entire population and not by certain segments only.

526. (c) To make the process of inclusive growth more effective the author suggests that we should not only concentrate on the poorer sections of society, but also ensure that the rich and middle class stand to gain certain points. In this way it will be possible to redistribute the economic gains made by these sections of society to those getting left behind.

527. (d) According to the passage eradication of poverty is not a sufficient condition for growth. So statement (1) is ruled out. Growth has to be treated as an instrument for ensuring prosperity for all. But this is yet to be attained. So India has to strive on. So statement (2) is also ruled out.

528. (b) If the price of crude oil is x and the exchange rate is y, and if such a transparent formula is set in place by the government the oil companies can make profits by innovating within the rules and regulations of anti-trust and other competition laws. To ensure greater profits they will also have to find out ways to cut costs. So statements (2) and (3) have been selected.

529. (a) According to the passage private oil companies can re-enter the oil producing market if a transparent rule based petrol pricing exists because they will be able to innovate, cut their costs and earn more profits which is an attractive incentive for any business.

530. (d) According to the passage due to the adverse impact of climatic change on the ecosystem can be a possible loss of certain species of animals and their habitats and also a decrease in the services of the ecosystem. (d) option is correct.

531. (b) The passage clearly states that the climatic change may have an adverse effect on the Himalayan ecosystem, by altering temperatures, changing precipitation patterns , leading to drought and consequently the death of several species of animals and plants including humans.

532. (b) The most important message conveyed in the passage is summed up in the last few lines. The idea is to shift the attention from merely the species-habitat focus to the entire biographical range meaning all the plants and animals including humans so that climatic adjustments can be taken care of more effectively.

533. (b) It is clear from the passage that not only human activity is causing environmental pollution, but also natural reasons can adversely affect climate systems. This is clearly stated in the first four lines of the passage.

534. (a) According to the passage government interference leads to distortions and inefficiency in the economy in the sense that there is room for corruption as well as a lack of interest in investment on the part of the entrepreneurs.

535. (c) The first paragraph states that the basic philosophy of globalization is to ensure absolute freedom for the markets, to set their prices, produce their goods, and distribute them as per their own criterion.

536. (c) The passage clearly states that in accordance with the conditions set by the WTO. etc. for globalization, public sectors should be privatized. So statement (1) is correct. Employment and wages should be conditioned by the free play of the market forces involved, otherwise it might discourage investment as stated in statement (3). Even social services like heath and education should welcome private players as is correctly expressed in statement (4).

537. (b) The entire passage focuses on the fact that the state should play a reducing role in the process of globalization. This is elaborated in the last few lines of the passage with particular reference to India.

538. (d) (a) is wrong as it states a fact mentioned in the passage. It does not sum up the passage.

   (b) is wrong as the passage does not restrict the problem to the developing countries only.

    (c) is wrong as the passage only says that the food production will have to double. It does not talk about food scarcity at all. Rather it talks about how to meet the required target.

    (d) correctly sums up the passage. Food security is increasingly a collective challenge and the passage suggests means to combat it.

539. (a) (a) is correct as the passage talks about the conflict between man and State. Moreover the passage confirms that this is a continuous tussle and is as old as the state history. The solution seems to be' still far off suggests that the conflict will remain unresolved.

    (b) and (d) are wrong as they present only the idea contained in the last line of the passage.

    (c) is wrong as the passage clearly mentions that old values and ideas constantly yield place to new ones which is contrary to what is mentioned in (c). Moreover it is not the author's viewpoint.

540. (b) (a) is wrong as it is a general statement and does present the crux of the passage.

    (c) is wrong as the opening line of the passage says that people talk about democracy (or understand democracy) but they have a weakness favouring their caste or community or religion.

    (d) is wrong as it projects an extreme situation which is out of the scope of the passage.

    (b) is the most appropriate statement as it talks about providing equal opportunities to all irrespective of the caste or community or religion. That's what is a True democracy.

541. (b) Clearly only 2 is correct. 1 is wrong as the passage says that 'Such access is not always available to all people in developing countries like India and more so, in rural areas.' This means that they are sometimes available.2 is correct as mentioned in the last sentence of the passage.

542. (d) The crucial message conveyed in the passage is to promote financial inclusion such that every citizen of the country has access to bank accounts and can save money so as to have better finances . Establishing more banks is a route to financial inclusion. Increasing the interest rate of bank deposits would promote savings. So (d) is correct.

543. (b) The passage suggests the biggest hurdle in the world agriculture is to maintain a demand - supply equilibrium. Based on the relevant information provided in the passage, it can be ascertained that regulating the pricing component for ensuring affordability to the poor and a proper marketing mix would be beneficial.

544. (d) The biggest challenge that has always haunted world agriculture is to achieve a balance the demand and supply for foods.

545. (c) To reduce hunger and starvation, ensuring equilibrium between demand and supply of food is mandatory, alongside ushering measures for Purchasing Power Parity, to help the poor consumers too.

546. (b) Since there is disparity in the sustainable provision and supply for food worldwide, this issue has gained significance.

547. (c) The key responsibility areas of the civil service officers need to be clearly defined and standardized, based on the political agendas. Lack of such clarity would lead to misgovernance. Also, striking equilibrium between external and internal accountabilities is mandatory for effective management.

548. (d) The passage does not provide relevant information on either of the provided options.

549. (d) Civil services, being an extremely reputed taskforce, should implement reforms to create benchmark in service and improve accountability of the office bearers.

550. (d) Seeking accountability through increased participation by individuals in the decision making process would not help increase internal accountability.

551. (a) Religious traditions, regardless of felicitating the Almighty or the Supernatural, ushers belief, ethics and a specific code of conduct in the society. Man being a social animal derives the value set from the society, important for maintaining relationships and goodwill. Thus, human relationships can be assumed to have been derived from the religious traditions.

552. (c) Fundamental rights, combined with duties, are mandatory for dispensing justice in a society.

553. (d) As per the passage, all the three options pose challenges to the utilization of biomass as fuel. Issues related to climatic variations, aggravation of carbon emissions due to liquid bio-fuels and competition between biomass and food production, have adverse effects.

554. (b) It is stated that unscrupulous cultivation of energy crops will lead to an unhealthy competition with food crops, thereby contributing to inflation and price hike for food crops.

555. (b) Technological intervention, with proper monitoring, could assist in using biomass for power generation and achieving negative emissions.

556. (a) As per the information provided in the 2nd paragraph, some energy models (unproven technology) might negate carbon emissions, thereby mitigating environmental pollution due to the greenhouse effect.

557. (a) The passage pertains to duty to vote.

558. (d) The passage denotes that despair sometimes leads to dictatorship in a country.

559. (b) The assumption that one of the aims of sustainable agriculture is to ensure minimal ecological imbalance can be made from the passage.

560. (c) Biopesticides are not hazardous to human health and they are essential to maintain the biodiversity of any ecosystem.

561. (c) The opening line of the passage says that 'universal access to education' is no longer enough. So, 1 is not of paramount importance. The second sentence says that 'facilities' or infrastructure is a prerequisite but 'insufficient' to fulfil the purpose of education So, 2 is not of paramount importance.

3 is mentioned in the second paragraph as being of paramount importance.

562. (d) Assumption 1 can be made from the sentence, 'Teacher accountability systems...

Assumption 2 follows from 'universal access to education' in the opening line.

Assumption 3 follows from, 'we must address the entire gamut ...,' which implies that India's 'demographic dividend' or 'huge young population across diversities' could be tapped.

563. (d) It is clearly mentioned in the first half of the second paragraph of the passage.

564. (c) The entire passage emphasises on giving quality education to all children. Options (a), (b) and (d) are true, but none conveys the essential message of the passage.

565. (b) It is clearly mentioned in the passage in the line "This theory is false, for the art of leadership can be acquired and can indeed be taught".

ENGLISH LANGUAGE COMPREHENSION SKILLS

INTRODUCTION

The success mantra in today's highly competitive world with ever expanding boundaries of knowledge, is "know the right thing at the right time, make right use of it and express it in just the right words"

Why do you think reading comprehension questions are asked from the primary level in school examinations to a level as high as competitive examinations for management or administrative work? Very simply put, in the present era which has a plethora of information, facts, knowledge, it is important for any officer, or manager' to be able to extract relevant information from the given draft in minimum possible time and use it for the execution of the assigned project in the best possible way. And this is what language comprehension exercises give you a practice in. Therefore, a student must consider this section not only as a preparatory exercise but also, as an exercise to build a skill that he/she will use for the rest of his/her life.

Make reading a habit to improve your expression and vocabulary. Each day list out the new words you come across. Classify them under subjects, Science, Sports, Politics, Literature. Learn their meanings and use them frequently. This will help you understand the jargon of different fields.

MUST Do_s FOR A GOOD READER

- ☐ Read about different fields, don't restrict yourself to one.
- ☐ Do intelligent reading, don't waste time reading junk information.
- ☐ Read only from good newspapers and magazines
- ☐ Utilise maximum time, read while travelling, waiting' etc.
- ☐ Try to indulge in a discussion everyday about what you read that day.
- ☐ Improve your passive vocabulary as you read and use the learnt words to build your active vocabulary.

For maximum utility of time, you can depend on News Channels. You can select certain talk shows aired on some good English news channels like NDTV, CNN IBN or TIMES NOW and watch them regularly. This will improve your general awareness, give you an analytical perspective, keep you updated with news from different sectors, and also improve your English.

An inquisitive mind is a gift for a student. Always maintain a desire to know more, keep yourself curious about every subject. Do not hesitate in discussing your opinions, asking questions, expressing your views with friends, teachers or experts. This kind of interaction and communication will greatly increase your interest and knowledge and you will be drawn towards reading more. Always keep in mind that developing these habits will help you reap long term benefits.

1. Practise solving more and more Reading Comprehension exercises. Start with shorter, simpler pieces on subjects of your interest and gradually move to heavier, more difficult passages. This will strengthen your confidence, as you build up your momentum, and prepare you better to deal with longer passages.

2. Self-monitor your reading. Mark every time you get distracted or lose concentration. In this manner you will be aware of the number of times you lost concentration in an hour; and with every passing hour, you will make a stronger effort to be more focussed. You will see that with each passing hour, the number of the marks will decrease. And, you will overcome the tendency to get distracted.

READING SPEED

From a competitive point of view, 'Time is money' The faster you read, the more time you will have for comprehension and analysis. But you must keep in mind certain points while trying to read fast. Students, in their attempt to read fast, Often increase their speed of reading without trying to understand or retain the information. Remember **Reading Comprehension = Reading + Comprehension.**

You must read at a fast speed but not at the cost of comprehension or understanding because in that case you'll have to read the passage again and, the time you saved by reading fast will be consumed in re-reading. So it will be a wasteful exercise.

1. Your reading speed is the number of words you can read as well as understand per minute. Remember, if you don't understand what you're reading, it is of no use.
2. Track your reading speed. In this manner you will be able to monitor your improvement.

RETAINING CAPACITY

This is the most important part of Reading. If a student is able to read well, read with concentration and read fast, but is not able to retain useful information of the data then all is lost. A good reader need not come back to the passage again and again to look for answers. The first reading of the passage should, therefore, be done with much care and attention so that most of the matter is retained.

You can follow some simple steps to improve your retaining capability. Every time you read a passage, make a mental note of the following :

(a) title of the passage
(b) basic theme of the passage
(c) the positions that the passage takes or the points that the passage makes
(d) conclusion of the passage.

READING APTITUDE

Reading Aptitude is different from reading skills. The points and factors discussed so far, constitute reading skill and pertain to the manner in which you read. Reading Aptitude is the natural ability to read and understand well. It gives an upper edge to a student in the RC section or even otherwise if developed properly.

WHAT IS READING APTITUDE?

Reading aptitude includes the approach that you take while reading; the mindset with which you read and the expectation you have from the piece. If you approach a reading piece only for the purpose of collecting facts to add to your existing store of knowledge; or, only as a practice to improve your reading speed; or, merely as an examination exercise; you would not receive the same results as you would if you read the passage with a different attitude.

HOW TO DEVELOP READING APTITUDE

Consider every piece of written information as a prospective useful draft.

Begin with the rule of WIIFM - what's in it for me. Once you have used your wisdom to decide if the passage is worth reading, approach the passage as a mystery novel. There are hidden clues you must look for. From the beginning stay a careful, clever reader. Remember the first reading itself should give you all you may need to have from a passage.

If there are facts in the passage, quickly decide, as you read, which of those are important enough to be memorized; and readily memorize them.

If there is an argument in the passage, keep a trail of how the argument proceeds; involve your mind with the passage and form an opinion about the argument.

If the passage is offering a philosophical perspective, got down a short summary of the philosophical theory in simple words.

If the essay describes a process or an event, then as you read on, form a chain of events in your mind.

Keeping these points in mind will improve your reading and retaining efficiency greatly. What you have to target and achieve is EFFECTIVE READING. A good reader may or may not be just as good at comprehension and analysis but an Effective Reader would definitely perform in comprehension and Analysis of data just as well. So, try and be an EFFECTIVE READER.

HOW TO APPROACH DIFFERENT TYPES OF COMPOSITION

Composition may be done in different styles as the following diagram shows.

(1) Narrative.

(2) Reflective

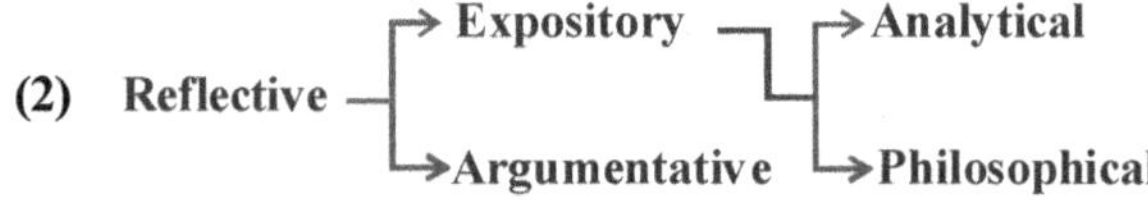

(3) Imaginative.

Let us now consider the different types of writing one may get to read and how one should deal with each.

1. Narrative Passage

A narrative passage usually tells a story which means a sequence of events. Thus, a narrative passage gives an orderly account of a series of related events or the successive particulars of an event. A narrative passage could be of various kinds: (1) Biography (2) History (3) Fiction (4) Execution of a process.

2. Reflective Passage

(a) Expository Passage

An expository passage is the most rigid and restricted form of composition. It is also the most common kind of writing. Its purpose is to explain, its language is clear and direct, mostly. Its appeal is to the intellect. What you would mostly come across in an expository essay will be definition, comparisons, contradictions. Expository passages can be either <u>analytical</u> or <u>philosophical</u> in approach. While the former is investigative, the latter, scholarly and sermonising.

(b) Argumentative Passage

An argumentative passage includes an argument and an argument is possible only about a subject that invites argument on conflicting opinions. Such an essay admits difference of opinions and, therefore, the purpose of an argumentative essay is to persuade the readers to adopt a certain idea, attitude or course of action and, if possible, to resolve the conflict implicit in the subject.

3. Imaginative passage

Imaginative passages are those that talk about something which does not exist in reality. These passages are **fictional** in nature; e.g., on conversation between two animals/trees, demons etc., or **fantasy**; e.g. imaginative creatures and situations.

Illustrations

PASSAGE-1

Read the following passages and answer the questions that follow :
Alzheimer's disease **impairs** a person's ability to recall memories, both distant and as recent as a few hours before. Although there is no cure yet for the illness, there may be hope for a cure with a protein called nerve growth factor. The protein is produced by nerve cells in the same region of the brain where Alzheimer's occurs. Based on this relationship, scientists from the University of Sweden and the University of California at San Diego designed an experiment to test whether doses of nerve growth factors could service the effects of memory loss caused by Alzheimer's. Using a group of rats with impaired memory, the scientists gave half of the rats doses of nerve growth factor while giving the other half a blood protein as a placebo, thus creating a control group. At the end of the four-week test, the rats given the nerve growth factor performed equally to rats with normal memory abilities. While experiments do not show that nerve growth factor can stop the general process of **deterioration** caused by Alzheimer's they do show potential as a means to slowing the process significantly.

Illustration – 1

This passage is mainly concerned with:

    (a)   **cures for Alzheimer's disease**

    (b)   **impaired memory of patients**
    (c)   **the use of rats as experimental subjects**
    (d)   **nerve growth factor as a cure for Alzheimer's**

Explanation :
This is a main theme question where you're to choose the basic idea of the given passage. The usual ambiguity in such questions is between main and supportive ideas mentioned in the passage and both given as prospective answers.

  (a)   This is a concern of the passage and can, therefore, be the answer. But the passage is more specific and factual. Therefore, we should eliminate this option in case of finding a more specific answer.

  (b)   This is only a connected allusion in the passage and not at all its central idea

  (c)   This again is mentioned in the passage but is not the main theme of the passage. This option can be eliminated.

  (d)   This is the right answer. This is more specific and accurate than option (a). The main theme of the passage is cure for Alzheimer's but this cure is through nerve growth factor and this is what the passage is concerned about chiefly.

Illustration – 2

According to the passage where is nerve growth factor produced in the body?

    (a)   **In the pituitary gland**
    (b)   **In nerve cells in brain**
    (c)   **In red blood cells in the circulatory system**
    (d)   **In nerve cells in the special column**

Explanation :
This is a factual question. Locate that part of the passage which gives the right fact, and information about the question. In this case the relevant line is "The protein is produced by nerve cells in the same region of the brain". Therefore, the right answer will be (b).

Illustration – 3

The word 'impairs' [underlined] is most similar to which of the following?

    (a)   **Affects**   (b)   **Destroys**
    (c)   **Enhances**   (d)   **Diminishes**

Explanation :
This is a 'Synonym' question.

  (a)   Affects- impairs means to weaken, which is affect negatively, affect is, therefore, an incomplete replacement for impairs and will not to be correct choice.

  (b)   Destroys is too strong a word to be similar to impair. To impair may mean to slow down the process of progress but not to destroy.

  (c)   Enhance- this is opposite to impair.

  (d)   Diminishes- This option is nearest to 'impair' in meaning in context of the passage, hence, the right answer.

Illustration – 4

Which of the following can be inferred from the passage?

    (a)   **Alzheimer's disease is deadly**

    (b)   **Though unsuccessful, the experiments did show some benefits derived from new growth factors**

    (c)   **The experiment did not show any significant benefits from nerve growth factor**

    (d)   **More work needs to be done to understand the effects of nerve growth factor**

Explanation :
This is an inference question. The obviously wrong options can be eliminated first in this type of passages.

  (a)   and (c) appear wrong from the first read itself. There is no mention of Alzheimer's disease being deadly, hence (a) is wrong.

  (b)   This is correct because though the experiment may be considered unsuccessful since no sure shot cure has yet been discovered, even nerve growth factor cannot cure Alzheimer's, it can only slow down the process of deterioration but the experiment showed some benefits from the protein.

  (c)   is factually incorrect because benefits from the nerve growth factor were seen after the experiment.

  (d)   This cannot directly be inferred from the given passage because it does not talk about further work in the field.

Illustration – 5

The passage most closely resembles which of the following patterns of organisation?

(a) Chronological
(b) Statement and illustration
(c) Alphabetical order
(d) None of the above

Explanation :

In this question you have to recognise the type of passage. Use Elimination technique.

(a) and (c) are wrong because the passage is neither chronological nor is there any alphabetical order in it.

(b) is the right answer. The passage makes statement about the disease and illustrates the experiment and its result.

Illustration – 6

Which of the following is closest in meaning to the word 'deterioration' (underlined) ? .

(a) Depression   (b) Deduction
(c) Decline   (d) Disconnection

Explanation :

Deterioration means becoming worse

(b) and (d) are not synonyms of deterioration

(a) Depression means 'low' but there is no gradual process of coming down suggested in the word depression. Deterioration is a comparative process. Depression is a state.

(d) This will be the right answer since decline is also a process of becoming worse or coming down, It is closest in meaning to the given word.

PASSAGE-2

Read the following passages and answer the questions that follows :

Today every major anthology of nineteenth century poetry includes examples of the work which Christina Rossetti produced during her long literary career. Born in 1830, she began composing verse at the age of eleven and continued to write for the remaining fifty-three years of her life. Her brother Dante Gabriel Rossetti, himself a poet and painter, soon recognised her genius and urged her to publish her poems. By the time of her death in 1894, Christina had written more than eleven hundred poems and had published over nine hundred of them. Although this work has earned her recognition as the greatest woman poet of the Victorian Age, there is still no authoritative edition of her poetry.

Illustration – 7

The word 'anthology' (line 1) probably means:

(a) writer   (b) collection
(c) poem   (d) poet

Explanation :

This is 'synonym' type question. 'Anthology' means a chronological collection.

(a), (c), (d) could easily be eliminated from the first read of line 'Anthology of poetry. It can only mean collection of poetry. Thus, (b) is the right answer.

Illustration – 8

Christina Rossetti began writing poetry :

(a)   only after her brother urged her to do so
(b)   when she was fifty three years old
(c)   when she was very young
(d)   when her genius was recognised

Explanation :

This is a factual question. First, locate the relevant lines in the passage. In this case, they are "She began composing verse at the age of eleven.

(a) Christina Rosetti started publishing her poetry when her brother urged her to do so but she had started writing much earlier. The question asks us about her 'writing' poetry and not 'publishing' poetry this is not the right answer, therefore.

(b) This is factually incorrect according to the passage and hence not the answer.

(c) This is true. The passage says she started writing when she was 11 years of age, which is quite young. This is a probable answer.

(d) This cannot be. Her genius was recognised only after she had written poetry. This is not the answer.

Thus, (b) is the right answer

Illustration – 9

Christina's brother was probably a good judge of her work because:

(a)   he loved his sister very much
(b)   he himself published poems
(c)   he was a poet
(d)   he was a famous painter

Explanation :

This is an inference question. The statements are not directly picked from the passage so their accuracy will be judged through inference and elimination.

(a) This cannot be the right answer as the passage does not link D.G. Rossetti's love for his sister with his judgement of her poetry.

(b) Though he published poems but it is not suggested anywhere that this is the reason why Dante Gabriel Rossetti was able to judge the poetic genius of his sister. Thus, this cannot be the right answer

(c) If we refer to the line 'Dante Rosseti, himself a poet and a painter soon recognised her genius..' then we can infer that Dante could judge the genius of his sister because he himself was a poet and could, therefore, recognise the abilities in his sister.

(d) This, obviously, is wrong. His being a painter has nothing to do with his judging Christina Rossetti's poetic genius.

Illustration 10

By 1894, Christina had:

(a) published only a few of the many poems she had written

(b) published all the poems she had written

(c) published more than eleven hundred poems

(d) published over nine hundred poems

Explanation :

This is a factual question. So, locate the relevant line in the passage before answering. "By the time of her death in 1894, Christina had written more than 1100 poems...."

(a) This is incorrect since Christina published 900 of the 1100 poems she had written.

(b) This is untrue because according to the passage, about 200 of her poems remained unpublished

(c) This is untrue again, she published over 900 poems, she had written over 1100 poems although

(d) This is true. Hence, this is the right answer.

Illustration 11

At the time this passage was written, Christina Rosetti's poetry :

(a) was almost unknown

(b) was rarely published

(c) had made her known as the greatest woman poet of the eighteenth century

(d) had not been collected in an authoritative edition

Explanation :

This is a factual question but not focussed on a single line. Each statement will have to be individually confirmed from the given passage.

(a) This is untrue since the very first sentence of the passage establishes that Christina Rossetti's poetry is included in all major anthologies of 19th century poetry. This is not the answer.

(b) This, also, is wrong for reasons the same as above.

(c) This statement is factually incorrect that Christina Rosseti lived and wrote poetry in the 19th century and not the 18th century. This is, then, not the answer.

(d) This is the right answer because the last sentence of the passage says that "there is still no authoritative edition of her poetry".

Exercise

Directions : *Read the given passages and answer the questions based on them.*

PASSAGE-1

The tree is beautiful the year around. It need not wait for a brief burst of blooming to justify itself, like the wild plum and the hawthorn. It is handsomer than most dressed only in its broad leaves, shining like dark polished jade, so that, when I am desperate for decoration, I break a few sprays for the house and find in them an ornament of which a Japanese artist would approve. The tree sheds some of its leaves just before it blooms, as though it shakes off old garments to be cleansed and ready for the new. There is a dry pattering to earth of the hard leaves, and for a brief time the tree is parched and drawn, the rosy-lichened trunk gray and anxious. Then pale green spires cover the boughs, unfolding into freshly lacquered leaves, and at their tips the blooms appear. When, in late April or early May, the pale buds unfold into great white waxy blossoms, sometimes eight or ten inches across, and the perfume is a delirious thing on the spring air, I would not trade one tree for a conservatory filled with orchids.

1. What is referred to as 'most dressed' as used in the passage?
    (a) A well dressed man looking at the tree
    (b) The author
    (c) Other trees
    (d) The wild plum and the hawthorn
2. The white waxy blossoms are
    (a) Huge   (b) Small
    (c) Pale green   (d) Most handsome
3. Why does the tree shed some of its leaves just before it blooms?
    (a) To bloom again
    (b) To appear beautiful throughout the year
    (c) To get decorated with new leaves
    (d) To convert the pale buds into white waxy blossoms

PASSAGE-2

We saw some horses that had been born and reared on top of the mountains, above the range of running water, and consequently they had never drunk that fluid in their lives but had been always accustomed to quenching their thirst by eating dew-laden or shower-wetted leaves. And now it was destructively funny to see them sniff suspiciously at a pail of water and then put in their noses and try to take a bite out of the fluid, as if it were a solid. Finding it liquid, they would snatch away their heads and fall to trembling, snorting, and showing other evidences of fright. When they became convinced at last that the water was friendly and harmless, they thrust in their noses up to their eyes, brought out a mouthful of water and proceeded to chew it complacently.

4. The horses expected water to be
    (a) Leaves   (b) Cold
    (c) Solid   (d) Hot
5. On the basis of the passage, it can be assumed that:
    (a) Horses are afraid of running water
    (b) Horses prefer quenching their thirst by eating dew-laden leaves
    (c) Horses are reared on mountainous regions
    (d) None of these
6. Which of the following is similar in meaning to the phrase 'destructive funny' as used in the passage?
    (a) Fortunately funny
    (b) Offensively funny
    (c) I could have died laughing
    (d) Aggressively funny

PASSAGE-3

There seems to be no chilly distance existing between the German students and the professor, but, on the contrary, a companionable intercourse, the opposite of chilliness and reserve. When the professor enters a beer hall in the evening where students are gathered together, these rise up and take off their caps and invite the old gentleman to sit with them and partake. He accepts, and the pleasant talk and the beer flow for an hour or two, and by and by the professor, properly charged and comfortable, gives a cordial good night, while the students stand bowing and uncovered, and then he moves on his happy way homeward with all his vast cargo of learning afloat in his hold. Nobody finds fault or feels outraged. No harm has been done.

7. What does the author mean by the phrase 'no chilly distance'?
    (a) Professor's home is not very far from the beer hall.
    (b) Students and the professor are very friendly with each other.
    (c) The weather is not very chilly in Germany.
    (d) The professor being very strict scares the students quite a few times as in the beer hall.
8. The writer in trying to defend:
    (a) Bowing
    (b) The virtues of beer
    (c) Friendliness between professor and students
    (d) The strictness of the professor
9. Find the false statements
    (a) The professor demanded utmost respect from the students in the beer hall.
    (b) There is an amiable relationship between the professor and the students.
    (c) The professor and the students drank beer for an hour or two.
    (d) Both (a) and (b)

PASSAGE-4

It was fairly dark a few minutes after we got within the wall, and we rode long distances through wonderfully crooked streets, eight to ten feet wide and shut in on either side by the high mud-walls of the gardens. At last we got to where lanterns could be seen flitting about here and there and knew we were in the midst of the curious old city. In a little narrow street, crowded with our pack mules and with a swarm of uncouth Arabs, we alighted and through a kind of a hole in the wall entered the hotel. We stood in a great flagged court with flowers and citron trees about us and a huge tank in the centre that was receiving the waters of many pipes. We crossed the court and entered the rooms prepared to receive four of us. In a large marble-paved recess between the two rooms was another tank of clear, cool water, which was kept running over all the time by the streams that were pouring into it from half a dozen pipes. Nothing, in this scorching, desolate land could look so refreshing as this pure water flashing in the lamp light, nothing could look so beautiful, nothing could sound so delicious as this mimic rain to ears long unaccustomed to sounds of such a nature.

10. What is the meaning of the word 'alighted' as used in the passage?
    (a) To ascend   (b) To descend
    (c) To run fast   (d) To take rest

11. What has been referred to as 'so refreshing' and 'so beautiful'?
    (a) The flagged court with flowers
    (b) The light flashing in the lamp
    (c) The mud wall of the garden
    (d) Another tank of clear and cool water

12. What did the author use to reach the hotel?
    (a) A mule
    (b) They were on foot
    (c) A horse
    (d) Not mentioned in the passage

PASSAGE-5

The inhabitants of Monmouth Street are a distinct class, a peaceable and retiring race who immure themselves for the most part in deep cellars or small back parlours and who seldom come forth into the world except in the dusk and coolness of the evening, when they may be seen seated in chairs on the pavement, smoking their pipes or watching the gambols of their engaging children as they revel in the gutter, a happy troop of infantine scavengers. Their countenances bear a thoughtful and a dirty cast, certain indications of their love of traffic, and their habitations are distinguished by that disregard of outward appearance and neglect of personal comfort so common among people who are constantly immersed in profound speculations and deeply engaged in sedentary pursuits.

13. To immure oneself is to
    (a) Hide oneself
    (b) Imprison oneself
    (c) Enclose oneself within walls
    (d) Burn oneself up

14. The scavengers are
    (a) Sweeping and cleaning up
    (b) Looking for food
    (c) Picking things up from the street
    (d) Making a game of walking in the gutter

15. The inhabitants
    (a) Love to keep things clean
    (b) Have no time for housekeeping
    (c) Are poor housekeepers
    (d) Enjoy shopping for new things

PASSAGE-6

Half our days we pass in the shadow of the earth, and the brother of death exacts a third part of our lives. A good part of our sleep is peered out [seen] with visions and fantastic objects, wherein we are confessedly deceived. The day supplies us with truths, the night, with fictions and falsehoods, which uncomfortably divide the natural account [story] of our beings. And, therefore, having passed the day in sober labors and rational inquiries of truth, we are fain [willing] to betake ourselves unto such a state of being wherein the soberest heads have acted [enacted] all the monstrosities of melancholy and which unto open eyes are no better than folly and madness.

16. What has been referred to as 'brother of death'?
    (a) Shadow
    (b) Sleep
    (c) Vision
    (d) Day

17. Find the true statement based on the passage:
    I. Nights have negative connotation
    II. We get deceived by our dreams
    III. Truths are supplied by the day
    IV. We are highly skeptical towards the day
    (a) Only I
    (b) Both III and IV
    (c) All I, II and III
    (d) All are true

18. Open eyes are:
    (a) Memories of dream
    (b) Being awake
    (c) Fictions and falsehood
    (d) Folly and madness

PASSAGE-7

In the guttering glare was the preacher, and for a while we could see no one else. He was an immensely tall and thin mountaineer in blue jeans, his collarless shirt open at the neck and his hair a tousled mop. As he preached he paced up and down under the smoking flambeaux, and at each turn he thrust his arms into the air and yelled "Glory to God!" We crept nearer in the shadow of the cornfield and began to hear more of his discourse. He was preaching on the Day of Judgment. The high kings of the earth, he roared, would all fall down and die. Only the sanctified would stand up to receive the Lord God of Hosts. One of these kings he mentioned by name, the king of what he called Greece-y. The king of Greece-y, he said, was doomed to Hell.

19. Who is a preacher?
  (a) A person who delivers a sermon or religious address to an assembled group of people.
  (b) A person who motivates others to follow a particular religion.
  (c) A person who advocates a particular religion or godliness.
  (d) A person who hunts animals on the mountains.

20. The sanctified are:
  (a) The sinners
  (b) All the congregation
  (c) Those free from sin
  (d) The priests

21. Find the false statement(s):
  I. The preacher was an immensely tall, thin and dark person.
  II. Lord God of Hosts would kill the high kings of earth on The Judgment Day.
  III. Only the pure and pious would be receiving the God of Hosts on Doomsday.
  (a) Only I
  (b) Both II and III
  (c) Both I and II
  (d) All I, II and III

PASSAGE-8

In fine weather, the old gentleman is almost constantly in the garden, and, when it is too wet to go into it, he will look out of the window at it by the hour together. He has always something to do there, and you will see him digging and sweeping and cutting and planting with manifest delight. In springtime, there is no end to the sowing of seeds and sticking little bits of wood over them, with labels, which look like epitaphs to their memory, and in the evening, when the sun has gone down, the perseverance with which he lugs a great watering pot about is perfectly astonishing. The only other recreation he has is the newspaper, which he peruses every day from beginning to end, generally reading the most interesting pieces of intelligence to his wife during breakfast.

22. What does the phrase 'by the hour' mean as used in the passage?
  (a) With someone   (b) With his wife
  (c) After every hour (d) For long hours

23. From the passage, it can be assumed that:
  I. The old gentleman is a nature loving person.
  II. The old gentleman lives alone in his house.
  III. The old gentleman loves reading newspapers more than anything else.
  (a) Only I   (b) Only III
  (c) Both I & III   (d) All I, II and III

24. Find the synonym of the word 'PERSEVERANCE'.
  (a) Grit   (b) Apathy
  (c) Indolence   (d) Lethargy

PASSAGE-9

We went on climbing, higher and higher, and curving hither and thither, in the shade of noble woods, with a rich variety and profusion of wild flowers all about us and glimpses of rounded grassy backbones below us occupied by trim chalets and nibbling sheep and other glimpses of far lower altitudes, where distance diminished the chalets to toys and obliterated the sheep altogether, and every now and then some ermined monarch of the Alps swung magnificently into view for a moment, then drifted past an intervening spur and disappeared again.

25. A spur is:
  (a) A sharp rock
  (b) A mountain trail
  (c) A ridge projecting from a mountain
  (d) A loop in a mountain trail

26. What are "backbones' referred to?
  (a) Trail of rocks   (b) Tall peaks
  (c) Long grasses   (d) Hill tops

27. The monarch is ermined because:
  (a) It is covered with snow
  (b) It is covered with forest
  (c) It's the home of animals
  (d) The hill are very high

28. The chalets were toys because:
  (a) They were fragile
  (b) They were very colourful
  (c) They were too far away
  (d) They were poorly constructed

PASSAGE-10

Medical knowledge in ancient Egypt had an excellent reputation, and rulers of other empires would ask the Egyptian pharaoh to send them their best physician to treat their loved ones. Egyptians had some knowledge of human anatomy, even though they never dissected the body. For example, in the classic mummification process, they knew how to insert a long hooked implement through a nostril, breaking the thin bone of the brain case and remove the brain. Egyptian physicians also were aware of the importance of the pulse and of a connection between pulse and heart. They developed their theory of "channels" that carried air, water and blood to the body by observing the River Nile. If the Nile became blocked, crops became unhealthy. They applied this theory to the body - if a person was unwell, they would use laxatives to unblock the "channels." Mostly, the physicians' advice for staying healthy was to wash and shave the body, including under the arms. This may have prevented infections. They also advised patients to look after their diet and avoid foods such as raw fish or other animals considered to be unclean.

Some practices were harmful. Many medical prescriptions contained animal dung, which contains products of fermentation and moulds. Some of them have curative properties, but they also contain bacteria, posing a threat of infection. Being unable to distinguish between the original infection and the unwholesome effects of the faeces treatment, they may have been impressed by the few cases when it did improve the patient's condition.

29. The passage basically talks about:
    (a) Ancient Egyptian physicians
    (b) The role of Nile in ancient Egypt
    (c) Medical knowledge in ancient Egypt
    (d) Infections and diseases in ancient Egypt
30. The brain was removed
    (a) To prevent infections
    (b) To unblock channels
    (c) During mummification
    (d) To keep the body clean
31. What does 'Pharaoh' mean?
    (a) Physicians   (b) Soldiers
    (c) Teachers   (d) Rulers

PASSAGE-11

It was Mary Leakey's 1959 discovery of a cranium at Olduvai Gorge in Africa that captured worldwide attention and made the Leakeys a household name. Building on this find, Louis and Mary attracted a multidisciplinary team of specialists to work at Olduvai and launched the modern science of paleoanthropology, the study of human origins. In 1978, Mary made what may have been her greatest find. Her team was exploring a site in Tanzania when they discovered a trail of remarkably clear ancient hominid footprints preserved in volcanic ash. It was a stunning glimpse of the world 3.6 million years ago.

32. The word paleo (as in paleoanthropology) means:
    (a) Stone   (b) Layer
    (c) Ancient   (d) Scientific
33. Anthropology is the scientific study of:
    (a) People around the world
    (b) Mankind
    (c) Skeletons
    (d) The origins and social relationships of human being
34. Hominid means:
    (a) Homo Sapiens
    (b) Primate
    (c) Primitive man
    (d) Primate family that includes modern human beings

PASSAGE-12

During the past 100 years, astronomers have discovered quasars, pulsars, black holes and planets orbiting distant suns. But all these pale next to the discoveries Edwin Hubble made in a few remarkable years in the 1920s. At the time, most of his colleagues believed the Milky Way galaxy made up the entire cosmos. But, peering deep into space from the chilly summit of Mount Wilson in Southern California, Hubble realized that the Milky Way is just one of millions of galaxies that dot an incomparably larger setting. Hubble went on to show that this galaxy-studded cosmos is expanding. He did nothing less, in short, than invent the idea of the universe and then provide the first evidence for the Big Bang theory. He discovered the cosmos and in doing so founded the science of cosmology.

35. What does Cosmos mean?
    (a) The solar system
    (b) Collection of galaxies
    (c) The Milky Way
    (d) Everything that exists anywhere
36. Hubble was the first to realize that:
    (a) The Milky Way is the entire cosmos
    (b) The Milky Way is only one of many galaxies
    (c) The universe is huge
    (d) Pulsars black holes and planets are part of our galaxy
37. The Big Bang is implied by
    (a) The universe
    (b) The cosmos
    (c) Galaxies beyond the Milky Way
    (d) The expanding universe

PASSAGE-13

Peter the Great ruled Russia and later the Russian Empire from 1682 until his death. He carried out a policy of Westernization and expansion that transformed the Czardom of Russia into the 3-billion acre Russian Empire, a major European power. He is cited as one of the greatest rulers in the 17th century, ranking alongside Louis XIV of France. In 1721, soon after peace was made with Sweden, Peter was acclaimed Emperor of All Russia. The State Chancellor was the first to add "the Great, Father of His Country, Emperor of All the Russias" to Peter's traditional title Czar. Peter's imperial title was recognized by the kings of Poland, Prussia, and Sweden but not by the other European monarchs. In the minds of many, the word emperor connoted superiority or pre-eminence over "mere" kings. Several rulers feared that Peter would claim authority over them, just as the Holy Roman Emperor had once claimed suzerainty over all Christian nations.

38. Find the false statement(s).
    I. Peter being a great dictator carried out a policy of Westernization and expansion that transformed Russia.
    II. Peter's imperial title was not recognized by other European monarchs as they considered him to be a cruel and dominant ruler.

III. Russian Empire emerged as a major European power during the reign of Peter the Great.

(a) Only II

(b) Both II and III

(c) Both I and II

(d) All I, II and III

39. Why was the title 'The Great' was given to Peter?

(a) Because he was the sole ruler of Europe

(b) Because it meant 'Father of his country'

(c) Because he was equivalent to Louis XIV

(d) None of these

40. Which of the following is most similar to the word 'CONNOTED' as used in the passage?

(a) Implied   (b) Hid

(c) Refrained   (d) Voiced

PASSAGE-14

Martin Luther King, Jr. was a prominent leader in the American civil rights movement. His main legacy was to secure progress on civil rights in the United States. King became a civil rights activist early in his career. He led the 1955 Montgomery Bus Boycott and helped found the Southern Christian Leadership Conference in 1957, serving as its first president. King's efforts led to the 1963 March on Washington, where he delivered his "I Have a Dream" speech. There, he raised public consciousness of the civil rights movement and established himself as one of the greatest orators in U.S. history. In 1964, King became the youngest person to receive the Nobel Peace Prize for his work to end racial segregation and racial discrimination through civil disobedience and other non-violent means. By the time of his death in 1968, he had refocused his efforts on ending poverty and opposing the Vietnam War, both from a religious perspective.

41. Who is an orator?

(a) A person who delivers a commentary accompanying a film or a piece of music etc.

(b) A person who leads or commands a group, organization or country.

(c) A public speaker, especially one who is eloquent or skilled.

(d) A person who is admired for his courage, outstanding achievement or noble qualities.

42. Civil rights are:

(a) Rights to hold office under the government

(b) Rights to legal, social and economic equality

(c) Right to become civil servants

(d) Right to bear arms

43. Find the true statement:

(a) King founded the Southern Christian Leadership Conference in 1957.

(b) King was the youngest recipient of Noble Prize for his contribution in ending racial segregation and racial discrimination through his orations.

(c) King was a prominent Civil Right activist of his time.

(d) King was one of the influential presidents of the USA.

PASSAGE-15

He created Mickey Mouse and produced the first full-length animated movie. He invented the theme park and originated the modern multimedia corporation. For better or worse, his innovations have shaped our world and the way we experience it. But the most significant thing Walt Disney made was a good name for himself. It was, of course, long ago converted into a brand name, constantly fussed over, ferociously defended, first by Disney and latterly by his corporate heirs and assigns. Serving as a beacon for parents seeking clean, decent entertainment for their children, the Disney logo — a stylized version of the founder's signature — more generally promises us that anything appearing beneath it will not veer too far from the safe, sound, and, above all, cheerful American mainstream, which it defines as much as serves. Which of the following statement(s) about the creator of Mickey Mouse is/are correct?

44. Which of the following statement(s) about the creator of Mickey Mouse is correct?

I. He originated the modern multimedia corporation.

II. He was the producer of first full-length animated movie.

III. His name was Walt Disney.

(a) Only I   (b) Only II

(c) Both I and II   (d) All I, II and III

45. What does 'significant' in the context of the passage mean?

(a) American   (b) Trivial

(c) Innovative   (d) Important

46. In the context of the passage, what does the phrase 'ferociously defended' mean?

(a) Walt Disney always defended his brand-name whenever his counterparts tried to defame him.

(b) Disney's heirs and assigns ferociously defended the allegations made by parents about the programs.

(c) Disney along with his corporate heirs and assigns successfully defended any attempt to defame his company.

(d) None of these

PASSAGE-16

Rationalism has been defined as the mental attitude which **unreservedly** accepts the supremacy of reason and aims at establishing a system of philosophy and ethics verifiable by experience and independent of all arbitrary assumptions or authority. This definition of rationalism was framed at the inauguration of the Rationalist Press Association (RPA) in London in the year 1899.

47. This paragraph best supports the statement that

(a) Ethics does not constitute a part of philosophy.

(b) One has to accept certain beliefs to find the final truth.

    (c)   Rationalism is a not a set of beliefs which is devoid of verification.

    (d)   Mental attitude is independent of all assumptions.

48. Which of the following words is most nearly the **SAME** in meaning as the word **unreservedly** as used in the paragraph?
    (a) Conditionally   (b) Fully
    (c) Partially   (d) Collectively

PASSAGE-17

In today's world where teachers have a busy schedule, it is noticed that only a few teachers have time for the student's learning experiences. One thing which is lacking in almost all classrooms is teachers motivating students to do better. What happens is that teachers would like to give attention to the students who have high intelligence and who are academically good. A larger portion of the student population is neglected. Teachers blame them for not trying to do their best.

49. The author would like the teachers to
    (a) motivate bright students to enhance their academic achievements.
    (b) improve their own academic standards to motivate students.
    (c) keep their schedule busy by carrying out various duties.
    (d) encourage and give planned learning experiences to all students.

50. According to the author, why are teachers not in a position to perform their expected role?
    (a) Majority of the students neglect classroom teaching.
    (b) The students are very busy and have less time to learn.
    (c) They are forced to spend more time in motivating good students.
    (d) None of these

PASSAGE-18

Due to the development of individualism and permissiveness, social norms have become slack and parents and teachers are unable to play their traditional role of shaping the character of their children and people. The growing complexity of society due to technological development and the **slackness** of social norms as a result of the growth of individualism and permissiveness are the two causes of the moral crisis of our time.

51. According to the author, which of the following is one of the outcomes of the present crisis of our time?
    (a) Inability of parents and teachers to develop value base of children
    (b) More than expected growth of science and technology
    (c) Increasing social cohesiveness IN SPITE OF violence and disturbances
    (d) Emergence of new social norms which obstruct growth of individualism

52. Which of the following words is most **OPPOSITE** in meaning of the word **slackness** as used in the paragraph?
    (a) Rigidity   (b) Vigorous
    (c) Sluggishness   (d) Business

PASSAGE-19

Marx, the founder of communism, had predicted the failure and eventual overthrow of capitalism because of what he **regarded** as its inherent contradiction. He visualised that capitalism would maintain the wages of labour at a low subsistence level, while progressively increasing its productivity by the employment of technologically advanced means of production. During the last many decades the real wages of workers in advanced capitalist countries have gradually and progressively increased. The prediction of Marx has not been borne out by history.

53. Which of the following supports the statement "the prediction ... borne out by history"?
    (a) Capitalism has just survived but not taken firm roots.
    (b) The salaries of the employees have gone up in advanced countries.
    (c) Technological development has not taken place in capitalist countries.
    (d) The salaries of all the employees have gone down in all the countries.

54. Which of the following words is most nearly the **SAME** in meaning to the word **regarded** as used in the paragraph?
    (a) Respected   (b) Valued
    (c) Related   (d) Thought

PASSAGE-20

Literature is a medium through which a person can convey his ideas towards or protest against different norms of society. Those works that deal with a moral issue are of particular importance in literature. They are written with a particular purpose in mind. A literary work with a moral issue will live on to be reinterpreted by different generations. These works involve the reader for he forms his own moral judgement towards the issue.

55. Why does the author consider write-ups 'that deal with a moral issue' more important in literature?
    (A) They are open for rethinking by coming generations.
    (B) They are written with a specific approach.
    (C) They help the reader in forming or consolidating his values and approaches.
    (a) Only A   (b) Both A and B
    (c) Both A and C   (d) Only C

56. The first sentence of the paragraph implies...
    (a) literature is not one of the best media of expression for a society.
    (b) society does not observe same standard for all its members.
    (c) only literature allows individuals to express their different views.
    (d) None of these

PASSAGE-21

The phenomena of child labour is quite complex. Children work because they belong to poor families who cannot survive without the benefit of the income which accrues to the family on account of child labour. Any attempt to abolish it through legal recourse would, under the circumstances, not be practical. The only alternative is to ban child labour in hazardous areas and to regulate and **ameliorate** the conditions of work in other areas. Many developing countries including India have accepted this approach.

57. According to the paragraph, abolishing child labour through legal means is most likely to result into...
    (a) dragging/pushing the family of the child in acute economic stress.
    (b) shortage of labour in other areas of work.
    (c) regulation of services of adult workers.
    (d) betterment of working conditions of adult labourers.

58. What can be inferred about the policy being followed about child labour in India?
    (A) Giving economic benefits to the families of child labourers.
    (B) Reducing/controlling child labour in unhealthy areas of work.
    (C) Monitoring and improving working conditions for children.
    (a) Only A and B   (b) Only B and C
    (c) Only A and B   (d) Only B

59. Which of the following words is most nearly the **SAME** in meaning to the word **ameliorate** as used in the paragraph?
    (a) Cover   (b) Adjust
    (c) Remove   (d) Mitigate

PASSAGE-22

In recent years, our society has shown readiness to **address** the educational and developmental needs of adolescents. Be it the Government or people in the community, there is a realisation that something needs to be done to build on the energy and enthusiasm of this crucial section of the population. Growing social unrest, violence, crime and increasing visibility of the young has contributed to this readiness.

60. Which of the following words is most **OPPOSITE** in meaning of the word **address** as used in the paragraph?
    (a) Discourage   (b) Ignore
    (c) Locate   (d) Disorganise

61. Which of the following is not a likely cause of readiness shown by people towards adolescents?
    (a) Increase in crime
    (b) Growing violence
    (c) Equality of opportunity
    (d) Physical presence of youth

PASSAGE-23

Recently, a study was made on the popularity of TV programmes and viewers' perception about their quality. The study of attitudes towards prime-time television programmes showed that programmes with identical ratings in terms of numbers of people watching them received highly **divergent** marks for quality from their viewers. This additional piece of information could prove valuable for advertisers who might be well advised to spend their advertising money for programmes that viewers **feel** are of high quality.

62. Which of the following is most nearly the same in meaning as the word **feel** as used in the passage?
    (a) Pour   (b) Sympathise
    (c) Perceive   (d) Evolve

63. Which of the following is most nearly opposite in meaning of the word **divergent** as used in the passage?
    (a) Pointed   (b) Similar
    (c) Heterogeneous   (d) Synonymous

64. Which of the following inferences can best be drawn from the above paragraph?
    (a) The number of viewers decided the quality of the programmes.
    (b) The viewers' perception about the quality of programmes is significant for advertisers.
    (c) The poor quality programmes have very few viewers.
    (d) Advertisers can derive benefit from the information about viewers' perception of quality of programmes.

65. Which of the following is/are the finding(s) of the study?
    A. The viewers decide the prime-time television programmes.
    B. The attitudes of viewers cannot be reliably assessed.
    C. The advertisers were benefitted from good quality programmes.
    (a) A only   (b) B only
    (c) C only   (d) None of these

66. Which of the following can be inferred from the contents of the paragraph?
    A. Advertisement can have some effect on the viewers' buying habits.
    B. Money spent on advertising with high quality programmes yields more profits.
    C. Different programmes with equal number of viewers can be rated differently as far as quality is concerned.
    (a) Only A   (b) Only B
    (c) Only A and B   (d) Only B and C

PASSAGE-24

Econometric models like the computable general equilibrium model are mostly valuable in policy formulation as they give some insight into how trade policy changes will affect the sectoral composition of output and employment. They are not in themselves designed to provide direct inputs but really to serve as background as to the sectors that will be most favourably or most unfavourably affected by policy. Besides, they render valuable help in policy matters regarding free trade.

Free trade has distinct benefits. These benefits are well accepted all over. However, there is a growing opposition to free trade. There is an increasing perception among certain groups of how international trading systems impact, especially how they affect low-wage workers and also have a degrading environmental impact. Yet it is difficult to accept that is the reason for any kind of protectionist move in the most advanced countries.

67. Most advanced countries are cautious about free trade/ because
 A. They prefer to have a protectionist approach.
 B. They feel degraded in international trading community.
 C. Their vested interests are thwarted.
 (a) A and B only (b) B and C only
 (c) A and C only (d) None of these

68. The author of the passage seems to be
 (a) in favour of use of econometric models but against free trade.
 (b) against both free trade as well as econometric models.
 (c) indifferent about both free trade and econometric models.
 (d) in favour of both econometric models and free trade.

69. Which of the following statements is definitely true in the context of the passage?
 A Despite the advantages of free trade, it is not whole-heartedly acclaimed by most advanced countries.
 B. Policy formulation should be solely dependent on econometric models.
 C. Reasons for model protectionist approach by advanced countries are not given in the passage.
 (a) Only A (b) Only B
 (c) Only C (d) A and B only

70. What is the contribution of econometric models?
 (a) They help develop insight into increasing output through less manpower.
 (b) They help in implementing new policies regarding free trade.
 (c) They help develop insight into how changes in policies influence certain sectors.
 (d) They ensure that policy changes have only positive impact on the economy.

71. Which of the following is the characteristic of econometric models?
 (a) They serve as a backdrop.
 (b) They are unfavourable to free trade.
 (c) They do not serve direct inputs.
 (d) Both (a) and (c)

72. The changes in economic policy are most likely to have
 (a) only desirable effect on all the sectors involved.
 (b) a mixed influence on all the sectors involved.
 (c) negative impact unless all the sectors are involved.
 (d) unfavourable effect on employment opportunities.

73. Free trade has been receiving escalating disapproval because
 (a) it unduly favours low-wage workers.
 (b) it leads to protectionist approach among advanced countries.
 (c) it affects international trading systems adversely.
 (d) None of these

PASSAGE-25

The young are those to whom we look for future strength and for future good; and the longer we live, the more anxious we become that they who are to be the fresh recruits should be morally of right stature. Around them are peculiar temptations and trials, witching, cunning, insidious and forceful: and we are obliged to see thousands falling by the way, whose fall seems needless. They, like ourselves, are to have but one chance in life. We who are somewhat advanced in years, seeing how many perils there are round about that one chance, feel an earnest desire that every advantage should be given to those who are coming onto fill our places. We can live but once; and life is usually moulded and takes its shape very early.   *[2007-I]*

74. Which one of the following is correct? The author looks upon the young as :
 (a) handsome and healthy
 (b) an embodiment of possibilities
 (c) strong and hardworking
 (d) a group of boys and girls who are obedient and dutiful

75. What does the phrase "morally of right stature" mean?
 (a) Being highly educated
 (b) Having a good personality
 (c) Having rectitude
 (d) Feeling superior to others

76. Which one of the following is correct?
 The failure of many a young men and women is
 (a) well deserved (b) unwarranted
 (c) fortuitous (d) sad

PASSAGE-26

When a bee, or an ant, beetle, moth or butterfly visits a flower for food, it simultaneously, and without knowing it, performs another vital function by carrying pollen from one plant to another. But not all flowers are visited by insects. A reliable guide to those that are, is their flamboyance. If the petals are large and colourful, if they smell sweet, it is because the plant needs to attract insects. Some plants have flowers which are graceful but not showy and therefore of no interest to insects. In this case the pollen is carried by the wind. Most flowers manufacture these minute grains called pollen which must be transferred to another flower of the same type before they can make seeds.

77. Which one of the following is correct?
 Plants that do not have showy flowers
 (a) get their pollen transferred to other flowers by wind
 (b) produce more pollen than others
 (c) don't reproduce easily
 (d) are very few in number

78. Which one of the following is correct?
    The fact that some flowers are flamboyant implies
    (a) that some plants do not need pollination
    (b) that we can distinguish between flowers pollinated by insects and those that are not
    (c) that flowers are more important to some plants than they are to others
    (d) that bright colours are important to all flowers
79. Which one of the following is correct?
    When insects carry pollen from one flower to another
    (a) they help the flowers to make seeds
    (b) the flowers become colourful and smell sweet
    (c) the insects find it easy to take food from the flowers
    (d) they help the plants to grow beautiful flowers
80. Which one of the following is correct?
    Insects carry pollen from one flower to another
    (a) deliberately　　　　(b) unconsciously
    (c) reluctantly　　　　(d) with extreme care
81. Which one of the following is correct?
    Insects visit flowers because they
    (a) want to carry pollen from one flower to another
    (b) are attracted by the bright colours
    (c) wish to obtain food
    (d) are in search of a mate

PASSAGE-27

Not all sounds made by animals serve for communication, and we have only to turn to that extraordinary discovery of echo-location in bats to see a case in which the voice plays a strictly utilitarian role. To get a full appreciation of what this means we must turn first to some recent human inventions. Everyone knows that if a person shouts in the vicinity of a wall or a mountainside, an echo will come back. The further off this solid obstruction, the longer time will elapse for the return of the echo. A sound made by tapping on the hull of a ship will be reflected from the sea bottom, and by measuring the time interval between the taps and the receipt of the echoes, the depth of the sea at that point can be calculated. So was born the echo-sounding apparatus, now in general use in ships. Every solid object will reflect a sound, varying according to the size of and nature of the object. A shoal of fish will do this. So it is a comparatively simple step from locating the sea bottom to locating a shoal of fish. With experience, and with improved apparatus, it is now possible not only to locate a shoal, but to tell if it is herring, cod, or other well-known fish, by the pattern of its echo.

A few years ago it was found that certain bats emit squeaks and by receiving the echoes they could locate and steer clear of obstacles or locate flying insects on which they feed. This echo-location in bats is often compared with radar, the principle of which is similar. *[2007-II]*

82. Which one of the following is correct?
    Echo-location was first discovered in
    (a) bats　　　　(b) cods
    (c) navigation　　　　(d) radars

83. Which one of the following is correct?
    An echo will come back if you shout near
    (a) solid obstruction　　　　(b) only wall
    (c) only a mountainside　　　　(d) the sea
84. Which one of the following is correct?
    In the first paragraph, the writer says that bats use sound for
    (a) communicating with one another
    (b) communicating with animals in general
    (c) some practical purpose
    (d) fun

PASSAGE-28

Wesward Ho!" we shouted as the sail of our crudely constructed raft, the Kon-Tiki caught the sind. The sail quickly filled and the Kon-Tiki began to move. The six of us were off to our great adventure.

As night fell, the troughs of the sea grew gradually deeper and our first duel with the elements began. Each time we heard the sudden deafening hiss of a roller close by and saw a white crest come towards us out of the darkness, we held on tight and waited for the worst. But invariably the Kon-Tiki calmly swung up her stern and rose skyward unperturbed.

85. What does the word 'duel' in the passage mean?
    (a) A battle　　　　(b) A fortification
    (c) A two-side contes　　　　(d) Divided in two
86. Which one of the following is correct? When big waves struck the raft the six people in it
    (a) started crying
    (b) showed courage and patience
    (c) acted in a rash manner
    (d) showed passiveness
87. How was the Kon-Tiki's performance on the high seas?
    (a) Very shaky　　　　(b) Extremely poor
    (c) Stable and resolute　　　　(d) Unpredicatable

PASSAGE-29

It was Sunday. As usual, there was a great rush of merry makers who had come to the river to swim or to bathe. Those who knew how to swim were jumping into the water from the high bridge or the banks of the deep river. Mohan did not know how to swim so he was merely watching others who were enjoying the fun of swimming. However on the insistence of his friend Swarn, he sat on his shoulders and both jumped into the water. Unable to carry Mohan along, Swarn left him in the flowing water. Mohan shouted for help. There were so many swimmers but nobody came to his rescue since they were indifferent to the plight of a stranger. I has just reached there, so I was in my full dress. Without undressing I jumped into the river and swam up to the drowning boy. Holding his left arm, I brought him out of water in a way that he might not hinder me from swimming safely. The boy was saved which won me great applause from the people. I had jumped into the water without any fear or hesitation as I knew the art of saving drowning persons. I has already saved a few lives from drowing.

88. Why did Swarn jump into the water carrying Mohan on his shoulders ?
    (a) Mohan had insisted to swim
    (b) He wanted to enjoy the fun of seeing a drowning man
    (c) He simply wanted to drown him in the river
    (d) Swarn felt that his friend should also enjoy the fun of swimming in the river

89. Why did Swarn leave his friend Mohan in the waters?
    (a) Mohan wanted to learn how to swim
    (b) He wanted Mohan to learn how to swim
    (c) Because he has sure that Mohan would be able to swim across the river
    (d) Because he found it difficult to in the river with his friend on his shoulders.

90. Although ther were many swimmers, why did nobody come forward to save the drowning boy ?
    (a) They wanted some financial reward
    (b) They did not know the art of saving a drowning person
    (c) They were not experts in the art of swimming
    (d) The river was very deep and they did not want to take a risk for a stranger

91. Why did the writer jump into the river without any fear or hesitation?
    (a) He was acquainted with Mohan
    (b) He could not bear the sight of a drowning person
    (c) He knew how to save a drowning person
    (d) He was called by the people present there

PASSAGE-30

Books are by far, the most lasting product of human effort. Temples crumble into ruins, pictures and statues decay, but books survive. Time does not destroy the great thoughts which are as fresh today as when they first passed through their author's minds ages ago. The only effect of time has been to throw out of currency the bad products, for nothing in literature can long survive but what is really good and of lasting value. Books introduce us into the best society; they bring us into the presence of the greatest minds that have ever lived, we hear what they said and did; we see them as if they were really alive, we sympathise with them, enjoy with them and grieve with them.

92. According to the passage, books live for ever because-
    (a) they have productive value
    (b) time does not destroy great thoughts
    (c) they are in printed form
    (d) they have the power to influence people

93. According to the passage, temples, pictures and statues belong to the same category because-
    (a) all of them are beautiful
    (b) all of them are substantial
    (c) all of them are likely to decay
    (d) all of them are fashioned by men

94. "Lasting value" in the passage means-
    (a) something which has survived the passage of time
    (b) something which has been lost with the passage of time
    (c) something which has relevance for the present
    (d) something which had relevance for the past

PASSAGE-31

In the fete, for a ticket costing eight annas you stood a chance of acquiring a variety of articles-pin-cushions, sewing machines, cameras or even a road engine. One evening they drew ticket number 1005, and I happened to own the other half of the ticket. They declared that I became the owner of a road engine! Don't ask me how a road engine came to be included among the prizes. It is more than I can tell you. I looked stunned. People gathered round and gazed at me as if were some curious animal. 'Fancy anyone becoming the owner of a road engine!' some persons muttered and giggled.

95. The writer purchased a ticket
    (a) to win a prize
    (b) to enter the fete
    (c) to buy some eatables in the fete
    (d) to play some games

96. 'they' in the paragraph stands for
    (a) the writer's friends
    (b) the organisers of the fete
    (c) the stall owners in the fete
    (d) the onlookers

97. The writer was stunned because
    (a) he did not win a prize
    (b) he was at a loss as to what to do with the prize
    (c) people giggled
    (d) the fete organisers were rude to him

PASSAGE-32

An old man with steel-rimmed spectacles and very dusty clothes sat by the side of the road. There was a pontoon bridge across the river and carts, trucks, and men, women and children were crossing it. The mule-drawn carts staggered up the steep bank from the bridge with soldiers helping to push against the spokes of the wheels. The trucks wound up and away heading out of it all. The peasants plodded along in the ankle-deep dust. But the old man sat there without moving.

98. The term "pontoon bridge" means
    (a) a temporary bridge constructed with the help of ropes
    (b) a bridge made by soldiers during a war
    (c) a bridge supported by floating flat bottomed boats
    (d) a bridge made with wooden planks

99. The soldiers were "helping to push against the spokes of the wheels" because
    (a) they wanted to stop the carts
    (b) the spokes of the wheels were broken
    (c) the mules refused to draw the carts
    (d) there was a steep elevation

100. The mule-drawn carts staggered up because
   (a) there were too many mule-carts
   (b) the mules were indisciplined
   (c) it was a steep uphill journey
   (d) the carts were blocked by the peasants
101. The reference to the old man in the beginning and the end of the passage indicates that
   (a) the writer wants to compare between the bridge and motionless old man
   (b) the description that takes place between the first sentence and the last sentence is irrelevant
   (c) there is an unnecessary repetition in the reference to the old man
   (d) the figure of the old man is brought under a sharp focus

PASSAGE-33

It was a very cold evening and so few people were seen out on the streets. I did not go out myself although it was my habit not to keep indoors after sunset. So I closed all the doors and windows of my room, took the book which had been lying opened on the table, and tried to read it. The cold was getting so severe that I started shivering, so I wrapped myself up with a bigger blanket. But I could continue reading the book because I was nearly rendered incapable of turning the pages.

102. The author's habit was to
   (a) read in the evening
   (b) sleep in the evening
   (c) go out in the evening
   (d) play in the evening
103. If it was not so cold the author would have
   (a) liked to work
   (b) liked to sit and look out to the streets
   (c) liked to read
   (d) liked to have a stroll
104. The author could not continue reading the book because
   (a) he did not like to
   (b) he, was feeling tired
   (c) he was feeling very cold
   (d) the lights had gone off
105. There were not many people outside because
   (a) it was a rainy evening
   (b) it was a cold evening
   (c) it was a dark evening
   (d) there was heavy snow outside

PASSAGE-34

One day my brother brought home a new song-bird. It was the smallest of them all, a tiny creature of a blue and a red that sparkled when brushed by the sun. But there was a problem: while the others sang, this new bird remained silent. My brother tried coaxing music out of him, in vain. He tried attacking with a stick, but the bird was unmoved. My brother first tried withholding food, but later when the incentive was offered the bird ignored it, and twice he knocked over his dish, scattering the seed.

106. One day the writer's brother brought home a bird
   (a) which never ate food
   (b) which flew so high it seemed to touch the sun
   (c) whose colours shone brightly in the sunlight
   (d) which was the largest of all the birds in his collection
107. At first his brother tried to get the bird to sing by
   (a) tempting with food
   (b) placing it in the company of the other birds while they sang
   (c) singing to the bird himself
   (d) with holding food
108. What does the word "coaxing" mean?
   (a) to behave rudely
   (b) to use violent means
   (c) to gently persuade.
   (d) to beg repeatedly

PASSAGE-35

"The doctor's coming in a minute, Inspector", said Miss Smith.
"Yes, thank you for phoning, Miss Smith. It was very kind of you ..... the lady's name is Mrs. West, you say, ..."
"Yes, that's right."
"And what about Mr. West?"
"Doctor West, Inspector."
"Oh, I see ..... Well, Doctor West, then. Do you know where he is?"
"Not exactly, Inspector. He never told Mrs. West where he was going. You see, they hated each other."
"What do you mean?"
"Well, Doctor West thought that Mrs. West was in love with another man, and everyone knows Doctor West went to see another woman."

109. The conversation appears to be taking place
   (a) in a street where an accident has just occurred
   (b) in a hotel where Mrs. West suddenly became ill
   (c) in Mrs. West's house where the police are enquiring into lady's murder
   (d) in Mrs. West's house where a theft has taken place the night before
110. The questions the Inspector asks are
   (a) inquisitive
   (b) foolish
   (c) disturbing
   (d) searching
111. "You see, they hated each other." "What do you mean?" The Inspector seems
   (a) to know Doctor West's secret
   (b) surprised to get the information
   (c) not to have understood Miss Smith
   (d) not impressed by Miss Smith's information

PASSAGE-36

There was a farewell ceremony on her last day at school, to which my parents and I were invited. It was a touching ceremony in a solemn kind of way. The City Corporation sent a representative and so did the two main political parties. There were many speeches and my grandmother was garlanded by a girl from every class. Then the head-girl, a particular favourite of hers, unveiled the farewell present the girls had bought for her by subscription. It was a large marble model of the Taj Mahal; it had a bulb inside and could be lit up like a table lamp. My grandmother made a speech too, but she couldn't finish it properly, for she began to cry before she got to the end of it and to stop to wipe away her tears. I turned away when she began dabbing at her eyes with a huge green handkerchief, and discovered, to my surprise, that many of the girls sitting around me were wiping their eyes too. I was very jealous, I remember. I had always taken it for granted that it was my own special right to love her; I did not know how to cope with the discovery that my right had been infringed by a whole school.

112. The farewell ceremony described in the passage is for the
   (a) author's mother used to teach at his/her school
   (b) mother of head-girl teaching at her school
   (c) grandmother of head-girl no longer teaching at her school
   (d) grandmother of the author who used to teach at his/her school

113. The farewell ceremony made everyone feel
   (a) sad   (b) unhappy
   (c) happy   (d) bad

114. Before the writer attended the ceremony he/she had thought
   (a) he/she was the only child who loved his/her grandmother
   (b) all the girls in the school loved his/her grandmother
   (c) only a few girls in the school loved his/her grandmother
   (d) only his/her parents loved his/her grandmother

PASSAGE-37

The psychological causes of unhappiness, it is clear, are many and various. But all have something in common. The typical unhappy man is one who, having been deprived in youth of some normal satisfaction, some come to value this one kind of satisfaction more than any other, and has therefore given to his life a one-sided direction, together with a quite undue emphasis upon the achievement as opposed to the activities connected with it. There is, however, a further development which is very common in the present day. A man may feel so completely thwarted that he seeks no form of satisfaction, but only distraction and oblivion. He then becomes a devotee of 'pleasure'. This is to say, he seeks to make life bearable by becoming less alive. Drunkenness, for example, is temporary suicide - the happiness that it brings is merely negative, a momentary cessation of unhappiness.

115. Who is a typical unhappy man ?
   (a) One who has been deprived of normal satisfaction in youth
   (b) One who finds life unbearable and attempts suicide
   (c) One who does not mind momentary unhappiness
   (d) One who seeks every form of satisfaction

116. "One sided direction" refers to the pursuit of which one of the following ?
   (a) Drinking and forgetfulness
   (b) The satisfaction one had been deprived of
   (c) Activities leading to happiness
   (d) Every form of psychological satisfaction

117. Which one of the following is the correct statement ? Drinking helps the unhappy only to
   (a) forget their dissatisfaction
   (b) get sublime happiness
   (c) get the motivational needs fulfilled
   (d) concentrate harder

118. What does "becoming less alive" imply?
   (a) Neglect of health
   (b) Decline in moral values
   (c) Living in a make believe world
   (d) Leading a sedentary way of living

PASSAGE-38

Once upon a time I went for a week's holiday in the Continent with an Indian friend. We both enjoyed ourselves and were sorry when the week was over, but on parting our behaviour was absolutely different. He was plunged in despair. He felt that because the holiday was overs all happiness was over until the world ended. He could not express his sorrow too much. But in me the Englishman came out strong. I could not see what there was to make a fuss about. It wasn't as if we were parting forever or dying. "Buck up", I said, "do buck up". He refused to buck up, and I left him plunged in gloom.

119. What is the Continent in the context of the passage ?
   (a) An island   (b) The countryside
   (c) Africa   (d) Europe

120. What does the author mean by 'buck up' ?
   (a) Buckle yourself up   (b) Stand up
   (c) Cheer up   (d) Shut up

121. Why was the Indian friend plunged in despair ?
   (a) He was hopeless
   (b) He experienced racial discrimination
   (c) He would never be so happy again
   (d) He had spent lot of money

122. What does 'But in me the Englishman came out strong' imply ?
   (a) He was a strong Englishman
   (b) He had the typical English character
   (c) The Englishman went out of him
   (d) He started following Indian traditions

123. What is the author's intention in the passage?
   (a) To contrast the Indian character with the English character
   (b) To show that an Indian is sorrowful
   (c) To ridicule the Indian traditions
   (d) To praise the Englishman

PASSAGE-39

The world is very full of people appallingly- full, it has never been so full before, and they are all tumbling over each other. Most of these people one doesn't know and some of them one doesn't like. Well, that is one to do There are two solutions. One of them is the Nazi solution. If you don't like people, kill them, banish them, and segregate them. The other way is much less thrilling, but it is on the whole the way of the democracies, and I prefer it.

If you don't like people, put up with them as well as you can. Don't try to love them : you can't, you'll only strain yourself. But try to tolerate them.

124. What does the author mean by 'appallingly'?
    (a) He is making an appeal to the leaders of the masses
    (b) In disconcertingly large numbers
    (c) Very interesting
    (d) Unpredictably
125. Which one of the following is the correct statement ? According to the writer Nazi solution is
    (a) the easiest solution
    (b) the readiest solution
    (c) the national solution
    (d) the Hitlerian solution
126. Which one of the following is the correct statement ? The author thinks that the other solution is much less thrilling because it is
    (a) dull
    (b) based on tolerance
    (c) not based on love
    (d) lacking in adventure
127. Which one of the following is the correct statement ? The author prefers the second solution because
    (a) he likes it
    (b) he is not a Nazi
    (c) he is essentially being a democrat
    (d) there is no other way

PASSAGE-40

We should preserve Nature to preserve life and beauty. A beautiful landscape, full of green vegetation, will not just attract our attention but will fill us with infinite satisfaction. Unfortunately, because of modernization, much of nature is now yielding to towns, roads and industrial areas. In a few places some Natural reserves are now being carved out to avert the danger of destroying Nature completely. Man will perish without Nature, so modern man should continue this struggle to save plants, which give us oxygen, from extinction. Moreover, Nature is essential to man's health.

128. What does 'Nature' in the passage mean ?
    (a) Countryside covered with plants and trees
    (b) Physical power that created the world
    (c) Inherent things that determine character
    (d) Practical study of plants and animals
129. Which one of the following is the correct statement ? According to the passage
    (a) beauty is only skin-deep
    (b) everything is beautiful in its natural state
    (c) there is beauty in Nature
    (d) Nature is a moray teacher
130. What does the writer suggest ?
    (a) We should not modernize, so that Nature can be preserved
    (b) While modernizing we should be careful not to destroy Nature completely
    (c) All Nature has been destroyed by modern living
    (d) Carving out Natural reserves will hamper the growth of industries

131. What does 'struggle' in the passage mean ?
    (a) Man's struggle to exist in the world
    (b) Man's struggle to save Nature
    (c) Man's struggle to catch up with modern trends
    (d) Man's struggle to conserve oxygen
132. Why a beautiful landscape 'will fill us with infinite satisfaction' ?
    (a) We love beauty
    (b) It is full of green vegetation
    (c) It will ensure our future existence
    (d) It will show our command over Nature

PASSAGE-41

Deriving your authority from the government, your position would secure the respect and consideration of everyone, especially in a service where official rank carries so much weight. This would secure to you every attention and comfort on your way and there, together with a complete submission to your orders.

I know these things are a matter of indifference to you except so far as they may further the great objects you have in view, but they are of importance in themselves, and of every importance to those who have a right to take an interest in your personal position and comfort.

133. The above passage most probably is a part of a
    (a) speech   (b) official communication
    (c) written report   (d) personal letter
134. The writer's attitude towards the person addressed is characterised by
    (a) officiousness   (b) flattery
    (c) humility   (d) arrogance
135. The person addressed is most likely a
    (a) social worker   (b) government servant
    (c) commercial agent (d) foreign dignitary
136. The writer is asking his reader to accept
    (a) great objects   (b) a respected position
    (c) an official rank (d) a significant assignment
137. 'The great objects' in the passage means
    (a) Significant items (b) Noble goals
    (c) Precious merchandise (d) Objects of praise

PASSAGE-42

While I stood drinking in the beauty of this placid scene, I became conscious of an alteration. In a moment, the sole porter emerged from his midday nap, operated a signal that clanked noisily into position, and then ambled slowly towards me for my return-half-ticket, whilst I remarked that his red amiable face and easygoing gait were in perfect harmony with the tranquil surroundings. A wisp of smoke on the horizon with a dark snake crawling beneath it announced the approach of the train. As it drew nearer, the deep silence of the place was gradually displaced by a creaking of brakes and a hissing of steam. Save for myself, no one entered the train and no one alighted. The porter with leisurely expertness, trundled a couple of milk churns on board, the door was slammed, the guard signalled to the driver, and we moved off, leaving the small station once more to its drowsy silence.

138. The meaning of drowsy is
    (a) Untidy   (b) Sleepy
    (c) Freezing   (d) Drugged
139. The central idea of the passage is
    (a) Leisure and Peace (b) Hurry and Noise
    (c) Activity   (d) The Porter

140. Who had a midday nap ?
     (a) The author   (b) The passenger
     (c) The Station-master   (d) The porter
141. Who/what does first break the silence of the station ?
     (a) The train   (b) The porter
     (c) The passenger   (d) Milk churns
142. What does the author suggest by the word 'placid' ?
     (a) The scene was filled with noise of the train
     (b) The place was filled with lively humanity
     (c) The place was quite and lonely
     (d) The horizon looked smoke laden

PASSAGE-43

It happened one day, about noon, going towards my boat, I was exceedingly surprised with the print of a man's naked foot on the shore, which was very plain to be seen in the sand. I stood like one thunder-struck, or as if I had seen an apparition. I listened, I looked round me, I could hear nothing, nor see anything. I went up the shore, and down the shore, but it was all one; I could see no other impression but that one. I went to it again to see if there were any more, and to observe if it might not be my fancy; but there was no room for that, for there was exactly the very print of a foot toes, heel and every part of a foot.   **[2008-II]**

143. The passage is full of short simple sentences. Their purpose is to
     (a) facilitate easy understanding
     (b) give a plain narration
     (c) convey breathless excitement
     (d) imply the inability of the author to write in a better way
144. Which one of these expressions best brings out the effect of the foot-print on the author?
     (a) Seen an apparition
     (b) Stood like one thunder-struck
     (c) Went up the shore
     (d) Looked round himself
145. How does the author convince himself that the foot-print is a real one ?
     (a) By finding the person who made it
     (b) By being told about it by a witness
     (c) By thinking about it for some time
     (d) By examining it carefully and noticing its details
146. Which one of the following words best describes the emotion evoked by the footprint in the author ?
     (a) Curiosity   (b) Indifference
     (c) Fear   (d) Surprise
147. On finding the foot-print on the shore, what did the author do ?
     (a) Did not pay much attention to it
     (b) Observed it with curiosity
     (c) Began to investigate its origin
     (d) Ran away in fear

PASSAGE-44

Ah! whatever could be said was said. All held him guilty. Even his own mother who claimed to understand him the best. All had betrayed him in his hour of need. Yet, there he was, still with a sparkling hope and knew that the truth must prevail. In the cold, dark and damp cell he never for a moment lost faith in God and goodness and was waiting anxiously for an to come, plead angel non guilty for him and free him of his miseries.

148. Three of the following statements indicate that he had a sparkling hope. Which statement does not?
     (a) He had never lost faith in God.
     (b) He was sure there was goodness.
     (c) He could have evidence in his favour.
     (d) He knew that the truth must prevail.
149. Whatever others said about him, he
     (a) Betrayed no one.
     (b) Thought over the problem.
     (c) Never lost faith in goodness.
     (d) Raised his voice against injustice.
150. In the dark dungeon he always waited for
     (a) His mother.
     (b) The jailer.
     (c) The verdict freeing him of his miseries.
     (d) The angle to come and plead for him.
151. The truth must prevail means
     (a) He was true
     (b) Angle will reveal truth
     (c) Truth always wins in the end
     (d) We must plead for the truth

PASSAGE-45

Once while travelling by the local bus, I got a seat beside a very strange man. He seemed interested in every passenger aboard. He would stare at a person, scribble some odd mathematical notations on his long notebook and then move on to the next. Being quite interested in what he was doing I asked him what all those notations meant and then came the starling reply. He saw a man's face not as a single unit but as thousands of squares put together. He was in fact a statistical expert and a budding artist learning the art of graphics.

152. The man was scribbling down
     (a) The figures of co-passengers
     (b) The details of thousands of squares put together
     (c) Some mathematical formulae and calculations
     (d) Some mathematical signs
153. The man caught author's attention because
     (a) He was sitting next to him.
     (b) He was staring at every person in the bus.
     (c) He would stare at every person and then scribble down some mathematical notation.
     (d) He was budding artist learning the art of graphics.
154. The author found that man's reply quite startling because
     (a) A statistical expert cannot be a budding scientist
     (b) A budding artist cannot be a statistical expert
     (c) Graphics is still a rare art form and he was learning in while travelling in a bus
     (d) The fact that "a man's face can be analysed as thousands of squares" was a strange concept.
155. From the passage we gather that
     (a) The author is very inquisitive.
     (b) The author tries to poke his nose in other people's business
     (c) The author is interested in mathematical notations.
     (d) The author wants to talk to fellow passengers in the bus.

PASSAGE-46

The unpleasant feeling passed and she glanced guardedly up at him. He was walking unmarked in moonlight, innocent of her reaction to him. She felt then – this thought had come to her before – that there might be more to him than she had imagined. She felt ashamed she had never thanked him for the help he had given her father.

156. She glanced at him when
    (a)   He walked alone and unnoticed in moonlight
    (b)   She was sure that she was not being noticed
    (c)   Her reactions did not have any effect on him
    (d)   The unpleasant feeling passed

157. Her unpleasant feeling passed when
    (a)   He did not take any notice of her
    (b)   The moonlight was beautiful
    (c)   She realized her sense of shame
    (d)   She looked carefully at him

158. She was ashamed because
    (a)   She was spying on him
    (b)   There was more to him than she had imagined
    (c)   A recurring thought came back to her
    (d)   She had never thanked him for his help to her father

PASSAGE-47

As I slung my pack onto my shoulders a big mosquito thudded against my cheek. There had been a few through the day, but it was early in the season – the ice had gone out just two weeks before – and I had scarcely noticed them. But now as I would down the ridge, the last breeze faded, and they were on me. Rising in clouds from the soggy tundra, they pelted against my face. I reached in my pocket for the repellent, and came up empty.

159. The traveller could not feel the breeze because
    (a)   The mosquito had bitten him.
    (b)   He was at the foot of the ridge.
    (c)   There was no ice on the mountain.
    (d)   There was no breeze on the tundra mountain.

160. The traveller carried with him
    (a)   Mosquito repellent
    (b)   A pack of food
    (c)   A sling
    (d)   A back-pack

161. When he was in the arctic, the time of the year was
    (a)   Middle of winter.   (b)   Early autumn
    (c)   Early spring   (d)   Middle of summer

PASSAGE-48

I was at the shop early. He was standing behind the counter and as soon as I saw him, I knew that there would be some unpleasantness. Mr. Higson is never at his best unshaven, in slippers and braces and smoking on the empty stomach. The atmosphere of the little shop was heavy with the bitter odour of fresh newspaper print and ink: stacks of crisp newspapers and magazines lay neatly on the counter, the Higson and the boy were making up the daily mend.

162. At the shop Mr. Higson appeared in
    (a)   his joy of smoking.
    (b)   his most slip-shod condition.
    (c)   the most unusual condition.
    (d)   in a strange mood.

163. The overall atmosphere in the shop was
    (a)   pleasant, wholesome and welcome.
    (b)   heavy with a lot of goods placed there.
    (c)   with the inactivity of the early morning.
    (d)   congenial and businesslike.

PASSAGE-49

The art of growing old is one which the passage of time has forced upon my attention. Psychologically there are two dangers to be guarded against in old age. One of these is undue absorption in the past. It does not do to live in memories, in regrets for the good old days. One's thoughts must be directed to the future. This is not always easy; one's past is a gradually increasing weight. The other thing to be avoided is clinging to youth on the hope of sucking vigour from its vitality.

164. "By the art of growing old", the author means
    (a)   some special skill by applying which one can grow old.
    (b)   that growing old is like creating a work of art.
    (c)   the acceptance of old age as a fact of life.
    (d)   the refusal on one's part to grow old.

165. The passage deals with the process of growing old. What does it describe?
    (a)   The decay of the senses in old age
    (b)   The psychological problems of old men
    (c)   The desire in man to grow old
    (d)   An old man's ability to recollect his past.

166. "It does not do to live in memories". This statement means that
    (a)   the past is not contained in memories.
    (b)   the old men are very forgetful.
    (c)   old men often think of the past.
    (d)   thinking of the past does no good to old men.

167. It is difficult for old men to think of the future because
    (a)   they are unable to think.
    (b)   they do not know what the future is like.
    (c)   the past occupies their minds.
    (d)   their feeling that the past was far more happier than the present grows stronger day by day.

PASSAGE-50

Punctually at midday he opened his bag and spread out his professional equipment, which consisted of a dozen cowrie shells, a square piece of cloths with obscure mystic charts on it, a note book, and a bundle of Palmyra writing. His forehead was resplendent with sacred ash and vermilion, and his eyes sparkled with a sharp abnormal gleam which was really an outcome of a continual searching look for customers, but which his simple clients took to be prophetic light and felt comforted. The power of his eyes was considerably enhanced by their position placed as they were between the painted forehead and the dark whiskers which streamed down his cheeks : even a half-wit's eyes would sparkle in such a setting. To crown the effect he wound a saffron-coloured turban around his head. This colour scheme never failed. People were attracted to him as bees are attracted to cosmos or dahila stalks.

168. From the description of this passage one can make out the person to be a :
    (a)   Snake Charmer   (b)   Footpath vendor
    (c)   Astrologer   (d)   Priest

169. The eyes of person is described as sparkled because :
    (a)   He was sitting under midday sun
    (b)   He was always looking for possible clients
    (c)   His forehead was bright with ash and vermilion
    (d)   He was full of joy

170. The person opened his bag
    (a) to search for something he needed
    (b) to indicate the start of his work
    (c) to keep his professional equipment
    (d) to take out things for display
171. The tone of the description is
    (a) sad   (b) neutral
    (c) ironic   (d) sympathetic

PASSAGE-51

Now a days we are amused by professionals. Why listen to your friends singing when you can hear the great singers of the world on the gramophone or the radio? Why read even a detective story if you can see one at the cinema, and why play football with players who are not very good when you can go, by train or car, to see some of the best players in your country playing an important match; if you have a television set, just sit comfortably at home and watch the same without the trouble of going outside ?

172. The primary criticism of the author about his contemporaries is that
    (a) they are unprofessional and unskilled.
    (b) they want to enjoy all the good things of life.
    (c) they waste all their time with amusements.
    (d) they have a lazy and mechanical attitude towards amusements.
173. The impression you get about the author is that he is
    (a) a cynic   (b) an old timer
    (c) a reformer   (d) a social critic

PASSAGE-52

A male jackdaw's courtship behaviour is astonishingly human. All his movements are consciously strained and his proudly reared head and neck are permanently in a state of self-display. He provokes the other jackdaws continually if the female jackdaw is looking on and he purposefully becomes embroiled in conflicts with otherwise deeply respected superiors. Above all, he seeks to impress his loved one with the possession of a potential nesting site, from which he drives all other jackdaws, irrespective of their rank.

174. A 'courtship behaviour' may best be described as
    (a) the behaviour of a jackdaw who shows off his feather.
    (b) the behaviour of a male bird to attract a female bird.
    (c) the behaviour by which a male bird displays its beauty to the female bird
    (d) the behaviour of any male to win a female of the same species
175. Which of the phrases best help to bring out the precise meaning of 'consciously strained'?
    (a) Proudly reared and exhibited
    (b) Permanently in a state of display
    (c) Purposefully put in a state of display
    (d) Possession of nesting sight
176. The most important 'trick' of the jackdaw to win his female is
    (a) displaying his head and neck
    (b) to be like a human being
    (c) to become embroiled with other birds
    (d) to possess a place for building a nest
177. The jackdaw fights with other jackdaws because
    (a) he does not respect the senior birds
    (b) he wants to fight with his rivals
    (c) he does not like to be challenged
    (d) he wants to show off

178. Which of the following statements best describes the central theme of the passage ?
    (a) The courtship behaviour of birds
    (b) The similarities between the courtship behaviour of birds and man
    (c) The astonishing facts about the jackdaw's love life
    (d) The scientific study of the jackdaw's life

PASSAGE-53

We shall go on to the end; we shall fight in France, we shall fight on the seas and oceans, we shall fight with growing confidence and strength in the air, we shall defend our island whatever the cost may be, we shall fight on the beaches, we shall fight on the landing grounds, we shall fight in the fields and in the streets, we shall fight in the hills. We shall never surrender, and even if this island or a large part of it were subjugated and starving, then our empire beyond the seas would carry on the struggle, until the New World steps forth to the rescue and the liberation of the Old.

179. On the basis of the passage which of the following statements may be said to be correct ?
    (a) The speaker is encouraging his men for the conquest of France.
    (b) The speaker is aggressive and maniacal war-monger.
    (c) The speaker is not satisfied with the conquest of the island.
    (d) The speaker is a patriot urging the defence of his mother-land.
180. The speaker in the passage wants to go on fighting because.
    (a) he is raving lunatic
    (b) he is in a state of utter despair
    (c) he expects help from other quarters
    (d) he is the leader of a suicide squad
181. Which of the following pairs of the phrases helps best to bring out the intention of the speaker ?
    (a) "go on to the end", "shall never surrender"
    (b) "growing confidence", subjugated and starving"
    (c) "subjugated and starving"; fight on the landing ground"
    (d) "fight in the streets", "subjugated and starving"

PASSAGE-54

One day a tea contractor, Mr. Sharma was working on an estate with his wife and daughter. He noticed a light movement on the edge of the jungle, so he stopped to watch for a moment. To his astonishment a large tigress appeared and came towards Mr. Sharma. The tea contractor was a very brave man. He told his wife and daughter to run towards a nearby road, while he stepped to fight the tigress with a knife.

The tigress sprang at Mr. Sharma and knocked him down, but he managed to wound it with his knife. As a result, the tigress and Mr. Sharma knocked each other unconscious. Luckily for Mr. Sharma, a friend heard the noise of the fight and came to investigate. He found Mr. Sharma and carried him to the road. Then he stopped a car and sent the injured man to a hospital, where he eventually recovered.

The tigress disappeared for a few days but was later hunted down and shot by a Game Ranger. The Game Ranger discovered that the tigress had injured her paw in a wire trap and had been unable to hunt wild animals in its normal manner.

182. When did Mr. Sharma's friend go to see what was wrong ?
    (a)   When he saw the tigress attacking his friend
    (b)   Just before the tigress was knocked down
    (c)   When the friend was knocked down
    (d)   When he heard something unusual
183. When Mr. Sharma saw the tigress, he was
    (a)   surprised   (b)   afraid
    (c)   nervous   (d)   angry
184. Mr. Sharma stayed on to fight the tigress for
    (a)   he wanted to try to protect his wife and daughter
    (b)   he was strong man who loved fighting
    (c)   he couldn't run as quickly as his wife
    (d)   he tigress caught him before he could run

PASSAGE-55

During his early days as editor of the popular magazine. Saturday Evening Post, George Lorimer did much of the reading of unsolicited stories. This meant endless hours of sitting at the desk, pouring over big stacks of manuscripts, trying to decide which were worthy of publication and which were not. Lorimer became an expert at making these decisions.

One day he received a huffy letter from a would-be writer who had a complaint. "Last week you rejected my story," she wrote. "I am positive you did not read it, because, as a test, I pasted together pages 14, 15 and 16. The manuscript came back with the pages still pasted. There is no question in my mind but that you are a sham and a disgrace to your profession."

Lorimer's reply was succinct: "Madam, at breakfast when I crack open an egg. I don't have to eat whole egg to know it is bad."

185. Lorimer did much reading of the stories
    (a)   if they were the solicited ones
    (b)   when they appeared to be bad
    (c)   when they were from women writer
    (d)   when they came unsolicited
186. Lorimer was a good editor because
    (a)   his reply to the angry writer was polite
    (b)   he apologized for rejecting the story without reading it
    (c)   he could find the worth of a story with a little effort
    (d)   he was prompt, in writing letters
187. The lady wrote a huffy letter because
    (a)   her story was rejected
    (b)   her story was rejected unread
    (c)   her story was rejected although it was good
    (d)   Lorimer was biased in his decision.
188. Lorimer's reply was
    (a)   irrelevant   (b)   rude
    (c)   witty   (d)   funny
189. Lorimer read the stories
    (a)   because he enjoyed reading them
    (b)   in order to publish them
    (c)   only to find fault with them
    (d)   in order to review them

PASSAGE-56

Cozette could have been a pretty child, but she was thin and pale and her eyes were stained with weeping. She was dressed in her thin torn cotton dress and she shivered all the time. Here and there on her body were blue marks from the beatings that her mistress had given her. Her naked legs were red and rough. When she spoke, her voice trembled. Everything about the child, her looks, her behaviour, her speech, her silence, every small gesture she made, showed a terrible fear. She was so afraid that, even though she was wet through, she dared not go near the fire to warm herself, but sat shivering in a corner of the room.

190. Cozette could not be a pretty child because
    (a)   she was pale and emaciated
    (b)   she was weeping
    (c)   she was scantily dressed
    (d)   she was trembling with fear
191. Cozette's voice trembled because
    (a)   she was feeling cold
    (b)   she was frightened
    (c)   there was no fire near her
    (d)   she was wearing a thin, cotton dress
192. Cozette's terrible fear is conveyed most vividly by the description of
    (a)   her constant shivering
    (b)   her tear-stained eyes
    (c)   her trembling voice
    (d)   her inability to go near the fire
193. The cause of Cozette's fear is explained by
    (a)   her pale appearance
    (b)   her torn dress
    (c)   the blue marks on her body
    (d)   her speech

PASSAGE-57

Discussions on drug addiction should also be concerned with the vast majority of people who are not addicts. Their homes and lives are insecure because our narcotics laws drive such people to crime. The drug addict is almost never dangerous when he is under the influence of drugs. What makes him dangerous is the desperate need for money to buy the next dose. Drugs are available only in an illegal black market. The costs are stupendous, and this is what drives the addict to steal, rob and even kill.

194. According to the author, discussions of drug addiction are generally concerned with
    (a)   addicts   (b)   non-addicts
    (c)   criminals   (d)   black marketers
195. Addicts take criminal acts because
    (a)   drugs make them lose self-control
    (b)   the habit of robbing and stealing is hard to break
    (c)   they need large sums of money to buy drugs
    (d)   law is powerless against them
196. The author seems to criticize the narcotics laws for
    (a)   being too lenient
    (b)   being too complicated
    (c)   being ineffective
    (d)   driving addicts to crime
197. The word 'stupendous" in the passage means
    (a)   very high   (b)   foolish
    (c)   shocking   (d)   illegal
198. With reference to the passage, consider the following statements :
    1.   Addiction to drugs is a criminal act.
    2.   Drug addicts cannot be rehabilitated.
    Which of the statements given above is/are correct?
    (a)   1 only   (b)   2 only
    (c)   Both 1 and 2   (d)   Neither 1 nor 2

PASSAGE-58

Our voyage was very prosperous, but I shall not trouble the reader with a journal of it. The captain called in at one or two parts and sent in his long-boat for provisions and fresh water, but I never went out of the ship till we came into the Downs, which was on the 3rd day of June, 1706, about nine months after my escape. I offered to leave my goods in security for payment of my freight, but the captain protested he would not receive one farthing. We took kind leave of each other, and I made him promise that he would come to see me at my house in Redriff. I hired a house and a guide for five shillings which I borrowed from the captain.

199. When the writer uses the word "prosperous" to describe the voyage, he means that
    (a)   it made him rich.
    (b)   it made him healthy.
    (c)   it was very pleasant
    (d)   it was uneventful.

200. On the voyage, the author
    (a)   left the ship at intervals.
    (b)   was not able to leave the ship because it did not stop.
    (c)   never left the ship at all.
    (d)   never left the ship till they came into the downs.

201. In the context of the passage, the word "provisions" means
    (a)   mainly food.
    (b)   mainly security.
    (c)   money.
    (d)   mainly ammunition.

202. For the payment of the author's freight, the captain
    (a)   kept his goods as security.
    (b)   refused to accept any money.
    (c)   protested against being paid only a farthing.
    (d)   accepted a sum of money.

203. From the passage, it is clear that the captain's attitude to the author was
    (a)   one of hostility.
    (b)   one of indifference.
    (c)   one of extreme friendliness and kindness.
    (d)   one of disgust and irritation.

PASSAGE-59

The man sat up in the snow for a moment and struggled for calmness. Then he pulled on his gloves by means of his teeth, and got upon his feet. He glanced down at first in order to assure himself that he was really standing up, for the absence of sensation in his feet left him unrelated to the earth. His erect position in itself started to drive the webs of suspicion from the dog's mind; and when he spoke peremptorily, with the sound of whip-lashes in his voice, the dog rendered its customary allegiance and came to him. As it came within reaching distance, the man lost his control. His arms flashed out to the dog and he experienced genuine surprise when he discovered that his hands could not clutch, that there was neither bend not feeling in the fingers. He had forgotten for the moment that they were frozen and that they were freezing more and more. All this happened quickly and before the animal could get away, he encircled its body with his arms. He sat down in the snow and in this fashion held the dog, while it snarled and whined and struggled.

204. From the passage, which group of words expresses the effect of snow upon the man's feet ?
    (a)   With the sound of whip-lashes in his voice.
    (b)   His arms, flashed out to the dog.

    (c)   The absence of sensation in his feet left him unrelated to the earth.
    (d)   The man sat up in the snow for a moment and struggled for calmness.

205. The statement that, the man experienced genuine surprise when he discovered that his hands could not clutch means that
    (a)   the man did not see anything to clutch.
    (b)   the man had nothing to clutch.
    (c)   the man was afraid of the dog.
    (d)   there was neither bend nor feeling in the fingers.

206. Which word of group of words shows the exact condition of being 'frozen'?
    (a)   Whip-lashes in his voice
    (b)   He pulled on his gloves
    (c)   His hands could not clutch
    (d)   Lost his control

PASSAGE-60

"Sit down", the Principal said, but Mr. Tagde continued to stand, gaining courage from his own straight-backed stance, because he was beginning to feel a little afraid now.
The Principal looked unhappy. He disliked being forced to perform this sort of an unpleasant task.
"I wish you would consider withdrawing this report", he said.
"I am sorry, Sir, I cannot do that" Mr. Tagde said. He was pleased with his unwavering voice and uncompromising words.
"It will be a very damaging report if put on record".
"It is a factual report on very damaging conduct".
"You are asking for the boy's expulsion from school. Don't you think the punishment is too harsh for a few boyish pranks" ?

207. Mr. Tagde did not sit down because
    (a)   he was angry with the Principal
    (b)   he was in a defiant mood
    (c)   he did not like the student
    (d)   he was in a hurry

208. He would not withdraw the report because
    (a)   he was arrogant and bitter
    (b)   it was an accurate report
    (c)   he wanted to create problems for the Principal
    (d)   he wanted to show his authority

209. The Principal was unhappy because he
    (a)   did not like to deal with an arrogant person
    (b)   was angry with Mr. Tagde
    (c)   could not enforce discipline in
    (d)   did not want to expel the boy

PASSAGE-61

It was a bitterly cold night, and even at the far end of the bus the east wind that raved along the street cut like a knife. The bus stopped, the two women and a man got in together and filled the vacant places. The younger woman was dressed in sealskin and carried one of those Pekinese dogs that women in sealskin like to carry in their laps. The conductor came in and took the fares. Then his eye rested with cold malice on the beady-eyed toy dog. I saw trouble brewing. This was the opportunity for which he had been waiting, and he intended to make the most of it.

210. The wind that blew on the night was
    (a)   mild   (b)   pleasant
    (c)   bitter   (d)   sharp

211. The younger woman was carrying the dog as
    (a) a necessity
    (b) a fashion
    (c) an expression of provocation
    (d) an escort
212. Which of the following statements best describes the nature of the conductor ?
    (a) He was dutiful
    (b) He was a law-abiding person
    (c) He liked dogs
    (d) He was unfriendly and malicious
213. It was a bitterly cold night, and even at the far end of the bus the east wind that raved along the street cut like a knife".
    This sentence gives us an idea of
    (a) a lonely night-bus journey
    (b) an unbearable cold night
    (c) the wind at the time that was still and cold
    (d) the hardship of author's journey

PASSAGE-62

Before an armed robber locked Mary Graves in the sweltering trunk of her car, she dialled an emergency number on her portable telephone and slipped it to her three-year-old daughter. Though confused, the little girl saved the day. She told emergency operators that her mother was locked in the trunk. Although she didn't know where she was, she provided some important clues: she could see airplanes and the sky, according to the transcript of the emergency phone call. The operator called Tampa international airport police, who searched the top floor of the airport parking garage where the car was parked. The operator told the girl to honk, enabling the police to locate the car and free Mrs. Graves.

214. The clues provided by the little girl suggest that the car was parked
    (a) outside but adjacent to the airport
    (b) by the main street of the city
    (c) at the airport
    (d) in a parking garage in the side-lane
215. The passage indicates that the girl was
    (a) clever and brave
    (b) had the maturity of an adult
    (c) coy and shy
    (d) worried and excited
216. The girl helped the police trace the car by
    (a) shouting loudly
    (b) making too much din
    (c) shrieking frightfully
    (d) sounding the horn

PASSAGE-63

Martin had many little tricks highly entertaining to his son. On an evening, returning from the market, he would buy a paper mask, the head of a hissing dragon. He would put it on and knock at the door. On opening the door, the boy would be terrified for a moment, but only for a moment, for he would soon remove it and the two would roll with laughter. Tom would, then, go out with the mask and knock at the door for his father to open. Martin had to act as if he was paralysed with fear.

217. Martin played his little tricks because
    (a) he was very much interested in them
    (b) he wanted to terrify his son
    (c) his son got pleasure from them
    (d) it was his habit to make tricks
218. Which of the following statements is the most appropriate description of the mask ?
    (a) It is a mask looking like a dragon with long tail and covering the whole body of Martin
    (b) It is mask looking like the head of a dragon with its tongue hanging out
    (c) It is mask looking like an animal with horns, wings and a pair of ferocious eyes emitting fire
    (d) It is a mask looking like the head of a king cobra
219. The father and son rolled with laughter after the
    (a) father put on the mask
    (b) opening of the door
    (c) son saw the mask
    (d) father removed the mask

PASSAGE-64

My father was passionate about two things: education and socialism. He was himself a born teacher. Indeed, he could never restrain himself form teaching, and as a small boy I was frequently embarrassed by his desire to instruct everybody – people in railway carriages, for instance – though I realized even then that it was an innocent desire, quite free from vanity. He was equally ready to receive instruction. Education, to men of his generation and temperament, was something it has largely ceased to be nowadays. It was the great golden gateway to the enchanted realms of the mind.

220. The author wants us to know that his father
    (a) was a school teacher
    (b) was an educationist and socialist
    (c) used to travel a lot
    (d) loved teaching
221. The author often felt embarrassed by the behaviour of his father because
    (a) he taught badly
    (b) he taught even at odd places
    (c) he wanted to show off his learning
    (d) he lost self-control while teaching
222. To the generation of the writer's father, education was
    (a) an old fashioned enterprise
    (b) the result of good teaching
    (c) an exploration of the world of imagination
    (d) one aspect of socialism
223. From the passage it is clear that the author
    (a) loved and admired his father
    (b) disapproved his father's love of teaching
    (c) thought of him as vain
    (d) considered his father's education inadequate.

PASSAGE-65

We started looking on the ground for blood hair, or a drag mark that would lead us to the deer killed by the tiger. We had proceeded a hundered yards, examining every foot of the ground and going dead slow, when Mothi, just as I turned may head to look at him, started backwards, screaming as he did so. Then he whipped round and ran for dear life, beating the air with his hands as if warding off a swarm of bees and continuing to scream as he ran.

The sudden and piercing scream of a human being in a jungle where a moment before all has been silent is terrifying to hear. Instinctively I knew what had happened. With his eyes fixed on the ground, looking for the blood or hair of the kill, Mothi had failed to see where he was going, and had walked towards the tiger.

224. Mothi and the narrator were scanning the ground because
 (a) they were looking for the tiger
 (b) the forest was full of unpleasant surprises
 (c) they were trying to discover the tiger's footprints
 (d) they were looking for marks left by the tiger's pray

225. Mothi began to scream when he
 (a) was attacked by a swarm of bees
 (b) was frightened by the sight of blood
 (c) came face to face with the tiger
 (d) stumbled on the tiger

226. In the context of the passage 'kill means'
 (a) the act of killing
 (b) an animal killed by the tiger
 (c) a human being killed by the tiger
 (d) a wounded tiger

227. Before Mothi screamed, the jungle was
 (a) quiet (b) dark
 (c) noisy (d) terrifying

PASSAGE-66

The first day out we met our first rhino, two of them, and I had the fright of my life. The pair had got our scent before we spotted them, and being bad tempered beasts, they rushed towards where they thought we were. Now it just happened that we were about fifty yards to one side of where they expected to find us – which was just as well, for I must say I did not like their look. As they thundered past, we crouched low and left them go. It did not strike me as a good opportunity for rhino photography. Anyhow. I was much too frightened to have been able to hold the camera steady.

228. From the above passage it appears that rhinos
 (a) run away they see human beings
 (b) rush to attack when they smell human scent
 (c) hide under the bushes at the sight of human beings
 (d) stand still if they are not attacked

229. When the author saw a rhino for the first time, he was
 (a) excited (b) frightened
 (c) charmed (d) surprised

230. The author could not take the photographs of the rhinos because
 (a) he was too far away from rhinos
 (b) he was not carrying a good camera
 (c) it did not occur to him that he had a chance to do so
 (d) he did not like the look of rhinos

PASSAGE-67

A well-dressed young man entered a big textile shop one evening. He was able to draw the attention of the salesmen who thought him rich and likely to make heavy purchases. He was shown the superior varieties of suit lengths and sarees. But after casually examining them, he kept moving to the next section where readymade goods were being sold and further on to the hosiery section. By then, the salesmen had begun to doubt his intentions, and drew the attention of the manager. The manager asked him what exactly he wanted and he replied that he wanted courteous treatment. He explained that he had come to the same shop in casual dress that morning and drawn little attention. His pride was hurt and he wanted to assert himself. He had come in good dress only to get decent treatment. Not for getting any textiles. He left without making any purchase.

231. The young man was well dressed because
 (a) it was his habit to dress well
 (b) it was his wedding day
 (c) he wanted to meet the manager of the shop
 (d) he wanted to impress the salesmen

232. The salesmen in the shop are described as people who pay attention to
 (a) only young men and women
 (b) pretty women
 (c) only rich customers
 (d) regular customers

233. The young man moved away to the hosiery section because he
 (a) was not interested in purchasing anything now
 (b) did not like the readymade clothes
 (c) wanted better clothes
 (d) was restless

234. The manager asked the young man what he wanted because
 (a) he would give him exactly what he was looking for
 (b) the salesman had drawn his attention to the indifferent attitude of the young man
 (c) he thought they could do more business which him that way
 (d) he thought the visitor was dissatisfied

235. The young man left without making purchases because he
 (a) did not have money
 (b) could not find any item of his choice
 (c) had come only to make a point about the indifferent attitude of the salesmen towards casually dressed customers
 (d) decided to come to make the purchases later on

PASSAGE-68

A large number of people had come to attend the meeting to be addressed by the gifted speaker. The organizers had a difficult time keeping the assembled people quiet as the meeting did not commence at the scheduled time. After some time the people lost their patience and began to shout and heckle. The organizers had great difficulty in assuaging the anger of the crowd when they were forced to cancel the meeting as the speaker had to be hospitalized due to sudden illness.

236. What was the actual reason for the organizers to have a difficult time ?
 (a) a large number of people had come to the meeting
 (b) the organizers could not make proper arrangements
 (c) the meeting could not be started in time
 (d) the speaker was ill

237. What does the word "assuaging" imply ?
 (a) accepting (b) tolerating
 (c) reducing (d) removing

238. Further delay resulted in the people
 (a) leaving the place
 (b) fighting with the organizers
 (c) making noise
 (d) making the speaker ill

PASSAGE-69

Those responsible for teaching young people have resorted to a variety of means to make their pupils learn. The earliest of these was the threat of punishment. This meant that the pupil who was slow, careless or inattentive risked either physical chastisement or the loss of some expected privilege. Learning was thus associated with fear. At a later period, pupils were encouraged to learn in the hope of some kind of reward. This often took the form of marks awarded for work done and sometimes of prizes given at the end of the year to the best scholar. Such a system appealed to the competitive spirit, but was just as depressing as the older system for the slow pupil.In the nineteenth century sprang up a new type of teacher, convinced that learning was worthwhile for its own sake and that the young pupil's principal stimulus should neither be anxiety to avoid a penalty nor ambition to win a reward, but sheer desire to learn. Interest, direct or indirect, became the keyword of instruction.

239. The educational system which caused fear in the pupil's mind was based on :
    (a)   rewards based
    (b)   labour
    (c)   punishment
    (d)   competition
240. The system based on rewards satisfied all except :
    (a)   the slow pupil
    (b)   the very intelligent pupil
    (c)   the laborious pupil
    (d)   the casual pupil
241. The system which appealed to the competitive spirit in the pupils was largely based on:
    (a)   punishment   (b)   marks
    (c)   chastisement   (d)   cash prizes

PASSAGE-70

During the summer I was introduced to the game of cricket, and I felt my inherent foreignness for the first time. The ball is far too hard for my taste. Even during my last games at the school, angry spectators would shout, "Butter fingers !" But I smiled. Everyone knew in their hearts that 'I was going to drop the ball anyway, and nobody expected me to be able to play the game.

242. The author first played cricket
    (a)   as a child in his own country
    (b)   when he was a school boy
    (c)   when he was a tourist
    (d)   when he returned home after his studies
243. "felt my inherent foreignness" means
    (a)   felt very strange
    (b)   felt very interested and excited
    (c)   enjoyed learning new games
    (d)   fely my superiority over others
244. Spectators would shout "Butter fingers" when the author was playing because
    (a)   he liked butter
    (b)   his fingers were like those of a lady
    (c)   he often dropped the ball
    (d)   he was very good at the game
245. 'Spectator' means
    (a)   glasses   (b)   onlooker
    (c)   watchman   (d)   player

PASSAGE-71

A man has two blacksmiths for his neighbours. Their names were Pengu and Shengu. The man was greatly troubled by the noise of their hammers. He decided to talk to them. The next day he called both of them and offered ₹100 each, if they found new huts for them selves. They took the money and agreed to find new huts for themselves. The next morning he woke up again to the sound of their hammers. He went out to see why the blacksmiths hadn't found new huts and he discovered that Pengu and Shengu had kept their promise. They had exchanged their huts.

246. The man was troubled because
    (a)   the blacksmiths always fought with each others
    (b)   the blacksmiths' hammers made a lot of noise
    (c)   he was afraid of blacksmiths
    (d)   the blacksmiths did not do their work properly
247. The man gave them money because
    (a)   the blacksmiths were poor
    (b)   the blacksmiths had asked him for money
    (c)   he did not want them to make a noise
    (d)   he wanted them to find new huts
248. The man went out of his house because
    (a)   he wanted to fight with the blacksmiths
    (b)   he wanted to ask the blacksmiths to stop the noise
    (c)   he wanted to find out why they hadn't found new huts
    (d)   he wanted his money back from the blacksmiths
249. The man came to know that
    (a)   the blacksmiths were not in their huts
    (b)   the blacksmiths had exchanged huts
    (c)   the blacksmiths were going away
    (d)   the blacksmiths had not kept their promise

PASSAGE-72

Much rhapsodical nonsense has been written about the "Mona Lisa" and her enigmatic smile, and there have been endless speculations as to her character and the meaning of her expression. It is all beside the mark. The truth is that the "Mona Lisa" is a study of modeling. Leonardo da Vinci had discovered that the expression of smiling is much more a matter of modeling of the cheek and of the forms below the eye than of the change in the line of the lips. It interested him to produce a smile wholly by these delicate changes of surface; hence the mysterious expression.

250. The word *rhapsodical* as used in the passage means
    (a)   plain   (b)   unreadable
    (c)   enthusiastic   (d)   uniformed
251. "Mona Lisa" is the name of
    (a)   a beautiful woman who made history in ancient Rome
    (b)   a famous painting
    (c)   the artist's mistress
    (d)   an art technique
252. The truth about the "Mona Lisa" is that it is a study in
    (a)   feminine psychology   (b)   facial expression
    (c)   feminine form   (d)   modelling
253. The painter was able to produce that strange smile on Mona Lisa's face by
    (a)   delicate changes on the surface of cheeks below the eyes
    (b)   using bright colours
    (c)   using a painting knife
    (d)   looking constantly at a smiling model while painting.
254. The author of the above passage has examined 'Mona Lisa' from
    (a)   an idealistic angle
    (b)   an imaginary point of View
    (c)   a purely artistic angle
    (d)   a scientific and realistic standpoint

PASSAGE-73

A profound terror, increased still by the darkness, the silence and his waking images, froze his heart within him. He almost felt his hair stand on end, when by straining his eyes to their utmost, he perceived through the shadows two faint yellow lights. At first he attributed these gradually to distinguish the objects around him in the cave. and he beheld a huge animal lying but two steps from him.

255. The opening of the passage suggests that
     (a) darkness, silence and waking images added to his already being in profound terror
     (b) a profound terror increased the waking images in his frozen heart
     (c) the person was frightened by darkness and silence
     (d) a profound terror was caused in him by the silence and darkness of the night

256. When he perceived through the shadows two faint lights.
     (a) he experienced a great strain
     (b) he felt his hair stand upright
     (c) his eyes felt strained to their utmost
     (d) his pupils dilated

257. The person in the story
     (a) imagined that he saw an animal
     (b) could not recognize the animal
     (c) saw the animal by chance
     (d) expected to see the animal

PASSAGE-74

When Jonathan (the seagull) came, it was well after dark, and he floated in moonlight on the surface of the ocean. His wings were ragged bars of lead, but the weight of failure was even heavier on his back. He wished, feebly, that the weight would be just enough to drag him gently down to the bottom, and end it all. But soon he came back to normal. He pushed wearily away from the dark water and few towards the land, grateful for what he had learned about work-saving low-altitude flying.

258. The word 'wearily' means
     (a) tireless   (b) exhausted
     (c) sadly   (d) unconscious

259. The seagull suffered because
     (a) he had tried to do something that other seagulls had not done.
     (b) probably he had been attacked by a stronger bird.
     (c) probably he had been attacked by some strong creature in the sea.
     (d) he had swooned and fallen into the water.

260. 'His wings were ragged bars of lead' means that
     (a) his wings were damaged and supported by bars of lead.
     (b) his wings were damaged and therefore very heavy.
     (c) he had rags and bars of lead on his wings.
     (d) his wings were broken like pieces of lead.

261. The lesson that he had learnt that day was about
     (a) not fighting with stronger birds.
     (b) flying carrying bars of lead on his wings.
     (c) diving too deep into the sea.
     (d) flying at low altitudes.

PASSAGE-75

Vacationing on a motorcycle, you see things in a way that is completely different from any other. In a car you are always in a compartment, and because you are used to it you do not realise that through that car window everything you see is just more TV. You are a passive observer and it is all moving by you boringly in a frame. On a motorcycle, however, the frame is gone. You are completely in contact with it all. You are in the scene, not just watching it anymore, and the sense of presence is overwhelming.

262. The writer likes travelling on the motorcycle. What is the most likely reason for this ?
     (a) The motorcycle has no windows.
     (b) The motorcycle does not go as fast as a car.
     (c) As the traveller is used to cars, travelling by motorcycle is a change.
     (d) Travelling by motorcycle, the writer feels that he is part of the scenery.

263. Which of the following statements is closest to the truth ?
     (a) The writer does not like TV as it gives a narrow view of things.
     (b) The writer likes TV but he does not like watching it from car windows.
     (c) The writer does not like TV because the picture is in a frame.
     (d) The writer does not like TV because the programmes are boring.

264. "In a car you are always in a compartment, and because you are used to it you do not realise that ...." In this sentence, 'it' refers to
     (a) travelling in a car.
     (b) always being in a compartment, e.g. one's room, office.
     (c) seeing the scenery through the window frame.
     (d) seeing so much TV at home.

265. In the last sentence, the writer talks of a 'sense of presence'. He is referring to the presence of
     (a) his own self as part of the scene.
     (b) the time that is now passing.
     (c) the scene and the beauty.
     (d) senses with which one feels.

266. The word 'overwhelming' means
     (a) very strong   (b) unavoidable
     (c) interesting   (d) humorous

PASSAGE-76

I was lying down in a dark, lonely compartment of the speeding train, trying to sleep. But, quite unusually, sleep eluded me. A vague uneasiness gripped me. It was pitch dark outside. A few points of light flashed by as we sped through a small station and in the dim light I thought I saw a hand gripping the bars of my window. Once again the train was swallowed up by the impenetrable darkness. My heart pounded. My mouth was parched. I could not get up. I do not know how long I remained thus before the train began to slow down. The reassuring bright lights of the station we were entering revealed no intruder. I breathed again.

267. The narrator could not sleep because
     (a) he usually found it difficult to fall asleep.
     (b) he could not find a place to lie down.
     (c) he was disturbed by some unspecified thoughts.
     (d) the people near him were disturbing' him.

268. In the dim light he saw
    (a) someone trying to climb into the train.
    (b) someone clinging to the bars of the window.
    (c) someone was attempting to steal his bag.
    (d) someone standing outside the window.
269. Which of the following words best describes the condition of the traveller ?
    (a) Cautious
    (b) Imaginative
    (c) Observant
    (d) Nervous

PASSAGE-77

I was abruptly awakened by a noisy scuffle. The sun, a mere fringe over the horizon, immediately chased away the grey half-darkness. I was too sleepy to notice what was happening. Yuri was rolling over on the ground. I ran up to him but was struck dumb. With his right hand he was holding a cobra by the neck. Two sharp fangs showed from its jaws. The battle was over in a few minutes. A hollow hissing and convulsive jerks were then only reminders of a just-ended tussle. The catcher half-opened the lid of the box and calmly put the quarry in.

270. When the writer saw Yuri holding a cobra by the neck, he was 'struck dumb'. This means that he was
    (a) extremely delighted.
    (b) very much helpless.
    (c) rather surprised.
    (d) absolutely shocked.
271. From the passage, Yuri appears to be a man who is
    (a) calm and courageous.
    (b) cunning and crafty.
    (c) noisy and dangerous.
    (d) active and jumpy.
272. With reference to the passage, the following assumptions have been made :
    1. The incident took place early in the morning.
    2. Yuri threw the snake away.
    Which of these assumptions is/are correct ?
    (a) 1 only
    (b) 2 only
    (c) Both 1 and 2
    (d) Neither 1 nor 2

PASSAGE-78

For many years, ship captains navigating the waters of Antarctica have been intrigued by sightings of emerald icebergs. Scientists have now explained their mystery. There icebergs are turned upside down. Icebergs are blocks of ice that have broken off huge slabs of frozen snow called ice shelves. Their green appearance results from sea water that has frozen at the bottom over hundreds of years. The frozen sea water has dissolved organic matter which givens it a yellow tone and the fresh water 'ice shelf' above has a blue tinge. When the iceberg turns upside down, it appears green through the visual mix of yellow with the blue from below.

273. What is the meaning of 'intrigued'?
    (a) Surprised
    (b) Fascinated
    (c) Muffled
    (d) Repulsed
274. What are ice shelves?
    (a) They are huge pieces of chunks of ice
    (b) They are frozen sea water
    (c) They are pieces of ice which look like shelves
    (d) They are huge pieces of ice which are very old
275. What are icebergs?
    (a) Huge chunks of ice floating on water
    (b) Frozen sea water
    (c) Green ice
    (d) Green yellow water below and blue above

276. When the iceberg turns upside down, it appears
    (a) green
    (b) yellow
    (c) blue
    (d) white

PASSAGE-79

To eat and not be eaten – that's the imperative of a caterpillar's existence. The leaf roller reduces its risks of being picked off by predators by silking together a temporary shelter in which to feed and rest. Adopting a different line of defense, the jelly slug extrudes a sticky translucent coating that may foul the mouth-parts of marauding ants. For its part, the aquatic larva, by its watery element, fashions a portable hideout from fragments of aquatic leaves. Cutting a serpentine trail as it feeds on tender young leaves, the minute citrus leaf miner spends its entire larval life inside its host plant, thus keeping its appetizing body safely under wraps.

277. Which varieties of caterpillars 'build' shelters to protect themselves?
    (a) Leaf roller and aquatic larva
    (b) Leaf roller and jelly slug
    (c) Jelly slug and aquatic larva
    (d) Jelly slug and citrus leaf miner
278. Which one of the following caterpillars produces a sticky covering?
    (a) Leaf roller
    (b) Jelly slug
    (c) Aquatic larva
    (d) Citrus leaf miner
279. Which one of the following pairs of words in the passage describes enemies of the caterpillar?
    (a) Serpentine and host
    (b) Predator and marauding
    (c) Serpentine and marauding
    (d) Predator and host
280. Which one of the following makes itself unpalatable?
    (a) Leaf roller
    (b) Jelly slug
    (c) Aquatic larva
    (d) Leaf miner
281. The main idea of the passage is that caterpillars
    (a) like to eat a lot
    (b) have to protect themselves while feeding
    (c) are good to eat
    (d) are not good to eat

PASSAGE-80

In Delhi, it was forbidden by the law, at one time, to take a Dog into a public vehicle. One day a lady, accompanied by a pet dog, entered a bus. Wishing to evade the law, she placed her tiny dog in her dress pocket. It so happened that the person next to this lady was a pick-pocket; and during the journey the carefully placed his hand into her pocket in search of her purse. Great was the horror to find instead a pair of sharp teeth inserted into his fingers. His exclamation of pain and surprise drew the attention of other passengers to him.

282. Once the law in Delhi did not permit the people to
    (a) carry dogs into private vehicles
    (b) board a bus without ticket
    (c) carry dogs into a public vehicle
    (d) carry animals with them

283. In order to evade the law, the lady
  (a) hid the dogs under the seat
  (b) got off the bus
  (c) gave the dog to a fellow passenger
  (d) put the dog in her pocket
284. The pick-pocket travelling with the lady
  (a) reported the matter to the conductor
  (b) put his hand in her pocket
  (c) took out the dog
  (d) asked the lady to get off
285. Which one of the following correctly expresses the meaning of "wishing to evade the law"?
  (a) Wish to avoid following the law
  (b) Desire to follow the law blindly
  (c) Reluctance to break the law
  (d) Wish to change the law
286. Why did the pick-pocket exclaim with pain?
  (a) He was hit by the lady
  (b) He was caught by the fellow-passengers
  (c) He was bitten by the dog
  (d) He fell of the bus

PASSAGE-81

Most people lead the lives that circumstances have thrust upon them. But Wilson had boldly taken the course of his life into his own hands. At 35, he had quit his job to lead a pleasant life on an exotic island with just enough money to last for twenty five years. Once, fifteen years after he had been on the island, I happened to meet him and enquired about his financial situation. He said, "It will carry me on till I am sixty." "But one cannot be sure of dying at sixty", I said, "Well..." he replied, "It depends on oneself, doesn't it?"   **[Prelim II-2010]**

287. According to the author most people
  (a) do not allow circumstances to affect their lives
  (b) have fatalistic attitude towards life
  (c) do not know how to cope with their situation
  (d) do nothing to change the condition they live in
288. Wilson's boldest decision was that he
  (a) took the course of his life into his own hands
  (b) saved a lot of money to lead a pleasant life
  (c) preferred to live in isolation
  (d) wanted to live without depending on others
289. '......depends on oneself' suggests that Wilson, at 60, would
  (a) depend on his own resources
  (b) surrender himself to destiny
  (c) take away his own life
  (d) carry on living in the same way

Directions : *Read the given passages and answer the question based on them.*

PASSAGE-82

I opened the bag and packed the boots in; and then, just as I was going to close it, a horrible idea occurred to me. Had I packed my tooth-brush? I don't know how it is, but I never do know whether I've packed my tooth-brush.

My tooth-brush is a thing that haunts me when I'm travelling, and makes my life a misery. I dream that I haven't packed it, and wake up in a cold perspiration and get out of bed and hunt for it. And, in the morning, I pack it before I have used it, and have to unpack again to get it, and it is always the last thing I turn out of the bag; and then I repack and forget it, and have to rush upstairs for it at the last moment and carry it to the railway station, wrapped up in my pocket-handkerchief.

[Prelim II-2011]

290. When he was going to close the bag, the idea that occurred to him was
  (a) unpleasant   (b) sad
  (c) fantastic   (d) amusing
291. What makes his life miserable whenever he undertakes travelling?
  (a) Going to the railway station
  (b) Forgetting his tooth-brush
  (c) Packing his bag
  (d) Bad dreams
292. His toothbrush is finally
  (a) in his bag
  (b) on his bed
  (c) in his handkerchief
  (d) lost

PASSAGE-83

He walked several miles that day but could not get anything to eat or drink except some dry bread and some water, which he got from cottagers and farmers. As night fell, he slept under a haystack lying in a meadow. He felt frightened at first, for the wind blew awfully over the empty fields. He felt cold and hungry, and was feeling more lonely than he had ever felt before. He, however, soon fell asleep, being much tired with his long walk. When he got up next day, he was feeling terribly hungry so he purchased a loaf of bread with a few coins that he had.   **[Prelim II-2011]**

293. When the night fell, he slept
  (a) in the open field
  (b) under a pile of dry grass
  (c) in a farmer's cottage
  (d) under a tree
294. He soon fell asleep because
  (a) he was exhausted
  (b) he was all alone
  (c) he had not slept for days
  (d) he was very frightened
295. With reference to the passage, consider the following statements
  1. He was walking through the countryside.
  2. The cottagers and farmers gave him enough food so that he could sleep at night without feeling hungry.

Which of the statement(s) given above is/are correct?

(a) Only 1   (b) Only 2

(c) Both 1 and 2   (d) Neither 1 nor 2

PASSAGE-84

In spring, polar bear mothers emerge from dens with three month old cubs. The mother bear has fasted for as long as eight months but that does not stop the young from demanding full access to her remaining reserves. If there are triplets, the most persistent stands to gain an extra meal and it may have the meal at the expense of others. The smallest of the litter forfeits many meals to stronger siblings. Females are protective of their cubs but tend to ignore family rivalry over food. In 21 years of photographing polar bears, I've only once seen the smallest of triplets survive till autumn. **[Prelim II-2011]**

296. Female polar bears give birth during

(a) spring   (b) summer

(c) autumn   (d) winter

297. Mother bears

(a) take sides over cubs

(b) let the cubs fend for themselves

(c) feed only their favourites

(d) see that all cubs get an equal share

298. With reference to the passage, the following assumptions have been made

1. Polar bears fast as long as eight months due to non-availability of prey.

2. Polar bears always give birth to triplets.

Which of the assumption(s) given above is/are valid?

(a) Only 1   (b) Only 2

(c) Both 1 and 2   (d) Neither 1 nor 2

PASSAGE-85

For fourteen and a half months I lived in my little cell or room in the Dehradun jail, and I began to feel as if I was almost a part of it. I was familiar with every bit of it, I knew every mark and dent on the whitewashed walls and on the uneven floor and the ceiling with its moth-eaten rafters. In the little yard outside I greeted little tufts of grass and odd bits of stone as old friends. I was not alone in my cell, for several colonies of wasp and hornets lived there, and many lizards found a home behind the rafters, emerging in the evenings in search of prey. **[Prelim II-2012]**

299. Which of the following explains best the sentence in the passage "I was almost a part of it"?

(a) I was not alone in the cell.

(b) I was familiar with every bit of the cell.

(c) I greeted little tufts of grass like old friends.

(d) I felt quite at home in the cell.

300. The passage attempts to describe

(a) the general conditions of the country's jails.

(b) the prisoner's capacity to notice the minute details of his surroundings.

(c) the prisoner's conscious efforts to overcome the loneliness.

(d) the prisoner's ability to live happily with other creatures.

301. The author of the passage seems to suggest that

(a) it is possible to adjust oneself to uncongenial surroundings.

(b) the conditions in Indian prisons are not bad.

(c) it is not difficult to spend one's time in a prison.

(d) there is a need to improve the conditions in our jails.

PASSAGE-86

We started pitching the highest camp that has ever been made. Everything took five times as long as it would have taken in a place where there was enough air to breathe; but at last we got the tent up, and when we crawled in, it was not too bad. There was only a light wind, and inside it was not too cold for us to take off our gloves. At night most climbers take off their boots; but I prefer to keep them on. Hillary, on the other hand, took his off and laid them next to his sleeping bag. **[Prelim II-2012]**

302. What does the expression "pitching the highest camp" imply?

(a) They reached the summit of the highest mountain in the world.

(b) Those who climbed that far earlier did not pitch any camp.

(c) So far nobody has ever climbed that high.

(d) They were too many climbers and needed to pitch a big camp.

303. They took a long time to finish the work because

(a) they were very tired.

(b) there was not enough air to breathe.

(c) it was very cold.

(d) it was very dark.

304. When they crawled into the tent

(a) they took off their gloves because it was not very cold.

(b) they could not take off their gloves because it was very cold.

(c) they took off their gloves though it was very cold.

(d) they did not take off their gloves though it was not cold.

PASSAGE-87

A local man, staying on the top floor of an old wooden house, was awakened at midnight by a fire. Losing his way in a smoke-filled passage, he missed the stairway and went into another room. He picked up a bundle to protect his face from the fire and immediately fell through the floor below where he managed to escape through a clear doorway. The "bundle" proved to be the baby of the Mayor's wife. The "hero" was congratulated by all. **[Prelim II -2012]**

305. The man went into another room because

(a) he did not know where exactly the stairway was.

(b) the passage was full of smoke.

(c) he was extremely nervous.

(d) he stumbled on a bundle.

306. The man was called a hero because he

(a) expressed his willingness to risk his life to save others.

(b) managed to escape from the fire.

(c) showed great courage in fighting the fire.

(d) saved a life.

PASSAGE-88

Seven-year-old Jim came home from the park without his new bicycle. "An old man and a little boy borrowed it," he explained. "They are going to bring it back at four o'clock". His parents were upset that he had given his expensive new bicycle, but were secretly proud of his kindness and faith. Came four o'clock, no bicycle. The parents were anxious. But at 4:30, the door bell rang, and there stood a happy man and a boy, with the bicycle and a box of chocolates. Jim suddenly disappeared into his bedroom, and then came running out. "All right," he said, after examining the bicycle. "You can have your watch back!" **[Prelim II-2013]**

307. When Jim came home without his bicycle his parents
 (a) were angry with him
 (b) were worried
 (c) did not feel concerned
 (d) were eager to meet the old man and the little boy.

308. Jim returned the watch to the old man and the little boy because
 (a) they gave him chocolates.
 (b) his father was proud of him.
 (c) he was satisfied with the condition of his bicycle
 (d) they were late only by 30 minutes.

PASSAGE-89

It was already late when we set out for the next town, which according to the map was about fifteen kilometers away on the other side of the hills. There we felt that we would find a bed for the night. Darkness fell soon after we left the village, but luckily we met no one as we drove swiftly along the narrow winding road that led to the hills. As we climbed higher, it became colder and rain began to fall, making it difficult at times to see the road. I asked John, my companion, to drive more slowly. After we had travelled for about twenty kilometers, there was still no sign of the town which was marked on the map. We were beginning to get worried. Then without warning, the car stopped and we found we had run out of pertrol. **[Prelim II-2013]**

309. The author asked John to drive more slowly because
 (a) the road led to the hills.
 (b) John was an inexperienced driver.
 (c) the road was not clearly visible.
 (d) they were in wilderness.

310. The travellers set out for the town although it was getting dark because
 (a) they were in a hurry.
 (b) the next town was a short distance away and was a hill-resort.
 (c) they were in wilderness.
 (d) the next town was a short distance away and promised a good rest for the night.

311. The travellers were worried after twenty kilometers because
 (a) it was a lonely countryside.
 (b) they probably feared of having lost their way.
 (c) the rain began to fall.
 (d) it was getting colder as they drove.

PASSAGE-90

A stout old lady was walking with her basket down the middle of a street in Petrograd to the great confusion of the traffic and no small peril to herself. It was pointed out to her that the pavement was the place for foot-passengers, but she replied "I'm going to walk where I like. We've got liberty now." It did not occur to the dear lady that if liberty entitled the foot-passenger to walk down the middle of the road it also entitled the taxi-driver to drive on the pavement, and that the end of such liberty would be universal chaos. Everything would be getting in everybody else's way and nobody would get anywhere. Individual liberty would have become social anarchy. **[Prelim II-2013]**

312. It was pointed out to the lady that she should walk on the pavement because she was
 (a) a pedestrian
 (b) carrying a basket
 (c) stout
 (d) an old lady

313. The lady refused to move from the middle of the street because
 (a) she was not afraid of being killed.
 (b) she felt that she is entitled to do whatever she liked.
 (c) she did not like walking on the payment.
 (d) she was confused.

314. The old lady failed to realise that
 (a) she was not really free.
 (b) her liberty was not unlimited.
 (c) she was an old person.
 (d) roads are made for motor vehicles only.

PASSAGE-91

In front of us was walking a bare-headed old man in tattered clothes. He was driving his beasts. They were all laden with heavy loads of clay from the hills and looked tired. The man carried a long whip which perhaps he himself had made. As he walked down the road he stopped now and then to eat the wild berries that grew on bushes along the uneven road. When he threw away the seeds, the bold birds would fly to peck at them. Sometimes a stray dog watched the procession philosophically and then began to bark. When this happened, my two little sons would stand still holding my hands firmly. A dog can sometimes be dangerous indeed. **[Prelim II-2014]**

315. The author's children held his hands firmly because
 (a) they were scared of the barking dogs.
 (b) they wanted him to pluck berries.
 (c) they saw the whip in the old man's hand.
 (d) the road was uneven.

316. The expression "a stray dog watched the procession philosophically" means that
 (a) the dog was restless and ferocious.
 (b) the dog stood aloof, looking at the procession with seriousness.
 (c) the dog looked at the procession with big, wondering eyes.
 (d) the dog stood there with his eyes closed.

PASSAGE-92

Cynthia was a shy girl. She believed that she was plain and untalented. One day her teacher ordered the entire class to show up for audition for the school play. Cynthia nearly died of fright when she was told that she would have to stand on stage in front of the entire class and deliver dialogues. The mere thought of it made her feel sick. But a remarkable transformation occurred during the audition. A thin, shy girl, her knees quaking, her stomach churning in terror, began to stun everyone with her excellent performance. Her bored classmates suddenly stopped their noisy chat to stare at her slender figure on the stage. At the end of her audition, the entire room erupted in thunderous applause.

[Prelim II-2014]

317. Cynthia was afraid to stand on stage because
    (a) she felt her classmates may laugh at her.
    (b) her stomach was churning.
    (c) she lacked self-confidence.
    (d) she did not like school plays.

318. Cynthia's classmates were chatting because
    (a) it was their turn to act next.
    (b) they were bored of the performances.
    (c) Cynthia did not act well.
    (d) the teacher had no control over them.

319. Cynthia's knees were quaking because
    (a) she felt nervous and shy.
    (b) the teacher scolded her.
    (c) she was very thin and weak.
    (d) she was afraid of her classmates.

320. The transformation that occurred during the audition refers to
    (a) the nervousness of Cynthia.
    (b) the eruption of the entire room in thunderous applause.
    (c) the surprise on\the faces of her classmates.
    (d) the stunning performance of Cynthia.

PASSAGE-93

Set against a rural backdrop, 'Stench of kerosene' is the story of a couple, Guleri and Manak, who have been happily married for several years but do not have a child. Manak's mother is desperate to have a grandchild to carry on the family name. Hence, she gets Manak remarried in Guleri's absence. Manak, who acts as a reluctant but passive spectator, is meanwhile, informed by a friend that Guleri, on hearing about her husband's second marriage, poured kerosene on her clothes and set fire to them. Manak is heartbroken and begins to live as if he were a dead man. When his second wife delivers a son, Manak stares at the child for a long time and blurts out, "Take him away ! He stinks of kerosene."

321. This is a sensitive issue-based story which tries to sensitise the readers about **[Prelim II-2015]**
    (a) Male chauvinism and infidelity
    (b) Love and betrayal
    (c) Lack of legal safeguards for women
    (d) Influence of patriarchal mindset

PASSAGE-94

The very first lesson that should be taught to us when we are of enough to understand it, is that complete freedom from the obligation to work is unnatural, and ought to be illegal, as we can escape our share of the burden of work only by throwing it on someone else's shoulders. Nature ordains that the human race shall perish of famine if it stops working. We cannot escape from this tyranny. The question we have to settle is how much leisure we can afford to allow ourselves.

322. The **main idea** of the passage is that **[Prelim II- 2017]**
    (a) it is essential for human beings to work
    (b) there should be a balance between work and leisure
    (c) working is a tyranny which we have to face
    (d) human's understanding of the nature of work is essential

PASSAGE-95

We have hard work ahead. There is no resting for any of us till we redeem our pledge in full, till we make all the people of India what destiny intends them to be. We are citizens of a great country, on the verge of bold advance, and we have to live up to that high standard. All of us, to whatever religion we may belong are equally the children of India with equal rights, privileges and obligations. We cannot encourage communalism or narrowmindedness, for no nation can be great whose people are narrow in thought or action.

323. The challenge the author of the above passage throws to the public is to achieve. **[Prelim II- 2017]**
    (a) a high standard of living, progress and privileges
    (b) equal privileges, fulfilment of destiny and political tolerance
    (c) spirit of adventure and economic parity
    (d) hard work, brotherhood and national unity

PASSAGE-96

"The individual, according to Rousseau, parts his person and all his power in common under the supreme direction of the General will and in our corporate capacity we receive each member as an indivisible part of the whole."

324. In the light of the above passage, the nature of General Will is **best described** as **[Prelim II-2017]**
    (a) the sum total of the private wills of the individuals
    (b) what is articulated by the elected representatives of the individuals
    (c) the collective good as distinct from private wills of the individuals
    (d) the material interests of the community

PASSAGE-97

Though I have discarded much of past tradition and custom, and am anxious that India should rid herself of all shackles that bind and contain her and divide her people, and suppress vast numbers of them, and prevent the free development of the body and the spirit; though I seek all this, yet I do not wish to cut myself off from that past completely. I am proud of that great inheritance that has been and is, ours and I am conscious that I too, like all of us, am a link in that unbroken chain which goes back to the dawn of history in the immemorial past of India.

325. The author wants India to rid herself of certain past bonds because **[Prelim II-2018]**
    (a) he is not able to see the relevance of the past
    (b) there is not much to be proud of
    (c) he is not interested in the history of India
    (d) they obstruct her physical and spiritual growth

Solutions

ANSWER KEY

1	(c)	34	(d)	67	(d)	100	(c)	133	(d)	166	(d)	199	(d)	232	(c)	265	(a)	298	(d)
2	(a)	35	(d)	68	(d)	101	(a)	134	(a)	167	(d)	200	(d)	233	(a)	266	(a)	299	(b)
3	(c)	36	(b)	69	(a)	102	(c)	135	(b)	168	(c)	201	(a)	234	(b)	267	(c)	300	(c)
4	(c)	37	(d)	70	(c)	103	(c)	136	(c)	169	(b)	202	(b)	235	(c)	268	(b)	301	(a)
5	(d)	38	(c)	71	(d)	104	(c)	137	(a)	170	(d)	203	(c)	236	(d)	269	(d)	302	(b)
6	(c)	39	(d)	72	(b)	105	(b)	138	(b)	171	(c)	204	(c)	237	(c)	270	(d)	303	(b)
7	(b)	40	(a)	73	(d)	106	(c)	139	(a)	172	(d)	205	(d)	238	(c)	271	(a)	304	(a)
8	(c)	41	(c)	74	(b)	107	(c)	140	(d)	173	(d)	206	(c)	239	(c)	272	(a)	305	(b)
9	(a)	42	(b)	75	(c)	108	(c)	141	(b)	174	(d)	207	(b)	240	(a)	273	(b)	306	(d)
10	(b)	43	(c)	76	(b)	109	(c)	142	(c)	175	(c)	208	(b)	241	(b)	274	(a)	307	(b)
11	(d)	44	(d)	77	(a)	110	(d)	143	(c)	176	(d)	209	(d)	242	(b)	275	(a)	308	(c)
12	(a)	45	(d)	78	(b)	111	(b)	144	(a)	177	(d)	210	(d)	243	(a)	276	(a)	309	(c)
13	(c)	46	(d)	79	(a)	112	(d)	145	(d)	178	(c)	211	(b)	244	(c)	277	(a)	310	(d)
14	(c)	47	(c)	80	(b)	113	(a)	146	(d)	179	(d)	212	(d)	245	(b)	278	(b)	311	(b)
15	(c)	48	(b)	81	(c)	114	(a)	147	(c)	180	(c)	213	(b)	246	(b)	279	(b)	312	(a)
16	(b)	49	(d)	82	(a)	115	(a)	148	(c)	181	(a)	214	(c)	247	(d)	280	(b)	313	(b)
17	(d)	50	(d)	83	(a)	116	(c)	149	(c)	182	(d)	215	(a)	248	(c)	281	(b)	314	(d)
18	(b)	51	(a)	84	(c)	117	(a)	150	(d)	183	(a)	216	(d)	249	(b)	282	(c)	315	(a)
19	(a)	52	(a)	85	(a)	118	(c)	151	(c)	184	(a)	217	(c)	250	(c)	283	(d)	316	(c)
20	(c)	53	(b)	86	(d)	119	(d)	152	(d)	185	(d)	218	(b)	251	(b)	284	(b)	317	(c)
21	(c)	54	(d)	87	(c)	120	(c)	153	(c)	186	(c)	219	(d)	252	(d)	285	(a)	318	(b)
22	(d)	55	(c)	88	(d)	121	(a)	154	(d)	187	(b)	220	(d)	253	(a)	286	(c)	319	(a)
23	(a)	56	(d)	89	(d)	122	(b)	155	(a)	188	(c)	221	(b)	254	(d)	287	(d)	320	(d)
24	(a)	57	(a)	90	(d)	123	(a)	156	(d)	189	(b)	222	(c)	255	(a)	288	(a)	321	(d)
25	(c)	58	(b)	91	(c)	124	(b)	157	(c)	190	(a)	223	(a)	256	(b)	289	(c)	322	(b)
26	(d)	59	(d)	92	(b)	125	(d)	158	(d)	191	(b)	224	(d)	257	(a)	290	(a)	323	(b)
27	(a)	60	(b)	93	(c)	126	(b)	159	(b)	192	(d)	225	(c)	258	(b)	291	(b)	324	(c)
28	(c)	61	(c)	94	(c)	127	(c)	160	(c)	193	(c)	226	(b)	259	(d)	292	(c)	325	(d)
29	(c)	62	(c)	95	(a)	128	(a)	161	(c)	194	(a)	227	(a)	260	(b)	293	(b)		
30	(c)	63	(b)	96	(b)	129	(c)	162	(c)	195	(c)	228	(b)	261	(d)	294	(a)		
31	(d)	64	(d)	97	(b)	130	(b)	163	(b)	196	(d)	229	(b)	262	(d)	295	(a)		
32	(c)	65	(d)	98	(d)	131	(b)	164	(c)	197	(a)	230	(c)	263	(a)	296	(d)		
33	(d)	66	(d)	99	(d)	132	(c)	165	(b)	198	(d)	231	(d)	264	(a)	297	(b)		

DETAILED EXPLANATIONS

1. (c) From the first line of the passage, it is clear that 'most dressed' is used for other trees that have broad leaves.

2. (a) From the line 'sometimes eight or ten inches across', it can be concluded that white waxy blossoms are huge.

3. (c) From the line 'The tree sheds some of its leaves.........ready for new one', it can be concluded that the tree sheds some of its leaves to get decorated with new leaves.

4. (c) Since the horses were in habit of quenching their thirst by eating dew-laden or shower-wetted leaves, they tried to take a bite of the water considering it to be as solid as dew-laden or shower-wetted leaves.

5. (d)

6. (c) None of the options other than option (c) appears similar to the phrase 'destructive funny' wherein 'death' and 'laughter' symbolizes 'destruction' and 'fun' respectively.

7. (b) The second part of the first sentence clearly states that the German students and the professor are quite friendly with each other and no strict relation

8. (c) whatsoever is seen between them which is generally seen between a professor and his students.

8. (c) It is evident from the passage.

9. (a) Nothing as such is mentioned in the passage.

10. (b) Alight means to descend from a train bus or other form of transport.

11. (d) It is clearly mentioned in the passage.

12. (a) It is clearly stated in the third sentence of the passage.

13. (c) Immure means to enclose or confine (someone) against their will.

14. (c) It can be clearly inferred from the passage.

15. (c) It is clearly mentioned in the passage.

16. (b) It is evident from the first and second sentence of the passage.

17. (d) All the given statements are true.

18. (b) It can be clearly inferred from the passage i.e. the reference in which the words 'open eyes' are used.

19. (a)

20. (c) Sanctified means free from sin; purify.

21. (c) Only III is mentioned in the passage. Statement I and II are incorrect in the context of the passage.

22. (d) The context in which the phrase 'by the hour' is used in the passage means 'for long hours'.

23. (a) It can easily be inferred from the first, second and third sentence of the passage that the old gentleman is a great lover of nature. Other two sentences are incorrect.

24. (a) Perseverance means persistence and tenacity etc. Therefore, 'grit' which means spirit and mettle is the correct synonym of the word perseverance.

25. (c)

26. (d) It can be inferred from the passage that as the author was climbing higher and higher, the hill (small mountains) tops with trees appeared to him as grassy backbone.

27. (a) The word 'ermine' means a stoat, especially, when in its white winter coat i.e. snow thus, option (a) goes correctly.

28. (c) The chalets looked like toys because they were too far away from where the author was looking at them. It can be inferred from the sentence '......... where distance diminished the chalets to toys ....).

29. (c) The whole passage is based on the medical knowledge of ancient Egyptians. The passage primarily deals with the medical practices prevalent in ancient Egypt.

30. (c) It is clearly mentioned in the passage.

31. (d) Pharaoh means rulers or kings

32. (c) Paleoanthropology is a branch of anthropology concerned with fossil hominids. 'Paleo' means 'older or ancient, especially relating to the geological past.'

33. (d)   34. (d)

35. (d)

36. (b) It is clearly stated in the fourth sentence.

37. (d) It is evident from the last three sentences.

38. (c) Both I & II are false and III is mentioned in the second sentence of the passage.

39. (d) No reason as such has been mentioned in the passage.

40. (a)

41. (c)

42. (b)

43. (c) It is clearly mentioned in the first sentence of the passage. Other sentences are incorrect in the context of the passage.

44. (d) All I, II and III are clearly mentioned in the passage.

45. (d) In the passage, 'significant' implies 'important'.

46. (d) All (a), (b) and (c) are wrong as neither are they mentioned in the passage nor can they be inferred from the passage

47. (c) 48. (b) 49. (d) 50. (d) 51. (a)

52. (a) 53. (b) 54. (d) 55. (c) 56. (d)

57. (a) 58. (b) 59. (d) 60. (b) 61. (c)

62. (c) 63. (b) 64. (d) 65. (d) 66. (d)

67. (d) 68. (d) 69. (a) 70. (c) 71. (d)

72. (b) 73. (d)

74. (b) The author looks upon the young, as an embodonient of possibilities, which is option (b). The line of the passage which gives clue regarding this is the very first line 'The young are those to whom we look for future strength and for future good.'

75. (c) The phrase 'morally of right stature' means having rectitude' which is option 'c'. The line of the passage which gives clue regarding this is 'that they who are to be the fresh recruits should be morally of right stature, this means that the youngsters should have rectitude which is moral and truth futures and spirit of go - getters.

76. (b) The failure of many a young men and women is unwarranted, which is option (b). The clue regarding this is mentioned in the following line of passage 'we are obliged to see thousands falling by the way whose fall seems headless. 'The word 'unwarranted' means 'unknowingly or without any justification or unnecessary.'

77. (a) Plants that do not have showy flowers, get their pollen transferred to other flowers by winds since insects do not get attracted towards them. They get attracted to those flowers whose petals are large and beautiful and also smells sweet.

78. (b) The fact that some flowers are flamboyant implies that we can distinguish between flowers pollinated by insects and those that are not. Flamboyance is a trait of insects which helps us in understanding pollination done by insects or by winds.

79. (a) When insects carry pollen from one flower to another they help the flowers to make seeds. That's what author of this para suggest, when insects carry pollen from one flowerplant to another it can help in developing seeds, through the pollen must be carried by insects to the same type of flower or insect.

Refer the last sentence for better understanding.

80. (b) Insects carry pollen from one flower to another unconsciously. Since insects visit plants/flowers in search of food and simultaneously they carry pollen grains from one flower to another. Option 'b' suggests/explains it all so, that would be the correct answer. 'Refers without knowing it' which means unconsciously'.

81. (c) Insects visit flowers because they are in search of food. That's how they obtain their food from visiting one flower to another. Option 'c' explains it all so that would be the correct answer. Just go through first sentence of this para.

82. (a) Writer explains in the intro of this passage that the extra-ordinary discovery of echo location was experienced in bats. So option 'a' would be correct answer.

83. (a) An echo comes back if a person shouts in the vicinity of a wall or solid obstruction. Though the further off this solid obstruction, the longer time will elapse for the return of the echo.

84. (c) In the first paragraph, the writer says that bats use sound for some practical purpose. Option 'c' explains it all so that would be the correct answer.

85. (a) In the second line of second para author says that 'our first duel with the elements began' which suggests of fight with the tides. So the word 'duel' in the passage mean 'a battle'.

86. (d) When author further describes the situation on the adventure trip, he says that all the six people on the raft held on tight and waited for the worst whenever they heard the sudden deafening hiss of a roller close by and saw a white crest came towards them. They did not do anything.

87. (c) Author says that the performance of the Kon-Tiki was unperturbed. Since that raft sailed through all the adversities.

88. (d) Swarn jump into the water carrying Mohan on his shoulders since Mohan was his friend and he did not know how to swim. And Swarn felt that his friend should also have fun of swimming in the water. So option 'd' would be the right answer.

89. (d) Refer line 9-10, Authors says that unable to carry Mohan along, swarn left him in the flowing water. Which explains the question of (Swarn leaing his friend in the water. So option 'd' would be the right answer.

90. (d) Refer line 11-12, In these lines author says clearly that there were so many swimmers but nobody came to his rescue since they were indifferent to the plight of a stranger.

91. (c) In the concluding line of this passage author says that he jumped into the water without any fear or hesitation as he knew the art of saving drowning persons. He had already saved few lives from drawning in the past.

92. (b) Refer to the third line of passage.

93. (c) Refer to the second line of passage.

94. (c) 'Lasting value' means something which has relevance for the present.

95. (a) Refer to the fourth sentence 'Don't ask me .... prizes'.

96. (b) Refer to the third sentence 'They declared .... engine!'.

97. (b) Refer to the para 'They declared that I became the .... looked stunned'.

98. (d) Pontoon Bridge is a bridge made with wooden planks; usually it is a floating type of bridge of short length.

99. (d) Soldiers were pushing against the steep elevation as mentioned in the passage. Carts were staggering on steep bank.

100. (c) Again the same sentence of the passage as in earlier question is having the answer. This is very easy question and direct one from the passage.

101. (a) A difficult blinder- option (b) is not correct as some relevance is evident, it cannot be completely negated, and this relevance is the purpose of passage. Option (c) also is incorrect as ample examples are needed to depict the scene. (d) is true but question is not about the focus. It about the comparison between the bridge and the old man.

102. (c) Second sentence of the passage is clearly about the author's habit of not be indoors after the sunset (evening).

103. (c) His habit was to remain outdoors but having a stroll (a leisure walk) is not mentioned. Second activity which interests him was 'reading' -hinted in passage from reference to 'opened book lying on his table' and he tried for it but due to so cold (shivering in blanket) he was unable to do that. Hence it is best option.

104. (c) Shivering due to cold rendered him incapable for reading as described in the passage. Being tired, no light, aversion to book has not been discussed in the passage.

105. (b) The passage begins on this note and reasons very cold outside for not coming out.

106. (c) Option (a) is not mentioned. Option (d) is opposite of what is mentioned in the passage. Option (b) is also not relevant. Only option (c) can be inferred from the passage.

107. (c) Coaxing in the passage is used to indicate that the brother of the author sings himself for inspiring music from the bird.

108. (c) Coaxing is to flatter/to persuade gently/ sycophancy / cajoling.

109. (c) in Mrs West's house where the police are enquiring into lady's murder

110. (d) searching

111. (b) surprised to get the information

112. (d) grandmother of the author who used to teach at his/her school.

113. (a) The farewell ceremony made everyone feel sad.

114. (a) he/she was the only child who loved his/her grandmother.

115. (a) According to the author a typical unhappy man is one who has been deprived of some normal satisfaction in youth.

116. (c) The author refers one-sided direction to those activities which lead to happiness.

117. (a) Drinking helps in a momentary cessation of unhappiness or to forget their dissatisfaction.

118. (c) According to author, becoming less alive implies living in a make believe world.

119. (d) The author narrates the story in the context of Europe.

120. (c) Buck up is an expression for the word cheer up.
121. (a) The Indian friend was being hopeless because the holiday was over.
122. (b) The author describes the typical English character.
123. (a) The author is trying to show the contrast between the Indian and Englishman.
124. (b) The word appalling means shockingly large number.
125. (d) Genocide of the Jews was the culmination of a decade of Nazi policy, under the rule of Adolf Hitler.
126. (b) The other solution requires patience and tolerance to put up with people.
127. (c) The author speaks in democratic tone.
128. (a) Nature here denotes a beautiful landscape, full of green vegetation – the countryside.
129. (c) The author is highlighting the nature's beauty.
130. (b) The author mentions the impact of modernization and that we should be more careful not to destroy nature while modernizing.
131. (b) The word struggle here refers to the efforts required to save the nature.
132. (c) If we preserve nature, it will ensure future existence.
133. (d) The passage seems to be a part of someone's personal letter as it is addressed at many places by the word 'you'.
134. (a) The tone of the author sounds quite official and serious.
135. (b) The writer is talking in context of government service.
136. (c) The writer asks his reader to accept 'an official rank'.
137. (a) The writer implies significant worldly items.
138. (b) The word drowsy means half-asleep or sleepy.
139. (a) The author talks about the leisure and peace he was experiencing.
140. (d) The author mentions "In a moment the sole porter emerged from his midday nap".
141. (b) The author mentions a reference to the porter by "operated a signal that clanked noisily into position".
142. (c) The word placid means pleasantly calm or peaceful; unruffled; tranquil; serenely quiet or undisturbed.
143. (c) The author sounds excited as he says "I was exceedingly surprised".
144. (a) The word apparition means "anything that appears, especially something remarkable or startling", thus best describing the author's feelings.
145. (d) The author says "I went to it again to see if there were any more".
146. (d) The author says "I was exceedingly surprised".
147. (c) The author was looking around to see where the foot prints came from.
148. (c) The speaker does not mention anything about the evidence in the passage.
149. (c) Whatever others said about him he never lost faith in goodness and he was sure that the truth must come out one day.
150. (d) In the dark dungeon he always waited for the angel to come and plead for him.
151. (c) The truth must prevail means truth always wins in the end.
152. (d) The man was scribbling down some odd mathematical notations.
153. (c) The man caught author's attention because he would stare at every person and then scribble down some mathematical notion. As the man was sitting next to the author, he caught his attention.
154. (d) The author found it quite amusing when the man was trying to analyse a man's face, not as a single unit but thousands squares put together.

155. (a) The passage shows the inquisitiveness or curiosity of the author.
156. (d) She glanced at him when the unpleasant feeling passed.
157. (c) The unpleasant feeling passed when she realized her sense of shame.
158. (d) She was ashamed because she had never thanked him for his help to her father. This thought had occurred to her before also, that's why she felt ashamed.
159. (b) The traveller could not feel the breeze as he was down the ridge.
160. (c) The traveller carried with him a sling.
161. (c) The traveler was traveling during Spring time.
162. (c) Mr. Higson was in his unusual self with unshaven, in slippers and braces and smoking
163. (b) The author mentions the atmosphere of the shop being heavy with bitter odour and filled with newspapers.
164. (c) The author emphasizes to accept old age as a fact of life.
165. (b) The author talks about the psychological problems faced by older people.
166. (d) The author is emphasizing the importance of living in the present and not giving too much importance to the past.
167. (d) The older people are psychologically more inclined towards their past.
168. (c) As the passage talks about professional equipment, a dozen cowrie shells, a square piece of cloth with obscure mystic charts on it, a note book, and a bundle of Palmyra writing; all these equipment are not used by a vendor, snake charmer or priest, hence the answer Astrologer.
169. (b) The author talks about attracting people's attention, as the protagonist was trying to lure possible clients.
170. (d) The astrologer is trying to catch people's attention by displaying all his work aids.
171. (c) The author describes the whole incident in a very satirical manner, hence the tone is very ironic.
172. (d) The author satirically criticizes the laid back attitude of the modern generation towards amusements.
173. (d) The author is criticizing the modern day generation's attitude towards socializing thus appears a social critic.
174. (d) The author tries to highlight the behaviour of any male species to win over the female species using the Jackdaw's example.
175. (c) The passage highlights Jackdaw's purposeful behaviour of showing off himself to attract the female species.
176. (d) In the end author describes the importance of holding a nesting place by a Jackdaw to attract the female.
177. (d) The author describes the purposeful behaviour of the Jackdaw to get involved in a conflict to attract the female.
178. (c) The author is highlighting the facts about Jackdaw's love life and his behaviour to attract a female.
179. (d) The speaker is motivating his fellowmen to fight for their country is a patriot urging defence of his motherland.
180. (c) As the speaker talks about the New World to step forth and rescue, he's expecting help from other parts of the world to arrive.
181. (a) The speaker is motivating his fellow men to continue highlighting the never give up attitude.

182. (d) Mr. Sharma's friend heard the noise of a fight.
183. (a) Mr. Sharma was astonished to see the Tigress.
184. (a) Mr. Sharma was concerned about his wife and daughter and was trying to protect them.
185. (d) when they came unsolicited
186. (c) He could find the worth of a story with a little effort.
187. (b) her story was rejected unread
188. (c) witty
189. (b) in order to publish them.
190. (a) She was pale and emaciated.
191. (b) She was frightened.
192. (d) Her inability to go near the fire.
193. (c) The blue marks on her body.
194. (a) Addicts
195. (c) They need large sums of money to buy drugs.
196. (d) Driving addicts to crime
197. (a) Very high
198. (d) Neither 1 nor 2
199. (d) By the word prosperous, the author means that the voyage was uneventful as the ship stopped only at two ports and was nothing to talk about.
200. (d) On the ship, the author never left the ship till they came into the downs.
201. (a) In the context of the passage, provisions means food. The author writes that the ship stopped at one or two ports for food and fresh water.
202. (b) For the payment of the author's freight, the captain refused to accept any money not even a single farthing.
203. (c) Since the captain did not take a single penny from the author and was very soft to him, it shows his friendliness and kindness towards the author.
204. (c) The words 'The absence of sensation in his feet left him unrelated to the earth'
205. (d) As a result of the cold from snow, his hands and fingers were freezing and could neither be bend nor had any sensation.
206. (c) His hands could not clutch depicts how frozen his hands and fingers are that they cannot be moved and felt.
207. (b) Mr. Tagde did not sit down because he was in a defiant mood (meaning bold resistant) and stood for a student's expulsion from the school for a prank.
208. (b) He did not wanted to take the report back because it was an accurate report based on the poor and damaging conduct of the student.
209. (d) The Principal was unhappy because he did not want to take the extreme step of expelling student from the school.
210. (d) The wind was very sharp and was cutting the skin like a knife on the bitterly cold night.
211. (b) The younger woman dressed in seal skin (fur coat) was carrying the dog as a fashion accessory. It is usually carried by women of high stature.
212. (d) The conductor was unfriendly and malicious with a ill will.
213. (b) The sentence describes the unbearable cold night and the sharp winds that were blowing at that moment.
214. (c) The little girl said that he she could see the airplanes and the sky. The airplanes can be seen only in the airport premises and not outside it.
215. (a) The passage shows that the girl was clever as she gave relevant clues to save her mother and was brave as she did not lose hope and was helpful throughout.

216. (d) The girl helped the police to trace the car by honking the car's horn.
217. (c) Martin played little tricks because his son was entertained and got pleasure from them.
218. (b) The paper mask is that of a hissing dragon face with his tongue out.
219. (d) The father and son rolled with laughter after the father removed the mask from his face.
220. (d) The author wants to say that his father had a strong desire to teach and this desire was without any vanity but full of innocence. This means that his father was passionate about teaching and loved it. Thus option d should be the correct answer as to what author wants to say.
221. (b) From the passage we get to know of an instance where his father started teaching even at railway carriages which made the author embarrassed. Thus, to question as to what made him embarrassed option b should be the answer, "even at odd places".
222. (c) The last sentence of passage conveys that for people of his father's time, education was a golden gateway of enchanted realms of mind. This means that education was a means to explore and sensitize the mind.
223. (a) Over all in the passage, we notice that the author describes his father's passion very lovingly and with pride. He glorifies his character in a profound manner. Thus option a that he loved and admired his father is the correct answer.
224. (d) The author was looking for all types of marks left by the tiger's prey a deer as it is mentioned in the first line of the passage.
225. (c) In the last sentence of the passage, it is revealed that Mothi was running to save his life from the tiger which had come face to face with him.
226. (b) We already know that the author was looking for the marks left by the tiger's prey, a deer. So, the prey only means a kill depicting the deer.
227. (a) The word used to describe the atmosphere before Mothi screamed was "silent". Silent also means quiet.
228. (b) From the passage, we get the idea that rhinos are aggressive beasts and they rushed to attack the narrator while smelling his scent. This means that rhinos attack humans on spotting them by their smell.
229. (b) In the passage, it was the first time the narrator had come across rhinos and he had a violent encounter. Thus naturally he was frightened.
230. (c) The author could not take photos of rhino because it is evident from the passage that he was too frightened to even do that. And in that course his mind went blank and it did not occur to him to take photos.
231. (d) As we see in the passage that the young man was disappointed in the morning when he had come in casual dress and had not received required attention from the salesmen. So he came back dressed in suit as he wanted attention from the salesmen. Thus we see that option (d) is the best explanation to this question.
232. (c) Salesmen generally give attention to rich customers. This thing is proved by the fact that the salesman had given him attention when he had arrived well dressed in the shop. Thus option (c) is the correct answer.
233. (a) From the passage, we get the idea that young man had already made up his mind not to buy anything as respect and attention was what he was asking for. Thus we can say that option (a) is the answer.

234. (b) It is indicated in the passage that after the customer was not buying anything the salesman had drawn the attention of the manager towards the young man. This is the reason why manager intervened. Thus option (b) is the correct answer.

235. (c) When the manger had asked the man, what he wanted, he replied by saying that he only came to assert his respect back. Thus, in this question, the correct option would be (c).

236. (d) In the passage, we find that crowd lost its patience when the speaker was not able to reach the venue as he was ill.

237. (c) Assuaging means reducing or abating thus option c is the answer.

238. (c) We see in the passage that people shouted and heckled when the speaker did not arrive.

239. (c) When the teaching was associated with punishment, it instilled fear in the minds of the students.

240. (a) When the teaching was associated with reward, it gave importance to only the best student and the slow pupil was left behind.

241. (b) The system which appealed to the competitive spirit in the pupils was largely based on marks.

242. (b) The author first played cricket when he was a school boy.

243. (a) The author explains how he felt strange to the game of cricket when he played it for the first time.

244. (c) The words butter fingers describes that how the author's always dropped the ball.

245. (b) Spectator means a person who watches at a show, game, or other event this the correct option is onlookers.

246. (b) The man was troubled by the noise made by the continuous beating of hammers of the blacksmiths.

247. (d) The man gave the blacksmiths ₹100 each as a bribe so that they find new huts and he doesn't get disturbed.

248. (c) The man after giving the blacksmiths money to find new huts was shocked to listen to the hammer noise the next day again and went outside to find why they hadn't found new huts.

249. (b) The man got to know that the blacksmiths have found new home and kept their promise as they both exchanged their huts.

250. (c) 'Rhapsodical' means enthusiastic expression of feeling.

251. (b) 'Mona lisa' is the name of a famous painting by Italian artist Leonardo da Vinci.

252. (d) The truth about the 'Mona Lisa' is that it is a study in modeling.

253. (a)   254. (d)

255. (a)   256. (b)   257. (a)

258. (b) The word 'wearily' means exhausted.

259. (d) The answer is given in the second and third sentences of the passage.

260. (b) 'This wings were ragged bars of lead' means his wings were damaged and therefore very heavy.

261. (d) The answer is given in the last sentences of the passage.

262. (d) The answer is given in last two sentences of the passage.

263. (a) It can be inferred from the passage.

264. (a) 'It' here, refers to 'travelling in a car'.

265. (a) By 'sense of presence', the author refers to his own self as a part of the scene.

266. (a) The word 'over whelming' means 'very strong'.

267. (c) The answer is given by third sentence of the passage.

268. (b) The answer is given in sixth sentence of the passage.

269. (d) It can be inferred from the passage that the traveller was nervous.

270. (d) 'Struck dumb' is an expression to indicate a state of absolute shock or surprise.

271. (a) It can be inferred after reading the passage that Yuri was calm and courageous.

272. (a) Only the first assumption has been made in the first and second sentences of the passage.

273. (b) 'Intrigued' means fascinated.

274. (a) Ice shelves are huge pieces of chunks of ice.

275. (a) Icebergs are huge chunks of ice floating on water.

276. (a) When the iceberg turns upside down, it appears green.

277. (a) This fact is clearly mentioned in the passage.

278. (b) It is clearly mentioned in the third line of the passage.

279. (b) It is clearly mentioned in the first and third line of the passage.

280. (b) It is mentioned in the third line of the passage that jelly slug extrudes a sticky translucent coating that may foul the mouth-parts of marauding ants.

281. (b) The main idea of the passage is that caterpillars are prone to attack thus, they try various things to protect themselves.

282. (c) It is clearly mentioned in the very first line of the passage.

283. (d) It is mentioned in the third line of the passage.

284. (b) It is mentioned in the fourth line of the passage

285. (a) Evade means to escape or avoid and according to the passage, the lady wished to avoid or ignore the law and boarded the bus with her dog. Option (a) is the correct explanation of the phrase 'wishing to evade the law'.

286. (c) It is mentioned in the second last line of the passage.

287. (d) The first sentence of the paragraph implies that this option is correct. The other options are not mentioned in the passage.

288. (a) Refer to sentence 2 of the passage. The other options are not mentioned in the passage.

289. (c) The line implies that after 60, when Wilson doesn't have money, he will take away his own life. The other options are neither mentioned nor implied in the passage.

290. (a) The idea is 'horrible' according to the passage, which means unpleasant.

291. (b) Whenever the author undertakes travelling, forgetting the toothbrush makes his life miserable.

292. (c) The toothbrush is finally in the handkerchief of the author.

293. (b) A haystack is a pile of dry grass. Sentence 2 states that this option is correct.

294. (a) The author soon fell asleep because he was too tired and exhausted (sentence 5).

295. (a) The second statement is not mentioned in the passage. Hence, option (a) is correct answer.

296. (d) By spring, cubs are 3 months old and hence they are born in winter.

297. (b) Mother bears 'tend to ignore family rivalry over food', as mentioned in sentence 5.

298. (d) Both statements 1 and 2 are not correct as statement 1 is not mentioned in the passage and sentence 3 says, 'If there are triplets...' meaning that statement 2 is also incorrect.

299. (b) When the narrator says that he was "almost a part of it" he means that he was familiar with every corner of the cell.

300. (c) The impression that comes across through the narrator's description is his untiring efforts to adjust to extreme loneliness. It is quite obvious that he was very lonely and that he was making friends with various types of insects, flowers, etc. to retain his sanity.
    (a) The general condition of the country jails is revealed in the passage but this is not the central idea of this passage.
    The same is true of options (b) and (d).

301. (a) (a) Since the central idea of the passage is loneliness and the author's struggle to adjust himself to rather difficult circumstances; option (a) is the right answer.
    (b) This obviously not correct.
    (c) This is true but it is not the central idea.
    (d) This is also true but that is not just what the author wants to suggest.

302. (b) The implication here is that even if anybody else had climbed this far earlier. They had not pitched any camp.
    (a) There is no reference to the building of any camp in this option.
    (c) It is implied that no camp had been built so high.
    (d) There is no mention of the manpower required to pitch the camp in the paragraph.

303. (b) They took a long time to finish the work because there was not enough air to breathe at such a high altitude. All the other three options (a), (c) and (d) are true, but they are not clearly stated in the passage as in the case of option (b).

304. (a) When they crawled in the tent they took off their gloves since it was not very cold.
    (b) The narrator says that is was not very cold at such a high altitude. So this option is ruled out.
    (c) The same argument as in (b) holds true.
    (d) The narrator says they took of their gloves. So, this option is not correct.

305. (b) The man went into another room because the passage was full of smoke. It was an old wooden house. There was a fire at midnight. The man who was staying on the top floor of the house was caught unawares. He stumbled out into the smoke filled passage and lost his way. So the root cause of his going into another room was the smoke filled passage.
    All the other three options (a), (c) and (d) are automatically cancelled in the height of the above context.

306 (d) The man was called a hero because he saved a life.
    (a) In the context of the passage he saved the life of a baby accidentally. So there is no question of his expressing his willingness to risk his life for others.
    (b) He did escape from the fire but that is no reason why he should be called a hero.
    (c) He just kept stumbling and falling from one spot to another; this does not call for courage.

307. (b) His parents were worried because the cycle was new and expensive.

308. (c) Jim has kept the watch from the old man and the little boy as a security for his new bicycle.

309. (c) As it was raining. Moreover it was dark so visibility was a problem.

310. (d) They expected to reach the town within a short time as the distance was only 15 km.

311. (b) They were supposed to reach their destination after a run of 15 km according to the map. After going 20 km and still not finding their destination they became worried as it was dark and rain had began to fall.

312. (a) If she did not walk on the pavement, she might face an accident.

313. (b) She felt so because she was arrogant and newly achieved liberty had gone into her head in a wrong way.

314. (d) The old lady failed to realise that the liberty given to her did not entitle her to walk on the roads as they were meant for motor vehicles only.

315. (a) Refer to last sentence of the passage. The two little boys feared the barwing dogs.

316. (c) The stray dogs looked at the procession curiously because everytime the old man threw seeds form the berries, the birds would fly to peck them.

317. (c) Cynthia was a shy girl and she believed that she was plain and untalented.

318. (b) It is because Cynthia's classmates were not interested in the previous performances.

319. (a) As Cynthia did not have confidence in herself and was frightened to perform in front of her class mates. She was trembling. So, her knees were quaking.

320. (d) Cynthia's remarkable performance attracted everybody's attention and everyone was stunned. After her performance ended, all the people in the room stood up and applauded for Cynthia.

321. (d) (a) is wrong as the passage is not at all related to Male chauvinism and infidelity
    (b) is wrong as Love and betrayal is not the issue the passage is trying to sentitise about. The passage is more about a mothers' influence on her child. How she governed his life?
    (c) is wrong as the passage is not at all related to Lack of legal safeguards for women. Guleri didn't resorted for any such protection.
    (d) is correct as discussed in (b). The real reason behind this situation was Manak's mother. He could not realise her wife's love as he was under the influence of her mother's mindset.

322. (b) The key point of the passage is that there should be a balance between work and leisure.

323. (b) The challenge the author throws to the public is to achieve equal privileges, fulfilment of destiny and political tolerance.

324. (c) The nature of General Will, in the passage, is best described as the collective good as distinct from Private Wills of the individuals.

325. (d) It can be inferred from the first sentence of the passage especially from the part ' India should rid herself ....development of the body and the spirit'.

Creation Charades

The heavens reveal God's creativity

AGE GROUP

Early Elementary

SCRIPTURE

Psalm 19:1-6

SUPPLIES

You'll need a Bible, a stack of index cards, pencils, and a hat.

PREPARATION

None needed.

Gather children in a circle or around tables. Open your Bible to Psalm 19:1-6. Show children the words and tell them the Bible is God's special book.

Say: **King David wrote a poem about how God's creation shows us that God is awesome—without using words.** (Read the Scripture.) **King David was amazed by how awesome the sky and the sun are. He wrote about how we can't look at them without being reminded of how awesome our creator God is.**

Ask:

- *What's your favorite part of creation? Maybe something you see in the sky, or your favorite animal, or something you might see in the woods or in the ocean?*
- *How does that piece of creation remind you of what God is like? (For example, if your favorite animal is an elephant, seeing one might remind you that God is big and strong.)*

Distribute the pencils and index cards. Have kids draw or write one or two of their favorite things God created on index cards, one per card. Collect the cards and place them in a hat.

Give kids instructions for Creation Charades. They'll take turns drawing a card and then silently acting out whatever is on that card. Help as needed. Once someone guesses the creation, invite children to share different ways that object reminds them about God.

Say: **When God created the world, he made it amazing! Everything he made is so wonderful that it reflects his nature.**

Closing Prayer
Strike a Pose

Have children strike a pose that best represents their favorite part of creation.

Say: **God, you are amazing. And we thank you that your creation reminds us of how wonderful you are.**

Instruct each child to offer a one-word praise to God that relates to the work of creation his or her pose represents. When everyone is finished, offer up a big closing together: **In Jesus' name, amen!**

Out of the Darkness

Jesus creates order from darkness

AGE GROUP

Upper Elementary

SCRIPTURE

John 1:1-5

SUPPLIES

You'll need a Bible. For each child, you'll need an "In the Beginning" handout, a paintbrush, a cup of water, watercolor paints, and a white crayon.

PREPARATION

None needed.

Have children sit around tables. Give each child a handout and set out the paintbrushes, white crayons, and watercolor paints on the table.

Say: **Let's pretend you had the job to write your best friend's life story. You love your friend and want to do a good job.**

Ask:

- *Where would you start your best friend's story?*
- *Why?*

Open your Bible to John 1:1-5. Show children the words and tell them the Bible is God's special book.

Say: **When Jesus' friend John decided to write Jesus' life story, he chose an unusual place to start. Instead of writing about Jesus' birth, he went back in time before God created anything, even the sun and stars.**

Maybe John picked this point in time because his people were living in a different type of darkness. Life was hard. God's people had been conquered by the Roman Empire and they were being treated badly.

Ask:

- *What kind of hard times do we deal with today that can make our lives feel dark?*

Say: **No matter what's happening around us, we also have to deal with the darkness caused by our sins. The Bible says when we're stuck in all the bad things we do, it's impossible to be friends with God. It's even hard to know he's right next to us.**

Ask:

- *How do you think our sins make it hard to be aware of God today?*

Say: **We live with a type of darkness just like people did in John's day. That's why John takes us back to the very beginning when *everything* was dark. Listen to this!**

Read John 1:1-3.

Say: **The Bible says that everything that was made was made by God the Father and his Son, Jesus. Take your white crayon and draw a picture of a few things Jesus created at the beginning of the world on your handout.** (Pause so children can work.) **Now use your white crayon to draw a picture of a cross. Jesus came to earth to create the way for us to become friends with God.** (Pause so children can work.) **Now draw a stick figure that represents you, because God loves you and created you to be friends with him!** (Pause so children can work.)

Say: **Let's read a bit further to see how Jesus deals with our darkness.** (Read John 1:4-5.) **The Bible says Jesus is the light, and darkness can't overcome him. Let's add some darkness to our pictures to see what this is like.**

Instruct the children to use their paintbrushes and watercolor paints to cover their entire paper with dark paint.

Ask:

- *What happened to your drawings?*
- *How is this like the power that Jesus has over the darkness in our lives?*

Say: **Jesus is the light that conquers every kind of darkness. He conquered the darkness that existed before creation. And he conquers the darkness caused by our sins and the hard times we go through.**

Closing Prayer

Conquering Darkness

Have the children hold their pictures, and turn off the lights.

Say: **Dear God, thank you for sending Jesus to conquer all of the darkness in our lives. Thank you for creating order from the darkness and for creating our world. Help us walk in your light. In Jesus' name, amen.**

In the Beginning

Moving Mountains

Jesus explains the power of faith

Have kids sit around tables. Then open your Bible to Matthew 21:21-22. Show children the words and tell them the Bible is God's special book.

Say: **In our Bible passage, Jesus had just performed an amazing miracle that stunned his disciples. When they asked him about what happened, he surprised them again with these words.**

Read the Scripture passage.

Ask:

- *What do you think it means to have faith in God?*
- *As a follower of Jesus, what do you think this verse means to you today?*

Say: **Let's do an activity to help us understand what this verse means. To do this, we're going to make mountains.**

Let kids make modeling dough from the flour, salt, and water. Have them mix the following ingredients together: 2 cups all-purpose flour, 1 cup of salt, and ½ to ¾ cup water. This makes enough dough for four children, so multiply the recipe as needed.

Split the dough equally among the children. Instruct them to each shape their dough into a mountain.

Say: **Think of a mountain-sized problem you might be facing today as you create your mountain.** (Allow time.) **If Jesus said we could move mountains, then we can certainly move the things that feel like mountains in our lives with God's power.**

Ask:

- *Think about the "mountain" in your life. What would it look like for you to use God's power to help you move that mountain?*
- *Why do you think Jesus didn't say God would move that mountain for you?*
- *What ways can we work with God to move mountains in our lives?*

Say: **God is willing to help us handle the challenges in our lives if we have faith in him. It's great to know that we don't have to move our mountains on our own.**

Closing Prayer
Peak Prayers

Have kids form a circle holding their mountains.

Say: **Dear God, we thank you that you are bigger than any mountains we face. Help us to trust you in all things and to remember that when we have faith in you, we can move those mountains. In Jesus' name, amen.**

Designs From Darkness

We trust God even in hard times

Have children sit around tables. Give each child a paper plate, a coffee filter, and a cup of water. Set the black watercolor markers on the table as well.

Open your Bible and read 2 Corinthians 5:7. Show children the words and tell them the Bible is God's special book.

Say: **"We live by believing and not by seeing." Those are some pretty interesting words Paul said. Let's do an experiment that'll help us understand what Paul meant.**

Instruct children to set their coffee filters on their plates and draw a black circle about an inch wide at the center of their coffee filters.

Say: **Let's pretend that the dark circle is a hard time you're going through.**

Ask:

- *Describe a hard time you or a friend has experienced.* (Be ready with your own example.)

Say: **Those sound like difficult times. Paul knew that when we face challenges, sometimes we focus on what's wrong and we stop believing that God is able to help us.**

Instruct children to dip their fingers into their cups and to flick water onto their coffee filters until they are completely damp. Their ink spots will bleed and reveal many colors as the ink separates.

Ask:

- *Explain how this experiment is like or unlike the way God transforms difficult times.*
- *How can we encourage each other to have faith that God will help us, even when all we can see is our hard time?*

Say: **We can trust God always—but especially when we're going through hard times. We can have confidence and faith in God, knowing that he's good and wants to help us.**

Closing Prayer

Delightful Designs

Have kids form a circle holding the plates with their art.

Say: **Dear God, we thank you that we can have faith that you'll help us, even when all we can see is our hard time. Help us make decisions based on our faith in you and not by the challenges we face. In Jesus' name, amen.**

Robe Repair

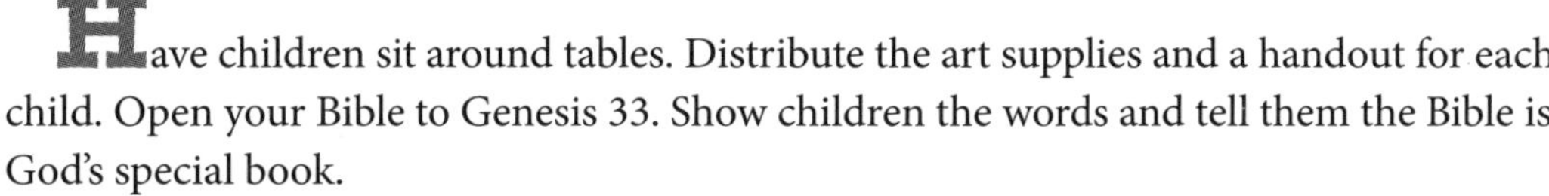

We forgive our family members

AGE GROUP

Early Elementary

SCRIPTURE

Passages from
Genesis 37–50

SUPPLIES

You'll need a Bible
and several rolls
of clear tape. For
each child, you'll
need a copy of the
"Joseph's Colorful
Coat" handout.
You'll also need art
supplies, such as
crayons, markers,
construction paper,
scissors, and glue
sticks.

PREPARATION

None needed.

Have children sit around tables. Distribute the art supplies and a handout for each child. Open your Bible to Genesis 33. Show children the words and tell them the Bible is God's special book.

Say: **The Bible tells us about a fight over a special piece of clothing, an expensive coat made of many different colors. You'll all make a coat so we can tell this story together.**

Have kids each cut out the picture of Joseph's coat and decorate it. Allow a few minutes for kids to work. Call time and begin the story.

Say: **As I tell you about a very large family in the Bible, I want you to tear off one piece of your coat whenever you hear me say something that would cause bad feelings between family members. But don't lose any of the pieces—you'll need them later.**

There was a man named Jacob. He had 12 sons. But Joseph was his favorite. Jacob made him an expensive, colorful coat. Boy, were his brothers jealous. (Pause.)

If that wasn't enough, God gave Joseph a special dream that he would rule over his brothers someday. Joseph made sure his brothers knew. (Pause.)

Then one day, Joseph told on his brothers because they were doing a bad job of taking care of the sheep. (Pause.)

Then his brothers got so mad at Joseph that they decided to kill him and threw him in a hole. (Pause.) **But then they changed their minds and sold him as a slave.** (Pause.)

Joseph lived for years as a slave in Egypt. But God was with him. After a wild series of events that only God could have arranged, Joseph became a ruler in Egypt. A great famine fell over the land, but God warned Joseph and had told him how to prepare, so the Egyptians had enough food. When Joseph's brothers heard there was food in Egypt, they traveled there to buy food. Imagine their surprise when they learned their brother Joseph was ruler and had the power to decide whether or not they would get food.

Joseph had a choice. He could get revenge on his brothers or work on fixing his relationship with his family. (Have children repair their coats using clear tape.)

Ask:

- *Explain whether your coat looks as nice as it did at the beginning.*
- *What does this experience tell you about protecting our family relationships?*
- *What do you think Joseph needed to do to help fix his relationship with his brothers?*
- *What did his brothers need to do to fix their relationship with Joseph?*

Say: **Joseph eventually forgave his brothers. It was hard at first, but they all learned to live with each other and trust each other again.**

Closing Prayer
Family Forgiveness

Have kids form a circle holding their coats.

Say: **Dear God, it can be hard work being in a family. We love each other, but sometimes we do things that hurt each other. Sometimes we get really mad at each other. Sometimes we're not nice to each other. Remind us to think of Joseph and his family. Remind us to be kind and forgiving to each other. In Jesus' name, amen.**

Joseph's Colorful Coat

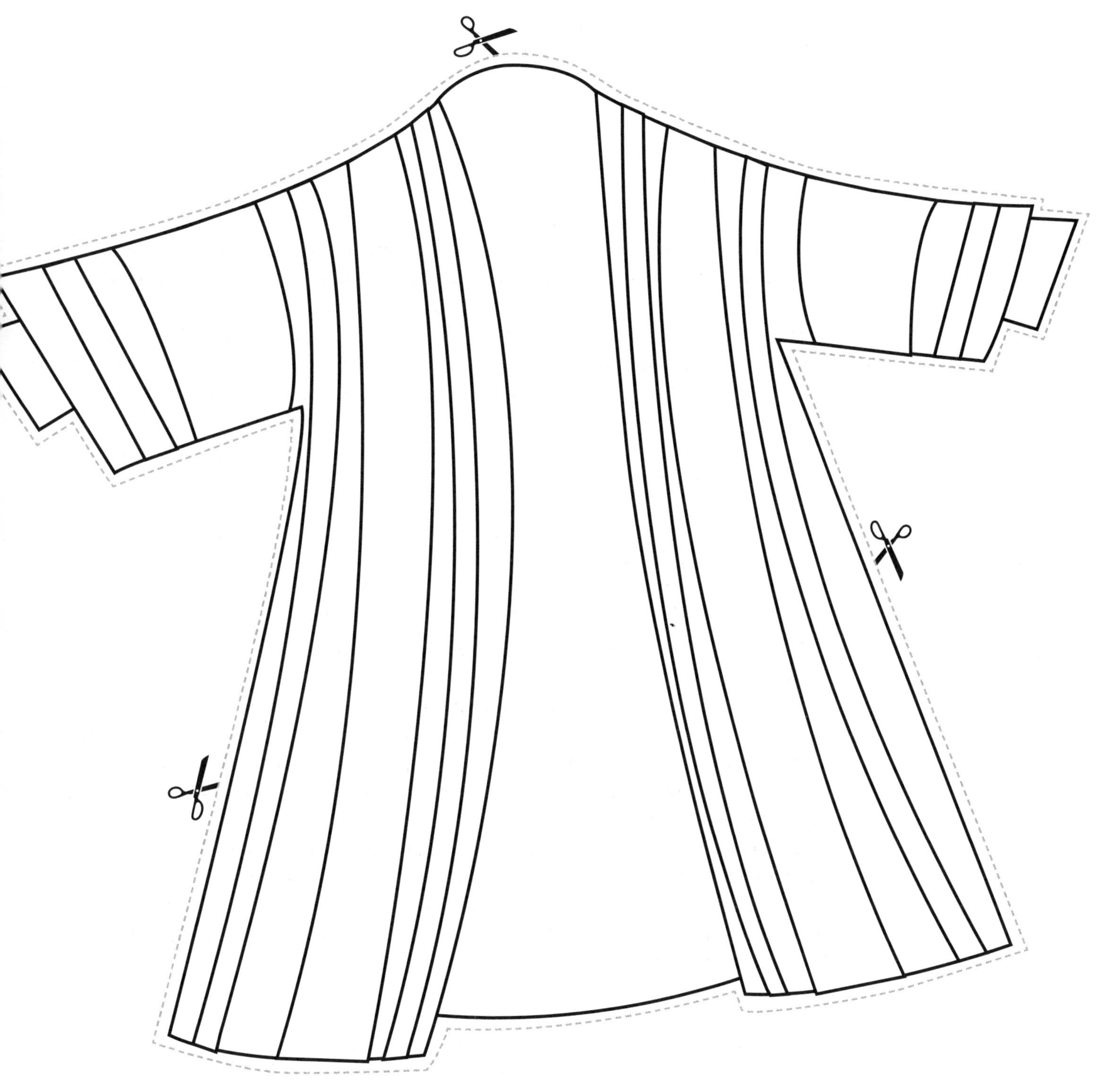

I've Got Your Back!

We are loyal to our families

AGE GROUP

Upper Elementary

SCRIPTURE

Ruth 1

SUPPLIES

You'll need a Bible, name tags, and markers.

PREPARATION

None needed.

Have children sit in a circle.

Say: **Have you ever heard someone say "I've got your back"? It's a way of telling someone that you're going to stay loyal, even when times are tough. Let's play a game to see what this is like.**

Have children each write their name on a name tag and place it on their back. Explain that when you say "Go!" the object is to take as many people's name tags as they can—without losing theirs. If someone loses his or her name tag, that person is out for the rest of that round. If you shout "Back-to-back!" children can choose to stand back-to-back with another child to protect each other's name tags. When you shout "Go!" again, kids play alone again.

Play several rounds, and then have the children sit in a circle.

Ask:

- *Explain whether you liked the game better when you had to protect yourself or when you were allowed to help each other.*
- *How was this game like what happens in real life when someone has your back?*
- *Who are the people in your life who have your back? What do they do?*

Open your Bible to Ruth 1. Show children the words and tell them the Bible is God's special book.

Say: **In our Bible passage, Naomi went through some difficult times. There was a famine in the land, so Naomi's family moved to a different country. Life was good for a while. Her two sons married local women, Orpah and Ruth. But life got really hard. Naomi's husband died. It was a sad time, but she had help from her sons and their wives. But then life got even sadder. Both of her sons died.**

Naomi was crushed. She felt like she had no family, so she decided to return to her hometown in her own country. She told her daughters-in-law that they should go back to their own families in their own country. Orpah listened to her, but Ruth did not. Ruth loved Naomi and decided that she would stay with her no matter what. Ruth decided that she would have Naomi's back no matter what.

Ask:

- *What do you think about Ruth's commitment to being Naomi's family?*
- *What does it look like for family members to have each other's backs today?*
- *What's one way you'd like your family to have your back this week?*
- *What's one thing you can do this week to show your family that you are committed to them?*

Say: **God wants families to have each other's backs during hard times. It's a good thing when we know we can count on our families.**

Closing Prayer
Family-Style Prayers

Have children stand back-to-back.

Say: **Dear God, we thank you that you gave us families so we can support each other when times are difficult. Thank you for the people in our lives who have our backs. Help us stay committed to our families and friends, even when life is hard. In Jesus' name, amen.**

Let It Go!

We give our worries to God

Have children gather around tables. Open your Bible to 1 Peter 5:7. Show children the words and tell them the Bible is God's special book.

Say: **Peter wrote a letter to a church and told them: "Give all your worries and cares to God, for he cares about you." Let's do an activity to help us understand why God doesn't want us to hold onto the things that worry us.**

Ask:

- *Describe a few things kids your age worry about.*

Set bowls of gravel on each table, as well as the crayons and paper.

Say: **Let's pretend that this gravel represents all of the things that worry us. Grab as much gravel as you can with each hand.** (Pause.) **I'm going to give you a series of simple instructions. Do just what I say while holding onto the gravel the entire time. Ready?**

Shake hands with the person next to you. (Pause.)

Wave to the person sitting across from you. (Pause.)

Use a crayon to write your name on a piece of paper. (Pause.)

As children work, they'll inevitably spill gravel on the table. Encourage them to stop, put the gravel back in their hands, and repeat the instructions. After allowing kids to struggle for a bit, have them return the gravel to the bowl.

Ask:

- *What was hard about this activity?*
- *How is this activity like attempting to go through life while holding onto our fears?*
- *Tell about a time you were worried about something. What did that feel like?*
- *Peter told us to give all our worries to God. How do you think we do that?*

Say: **We give our worries to God when we pray and tell him about the things that worry us. God is waiting for us to tell him about those things so he can help us.**

Closing Prayer

Give It Away

Instruct each child to pick up a handful of gravel.

Say: **Dear God, we thank you for wanting to hear about our worries. Thank you for loving us. Thank you for giving us peace to know you'll help us.** (Tell children to think about one thing they're worried about now. Tell them that when they're ready to give that fear to God, they can drop their gravel in the empty bowl.) **Thank you, God, for letting us give our worries to you. In Jesus' name, amen.**

"Egg-stra" Protection

God promises to guard our hearts

Set the plastic tablecloth on the ground and have children sit around it. Open your Bible to Philippians 4:6-7. Read the verses to the children and remind them the Bible is God's special book.

Say: **In these verses, we learn God promises to protect our hearts when we tell him about the things that make us worried.**

Give an uncooked egg to each child. Instruct kids to carefully hold the eggs in their hands—it's their job to keep the eggs safe.

Say: **Imagine that these eggs are like our hearts—holding our most precious thoughts and feelings. They can seem fragile and tender.**

Ask:

- *What things worry our hearts?*
- *What do you think can happen if our hearts are filled with worry for too long?*

Say: **God made our hearts strong. But they weren't designed to deal with worry and stress for a long time. If we don't do something about the things that worry us, our hearts can start to get cracks, just like an egg.**

The good news is, God promises to protect our hearts from worry. Let's do an activity to help us understand what that is like.

Instruct children to stand on the edge of the plastic tablecloth and gently toss their eggs into the air and catch them again.

Ask:

- *Describe what you were thinking when you tossed your egg.*
- *What stopped you from tossing your egg higher?*

Say: **Let's try again, but this time we're going to give our eggs some protection.**

Show children how to tightly pack two foam cups full of cotton balls. Instruct them to place the egg in one cup and then turn the second cup upside down on top of the first cup. Have them tightly fasten the two cups together with packing tape. (If you have limited supplies, you can do one egg for your entire group.)

When kids have finished making their "egg armor," invite them to toss their eggs into the air and catch them again. Encourage them to toss the containers as high as they can and still be able to safely catch them. After kids have had two or three chances to toss and catch their eggs, have them return to their seats.

Ask:

- *What did you expect to happen when you tossed the egg higher this time?*
- *What made you willing to toss your egg so high?*
- *How is this experience like knowing God guards our hearts from worry?*

AGE GROUP

Upper Elementary

SCRIPTURE

Philippians 4:6-7

SUPPLIES

You'll need a Bible, cotton balls, packing tape, and a plastic tablecloth. For each child you'll need 1 raw egg in the shell and 2 foam cups.

PREPARATION

Set aside the empty egg cartons for the Closing Prayer.

ALLERGY ALERT!
See page 8

Say: **God guards our hearts and our minds from worry. All we have to do is give our worries to him through prayer, and he promises to do the rest.**

Closing Prayer
Prayer for Peace

Have children open up their containers so they can hold their eggs. Set the empty egg cartons in the center of the tablecloth.

Say: **Dear God, we thank you for agreeing to protect our hearts and minds from all the things that worry us. We're so glad we can trust you.** (Have children take turns carefully returning their eggs to the carton.) **We love you! In Jesus' name, amen.**

The Navigator

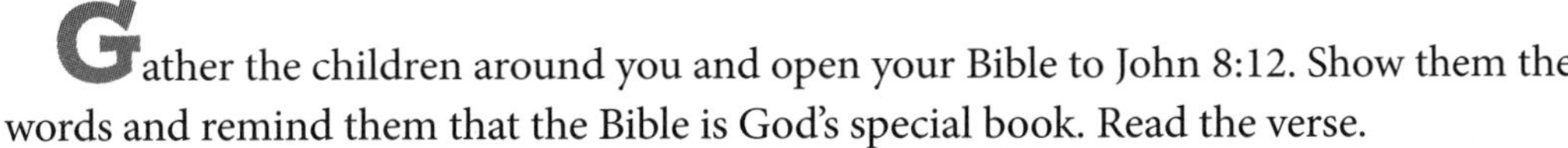

Jesus brings light to our lives

AGE GROUP

Early Elementary

SCRIPTURE

John 8:12

SUPPLIES

You'll need a Bible and several blindfolds.

PREPARATION

None needed.

Gather the children around you and open your Bible to John 8:12. Show them the words and remind them that the Bible is God's special book. Read the verse.

Say: **Let's do an activity that'll help us understand why it's important to have Jesus be our light.**

Instruct children to help make an obstacle course out of the items in your room. Allow them to rearrange desks or tables, chairs, and objects such as toy boxes and piles of books.

Ask:

- *What obstacles or challenges do you face at school?*
- *What about in the neighborhood when you're playing with friends?*
- *What about at home?*

Say: **Life is good, but it can be filled with some tricky obstacles, too. We'll come back to real life in a moment. But for now, let's test out our obstacle course.**

Ask for a volunteer to go first. Surprise your volunteer by pulling out a blindfold. Have children walk through the obstacle course, one by one, until everyone has a chance to navigate it in the dark. Have everyone take a seat.

Ask:

- *What would've made this activity easier?*
- *How was this activity like trying to navigate life's obstacles without Jesus?*
- *What does it mean to follow Jesus?*
- *How does following Jesus add light to our paths?*

Say: **Our lives will have obstacles in them whether we choose to follow Jesus or not. But when we listen to Jesus and do things his way, life makes more sense. We can see challenges coming and get Jesus' advice on how we can handle them.**

Closing Prayer
Travel Prayer

As you pray, have the children navigate the course with their eyes open.

Say: **Dear God, we thank you that Jesus is the light of the world. Help us follow you, even when there are obstacles in our lives. Help us obey you so we can see the path want us to take. In Jesus' name, amen.**

"Big Stuff" Is Small

We don't have to impress God

Have children sit around tables.

Say: **Before we get started with our lesson, we have a little work to do. In our Bible passage, we're going to meet people who felt like they were bigger than they really were, so we're going to make a person who can grow and shrink as needed.**

Give each child a handout and a strip of construction paper. Distribute crayons, scissors, and glue sticks. Have children color their characters any way they wish and then cut along the dotted lines; characters will be cut in half. Show them how to accordion-fold the construction paper and fasten each end to the top and bottom of their characters.

Say: **Perfect! We're ready to get started!**

Open your Bible to Luke 5:27-31. Show children the words and tell them the Bible is God's special book.

Say: **Many of you have probably gone to an amusement park to ride the rides. If you have, you have probably seen those measuring sticks with the sign that says "You must be this tall to ride this ride."**

Ask:

- *When you were younger and weren't sure whether you were tall enough, what did you do when you stood up against the ruler?*

Say: **That's right. Some of us would stand as tall as we could and maybe even try to stand on our tiptoes to look bigger than we were. Now, in our Bible passage there were some who thought people needed to be a different kind of big. There were people who thought that they could be "big stuff" and impress God with all the good things they did.**

Ask:

- *What are things that people might to do look big in God's eyes?* (As the kids supply answers, show them how to make the figure taller and taller by stretching the accordion fold.)

Say: **These people who thought they were big stuff were called Pharisees. They impressed everyone around them by doing good things and by talking about God a lot.**

But then there was a man named Levi. The Pharisees didn't think he was big stuff in God's eyes. He didn't follow their rules. (Have the children shrink their characters a little.) **He didn't know as many stories about God as they did.** (Have the children shrink their characters a little more.) **In fact, a lot of his friends weren't very big in the Pharisees' eyes either. Some of Levi's friends did bad things.** (Shrink the character all the way.) **Levi may have believed that his goodness wasn't as big as the Pharisees' goodness.**

The Pharisees were *certain* they were bigger than Levi and his friends in God's eyes. (Have them make their characters bigger.) **So imagine their surprise when Jesus came to town and invited Levi to follow him—and didn't invite them.**

Ask:

- *Why do you think Jesus chose Levi to follow him instead of the Pharisees?*
- *What does this passage tell you about Levi? the Pharisees? Jesus?*

Say: **The reason Jesus didn't care who was bigger in "goodness" was he knew nobody was as tall as he was when it came to doing the right thing. The Pharisees thought they were tall enough to make God happy, so they didn't think they needed Jesus' help. Levi, on the other hand, knew he only had a small amount of goodness, so he was happy to follow Jesus and get his help.**

Closing Prayer
Taller!

Have kids hold their characters. Instruct them to stretch their characters when they hear the word "tall" and shrink them when they hear the word "small."

Say: **Dear God, we thank you that we don't need to be "tall" (pause) in our goodness to follow you. We thank you that even though our goodness is "small" (pause), your goodness is tall enough for all of us. Thank you. In Jesus name, amen.**

Do We Measure Up?

THE **GIANT** BOOK OF CHILDREN'S MESSAGES

Washed Clean

Only God can wash our sins away

AGE GROUP

Early Elementary

SCRIPTURE

Zechariah 3:1-5

SUPPLIES

You'll need a Bible, 2 old white dress shirts, a plastic tablecloth, dark washable craft paint, a large paintbrush, and a plastic dish tub filled with water.

PREPARATION

None needed.

Set the plastic tablecloth on the ground and have children find a place to sit on it. Open your Bible to Zechariah 3:1-5. Show children the words and tell them the Bible is God's special book.

Say: **In today's Bible passage, God gave Zechariah a special dream to understand what God's forgiveness is like. In the dream, Joshua the high priest was wearing a filthy robe to represent all the bad things he did that didn't make God happy.** (Show the children one of the white shirts.) **Let's see what that might look like.**

Ask:

- *Tell about some wrong things we do today that don't make God happy.* (Every time a child answers, allow that person to take the brush and add some dark paint to the shirt. Allow for several responses.)

Ask:

- *How is this shirt like what our lives look like when we sin?*

Say: **Joshua had a big problem. He was the high priest, and God gave him the job to offer sacrifices so God would forgive people's sins. But he was the only high priest. There was no one who could make sacrifices for *his* sin. Let's try something. Maybe we can clean the sins off his robe for him.** (Help the children carefully dip the dirty shirt in the water and wring it out. Hold the shirt up for everyone to see.) **Oh no! The shirt is still dirty.**

Ask:

- *What ways do you think people try to clean up their own sins?*
- *What does this shirt remind us about our ability to wash away our own sins?*

Say: **Joshua knew that he wasn't able to clean his own robes. He knew he needed God's help. In the dream, angels took away his dirty clothes and replaced them with brand new clothes.** (Hide the dirty shirt from view and replace it with a clean shirt.)

Closing Prayer

Nice and Clean

Have kids each put a hand on the clean shirt.

Say: **Dear God, thank you for forgiving our sins. We know we aren't able to wash away the stains of the bad things we do. Thank you for making us clean again. In Jesus' name, amen.**

Time Machine

God promises to forgive his people

Gather children around you and show them the hula hoop.

Say: **Now this might look like your average hula hoop, but it's actually a time machine. Whenever you step through the hula hoop, you'll end up at a different time—in the past or the future. Right now, I have this time machine set to the past. To be precise, I have it set for the day when God made all the animals. Let's go back in time.**

Hold up the hula hoop and have all of the children step through it. (If you have a large group, have volunteers hold up additional hula hoops to keep everyone active). Once everyone has "time traveled," have children share what they might see or hear that day. Allow a few children to pick different points in history that they want to visit in the time machine. Allow time to imagine what it might be like to actually have been there.

Say: **Okay, that's enough traveling into the past. Now I'm going to send you into the future— your future!** (Have everyone pass through the time machine into the future and then sit in a circle.) **Let's play a "what-if" game about the future. Ready?**

Here's one: You travel in time and learn that if you study hard today, you'll become a famous scientist.

Ask:

- *Tell whether this information would change how you approach school, and why.*

Say: **Here's another one. If you practice the guitar for an hour every day starting today, you're guaranteed to be a world-famous rock star in the future.**

Ask:

- *Would you do it? Why or why not?*

Say: **Last one: You travel into the future and learn that your best friend is horrible to you and gossips about you until you lose all of your other friends.**

Ask:

- *Would you still be friends with that person today? Why or why not?*

Say: **God faced that last situation. Let's see how he handled it.**

Open your Bible to 2 Chronicles 7:11-16. Show children the words and tell them the Bible is God's special book.

Say: **God's people had just finished building the Temple. It was a building similar to a church, where people would meet God so they could worship him and be his friend.**

God knows everything that happens in the future. He knew his people would be bad friends. They would stop following his rules and would start worshipping false gods. God knew this would happen, and still he chose to be their friend. So listen to what God said.

Read the passage aloud.

Ask:

- *Why do you think God would still be friends with his people, even when he knew they would disappoint him?*
- *Why does God promise to forgive us for the future wrongs he knows we will do?*

Say: **God is amazing. He promises to forgive us, even for the wrong things we haven't done yet, if we ask his forgiveness. He knows we're going to do things that hurt our friendship with him, and still he wants to be our friend. That's wonderful.**

Closing Prayer
future forgiveness

Have each of the children hold onto a hula hoop.

Say: **Dear God, thank you for forgiving us. Thank you for still being our friend even though you know all the wrong things we've already done and will do in the future. We are so grateful. In Jesus' name, amen.**

Fruitful Friendships

Our friendships can honor God

Have children sit in a circle or around tables. Open your Bible to Daniel 1:8-20. Show children the words and tell them the Bible is God's special book.

Say: **Our Bible passage is about good friends who helped each other obey God even when it was hard. A bad king had taken God's people into captivity. They lived far from home and had to follow their new king's rules. The king made some of God's people go to a special school to learn to become servants of the king.**

Daniel and his friends were chosen to be in that school. But they discovered the king wanted them to eat foods God didn't want them to eat.

Ask:

- *When have you found yourself in a situation where the people around you didn't obey God's rules?*
- *What was that experience like for you?*

Say: **Daniel and his friends probably had those feelings, too. But they wanted to please God. So Daniel asked permission for him and his friends to eat fruits and vegetables while everyone else ate the king's food.**

Ask:

- *Explain whether you think it was easy for Daniel and his friends to be different from everyone else in their school.*
- *What are ways they could help each other do the right thing?*
- *How could you use those ideas today to help you and your friends obey God?*

Say: **Daniel and his friends obeyed God and only ate the fruits and vegetables. After 10 days, their leader was impressed. Daniel and his friends looked healthier than anyone else in their class.**

Tell the children that they'll work together as friends to make a fruit salad like Daniel and his friends might have eaten. Form groups of four. Have a representative from each group get a bowl of apples, a second person get the orange pieces, a third get the raisins, and the fourth get the cantaloupe. Instruct each person to share with the group until everyone has all the ingredients. Let children enjoy their snacks.

Say: **You had to work together to make the fruit salad. And sometimes we must work together to help each other obey God.**

Ask:

- *When do you struggle with obeying God?*
- *How can your friends here help you in that situation?*

Say: **God knows it's not always easy to obey him. That's one of the reasons God gives us Christian friends—so we can encourage each other to do the right thing, even when it's difficult.**

Closing Prayer
Delightful Thanks

Have kids form a circle and link arms.

Say: **Dear God, sometimes following you means we have to live differently than the people around us. Thank you for Christian friends who can encourage us to do the right thing. In Jesus' name, amen.**

On-Target Friendships

We can choose to be good friends

Have children sit in a circle or around tables. Open your Bible to 1 Samuel 20. Show children the words and tell them the Bible is God's special book.

Say: **These events took place in a scary time during David's life. King Saul knew that David was going to take his place on the throne someday, and he was not happy about it. He wanted his son Jonathan to be the next king, so he decided he was going to kill David. However, David and Jonathan were best friends. They did everything together.**

The king invited David to a feast. The two friends suspected it was trap so the king could kill David. They agreed that David would skip the first three days of the feast. If the king became mad, they would know that it was because his plot was ruined.

Sure enough, after three days, King Saul became furious that David wasn't there. Jonathan knew that his father wanted to kill David. So he took his servant to a field where David was hiding in the bushes. He shot three arrows past a target and shouted, "Behold, the arrows went past the target!" This was David's signal that the king was mad at him. So David was able to run away and be safe because his good friend helped him.

Ask:

- *What do you think made Jonathan a good friend?*
- *What qualities do you look for in a friend?*
- *How can our friends help us be better friends with God?*

Say: **Let's make a craft to remind us of things that make a good friend.**

Distribute the supplies. Have kids use markers to create a design on their half-sheets of card stock. Then show them how to create an archer's quiver by rolling the card stock into a tube and stapling the sides and bottom.

Next help them attach their chenille wires as handles.

Have children cut out the arrows from their handouts and write one quality they think makes a good friend on each arrow. Ask them to insert their arrows into their quivers.

Ask:

- *What can you do to be a good friend to others?*

Say: **It's important to have good friends that help each other, just like Jonathan helped David. We can choose friends with the qualities we listed. And we can choose to be a friend with those qualities, too.**

Closing Prayer
Pointed Prayers

Have kids pretend to draw a bow and hold that pose as you pray.

Say: **Dear God, thank you for the example of the friendship between David and Jonathan. Help each of us be good and loving friends like those two were. And thank you for being our friend, too. In Jesus' name, amen.**

Friendship Arrows

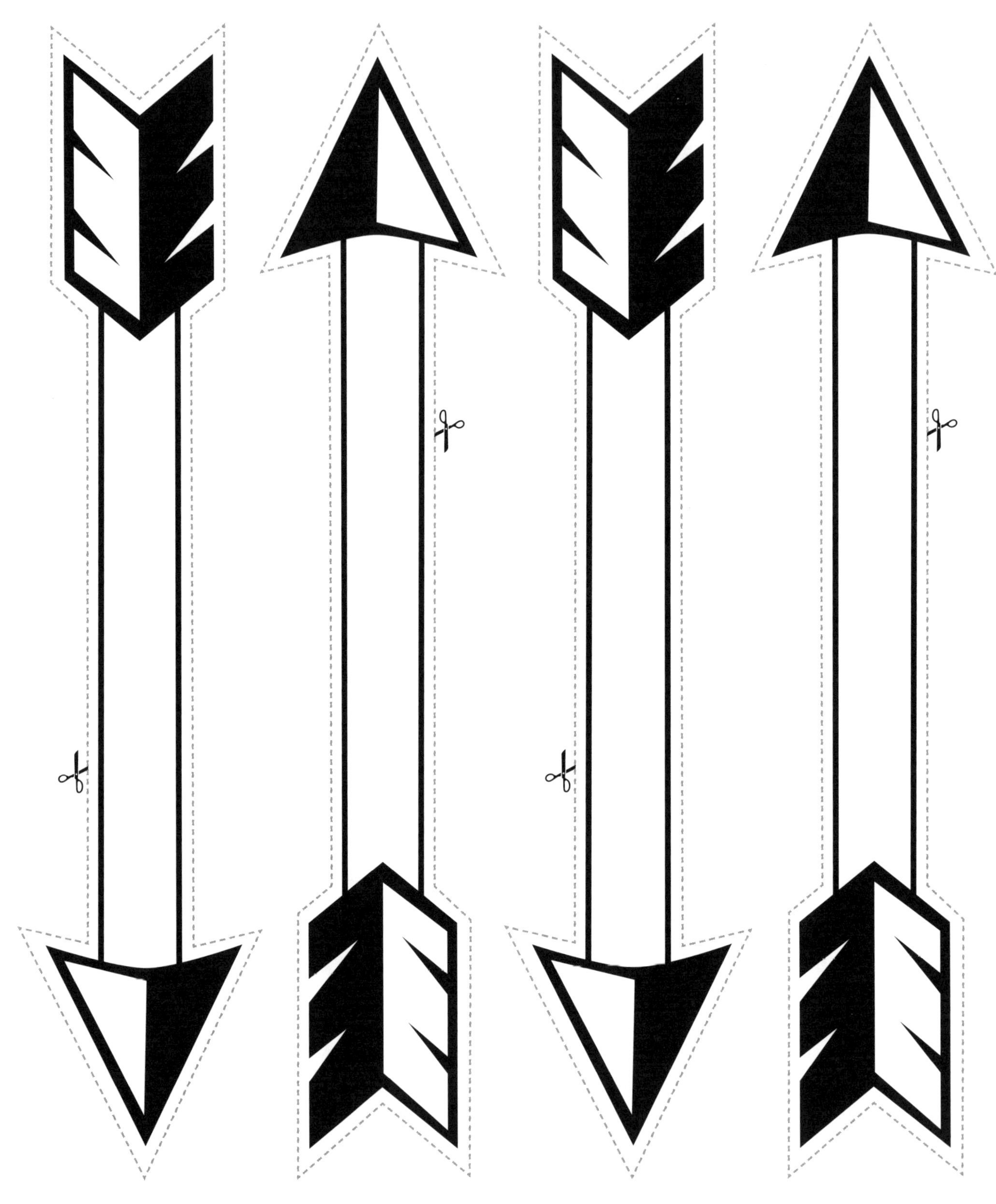

THE **GIANT** BOOK OF CHILDREN'S MESSAGES

Gift Hunters

Everyone has spiritual gifts for serving God

Gather children together. Open your Bible to 1 Peter 4:10-11. Show children the words and tell them the Bible is God's special book. Read the passage aloud.

Say: **Peter wrote a letter to a church that was having hard times. He reminded them that God gave all the people in the church something special they were good at that they could use to help each other become better followers of Jesus. Peter only mentioned a few of these gifts, like speaking and serving. Let's search our church for other examples of how people can use their strengths to make the church strong.**

Lead children on a quiet tour of the church. Have them raise their hands to point out to the whole group when they see someone serving. When appropriate, have your group approach a volunteer and have that person explain how he or she serves others. Have kids take turns giving volunteers a piece of candy to thank them for using their spiritual gifts. After you've returned to your room, have everyone sit in a circle.

Ask:

- *What might happen in our church if people stopped using their spiritual gifts?*
- *Out of all the different ways you saw people serving, which do you think would be the most fun to do? Why?*

Say: **God gave each of you a spiritual gift, too. Let's help each other figure out what our gifts might be.**

Distribute the handouts and pencils. Have kids each write their name on the top of the page. Then have them pass their papers to the person on the right. Have kids look at the name on the paper in front of them and write one thing they think that person is good at. Help as needed. Repeat until kids have their own papers back in front of them.

Ask:

- *What thoughts do you have when you read all of the strengths your friends see in you?*
- *How might you use those gifts to help others know, love, and serve Jesus?*

Say: **It's great to know that every one of us has a spiritual gift we can use to strengthen the church and serve God.**

Closing Prayer
Gift Thanks!

Have kids hold their hands out, palms up. As you pray, walk around the circle and give each child a sweet gift from the bag of candy.

Say: **Dear God, we thank you for giving each of us a spiritual gift we can use to make the church stronger. We know when we use our gifts, the church becomes a sweeter place. In Jesus' name, amen.**

AGE GROUP

Early Elementary

SCRIPTURE

1 Peter 4:10-11

SUPPLIES

You'll need a Bible and a bag of candy. For each child, you'll need a copy of the "My Gift" handout and a pencil.

PREPARATION

Get any necessary permission to take kids on a walk around your church. Let parents know you'll be away from the room so they aren't alarmed if they find an empty room.

My Gift

"God has given each of you a gift
from his great variety
of spiritual gifts. Use them well
to serve one another."

(1 Peter 4:10)

Gifted to Build

Every gift matters

Have children sit in a circle or around tables.

Say: **Let's pretend that we are on the leadership team of our church. It's our job to come up with a list of all the skills and talents we need to help people worship God.**

Ask:

- *What gifts and talents do we need to help people worship God?*
- *What would you do if you wanted to help people worship, but your talent wasn't on the list?*

Say: **Let's see what happened to two people in today's Bible passage.** (Open your Bible to Exodus 31:1-6. Show children the words and tell them the Bible is God's special book.) **Oholiab and Bezalel were two men who loved God deeply. They wanted to help God's people worship. But there was one problem. Neither was good at playing a musical instrument, singing, or even preaching. Bezalel and Oholiab had different talents. The Bible said they were smart men who were good at working with wood, metal, and stone. They were master craftsmen, but they didn't have the skills to lead God's people in worship. They loved God, but it didn't seem like they had any talents God needed.**

One day, God told Moses he wanted to build a special place for God's people to worship him. God told Moses about Oholiab and Bezalel and how good they were at making things. So Moses approached them and asked them to make God's special place of worship.

Form groups of three or four. Distribute the gumdrops and toothpicks. Have kids take on the role of Oholiab and Bezalel and work together to design God's special place of worship. Allow kids several minutes to design and present their structures.

Ask:

- *What does it mean to you that God wanted to use Oholiab and Bezalel's unusual gifts to help people worship?*
- *What unusual gifts do you have? How could you use them to help people worship God?*

Say: **God knows how to make his people strong. He gives the right people the right gifts at the right time. It doesn't matter if your gifts seem "normal" or not. There's a way for you to use your gifts to help God's people.**

Closing Prayer

Gifts That Give

Have kids form a circle within their groups and hold their buildings.

Say: **Dear God, we thank you for giving us each amazing and sometimes unusual gifts. Remind us that our gifts are never wasted, especially when we use them to serve you, our church, and people outside our church. In Jesus' name, amen.**

Eyes on the Prize

Our goals can honor God

AGE GROUP

Early Elementary

SCRIPTURE

Philippians 3:12-14

SUPPLIES

You'll need a Bible, an old trophy, and masking tape.

PREPARATION

Make 2 tape lines on the floor about 4 feet apart. Make another tape line on the wall, within jumping reach of the children you work with.

Have children sit in a circle or around tables. Open your Bible to Philippians 3:12-14. Show children the words and tell them the Bible is God's special book. Read the verse.

Say: **Goals are something we focus on accomplishing over the course of time—a week, month, year, or even lifetime. Goals are important because they help us stay focused on what's really important to us. They help us to not lose sight of what matters.**

Show the kids the trophy and explain how you (or someone else) got it.

Say: **Trophies are prizes we sometimes win for accomplishing a goal. Our Scripture is a reminder that our ultimate goal isn't to win a prize here on earth, but to aim toward heaven. Each goal we set can help us accomplish that.**

Say: **I have three goals for today. I want some people to jump from this line to this line.** (Show the two tape lines on the floor.) **I want some people to jump up and touch this mark on the wall.** (Show the tape line on the wall.) **And I want some people to each compliment three other people in the room. You can choose one goal to accomplish in the next minute. Ready? Go!**

Allow time.

Ask:

- *How did you choose which goal to aim for?*
- *How do you think setting goals helps us in real life?*
- *What does the Bible verse tell us about setting goals?*

Say: **Goals can help us get closer to God. When we make a goal, our focus isn't only on the prize or trophy at the end, but on accomplishing that goal for God.**

Closing Prayer

The Ultimate Goal

Say: **God, thank you for helping us want to achieve great things by setting goals. Please help us reach our goals—and more importantly to choose goals that guide us closer to you. In Jesus' name, amen.**

God-Pleasing Goals

Our ultimate goal is to please God

AGE GROUP

Upper Elementary

SCRIPTURE

2 Corinthians 5:6-10

SUPPLIES

You'll need a Bible, a beach ball, and a ping-pong ball. For each child, you'll need a copy of the "My Goals" handout.

PREPARATION

None needed.

Have children sit in a circle or around tables. Open your Bible to 2 Corinthians 5:6-10. Show children the words and tell them the Bible is God's special book.

Say: **Every year, people set goals for themselves. Some people do this at the beginning of the year for things they want to accomplish that coming year. Others set goals during each month or season, depending on what they want to do.** (Distribute handouts and pencils.) **You have a paper in front of you. Think of five goals for yourself, for this week, this month, or this year. A goal can be anything that you want to try hard to accomplish—from earning straight A's to not fighting with your sister. One of my goals for this year is...** (name a non-spiritual goal you're working on).

Ask:

- *What are some goals you're working on at school?*
- *What are goals you have at home?*
- *Why do you think it's important to set goals?*
- *What happens when we don't set goals?*

Allow time for kids to write five goals.

Say: **The Scripture we're talking about today encourages us to make goals that please God. Now let's take a look at those lists again. In the second column, write five spiritual goals for this week, month, or year that you want to accomplish that honor God. One of my spiritual goals for this year is...** (name a spiritual goal you're working on).

Allow time for kids to write five goals.

Ask:

- *How is setting spiritual goals different from setting regular goals?*
- *Why is it important to set specific spiritual goals?*

Say: **Some goals are easy and some are hard. Line up single file and make a tunnel with your legs.** (Pause.) **I'm going to roll this large ball down the tunnel to see how far it gets. Then I'm going to roll the little ball down the tunnel to see how far it gets.**

Roll the beach ball and then the ping-pong ball. In most cases the little ball goes the farthest.

Ask:

- *What, if anything, surprised you about which ball went the farthest?*
- *How was this experiment like or unlike what happens when we make goals that are hard or easy?*
- *Which spiritual goal on your list will you need the most help with?*

Say: **Goals are valuable because they focus us on what's important. Some goals are easier than others, like the way the little ball rolled right down the tunnel. Other goals are** not easy and we need help to accomplish them. For the bigger ball to get down the tunnel, we needed everyone to make a wider tunnel. That ball needed assistance! But to achieve success with any goal, let's remember to honor God with our efforts.

Closing Prayer
Our Efforts Can Please God

Have kids sit in a circle and roll the beach ball across the circle to each other as you pray.

Say: **God, thank you for helping us set goals that honor you. You know our lists of goals, whether they're from everyday life or from our spiritual life with you. Please help us meet these goals over this week, month, and year. Help us honor you in our efforts to meet our goals. We hope our efforts please you. In Jesus' name, amen.**

My Goals

Personal Goals

1.

2.

3.

4.

5.

Goals for God

1.

2.

3.

4.

5.

Big, Delicious Love

God's big love is for us

Have children sit in a circle or around tables. Open your Bible to 1 John 4:7-10. Show children the words and tell them the Bible is God's special book. Read the passage.

Say: **You all have lots of people who love you. Your family loves you, your friends love you, you love each other, and I love you. I love each of you so much that I even brought a snack for you.**

Give one small chocolate chip cookie to each child.

Say: **In God's special book, we learned that God is love. He loves us always because he is love. This cookie I gave you today** (show small cookie) **is like how much everyone loves you—me, your friends, your parents. But this cookie** (show the giant cookie cake) **is how much God loves you.**

Ask:

- *What does it mean to you that God loves you so much?*

Say: **God's love is bigger than anything we can imagine. He loved you when he created the world. He loved you when you were born, even before you were born. He loved you when he provided food for your meals. He loved you when he created colors, flowers, rain, trees, animals, waterfalls, and everything else. God created it all, because he loves you. He even gave us his Son, Jesus, because he loves us so much.**

Give a piece of the big cookie cake to each child.

Ask:

- *Tell about a time someone showed you love.*
- *What are ways you show love to others?*
- *Tell about a time you felt loved by God. How can you share that great big love with others?*

Say: **God is love, God shows love, and God loves you. He loves all of us because we're very special to him. Because God loves us first, he wants us to share his love with those around us.**

Closing Prayer

Thankful for Love

Say: **God, thank you for always loving us. Thank you for being love and teaching us how to love others. Please show us your love this week so we can show it to the people around us. In Jesus' name, amen.**

Bridge of Love

God's love never leaves us

AGE GROUP

Upper Elementary

SCRIPTURE

Romans 8:39

SUPPLIES

You'll need a Bible.

PREPARATION

None needed.

Have children sit in a circle or around tables. Open your Bible to Romans 8:39. Show children the words and tell them the Bible is God's special book. Then read the verse.

Say: **Wow! This verse tells us nothing will separate us from God's love. Absolutely nothing. Nothing in creation can separate us from God, like being in the lowest part of the Grand Canyon, or the highest part of Mount Everest. No one can separate us from God's love—not our parents, not our friends, and not even ourselves. God's love is bigger than everything. There is nowhere we can go, or anything we can do, that is going to change the fact that God loves us.**

Say: **Let's put this into action. We're going to make human bridges. Find a partner who's about as tall as you.** (Help kids each find a partner, switching them around if needed so all have a partner close in height. If you have an odd number of children, partner with the tallest or do two different rounds of the game.)

Say: **Please face each other with your feet touching toe-to-toe and hold hands. Okay! You are now a human bridge. Each time I say so, both of you will take one step backward, but you can't let go of each other's hands. We're going to see who can remain a human bridge the longest. If your hands let go, your team is out. Ready? Take a step backward.** (Continue having pairs take a step backward until you only have one team left.)

Congratulate kids and ask them to gather for discussion.

Ask:

- *Did you think this challenge would be easy or hard—and why?*
- *How was this experience like or unlike the fact that nothing can ever separate us from God's love?*
- *How does knowing God's love will always be with you change the way you view life?*

Say: **God loved you first, because he created you. And he loves you so much that nothing will ever change that. God made us that promise, and we can trust him.**

Closing Prayer

Unbreakable Love

Have kids form a circle and link arms.

Say: **God, thank you for loving us so much that nothing can ever break that. Thank you for never being far from us. In Jesus' name, amen.**

Follow and Trust

God's plan is for our good

AGE GROUP

Early Elementary

SCRIPTURE

Jeremiah 29:11

SUPPLIES

You'll need a Bible, soccer ball, a goal (a box or hula hoop works well), and a copy of the "Follow the Plan" handout for every two kids.

PREPARATION

Place the soccer ball and goal somewhere visible in room.

Have children sit in a circle or around tables. Open your Bible to Jeremiah 29:11. Show children the words and tell them the Bible is God's special book. Read the Scripture.

Say: **God has a plan for you, and his plan is for good things for your life. That's great news! But one thing we may not think is so great is that while God has a plan, we often don't see it. We may know that God has it all worked out for us because we can trust him. But in those moments when it seems like things aren't working out well, we can struggle. The truth is, no matter what's happening around us, we can have faith, trust, and comfort in knowing his plans for us are good. Let's dig into this a little more.**

Help kids find partners. If you have an odd number, pair up with one of the kids. Each pair will need at least one reader. Distribute handouts—just one per pair.

Say: **One partner will read the map, and the other partner will act out the instructions without seeing the map.** (For variety in the room, consider having each pair start at a different number on the map.)

Allow time for partners to follow the steps.

Say: **You guys did great! And you all made it back to your starting point in one piece.**

Ask:

- *What was it like to be able to see the map and know what each next step would be throughout the activity?*
- *What was it like to complete each action, not knowing what was next?*
- *What is the hardest part about trusting God with his plan for your life when you can't see what's next?*

Say: **Trusting God with his plan for your life can be a little like trusting your partner with getting you around this room. It can be hard, exhausting, and fun all at the same time. But in the end, we can remember that God really does want good things for us and he already has the plan worked out.**

Closing Prayer

God Holds the Plan

Have kids each put a hand on the soccer goal as you pray.

Say: **God, thank you for having a plan for each of us. We know your plan is a good one, even when it doesn't seem like it and we feel confused by what's happening. Please continue to guide us each and every day through your plan for us and guide us to trust you. In Jesus' name, amen.**

Follow the Plan

Guide your partner with the directions on this map. Do not show the map to your partner.

No Accidents

God has a plan for your family

AGE GROUP

Upper Elementary

SCRIPTURE

Matthew 1:1-17

SUPPLIES

You'll need a Bible and a whiteboard or poster board and marker. For each child, you'll need a copy of the "Family Tree" handout and a pencil.

PREPARATION

Following the model of the handout, write your own family tree on a whiteboard or poster board for everyone to see.

Have children sit in a circle or around tables.

Say: **God created Adam and Eve in the Garden of Eden, and they were the first humans. Unfortunately they sinned. They ate from a tree that God had made off-limits. The punishment for sin is death, so Adam and Eve got kicked out of the Garden of Eden. From the moment that sin happened, God had a plan to save them—and all of us. He was going to send his Son, Jesus, to earth, to save them.**

Distribute the handouts and pencils. Open your Bible to Matthew 1:1-17. Show children the words and tell them the Bible is God's special book.

Say: **Our Bible passage today tells us the family history of Jesus. It starts with Abraham, who was considered the father of the Jewish people. As we go through this passage, write down some of Jesus' key relatives.**

Read the passage, pointing out Abraham, Rahab, Boaz, Ruth, Jesse, David, Solomon, Joseph, Mary, and any others kids may have read about before.

Say: **Jesus came from a big family—a family that was written about throughout the Bible. But you come from an important family, too—one that's also a part of God's plan.**

Have kids fill out their portion of the family tree. Show them yours on the whiteboard or poster board for ideas.

Ask:

- *Who, if anyone, from Jesus' family was a surprise to you?*
- *What's something surprising about your family?*
- *What surprises you about God's plan?*

Say: **God had a plan for all of us and for Jesus to come to earth. Part of that plan included you. He gave you to your family for a reason, but he also wanted you to become a part of God's bigger family.**

Closing Prayer
Thankful for family

Have kids hold their family tree handouts to their hearts as you pray.

Say: **God, thank you for having a plan for each one of us. Thank you for Jesus' family, and thank you for our family. Thank you for having a plan for us just as you had for Jesus. Thank you for letting us be part of your family. In Jesus' name, amen.**

Family Tree

Grandparents
Dad
Grandparents
Mom
Me

Key Relatives
Dad
Mom
Jesus

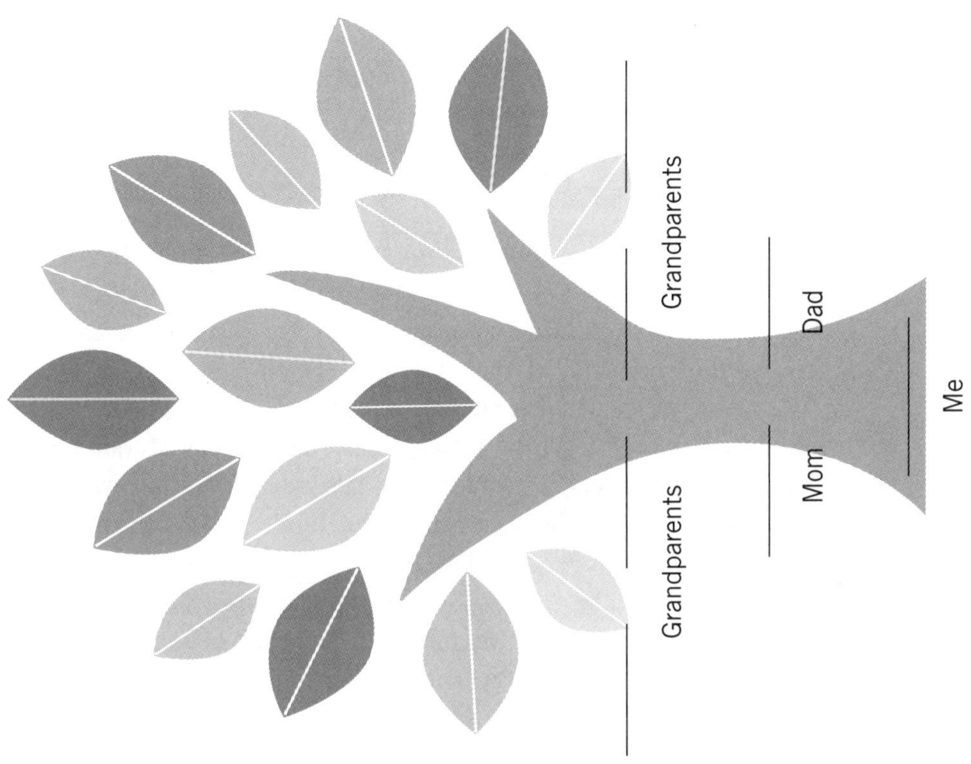

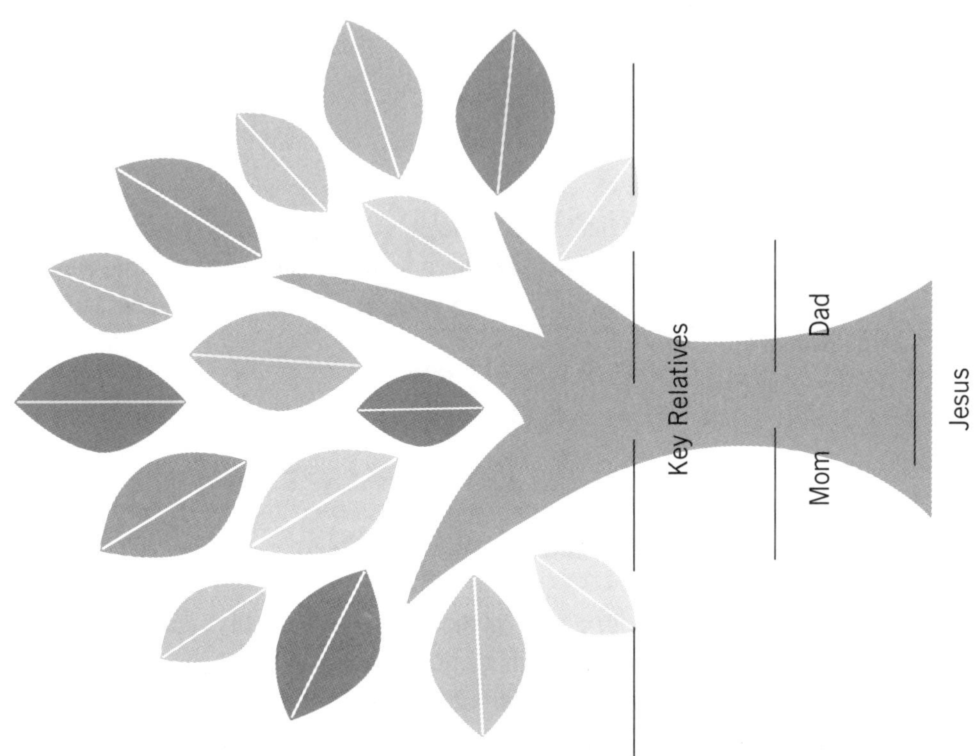

Unlimited Power

God is powerful

AGE GROUP

Early Elementary

SCRIPTURE

1 Corinthians 2:3-5

SUPPLIES

You'll need a Bible, a AAA battery, a C battery, a lamp that takes a 100-watt light bulb, and a 100-watt light bulb.

PREPARATION

Set the items on a table and plug in the lamp.

Have children sit in a circle or around tables. Open your Bible to 1 Corinthians 2:3-5. Show children the words and tell them the Bible is God's special book. Read the Scripture.

Say: **This passage explains that our faith doesn't rely on our wisdom or strength, but on God's power. God's power is greater than anything. Take a look at what I have up here on this table. I have this AAA battery, a C battery, and this lamp, which is powered by a 100-watt light bulb.** (Show each item as you go, describing what kinds of electronics each battery might power and how the lamp is powered by electricity from the outlet. Explain how the batteries and electrical outlets are the power sources that make various items work.)

Say: **Each of these items has power behind it. And each of us puts out power, too. One AAA battery puts out 1.41 watts of energy; one C battery puts out 9.56 watts of energy; one 100-watt light bulb puts out 100 watts of energy. And guess what? One human puts out about 100 watts of energy, too!**

Human wisdom created electricity, light bulbs, and batteries. But if a human *created by God* can put out the same amount of energy as one light bulb, imagine how much power God has!

Ask:

- *Describe some items that need power to work.*
- *What do you think the difference is between power and wisdom?*
- *What do you think the verse we read tells us about relying on our own power versus relying on God's power?*

Say: **God's power isn't limited to wattage, volts, electricity, or batteries. God's power is *unlimited*—beyond anything we have here in this room or even in this world. Because of that, our faith in God can go beyond what we understand and be cemented in God's power—not our own wisdom or power.**

Closing Prayer

Resting in God's Power

Gather kids around the lamp and let them take turns turning the lamp on and off as you pray.

Say: **Thank you, God, for giving us the power we need to create things and harness the power and electricity to make things work. Thank you for giving each of us our own energy. We're most thankful that your power isn't limited to light bulbs and batteries. Your power is unlimited! We rest in your power today, God. In Jesus' name, amen.**

Freeze Dance

When we understand God's power, everything makes sense

AGE GROUP

Upper Elementary

SCRIPTURE

1 Corinthians 1:18-19

SUPPLIES

You'll need a Bible, a music player, and upbeat kids' music.

PREPARATION

Set up the music player for a game of Freeze Dance.

Have children sit in a circle or around tables. Open your Bible to 1 Corinthians 1:18-19. Show children the words and tell them the Bible is God's special book. Read the passage.

Say: **Christmas is a special holiday because we celebrate the birth of Jesus. Easter is another special holiday because we celebrate Jesus' resurrection. For Christians, those two holidays are very meaningful because they celebrate what Jesus did for us. But for people who aren't Christians and don't believe in Jesus, these are just fun holidays for time with family. This passage of Scripture reminds us that for some people, the idea that Jesus died on the cross and rose from the dead is foolish. For us, we know this passage shows just how powerful God really is.**

Say: **We're going to play a game of Freeze Dance. You get to dance like crazy until the music stops; then freeze in place until it starts again.**

Tell kids to get ready, and then say "Go!"—but don't play any music. Occasionally yell out "Freeze!" Then say "Go!" again. Do this three to five times.

Say: **You did great! Wasn't that fun?** (Allow a few kids to respond to the odd game.) **Okay, let's add music this time.**

Play the game again, this time using music.

Ask:

- *Describe what you were feeling when we played Freeze Dance without music.*
- *What was it like when we added music?*
- *Which version of the game would you like to play again?*

Say: **It was kind of foolish playing Freeze Dance without any actual music. But when we added the music, the game was more powerful—and fun. For some people, hearing about Jesus is like playing Freeze Dance with no music; they don't really get it. But when people truly understand what Jesus did for them and how much he loves them, it's like adding the music to the game. They get it! It makes sense! And it's powerful!**

God is so powerful that he defeats death. He wants us to understand his power and teach others about it so they can understand it, too.

Closing Prayer
Sharing God's Power

Play the music again. This time when you stop it, have kids hold that pose as you pray.

Say: **God, thank you for helping us understand why you sent Jesus to die and defeat death for us. Thank you for your power. Remind us to share your power with people who don't yet understand. In Jesus' name, amen.**

Surprise Provision

God provides for us every day

AGE GROUP

Early Elementary

SCRIPTURE

Isaiah 48:21

SUPPLIES

You'll need a Bible,
2 buckets of water,
2 empty buckets,
1 rock, and 1 sponge.

PREPARATION

Put the 2 buckets of
water with the rock
and sponge on one
end of the room and
the 2 empty buckets
on the other side of
the room.

Have children sit in a circle or around tables. Open your Bible to Isaiah 48:21. Show children the words and tell them the Bible is God's special book. Read the Scripture.

Say: **This passage is about a time that God provided for the Israelites in the desert. They were thirsty but there were no rivers or water sources near them. They called out to God, and he provided water for them by asking Moses to split the rock open with his staff. When he did, water came gushing out for the Israelites to drink.**

Water doesn't normally come from rocks, but we're going to see how much water we can pull from one. (Form two teams. One team will stand by the bucket with the rock, and the other team will stand by the bucket with the sponge.) **Each team gets a bucket of water at one end and an empty bucket at the other end. One team has a sponge and the other team has a rock. Each person in line will dip the team's item into the bucket of water, carry it to the empty bucket to ring out the water, then run back and pass the item to the next person in line and sit down. The team with the most water in its bucket at the end wins. Ready? Go!**

Once play is over, have everyone sit in a circle.

Say: **The winning team is—no surprise here—the team with the sponge. Rocks don't hold water well, do they? Still, God used them to provide water for his people. God uses all different ways to provide for us, sometimes surprising ways like bringing water from rocks.**

Ask:

- *What, if anything, surprised you about our relay?*
- *What does it mean to you that God provided water for his people—who were in need—in such a surprising way?*
- *What are some surprising ways God has provided for you or your friends?*

Say: **God uses different ways to provide for our needs, but he always provides. We can be on the lookout for the many surprising ways God provides for us every day.**

Closing Prayer

God's Surprising Provision

Pass around the bucket and sponge and let kids each squeeze water from the sponge as you pray.

Say: **God, thank you for providing water for the Israelites from rocks. Thank you for using surprising ways to provide for us. Please continue to provide for our needs in surprising ways. In Jesus' name, amen.**

Help Is on the Way

God still provides for our needs

AGE GROUP

Upper Elementary

SCRIPTURE

Nehemiah 9:19-21

SUPPLIES

You'll need a Bible, name tags, and markers.

PREPARATION

Create two sets of tags: one for needs, the other for provisions. Each child will need a tag. For the set of needs, write one word on each tag: *hungry, thirsty, tired, sad, poor, sick, shoeless, worn-out clothes, lonely*. For the set of provisions, write one word on each tag: *food, water, a bed, joy, money, medicine, new shoes, new clothes, friends*. If you have a large group, duplicate the terms.

Have children sit in a circle or around tables. Open your Bible to Nehemiah 9:19-21. Show children the words and tell them the Bible is God's special book.

Say: **The Bible tells us about Moses, who was the leader of the Israelites. The Israelites were wandering around the desert in search of the Promised Land. But they were thirsty and hungry. God provided for them by giving them manna to eat and making water spring from rocks for them to drink. The Israelites were in great need, and when they called out to God, he provided for them, even in the middle of the desert.**

Read the Scripture.

God provides for us too, each and every day. Sometimes he provides for us through other people, like our parents, teachers, doctors, and friends. We're going to learn more about this by playing a game. You'll all get a mystery tag on your back for a need or for a provision. (Put a tag on each child's back.) **You can ask each other only yes-or-no questions to figure out what need or provision you are. Once you know what you are, you must find your corresponding need or provision. Ready? Go!**

Allow time to play.

Ask:

- *Describe what it was like to try to figure out your need or provision. How is that like or unlike what happens when we have needs or provisions in real life?*
- *What needs do you or your friends have right now?*
- *Tell about a time God provided for your needs.*

Say: **God provided for Moses and the Israelites when they were in need. He provides for us today, too. God wants us to ask for help when we need it, and he will respond.**

Closing Prayer
Thankful Today

Have kids sit with their partners that they found in the previous activity. Ask them to stick their needs and provisions tags together and hold them as you pray.

Say: **God, thank you for your remarkable provision for Moses and the Israelites so long ago. Thank you for listening to our needs and for providing for us today. Help us see the everyday ways you provide for us—through meeting our physical needs like hunger and thirst and the emotional ones like our need for friends and joy. Please provide for the needs of our families and friends. In Jesus' name, amen.**

Can't Win This

We can't earn God's forgiveness

AGE GROUP

Early Elementary

SCRIPTURE

Luke 15:11-20;
Romans 5:8

SUPPLIES

You'll need a Bible,
1 wrapped piece of
candy for each child,
and a stopwatch.

PREPARATION

None needed.

ALLERGY ALERT!
See page 8

Have children sit in a circle. Open your Bible to Luke 15:11-20. Show children the words and tell them the Bible is God's special book. Read the passage aloud.

Say: **When the younger son deserved to be treated like a servant, his father treated him like a son. That's called grace. Let's dig into grace more.**

Tell kids that in order to get a piece of candy, they must complete a series of tasks in under 60 seconds. For example, kids could run back and forth across the room three times, spin around 10 times, and sing the ABCs. The tasks should be almost impossible to complete in the time limit. After kids understand the challenge, give kids 60 seconds to complete them.

Say: **Even though some** (or all) **of you weren't able to complete the challenge, I'll give you a treat anyway.** (Give kids a treat, but don't let them eat it until prayer time.) **Just as the younger son received grace when his father welcomed him home with open arms, you received grace when I gave you a treat you didn't deserve.**

Ask:

- *What was it like to receive a reward that you didn't deserve?*
- *Tell about a time someone showed you grace in your daily life.*

Read Romans 5:8.

Ask:

- *How has God shown grace to you?*
- *What is one way you can show grace to others this week?*

Say: **God showed us grace by sending Jesus to die for our sins while we were still sinners. We don't deserve and we can't earn God's forgiveness. However, God loves us so much that he offers us forgiveness anyway.**

Closing Prayer
Sweet Prayer

Have kids unwrap the candy and place it in their mouths so they can enjoy it as you pray.

Say: **Dear God, thank you for your sweet grace. We can't earn your forgiveness and don't deserve anything you give us. Help us remember that it's only by your grace that we can be forgiven. In Jesus' name, amen.**

Sand Sketch

God offers grace to all

O pen your Bible to John 8:1-11. Show children the words and tell them the Bible is God's special book. Read the passage aloud.

Say: **Jesus offered forgiveness to a woman who had been caught in sin and deserved punishment. Let's close our eyes for a moment and think about the different ways we sin and what we deserve for those sins.**

Have kids open their eyes. Give each child a container with sand.

Say: **Let's use our fingers to write in the sand like Jesus did. Think about a sin you've been caught in. Draw a picture or write a word in the sand as you confess that sin to God.** (Allow time.)

Jesus told the accusers that anyone who had never sinned could throw the first stone. Then he wrote in the dust again. Think about a sin that no one other than God knows about. Draw in the sand as you ask God to help you with that sin. (Allow time.)

Jesus told the woman he didn't condemn her. Smooth out the sand as you thank God for his forgiveness. (Allow time.)

Ask:

- *Tell about a time someone caught you in sin.*
- *How was smoothing out the sand like or unlike how God wipes out our sin?*
- *Tell about a time someone showed you grace.*

Say: **Just as the woman caught in sin didn't deserve forgiveness, we also don't deserve forgiveness. The amazing thing is God offers us grace anyway.**

Closing Prayer

Words in the Dust

Say: **As Jesus knelt in the dust, there were all sorts of things he could've been writing. Let's use our handouts to discover what words God might have for us.**

Give each child a "Jesus' Words" handout. Have kids trace glue along the lines of the handout and then pour sand over the glue. As they do, the words "Forgiven" and "Grace" will appear.

Say: **Jesus, thank you that just as you forgave the woman caught in sin, you show us grace and forgive us. Help us remember there is nothing we can do to earn your love and grace. You give it to us because you want to. In Jesus' name, amen.**

AGE GROUP

Upper Elementary

SCRIPTURE

John 8:1-11

SUPPLIES

You'll need a Bible. For each child, you'll need a copy of the "Jesus' Words" handout, a pencil, glue, a cup of sand, and a shallow container or paper plate.

PREPARATION

Pour sand into each container.

Jesus' Words

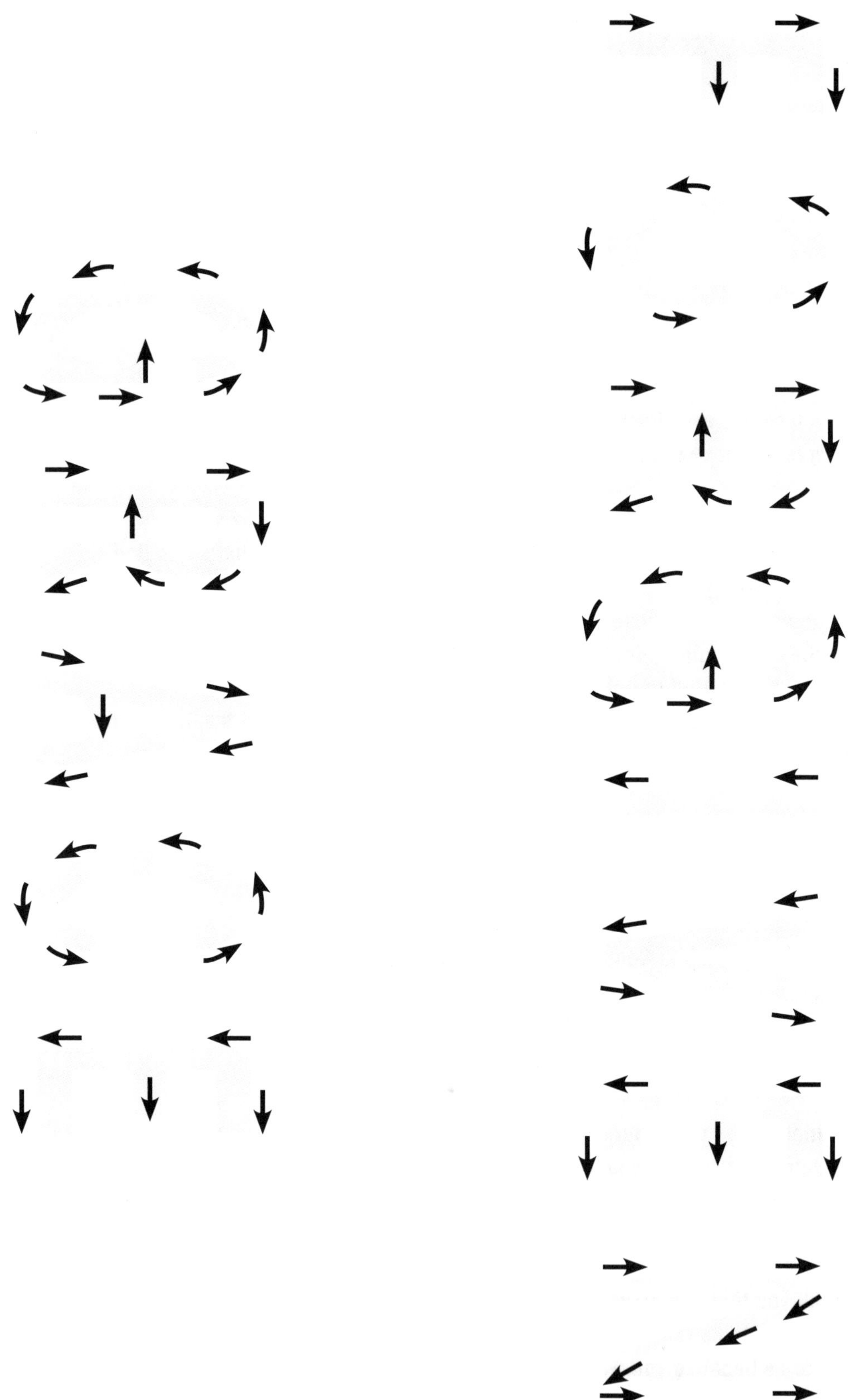

Brush It Away

Jealousy eats away at us

AGE GROUP

Early Elementary

SCRIPTURE

Proverbs 14:30

SUPPLIES

You'll need a Bible, a foam cup, nail polish remover with acetone, an aluminum tray, a trash can, and 4 handheld dust brooms. For each child, you'll need a copy of the "Jealous Thoughts" handout and a pencil.

PREPARATION

None needed.

Have children sit in a circle or around a table with the supplies.

Say: **This foam cup represents us.** (Place the foam cup in the tray.) **Sometimes we have jealous thoughts, like when we wish we were as smart as someone else or when we want a gift someone else received.** (Pour a few drops of acetone nail polish remover over the foam cup.)

Ask the following discussion questions as you watch the nail polish remover melt the foam cup.

Ask:

- *Tell about a time you were jealous of someone else.*
- *What do you think jealousy does to our hearts and bodies?*

Say: **Look at how the jealous thoughts are eating away at us!**

Open your Bible to Proverbs 14:30. Show children the words and tell them the Bible is God's special book. Read the Scripture.

Say: **Jealous thoughts eat away and rot our bones. They are like cavities!**

Give each child a copy of the "Jealous Thoughts" handout. Have them each write or draw a jealous thought on their paper and crumple it into a ball.

Say: **Just like we brush our teeth to prevent cavities, we're going to brush away our jealous thoughts.**

Form four groups, and give each group a handheld dust broom. Line the children up for a relay race. Show them how to brush their "jealous thoughts" across the room using the broom and then run back to tag the next person in line.

Closing Prayer
Sparkly White

Have children hold their "Jealous Thoughts" crumpled papers while you pray.

Say: **Dear God, we know jealousy is rotten and eats away at us. We thank you for forgiving us and making us shine brightly. Help us brush away jealous thoughts forever. In Jesus' name, amen.**

Have children throw their papers into the trash can.

Jealous Thoughts

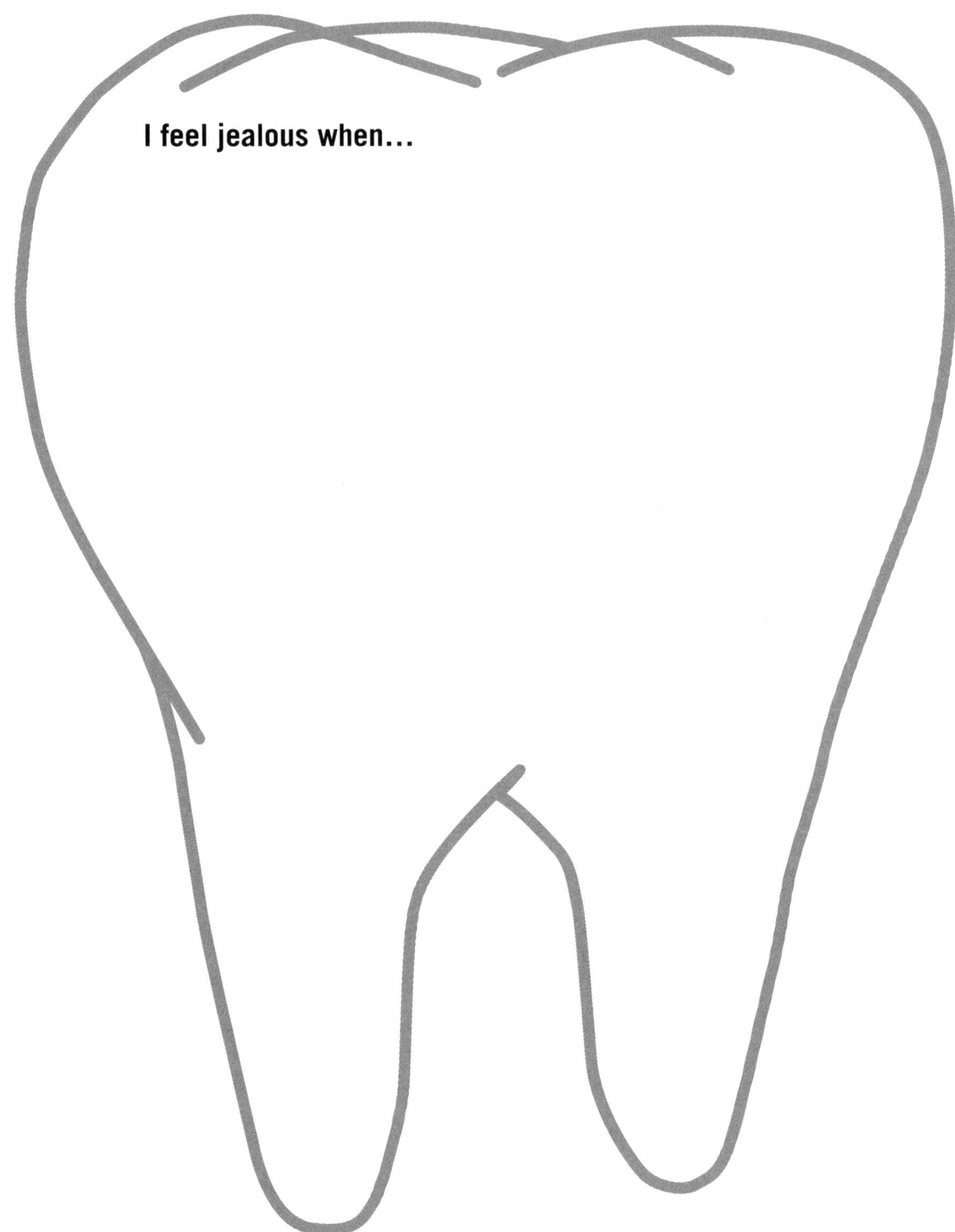

THE **GIANT** BOOK OF CHILDREN'S MESSAGES

Disorderly Conduct

Jealousy leads to disorder and mess

AGE GROUP

Upper Elementary

SCRIPTURE

James 3:16-18

SUPPLIES

You'll need a Bible, a small hand shovel, a small flower pot and a large flower pot, large bucket of dirt, a pitcher of water, small seeds, and a garbage bag. You'll also need one seed for each child for the Closing Prayer.

PREPARATION

Lay a garbage bag on the ground for easy clean up.

Have children sit in a circle around the garbage bag.

Say: **We're going to work together to plant some flowers. You'll need to follow my directions.** (Give kids the various supplies for planting.) **But, uh-oh, jealousy is taking over!**

What if the person with the dirt is jealous of the person who goes first? (Have a child pour some dirt onto the hand shovel.) **What if the person with the large flowerpot is jealous of the small pot?** (Have a child pour the large bucket of dirt into the small pot, allowing the dirt to overflow.) **What if the person with the seeds is jealous of the person with the water?** (Put the seeds into the pitcher of water. Pour the seeds and water onto the dirt.) **We've made quite a mess!**

Open your Bible to James 3:16-18. Show children the words and tell them the Bible is God's special book. Read the Scripture passage aloud.

Ask:

- *How will jealousy affect our flowers' ability to grow?*
- *How does our jealousy mess up God's plans?*
- *What are some ways you can plant seeds of peace in your life?*

Say: **God has a plan for each of us, and he gives each of us special gifts to use for his plans. When we're jealous of other people, it creates disorder and makes a mess of God's perfect plans.**

Closing Prayer

Seeds of Peace

Give each child one flower seed.

Say: **As I pray, I want you to think of you how you're going to plant seeds of peace in your life. When you're finished praying, toss your seed into the flower pot.**

Dear God, we thank you for having a plan for each of us. We know your plans are perfect. We apologize for the times our jealousy messes it up. Help us to plant seeds of peace. In Jesus' name, amen.

The Main Attraction

Jesus came to draw us to God

Have children sit around tables. Open your Bible to Matthew 1:18-23. Show children the words and tell them the Bible is God's special book. Then read the passage aloud.

Say: **Jesus was called Immanuel, which means "God is with us." Jesus came to earth to create a way for us to have a relationship with God.**

Place two magnets on the table in front of each child with the words *God* and *Sin* facing up. Tell kids that without turning over the magnets or lifting them off the table, their goal is to bring the two magnets together. Allow time. Then have kids push the magnets off to the side.

Give each child a "Baby Jesus" handout, markers, and scissors. Have kids cut out the picture of the baby Jesus. Ask kids to think about all the names they know for Jesus and write the names across the picture of Jesus.

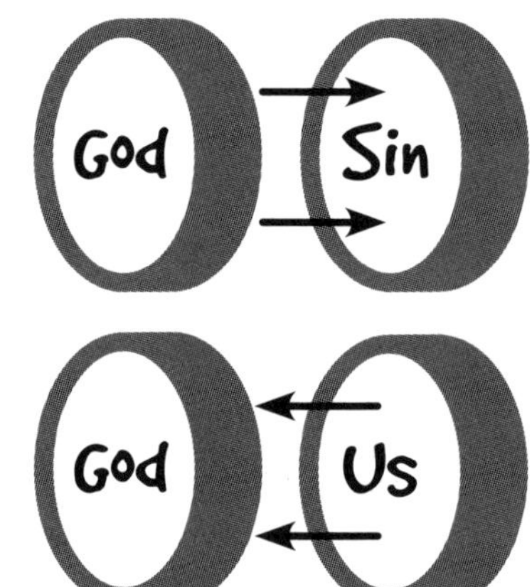

Then ask kids to hold the picture of Jesus vertically between the two magnets. Encourage kids to flip over the Sin magnet so they now see the word *Us*. Allow time for kids to see how the magnets are drawn together with the picture of Jesus between them.

Ask:

- *What did you learn from the magnets that repelled or attracted each other?*
- *How does knowing Jesus bring you closer to God?*

Say: **God is holy and perfect. We are sinful. Because of our sin, we can never be with God on our own, just as your two magnets could never meet up. However, with Jesus' birth, God is with us, and we now have a way to live eternally with God.**

Closing Prayers

Magnetic Prayers

Have kids hold the magnets so they repel each other.

Say: **God, we're sorry for our sin that separates us from you. Please forgive us.** (Have kids turn the magnets so they attract each other.) **Thank you for sending Jesus to provide a way so we could be with you. In Jesus' name, amen.**

Baby Jesus

Birth Announcements

We share the good news of Jesus' birth

AGE GROUP

Upper Elementary

SCRIPTURE

Luke 2:1-14

SUPPLIES

You'll need a Bible. For each group of three children, you'll also need a Bible, a copy of the "Good News" handout, and a marker.

PREPARATION

None needed.

Have children gather around you. Open your Bible to Luke 2:1-14. Show children the words and tell them the Bible is God's special book. Then read the passage aloud.

Say: **When Jesus was born, an angel of God appeared to the shepherds announcing good news. Let's make our own good news announcements about this major event.**

Have kids form groups of three or four. Give each group a Bible, a handout, and markers. Encourage groups to look back over Luke 2:1-14 to create a good news announcement of their own.

Once groups have completed their announcements, have one group at a time stand and share its good news with the rest of the group. Then encourage the larger group to respond to the news by reading Luke 2:14 out loud. Continue with groups reading and responding the same way the armies of heaven responded to Jesus' birth.

Ask:

- *How does Jesus being born impact your life?*
- *How can you share this good news like the angel did?*
- *Who do you need to share this good news with?*

Say: **God sent his Son to be born, to live a sinless life, and to die on the cross for our sin. The armies of heaven celebrated because they realized that Jesus' birth meant that we could one day live in heaven with God. Jesus' birth is good news that we can share with everyone.**

Closing Prayer
Passing Praise

Have kids form a single-file line. Explain to kids that you're going to play Telephone as you share good news with one another. Start by telling the first child in line: "Jesus was born in Bethlehem." Once kids have whispered the message into each other's ears all the way down the line, start again. This time, tell the first child in line: "He is the Messiah, the Lord."

Say: **God, thank you for the good news of Jesus' birth. Help us to shout it out like the armies of heaven did. We don't want to keep the good news to ourselves. In Jesus' name, amen.**

Good News

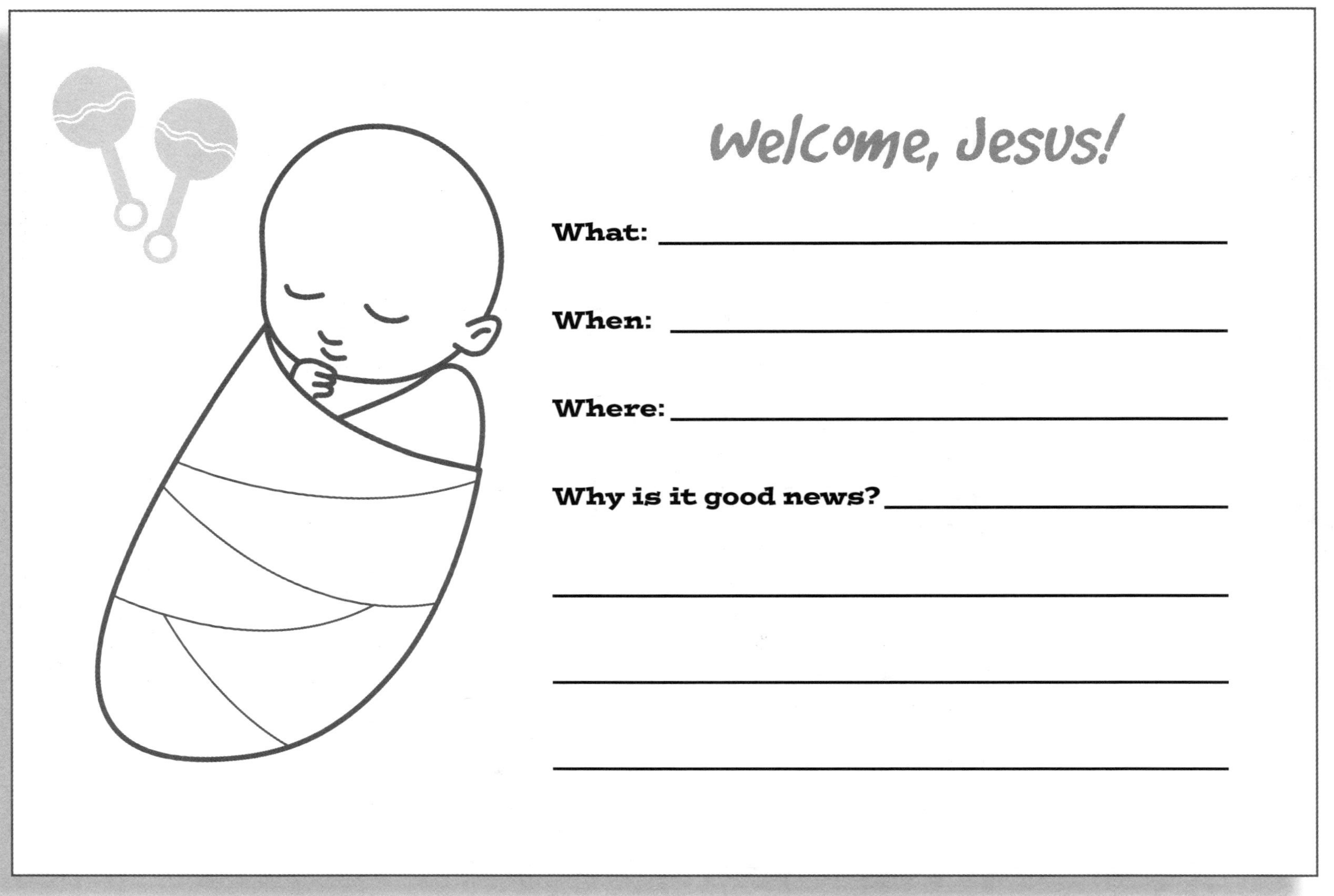

Storm Commands

Like the wind and the waves, we obey Jesus

AGE GROUP

Early Elementary

SCRIPTURE

Matthew 8:23-27;
22:37-39

SUPPLIES

You'll need a Bible,
1 chenille wire and a
handful of red beads
for each child, and
scissors.

PREPARATION

Cut the chenille
wires in half. Beads
need to be large
enough to fit on the
chenille wire; try
the plastic beads
commonly known as
"pony beads," found
at craft stores.

Have children sit in a circle. Open your Bible to Matthew 8:23-27. Show children the words and tell them the Bible is God's special book. Explain to kids that as you read through the passage, you'll pause and give commands.

Read verse 23. Command children to pretend they're rowing a boat.

Read verse 24. Command children to stomp and clap like a loud storm.

Read verse 25. Command kids to shout, "Lord, save us!"

Read verse 26. Command kids to lie down and be still.

Read verse 27. Command kids to show you an expression of amazement.

Say: **Just as you obeyed my commands, the disciples discovered that even the winds and the waves obeyed Jesus. We obey Jesus' commands, too.**

Ask:

- *What are some commands Jesus gives us?*
- *When is it hard for you to obey Jesus' commands?*

Say: **The two greatest commandments Jesus gives us are in Matthew 22:37-39.** (Read the verses aloud.) **God commands us to love him and love others. Let's make a craft to help us remember that.**

Give each child two halves of a chenille wire and a handful of red beads. As kids put beads on the first chenille wire, have them talk about what it looks like to obey God by loving him. As kids put beads on the second chenille wire, have them talk about what it looks like to obey God by loving others. Once both chenille wires have beads on them, show kids how to connect the beaded wires and form them into the shape of a heart.

Closing Prayer

Loving Commands

Say: **Take your beaded hearts home as a reminder to obey Jesus' commands by loving God and loving others.**

Have kids hold their hands open with their beaded hearts resting in their hands.

Say: **God, we want to obey you just like the wind and the waves. Help us to love you and others. Give us hearts that long to obey you. In Jesus' name, amen.**

Tears in a Bottle

Jesus cares about our tears

AGE GROUP

Upper Elementary

SCRIPTURE

Psalm 56:8;
Luke 7:11-17

SUPPLIES

You'll need a Bible,
food coloring, a cup
of water, a clear
bottle with a cup of
bleach in it, and an
eye dropper.

PREPARATION

Place several drops
of food coloring in
the cup of water.

Have children sit in a circle. Open your Bible to Luke 7:11-17. Show children the words and tell them the Bible is God's special book. Then read the passage aloud.

Say: **Just as Jesus had compassion on the mother, God cares about our tears, too. In fact, God keeps track of our sorrows.**

Read Psalm 56:8 aloud.

Say: **The Bible says that God collects our tears in bottles because he cares about the hard things we go through.**

Set the cup of water, the eye dropper, and the bottle out on a table. Ask kids to take a moment to think about sad or hard things they're going through. Then, one at a time, encourage kids to use the eye dropper to drop a couple drops of water into the bottle with bleach. As they do, have kids silently talk to God about what they're going through. When everyone has dropped tears into the bottle, hold up the bottle for the children to see.

Ask:

- *Like the woman whose son died, we all go through hard things. What hard things are you going through?*
- *What are things you talked to God about as you dropped the tears in the bottle?*
- *What does it mean to you to know that God keeps track of your tears?*

Say: **Jesus performed a miracle and brought the woman's son back to life because his heart overflowed with compassion for her. In the same way, God's heart for us overflows with compassion. God keeps track of our sorrow and cares about our tears.**

Closing Prayer
Sorrowful Prayers

Have kids form a circle. Pass the tear bottle around. As each child holds the bottle, encourage him or her to pray aloud a simple prayer before passing the bottle to the next child until it comes back to you.

Say: **God, thank you that Jesus performed a miracle and brought the woman's son back to life. Thank you for caring when we're sad, too. Help us trust that you see every tear and hear every cry of our hearts. In Jesus' name, amen.**

Run and Tell

We tell others Jesus is alive

AGE GROUP

Early Elementary

SCRIPTURE

Matthew 28:1-8

SUPPLIES

You'll need a Bible, a whiteboard, and whiteboard markers. For each child, you'll need a copy of the "Empty Tomb" handout and a pencil.

PREPARATION

None needed.

Have children sit in a circle. Open your Bible to Matthew 28:1-8. Show children the words and tell them the Bible is God's special book. Then read the passage aloud.

Say: **The angel told Mary to go quickly and tell the disciples that Jesus had risen from the dead. Let's practice going and telling others about Jesus.**

Stand next to a whiteboard. Have kids form a single-file line at the opposite end of your meeting area. One at a time, have kids run quickly to you and tell you one important thing they know about Jesus. Write down what the child tells you. Then have the child run back to the end of the line as the next child runs to you. Once every child has completed the running relay, have kids join you at the whiteboard.

Give everyone a handout and a pencil. Encourage kids to choose the two most important things from the whiteboard that they think other people need to know about Jesus. Have kids write the two things they chose on the empty tomb. (Pair writers with nonwriters as necessary.) Then next to the word *Go,* have kids write the name of one person who needs to hear about Jesus this week.

Ask:

- *Tell about a time you told others about Jesus like Mary did.*
- *What two things did you choose as the most important to tell others about Jesus?*
- *Why is it important to tell others about Jesus and his resurrection?*

Say: **God also tells us to go and tell others about who Jesus is and what he has done, just like he told Mary. Use your handout to help you remember what you've learned about Jesus.**

Closing Prayer

Cupped Hands

Have kids cup their hands together. Then ask kids to look inside their hands and tell you what they find.

Say: **God, thank you that just as our cupped hands are empty, Jesus' tomb was empty. Please help us to be like Mary as we go and tell others that Jesus is alive. In Jesus' name, amen.**

Empty Tomb

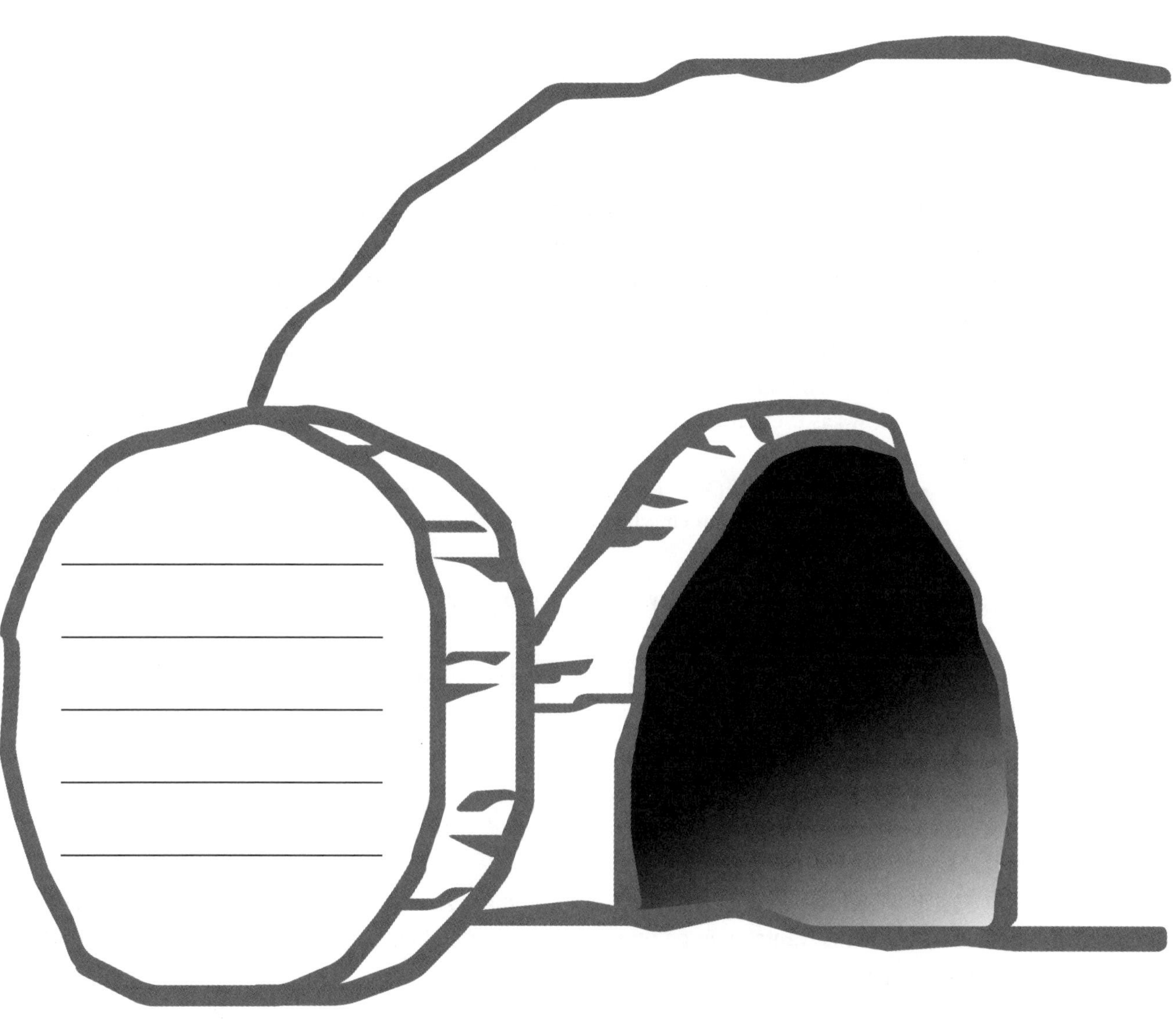

GO: ____

Breathe and Go

Jesus sends us to tell others

Have children sit in a circle. Open your Bible to John 20:19-22. Show children the words and tell them the Bible is God's special book. Read the passage aloud.

Say: **After Jesus died and rose again, he appeared and showed the disciples his wounds. He then told the disciples that just as the Father sent him, he was also sending the disciples. Then he breathed on them and they received the Holy Spirit. Let's think more about Jesus sending us, just as he sent his disciples.**

Have kids gather around windows in your meeting area or give children handheld mirrors. Explain to kids that you'll ask them some questions, and in response they'll breathe and draw on the windows as they think about Jesus breathing on the disciples.

Ask:

- *Where do you think God might be sending you?* (Encourage kids to breathe on the window and draw a place, such as their school.)

Ask:

- *Who might God be sending you to?* (Encourage kids to write someone's name.)

Ask:

- *When is God sending you?* (Ask kids to write in response.)

Then gather kids back together.

Ask:

- *How is God sending you like he sent his disciples?*
- *What's one thing you'll do this week as a result of what you thought about during this breathing exercise?*

Say: **Just as Jesus sent the disciples to tell others about his death and resurrection, Jesus is sending us. Jesus wants us to go into our schools, neighborhoods, and homes and tell people who he is and what he's done.**

Give kids window cleaner and paper towels and have them wipe down the windows.

Closing Prayer
Breathless Prayers

Have kids take a deep breath and hold it.

Say: **God, without you our lives are meaningless.** (Have kids let out a long breath.) **Thank you for breathing on your disciples and sending them. Thank you for sending us, too. Help us faithfully share the good news of your resurrection with the people around us. In Jesus' name, amen.**

Overflowing Joy

Jesus offers living water

Have children sit around tables. Give each child a cup full of water and a straw.

Open your Bible to John 4:6-15. Show children the words and tell them the Bible is God's special book. Read the passage aloud.

Say: **Jesus offered the woman at the well living water, and he wants to offer us the same thing. Sometimes our lives are full and joyful like this cup. Other times, it seems like the joy is being sucked right out of our lives. Think of something that sucks away your joy. Then, call it out and suck a big drink of water through your straw.**

Continue until every child's cup is empty. Save the straws for the Closing Prayer. Then read John 10:10.

Say: **The Bible also says that God wants to give us a rich and satisfying life—like a cup that overflows.**

Pour some of the unlabeled vinegar into each child's cup. (Tell kids not to drink from the cup.) Then as you add baking soda to each cup, encourage children to call out ways God has brought overflowing joy to their lives. The combination will create a chemical reaction that bubbles up out of the cup. Use paper towels for cleanup.

Ask:

- *Explain whether you feel more like a straw sucking away your joy or a cup overflowing, and why.*
- *In what areas of your life do you need to ask God to help you have joy?*

Say: **We can let hard things suck the life out of us like we sucked the water out of our cups. Or we can be filled with joy that comes from trusting God. God wants to overflow our lives with joy.**

Closing Prayer
Straw Prayers

Have kids hold the straws up to their mouths and suck in air as you pray.

Say: **God, thank you that having a friendship with you doesn't mean you suck the fun out of our lives. We're so grateful that you want to fill and overflow our lives with joy. Help us trust you and praise you in hard times so we can be joyful no matter what. In Jesus' name, amen.**

A New View

God is in Control

Gather children around you.

Ask:

- *What do you usually think about when you hear the word* joy?

Open your Bible to James 1:2-3. Show children the words and tell them the Bible is God's special book. Then read the passage aloud.

Say: **The Bible says there's joy in suffering, and when troubles come our way we should look at them as opportunities for joy.**

Ask:

- *When is it hard for you to be joyful?*

Say: **The Bible also says that Jesus willingly went through pain, suffering, and death on the cross because of the joy before him. That joy was that he was providing the offer of forgiveness for sin to live eternally with God.**

Joy is *not* being happy all the time—joy is trusting that God is in control of every situation and choosing to praise him no matter what.

Let's use our handouts to help us remember to look for joy in every situation.

Give each child a handout, scissors, glue, and a piece of cellophane. Have kids cut out the magnifying glass and then glue the cellophane over the open center of the magnifying glass. Allow time for kids to explore your meeting area using their colored magnifying glasses.

Ask:

- *How do things look different through the lens of your magnifying glass?*
- *How will you look at a situation you're going through right now differently knowing that God is in control?*
- *What does it look like for you to praise God and be joyful in that specific situation?*

Say: **Just like our magnifying glasses change the way our meeting area looks, choosing to trust and praise God changes how we view our lives. We can have joy in hard situations knowing that God is in control.**

Closing Prayer

Joy Magnified

Have kids hold up their magnifying glasses to their eyes as you pray.

Say: **God, thank you for helping us see things differently. Help us trust you more so that we can be joyful in hard times. In Jesus' name, amen.**

Joyful Vision

The King's Kindness

We can always be kind to others

AGE GROUP

Early Elementary

SCRIPTURE

2 Samuel 9:1-7;
19:24-30

SUPPLIES

You'll need a Bible
and pictures of
a crown, a happy
face, two boys as
friends, and a boy on
crutches.

PREPARATION

None needed.

Have the children sit in a circle or around tables. Open your Bible to 2 Samuel 9:1-7; 19:24-30. Show children the words and tell them the Bible is God's special book.

Say: **This Bible passage says that King David fought a lot of wars to protect all the people of Israel.** (Show children the crown.) **But when the wars were over, there was a time of happiness and peace.** (Show the happy face.) **When David was younger, he had a best friend named Jonathan who was the son of King Saul. David liked to remember all the great times he and his friend had had together.** (Show the two boys as friends.)

David also remembered that he had promised Jonathan he'd take care of Jonathan's children. Jonathan had a son named Mephibosheth. When Mephibosheth was little, he had an accident and he couldn't walk. (Show the boy on crutches.) **David kept his promise to his best friend Jonathan, and Mephibosheth got to sit at King David's table. He got to have all the wonderful good things that a king would eat. In his kindness, David promised Mephibosheth that he would always take care of him for the rest of his life.**

Let's practice showing kindness to others this week like King David did.

Ask:

- *What do you think it means to show kindness to others?*
- *Tell about a time someone showed kindness to you.*
- *When have you showed kindness to others?*

Say: **David's kindness to Mephibosheth was also a kindness to his friend Jonathan because he kept his promise from long ago. King David was faithful to God because God wants us to be kind to one another and he wants us to keep our promises.**

Closing Prayer

Commitment to Kindness

Have children form a circle holding hands.

Say: **Dear God, thank you for being so kind to us. Help us be kind to others, even when we don't feel like it. Remind us to follow King David's example of keeping our promises and treating others with kindness. In Jesus' name, amen.**

Boiling Mad Rescue

Kindness can help in bad situations

AGE GROUP

Upper Elementary

SCRIPTURE

1 Samuel 25:2-42

SUPPLIES

You'll need a Bible, a small bowl, a casserole dish, 1 tbsp baking soda, dish soap, 3 drops red food coloring, 1 tsp of water, and vinegar in a squeezeable container.

PREPARATION

Place the small bowl inside the casserole dish. Place baking soda in the small bowl with one squirt of dish soap. Mix the food coloring and water, and then add the mixture to the small bowl.

Have kids sit around the bowl you prepared. Open your Bible to 1 Samuel 25:2-42. Show children the words and tell them the Bible is God's special book.

Say: **In this Bible passage, there's a situation where kindness is important. Nabal was a very wealthy man who owned lots of sheep and goats. He was unkind to others, but his wife Abigail was a kind person who cared about people. During a celebration where people sheared sheep, a man named David sent men to Nabal to ask him to share his wealth. Nabal said, "Who is this man who thinks he can ask for some of my wealth?" He was very mad. The men went back and told David what Nabal said. David became angry and told 400 of his men to go with him and attack Nabal. Both men were so angry, they didn't stop and think about their actions. Anger is ugly and messy.**

Squirt vinegar in the small bowl, and watch the fizz dramatically boil over.

One of Nabal's servants told Abigail what her husband had said. "David's men have been kind and protected us from our enemies," the servant said. "I'm afraid David is very angry." Without Nabal's knowledge, Abigail quickly gathered loaves of bread, wine, sheep, grain, raisins, and fig cakes and packed them on donkeys.

When she saw David, Abigail got off her donkey, fell at his feet, and said, "I accept all blame in this matter, my lord. Nabal is wicked! Please do not listen to him! Here is a peace offering that I have brought for you and your men."

David was surprised and said, "Praise God, he sent you to meet me today to prevent me from doing a horrible thing. Thank you for your kindness and for stopping me from harming Nabal. Return home in peace."

Ask:

- *Why do you think Nabal may have been unkind to David?*
- *Describe some of Abigail's traits from this passage.*
- *Is there a situation in your life now where you could be more like Abigail than Nabal?*

Say: **Anger is messy, just like that fizz. It can create all kinds of problems. We have to stop and think about the consequences of our actions. Abigail was kind and wanted to protect her family from harm. She selflessly protected her family by going and delivering food and goods to David. She is a great example of how kindness can help in bad situations.**

Closing Prayer

Practice kindness

Say: **Dear God, thank you for helping us learn from others' mistakes like Nabal and David, and for showing us the example of Abigail's kindness. Thank you for always being kind to us. Remind us to be kind like Abigail in all situations. In Jesus' name, amen.**

Lonely Links

We can call on God when we're alone

AGE GROUP

Early Elementary

SCRIPTURE

Psalm 25:15-20

SUPPLIES

You'll need a Bible.

PREPARATION

None needed.

Say: **King David was the king of Israel. He was a mighty warrior and a man after God's own heart. Despite all of this, King David still dealt with loneliness.**

Open your Bible to Psalm 25:15-20. Show children the words and tell them the Bible is God's special book. Then read the verses aloud.

Say: **When David felt lonely, he cried out to God. In the same way, we can cry out to God when we feel alone. Let's see what that might be like.**

Have kids spread out around the room and close their eyes. Explain that the object of the game is for kids to find a partner and link arms. Kids will do this by calling out things like "I'm lonely" or "I need someone." Kids will listen for others calling out and they'll walk with eyes closed toward other people until they each link up with someone else who is alone. The game ends once every child is linked up with one other partner.

Ask:

- *How is calling out in this game like or unlike calling out to God when you're feeling lonely in your daily life?*
- *Tell about a time you were lonely.*
- *What's one thing you learned from this activity that can help you the next time you feel alone?*

Say: **Like King David, we all get lonely. When we do, we can talk to God about our loneliness. We can also talk to other people around us because chances are, they might be lonely, too. God wants to comfort us when we're lonely.**

Closing Prayer

Lonely Prayers

Have kids spread out around the room and assume a prayerful posture. Allow time for kids to pray by themselves as they talk to God about being lonely. After a few minutes, gather kids together in a huddle.

Say: **God, we all struggle with loneliness. Help us remember that we're never truly alone because you're always with us. Remind us each day of your love and your presence in our lives. In Jesus' name, amen.**

Blanket of Loneliness

Jesus knows what it's like to be lonely

AGE GROUP

Upper Elementary

SCRIPTURE

Deuteronomy 31:8;
Matthew 27:45-50

SUPPLIES

You'll need a Bible and a blanket or bedsheet. For each child, you'll need one strip of the "Lonely" handout.

PREPARATION

None needed.

Give each child a pencil and a slip of paper cut from the handout. Ask kids to complete the sentence on the slip, and then collect them. Shuffle the papers, and without revealing who wrote what, read each statement aloud.

Say: **There wasn't a single blank handout because everyone feels lonely at times. Even Jesus experienced loneliness.**

Open your Bible to Matthew 27:45-50. Show children the words and tell them the Bible is God's special book. Read the passage aloud.

Say: **When Jesus was on the cross, he felt lonely and abandoned by God. Let's experience the truth about loneliness.**

Form a circle, and have one child sit in the center. Cover that child with a blanket. Remind the child that even though all he or she can see is the blanket, the child is still surrounded by people who care. Go around the circle and encourage everyone to call out affirmations such as, "You're not alone" and "You're my friend." Then read Deuteronomy 31:8 aloud. Take turns so each child gets to sit under the blanket.

Ask:

- *What did you learn about loneliness from this experience?*
- *How can what you just learned help when you feel lonely?*

Say: **When we're lonely, we feel like some of you probably did under the blanket. We feel separated and disconnected from everyone—even sometimes God. The truth is, just like God never abandoned Jesus on the cross, God promises to never abandon us. We can trust that God is with us when we feel lonely.**

Closing Prayer

Togetherness Prayers

Form a circle. Encourage kids to sit with their eyes closed as you begin to pray. Tell kids that as you pray, you'll pause after each sentence. When you do, ask kids to look up and mimic your actions.

Say: **God, help me when I'm lonely.** (Stand with your hands by your sides and stare at the ground.) **Remind me that you're always with me.** (Wrap your arms around yourself.) **Thank you for placing people in my life who love me.** (Loop your arms through the arms of the people on either side of you.) **In Jesus' name, amen.**

Lonely

"I feel lonely when..."

"I feel lonely when..."

"I feel lonely when..."

"I feel lonely when..."

"I feel lonely when..."

"I feel lonely when..."

"I feel lonely when..."

Dinner With a Sinner

Jesus shows love to everyone

AGE GROUP

Early Elementary

SCRIPTURE

Luke 19:1-10

SUPPLIES

You'll need a Bible.

PREPARATION

None needed.

Have kids sit in a circle or around tables. Open your Bible to Luke 19:1-10. Show children the words and tell them the Bible is God's special book.

Say: **In this passage we learn about Zacchaeus, a tax collector in Jericho. Not many people liked him. He worked for the Romans, who were mean to the Jews. Tax collectors would take money from the Jews to pay the Romans, but they also cheated the people and took lots of money for themselves. Zacchaeus was different, and people didn't like him because of that.** (Have everyone stand.) **I want everyone who's wearing something blue to sit down.** (Pause.) **Now everyone with tennis shoes on, sit down.** (Pause.) **If you have green on, stand up.** (Pause.) **Now everyone, please sit back in our circle.** (Pause.)

Ask:

- *Describe what it was like when you had to stand or sit because of your differences.*
- *Tell about a time you were different from others and everyone knew it.*

Say: **The Jews did not like people who were different, like Zacchaeus. One day, Jesus was in town. Whenever he came, large groups of people gathered around to hear him talk. Zacchaeus wanted to hear him but couldn't see over all the people. He was too short. He found a nearby sycamore tree and climbed up it to see Jesus. When Jesus saw Zacchaeus, he told him to come down. "Quick," Jesus said, "for I am going to be a guest in your house today." Zacchaeus was excited that Jesus wanted to come to his house. But the crowd around Jesus wasn't happy because Jesus was going to the home of a sinner. Jesus knew this would upset the people, and he told them, "Salvation has come to this home today. For the Son of Man came to seek and save those who are lost."**

Ask:

- *Tell about a time someone did something to you that you didn't like.*
- *Why can it be hard to love people who do things we don't like?*
- *How can we show love to the people in our lives who've upset us?*

Say: **Jesus loved Zacchaeus even though he wasn't a good person and he cheated people out of money. But Jesus knew Zacchaeus could change by becoming a Christian and following him.**

Closing Prayer

Example of Love

Say: **Dear God, we thank you so much for Jesus. We know he's a great example of love. Jesus loved others even when no one else loved them. Please help us learn to be more like Jesus each and every day. In Jesus' name, amen.**

A Basket Ride to Safety

Telling others about Jesus is loving

Have children sit in a circle or around tables. Open your Bible to Acts 9:19-31. Show kids the words and tell them the Bible is God's special book.

Say: **This part of the Bible tells us that being a Christian during Saul's time was very dangerous. Many were put in prison and some were killed. Saul had once been an enemy of Christians, searching for them and putting them in prison. But when he became a Christian, he was so excited that he started telling everyone about Jesus. Many people argued with Saul and became angry with him. They were so mad, they wanted to capture and kill Saul. When Saul heard that, he wasn't afraid because he knew God would take care of him. Other Christians came up with a plan to help Saul escape. There was a big wall all around the city. Some people lived next to the wall and had windows.** (Have kids pass around the picture of a window.) **They could look out those windows—and maybe even escape through them!** (Next, let kids pass around the basket and encourage them to feel its texture. Then distribute a small piece of rope or twine to each child.) **Saul's friends helped him escape from the city by lowering him down the wall in a basket with ropes.**

Ask:

- *Imagine you were looking out a window in your house right now. What kinds of things would you see? When we look out our window and see people who don't know about Jesus, what do you think we could do?*
- *When you think about the rough texture of the basket, that's kind of like the rough time Saul had. How do you think he was so brave even when people wanted to kill him for talking about Jesus?*
- *When you think about the rope and how strong it had to be to lower a big man to the ground and let him fall, how do you think that's like or unlike how God protects us?*

Say: **Saul knew others needed to hear the good news about Jesus. But he also needed the support and love of his fellow Christians and trust in God's protection to keep him safe.**

Closing Prayer
Loving Links

Have children stand in a circle, shoulder to shoulder.

Say: **Dear God, help us to remember how you work in our lives. Remind us to follow Saul's example and love others, even when it's risky.** (Have kids link arms.) **Please help us have faith in your strong protection, just as you protected Saul. Remind us to look for opportunities to share your love with others and take care of them. In Jesus' name, amen.**

Two Coins and a Big Heart

We give our best to God

AGE GROUP

Early Elementary

SCRIPTURE

Mark 12:41-44

SUPPLIES

You'll need a Bible, 3 sacks, lots of coins, and an open box.

PREPARATION

Put many coins in two sacks so they jingle loudly. Put two coins in the third sack.

Have kids sit in a circle or around tables. Open your Bible to Mark 12:41-44. Show kids the words and tell them the Bible is God's special book.

Say: **Jesus was in the Temple, watching people drop their money in a box as an offering.** (Set the box in front of kids.) **Many of those who put in a lot of money were rich.** (Walk by the box jingling the money in the two bags and drop a small handful of coins from one bag into the box. Make a big deal of this.) **Then a woman whose husband had died came into the Temple. She was poor and had hardly any money to live on. When she came by the box, she dropped in two coins.** (Approach the box as you jingle the sack with two coins; then empty both coins into the box.)

Ask:

- *In your opinion, who do you think gave more to Jesus, and why?*

Say: **Let's see what Jesus said about this situation. He told the disciples, "I tell you the truth, this poor widow has given more than all the others!"**

The rich people gave money after they bought everything they needed, while the widow gave God all she had.

Ask:

- *Explain what you think Jesus meant when he said that.*
- *What's the difference between giving some and giving all—whether it's money, effort, or love?*
- *Tell about a time you gave all you had.*

Say: **Giving our all to God is important, and sometimes it means giving up some of our comforts to help God's kingdom. God asks us to give just like the widow gave.**

Closing Prayer

Giving All

If you'd like to donate the coins from this activity to your church, then distribute them to the kids and pass around the box as you read the Closing Prayer. Encourage kids to drop the coins in the box. Then bring the box to the church office.

Say: **Dear God, you've blessed us with so much. We have food to eat, clothes to wear, and a roof over our heads. Help us to find ways to give back to you so that we can bless others around us. In Jesus' name amen.**

Greedy Gehazi

Love of money can have terrible consequences

AGE GROUP

Upper Elementary

SCRIPTURE

2 Kings 5:5, 20-27

SUPPLIES

You'll need a Bible and a paper bag with flour inside. For each child, you'll also need 1 small paper bag with coins or dry beans inside.

PREPARATION

None needed.

Have kids sit in a circle or around tables. Open your Bible to 2 Kings 5:5, 20-27. Show kids the words and tell them the Bible is God's special book.

Distribute sacks of coins (or dry beans) for kids to hold. Instruct them that each time you say "Gehazi" as you retell the passage, they'll shake their bag of coins.

Say: **Gehazi** (shake bags) **was the servant of the prophet Elisha. He saw many miracles that Elisha performed. Gehazi** (shake bags) **was a good helper for Elisha—but he was also greedy and deceitful. That means he wanted more than his share and he didn't always tell the truth.**

When Elisha healed Naaman's sickness, Naaman wanted to pay Elisha with gifts of gold, silver, and fine clothes. But Elisha refused the gifts. After Naaman left, Gehazi (shake bags) **followed Naaman and said Elisha changed his mind about the gifts. But Gehazi** (shake bags) **was lying. He wanted the gifts for himself. Naaman gave the gifts to Gehazi** (shake bags)**, and Gehazi** (shake bags) **hid them in his room. But Elisha knew what had happened.**

Reach into the bag of flour like you're reaching for coins. Cover your hand in flour and hold it up for kids to see, as if you have leprosy.

Say: **Elisha said because of his greed, Gehazi** (shake bags) **and his family would have Naaman's sickness of leprosy forever.** (Hold up your hand again.) **He immediately got sick and the Bible tells us his skin was as white as snow.**

Ask:

- *What surprised you about Gehazi's greed?*
- *Tell about a time you wanted something so badly you considered lying to get it. What did you do?*
- *Why do you think people sometimes like money so much they'll lie to get it?*

Say: **Greed for money was the reason Gehazi lied and stole from Naaman. Even though he'd seen all the wonderful things God did through Elisha's miracles, he still gave into a desire for money. Gehazi wasn't listening to God—he was listening to greed!**

Closing Prayer

Guide against greed

Have children form a circle holding hands and the bags of coins at the same time.

Say: **Dear God, thank you for taking care of us each and every day and providing for what we need. Guide us to not give into greed and the desire for things we don't need. Remind us to listen to you, not to greed. In Jesus' name, amen.**

I See Water

Obeying God is wise

AGE GROUP

Early Elementary

SCRIPTURE

Jonah

SUPPLIES

You'll need a Bible. For each child, you'll need a 12oz bottled water. You'll also need an assortment of small rocks and twigs that'll fit into the bottles, blue food coloring, blue glitter, and small craft foam fish. inside.

PREPARATION

Remove the labels from the bottled water.

Have kids sit in a circle or around tables. Open your Bible to the book of Jonah. Show children the words and tell them the Bible is God's special book.

Say: **In this passage of the Bible, we'll learn about Jonah, a man who didn't obey God very well. You can help me tell what happened to Jonah.** (Give kids their water bottles.)

"Go to the town of Nineveh and tell the people there about me," God told Jonah. But Jonah didn't want to go to the town because it wasn't a very nice place. Instead he got on a ship headed the opposite direction from Nineveh. (Help kids add glitter and food coloring to their water bottles.) **But God always knew where Jonah was—far from land in the middle of the sea.** (Help kids add small twigs, rocks, and foam fish to their bottles and then tightly screw on the lids.) **While Jonah was on the ship, God sent a terrible storm.** (Have kids shake their bottles and continue until the storm stops.) **The ship was about to sink. The sailors were afraid, so they began throwing things overboard. When the captain found Jonah, he asked him to pray for God to stop the storm.**

"I'm running from God," Jonah said. "This is my fault. You must throw me into the sea." So they threw Jonah into the sea, and the storm stopped right away. (Hold bottles still.)

God had prepared a great big fish to come and swallow Jonah after he was thrown into the sea. Jonah was inside the fish for three nights. During that time, Jonah prayed to God to save him. Then God ordered the big fish to spit out Jonah, and Jonah was safe. He then went to Nineveh as God had told him, and he told the people there about God. Everyone in Nineveh believed Jonah and asked God for forgiveness.

Ask:

- *What do you think it means to be obedient to God?*
- *Describe a time it was difficult for you to obey someone.*
- *Why do you think it's a good idea to obey God's commands?*

Say: **Even though Jonah disobeyed God, God loved him anyway. God got Jonah's attention in a big way. When Jonah thought about it, he knew it was wise to obey God because God knows what he's doing. We're all like Jonah sometimes and we need God's love and patience as we learn to obey him.**

Closing Prayer

Love and Obey

Say: **Dear God, it's hard for us to obey your commands at times. It's also hard to obey our parents, teachers, and other adults when we feel like disobeying.** (Have kids close their eyes and think of one way it's hard for them to obey as they rock their bottles to make waves.) **Remind us of the love and patience you had with Jonah when he didn't obey and remind us that your ways are the best ways. In Jesus' name, amen.**

Moses and the Bronze Snake

God shows mercy when we disobey

AGE GROUP

Upper Elementary

SCRIPTURE

Numbers 21:4-9

SUPPLIES

You'll need a Bible and bronze paint. For each child, you'll need an empty paper towel roll, a paintbrush, scissors, markers, glue, and a set of googly eyes.

PREPARATION

None needed.

Have kids sit in a circle or around tables. Open your Bible to Numbers 21:4-9. Show children the words and tell them the Bible is God's special book.

Say: **In this Bible passage, we learn how the Israelites were God's chosen people. Through them, God's plan was to save the sinful world. But just like us today, the Israelites kept sinning and messing up, even when God told them to stop. The people of Israel were taking the road to the Red Sea when they got angry and impatient from the long journey. They began to complain. They whined about God bringing them out of Egypt just to let them die in the wilderness. They griped about the food God had given them. The Israelites were unhappy and blamed God. Finally, God had had enough of their disobedience. He sent poisonous snakes, and many people were bitten and died. The people cried to Moses for help. Moses prayed for God to forgive the people and to take away the snakes.**

God did forgive them. He told Moses to make a bronze snake and to put it on a pole. Whoever looked at the bronze snake would be healed.

Ask:

- *Tell about a time you acted similar to how the Israelites were acting.*
- *When have you disobeyed God?*
- *What does it mean to you that God forgave the Israelites' disobedience?*

Say: **We're going to make bronze snakes to remind us of God's forgiveness and mercy.**

Have kids cut a snake coil out of a tube starting from one end and cutting in a spiral around to the other end of the tube. Have kids cut out a notch on one end for the snake's tongue. Have kids paint or color their snake bronze. Allow them to dry. Then kids can use markers to decorate the snake, and add googly eyes. Tell kids to place their snakes somewhere to remind them that God forgave the Israelites even though they kept disobeying him, and he'll forgive us when we ask, too.

Say: **The Israelites were constantly complaining, even though God was taking care of them. There were consequences for their disobedience. But even though they disobeyed, God never stopped loving them. He forgave them and showed mercy, and he does the same for us.**

Closing Prayer

Follow Jesus' Footsteps

Have kids form a circle with their snakes in their left hand and the other hand on the shoulder of the person to their right.

Say: **Dear God, thank you for forgiving us when we sin and disobey you. Thank you for showing mercy to the Israelites through the bronze snake. Please guide us to be obedient to your commands and to follow in Jesus footsteps. In Jesus' name, amen.**

Don't Get Burned

We don't have to follow everyone else

AGE GROUP

Early Elementary

SCRIPTURE

Daniel 3

SUPPLIES

You'll need a Bible, a whiteboard, and dry-erase markers.

PREPARATION

Write at the top of the whiteboard: "Advice, please."

Have kids sit in a circle or around tables. Open your Bible to Daniel 3. Show them the words and tell them the Bible is God's special book.

Say: **The Bible tells us King Nebuchadnezzar was a king who didn't love God. He made a huge statue of gold and told his people to bow down to it when they heard musical instruments. If anyone refused, the king would have that person thrown into the fiery furnace. That was a lot of peer pressure! Many people knew it was wrong to do, but they followed the king's orders anyway because everyone else was doing it and they didn't want to be put in the furnace.**

Show kids the whiteboard with the words "Advice, please."

Say: **In news magazines and on the Internet, there are lots of advice columns. An advice column is where readers write in to ask questions and a columnist responds with advice. Let's be the columnist and answer a reader's question. Here's the question: "Today I was told by the king to either bow down to a gold statue or be thrown into a fiery furnace. What should I do?" Let's come up with encouraging answers to this question.**

Allow time for kids to each give their advice. Write a summarization of each child's answer on the board.

Say: **At the sound of the instruments, everyone bowed down to worship the statue. Well, that is everyone except Shadrach, Meshach, and Abednego. This made the king angry and he ordered them to come at once. When they arrived, he asked if they were going to bow down. They said that they wouldn't worship him or any other false god because they only served God. This made the king even angrier and he ordered the guards to make the fire in the furnace three times hotter. Then he threw them into the fire!**

When the king and his men looked inside the furnace, they saw four men instead of three, and they were alive! Confused, the king brought them out of the furnace. They weren't burned at all! Everyone was amazed. It was incredible. King Nebuchadnezzar said, "Praise to the God of Shadrach, Meshach, and Abednego! He sent an angel (the man in the furnace with them) to rescue his servants who trusted him." The king then set a decree that no one could speak against God or the three men.

Ask:

- *Look back on the advice you gave a few minutes ago. Explain whether you would change it— and how—now that you know the whole story.*
- *Tell about a time you did something just because all of your friends were doing it. What happened?*
- *When you feel pressured to do something you know is wrong, what can you do?*

Say: **It's easy to give advice to someone, but sometimes it's hard to follow good advice. These three friends faced something really scary together if they didn't follow what everyone else was doing. The choice to stand up to the king could have gotten them killed. But they showed us how to follow God's will—and not get burned!**

Closing Prayer
Stand Up for What's Right

Have kids form a circle on the floor, facing outward so they're not looking at each other.

Say: **Dear God, it's easy to want to be part of the group, even when the group is doing things that we know you don't want us to do. Please remind all the kids here today that you want us to follow you, not the group. Please give kids your strength and courage to face peer pressure as you did the three friends. Remind them to always stand up for what's right. In Jesus' name, amen.**

Standing Strong

Jesus gives us strength to do what is right

**ave kids sit in a circle or around tables. Open your Bible to John 18:15-18, 25-27.
Show kids the words and tell them the Bible is God's special book.

Say: **The Bible tells us about Peter, one of Jesus' disciples. Peter was faced with a very
tough decision.** (Give each child a stone.) **In Matthew 16:18, Jesus told Peter he was Jesus'
rock. Jesus knew Peter loved him very much. And later on when Jesus was arrested, Peter told
Jesus he'd never deny knowing Jesus if someone asked. But Jesus told Peter that even before
the rooster crowed, he would deny Jesus three times. Peter was shocked. He told Jesus he
would never do such a thing! When the soldiers arrested Jesus, Peter followed at a distance
to see what would happen. He waited outside the gate, and a servant girl approached him.
"Aren't you Jesus' disciple?" she asked. Suddenly, Peter was afraid. What might happen to
him if he said yes? "No!" Peter said. Two more times people asked whether Peter was a disciple of Jesus, and two more times Peter answered "No! I am not!" Immediately after the last
time, a rooster crowed and Peter remembered what Jesus had said. He cried when he realized
what he had done because he was afraid of what others would think and do.**

Ask:

- *Tell about a time you made a bad decision because you were afraid of what people would think.*
- *Why do you think Peter may have denied knowing Jesus?*
- *What can you do the next time you're afraid of what others think about you?*
- *What's one way Jesus helps you stay strong when you feel weak?*

Set out markers. Say: **We're going to write "Strong" on our rocks to remind us to be strong
and have faith in Jesus when we are afraid.** (Allow time.) **Keep your stone in your pocket or
bag. The next time you feel pressured or afraid of what others will think, the rock can remind
you to stay strong.**

**Remember: Peter had good intentions, but intentions aren't enough. It's our actions that
count. Peter learned from his mistake and became a great leader for Jesus. We can remember that if we follow Jesus, we don't have to be worried about what others think or do. Jesus
gives us the strength to do what's right if we trust in him.**

Closing Prayer
Rock Solid

Have kids hold their stones as you pray.
Say: **Dear God, we can always trust in you and not worry about what others think or do.
Remind us to focus always on what you want us to do, not what others tell us we should do.
Give us the strength to do what's right and to share your love with others. In Jesus' name,
amen.**

Breaking Free

Our worship during difficulty encourages others

Have kids sit in a circle or around tables. Open your Bible to Acts 16:16-34. Show children the words and tell them the Bible is God's special book.

Say: **The Bible tells us God wants us to praise and worship him in all situations. Praising God is good for us because it helps us focus on him. And as we worship God, it encourages others to worship him, too.**

Paul and Silas experienced how worshipping God was an encouragement to others. In Acts 16:16-34, we read about when Paul and Silas were going to pray and they met a slave girl who had an evil spirit. They healed her, but that made her owner angry because she made money for him. Paul and Silas were arrested, beaten, and then put into prison where a jailer was ordered to watch them. It was close to midnight, and Paul and Silas were praying and singing hymns to God. The other prisoners listened to them sing, but the jailer had fallen asleep.

Suddenly, there was an earthquake. All the doors in the prison opened and the chains fell off the prisoners. When the jailer woke and saw the doors open, he was terrified and thought the prisoners had escaped. He was about to hurt himself when Paul yelled at him, "Stop! We are here!" The jailer found them and, amazed, asked, "What must I do to be saved?" They shared the gospel with him—and he and his entire family became followers that night.

Ask:

- *Why is it important to you to praise and worship God?*
- *Paul and Silas were in trouble and in prison. Why do you think singing praise to God may have helped in that situation?*
- *Tell about a time you were afraid to worship God but did so anyway.*

Say: **The Bible tells us it's important to praise God—not just because he enjoys it, but because it benefits us, too. He wants our praise in all situations, good and bad. When we're sad and lonely and scared, we can sit and reflect with God. Our focus on God during good and bad times will encourage us—and the people who see that we rely on God.**

Closing Prayer
Strength in Praise

Have kids stand in a circle and link arms.

Say: **Dear God, thank you for blessing us with the ability to worship and praise you like Paul and Silas did. We know our praise is sweet music to your ears—and ours! Give us the strength and desire to praise you everyday in all situations. Let our praise of you be an encouragement to others and to us, as well. In Jesus' name, amen.**

Believing Is Seeing

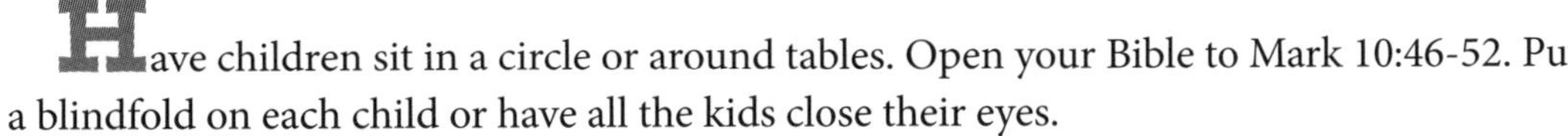

We praise Jesus and ask for his help

AGE GROUP

Upper Elementary

SCRIPTURE

Mark 10:46-52

SUPPLIES

You'll need a Bible, a blindfold for each child (optional), and a pair of shoes.

PREPARATION

Clear an area of obstacles for this activity.

Have children sit in a circle or around tables. Open your Bible to Mark 10:46-52. Put a blindfold on each child or have all the kids close their eyes.

Say: **The Bible tells us Bartimaeus was a blind man who had to beg for food and money outside the city of Jericho. One day, Jesus, his disciples, and a crowd of people were walking along the road.** (Use shoes to make the sound of people walking by.) **Bartimaeus heard all the noise. When he found out it was Jesus, he called out, "Jesus, Son of David, have mercy on me!"**

People around Bartimaeus told him to be quiet, but he refused. He kept calling out and praising him until Jesus heard it. Jesus came over and asked what Bartimaeus wanted. Bartimaeus said simply, "I want to see."

Then Jesus touched his eyes and told him his faith had made him well. (Have kids uncover their eyes.) **Instantly, Bartimaeus could see. He followed Jesus and praised God as he went.**

Say: **Let's explore what this might have been like for Bartimaeus.**

Have kids put their blindfolds back on or close their eyes and then get on the floor on their hands and knees. Ensure there are no major obstacles in your area, such as chairs and tables. Tell kids you're going to take the shoes and go to another part of your room. You'll "walk" the shoes on the floor as if Jesus is coming along the path. They must crawl over to find the path where Jesus is and cry out, "Jesus, Son of David, have mercy on me!" until all of them reach you. Play a couple rounds if you have time.

Ask:

- *What was this experience like for you?*
- *How easy or difficult do you imagine Bartimaeus' life might have been, and why?*
- *What do you think it means to praise God no matter what's happening in our life?*
- *Tell about a time you didn't feel like praising God.*
- *What do you think Bartimaeus' experience tells us about Jesus?*

Say: **Bartimaeus was a poor, blind man, but he still had faith in Jesus and proclaimed it loudly. And he wasn't afraid to ask Jesus for help. No matter what our situation is, we can all praise Jesus and ask him to help us. Jesus wants us to praise him and ask him to come into our lives, just as Bartimaeus did.**

Closing Prayer
Praise God always

Have kids form a circle and put their blindfolds back on.

Say: **Dear God, we know life isn't always easy. Sometimes it's very hard and challenging and it can be easy to forget to praise you during those times. Please forgive us for forgetting to praise you in all situations, and give us the courage to seek your help when we need it. We know you love us and have good things for us. Remind us to always praise your name for the wonderful life you've given us. In Jesus' name, amen.**

God's Listening

God wants to hear our prayers

AGE GROUP

Early Elementary

SCRIPTURE

Philippians 4:4-7

SUPPLIES

You'll need a Bible. For each child, you'll need a copy of the "Pray About Everything" handout and markers.

PREPARATION

None needed.

Have children sit in a circle or around tables. Open your Bible to Philippians 4:4-7. Show children the words and tell them the Bible is God's special book.

Say: **Jesus' disciple Paul wrote a letter encouraging people to pray.**

Read the passage. Then say: **God wants us to pray all the time, for everything, so we can connect with God and build a relationship with him.**

Hold up the handout.

Say: **God wants us to be thankful for everything.** (Point to the "THANK YOU" on the handout.) **God wants us to ask for things we need.** (Point to the "I NEED.") **God wants us to say we're sorry for times when we disobey him or when we do something that hurts ourselves or others.** (Point to the "I'M SORRY.")

Now let's spend some time in groups drawing pictures to remind us of things we're thankful for, things we need, and things we're sorry about.

Give each child a handout and form three groups. Assign each group one of the prayer types, and have kids circle it on their handouts. Then ask them to flip their handouts over and write about or draw pictures of things based on the prayer topic you gave them: things they're thankful for, things they want and need, or things they're sorry for. Encourage them to talk with each other about what they're drawing.

After completing the handout, have everyone sit in a circle or around tables and share their drawings with the rest of the group.

Ask:

- *What does it mean to you to be thankful?*
- *Why do you think God sometimes says "No" when we ask for something we want or need?*
- *Why is it important to say we're sorry to God?*

Say: **God wants us to be thankful, ask for things, and say we're sorry when we mess up. No matter what, God wants us to tell him everything.**

Closing Prayer

Pray-for-Everything Prayer

Lead kids in motions while you pray, starting with prayer hands.

Say: **Dear God, we thank you for sending your Son, Jesus, for being an incredible God, and for listening to us** (cups hands around ears). **We know we have so many needs** (hold hands out, palms up). **Please continue to meet our needs and answer our prayers** (put your hands on your heart). **We're sorry for hurting others and disobeying you. We love you. In Jesus' name, amen.**

THANK YOU

I NEED

I'M SORRY

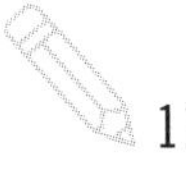

Praying A.C.T.S. to God

We can pray the Lord's Prayer

AGE GROUP

Upper Elementary

SCRIPTURE

Matthew 6:5-15

SUPPLIES

You'll need a Bible, classical or worship music and music player, and flicker lights. For each child, you'll need a copy of the "A.C.T.S." handout and a pencil.

PREPARATION

None needed.

Have children sit in a circle or around tables. Open your Bible to Matthew 6:5-15. Show children the words and tell them the Bible is God's special book.

Say: **The Bible tells us that God wants to have a relationship with us. As in any relationship, having conversations helps build a bond and talking nurtures the relationship. Prayer is simply talking with God and having a relationship with him.** Show the handout.

Say: **First, God wants us to ADORE him and worship him for being God.** (Point to the "A" on the handout.) **We are to love God not for what he gives us but simply because he is God.**

Second, God wants us to CONFESS our sins. (Point to the "C.") **Everyone sins, disobeys God, and makes mistakes. God wants us to admit when we've done something wrong. It helps us reconnect with our Lord.**

Third, we connect with God by being THANKFUL. (Point to the "T.") **Recognizing our blessings and expressing gratitude helps us remember that God cares and provides for us.**

Finally, we offer SUPPLICATION to God. (Point to the "S.") **Supplication means we are humbly asking God for something. God wants to provide for us, but he wants us to ask. We can ask God for healing, food, love, and other things.**

Say: **Jesus said that when we pray, we are to go into our rooms, close the door, and pray alone. Let's spend some time filling out this handout and then praying alone today.**

Give each child a handout. Have them write things they ADORE about God next to the "A" on the handout, things they need to CONFESS next to the "C" on the handout, things they're THANKFUL for next to the "T" on the handout, and things they want to SUPPLI-CATE next to the "S" on the handout. While children fill out the handout, play some soft music and turn on the flicker lights. Have the children pray silently as they write. After some time of silent prayer, have children sit in a circle or around the table.

Ask:

- *How can adoring God, thanking God, and confessing your sins to God bring you closer to God?*
- *Why do you think God wants us to come to him in prayer?*

Say: **By adoring God, confessing our sins to God, thanking God, and asking God to meet our needs, we build our relationship with God and connect to him daily.**

Closing Prayer

Acts

Ask kids to form their hands in the shape of either A, C, T, or S as you pray.

Say: **Dear God, we adore you for being you. Please forgive our sins and help us to always be grateful for everything you've given us. Please hear our needs and continue to provide for us. In Jesus' name, amen.**

A.C.T.S.

A.

C.

T.

S.

Simon Says Stand Up

God stands with us under pressure

AGE GROUP

Early Elementary

SCRIPTURE

Daniel 6:1-28

SUPPLIES

You'll need a Bible.

PREPARATION

None needed.

Gather children in a circle. Have them stand arms' width apart.

Say: **We're going to play Simon Says. Remember the one main rule: Only do what I say if I say "Simon says." If I don't say "Simon says," stand still. Ready?**

Begin with normal Simon Says actions, like jumping on one foot and patting your head. Continue playing the normal way for a few minutes.

Then use the following commands:

- **Simon says, kneel on the ground.**
- **Don't pray.**
- **Simon says, don't pray.**
- **Stand up.**
- **Simon says, stand up.**
- **Simon says put both hands in the air.**
- **Simon says, don't worship God.**

Tell kids the game is over and ask them to sit down exactly where they are. You may have to say, "Simon says, sit down where you are because the game is over."

Ask:

- *Describe what this game was like for you.*
- *What were you thinking when I told you to do things you might not feel comfortable with?*
- *How was our game like or unlike what happens in real life with friends sometimes?*

Say: **Sometimes we're pressured into doing things we don't want to do or things that go against what we believe to be right. Kids at school may be bullying someone and may pressure you not to tell on them. Someone may pressure you to cheat or lie. God wants us to know that he'll always be with us no matter how much pressure we are under.**

Open your Bible to Daniel 6:1-28. Show children the words and tell them the Bible is God's special book.

Say: **This part of the Bible tells about Daniel. People were jealous of Daniel's important job, so they convinced the king to make a law that anyone caught worshipping or praying to anyone other than the king would be thrown into the lions' den with a bunch of hungry lions! They knew that Daniel worshipped God and that this would get him in trouble.**

Their plan worked...kind of. The king signed the law, and Daniel was caught breaking the law because he was praying to God. The king was sad because he liked Daniel, but this was a law that he had signed. So he had Daniel thrown into the lions' den. The next day when the king went to check on Daniel, he found him alive! Daniel said, "My God sent his angel to shut the lions' mouths so that they would not hurt me."

Ask:

- *How do you normally deal with pressure at school?*
- *How can God help you with school pressures?*
- *How does knowing God is always with you help you to stand up to school pressure?*

Say: **God stood with Daniel and gave him the strength to keep praying even when the king told him not to pray. God also stood by Daniel and gave him the strength to stand firm in the lions' den. God will stand by us, too, and give us strength when we face pressures to do things that go against what we believe to be right and good.**

Closing Prayer
In the Den of Lions

Have kids stand tall as you pray.

Say: **Dear God, our young people face so many pressures every day at school. Kids may pressure them to disobey you or do things that'll displease you. Help them to stand up to others in the same way Daniel stood up to his enemies—and to the lions in the den. In Jesus' name, amen.**

Taking the Heat

God helps us stand firm

AGE GROUP

Upper Elementary

SCRIPTURE

Daniel 3:1-18

SUPPLIES

You'll need a Bible.

PREPARATION

None needed.

Have children form two groups.

Say: **We are going to have a relay race with a twist. Each group needs to come up with three rules the other team members must obey to win a relay race, such as hopping on one foot, closing their eyes, and patting their head.**

After each group comes up with its three rules, have them share their rules with the other team. Then announce this additional rule for both teams: They must also run the entire relay race facing backward.

After the race, gather kids for discussion.

Ask:

- *Describe what it was like for you to follow the rules your team was given.*
- *What was the worst thing about this game, and why?*

Say: **This race was fun, and maybe you were asked to do some things you didn't really want to do. Sometimes we're pressured to do things we don't want to do or to do things that go against God's will. God will always be with us and will never abandon us, but when we are pressured at school, it can be very hard to resist and stay strong. Let's see about what some friends faced during the time of King Nebuchadnezzar.**

Open your Bible to Daniel 3:1-18. Show children the words and tell them the Bible is God's special book. Read the passage aloud.

Ask:

- *What are some specific pressures you face at school?*
- *How does God help you with those school pressures?*
- *How do you stand against pressures that go against God and God's will?*

Say: **When Shadrach, Meshach, and Abednego stood up for their faith and resisted pressure, they were thrown into a fiery furnace, but God stood with them, gave them strength, and sent an angel to save them from the fire. God will help you withstand the fires of school pressure as well. Trust in God and he'll help you stand firm.**

Closing Prayer

The Fiery Pressure Furnace

Have kids put their arms up over their heads, hands together as if making a flame.

Say: **Dear God, every day we encounter the fiery furnaces of school pressure. Sometimes our friends and classmates can try to pressure us into doing things we feel are wrong or that go against you and your will. Help us stand firm in the face of pressure and remind us that you'll never leave us. In Jesus' name, amen.**

White as Snow

Jesus gave his life to make us clean

AGE GROUP

Early Elementary

SCRIPTURE

Isaiah 1:18;
Romans 6:23

SUPPLIES

You'll need a Bible, a pitcher half full of plain tap water, iodine, and a pitcher half full of water and bleach (adult use only). For the Closing Prayer, you'll need a new pitcher of drinking water and cups.

PREPARATION

Test this experiment beforehand to ensure the mixture of bleach and water is enough to clear the pitcher of water and iodine. Set all the ingredients out of kids' reach and take precautions so they can't get to it.

Have children sit in a circle or around tables.

Say: **When God created humans, he created them perfect with no sin.** (Show the pitcher with clear tap water.) **When Adam and Eve disobeyed God, sin entered the world. Adam and Eve and every human being after them sinned and were unclean.** (Pour some iodine in the pitcher of clear tap water.) **People couldn't connect with God or be near God. They had to be punished for their sin, and people would eventually die because of their sin. In order to be protected from their punishment and death, people needed to be clean, but they couldn't clean themselves. So God sent his only Son, Jesus, to clean them up.**

Open your Bible to Isaiah 1:18. Show children the words and tell them the Bible is God's special book. Read the Scripture aloud. Then pour the bleach water into the pitcher to make it clear again.

Say: **Jesus died on the cross to take away our sins and receive our punishment. God loves us so much and wants us to live with him forever in heaven; that's why God sent Jesus to die for us.**

Next read Romans 6:23.

Ask:

- *How does your sin separate you from God?*
- *What does it mean to you that Jesus died for your sins and made you clean again?*
- *What do you think it means to have eternal life?*

Say: **God sent Jesus to die for our sins, make us clean, and give us eternal life in heaven. God wants us to love him and stay connected to him.**

Closing Prayer

Clear as Water

Give each child a cup of fresh water.

Say: **Dear God, we thank you for sending Jesus and making us clean. Thank you for making it possible for us to live with you forever in heaven. In Jesus' name, amen.**

Have kids drink their clear water.

Triumph Over Sin

Jesus died so we can have eternal life

AGE GROUP

Upper Elementary

SCRIPTURE

Romans 3:22-25;
Colossians 2:13-15

SUPPLIES

You'll need a Bible,
note cards, markers,
thumbtacks, and
a big cross made
out of poster board.
For the Closing
Prayer, you'll need a
medium-sized nail
for each child.

PREPARATION

Create a cross out
of poster board in
advance.

Have children gather around the large cross you prepared. Set out a stack of note cards, markers, and thumbtacks.

Say: **We all sin and disobey God. Think of some specific sins you struggle with, like being jealous of someone or lying or cheating. Spend some time thinking about those sins and write them down on separate note cards.**

Allow a few minutes, and then say: **God sent his only Son, Jesus, to die for our sins and make it so we don't have to be punished for them anymore. Jesus took our sins away and nailed them to the cross, just like we are going to do right now.**

Open your Bible to Colossians 2:13-15. Show children the words and tell them the Bible is God's special book. Read the passage aloud. Then read it a second time while children use thumbtacks to stick their cards to the cross.

Say: **Jesus was innocent and didn't sin, but he died so that all people could have their sins forgiven.**

Read Romans 3:22-25.

Ask:

- *How does your sin separate you from God?*
- *What does it mean to you that Jesus died and nailed your sins to the cross?*
- *What do you think it means to be made right with God?*

Say: **God sent Jesus to die on the cross, nail our sins to the cross, and make it possible for us to live forever with God in heaven. God wants us to love him and stay connected to him.**

Closing Prayer

Nailed to the Cross

Give each child a medium-sized nail.

Say: **Dear Jesus, thank you for dying for our sins and nailing them to the cross. Thank you for giving us new life and removing our sins. In Jesus' name, amen.**

Have kids each push their nail in the center of the poster board cross, making the shape of a heart.

Bag of Burdens

God knows what it's like to be sad

AGE GROUP

Early Elementary

SCRIPTURE

Matthew 26:36-39;
Galatians 6:2

SUPPLIES

You'll need a Bible,
heavy books, and
large cloth bags with
handles.

PREPARATION

None needed.

Gather kids together. Open your Bible to Matthew 26:36-39. Show children the words and tell them the Bible is God's special book. Read the verses aloud.

Say: **Sadness is something everyone experiences. In fact, the Bible even describes Jesus as being so sad that his soul was "crushed with grief." Let's think more about what that feels like.**

Have kids place their hands on the ground with their palms up. Place a heavy book in each child's hands. Invite children to share about a time sadness felt like it was weighing them down or crushing them like the book feels in their hands.

Then read Galatians 6:2 aloud.

Say: **One way God helps us deal with sadness is by putting people in our lives who bear our burdens with us. This means people who pray for us, listen to us, or just give us a hug when we're sad.**

Help kids experience what bearing others' burdens is like by having them place several of the books in a cloth bag and try to carry the bags themselves. Then have kids form partners and each take a handle of the cloth bag as they bear each other's burdens. Depending on the number of books and bags you have, they may need to take turns.

Ask:

- *What did you learn about bearing each other's burdens from this activity?*
- *What's one way you can bear someone else's burden this week?*

Say: **Just like Jesus, we too will deal with sadness and crushing grief. Like Jesus, we can cry out to God and share our burdens with others when we are overwhelmed with sadness.**

Closing Prayer

Book Prayers

Have kids hold the books in their hands.

Say: **Dear God, thank you for knowing what it's like to be crushed with grief so we don't feel so alone when we're sad. Help us to cry out to you and share our burdens with others so sadness doesn't weigh us down. In Jesus' name, amen.**

Have kids stack the books together as a reminder that it's easier to deal with sadness in our lives when we do it together.

The Face of Sadness

We pour out our tears to God

AGE GROUP

Upper Elementary

SCRIPTURE

1 Samuel 1:8-18

SUPPLIES

You'll need a Bible, a large bowl, and a pitcher of water. For each child, you'll need a copy of the "Sadness" handout, markers, and a paper cup.

PREPARATION

Fill paper cups with water for the Closing Prayer.

Choose three children to play Hannah, Elkanah, and Eli. Explain that you'll pause after each verse in today's Bible passage for them to silently act out what they've heard without using any words or sounds.

Open your Bible to 1 Samuel 1:8-18. Show children the words and tell them the Bible is God's special book. Then read the passage, pausing after each verse to allow the kids time to act.

Say: **Just as Hannah prayed and no sound came out, our actors did great with their silent actions.**

When Hannah was sad, she asked God to look upon her sorrow and answer her prayer. Let's think more about what sorrow looks like in our own lives.

Set out markers and give each child a "Sadness" handout. Have children complete the sentence on the handout. Then encourage children to draw self-portraits of what they look like when they're sad. Allow time.

Ask:

- *Tell about a time you felt sad like Hannah.*
- *What does sadness look like for you?*
- *How can you respond like Hannah did the next time you're sad?*

Say: **Sadness looks different for everyone. Some people get really quiet, some people cry bitterly like Hannah, and some people even get mad. No matter what our sadness looks like, our response can be the same as Hannah's. Like Hannah, we pour out our tears to God because God hears us.**

Closing Prayer

Pouring Out Sadness

Place the bowl at the front of the room. Give each child a cup of water. Explain to kids that the water in the cup represents their tears. Encourage kids one at a time to come up to the bowl and silently cry out to God as they pour their "tears" into the bowl.

Say: **Dear God, thank you for looking upon us just like you looked upon Hannah. Thank you for caring about our tears and the things that make us sad. Remind us to bring our tears to you because we know you answer prayer. In Jesus' name, amen.**

Sadness

"I feel sad when..."

THE **GIANT** BOOK OF CHILDREN'S MESSAGES

Blocks of Self-Esteem

God made us to be wonderful

Have children sit around your pile of blocks. Set a few of the larger blocks behind you.

Say: **Let's all build a tower with these blocks.**

When kids are finished building their tower, take the bigger blocks and set them on top, making sure the tower falls under the weight.

Say: **Sometimes kids say things to us that are bad and mean, and they tear us down like this big block broke down the tower.**

Open your Bible to Psalm 139:13-18. Show children the words and tell them the Bible is God's special book. Read the passage aloud. Then show them 2 Corinthians 5:17 and read the passage.

Say: **God values us, and our faith in Jesus makes us strong and whole. Jesus is like a strong, solid foundation to our tower. Let's build a tower again, only this time let's start with the bigger blocks and end with the smaller blocks.**

Have kids build the tower again. As they build, say: **With each block on our tower, call out one positive thing about yourself as a reminder of who you are in Jesus.**

Ask:

- *What are big blocks in your life that seem to knock you down?*
- *How can we overcome those blocks and not let them hurt us?*
- *How does God see you? What does it mean to be a new creation?*

Say: **God sees us as precious, and he made us to be wonderful. Because of Jesus, we are a new creation, pure, and beautiful.**

Closing Prayer
Blocks of Beauty

Have kids form a circle. Let them each find one block to hold.

Say: **Dear God, thank you for making us to be wonderful and beautiful. We know you value us; help us value ourselves and help us overcome those big blocks in our lives that try to tear us down. In Jesus' name, amen.**

AGE GROUP

Early Elementary

SCRIPTURE

Psalm 139:13-18;
2 Corinthians 5:17

SUPPLIES

You'll need a Bible and a pile of wooden blocks in different sizes. (Two or three should be significantly larger.)

PREPARATION

None needed.

Self-Esteem Towers

We are holy and blameless in God's sight

AGE GROUP

Upper Elementary

SCRIPTURE

Ephesians 1:3-10

SUPPLIES

You'll need a Bible, a large supply of index cards, masking tape, scissors, a pile of scrap paper, a trash can, and pencils or markers.

PREPARATION

Put a line of masking tape down the middle of the room.

Have kids form two teams. Give each team a pile of index cards and send the teams to opposite sides of the room. Say: **Work together with your team to build a tower with index cards. Fold them any way you'd like. Build your tower as strong as you can.**

Allow several minutes.

Say: **Those are some nice towers. Unfortunately, the next part of this activity is to try to knock down the other team's tower from across the room. First, you'll need to make weapons.** (Set out a stack of scrap paper and pencils or markers.) **On each paper, write words or draw things that tear people down. Then crumple the paper and throw it at the other team's tower. Don't step past the masking tape line or you'll be disqualified.**

Allow several minutes. Leave the papers on the floor for the Closing Prayer.

Then open your Bible to Ephesians 1:3-10. Show children the words and tell them the Bible is God's special book. Read the passage aloud.

Have children form groups of three. Give each group one sheet of paper and a pencil or marker. Have tape and scissors available.

Say: **Take turns writing something good about each person in your group on the paper until you have at least 20 things written. Then work on folding the paper into a block or a cube, together with your group. Your block can look or work any way you wish. Once your block is finished, talk with your group about the insults on the crumpled paper that tear down our self-esteem compared to the words on your block.**

Ask:

- *How do insults affect how you feel about yourself?*
- *How does God see you?*
- *How can God's view of us change how we view ourselves?*

Say: **God sees us as precious and he made us to be wonderful. Because of Jesus, we are a new creation, pure, and beautiful.**

Closing Prayer
God's Creation

Have kids collect the crumpled papers and gather in a circle with a trash can in the center. Let them gently toss the papers into the trash before you pray.

Say: **Dear God, we know that you see us as special and beautiful. Thank you for valuing us and sending Jesus to die for us and making us pure and blameless. Help us to always know that we are special. In Jesus' name, amen.**

The First Must Be Last

Humble yourself to serve

AGE GROUP

Early Elementary

SCRIPTURE

Mark 10:35-45

SUPPLIES

You'll need a Bible; blue, red, and white construction paper; a stopwatch; crayons; scissors; paper; and pencils.

PREPARATION

Set up an obstacle course.

Gather children around the obstacle course you created.

Say: **We're going to have a fun race through this obstacle course. But first we need to design the prizes.**

Have the children form three groups. Give group 1 the blue construction paper, group 2 the red construction paper, and group 3 the white construction paper. Have scissors, crayons, and pencils available.

Say: **The group with the blue paper is going to design a first-place ribbon. The group with the red paper is going to design a second-place ribbon. And the group with the white paper is going to design a third-place ribbon.**

Allow a few minutes. Then let groups show their ribbon creations.

Say: **Each person will go through the obstacle course one at a time. I'm going to time you to see who wins.**

Have each kid race through the obstacle course, while you time and record each performance. Make a big deal out of your last-place finishers.

Say: **Now, I'll announce the winners!**

Give the person who finished last the first-place ribbon, second to last the second-place ribbon, and third to last the third-place ribbon. Allow a minute for kids to process this.

Open your Bible to Mark 10:35-45. Show children the words and tell them the Bible is God's special book. Read the passage aloud.

Ask:

- *What surprised you about the results of our race?*
- *Tell about a time you won something and how that felt.*
- *Tell about a time you didn't win something and how that felt.*
- *What do you think it means that the "first shall be last"?*

Say: **Jesus stressed that in order to serve, we must humble ourselves and serve selflessly.** (Give each child paper and a writing utensil.) **I want you to each draw a picture of someone you can serve this week without getting anything in return.**

Allow time for kids to draw.

Ask:

- *Why do you think Jesus stressed the first being last?*
- *How can you serve someone selflessly?*
- *Why do you think it's important to be humble when we serve?*

Say: **Jesus made the point that to truly serve others, we must be humble. We must be willing—and even glad—to be last. He wants us to put selfishness aside and focus on serving others because that's what he did for us.**

Closing Prayer
Selfless Service

Gather kids in a circle. Let them pass around the three ribbons as you pray.

Say: **Dear God, when James and John fought about having a place next to you in heaven, you told them to serve humbly and stop worrying about being first. Help us to serve others as well and to know that when we follow you, we should always focus on living a selfless life and not trying to be first all the time. In Jesus' name, amen.**

Washing and Serving

Jesus tells us to put others first

AGE GROUP

Upper Elementary

SCRIPTURE

John 13:1-17

SUPPLIES

You'll need a Bible, a basin or big bowl, several towels, paper, and pencils.

PREPARATION

Fill the basin or big bowl with warm soapy water.

Gather children in a circle around the basin of water and towels. Open your Bible to John 13:1-17. Show children the words and tell them the Bible is God's special book. Read the passage aloud.

Say: **We're going to wash each other's hands to remember Jesus washing his disciples' feet. After I'm finished washing the hands of my neighbor, that person will then wash the hands of his or her neighbor to the right, dry the hands with a towel, and so on. Everyone will wash the hands of the person to the right.**

Begin by washing one child's hands and then drying them with a towel. Have kids go all the way around the circle washing their neighbor's hands until the final person's hands are washed, and then that person will wash your hands.

Say: **Jesus washed his disciples' feet to show them that there isn't a single person who is too important to serve others. Jesus was the Son of God and the promised Messiah, yet he washed his disciples' feet. Every one of us can serve others. No one is too important.**

Give each child paper and a pencil, and ask them to get into groups of two or three.

Say: **Trace your feet on the paper. Inside your left foot, write how you'll serve one person next week. You can work with your group to come up with ideas. Keep your paper with you this week. Then inside the right foot, you'll write what happened when you served the person.**

Allow time for kids to work.

Ask:

- *Why is it important to remember to be humble in all situations?*
- *What does it mean to you that Jesus was humble and selfless as he served others?*
- *Why do you think Jesus had to demonstrate humility to his disciples?*

Say: **Jesus showed us what it looks like to be humble and how it makes others feel.**

Closing Prayer

Washing Feet

Sit cross-legged with kids in a tight-knit circle. Have everyone reach out and grasp the tops of the shoes of their neighbors and hold them as you pray.

Say: **Dear God, Jesus' disciples had really dirty feet, and Jesus knelt in front of them and washed their feet. Jesus is your Son and he came to save the world, yet he still served others. Remind us to be humble and serve others without expectations. In Jesus' name, amen.**

Beads of Sharing

God wants us to share with others

AGE GROUP

Early Elementary

SCRIPTURE

Deuteronomy 24:17-22

SUPPLIES

You'll need a Bible. For each child you'll need an 18-inch length of string or yarn and 6 beads (including 1 bead each for the Closing Prayer).

PREPARATION

Cut one extra string for the Closing Prayer.

Have children sit in a circle or around tables. Give each child a string and anywhere from zero to 10 beads. Be random about how many beads each child receives, but make sure you start with enough beads that everyone will eventually have five beads after they share.

Say: **We're going to make beaded necklaces. Each necklace needs to have exactly five beads on it. You'll need to go around and ask for beads if you need them and share your beads if you have too many. You'll have three minutes to make your necklaces.**

Help as necessary. Then after three minutes, gather kids together. Let them help each other put their necklaces on.

Open your Bible to Deuteronomy 24:17-22. Show children the words and tell them the Bible is God's special book. Read the passage aloud.

Ask:

- *How was sharing important in making your beaded necklaces?*
- *Why do you think sharing is important to God?*
- *What are ways you could share in your everyday life?*

Say: **God wants us to remember that when we have more than we need, we can share it with others.**

Closing Prayer
Prayer Beads

Gather kids in a circle and give them each one bead. Put a knot in one end of the extra string.

Say: **Let's each think of someone specific that we can share with this week. I'll pass this string around, and when it comes to you, say a prayer asking God to help you share with that person as you put your bead on the string. Then pass it to the person on your right.**

Start with your own prayer request and bead. When you receive the necklace back with all the beads, finish the prayer.

Dear God, help us keep these commitments to share with others. Thank you for blessing us, and give us the courage and strength to share. In Jesus' name, amen.

Tell kids you'll use the necklace as a reminder to pray for each of them this week, asking God to help you all share.

Sharing Musical Chairs

We can share and show compassion to others

AGE GROUP

Upper Elementary

SCRIPTURE

Luke 16:19-31

SUPPLIES

You'll need a Bible, music and a music player, and a chair for every child (minus 1).

PREPARATION

Set up a circle of chairs. If you have a large and energetic group, set up one circle for boys and one for girls.

Have children sit in a circle or around tables. Open your Bible to Luke 16:19-31. Show children the words and tell them the Bible is God's special book. Read the Scripture aloud.

Say: **Let's find out more about what this passage means. We're going to play Sharing Musical Chairs. This game is just like Musical Chairs, but instead of being eliminated, the person without a chair needs to sit on someone's lap. You will each get 1 point, but if you have another person on your lap, you get 2 points and the person on your lap gets 1 point. If there are three people sitting on your lap, you get 3 points, the next person gets 2 points, and the top person gets 1 point.**

Begin the music and then stop it. Once it stops, make sure one person is sitting on someone's lap. Then remove a chair and play the music again. Have kids keep track of their own scores. By the end there will be one chair and everyone will be sitting on someone else's lap.

Ask:

- *How was sharing an important element to this game?*
- *What did our Scripture passage tell you about why it's important to share and show compassion?*
- *How were you rewarded for sharing in our game?*
- *How can you share better at school and at home?*

Say: **When God gives us more than we need, he expects us to share it with others.**

Closing Prayer
Share Prayer

Have kids pair up and share chairs.

Say: **Dear God, the rich man didn't share with Lazarus and he regretted it later. Guide us to always be mindful of the needs of others. Thank you for blessing us and help us show our gratitude by sharing those blessings with others as well as showing compassion to those less fortunate. In Jesus' name, amen.**

Put Your Light on a Stand

Let your faith shine to glorify God

AGE GROUP

Early Elementary

SCRIPTURE

Matthew 5:15-16

SUPPLIES

You'll need a Bible, a lamp with a lampshade, and several small flashlights.

PREPARATION

Turn off all the lights and have a lamp with a lampshade lit in the middle of the room.

Have children sit around the lamp. You should have just enough light to read. Open your Bible to Matthew 5:15-16. Show children the words and tell them the Bible is God's special book. Read the passage aloud.

Say: **We all have a light inside of us—it's Jesus' love.**

Have kids get into small groups, and hand out a flashlight to each group. Say: **Now, turn on your flashlights and cover them with your hands. God wants us to share our light with everyone and never hide it.**

Switch off the lamp so the room is in darkness. Say: **When we hide our love for Jesus, everyone else is in darkness—like we are now.**

Switch the lamp back on, and leave the lampshade in place. Say: **Keep covering your flashlights. Sometimes we tell others about Jesus and shine our lights, but we don't share everything. We sometimes hold back. That's like having a shade on our lights.**

Remove the lampshade from the lamp and have kids remove their hands from their flashlights. Say: **When we share our love for Jesus fully with everyone and shine brightly for all to see, the light of our love fills the room and the world.**

Ask:

- *Tell about a time you shaded your light in the past.*
- *What's one way you can shine your light fully like it's on a pedestal or a stand?*
- *How do you think sharing our faith in Jesus can impact others?*

Say: **There's a lot of darkness in the world, but we can shine a light by sharing our faith.**

Closing Prayer

Flashlight Prayers

Still in their small groups, have kids turn on their flashlights but cover them with their hands.

Say: **Dear God, sometimes we're afraid to share our love for Jesus and our faith in you with others. When we don't share our faith, the world will continue to live in darkness.** (Have kids remove their hands from covering their flashlights.) **Help us to shine our lights clearly so the world will know Jesus and will see our love for you and our faith in you clearly. In Jesus' name, amen.**

Targeted Faith

Share God's love with everyone

AGE GROUP

Upper Elementary

SCRIPTURE

Acts 1:1-11

SUPPLIES

You'll need a Bible, a whiteboard or poster board, markers, paper, and masking tape.

PREPARATION

On the whiteboard, draw a giant target with a bullseye, a second ring, and third ring. Hang the target on the wall. Put a tape line on the floor 10 feet away.

Have children sit in a circle or around tables. Open your Bible to Acts 1:1-11. Show children the words and tell them the Bible is God's special book.

Say: **In this part of the Bible we learn how Jesus told his disciples to tell the news about him to people in Jerusalem. Jerusalem was right in their backyard.** (Write "BACKYARD" in the bullseye.) **Jesus then told his disciples to tell his story to people in Judea and Samaria. Judea and Samaria was similar to our neighborhoods and towns.** (Write "TOWN" in the second ring.) **Jesus finally told his disciples to tell his story to the ends of the earth.** (Write "WORLD" in the third ring.) **Jesus wanted all his disciples to share his story, and we're his disciples as well.**

Give a sheet of paper to each child. Say: **Everyone, crumple up your paper and line up behind the line on the floor. We're going to throw our paper balls at the target. If you hit the bullseye, name someone in your own backyard you're going to share Jesus with. If you hit the second ring, name someone in your town you're going to share Jesus with. If you hit the third ring, name someone in the world you're going to share Jesus with.**

Allow time so everyone gets a chance.

Ask:

- *Explain whether you think it matters that we share our faith.*
- *Why do you think it mattered that Jesus told his disciples specifically where to share their faith?*
- *What are ways you can share your faith with your family, your friends, your neighbors, and the world?*

Say: **Just like the disciples, we too can share about Jesus with everyone.**

Closing Prayer
Paper Prayers

Gather everyone in a circle. You'll need one of the crumpled papers.

Say: **Let's pray to God about sharing our faith. I'm going to start and finish. After I start, I'll toss the paper ball to someone else, and that person will ask God for help sharing faith with another person. If you don't want to pray aloud, just toss the paper ball to someone else. When we're finished, pass the paper ball to me and I'll close.**

Dear God, I know how important it is to you for us to share our faith in Jesus and Jesus' message with others. Guide me to share my faith with...(Fill in a person, such as "my brother" or "Bob who lives down the street." Then toss the paper ball to someone else and let the prayers flow until you have the paper ball back in hand.) **Give us the strength to commit to sharing our faith and our love for Jesus with others. In Jesus' name, amen.**

God Loves Us, Cracks and All

Despite sin, we're still sweet to God

Have children sit in a circle or around tables. Open your Bible to Proverbs 3:1-8. Show children the words and tell them the Bible is God's special book. Read the passage aloud.

Hand out a lollipop and a resealable sandwich bag to each child.

Say: **God created us whole and perfect, just like your lollipop. But when Adam and Eve disobeyed God and ate the fruit from the tree, sin entered the world, causing all people to have a broken relationship with God and each other. Because of sin, we're now all broken.**

Help children break the lollipop inside the bag. They seal the lollipop inside the bag; you control the hammer.

Say: **Even though we're all broken because of sin, God sent Jesus to make us whole again. We may be broken, but we're still sweet to God.**

Have kids open their bags and taste the broken lollipops.

Ask:

- *How do our sins break our relationship with God? with each other?*
- *How does Jesus make us whole?*
- *What does it mean to you that God values you so much?*

Say: **When we put our trust in God, he can heal us and make us whole again.**

Closing Prayer
Whole Again Prayer

Give each child a whole lollipop.

Say: **Dear God, thank you for creating us whole and perfect. We know sin broke our relationship with you and with each other, but we also know you made us whole again by sending Jesus to die for us. Thank you for seeing us as whole and sweet people anyway. In Jesus' name, amen.**

Racing After Jesus

We can make a commitment to God

Have children gather at the opposite end of the room from the Bibles. Open your Bible to Hebrews 12:1-3. Show children the words and tell them the Bible is God's special book. Read the passage.

Say: **We're going to have a relay race to help us think about the endurance race that God sets before us.**

Point out the two Bibles at the other end of the room. Explain that within the Bibles are strips of paper. The first racers in each line must look at the first verse you give them, run down and locate that verse in the Bible. In that location, they'll find the next verse slip. They'll run back to their team with that verse strip in hand and give it to the next person in line, who'll run down to look up the next verse and find the next slip. Teams will race until they find the strip of paper that reads, "YOU WON!"

Say: **Excellent job. You all ran a wonderful race just now. The Bible compares our faith journey to running a race. We're committed to race after Jesus by studying the Bible, praying, following Jesus, and serving others. It takes training and endurance, but God will keep us strong as we race after Jesus.**

Distribute the handout and have kids form pairs. Say: **With your partner, read through the verses on your handout and talk about how you can apply these verses to your spiritual race to Jesus.**

Ask:

- *How do you keep your eyes on Jesus?*
- *How do you think Jesus helps us grow in our faith?*
- *What are ways we can encourage each other to run the race toward Jesus?*

Say: **The Bible helps us keep our eyes focused on Jesus and not give up.**

Closing Prayer

Racing Prayer

Have kids very quietly jog in place as your pray.

Say: **Dear God, thank you for sending Jesus as our leader and pace setter in this race of faith we're all running. Keep us strong as we run after Jesus and strengthen us to endure through trials and sin. Guide us to finish strong and continue to chase after Jesus. In Jesus' name, amen.**

You Won!

Three Minds Are Better Than One

God tells us to work together

AGE GROUP

Early Elementary

SCRIPTURE

Exodus 17:8-13

SUPPLIES

You'll need a Bible; 25 common items such as a shoe, a pencil, a toothbrush, and so on; a dark bedsheet; a timer or stopwatch; 2 sheets of paper per child; and pencils.

PREPARATION

Place the 25 items on the table and cover them with the bedsheet.

Gather children around the table of covered items.

Say: **We are going to play a memory game. In a few seconds, I'm going to remove this sheet to reveal 25 items. You'll have 20 seconds to memorize as many items as possible. Ready?** (Reveal the items for 20 seconds; then cover them with the sheet again. Give paper and a pencil to each child.) **You'll now have 60 seconds to write or draw as many items as you can. Ready?** (Allow 60 seconds.) **Write your name on your paper and hand it in.** (Collect the papers.) **Now form groups of three and see how many items you can recall together as a group.** (Give each group another sheet of paper.) **You have 60 seconds to work with your teammates and recall as many items as you can.** (After 60 seconds, collect the papers.)

Ask:

- *How much more successful were you by working together?*

Say: **Let's see what the Bible tells us about a time people worked together.**

Open your Bible to Exodus 17:8-13. Show children the words and tell them the Bible is God's special book. Read the Bible passage.

Ask:

- *Tell about a time you needed help but didn't get it. What happened?*
- *When have you stepped in to help someone else?*
- *Why do you think it's important that we help and support each other?*

Say: **God wants us to work together like Moses and his friends in the Bible passage. He wants us to help and support each other because we can accomplish so much more when we work together than we could ever do apart.**

Closing Prayer
Teamwork Prayers

Have groups of three stand together with one person in the middle and the other two holding up one hand of the middle person.

Say: **Dear God, Moses needed Aaron and Hur to hold up his hands during battle. God knew Moses couldn't do everything alone, that even a great leader like Moses needed help. We too need help, and we need to help each other. Give us the strength to work together as a team. Guide us to love, support, and care for one another. In Jesus' name, amen.**

Just for Kicks

We all have a purpose

Gather children together. Open your Bible to 1 Corinthians 12:12-26. Show children the words and tell them the Bible is God's special book. Read the passage.

Say: **We're going to learn more about what this passage means by playing a game.**

Have kids form groups of three, and give each group a balloon and a blindfold.

Say: **Inflate your balloon and choose one of your teammates to wear a blindfold. For round one, your blindfolded teammate will kick the balloon from one end of the room to the other. You can't help your teammate in any way. Your blindfolded teammate must kick the balloon in complete silence.** On "Go," have every blindfolded teammate kick a balloon to the end and back…or at least try.

Say: **Now, for round two, you can help your blindfolded teammate kick the balloon by giving verbal instruction. You can't touch your teammate.** On "Go," have every blindfolded teammate kick the balloon to the end and back while the other two teammates give verbal instructions.

Say: **For round three, you can help your blindfolded teammate kick the balloon by speaking and guiding him or her with your hands.** On "Go," have every blindfolded teammate kick the balloon to the end and back while the other two teammates give verbal instructions and guide their teammate with their hands.

Ask:

- *How was each round of this game different for you and for your team?*
- *Tell about a time working with a team made things better for you.*
- *Why do you think teamwork is part of God's plan for our lives?*

Say: **The Bible passage reminds us that just like the human body has many parts that need to work together, "so it is with the body of Christ."**

Closing Prayer

Team Time

Have kids stand in a circle. Tell kids you'll call each person's name during the prayer, starting with the person on your right. Give that person a high-five, then thank God for the next person. The child you high-fived will high-five that person.

Say: **Dear God, please help us recognize our gifts and use those gifts to help others. Thank you for letting us be part of your team. Thank you for...** (Say child's name. Continue around the circle and say each child's name.) **Thank you for the teamwork of everyone in this circle. In Jesus' name, amen.**

Nothing too Small

We can be thankful for everything

AGE GROUP

Early Elementary

SCRIPTURE

Psalm 136

SUPPLIES

You'll need a Bible and a box full of random things we're not normally thankful for, like a bow, string, ball, dirty sock, and so on. You'll need at least 1 item per person.

PREPARATION

None needed.

Have children sit in a circle or around tables. Open your Bible to Psalm 136. Show children the words and tell them the Bible is God's special book.

Say: **In this passage from the Bible, it tells us that no matter what's happening in our lives, God always loves us and his love conquers everything. It says he provides everything for us because he loves us so. That's why God wants us to be thankful for everything, even the small things in life. Even things we may not even think about being thankful for.**

In this box, I have several random items. I'm going to pull out each item one at a time. When I do, I'll call on someone to come up with one reason you can be thankful for that item. For example, if I pull out a bow, you could say that the bow was taken from a birthday gift and we're thankful for presents.

Play this until your box of items is empty.

Ask:

- *What are some weird things you're thankful for, and why?*
- *Why do you think it's important to be thankful for everything?*
- *What's one thing you can be grateful for this week that you haven't thought much about before?*

Say: **We can be thankful to God for all things, all the time, because he loves us so much.**

Closing Prayer
Prayer of Thanksgiving

Have children form a circle on the floor. Have them bow their heads as you pray, and give them a few seconds to silently think of something ordinary or unusual that they're thankful for. Tell them you'll give time for them to call out those things during the prayer.

Say: **Dear God, you've given us some many things. We're so blessed. We have big things like food, clothing, and a roof over our heads. We also have small things like socks, string, and toothpaste. We have other things like**... (Allow kids to call out the items they're thankful for.) **Remind us to be thankful for the big things and the small things. Remind us to be thankful for everything, especially your enduring love. In Jesus' name, amen.**

Worry Knot

God wants us to be grateful and not worry

AGE GROUP

Upper Elementary

SCRIPTURE

Matthew 6:25-34

SUPPLIES

You'll need a Bible and a large bag of mini pretzel knots (traditionally shaped pretzels).

PREPARATION

None needed.

ALLERGY ALERT!
See page 8

Have children sit in a circle or around tables. Open your Bible to Matthew 6:25-34. Show children the words and tell them the Bible is God's special book. Read the passage aloud.

Say: **This passage in the Bible tells us God wants us to trust him and to not worry about anything. God will always provide. Part of trusting God is recognizing what God's already done for us. God wants us to be thankful for everything.**

Think for a moment about what you're wearing today. What's one item you have on and why are you thankful for it? It must be something on your body—perhaps your clothing, something in your pockets, or your clean teeth.

Allow time for kids to decide on one thing. After kids discuss things they're thankful for, have them find a partner. Give everyone three pretzels. Show kids how the pretzels are shaped like knots, and talk about how worry makes us feel like our stomach is in knots.

Say: **With your partner, share three things you worry about—one for each pretzel. Things that worry us could be things like our grades, sickness, or money. Then share about how you can trust God to provide for you and how you can be thankful for his provision.**

After a few minutes, gather kids for discussion.

Ask:

- *How do you think worrying can affect your gratefulness?*
- *Tell about a time something you were worried about actually turned into a good thing.*
- *Why do you think it's important to be thankful for everything—even things that seem bad at the time?*
- *How can you focus this week on being happy rather than being worried?*

Say: **Rather than worry, God wants us to have faith that he will provide for all our needs, as he has done already.**

Closing Prayer

Prayer of Thanksgiving

Let kids quietly nibble pretzels as you pray.

Say: **Dear God, you've given us so many things, including our lives. We know you care for lilies and birds, so why wouldn't you care for us? Help us to not worry about what we wear or what we'll eat, but instead be thankful for everything we have. Thank you for providing for us and for sending Jesus to save us. Help us to be thankful for everything. In Jesus' name, amen.**

A Salty Truth

Small lies are still lies

AGE GROUP

Early Elementary

SCRIPTURE

Psalm 15:1-2

SUPPLIES

You'll need a Bible. For every five children, you'll need a small bowl of salt. And for each child, you'll need a cup of water.

PREPARATION

None needed.

Have children sit in groups of five. Give each child a cup of water. Set out bowls of salt.

Say: **The Bible tells us that lying is disobeying God. But some people think it's okay if we tell just a teeny-tiny lie. They may call it a "white lie." A little lie may not actually hurt anyone, and it may seem innocent at first. Like maybe your mom asks if you put your dishes in the dishwasher like she asked you to. And you say yes, even though you haven't, because you plan to do it later. We may hardly even notice telling a little lie like that because we don't really mean to hurt anyone.**

Have kids drop a grain of salt into their cups.

Ask:

- *What are some examples of a little lie?* (Be ready to offer examples.)

Say: **A teeny-tiny lie might not hurt anyone or cause a big problem right away, but these lies have a way of growing. Sometimes when we get caught in a lie, we lie again to cover it up.** (Have kids drop another grain of salt into their cups of water). **It still seems harmless, right? But the more we tell little lies, the more lying becomes easier for us to do.** (Add several grains of salt.) **We may tell lies more and more frequently.** (Add a pinch of salt.) **Or we may tell even bigger lies.** (Have kids add two pinches of salt.)

Ask if any of the children would like to taste their water. Open your Bible to Psalm 15:1-2. Show children the words and tell them the Bible is God's special book. Read the Scripture.

Ask:

- *What do you think it means to be blameless?*
- *Tell about a time you told a lie. What happened, and how did you feel?*
- *What happened to our pure water?*
- *How is the salt in our water like our life when we tell lies?*

Say: **God wants us to lead blameless or pure lives, which means speaking the truth in every situation. A small lie is still a lie. Small lies most often turn into bigger and bigger lies. Lying, no matter how big or how small, is disobeying God.**

Closing Prayer

Sincere Hearts

Have kids each place one hand over their heart and one hand over their mouth.

Say: **Dear God, thank you for always telling us the truth through your Son, Jesus, and through your Word. We know you want us to lead blameless and pure lives. Remind us in every situation that you want us to be truthful. Guide us to speak truth from sincere hearts. In Jesus' name, amen.**

Lies Come to Light

Lies are always exposed

Have children sit in a circle or around tables. Open your Bible to Proverbs 12:19. Show children the words and tell them the Bible is God's special book.

Say: **We never think we'll get caught lying, do we? We think it will stay a secret.** (Read the Scripture.) **The Bible says that lies are exposed over time. I'm going to tell you three statements about myself. Two statements are true, and one is a lie. You have to guess which one is the lie. After you guess, I'll expose the lie.**

Share two true statements and one false statement about yourself, such as your favorite color or a place you've visited. (The false statement should be the one you've written in lemon juice on the paper beforehand.) After kids have guessed, hold the paper to the lamp. The heat from the lamp will cause the lemon juice to darken, exposing the message.

Say: **Now it's your turn to play the game.**

Form groups of three, and give everyone a copy of the handout, a pencil, a cotton swab, and a cup of lemon juice. Have kids write their statements at the top of the page, and show them how to write the lie in lemon juice on the bottom. Allow time for everyone to play the game. Help kids expose the lies in the lamp light.

Ask:

- *How did you figure out which statements were truth or lies?*
- *Tell about a time a lie you told was exposed. What happened?*
- *How did you feel having to lie about yourself in this game?*
- *How does Jesus, the light of the world, expose our lies?*

Say: **The Bible is our source of truth, and Jesus is the light. When we tell lies, they'll always come before the light. We can't lie to God or Jesus. And God doesn't want us to lie to anyone, ever. He tells us to be truthful in all situations. When we've lied, God wants us to ask for forgiveness and stop lying.**

Closing Prayer
Looking for Lies

Say: **Let's take a moment to search our hearts for any lies that we need to have exposed and forgiven.** (Have children silently pray for one minute.)

Dear God, we thank you that your truth, the Word, stands the test of time. We know you want us to always speak the truth. Expose any lies we may have said and forgive us of our sin. Guide us to be truthful and pure. In Jesus' name, amen.

Two Truths and a Lie

Write three statements about yourself, two that are true and one that is a lie.

1.

2.

3.

- -

My lie:

Faith, Trust, and a Hula Hoop

We can always put our trust in God

AGE GROUP

Early Elementary

SCRIPTURE

Proverbs 3:5

SUPPLIES

You'll need a Bible, 1 adult-size chair to sit in, and 1 hula hoop and ball for every pair of children.

PREPARATION

None needed.

Have children sit in a circle or around tables. Open your Bible to Proverbs 3:5. Show children the words and tell them the Bible is God's special book.

Say: **To trust someone means you believe him or her, you have faith in that person, and you don't doubt the person. Our passage today reminds us that we can each trust in God with all of our heart. We don't have to overthink it.** (Read the passage aloud.)

Let's learn more about what this means. I have a chair in front of me that I'm going to sit on. I trust this chair. I really do. When I go to sit on the chair, I trust that it'll hold me up. I don't have to think about it; I just believe it'll do what it's supposed to do. I don't have to inspect the chair thoroughly to make sure it'll hold me. I don't have to bring my own chair with me everywhere I go. Let's see what happens when I trust the chair.

Stand in front of the chair as if you're about to sit. Then close your eyes and sit down. Open your eyes. Say: **I was right to trust the chair!**

Have kids each find a partner. If you have an odd number, form a group of three. Give one person in each pair a hula hoop and the other person a ball.

Say: **In a moment, if you're holding a hula hoop, I want you to hold it up in front of yourself. If you're holding a ball, you'll try to make a basket by tossing the ball through the hula hoop. Take three tries, and then trade items. Ready? Go!**

Allow time. Then say: **Each of you trusted your friend to not throw the ball in your face when you held up the hula hoop. You also trusted your friend to keep the hula hoop in the air.**

Ask:

- *Explain whether it was easy to trust your partner. How might it have been different if I had chosen your partner for you?*
- *What are some things or people that you put your trust in?*
- *What do you think it means to trust God?*

Say: **It was easy to trust your friend because you could see him or her. It was easy to trust the chair because it's always held me up before. We can trust God in the same way, because he loves us no matter what and he's always there, every day. We can always talk with him, give our worries to him, and have faith that he'll provide for us.**

Closing Prayer

Learning to Trust

Have kids form a line and hold up their hula hoop or ball.

Say: **Dear God, we're learning to trust you every day. Please remind us that we can always put our faith in you. We can always know that you're there, listening to us, helping us, providing for us, and loving us. In Jesus' name, amen.**

God or Chariots?

We put our trust in God alone

AGE GROUP

Upper Elementary

SCRIPTURE

Psalm 20:7

SUPPLIES

You'll need a Bible. For each child, you'll need an index card and colored pencils.

PREPARATION

None needed.

Have children sit in a circle or around tables. Open your Bible to Psalm 20:7. Show children the words and tell them the Bible is God's special book. Read the Scripture aloud.

Say: **This passage talks about how people will trust other things over God. A long time ago, people even trusted their chariots and horses more than they did God. "Chariots and horses" at that time could have represented transportation, government, war, and armies. God's Word in this passage challenges us not to trust the things of this world over God.**

Have kids pair up with someone who's close in height.

Say: **We're going to do a trust exercise to learn more about what it means to trust God.**

Have partners stand one behind the other, facing in the same direction. Check partners to ensure kids are fairly equal in size. If you see mismatched partners, switch kids around.

Say: **When I count to three, the partner standing in front will fall back. The partner behind you will catch you.** (Count to three.) **Great catches!** (Have kids switch places and go again.) **Nice job! You trusted your friend to catch you, and your friend trusted you.**

Ask:

- *Describe what it was like for you to fall backward.*
- *What was it like to catch your friend?*
- *How easy or difficult was it to trust in this activity versus what it's like to trust in real life?*
- *How is trusting God different from this experience?*

Say: **Friends are an important group of people to trust. When you fell, you really trusted your friend. If God had been in your friend's place, would you still have fallen?** (Allow for responses.) **More than any thing—any vehicle, building, toy, game, and even person—we can trust in God. God is for us always, and he wants us to put our trust in him.**

Closing Prayer

Trusting Today

Distribute index cards and colored pencils.

Say: **Take a moment to write or draw what you can trust God with this week. Then hold that sheet of paper in your hand as we pray.**

Allow time. Then pray:

Dear God, we give you these things in our hands. We're choosing today to trust you with them. Please remind us to always put our trust in you above all things. In Jesus' name, amen.

Idols Away!

God helps us make wise choices

Have kids sit in a circle or around tables. Open your Bible to 2 Kings 22–23. Show kids the words and tell them the Bible is God's special book.

Say: **Josiah was a young king. He became the king of Judah when he was only 8 years old. Can you imagine being in charge of an entire kingdom at age 8? He was actually very wise for his age.**

One day, though, the high priest came to the king and said, "I have found the Book of the Law in the Lord's Temple!" He gave the scroll to the king to read it. When the king finished reading, he was upset. He realized his kingdom wasn't doing what God wanted, because they had many idols they worshipped all the time. An idol is a picture or item that people worship instead of God.

Josiah went to the Temple and gathered all the people and read them the lost scroll. King Josiah then made a promise to God to obey his commands, and his people promised to do the same. Josiah then went around the entire kingdom destroying altars and temples that other kings had set up.

Ask:

- *Describe what an idol might be.*
- *Why do you think it's important that we don't let idols distract us from God?*

Say: **You may have noticed something unusual in our room. I've set up some idols we have today. You're going to follow King Josiah's example and knock down those idols!**

Place the bean bags or balled-up socks in the center of the room. Tell kids they can grab one bean bag or pair of socks at a time and then go find an idol to knock down. Remind kids to be gentle and not to throw if someone is in the way. As they knock down idols, go around the room and set them up. Play for two or three minutes.

Say: **Josiah was a wise king who loved God and wanted to please him in every way possible. Great job on knocking down idols like wise Josiah did!**

Ask:

- *What idols do you have in your life?* (Be ready with your own examples.)
- *What are ways you can get rid of idols?*
- *Why do you think it's important to worship only God?*
- *Why do you think Josiah was wise?*

Say: **Just like Josiah, we can make wise decisions. If we trust and rely on God and listen to his Word, he'll give us the strength we need to make wise decisions.**

Closing Prayer

Wisdom Wish

Have kids gather the "idols" from your game, and then sit in a circle with the idols in the center.

Say: **Dear God, we're so thankful for examples in the Bible like King Josiah. He was young but wise. Please give us the wisdom like he had to make good decisions in our lives.** (Have kids place all the idols outside the circle.) **Thank you for sharing your wisdom with us. In Jesus' name we pray, amen.**

Build on the Rock

God's Word is a solid foundation

AGE GROUP

Upper Elementary

SCRIPTURE

Matthew 7:24-29

SUPPLIES

You'll need a Bible, 1 medium-sized rock, 1 or 2 cups of sand, 2 paper cups, markers, 1 large casserole dish, and 1 large cup of water.

PREPARATION

Draw windows and doors on paper cups to make them look like houses.

Have kids sit in a circle or around tables. Open your Bible to Matthew 7:24-29. Show kids the words and tell them the Bible is God's special book.

Place the empty casserole dish in front of you. Say: **Jesus told a story about two people who were going to build houses. There was a wise builder and a foolish builder. Jesus said anyone who hears what he says and obeys is like a person who builds his house on rock.** (Put the rock on one side of the casserole dish.) **He also said anyone who hears what he says and doesn't obey is like a person who builds his house on sand.** (Pour sand in the casserole dish forming a "mound.") **Jesus was telling us that we need to build our lives on the solid foundation of God's Word and listen and do what he says.** (Place a paper cup house on the rock and one on the sand.) **Jesus said when the rain came and wind blew and beat on the houses, something happened.** (Pour water around the house on the rock.) **The house built on the rock didn't fall.** (Pour water around the house on the sand. Tip the house over.) **The house built on sand fell. Jesus said if we build our lives on anything other than him, our lives won't stand up when storms and troubles come.**

Read the passage aloud.

Say: **When we build our lives on Jesus, we gain wisdom that helps us through tough times and helps us make good choices in life.**

Ask:

- *What does it mean to be wise?*
- *Tell about a time you made a wise choice.*
- *Tell about a time you made a foolish choice.*
- *How is listening to Jesus being wise?*

Say: **Jesus reminded us that God is good and loves us. God wants what's best for us. He wants us to build our lives on rock because he'll take care of us. We're stronger when we wisely trust in Jesus and follow his instructions for our lives.**

Closing Prayer

Get Wise

Tell kids to follow you as you do actions during this prayer.

Say: **Dear God** (clasp hands in prayer), **thank you for sending Jesus** (raise hands to sky) **to teach us lessons about how to be wise** (tap head). **Remind us to be wise** (tap head) **and build** (hammer into palm) **our house** (make a roof over your head) **on the rock—you!** (Raise hands to sky.) **In Jesus' name, amen.**

Tomb Stone

Jesus defeats death

AGE GROUP

Early Elementary

SCRIPTURE

John 20:1-10

SUPPLIES

You'll need a Bible, a small ball, 1 stone for each child, and permanent markers.

PREPARATION

None needed.

Have children sit in a circle. Open your Bible to John 20:1-10. Show children the words and tell them the Bible is God's special book. Read verse 1 aloud. Then hold up the ball.

Say: **This ball represents the tombstone that was rolled away from Jesus' tomb. As I continue reading, I'll pause after each verse. Then I'll roll the "stone" to one of you and have you retell me in your own words what the verse says or means to you. Ready?**

Read verse 2 and then pause and roll the ball to a child in the circle. After the child has shared what verse 2 means, have the child roll the ball back to you. Then continue reading each verse and pausing until you've finished the passage.

Give each child a small stone and a permanent marker. Ask children to take a moment to silently roll the stone around in their hands as they reflect on what the stone being rolled away at Jesus' tomb means to them. Then encourage kids to write a word or draw a simple picture on the stone as a reminder of what they thought about.

Ask:

- *Explain what you drew or wrote on your stone.*
- *Why does it matter to you that the stone was rolled away?*
- *How will you live differently this week knowing that Jesus is alive?*

Say: **The stone being rolled away means that Jesus beat death and conquered sin. We can know for sure that our sins are forgiven and we can one day bow before God in heaven.**

Closing Prayer
Rolling Prayers

Ask kids to spread out around the room and get on their hands and knees. As you pray out loud, encourage kids to gently roll their stones.

Say: **Dear God, without Jesus dying and coming back to life, we would have no hope. Thank you for sending your Son to pay for our sin. Help us to live each day focused on the gift of eternal life you offer each of us. In Jesus' name, amen.**

Hidden Treasure

Jesus is alive

AGE GROUP

Upper Elementary

SCRIPTURE

John 20:11-18

SUPPLIES

You'll need a Bible for every four kids, a small object like a bouncy ball or a tube of lip balm, and a copy of the "Finding Treasure" handout and a pencil for each child.

PREPARATION

Before kids arrive, hide the small object somewhere in your meeting space.

Without telling children what object you've hidden, encourage them to search the room. Ask kids to stop and stand next to an object when they think they've discovered what you've hidden. Allow time. Then gather kids together and show them which object you hid.

Say: **Most of you didn't recognize or find what I hid because you didn't know what to look for. In our passage today, Mary didn't recognize Jesus. Let's find out more.**

Open your Bible to John 20:11-18. Show children the words and tell them the Bible is God's special book. Read the passage aloud. Then play the game again; have kids cover their eyes as you hide the same or another object. This time tell kids what object to look for.

Then give each child a handout and a pencil. Have kids form four groups, and assign each group one of the four verses. Give each group a Bible. Encourage groups to work together to write a short description of Jesus based on what they've read.

Afterward, gather groups together to share what they've learned with the larger group so that all kids can complete their handouts based on the other groups' findings.

Ask:

- *Like Mary, when have you not recognized Jesus in your life?*
- *What have you learned from these verses that will help you better recognize Jesus?*
- *What's one thing you can tell someone else this week that will help that person better recognize and understand who Jesus is?*

Say: **Like Mary, sometimes we don't recognize Jesus in our lives because we don't know who Jesus truly is. Jesus is the Son of God. He came to earth, lived a sinless life, and willingly died on a cross to take the punishment for all our sins. These truths will help us know and recognize Jesus.**

Closing Prayer

Open Our Eyes

Encourage kids to look up at the ceiling and keep their eyes open wide while you pray aloud.

Say: **God, help us to see and recognize you. Show us the truth of who you are and what you've done for us. We are so thankful that you came and died for us. In Jesus' name, amen.**

Finding Treasure

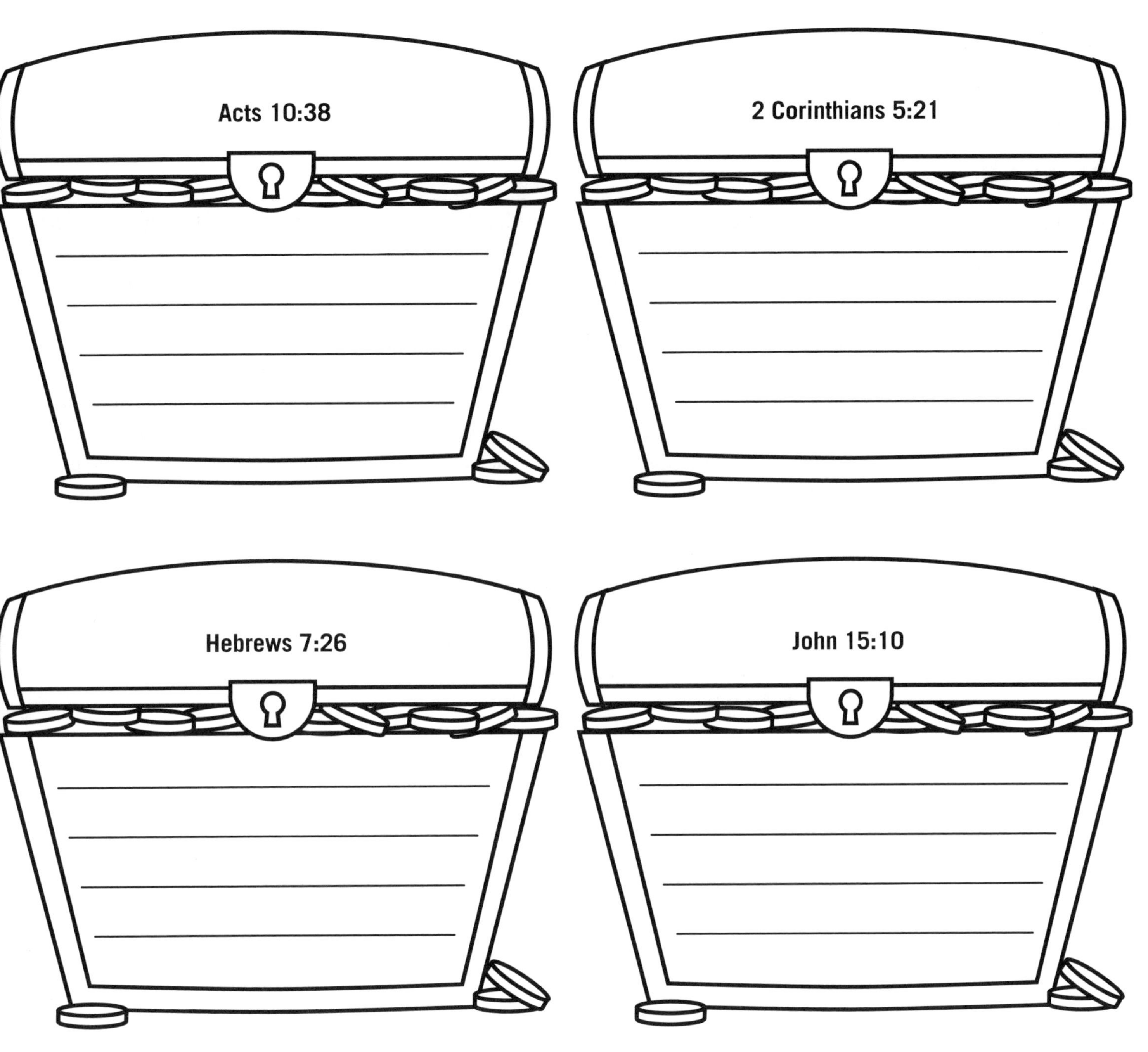

Thanksgiving Feast

We give thanks for our blessings

Say: **Although we've been celebrating Thanksgiving for a couple hundred years, God told his people to celebrate and give thanks thousands of years before.**

Open your Bible to Nehemiah 8:6-12. Show children the words and tell them the Bible is God's special book.

Read verse 6 aloud. Have kids bow down and worship God by telling him what they're thankful for.

Read verses 7-8 aloud. Explain to kids what you're reading about, just as the Levites helped the people understand the Book of the Law of God. Say: **The Israelites had been in captivity for many generations. During this time, the Israelites stopped obeying God. As Ezra and the Levites began reading God's words to them, people heard and understood what God planned for his people.**

Read verse 9 aloud. Say: **Instead of weeping over their sin, God wanted the Israelites to celebrate because they were coming back to God.** Have kids give each other high fives and cheer.

Read verses 10-12 aloud. Have kids wash their hands with anti-bacterial gel. Then give kids cups of juice to represent the sweet drinks and donut holes and fruit to represent the rich foods the Israelites ate.

Ask:

- *How is what you're thankful for similar to or different from what the Israelites were thankful for?*
- *What can you learn from the Israelites about thankfulness?*
- *How will you demonstrate your thankfulness to God this week?*

Say: **The Israelites celebrated and thanked God because they heard his words and understood them. Like the Israelites, we can be thankful that we can read the Bible each day and learn more about God whenever we want to.**

Closing Prayer
Bible Prayers

Have kids gather around the Bible and place a hand on top of it.

Say: **God, we are thankful for everything you give us. We're reminded how wonderful it is that we can hold your living words in our hands. Help us to want to read your words and teach us to understand them more each day. In Jesus' name, amen.**

Jar of Thanks

It's important to give thanks to God

Have children sit in a circle. Open your Bible to Luke 17:11-19. Show children the words and tell them the Bible is God's special book. Read the passage aloud.

Say: **Leprosy is a sickness that creates red sores on the skin. The Bible says that 10 men who had leprosy asked Jesus to heal them. Jesus healed every one of them, but only one returned to thank Jesus.**

Next read 1 Thessalonians 5:18 to the kids.

Say: **The Bible tells us to be thankful in all circumstances. That means whether we are being healed from leprosy or having a really hard day, we can still find something to thank God for.**

Give each child a mason jar, 10 red construction paper circles, and a pencil. Allow time for kids to each think of one thing they can be thankful for. Have kids write that thing on one of their circles and place that circle and the other nine circles in their jars.

Ask:

- *When have you been thankful like the Samaritan leper was?*
- *When have you been like the other nine lepers and forgotten to thank God?*
- *How can you show your thanks to God for what he has done?*

Say: **Take your jars home with you. For the next nine days, find one thing you can be thankful for and write it on one of the red circles. Like the Samaritan leper, we remember to thank God for the big and small things he does in our lives.**

Closing Prayer
Thankful Prayers

Say: **Dear God, we want to remember to thank you like the leper did. No matter what is going on in our lives, we know we can find something to be thankful for. So right now, we thank you for...** (Name something you're thankful for. Encourage kids to each to read aloud what they wrote on their red dot. Then end the prayer.) **God, please teach us to be thankful in all circumstances. In Jesus' name, amen.**

The Shepherds and Angels

Jesus is our miracle

AGE GROUP

Early Elementary

SCRIPTURE

Luke 2:15-20

SUPPLIES

You'll need a Bible, a piece of thin cloth, sparkly gold chenille wires, and craft faux fur. For each child, you'll also need a copy of the "In the Heart" handout, scissors, and a glue stick.

PREPARATION

Cut the cloth into thin strips about 1-inch long. Cut the chenille wires into 1½-inch lengths; then form each wire into a small circle and twist the ends together. Cut the craft faux fur into 1-inch squares.

Give each child a handout, a glue stick, and scissors. Demonstrate for kids how to follow the instructions on the handout. Help as needed.

Say: **The Bible says Jesus' mother, Mary, hid in her heart all the things that the angels said. As I read the passage, I'll pause and give you time to glue things inside your heart.**

Open your Bible to Luke 2:15-20. Show children the words and tell them the Bible is God's special book.

Read verses 15-16. Give each child a small piece of cloth to represent Jesus' swaddling cloth. Have kids glue the cloth inside their hearts.

Read verses 17-18. Give kids the halo-shaped chenille wire to represent the angels. Allow time for gluing.

Read verses 19-20. Give kids the faux fur as a reminder of the shepherds. Allow time for gluing. Then have kids form pairs.

Say: **Based on what you've hidden in your heart, take turns retelling the story of Jesus' birth.** Allow time.

Ask:

- *Like Mary, what's something that's happened to you that you think about often?*
- *Why is it important to hide the words of Jesus' birth in your heart?*
- *How can you share about what Mary hid in her heart this week?*

Say: **Jesus coming to earth as a human person to die for our sin is the most important truth we can hide in our hearts. Like Mary, we can think often about what Jesus' birth means for how we live every single day.**

Closing Prayer

Heartfelt Prayers

Have kids hold their paper hearts against their chests.

Say: **God, just like Mary, we want to hide your words in our heart. Help us to think often about who you are and what you've done for us.** (Pause and have kids lay their hearts on the ground with the flaps open wide.) **Help us also to open our hearts to those around us so we can share the good news that Jesus' birth brings to everyone. In Jesus' name, amen.**

In the Heart

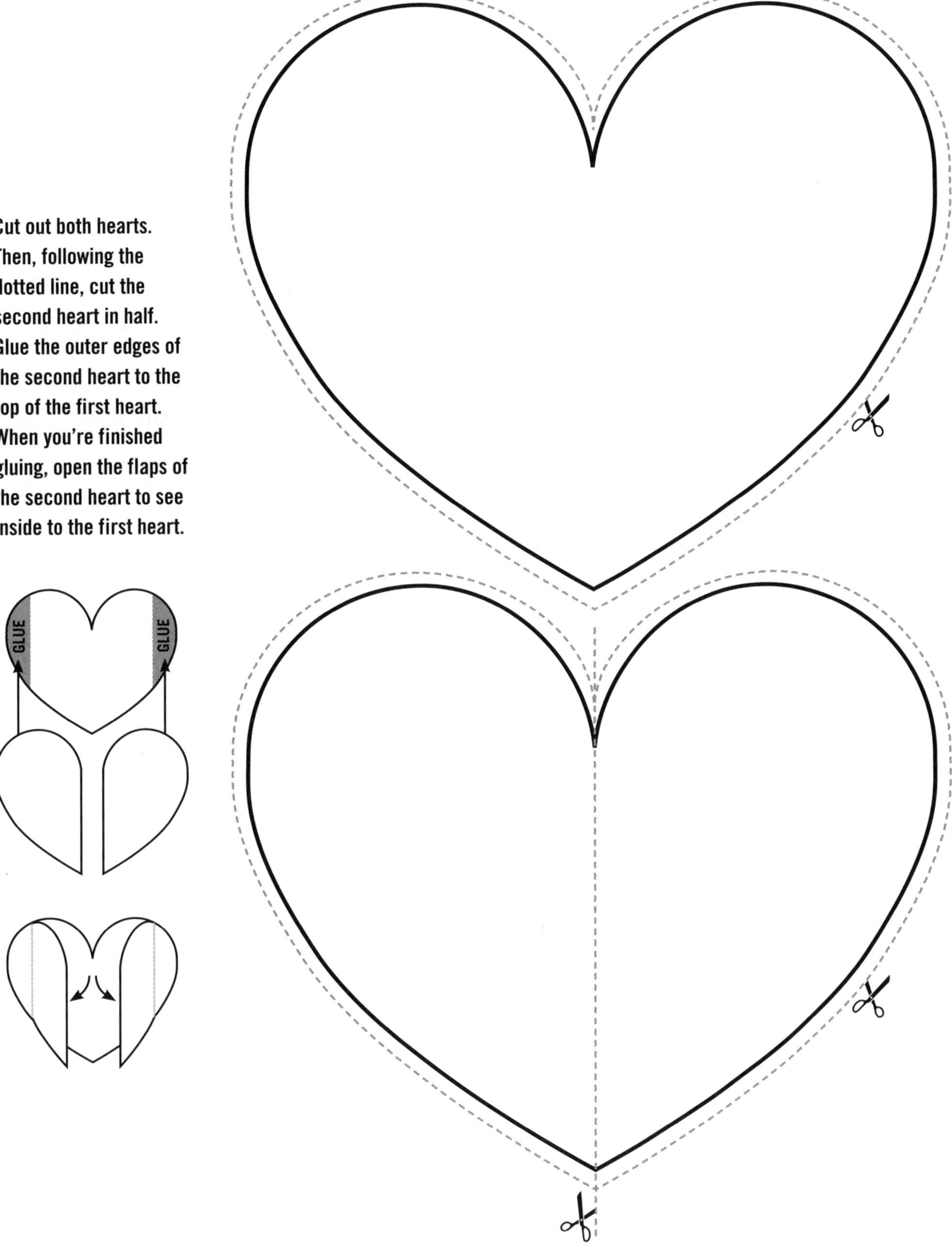

Cut out both hearts. Then, following the dotted line, cut the second heart in half. Glue the outer edges of the second heart to the top of the first heart. When you're finished gluing, open the flaps of the second heart to see inside to the first heart.

Follow the Star

Jesus is born

AGE GROUP

Upper Elementary

SCRIPTURE

Matthew 2:1-11

SUPPLIES

You'll need a Bible, 3 craft sticks per child, thin-tipped permanent markers, and gold and silver glitter glue.

PREPARATION

None needed.

Open your Bible to Matthew 2:1-11. Show children the words and tell them the Bible is God's special book. Then read the passage aloud.

Say: **The wise men followed the star as it rose. When they followed the star it led them to Jesus. Just as the wise men followed the star long ago, we follow Jesus.**

Ask:

- *What can you learn from the wise men following the star that will help you to better follow Jesus?*
- *In what ways do you struggle to follow Jesus?*

Give each child three craft sticks and a permanent marker. Encourage kids to write a word or phrase on each craft stick that represents one thing that gets in the way of them following Jesus. For example, kids might write the word *friends* if they struggle to follow Jesus because of who they hang out with.

After kids have written three things, show them how to create a star by stacking the three craft sticks and then fanning them out from the center. Have kids glue the sticks together in the shape of a star. Then encourage kids to decorate the star with the glitter glue.

Ask:

- *What's one way you'll commit this week to following Jesus like the wise men followed the star?*

Say: **Take your star home and hang it somewhere in your room as a reminder to follow Jesus like the wise men followed the star.**

Closing Prayer

Starry Prayers

Have kids gather on one end of your meeting space. Encourage them to hold their stars stretched out in front of them. Ask kids to walk across the room, following their stars as you pray.

Say: **Dear God, thank you for the example of the wise men who were eager to know you and worship you. Help us to faithfully follow you just as the wise men followed the star. We love you and we need you. In Jesus' name, amen.**

THE GIANT
BOOK
of
Children's
MESSAGES
Scripture
Index

THE **GIANT** BOOK OF CHILDREN'S MESSAGES

Upper Elementary

More than 200 GIANT-SIZED games to maximize your impact!

The Giant Book of Games for Children's Ministry

This JAM-PACKED, CHOCK-FULL book of more than 200 GIANT-SIZED games will fill your ministry with TONS of fun and laughter! With a variety of games for preschoolers through preteens, you'll find the perfect game for every occasion!

Each of these fun-filled games is tied to a different topic, with a Scripture connection and discussion to help kids understand the Bible point. You'll bring more depth and learning to topics including The Body of Christ, Salvation, Faith, Creation, Fear, Following Jesus, Trust, Forgiveness, Friendship, God's Love, Jesus' Birth and Resurrection, Grace, Prayer, Thankfulness, and so many more!

Every game includes an overview that details the game's energy level, supply level, age level, and preparation needed, so you'll be able to find the best fit for your lesson and time slot. Plus these relational, cooperative games can be used anytime…wherever they fit into your schedule or to fill an on-the-spot need!

Reinforce your lessons with these 200+ must-have games that'll help kids actually remember what they learned!

▶ ISBN 978-1-4707-0424-7 • $29.99

Order today! Visit group.com or your favorite Christian retailer.

Tons of IDEAS TO MAXIMIZE preschool ministry!

Make God's Word come alive with loads of active fingerplays!

The Giant Book of Bible Fingerplays for Preschoolers

▶ ISBN 978-1-4707-4478-6 • $24.99

This Giant Book of Bible Fingerplays for Preschoolers includes a Bible verse and story to read, and a Bible fingerplay that children can say and act out. Imagine a Bible learning time with listening, speaking, and action. Sounds like fun!

This book:

• teaches Bible passages on a simple level

• lists the Bible basis for each passage

• features a key Bible verse from the passage

• includes 101 fingerplays

What is a fingerplay?

A fingerplay is a short verse, poem, or rhyme where hand and body movements act out the words being said. Fingerplays are performed with young children, both girls and boys. Young children enjoy actively engaging in telling the story along with you. Acting out the passage helps children remember the details while keeping them interested and having fun!

Fingerplays in this book:

• are easy to learn and remember

• are fun, fast, attention-getters

• can be sung to the tune *Frère Jacques*

• contain short versions of Bible passages from the Old and New Testaments

Order today! Visit group.com or your favorite Christian retailer.